C# 8 and .NET Core 3 Projects Using Azure

Second Edition

Build professional desktop, mobile, and web applications that meet modern software requirements

Paul Michaels
Dirk Strauss
Jas Rademeyer

Packt>

BIRMINGHAM - MUMBAI

C# 8 and .NET Core 3 Projects Using Azure
Second Edition

Commissioning Editor: Richa Tripathi
Acquisition Editor: Alok Dhuri
Content Development Editor: Digvijay Bagul
Senior Editor: Rohit Singh
Technical Editor: Pradeep Sahu
Copy Editor: Safis Editing
Project Coordinator: Francy Puthiry
Proofreader: Safis Editing
Indexer: Priyanka Dhadke
Production Designer: Alishon Mendonsa

First published: March 2018
Second edition: December 2019

Production reference: 1301219

Published by Packt Publishing Ltd.
Livery Place
35 Livery Street
Birmingham
B3 2PB, UK.

ISBN 978-1-78961-208-0

`www.packt.com`

To my daughter, Abigail, who is generous, honourable, sharp-witted, funny, and who believes in me; and to my son, Dylan, who is far cleverer than me, kind, gentle, and always smiling. I consider myself to be the richest person alive to call you both my children, and I am proud of you both!

- Paul Michaels

Contributors

About the authors

Paul Michaels is a Lead Developer with over 20 years experience. He likes programming, playing with new technology and solving problems. When he's not working, you can find him cycling or walking around The Peak District, playing table tennis, or trying to cook for his wife and two children. You can follow him on twitter at `@paul_michaels`, or find him on LinkedIn by searching for pcmichaels. He also writes a blog for which the link is available on both his LinkedIn and Twitter profiles.

A special thanks to Abigail Michaels, who provided the artwork for this book.

Dirk Strauss is a full-stack developer with Embrace. He enjoys learning and sharing what he learns with others. Dirk has published books on C# for Packt as well as ebooks for Syncfusion. In his spare time, he relaxes by playing guitar and trying to learn Jimi Hendrix licks. You can find him at `@DirkStrauss` on Twitter.

I would like to thank my wife, my son, and my daughter for supporting me and always being there for me. I love you with all that I am.

Jas Rademeyer has been a part of the IT industry for over 15 years, focusing on the software side of things for most of his career. With a degree in information science, specializing in multimedia, he has been involved in all facets of development, ranging from architecture and solution design to user experience and training. He is currently plying his trade as a technical solutions manager, where he manages development teams on various projects in the Microsoft space. A family man and a musician at heart, he spends his free time with his wife and two kids and serves in the worship band at church.

About the reviewer

Alvin Ashcraft is a developer living near Philadelphia. He has spent his 23-year career building software with C#, Visual Studio, WPF, ASP.NET, and more. He has been awarded the Microsoft MVP title nine times. You can read his daily links for .NET developers on his blog, *Morning Dew*. He works as a principal software engineer for Allscripts, building healthcare software. He has previously been employed by software companies, including Oracle. He has reviewed other titles for Packt Publishing, such as *Mastering ASP.NET Core 2.0*, *Mastering Entity Framework Core 2.0*, and *Learning ASP.NET Core 2.0*.

I would like to thank wonderful wife, Stelene, and our three amazing daughters for their support. They were very understanding when I was reading and reviewing these chapters on evenings and weekends to help deliver a useful, high-quality book for .NET developers.

Packt is searching for authors like you

If you're interested in becoming an author for Packt, please visit `authors.packtpub.com` and apply today. We have worked with thousands of developers and tech professionals, just like you, to help them share their insight with the global tech community. You can make a general application, apply for a specific hot topic that we are recruiting an author for, or submit your own idea.

Table of Contents

Preface

.NET Core is a general-purpose, modular, cross-platform, and open source implementation of .NET. The latest release of .NET Core 3 comes with improved performance along with support for desktop applications. .NET Core 3 should not only entice new developers to start learning the framework but also convince legacy developers to start migrating their apps.

This book is the second edition of *C# 7 and .NET Core 2.0 Blueprints*, updated with the latest features and enhancements of C# 8 and .NET Core 3.0. This book is a comprehensive guide delivering 10 real-world enterprise applications. It will help you learn and implement the concepts simultaneously and advance by building effective applications on ASP.NET Core and Azure that meet modern software requirements.

We'll work with relational data using Entity Framework Core 3 and use ASP.NET Core to create a real-world web application. We'll see how readers can upgrade their old WinForms app to the latest version of .NET Core. We'll also create a real-time chat application with SignalR. Finally, we'll learn about serverless computing with Azure Storage and how to build a load-balanced order processing microservice using Docker and Kubernetes.

To sum it up, this book will teach you the core concepts of web applications, serverless computing, and microservices using various projects and applications. Following this step-by-step guide, you will be able to create an ASP.NET Core MVC application and build modern applications using cutting-edge services from Microsoft Azure.

Who this book is for

This book is for amateur developers/programmers as well as professionals who wish to build real-world projects and learn the new features of .NET Core 3. It would be also useful for developers working on legacy desktop software who wish to migrate to .NET Core 3. Basic knowledge of .NET Core and C# is assumed.

What this book covers

`Chapter 1`, *Ebook Manager and Catalogue App – .NET Core 3 on Windows Desktop*, introduces the key features of .NET Core 3 – the headline feature being support for desktop applications in .NET Core. You will create a WinForms application based on the previous version of this book and upgrade it to use .NET Core 3. Then we will introduce XAML Islands and create a new desktop control using UWP and add it to the existing WinForms application.

`Chapter 2`, *Task Bug Logging ASP.NET Core MVC App Using Cosmos DB*, focuses on creating an ASP.NET Core MVC application that allows the user to capture tasks and log issues. The application will allow you to view captured tasks and to action them.

`Chapter 3`, *ASP.NET Azure SignalR Chat Application*, creates a real-time chat application using ASP.NET SignalR. Real-time web functionality is the ability of server-side code to push content to connected clients as it happens in real time. Once created, we'll create an Azure App Service instance and host the application there.

`Chapter 4`, *Web Research Tool with Entity Framework Core*, introduces you to Entity Framework Core and shows you how to create an ASP.NET Core MVC application that can be used to save links and social media posts for research purposes. Many such applications exist, such as Instapaper and Evernote. This application, however, will show you how to roll your own and add specific functionality.

`Chapter 5`, *Building a Twitter Automated Campaign Manager Using Azure Logic Apps and Functions*, investigates Logic Apps from Azure. The chapter guides you through the creation of a logic application, integrating the application to Twitter, and allowing the user to enter data into a spreadsheet, and have it automatically posted on Twitter.

`Chapter 6`, *Stock Checker Using Identity Server and OAuth 2*, illustrates the concept of authentication using the Identity Server OSS as a template. The chapter guides you through creating your own identity server and then logging into it from a UWP application.

`Chapter 7`, *Building a Photo Storage App Using a Windows Service and Azure Storage*, illustrates the concept of serverless computing. You will create an application that will back up photos on a user's PC to Azure Storage. There are many backup services available to users these days. Azure Blob storage is but one such service that allows developers to create applications that utilize Microsoft's servers to store files.

`Chapter 8`, *A Load-Balanced Order Processing Microservice Using Docker and Azure Kubernetes Service*, starts by covering the concept of microservices with an explanation of what they are and why you would use them. In this chapter, we'll introduce the concept of distributed systems. We'll build a microservice, configure a Kubernetes cluster on Azure Kubernetes, and use storage queues to interface with our microservice.

`Chapter 9`, *Emotion Detector Mobile App Using Xamarin Forms and Azure Cognitive Services*, creates a mobile application using Xamarin.Forms. In this chapter, we'll integrate with Azure Cognitive Services and the camera on the device, allowing the user to take a picture of a face, and have Azure come back with a rating of that person's emotions. We'll then display on the screen what we think that person is feeling. We'll cross-compile this to Android.

`Chapter 10`, *Eliza for the 21st Century – UWP and MS Bot Framework*, sets up a new UWP application using .NET Core 3. This will be a simple chat application but will interface with LUIS and an MS chat bot intended to pass the Turing test.

`Appendix A`, *WebAssembly*, covers WebAssembly, which has recently been integrated into all the main browsers, and allows code to be compiled down to WASM (a sort of IL for the browser). Microsoft has recently released a preview of something called Blazor, allowing Razor syntax to run in place of JavaScript.

To get the most out of this book

These are the prerequisites that you need to be equipped with in order to follow the instructions given in this book:

- Azure subscription
- Visual Studio
- Copy of Excel/Office Online
- OneDrive account
- Twitter
- Postman

Download the example code files

You can download the example code files for this book from your account at `www.packt.com`. If you purchased this book elsewhere, you can visit `www.packt.com/support` and register to have the files emailed directly to you.

You can download the code files by following these steps:

1. Log in or register at `www.packt.com`.
2. Select the **SUPPORT** tab.
3. Click on **Code Downloads & Errata**.
4. Enter the name of the book in the **Search** box and follow the onscreen instructions.

Once the file is downloaded, please make sure that you unzip or extract the folder using the latest version of:

- WinRAR/7-Zip for Windows
- Zipeg/iZip/UnRarX for Mac
- 7-Zip/PeaZip for Linux

The code bundle for the book is also hosted on GitHub at `https://github.com/PacktPublishing/C-8-and-.NET-Core-3-Projects-Using-Azure-Second-Edition`. In case there's an update to the code, it will be updated on the existing GitHub repository.

We also have other code bundles from our rich catalog of books and videos available at `https://github.com/PacktPublishing/`. Check them out!

Download the color images

We also provide a PDF file that has color images of the screenshots/diagrams used in this book. You can download it here: `https://static.packt-cdn.com/downloads/9781789612080_ColorImages.pdf`.

Conventions used

There are a number of text conventions used throughout this book.

`CodeInText`: Indicates code words in text, database table names, folder names, filenames, file extensions, pathnames, dummy URLs, user input, and Twitter handles. Here is an example: "Open the `Document.cs` file and add the following code to the class."

A block of code is set as follows:

```
public class Document
{
  public string Title { get; set; }
  public string FileName { get; set; }
  public string Extension { get; set; }
  public DateTime LastAccessed { get; set; }
  public DateTime Created { get; set; }
  public string FilePath { get; set; }
  public string FileSize { get; set; }
}
```

When we wish to draw your attention to a particular part of a code block, the relevant lines or items are set in bold:

```
public class Document
{
  public string Title { get; set; }
  public string FileName { get; set; }
  public string Extension { get; set; }
  public DateTime LastAccessed { get; set; }
  public DateTime Created { get; set; }
  public string FilePath { get; set; }
  public string FileSize { get; set; }
}
```

Bold: Indicates a new term, an important word, or words that you see onscreen. For example, words in menus or dialog boxes appear in the text like this. Here is an example: "There are other options that the **Nullable** option can be configured for."

Warnings or important notes appear like this.

Tips and tricks appear like this.

Get in touch

Feedback from our readers is always welcome.

General feedback: If you have questions about any aspect of this book, mention the book title in the subject of your message and email us at `customercare@packtpub.com`.

Errata: Although we have taken every care to ensure the accuracy of our content, mistakes do happen. If you have found a mistake in this book, we would be grateful if you would report this to us. Please visit `www.packt.com/submit-errata`, selecting your book, clicking on the Errata Submission Form link, and entering the details.

Piracy: If you come across any illegal copies of our works in any form on the Internet, we would be grateful if you would provide us with the location address or website name. Please contact us at `copyright@packt.com` with a link to the material.

If you are interested in becoming an author: If there is a topic that you have expertise in and you are interested in either writing or contributing to a book, please visit `authors.packtpub.com`.

Reviews

Please leave a review. Once you have read and used this book, why not leave a review on the site that you purchased it from? Potential readers can then see and use your unbiased opinion to make purchase decisions, we at Packt can understand what you think about our products, and our authors can see your feedback on their book. Thank you!

For more information about Packt, please visit `packt.com`.

1

Ebook Manager and Catalogue App - .NET Core for Desktop

.NET Core 3 marks a significant release in the reboot of .NET. Now that the fundamental framework is in place, Microsoft has been able to look at technologies that, while no longer en vogue, are running on millions of machines around the world.

WinForms and WPF have been victims of their own success: Microsoft simply dare not change the framework around them and risk breaking applications that may have been running successfully for several years.

C# 8 has a similar theme in that it introduces features such as nullable reference types, and interface implementations that are designed to improve legacy code bases.

> A legacy code base is any code that has already been written, whether that was 10 years or 10 minutes ago!

In this, the first chapter, we'll create the Ebook Manager application. Following this, we'll pick up our Ebook Manager built with .NET Core 2 and migrate it over to .NET Core 3.

In .NET Core 2, a number of significant performance enhancements were made, and so there is a real drive to upgrade existing WinForms apps to .NET Core 3. Microsoft has boasted that .NET Core 2.1 had over 30% performance boost for Bing.

The topics that we'll cover are as follows:

- Creating a new WinForms application in .NET Core 3.0
- Migrating an existing WinForms application to .NET Core 3.0
- Nullable reference types
- XAML Islands, and how they can be used to add functionality to existing WinForms applications
- Tree shaking and compilation

Technical requirements

To follow along with the first part of the chapter, you'll need the WinForms designer. At the time of writing, this is in pre-release and can be downloaded from `https://aka.ms/winforms-designer`.

For the XAML Islands section, you will need to be running Windows 10 1903 or later. By the time this book is published, it is expected that the 1903 release will have been delivered automatically to all Windows 10 machines; however, if you are running an earlier version, then you can force an update by visiting the following link: `https://www.microsoft.com/en-us/software-download/windows10`.

TIP

At the time of writing, this WinForms designer was nowhere near ready for production. Try it out while following the chapter; however, if you find that it is too glitchy, feel free to copy the designer code from the GitHub project.

Creating a new WinForms application

Let's start by creating a new .NET Core 3.0 WinForms application and later we'll also see how to upgrade an old .NET Core WinForms app to 3.0, so that we can show both ways of achieving this.

> To follow this section, you'll need to install the WinForms designer described in the *Technical requirements* section. It's worth pointing out that this tool is in preview at the time of writing and therefore has a number of limitations, so the instructions have changed in order to cater to those limitations.

Using Visual Studio 2019, we will create a simple **Windows Forms App** template project. You can call the application anything you like, but I called mine `eBookManager`:

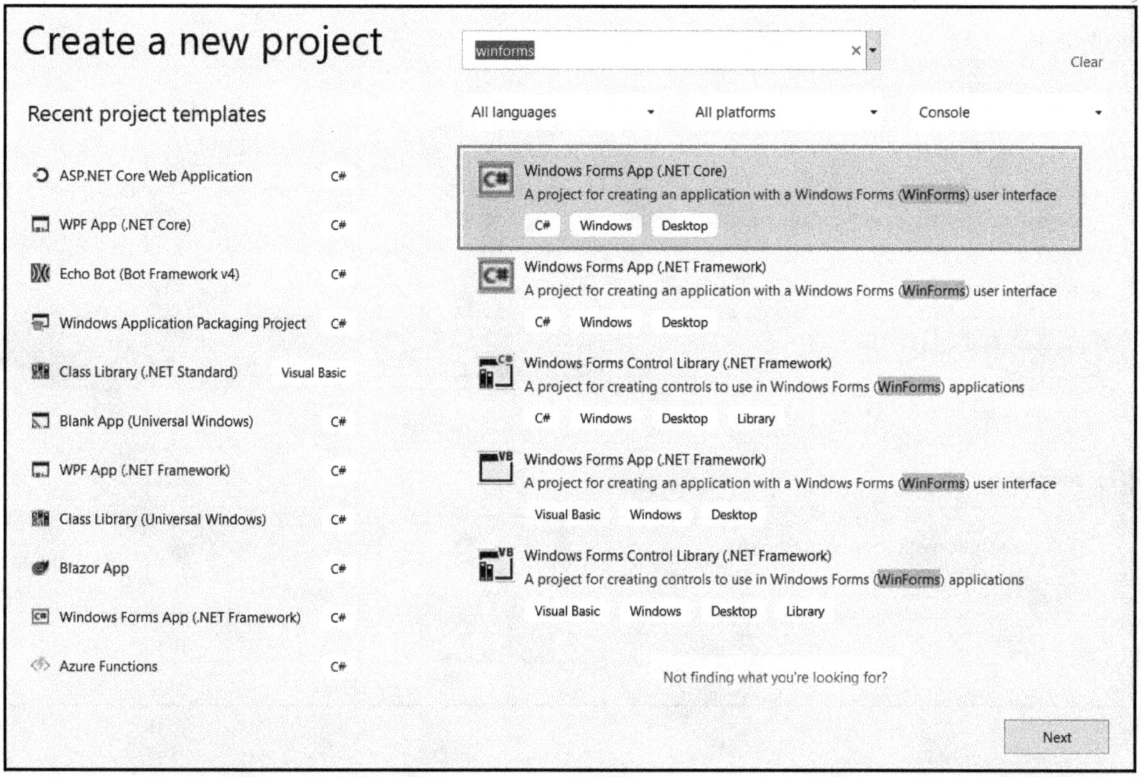

The process of creating a new project has changed slightly in Visual Studio 2019, and you are required to select the type of application, followed by where to create it:

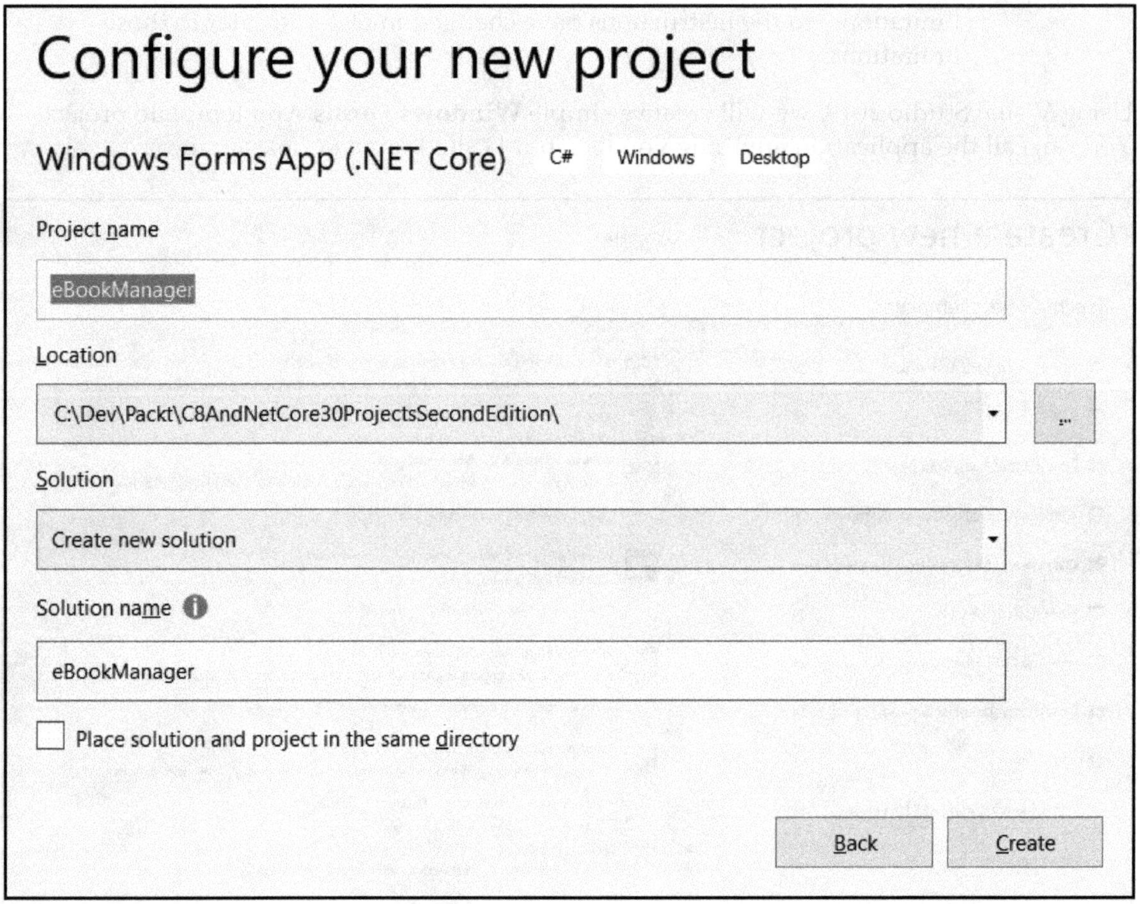

The project will be created and will look as follows:

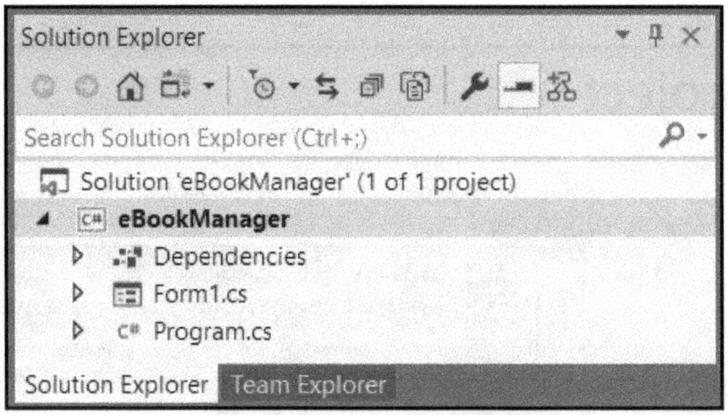

TIP

Since this is .NET Core, you can do all of this from the command line. In PowerShell, running the following command will create an identical project: `dotnet new winforms -n eBookManager`.

Our solution needs a class library project to contain the classes that drive the `eBookManager` application. In .NET Core 3.0, we have the option of creating either a .NET Core class library or a .NET Standard class library.

.NET Standard is a bit of a strange concept. In and of itself, it is not a technology, but a contract; creating a .NET Standard class library simply prevents you from using anything that is .NET Core—(or framework—) specific, and does not adhere to .NET Standard. The following document illustrates the .NET Standard versions, and what releases of Core and Framework support them: `https://github.com/dotnet/standard/blob/master/docs/versions.md`.

Add a new **Class Library (.NET Standard)** project to your solution and call it `eBookManager.Engine`:

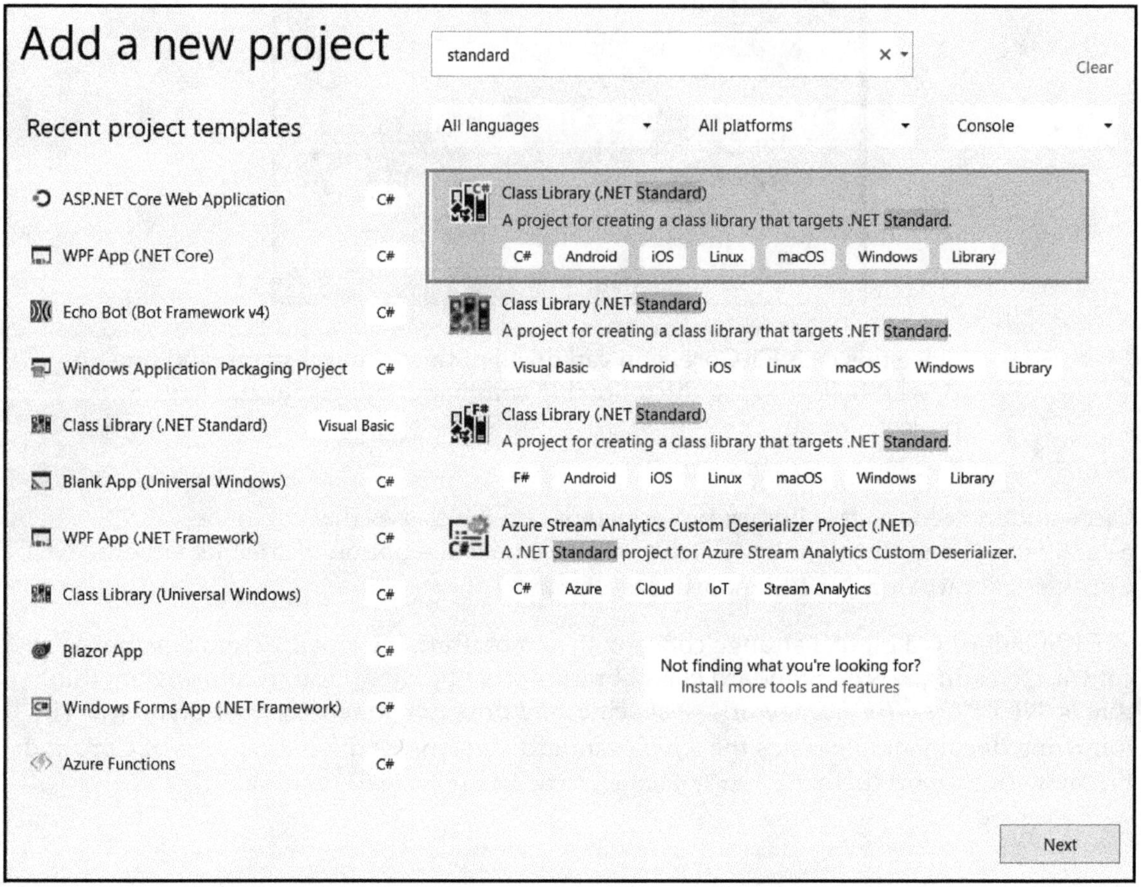

A class library project is added to the solution with the default class name. Change this class to `Document`:

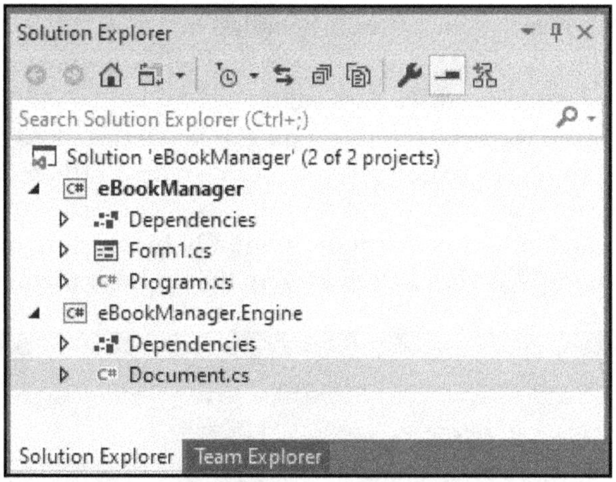

The `Document` class will represent a single eBook. When thinking of a book, we can have multiple properties representing a single book, but that would be representative of all books. An example of this would be the author. All books must have an author; otherwise, they would not exist.

The properties I have added to the class are merely my interpretation of what might represent a book. Feel free to add additional code to make this your own. Open the `Document.cs` file and add the following code to the class:

```
public class Document
{
    public string Title { get; set; }
    public string FileName { get; set; }
    public string Extension { get; set; }
    public DateTime LastAccessed { get; set; }
    public DateTime Created { get; set; }
    public string FilePath { get; set; }
    public string FileSize { get; set; }
    public string ISBN { get; set; }
    public string Price { get; set; }
    public string Publisher { get; set; }
    public string Author { get; set; }
    public DateTime PublishDate { get; set; }
    public DeweyDecimal Classification { get; set; }
    public string Category { get; set; }
}
```

You will notice that I have included a property called `Classification` of type `DeweyDecimal`. We have not added this class yet and will do so next. To the `eBookManager.Engine` project, add a class called `DeweyDecimal`. If you don't want to go to this level of classification for your eBooks, you can leave this class out. I have included it for the sake of completeness. We're going to introduce a neat little feature that's been in Visual Studio for some time: if you hover over the `DeweyDecimal` text, you'll see a lightbulb appear (you can bring this menu up manually by holding the Ctrl key and the dot key (*Ctrl* + .). I will be using this shortcut profusely throughout the rest of the book!):

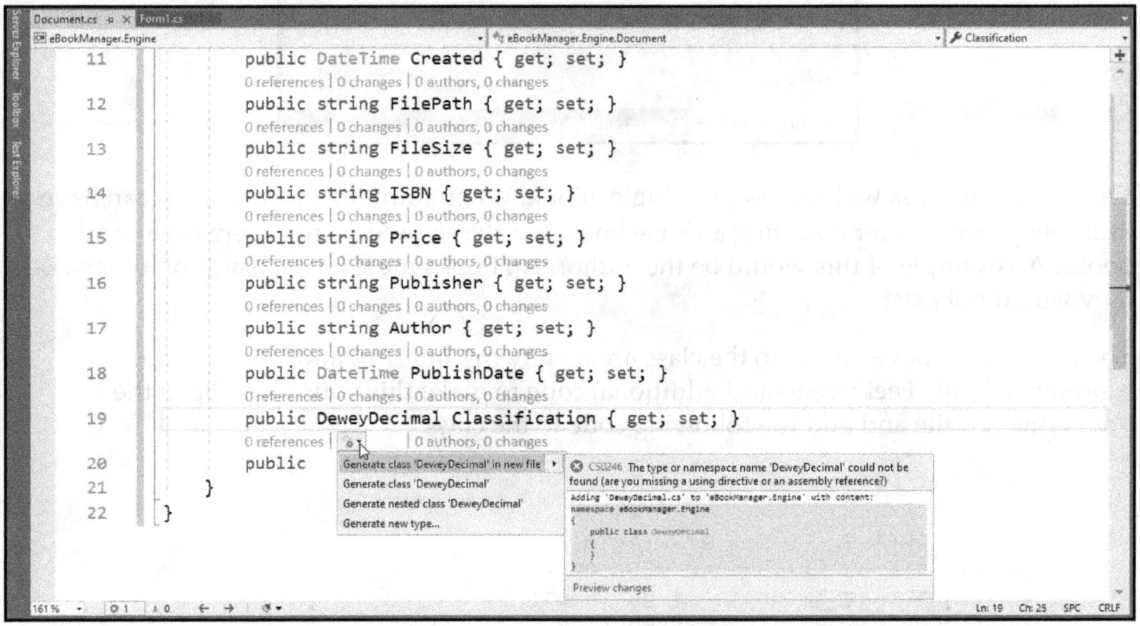

This allows us to create a new class with a couple of keystrokes. It also means that the name of the class will match the class name in the calling code.

> **TIP:** You can use the lightbulb menu to create methods, add using statements, and even import NuGet libraries!

The `DeweyDecimal` system is quite big. For this reason, I have not catered for every book classification available. I have also assumed that you only want to be working with programming eBooks. In reality, however, you may want to add other classifications, such as literature, the sciences, the arts, and so on. It is up to you:

1. Open up the `DeweyDecimal` class and add the following code to the class:

```
public class DeweyDecimal
{
    public string ComputerScience { get; set; } = "000";
    public string DataProcessing { get; set; } = "004";
    public string ComputerProgramming { get; set; } = "005";
}
```

Word nerds may disagree with me here, but I would like to remind them that I'm a code nerd. The classifications represented here are just so that I can catalog programming- and computer science-related eBooks. As mentioned earlier, you can change this to suit your needs.

2. We now need to add in the heart of the `eBookManager.Engine` solution. This is a class called `DocumentEngine` and will contain the methods you need in order to work with the documents:

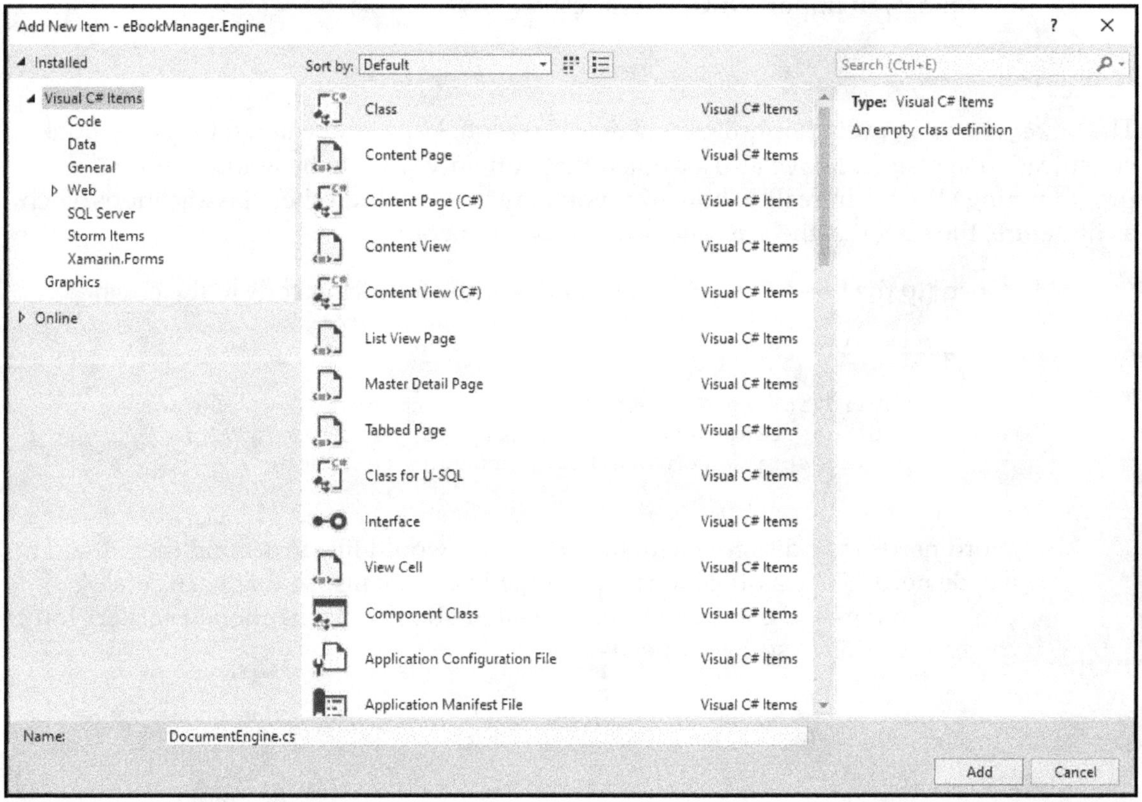

Your `eBookManager.Engine` solution will now contain the following classes:

- `DeweyDecimal`
- `Document`
- `DocumentEngine`

3. We now need to add a reference to `eBookManager.Engine` from the `eBookManager` project:

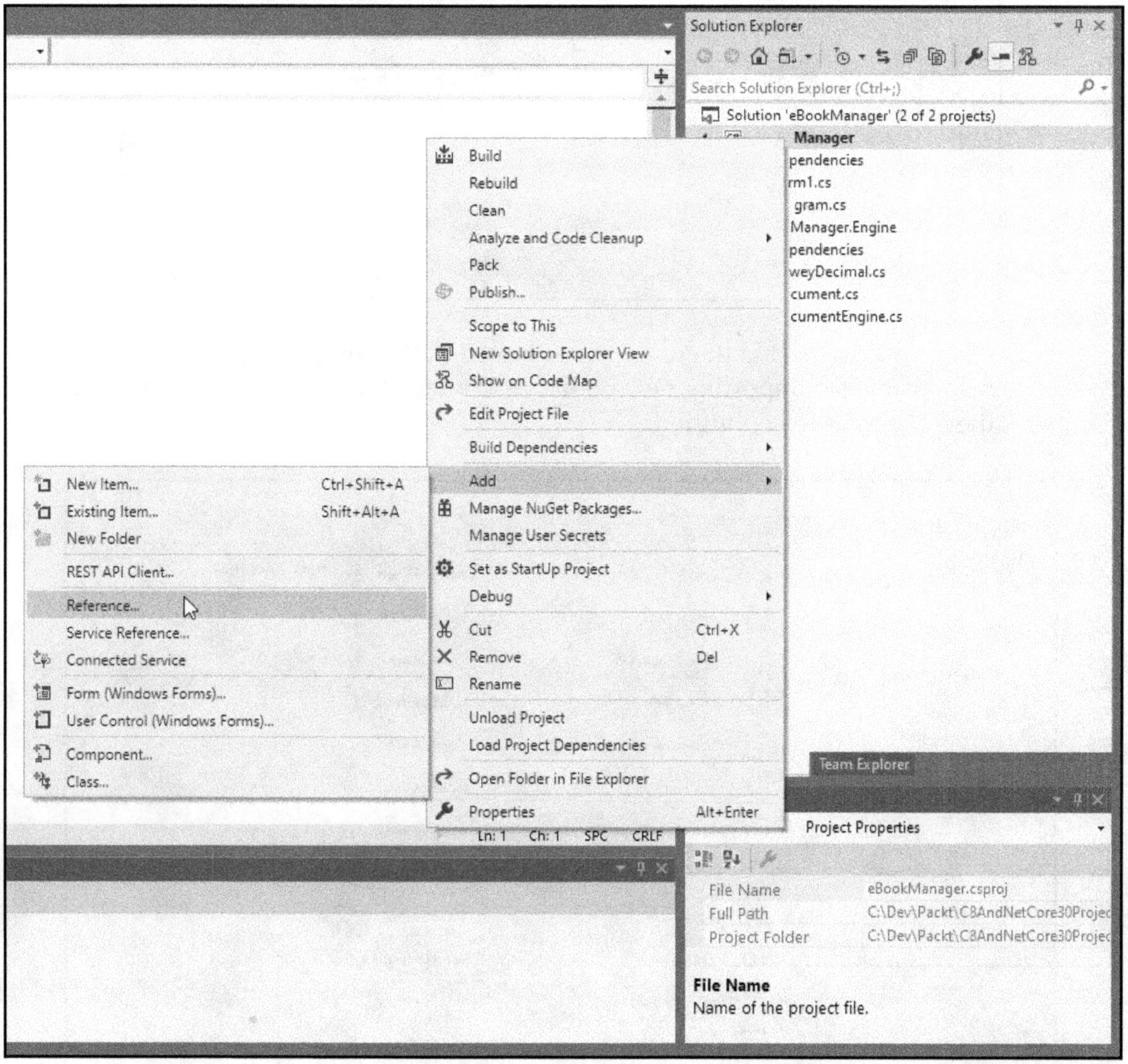

The `eBookManager.Engine` project will be available in the **Projects** section in the **Reference Manager** screen:

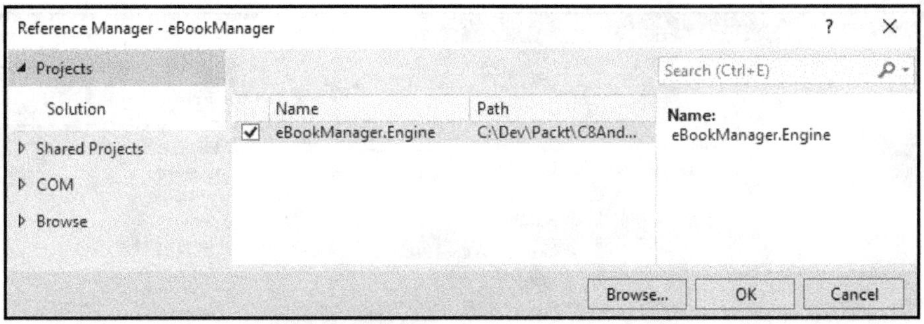

4. Once we have added the reference, we need a Windows Form that will be responsible for importing new books. Add a new form called `ImportBooks` to the `eBookManager` solution:

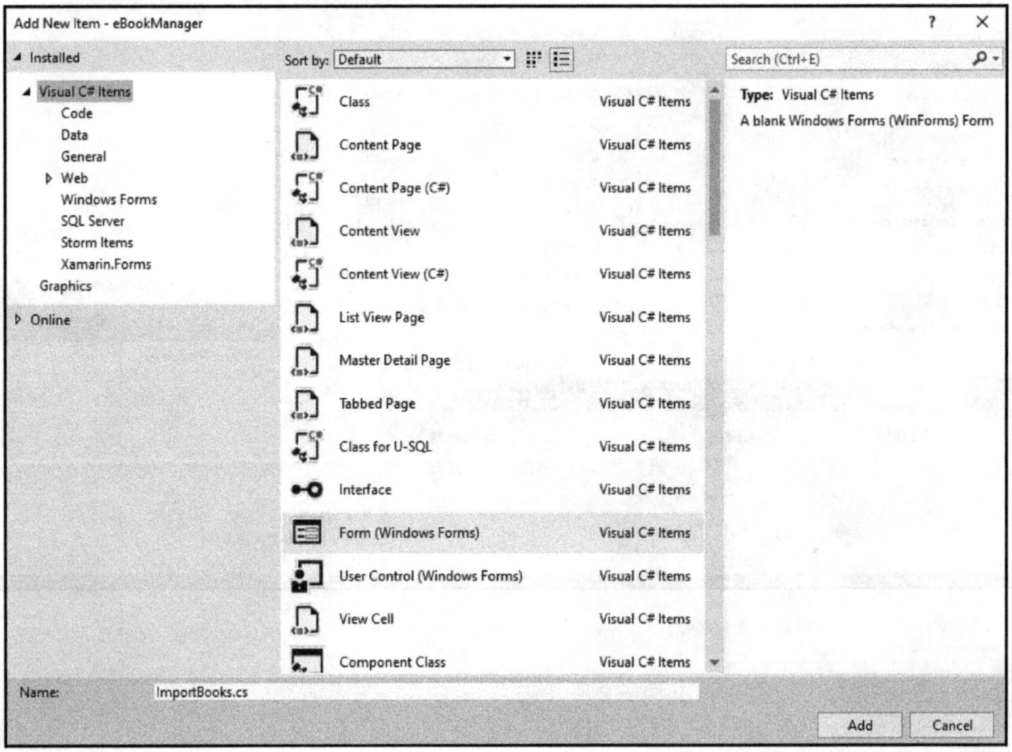

5. We'll create a separate project for extension methods. Add the `eBookManager.Helper` class library project (again, as a .NET Standard class library project):

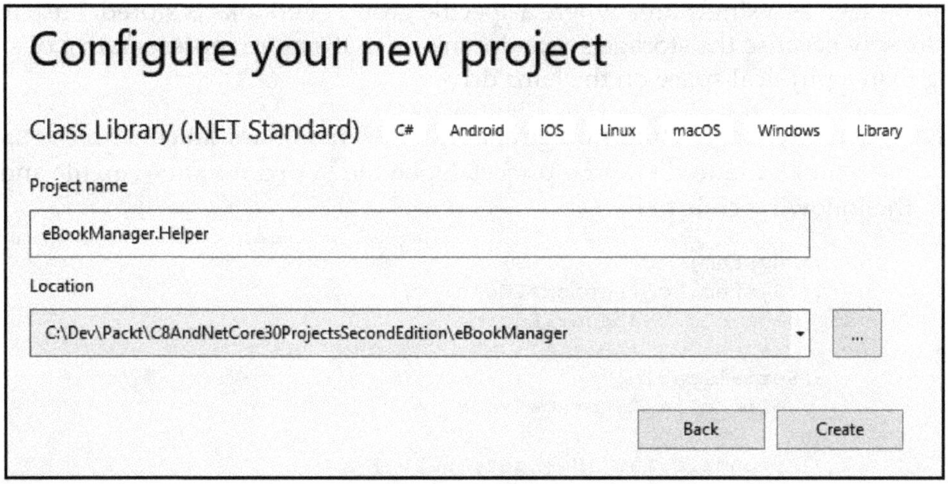

6. We'll reference that from our main project (as before):

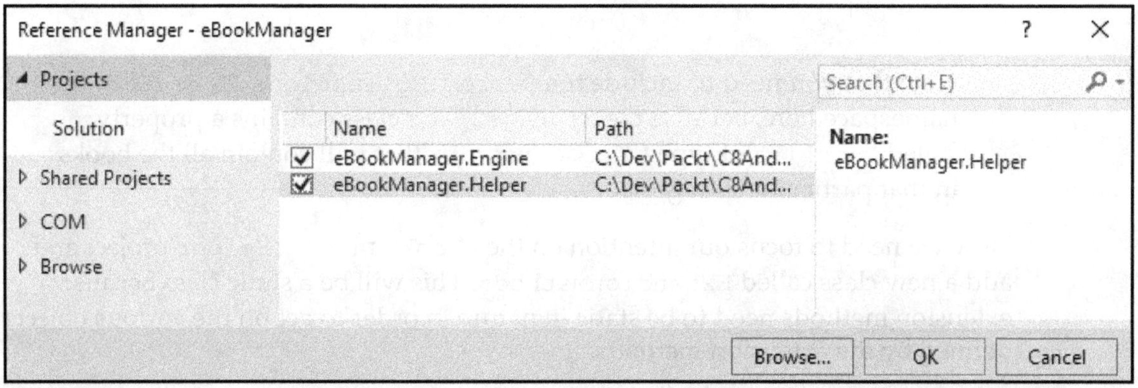

We've now set up the basics needed for our `eBookManager` application. Next, we will venture further into the guts of the application by writing some code.

Virtual storage spaces and extension methods

Let's start by discussing the logic behind virtual storage space. This is a single virtual representation of several physical spaces on your hard drive (or hard drives). A storage space will be seen as a single area where a specific group of eBooks is stored. I use the term "stored" loosely because the storage space doesn't exist. It's more representative of a grouping than a physical space on the hard drive:

1. To start creating virtual storage spaces, add a new class called `StorageSpace` to the `eBookManager.Engine` project. Open the `StorageSpace.cs` file and add the following code to it:

```
using System;
using System.Collections.Generic;
namespace eBookManager.Engine
{
    [Serializable]
    public class StorageSpace
    {
        public int ID { get; set; }
        public string Name { get; set; }
        public string Description { get; set; }
        public List<Document> BookList { get; set; }
    }
}
```

> Note that you need to include the `System.Collections.Generic` namespace here, because the `StorageSpace` class contains a property called `BookList` of type `List<Document>` that will contain all the books in that particular storage space.

Now we need to focus our attention on the `eBookManager.Helper` project and add a new class called `ExtensionMethods`. This will be a static class because extension methods need to be static in nature in order to act on the various objects defined by the extension methods.

2. The new `ExtensionMethods` class will initially look as follows:

```
public static class ExtensionMethods
{
}
```

Let's add the first extension method to the class called `ToInt()`. What this extension method does is take a string value and try to parse it to an integer value. I am too lazy to type `Convert.ToInt32(stringVariable)` whenever I need to convert a string to an integer. It is for this reason that I use an extension method.

3. Add the following static method to the `ExtensionMethods` class:

```
public static int ToInt(this string value, int defaultInteger = 0)
{
    try
    {
        if (int.TryParse(value, out int validInteger))
        {
            // Out variables
            return validInteger;
        }
        else
        {
            return defaultInteger;
        }
    }
    catch
    {
        return defaultInteger;
    }
}
```

The `ToInt()` extension method acts only on strings. This is defined by `this string value` in the method signature, where `value` is the variable name that will contain the string you are trying to convert to an integer. It also has a default parameter called `defaultInteger`, which is set to `0`. Unless the developer calling the extension method wants to return a default integer value of `0`, they can pass a different integer to this extension method (`-1`, for example).

The other methods of the `ExtensionMethods` class are used to provide the following logic:

- Read and write to the data source
- Check whether a storage space exists
- Convert bytes to megabytes
- Convert a string to an integer (as discussed previously)

The `ToMegabytes` method is quite easy. To avoid having to write this calculation all over the place, defining it inside an extension method makes sense:

```
public static double ToMegabytes(this long bytes) =>
    (bytes > 0) ? (bytes / 1024f) / 1024f : bytes;
```

We also need a way to check whether a particular storage space already exists.

> TIP: Be sure to add a project reference to `eBookManager.Engine` from the `eBookManager.Helper` project.

What this extension method also does is return the next storage space ID to the calling code. If the storage space does not exist, the returned ID will be the next ID that can be used when creating a new storage space:

```
public static bool StorageSpaceExists(this List<StorageSpace> space, string
nameValueToCheck, out int storageSpaceId)
{
    bool exists = false;
    storageSpaceId = 0;
    if (space.Count() != 0)
    {
        int count = (from r in space
                     where r.Name.Equals(nameValueToCheck)
                     select r)
            .Count();
        if (count > 0) exists = true;
        storageSpaceId = (from r in space
                          select r.ID).Max() + 1;
    }
    return exists;
}
```

> TIP: If you're pasting this code in, remember the *Ctrl* + . tip from earlier. Wherever you see code that is not recognized, simply place the cursor there and press *Ctrl* + ., or click the lightbulb, and it should bring in the necessary references.

We also need to create a method that will write the data we have to a file after converting it to JSON:

```
public async static Task WriteToDataStore(this List<StorageSpace> value,
string storagePath, bool appendToExistingFile = false)
{
    using (FileStream fs = File.Create(storagePath))
```

```
        await JsonSerializer.SerializeAsync(fs, value);
    }
```

Essentially, all we're doing here is creating a stream and serializing the `StorageSpace` list into that stream.

> Note that we're using the new syntactical sugar here from C# 8, allowing us to add a `using` statement with an implicit scope (that is, until the end of the method).

You'll need to install `System.Text.Json` from the package manager console:

```
Install-Package System.Text.Json -ProjectName eBookManager.Helper
```

This allows you to use the new .NET Core 3 JSON serializer. Apart from being more succinct than its predecessor, or even third-party tools such as Json.NET, Microsoft claims that you'll see a speed improvement, as it makes use of the performance improvements introduced in .NET Core 2.x.

Lastly, we need to be able to read the data back again into a `List<StorageSpace>` object and return that to the calling code:

```
public async static Task<List<StorageSpace>> ReadFromDataStore(this
List<StorageSpace> value, string storagePath)
{
    if (!File.Exists(storagePath))
    {
        var newFile = File.Create(storagePath);
        newFile.Close();
    }

    using FileStream fs = File.OpenRead(storagePath);
    if (fs.Length == 0) return new List<StorageSpace>();

    var storageList = await
JsonSerializer.DeserializeAsync<List<StorageSpace>>(fs);

    return storageList;
}
```

The method will return an empty list, that is, a `<StorageSpace>` object, and nothing is contained in the file. The `ExtensionMethods` class can contain many more extension methods that you might use often. It is a great way to separate often-used code.

TIP

As with any other class, you should consider whether your extension method class is getting too large, or becoming a dumping ground for unrelated functionality, or functionality that may be better extracted into a self-contained class.

The DocumentEngine class

The purpose of this class is merely to provide supporting code to a document. In the `eBookManager` application, I am going to use a single method called `GetFileProperties()` that will (you guessed it) return the properties of a selected file. This class also only contains this single method. As the application is modified for your specific purposes, you can modify this class and add additional methods that are specific to documents.

Inside the `DocumentEngine` class, add the following code:

```
public (DateTime dateCreated, DateTime dateLastAccessed, string fileName,
string fileExtension, long fileLength, bool error) GetFileProperties(string
filePath)
{
    var returnTuple = (created: DateTime.MinValue,
    lastDateAccessed: DateTime.MinValue, name: "", ext: "",
    fileSize: 0L, error: false);
    try
    {
        FileInfo fi = new FileInfo(filePath);
        fi.Refresh();
        returnTuple = (fi.CreationTime, fi.LastAccessTime, fi.Name,
                       fi.Extension, fi.Length, false);
    }
    catch
    {
        returnTuple.error = true;
    }
    return returnTuple;
}
```

The `GetFileProperties()` method returns a tuple as `(DateTime dateCreated, DateTime dateLastAccessed, string fileName, string fileExtension, long fileLength, bool error)` and allows us to inspect the values returned from the calling code easily.

Before getting the properties of the specific file, the tuple is initialized by doing the following:

```
var returnTuple = (created: DateTime.MinValue, lastDateAccessed:
DateTime.MinValue, name: "", ext: "", fileSize: 0L, error: false);
```

If there is an exception, I can return default values. Reading the file properties is simple enough using the `FileInfo` class. I can then assign the file properties to the tuple by doing this:

```
returnTuple = (fi.CreationTime, fi.LastAccessTime, fi.Name, fi.Extension,
fi.Length, false);
```

The tuple is then returned to the calling code, where it will be used as required. We will have a look at the calling code next.

The ImportBooks form

The `ImportBooks` form does exactly what the name suggests. It allows us to create virtual storage spaces and to import books into those spaces. The form design is as follows:

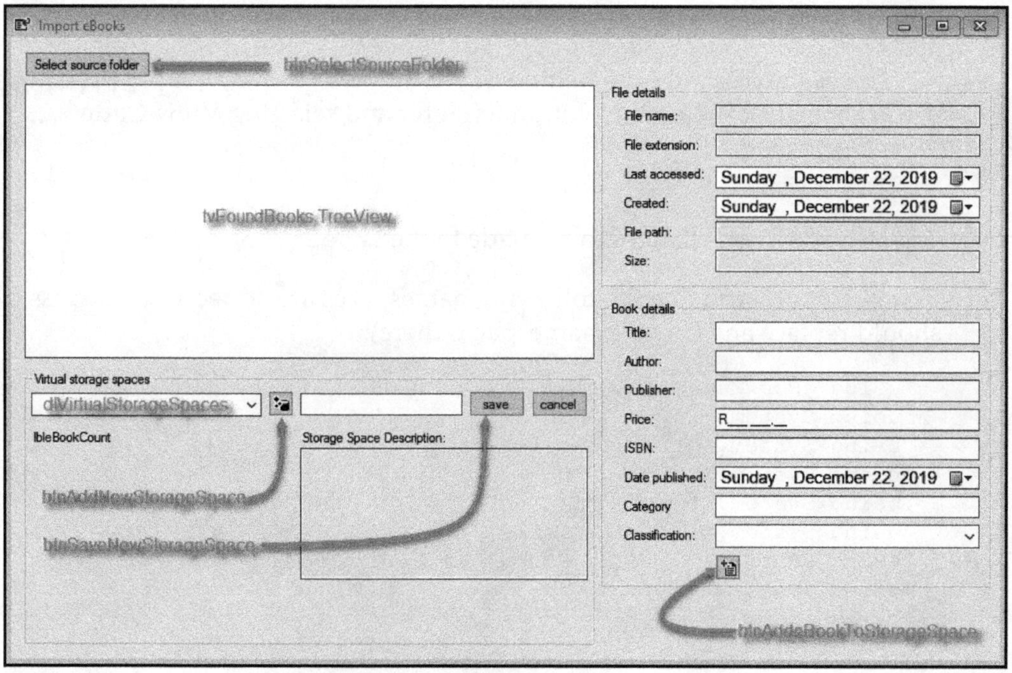

TreeView controls are prefixed with `tv`, buttons with `btn`, combo boxes with `dl`, textboxes with `txt`, and date time pickers with `dt`.

TIP

Although this kind of prefixing isn't widely used today, this used to be a common practice for WinForms developers. The reason behind it is that WinForms never really lent itself very well to a separation of business and presentation layers (there have been attempts to rectify this, notably with the MVP pattern), meaning that referencing controls directly from code-behind was a common practice and, as such, it made sense to indicate the type of control you were dealing with.

When this form loads, if any storage spaces have been defined then they will be listed in the `dlVirtualStorageSpaces` combo box. Clicking on the **Select source folder** button will allow us to select a source folder in which to look for eBooks.

If a storage space does not exist, we can add a new virtual storage space by clicking the `btnAddNewStorageSpace` button. This will allow us to add a name and description for the new storage space and click on the `btnSaveNewStorageSpace` button. Selecting an eBook from the `tvFoundBooks` TreeView will populate the **File details** group of controls to the right of the form. You can then add additional **Book details** and click on the `btnAddeBookToStorageSpace` button to add the book to our space.

TIP

You can access the code-behind of a Windows Form by simply pressing *F7*, or right-clicking in Solution Explorer and selecting **View Code**.

The following steps describe changes to be made to the `ImportBooks` code-behind:

1. You need to ensure that the following namespaces are added to your class (these should replace any existing namespaces there):

```
using eBookManager.Engine;
using System;
using System.Collections.Generic;
using System.IO;
using System.Linq;
using System.Windows.Forms;
using static eBookManager.Helper.ExtensionMethods;
using static System.Math;
```

2. Next, let's start at the most logical place: the `ImportBooks()` constructor and the class-level variables. Add the following declarations above the constructor:

```
private string _jsonPath;
private List<StorageSpace> _spaces;
private enum _storageSpaceSelection { New = -9999, NoSelection = -1
}
```

The usefulness of the enumerator will become evident later on in the code. The `_jsonPath` variable will contain the path to the file used to store our eBook information.

> **TIP:** Some people, including myself, like to prefix private class-level variables with an underscore (as in this example). This is a personal preference; however, there are settings in Visual Studio that will aid in the auto-generation of such variables if you tell it what your preference is.

3. Modify the constructor as follows:

```
public ImportBooks()
{
    InitializeComponent();
    _jsonPath = Path.Combine(Application.StartupPath,
"bookData.txt");
}
```

`_jsonPath` is initialized in the executing folder for the application and the file is hardcoded to `bookData.txt`. You could provide a settings screen to configure these settings if you chose to improve this project.

4. Because we want to load some data when the form loads, we'll attach the `Form_Load` event. An easy way to create an event handler in WinForms is to select the event in the form designer and simply double-click next to the event that you wish to handle:

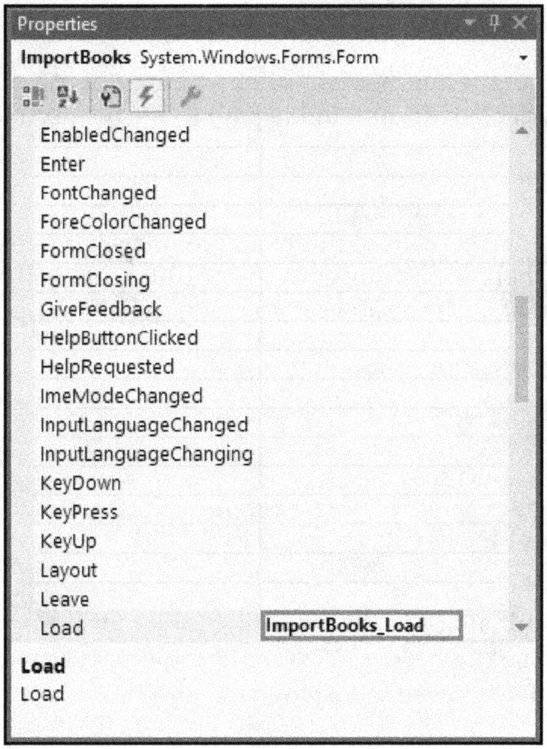

The new event should load the following code from the data store asynchronously:

```
private async void ImportBooks_Load(object sender, EventArgs e)
{
    _spaces = await _spaces.ReadFromDataStore(_jsonPath);
}
```

5. Next, we need to add another two enumerators that define the file extensions that we will be able to save in our application:

```
private HashSet<string> AllowedExtensions => new
HashSet<string>(StringComparer.InvariantCultureIgnoreCase)
{ ".doc", ".docx", ".pdf", ".epub", ".lit" };
```

```
        private enum Extension { doc = 0, docx = 1, pdf = 2, epub = 3, lit
        = 4 }
```

We can see the implementation of the `AllowedExtensions` property when we look at the `PopulateBookList()` method.

Populating the TreeView control

All that the `PopulateBookList()` method does is populate the `TreeView` control with files and folders found at the selected source location. Consider the following code in the `ImportBooks` code-behind:

```
public void PopulateBookList(string paramDir, TreeNode paramNode)
{
    DirectoryInfo dir = new DirectoryInfo(paramDir);
    foreach (DirectoryInfo dirInfo in dir.GetDirectories())
    {
        TreeNode node = new TreeNode(dirInfo.Name);
        node.ImageIndex = 4;
        node.SelectedImageIndex = 5;
        if (paramNode != null)
            paramNode.Nodes.Add(node);
        else
            tvFoundBooks.Nodes.Add(node);
        PopulateBookList(dirInfo.FullName, node);
    }
    foreach (FileInfo fleInfo in dir.GetFiles()
        .Where(x => AllowedExtensions.Contains(x.Extension)).ToList())
    {
        TreeNode node = new TreeNode(fleInfo.Name);
        node.Tag = fleInfo.FullName;
        int iconIndex = Enum.Parse(typeof(Extension),
        fleInfo.Extension.TrimStart('.'), true).GetHashCode();
        node.ImageIndex = iconIndex;
        node.SelectedImageIndex = iconIndex;
        if (paramNode != null)
            paramNode.Nodes.Add(node);
        else
            tvFoundBooks.Nodes.Add(node);
    }
}
```

The first place we need to call this method is obviously from within itself, as this is a recursive method. The second place we need to call it is from the `btnSelectSourceFolder` button click event (again, as before, select the click property and double-click):

```
private void btnSelectSourceFolder_Click(object sender, EventArgs e)
{
    try
    {
        FolderBrowserDialog fbd = new FolderBrowserDialog();
        fbd.Description = "Select the location of your eBooks and
documents";
        DialogResult dlgResult = fbd.ShowDialog();
        if (dlgResult == DialogResult.OK)
        {
            tvFoundBooks.Nodes.Clear();
            string path = fbd.SelectedPath;
            DirectoryInfo di = new DirectoryInfo(path);
            TreeNode root = new TreeNode(di.Name);
            root.ImageIndex = 4;
            root.SelectedImageIndex = 5;
            tvFoundBooks.Nodes.Add(root);
            PopulateBookList(di.FullName, root);
            tvFoundBooks.Sort();
            root.Expand();
        }
    }
    catch (Exception ex)
    {
        MessageBox.Show(ex.Message);
    }
}
```

This is all quite straightforward code. Select the folder to recurse and populate the *TreeView* control with all the files found that match the file extension contained in our `AllowedExtensions` property. We also need to look at the code when someone selects a book in the `tvFoundBooks TreeView` control. When a book is selected, we need to read the properties of the selected file and return those properties to the file details section:

```
private void tvFoundBooks_AfterSelect(object sender, TreeViewEventArgs e)
{
    DocumentEngine engine = new DocumentEngine();
    string path = e.Node.Tag?.ToString() ?? "";
    if (File.Exists(path))
    {
        var (dateCreated, dateLastAccessed, fileName, fileExtention,
fileLength, hasError) = engine.GetFileProperties(e.Node.Tag.ToString());
```

```
        if (!hasError)
        {
            txtFileName.Text = fileName;
            txtExtension.Text = fileExtention;
            dtCreated.Value = dateCreated;
            dtLastAccessed.Value = dateLastAccessed;
            txtFilePath.Text = e.Node.Tag.ToString();
            txtFileSize.Text = $"{Round(fileLength.ToMegabytes(),
2).ToString()} MB";
        }
    }
}
```

You will notice that it is here that we are calling the `GetFileProperties()` method on the `DocumentEngine` class that returns the tuple.

Populating the storage space list

The next stage is to populate our list of storage spaces:

```
private void PopulateStorageSpacesList()
{
    List<KeyValuePair<int, string>> lstSpaces =
        new List<KeyValuePair<int, string>>();
    BindStorageSpaceList((int)_storageSpaceSelection.NoSelection, "Select
Storage Space");

    void BindStorageSpaceList(int key, string value) =>
        lstSpaces.Add(new KeyValuePair<int, string>(key, value));

    if (_spaces is null || _spaces.Count() == 0) // Pattern matching
    {
        BindStorageSpaceList((int)_storageSpaceSelection.New, " <create
new> ");
    }
    else
    {
        foreach (var space in _spaces)
        {
            BindStorageSpaceList(space.ID, space.Name);
        }
    }
    dlVirtualStorageSpaces.DataSource = new
        BindingSource(lstSpaces, null);
    dlVirtualStorageSpaces.DisplayMember = "Value";
    dlVirtualStorageSpaces.ValueMember = "Key";
}
```

The `PopulateStorageSpacesList()` method is using a *local function,* essentially allowing us to declare a piece of functionality that is accessible *only* from within its parent.

Let's add the call to this new method to the `ImportBooks_Load` method:

```
private async void ImportBooks_Load(object sender, EventArgs e)
{
    _spaces = await _spaces.ReadFromDataStore(_jsonPath);
    PopulateStorageSpacesList();
    if (dlVirtualStorageSpaces.Items.Count == 0)
    {
        dlVirtualStorageSpaces.Items.Add("<create new storage space > ");
    }
    lblEbookCount.Text = "";
}
```

We now need to add the logic for changing the selected storage space. The `SelectedIndexChanged()` event of the `dlVirtualStorageSpaces` control is modified as follows:

```
private void dlVirtualStorageSpaces_SelectedIndexChanged(object sender,
EventArgs e)
{
    int selectedValue =
dlVirtualStorageSpaces.SelectedValue.ToString().ToInt();
    if (selectedValue == (int)_storageSpaceSelection.New) // -9999
    {
        txtNewStorageSpaceName.Visible = true;
        lblStorageSpaceDescription.Visible = true;
        txtStorageSpaceDescription.ReadOnly = false;
        btnSaveNewStorageSpace.Visible = true;
        btnCancelNewStorageSpaceSave.Visible = true;
        dlVirtualStorageSpaces.Enabled = false;
        btnAddNewStorageSpace.Enabled = false;
        lblEbookCount.Text = "";
    }
    else if (selectedValue != (int)_storageSpaceSelection.NoSelection)
    {
        // Find the contents of the selected storage space
        int contentCount = (from c in _spaces
            where c.ID == selectedValue
            select c).Count();
        if (contentCount > 0)
        {
            StorageSpace selectedSpace = (from c in _spaces
```

```
                where c.ID == selectedValue
                select c).First();
            txtStorageSpaceDescription.Text = selectedSpace.Description;
            List<Document> eBooks = (selectedSpace.BookList == null)
                ? new List<Document> { }
                : selectedSpace.BookList;
            lblEbookCount.Text = $"Storage Space contains { eBooks.Count()}
{(eBooks.Count() == 1 ? "eBook" : "eBooks")}";
        }
    }
    else
    {
        lblEbookCount.Text = "";
    }
}
```

I will not go into a detailed explanation of the code here as it is relatively obvious what it is doing.

We also need to add code to save a new storage space. Add the following code to the *Click* event of the `btnSaveNewStorageSpace` button:

```
private void btnSaveNewStorageSpace_Click(object sender, EventArgs e)
{
    try
    {
        if (txtNewStorageSpaceName.Text.Length != 0)
        {
            string newName = txtNewStorageSpaceName.Text;
            bool spaceExists =
                (!_spaces.StorageSpaceExists(newName, out int nextID))
                ? false
                : throw new Exception("The storage space you are trying to
add already exists.");
            if (!spaceExists)
            {
                StorageSpace newSpace = new StorageSpace();
                newSpace.Name = newName;
                newSpace.ID = nextID;
                newSpace.Description =
                txtStorageSpaceDescription.Text;
                _spaces.Add(newSpace);

                PopulateStorageSpacesList();
                // Save new Storage Space Name
                txtNewStorageSpaceName.Clear();
                txtNewStorageSpaceName.Visible = false;
                lblStorageSpaceDescription.Visible = false;
```

```
                    txtStorageSpaceDescription.ReadOnly = true;
                    txtStorageSpaceDescription.Clear();
                    btnSaveNewStorageSpace.Visible = false;
                    btnCancelNewStorageSpaceSave.Visible = false;
                    dlVirtualStorageSpaces.Enabled = true;
                    btnAddNewStorageSpace.Enabled = true;
                }
            }
        }
        catch (Exception ex)
        {
            txtNewStorageSpaceName.SelectAll();
            MessageBox.Show(ex.Message);
        }
    }
```

The last few methods deal with saving eBooks in the selected virtual storage space. Modify the *Click* event of the `btnAddBookToStorageSpace` button. This code also contains a throw expression. If you haven't selected a storage space from the combo box, a new exception is thrown:

```
    private async void btnAddeBookToStorageSpace_Click(object sender, EventArgs
    e)
    {
        try
        {
            int selectedStorageSpaceID =
                dlVirtualStorageSpaces.SelectedValue.ToString().ToInt();
            if ((selectedStorageSpaceID !=
    (int)_storageSpaceSelection.NoSelection)
                && (selectedStorageSpaceID != (int)_storageSpaceSelection.New))
            {
                await UpdateStorageSpaceBooks(selectedStorageSpaceID);
            }
            else throw new Exception("Please select a Storage Space to add your
    eBook to"); // throw expressions
        }
        catch (Exception ex)
        {
            MessageBox.Show(ex.Message);
        }
    }
```

If you enter this code, you'll notice that the `UpdateStorageSpaceBooks` method does not yet exist; let's rectify that.

Saving a selected book to a storage space

The following code basically updates the book list in the selected storage space if it already contains the specific book (after confirming this with the user). Otherwise, it will add the book to the book list as a new book:

```
private async Task UpdateStorageSpaceBooks(int storageSpaceId)
{
    try
    {
        int iCount = (from s in _spaces
                      where s.ID == storageSpaceId
                      select s).Count();
        if (iCount > 0) // The space will always exist
        {
            // Update
            StorageSpace existingSpace = (from s in _spaces
                                          where s.ID == storageSpaceId
                                          select s).First();
            List<Document> ebooks = existingSpace.BookList;
            int iBooksExist = (ebooks != null)
                ? (from b in ebooks
                   where
$"{b.FileName}".Equals($"{txtFileName.Text.Trim()}")
                   select b).Count()
                : 0;
            if (iBooksExist > 0)
            {
                DialogResult dlgResult = MessageBox.Show($"A book with the
same name has been found in Storage Space {existingSpace.Name}. Do you want
to replace the existing book entry with this one ?", "Duplicate Title",
                    MessageBoxButtons.YesNo,
                    MessageBoxIcon.Warning,
                    MessageBoxDefaultButton.Button2);
                if (dlgResult == DialogResult.Yes)
                {
                    Document existingBook = (from b in ebooks
                                             where $"{
b.FileName}".Equals($"{txtFileName.Text.Trim()}")
                                             select b).First();
                    SetBookFields(existingBook);
                }
            }
            else
            {
                // Insert new book
                Document newBook = new Document();
                SetBookFields(newBook);
```

```
                if (ebooks == null)
                    ebooks = new List<Document>();
                ebooks.Add(newBook);
                existingSpace.BookList = ebooks;
            }
        }
        await _spaces.WriteToDataStore(_jsonPath);
        PopulateStorageSpacesList();
        MessageBox.Show("Book added");
    }
    catch (Exception ex)
    {
        MessageBox.Show(ex.Message);
    }
}
```

We call a helper method in the preceding method, called `SetBookFields`:

```
private void SetBookFields(Document book)
{
    book.FileName = txtFileName.Text;
    book.Extension = txtExtension.Text;
    book.LastAccessed = dtLastAccessed.Value;
    book.Created = dtCreated.Value;
    book.FilePath = txtFilePath.Text;
    book.FileSize = txtFileSize.Text;
    book.Title = txtTitle.Text;
    book.Author = txtAuthor.Text;
    book.Publisher = txtPublisher.Text;
    book.Price = txtPrice.Text;
    book.ISBN = txtISBN.Text;
    book.PublishDate = dtDatePublished.Value;
    book.Category = txtCategory.Text;
}
```

Lastly, as a matter of housekeeping, the ImportBooks form contains the following code for displaying and enabling controls based on the button click events of the `btnCancelNewStorageSpace` and `btnAddNewStorageSpace` buttons:

```
private void btnCancelNewStorageSpaceSave_Click(object sender, EventArgs e)
{
    txtNewStorageSpaceName.Clear();
    txtNewStorageSpaceName.Visible = false;
    lblStorageSpaceDescription.Visible = false;
    txtStorageSpaceDescription.ReadOnly = true;
    txtStorageSpaceDescription.Clear();
    btnSaveNewStorageSpace.Visible = false;
    btnCancelNewStorageSpaceSave.Visible = false;
```

```
        dlVirtualStorageSpaces.Enabled = true;
        btnAddNewStorageSpace.Enabled = true;
    }

    private void btnAddNewStorageSpace_Click(object sender, EventArgs e)
    {
        txtNewStorageSpaceName.Visible = true;
        lblStorageSpaceDescription.Visible = true;
        txtStorageSpaceDescription.ReadOnly = false;
        btnSaveNewStorageSpace.Visible = true;
        btnCancelNewStorageSpaceSave.Visible = true;
        dlVirtualStorageSpaces.Enabled = false;
        btnAddNewStorageSpace.Enabled = false;
    }
```

All that remains now is for us to complete the code in the `Form1.cs` form, which is the startup form.

Creating the main eBookManager form

Start off by renaming `Form1.cs` to `eBookManager.cs`. This is the startup form for the application, and it will list all existing storage spaces that were previously saved:

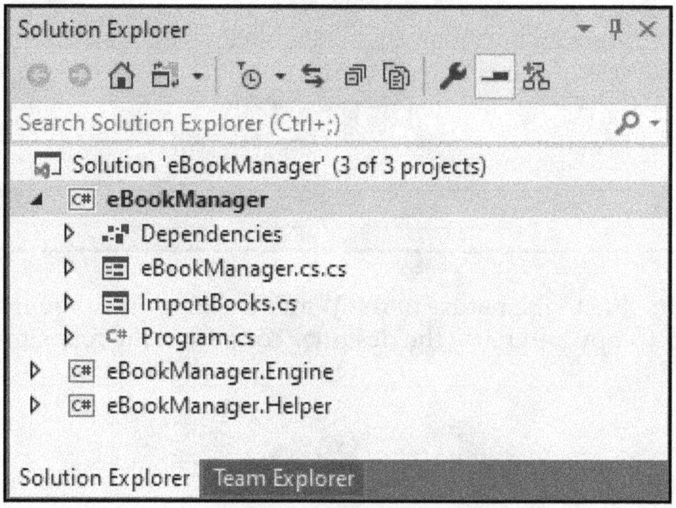

Design your `eBookManager` form as follows:

- A ListView control for existing storage spaces
- A ListView for eBooks contained in the selected storage space
- A button that opens the file location of the eBook
- A menu control to navigate to the ImportBooks.cs form
- Various read-only fields to display the selected eBook information:

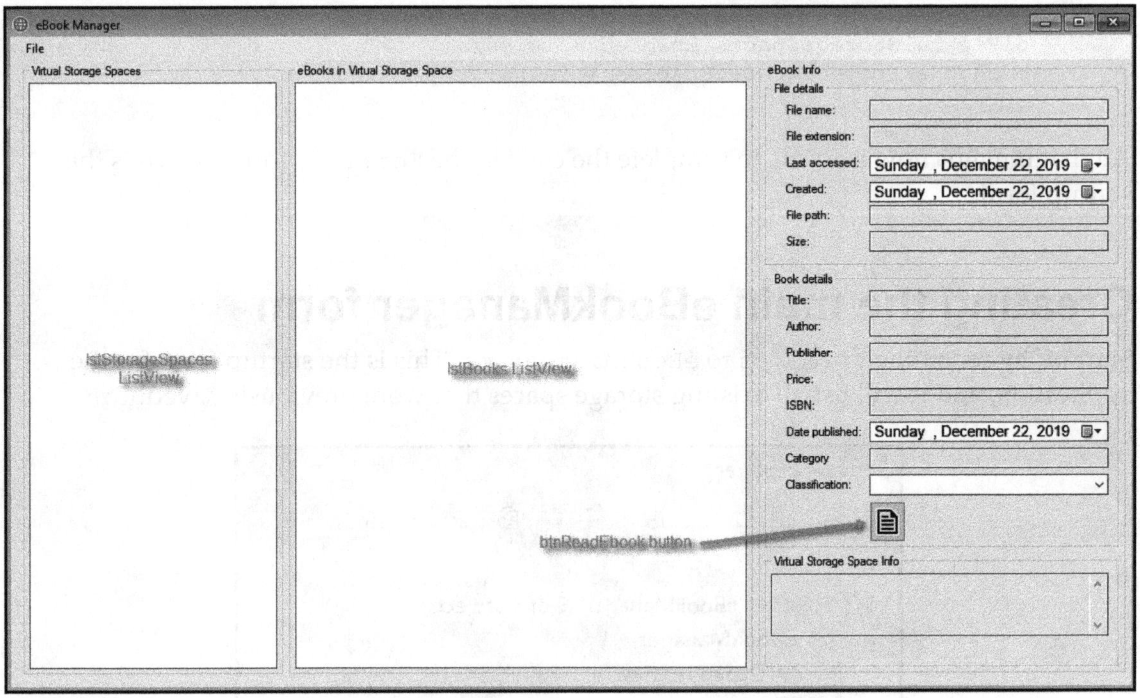

Again, due to the nature of the WinForms designer, you may choose to simply copy and paste the designer code from the repository.

The following `using` statements will be needed in this section:

```
using eBookManager.Engine;
using eBookManager.Helper;
using System;
using System.Collections.Generic;
using System.IO;
```

```
using System.Windows.Forms;
using System.Linq;
using System.Diagnostics;
```

> **TIP**
>
> As demonstrated earlier, you may choose to omit this and then press *Ctrl* + . each time a particular method or namespace isn't recognized.
>
> Bear in mind that you won't be able to use this to include libraries with extension methods, so you'll need to include `eBookManager.Helper` manually.

Let's now start designing our `eBookManager` form with the help of the following steps:

1. The constructor and load methods are quite similar to those in the `ImportBooks.cs` form. They read any available storage spaces and populate the storage spaces list view control with the previously saved storage spaces:

```
private string _jsonPath;
private List<StorageSpace> _spaces;

public eBookManager()
{
    InitializeComponent();
    _jsonPath = Path.Combine(Application.StartupPath,
        "bookData.txt");
}

private async void eBookManager_Load(object sender, EventArgs e)
{
    _spaces = await _spaces.ReadFromDataStore(_jsonPath);

    // imageList1
    this.imageList1.Images.Add("storage_space_cloud.png",
Image.FromFile("img/storage_space_cloud.png"));
    this.imageList1.Images.Add("eBook.png",
Image.FromFile("img/eBook.png"));
    this.imageList1.Images.Add("no_eBook.png",
Image.FromFile("img/no_eBook.png"));
    this.imageList1.TransparentColor =
System.Drawing.Color.Transparent;

    // btnReadEbook
    this.btnReadEbook.Image = Image.FromFile("img/ReadEbook.png");
    this.btnReadEbook.Location = new System.Drawing.Point(103,
227);
    this.btnReadEbook.Name = "btnReadEbook";
```

```
        this.btnReadEbook.Size = new System.Drawing.Size(36, 40);
        this.btnReadEbook.TabIndex = 32;
        this.toolTip1.SetToolTip(this.btnReadEbook, "Click here to open
    the eBook file location");
        this.btnReadEbook.UseVisualStyleBackColor = true;
        this.btnReadEbook.Click += new
    System.EventHandler(this.btnReadEbook_Click);

        // eBookManager Icon
        this.Icon = new System.Drawing.Icon("ico/mainForm.ico");

        PopulateStorageSpaceList();
    }

    private void PopulateStorageSpaceList()
    {
        lstStorageSpaces.Clear();
        if (!(_spaces == null))
        {
            foreach (StorageSpace space in _spaces)
            {
                ListViewItem lvItem = new ListViewItem(space.Name, 0);
                lvItem.Tag = space.BookList;
                lvItem.Name = space.ID.ToString();
                lstStorageSpaces.Items.Add(lvItem);
            }
        }
    }
```

2. If the user clicks on a storage space, we need to be able to read the books contained in that selected space:

```
    private void lstStorageSpaces_MouseClick(object sender,
    MouseEventArgs e)
    {
        ListViewItem selectedStorageSpace =
        lstStorageSpaces.SelectedItems[0];
        int spaceID = selectedStorageSpace.Name.ToInt();
        txtStorageSpaceDescription.Text = (from d in _spaces
            where d.ID == spaceID
            select d.Description).First();
        List<Document> ebookList =
            (List<Document>)selectedStorageSpace.Tag;
        PopulateContainedEbooks(ebookList);
    }
```

3. We now need to create the method that will populate the `lstBooks` list view with the books contained in the selected storage space:

```
private void PopulateContainedEbooks(List<Document> ebookList)
{
    lstBooks.Clear();
    ClearSelectedBook();
    if (ebookList != null)
    {
        foreach (Document eBook in ebookList)
        {
            ListViewItem book = new ListViewItem(eBook.Title, 1);
            book.Tag = eBook;
            lstBooks.Items.Add(book);
        }
    }
    else
    {
        ListViewItem book = new ListViewItem("This storage space
contains no eBooks", 2);
        book.Tag = "";
        lstBooks.Items.Add(book);
    }
}
```

4. We also need to clear the selected book's details when the selected storage space is changed. I have created two group controls around the file and book details. This code just loops through all the child controls; if the child control is a textbox, it clears it:

```
private void ClearSelectedBook()
{
    foreach (Control ctrl in gbBookDetails.Controls)
    {
        if (ctrl is TextBox)
            ctrl.Text = "";
    }
    foreach (Control ctrl in gbFileDetails.Controls)
    {
        if (ctrl is TextBox)
            ctrl.Text = "";
    }
    dtLastAccessed.Value = DateTime.Now;
    dtCreated.Value = DateTime.Now;
    dtDatePublished.Value = DateTime.Now;
}
```

5. The `MenuStrip` that was added to the form has a click event on the `ImportEbooks` menu item. It simply opens up the `ImportBooks` form:

```
private async void mnuImportEbooks_Click(object sender, EventArgs
e)
{
    ImportBooks import = new ImportBooks();
    import.ShowDialog();
    _spaces = await _spaces.ReadFromDataStore(_jsonPath);
    PopulateStorageSpaceList();
}
```

6. The following method wraps up the logic to select a specific eBook and populate the file and eBook details on the `eBookManager` form:

```
private void lstBooks_MouseClick(object sender, MouseEventArgs e)
{
    ListViewItem selectedBook = lstBooks.SelectedItems[0];
    if (!String.IsNullOrEmpty(selectedBook.Tag.ToString()))
    {
        Document ebook = (Document)selectedBook.Tag;
        txtFileName.Text = ebook.FileName;
        txtExtension.Text = ebook.Extension;
        dtLastAccessed.Value = ebook.LastAccessed;
        dtCreated.Value = ebook.Created;
        txtFilePath.Text = ebook.FilePath;
        txtFileSize.Text = ebook.FileSize;
        txtTitle.Text = ebook.Title;
        txtAuthor.Text = ebook.Author;
        txtPublisher.Text = ebook.Publisher;
        txtPrice.Text = ebook.Price;
        txtISBN.Text = ebook.ISBN;
        dtDatePublished.Value = ebook.PublishDate;
        txtCategory.Text = ebook.Category;
    }
}
```

7. Lastly, when the book selected is the one you wish to read, click on the **Read eBook** button to open the file location of the selected eBook:

```
private void btnReadEbook_Click(object sender, EventArgs e)
{
    string filePath = txtFilePath.Text;
    FileInfo fi = new FileInfo(filePath);
    if (fi.Exists)
    {
        Process.Start("explorer.exe",
Path.GetDirectoryName(filePath));
```

```
        }
    }
```

This completes the code logic contained in the `eBookManager` application.

> **TIP:** You can further modify the code to open the required application for the selected eBook instead of just the file location. In other words, if you click on a PDF document, the application can launch a PDF reader with the document loaded. Lastly, note that classification has not been implemented in this version of the application.

It is time to fire up the application and test it out.

Running the eBookManager application

To run the application, please perform the following steps:

1. When the application starts for the first time, there will be no virtual storage spaces available. To create one, we will need to import some books. Click on the **Import eBooks** menu item:

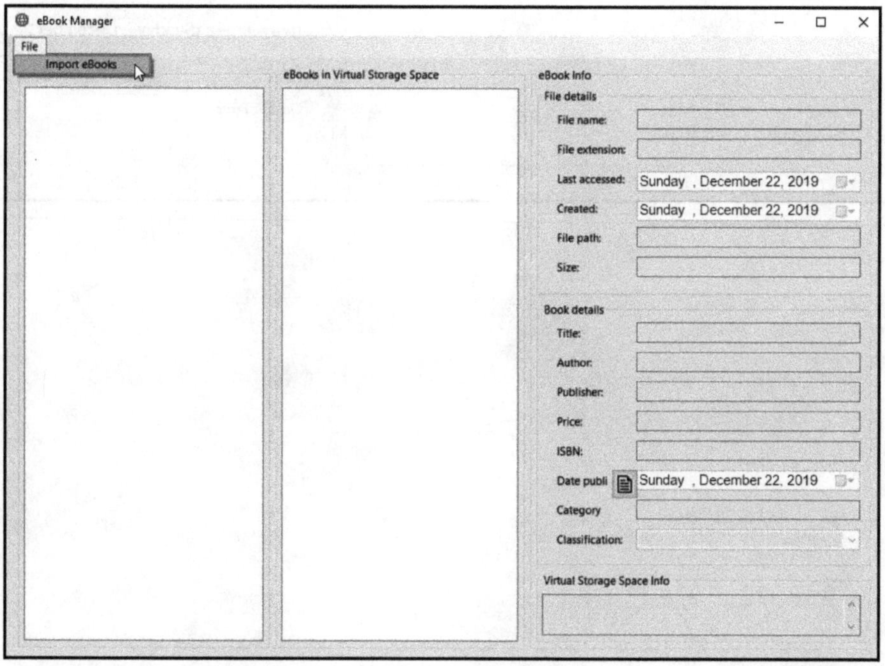

2. The **Import eBooks** screen opens. You can add a new storage space and select the source folder for eBooks:

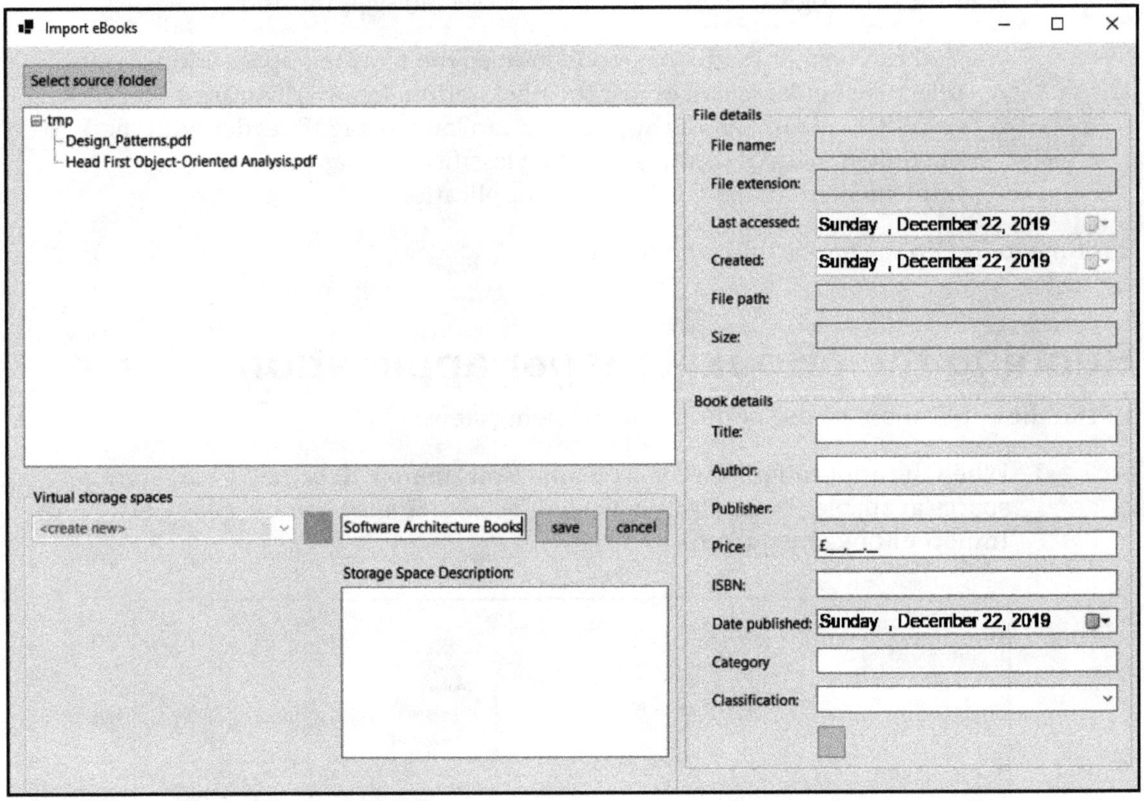

3. Once you have selected an eBook, add the information about the book and save it to the storage space. After you have added all the storage spaces and eBooks, you will see a list of virtual storage spaces. As you click on a storage space, the books it contains will be listed:

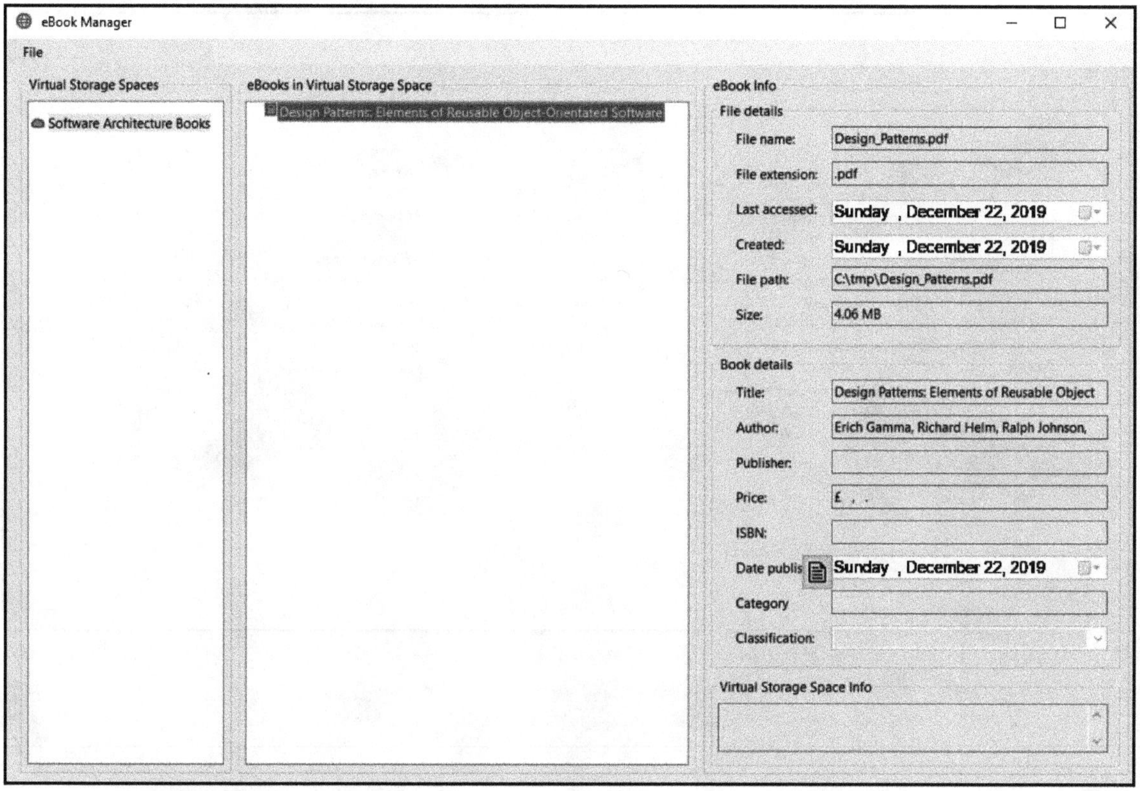

4. Selecting an eBook and clicking on the **Read eBook** button will open up the file location containing the selected eBook.
5. Lastly, let's have a look at the JSON file generated for the *Ebook Manager* application. Initially, this will be stored in the output location of the project:

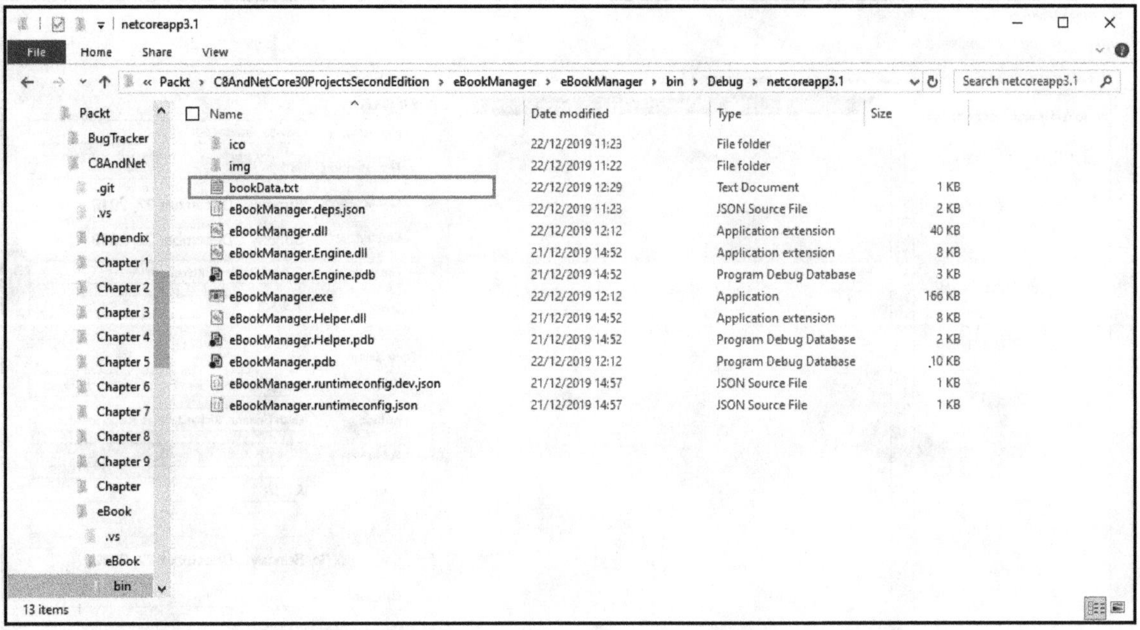

In the following, I've used VS Code to nicely format the JSON:

```
[
    {
        "ID": 0,
        "Name": "Software Architecture Books",
        "Description": "",
        "BookList": [
            {
                "Title": "Design Patterns: Elements of Reusable Object-Orientated Software",
                "FileName": "Design_Patterns.pdf",
                "Extension": ".pdf",
                "LastAccessed": "2019-12-22T12:22:53.5985254+00:00",
                "Created": "2019-12-22T12:22:53.5545254+00:00",
                "FilePath": "C:\\tmp\\Design_Patterns.pdf",
                "FileSize": "4.06 MB",
                "ISBN": "",
                "Price": "\u00A3    ,    .",
                "Publisher": "",
                "Author": "Erich Gamma, Richard Helm, Ralph Johnson, John Vlissides",
                "PublishDate": "2019-12-22T12:22:06.0479953+00:00",
                "Classification": null,
                "Category": ""
            }
        ]
    }
]
```

TIP

The keyboard shortcut to format JSON in VS Code is *Shift* + *Alt* + *F*.

As you can see, the JSON file is quite nicely laid out, and it is easily readable.

Now let's see how to upgrade an existing WinForms app to .NET Core 3.

Upgrading to .NET Core 3

In order to follow this section, you won't *need* the WinForms app from the first edition—any WinForms app will do; however, it is recommended that you use that application, especially for the later section where we will discuss C# 8 features.

You can download the original project from the following location:

`https://github.com/PacktPublishing/CSharp7-and-.NET-Core-2.0-Blueprints`

If you download and run the application, you should see that it still works fine:

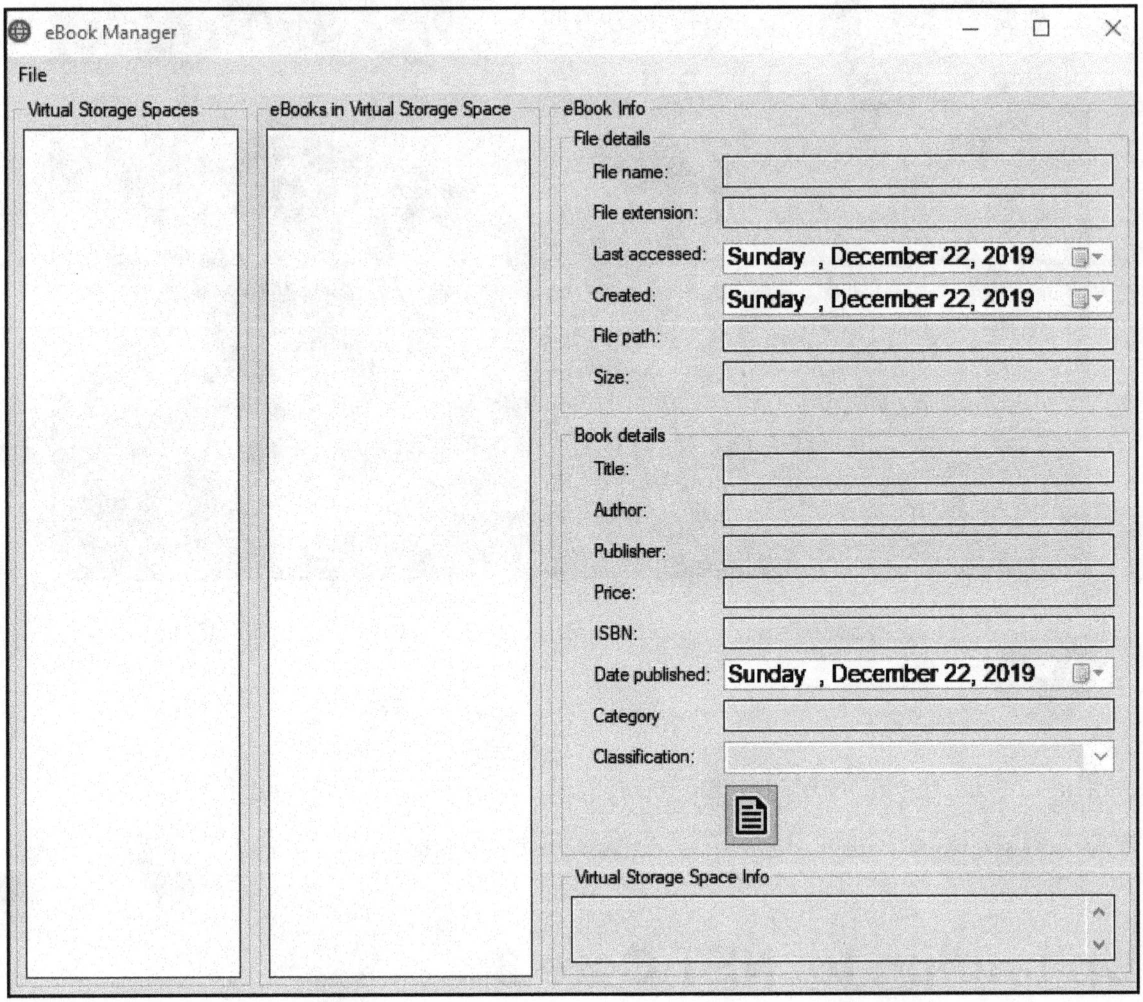

Let's now investigate how we can run this exact same code base under .NET Core 3. We'll start with the project file. Basically, we need to tell Visual Studio that we now have a .NET Core 3 project, and not a Framework one.

If you have PowerTools installed (`https://marketplace.visualstudio.com/items?itemName=VisualStudioProductTeam.ProductivityPowerPack2017`), you can do this from within Visual Studio; if not, then simply open the `.csproj` file using your favorite text editor:

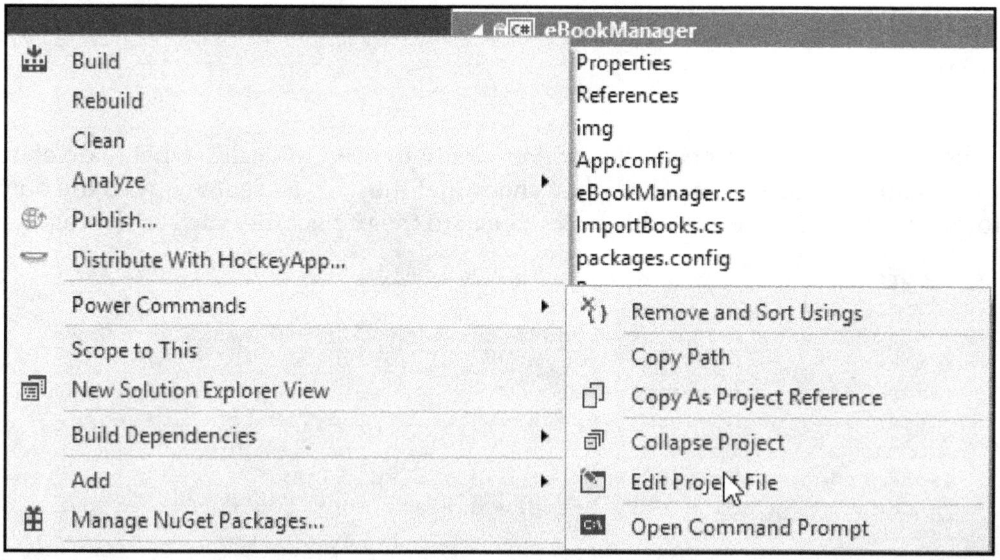

Change the contents of the `.csproj` file to the following:

```
<Project Sdk="Microsoft.NET.Sdk.WindowsDesktop">

  <PropertyGroup>
    <OutputType>WinExe</OutputType>
    <TargetFramework>netcoreapp3.0</TargetFramework>
    <LangVersion>8.0</LangVersion>
    <AssetTargetFallback>uap10.0.18362</AssetTargetFallback>
    <UseWindowsForms>true</UseWindowsForms>
  </PropertyGroup>

  <ItemGroup>
    <PackageReference Include="Newtonsoft.Json" Version="12.0.2" />
  </ItemGroup>

  <ItemGroup>
```

```
    <ProjectReference
  Include="..\eBookManager.Controls\eBookManager.Controls.csproj" />
    <ProjectReference
  Include="..\eBookManager.Engine\eBookManager.Engine.csproj" />
    <ProjectReference
  Include="..\eBookManager.Helper\eBookManager.Helper.csproj" />
  </ItemGroup>

  <ItemGroup>
    <Reference Include="System">
      <HintPath>System</HintPath>
    </Reference>
  </ItemGroup>
</Project>
```

This is, essentially, all that's needed; however, you will need to decide what to do about the project's resources. You can manually just check that they are all set to copy to the output directory; alternatively, we can add an *ItemGroup* to the project file, such as the following:

```
  <ItemGroup>
    <None Update="ico\importBooks.ico">
      <CopyToOutputDirectory>PreserveNewest</CopyToOutputDirectory>
    </None>
    <None Update="ico\mainForm.ico">
      <CopyToOutputDirectory>PreserveNewest</CopyToOutputDirectory>
    </None>
    <None Update="img\add_ebook_to_storage_space.png">
      <CopyToOutputDirectory>PreserveNewest</CopyToOutputDirectory>
    </None>
    <None Update="img\add_new_storage_space.png">
      <CopyToOutputDirectory>PreserveNewest</CopyToOutputDirectory>
    </None>
    <None Update="img\docx16.png">
      <CopyToOutputDirectory>PreserveNewest</CopyToOutputDirectory>
    </None>
    <None Update="img\docxx16.png">
      <CopyToOutputDirectory>PreserveNewest</CopyToOutputDirectory>
    </None>
    <None Update="img\eBook.png">
      <CopyToOutputDirectory>PreserveNewest</CopyToOutputDirectory>
    </None>
    <None Update="img\epubx16.png">
      <CopyToOutputDirectory>PreserveNewest</CopyToOutputDirectory>
    </None>
    <None Update="img\folder-close-x16.png">
      <CopyToOutputDirectory>PreserveNewest</CopyToOutputDirectory>
    </None>
    <None Update="img\folder_exp_x16.png">
```

```
      <CopyToOutputDirectory>PreserveNewest</CopyToOutputDirectory>
    </None>
    <None Update="img\image sources.txt">
      <CopyToOutputDirectory>PreserveNewest</CopyToOutputDirectory>
    </None>
    <None Update="img\no_eBook.png">
      <CopyToOutputDirectory>PreserveNewest</CopyToOutputDirectory>
    </None>
    <None Update="img\pdfx16.png">
      <CopyToOutputDirectory>PreserveNewest</CopyToOutputDirectory>
    </None>
    <None Update="img\ReadEbook.png">
      <CopyToOutputDirectory>PreserveNewest</CopyToOutputDirectory>
    </None>
    <None Update="img\storage_space_cloud.png">
      <CopyToOutputDirectory>PreserveNewest</CopyToOutputDirectory>
    </None>
  </ItemGroup>
```

As you can see, the whole thing is a great deal simpler than the previous version of the file.

> At the time of writing, the first preview of a WinForms editor was released. The following article details what it is currently capable of: `https://devblogs.microsoft.com/dotnet/introducing-net-core-windows-forms-designer-preview-1/`.
>
> Unfortunately, *Preview 1* was not stable enough to make the changes necessary for this chapter, and so we are bypassing the designer.

The next step is to delete the following files, found under `Properties`:

- `AssemblyInfo.cs`
- `Settings.Designer.cs`
- `Settings.settings`

In fact, by the end of this chapter, the entire `Properties` folder will be gone.

Actually, that's it. Simply reload the project and hit *F5*. The app is now running under .NET Core. However, it's very likely you'll get an error at this point. The reason is that we have two other projects that are still running under .NET Framework:

- `eBookManager.Engine`
- `eBookManager.Helper`

We'll need to migrate each project in a similar way; let's start with `eBookManager.Engine`. As before, edit the project file and replace what you find there with the following:

```
<Project Sdk="Microsoft.NET.Sdk">
  <PropertyGroup>
    <TargetFramework>netcoreapp3.0</TargetFramework>
  </PropertyGroup>
</Project>
```

As you can see, this is even simpler than before. In fact, it is not necessary to have this target 3.0; we could target 2.2, or even 2.1 if we so chose. Again, we'll delete `AssemblyInfo.cs`.

Finally, we come to `eBookManager.Helper`. Edit the project file again to match the following:

```
<Project Sdk="Microsoft.NET.Sdk">
  <PropertyGroup>
    <TargetFramework>netcoreapp3.0</TargetFramework>
  </PropertyGroup>

  <ItemGroup>
    <PackageReference Include="Newtonsoft.Json" Version="11.0.2" />
  </ItemGroup>

  <ItemGroup>
    <ProjectReference
Include="..\eBookManager.Engine\eBookManager.Engine.csproj" />
  </ItemGroup>
</Project>
```

Again, we'll delete `AssemblyInfo.cs`. We'll also need to remove a stray reference to `System.Windows.Forms` in `ExtensionMethods.cs`.

Fixing compilation errors

Finally, we'll need to restructure some of the code that depends on embedded image resources. If you run the code as-is, you'll likely get an error similar to the following:

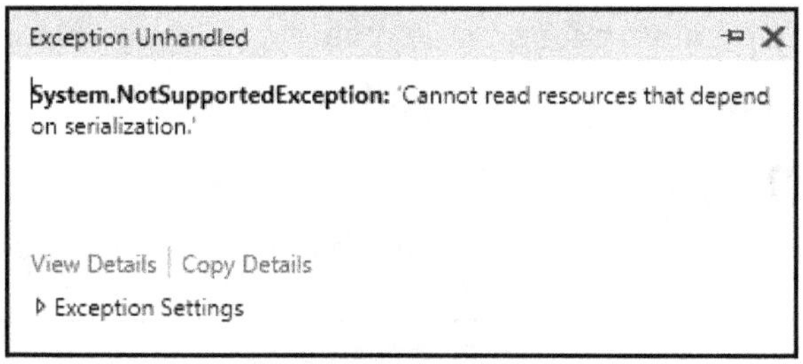

At the time of writing, WinForms on .NET Core 3.0 doesn't support binary serialization. As a result, we need to make a few small changes.

Resource files

The first thing we'll need to do is to read the files from the output directory, so we'll change the **Copy to Output Directory** setting on the image and icon files; highlight all the files, and then change the **Copy to Output Directory** action to **Copy if newer**:

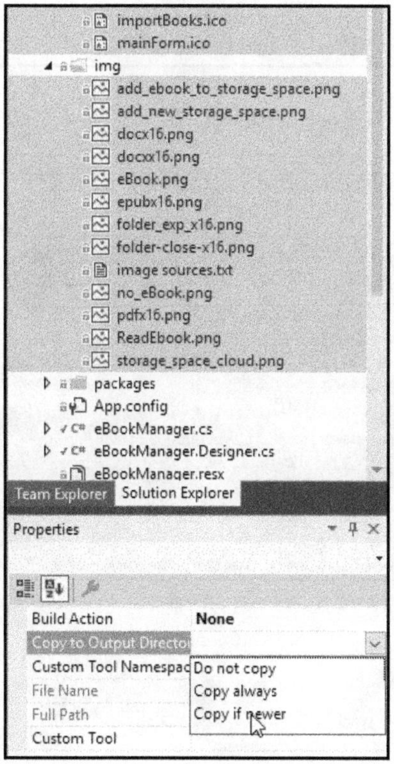

The next step is to go to the `eBookManager` screen.

The eBookManager screen

In the `eBookManager.Designer.cs` file, remove the `imageList1` section:

```
this.lstStorageSpaces.TabIndex = 1;
this.lstStorageSpaces.UseCompatibleStateImageBehavior = false;
this.lstStorageSpaces.View = System.Windows.Forms.View.Tile;
this.lstStorageSpaces.MouseClick += new System.Windows.Forms.MouseEve
//
// imageList1
//
this.imageList1.ImageStream = ((System.Windows.Forms.ImageListStreame
this.imageList1.TransparentColor = System.Drawing.Color.Transparent;
this.imageList1.Images.SetKeyName(0, "storage_space_cloud.png");
this.imageList1.Images.SetKeyName(1, "eBook.png");
this.imageList1.Images.SetKeyName(2, "no_eBook.png");
//
// groupBox1
//
this.groupBox1.Anchor = ((System.Windows.Forms.AnchorStyles)(((System
| System.Windows.Forms.AnchorStyles.Left)));
```

Also remove the `btnReadEbook` section:

```
this.txtStorageSpaceDescription.TabIndex = 6;
//
// btnReadEbook
//
this.btnReadEbook.Image = global::eBookManager.Properties.Resources.R
this.btnReadEbook.Location = new System.Drawing.Point(103, 227);
this.btnReadEbook.Name = "btnReadEbook";
this.btnReadEbook.Size = new System.Drawing.Size(36, 40);
this.btnReadEbook.TabIndex = 32;
this.toolTip1.SetToolTip(this.btnReadEbook, "Click here to open the e
this.btnReadEbook.UseVisualStyleBackColor = true;
this.btnReadEbook.Click += new System.EventHandler(this.btnReadEbook_
//
// toolTip1
//
this.toolTip1.ToolTipIcon = System.Windows.Forms.ToolTipIcon.Info;
```

And finally, remove the `this.Icon` assignment in the `eBookManager` section:

```
//
// eBookManager
//
this.AutoScaleDimensions = new System.Drawing.SizeF(6F, 13F);
this.AutoScaleMode = System.Windows.Forms.AutoScaleMode.Font;
this.ClientSize = new System.Drawing.Size(1113, 643);
this.Controls.Add(this.groupBox3);
this.Controls.Add(this.groupBox2);
this.Controls.Add(this.groupBox1);
this.Controls.Add(this.menuStrip1);
this.Icon = ((System.Drawing.Icon)(resources.GetObject("$this.Icon"))
this.MainMenuStrip = this.menuStrip1;
this.Name = "eBookManager";
this.Text = " eBook Manager";
this.Load += new System.EventHandler(this.Form1_Load);
```

We'll move the code that has been removed into the `Form_Load` event of `eBookManager.cs`:

```
private void Form1_Load(object sender, EventArgs e)
{
    System.ComponentModel.ComponentResourceManager resources = new
System.ComponentModel.ComponentResourceManager(typeof(eBookManager));

    this.components = new System.ComponentModel.Container();

    // imageList1
    //this.imageList1.ImageStream =
((System.Windows.Forms.ImageListStreamer)(resources.GetObject("imageList1.I
mageStream")));
    this.imageList1.Images.Add("storage_space_cloud.png",
Image.FromFile("img/storage_space_cloud.png"));
    this.imageList1.Images.Add("eBook.png",
Image.FromFile("img/eBook.png"));
    this.imageList1.Images.Add("no_eBook.png",
Image.FromFile("img/no_eBook.png"));
    this.imageList1.TransparentColor = System.Drawing.Color.Transparent;

    // btnReadEbook
    this.btnReadEbook.Image = Image.FromFile("img/ReadEbook.png");
    this.btnReadEbook.Location = new System.Drawing.Point(103, 227);
    this.btnReadEbook.Name = "btnReadEbook";
    this.btnReadEbook.Size = new System.Drawing.Size(36, 40);
    this.btnReadEbook.TabIndex = 32;
    this.toolTip1.SetToolTip(this.btnReadEbook, "Click here to open the
```

```
eBook file location");
    this.btnReadEbook.UseVisualStyleBackColor = true;
    this.btnReadEbook.Click += new
System.EventHandler(this.btnReadEbook_Click);

    // eBookManager Icon
    this.Icon = new System.Drawing.Icon("ico/mainForm.ico");

    PopulateStorageSpaceList();
}
```

importBooks screen

A similar change is needed for `importBooks.Designer.cs`. The following section should be removed:

```
this.tvFoundBooks.AfterSelect += new System.Windows.Forms.TreeViewEve
//
// tvImages
//
this.tvImages.ImageStream = ((System.Windows.Forms.ImageListStreamer)
this.tvImages.TransparentColor = System.Drawing.Color.Transparent;
this.tvImages.Images.SetKeyName(0, "docx16.png");
this.tvImages.Images.SetKeyName(1, "docxx16.png");
this.tvImages.Images.SetKeyName(2, "pdfx16.png");
this.tvImages.Images.SetKeyName(3, "epubx16.png");
this.tvImages.Images.SetKeyName(4, "folder-close-x16.png");
this.tvImages.Images.SetKeyName(5, "folder_exp_x16.png");
//
// label1
//
this.label1.AutoSize = true;
```

Remove the setter for the `btnAddeBookToStorageSpace` image in the same file:

```
//
// btnAddeBookToStorageSpace
//
this.btnAddeBookToStorageSpace.Image = global::eBookManager.Propertie
this.btnAddeBookToStorageSpace.Location = new System.Drawing.Point(10
```

Remove the image for `btnAddNewStorageSpace` (again, in the same file):

```
this.txtStorageSpaceDescription.TabIndex = 5;
//
// btnAddNewStorageSpace
//
this.btnAddNewStorageSpace.Image = global::eBookManager.Properties.Re
this.btnAddNewStorageSpace.Location = new System.Drawing.Point(219, 1
this.btnAddNewStorageSpace.Name = "btnAddNewStorageSpace";
```

Finally, remove the icon setter for the form:

```
//
// ImportBooks
//
this.AutoScaleDimensions = new System.Drawing.SizeF(6F, 13F);
this.AutoScaleMode = System.Windows.Forms.AutoScaleMode.Font;
this.ClientSize = new System.Drawing.Size(891, 556);
this.Controls.Add(this.groupBox3);
this.Controls.Add(this.groupBox2);
this.Controls.Add(this.groupBox1);
this.Controls.Add(this.tvFoundBooks);
this.Controls.Add(this.btnSelectSourceFolder);
this.Icon = ((System.Drawing.Icon)(resources.GetObject("$this.Icon"))
this.Name = "ImportBooks";
this.Text = " Import eBooks";
this.Load += new System.EventHandler(this.ImportBooks_Load);
```

We'll move this into the `Form_Load` event of `ImportBooks.cs`, which should now look as follows:

```
private void ImportBooks_Load(object sender, EventArgs e)
{
    // tvImages
    this.tvImages.Images.Add("docx16.png",
Image.FromFile("img/docx16.png"));
    this.tvImages.Images.Add("docxx16.png",
Image.FromFile("img/docxx16.png"));
    this.tvImages.Images.Add("pdfx16.png",
Image.FromFile("img/pdfx16.png"));
    this.tvImages.Images.Add("epubx16.png",
Image.FromFile("img/epubx16.png"));
    this.tvImages.Images.Add("folder-close-x16.png",
Image.FromFile("img/folder-close-x16.png"));
    this.tvImages.Images.Add("folder_exp_x16.png",
Image.FromFile("img/folder_exp_x16.png"));
    this.tvImages.TransparentColor = System.Drawing.Color.Transparent;
```

```
    // btnAddeBookToStorageSpace
    this.btnAddeBookToStorageSpace.Image =
Image.FromFile("img/add_ebook_to_storage_space.png");
    // btnAddNewStorageSpace
    this.btnAddNewStorageSpace.Image =
Image.FromFile("img/add_new_storage_space.png");

    // ImportBooks
    this.Icon = new System.Drawing.Icon("ico/importBooks.ico");


    PopulateStorageSpacesList();
    if (dlVirtualStorageSpaces.Items.Count == 0)
    {
        dlVirtualStorageSpaces.Items.Add("<create new storage space>");
    }

    lblEbookCount.Text = "";
}
```

ProcessStartInfo

Finally, the following will need to be changed in `eBookManager.cs`:

```
private void btnReadEbook_Click(object sender, EventArgs e)
        {
            string filePath = txtFilePath.Text;
            FileInfo fi = new FileInfo(filePath);
            if (fi.Exists)
            {
                var processStartInfo = new ProcessStartInfo(filePath,
Path.GetDirectoryName(filePath))
                {
                    // Change in .NET Core - this defaulted to true in
WinForms
                    UseShellExecute = true
                };
                Process.Start(processStartInfo);
            }
        }
```

The reason is that `ProcessStartInfo` in .NET Framework used to default to `UseShellExecute = true`. However, in .NET Core, it now defaults to `false`, and will therefore fail without this change.

That's it! If you run the app, you're now running it under .NET Core 3. It's the same application (albeit with some minor code changes), but now it's running the .NET Core runtime!

Benefits of upgrading to .NET Core

Let's start with the elephant in the room. You can't now take Ebook Manager and run it on Linux—it is *not* now cross-platform. WinForms always was, still is, and probably always will be, a Windows-specific technology.

Upgrading essentially gives you three benefits:

- **Speed**: .NET Core 2.1 saw some significant speed improvements. Your mileage may vary with this, and it's likely that it will depend on exactly what your application is doing. For example, the Ebook Manager application scans the hard drive to retrieve books: it's unlikely that the memory allocation improvements made in .NET Core 2.1 are going to make a huge difference to the speed of that.
- **Support**: Once you've upgraded to .NET Core, your app will now be running on a far more active piece of technology; in the future, Microsoft is less likely to change .NET Framework, except for security bug patches, but .NET Core has an active road-map.
- **Enthusiasm**: It's hard to get people excited about (or to get people at all) working on a WinForms application written fifteen years ago.

From the announcement with build 2019, it looks like .NET Framework will shortly be swallowed by .NET Core (to be known as .NET 5 at the time of writing). This means that, if you haven't converted by then, you may be on a train that ends (albeit in a few years) with Microsoft withdrawing support for the framework.

C# 8 brings a host of new features to the table, including the following:

- Nullable reference types
- Default implementations of interfaces
- Records
- Recursive patterns
- Async streams

- Ranges
- Static local functions
- Using declarations

Taking the top two headline features from that list, it's clear that there is synergy between being able to run legacy code in .NET Core 3 and being able to apply some of these features to help to update and maintain legacy code.

Understanding nullable reference types

In .NET Core 2.1 (or any previous version of .NET), we could legitimately type the following code and run it:

```
string test = null;
Console.WriteLine(test.Length);
```

And, of course it would crash. Obviously, no-one familiar with the language would write this; however, they might write something as follows:

```
string test = FunctionCanReturnNull();
Console.WriteLine(test.Length);
```

Nullable reference types are an opt-in feature (that is, you have to explicitly turn it on) that simply gives a warning to say that you have a potential for a reference type to be `null`. Let's try turning this on for our Ebook Manager. It can be turned on a class-by-class basis by adding the following directive to the top of a file:

```
#nullable enable
```

However, you can also switch it on for the entire project by adding the following line to the `.csproj` file:

```
<PropertyGroup>
    <TargetFramework>netcoreapp3.0</TargetFramework>
    <LangVersion>8.0</LangVersion>
    <Nullable>enable</Nullable>
</PropertyGroup>
```

> **TIP**
> At the time of writing, this property will be automatically added to the `.csproj` file.

> **INFO**
> There are other options that the `Nullable` option can be configured for; for further information, see the following URL:
>
> `https://docs.microsoft.com/en-us/dotnet/csharp/nullable-references`

This is a granular feature, so it can be turned off or on for specific sections of code. There are a few warnings that pop up, so let's focus on `StorageSpace.cs`:

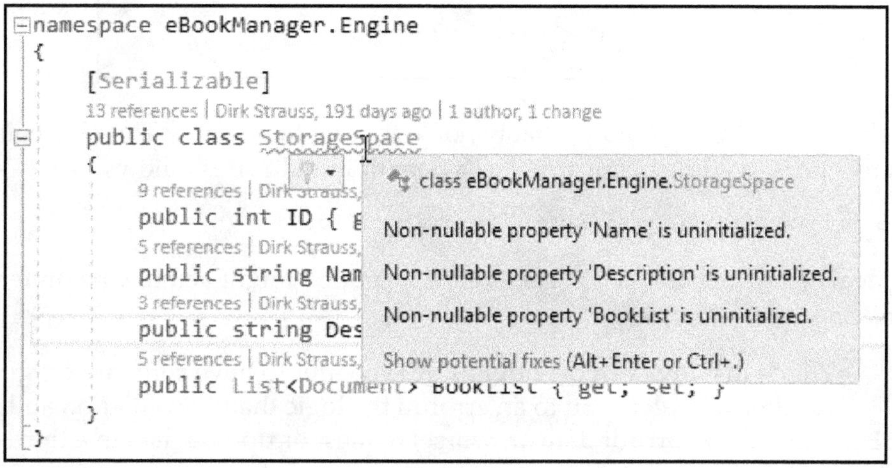
namespace eBookManager.Engine
{
[Serializable]
13 references | Dirk Strauss, 191 days ago | 1 author, 1 change
public class StorageSpace
{
9 references | Dirk Strauss,
public int ID {
5 references | Dirk Strauss,
public string Nam
3 references | Dirk Strauss,
public string Des
5 references | Dirk Strauss,
public List<Document> BookList { get; set; }
}
}
class eBookManager.Engine.StorageSpace
Non-nullable property 'Name' is uninitialized.
Non-nullable property 'Description' is uninitialized.
Non-nullable property 'BookList' is uninitialized.
Show potential fixes (Alt+Enter or Ctrl+.)

So, what exactly is this telling us?

To answer that, let's look first at `ID`. `ID` is a value type, and therefore cannot be `null`. If nothing is assigned to `ID`, it will have the default value: `0`. `Name`, however is a string (which is a reference type), and therefore *can* be `null` and, in fact, *will* be `null` unless we set it otherwise. If we want one of these fields to be nullable, then we can certainly do that (and in the case of `Description`, we probably should):

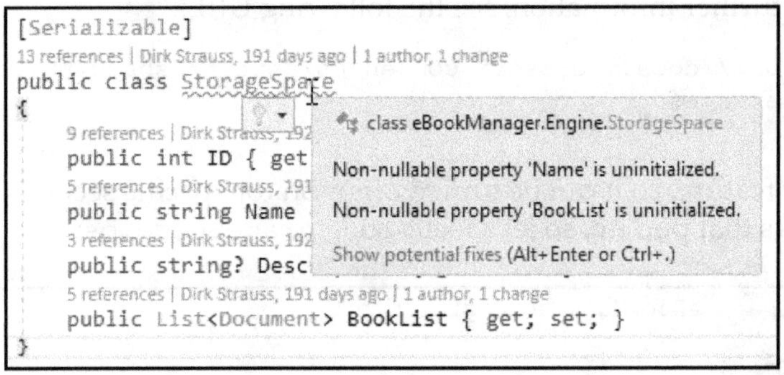
[Serializable]
13 references | Dirk Strauss, 191 days ago | 1 author, 1 change
public class StorageSpace
class eBookManager.Engine.StorageSpace
Non-nullable property 'Name' is uninitialized.
Non-nullable property 'BookList' is uninitialized.
Show potential fixes (Alt+Enter or Ctrl+.)
public int ID { get
public string Name
public string? Desc
5 references | Dirk Strauss, 191 days ago | 1 author, 1 change
public List<Document> BookList { get; set; }

But what about `Name`? We would probably not want that to be `null`. There's a couple of options here; one is to add a blank string as a default initializer as follows:

```
public string Name { get; set; } = string.Empty;
```

This isn't ideal. In fact, getting a `null` reference exception might actually be preferable to it being blank and bypassing that.

> **TIP:** This is just my opinion, but it is much better to have software crash at runtime and alert you to an error in the logic than to soldier on and potentially corrupt data or, worse, request or update data in a third-party system!

Another option is to add a constructor. The following is an example:

```
[Serializable]
public class StorageSpace
{
    public StorageSpace(string name)
    {
        Name = name;
    }
    public int ID { get; set; }
    public string Name { get; set; }
    public string? Description { get; set; }
    public List<Document>? BookList { get; set; }
}
```

This clears up the warnings and ensures that anyone creating the class provides a name, which we are saying can never be `null`. This is instantiated in `ImportBooks.cs`, so now we'll have to provide that parameter:

```
private void btnSaveNewStorageSpace_Click(object sender, EventArgs e)
{
    try
    {
        if (txtNewStorageSpaceName.Text.Length != 0)
        {
            string newName = txtNewStorageSpaceName.Text;

            // null conditional operator:
"spaces?.StorageSpaceExists(newName) ?? false"
            // throw expressions: bool spaceExists = (space exists = false)
? return false : throw exception
            // Out variables
            bool spaceExists = (!spaces.StorageSpaceExists(newName, out int
nextID)) ? false : throw new Exception("The storage space you are trying to
add already exists.");
            if (!spaceExists)
            {
                StorageSpace newSpace = new StorageSpace(newName);
                newSpace.ID = nextID;
                newSpace.Description = txtStorageSpaceDescription.Text;
                spaces.Add(newSpace);
```

Now we know that the `Name` property can never be `null`, it's worth remembering that the warnings that you get here are just that, warnings; and, like all warnings, it is your prerogative to ignore them. However, C# 8 does have a feature (which I've heard referred to as the dammit operator) that allows you to insist that, despite what the compiler believes, you know the variable will not be `null`; it looks as follows:

```
string test = null;

Console.WriteLine(test!.Length);
Console.ReadLine();
```

Obviously, if you do this, the preceding code will crash, so if you do decide that you know better than the compiler, be sure!

Exploring XAML Islands

For this section, you will need to be running Windows 10 1903 or later. By the time this book is published, it is expected that the 1903 release will be delivered automatically to all Windows 10 machines; however, if you are running an earlier version, then you can force an update by visiting the following link: `https://www.microsoft.com/en-us/software-download/windows10`.

In 2019, when this chapter was written, we noted that the `TreeView` in the import books section looks a little dated. In fact, you'd think it was a `TreeView` from 2005 when WinForms was all the rage! Also, we'd like to bind our data to the `TreeView`, rather than build it up separately. While there are some data binding capabilities in WinForms, we are stuck with the general appearance of `TreeView`.

Unless, that is, we use one of the nice new UWP controls in WinForms. That's exactly what XAML Islands gives us! We can take an existing UWP control, or even create our own, and use it directly from an existing WinForms application.

Let's try and use the `TreeView` from the UWP Community Toolkit inside our WinForms application.

UWP TreeView

There are a number of setup requirements for this, which I'll detail later.

TIP

By the time this is published, the process for setting this up may have been simplified considerably; please refer to the linked articles for the most recent advice.

The first step is to ensure (as detailed in the *Technical requirements* section) that you're running Windows 10, version 1903 or later. Please follow the information in that section if you are not. The second step is to install the Windows 10 SDK; for this, you can use the following link: `https://developer.microsoft.com/en-us/windows/downloads/windows-10-sdk`.

We will be performing the following article for the next step: `https://docs.microsoft.com/en-us/windows/apps/desktop/modernize/desktop-to-uwp-enhance#set-up-your-project`.

Add the following NuGet package to your WinForms project:

```
Microsoft.Windows.SDK.Contracts
```

Install the `XamlHost` NuGet package into the WinForms app:

```
Install-Package Microsoft.Toolkit.Forms.UI.XamlHost
```

Now we can replace our existing `TreeView` with the UWP one.

> TIP: You'll notice that I've fully qualified all the XAML controls. Since we're dealing with two disparate frameworks, this kind of change makes it very easy to get confused and mix up which control you're dealing with.

> In the following code samples, I've included class-level variables with the code samples for clarity. I, personally, would suggest that these actually go at the top of your class file. Of course, it makes no functional difference.

The first thing that we need to consider is `XamlHost`.

WIndowsXamlHost

Let's create our `TreeView`; we'll do this in the code-behind for `ImportBooks.cs`. We're going to add some code to the constructor, which will now look as follows:

```
private readonly Microsoft.Toolkit.Forms.UI.XamlHost.WindowsXamlHost
_windowsXamlHostTreeView;

public ImportBooks()
{
    InitializeComponent();
    _jsonPath = Path.Combine(Application.StartupPath, "bookData.txt");
    spaces = spaces.ReadFromDataStore(_jsonPath);

    var windowsXamlHostTreeView = new WindowsXamlHost();
    windowsXamlHostTreeView.InitialTypeName =
"Windows.UI.Xaml.Controls.TreeView";
    windowsXamlHostTreeView.AutoSizeMode =
System.Windows.Forms.AutoSizeMode.GrowOnly;
    windowsXamlHostTreeView.Location = new System.Drawing.Point(12, 60);
    windowsXamlHostTreeView.Name = "tvFoundBooks";
    windowsXamlHostTreeView.Size = new System.Drawing.Size(513, 350);
    windowsXamlHostTreeView.TabIndex = 8;
    windowsXamlHostTreeView.Dock = System.Windows.Forms.DockStyle.None;
```

```
    windowsXamlHostTreeView.ChildChanged +=
windowsXamlHostTreeView_ChildChanged;

    this.Controls.Add(windowsXamlHostTreeView);
}
```

Let's quickly review what we've done here (it's actually not that much). Firstly, we've created a new `WIndowsXamlHost` object. This is the basis for XAML Islands; it acts as a wrapper around your UWP control, so it will work in a WinForms context.

> **TIP:** Although this chapter discusses WinForms, the same is true for WPF and, while the exact syntax may differ slightly, the basic principle is the same.

The things to notice on this code sample are as follows:

- We're setting the name to `tvFoundBooks`, which is the same name as our WinForms app had.
- We're listening to the `ChildChanged` event: this is so that we can set some specifics on the control itself (we'll come back to this shortly).
- The `InitialTypeName` is how XAML Islands knows which UWP control to invoke.
- We're adding the host control to the current form (we also set the location).

ItemTemplate

Now that we've set up the host control, we can have a look at the `ChildChanged` event that we mentioned; this is where we set up the UWP control (rather than the host control):

```
private Windows.UI.Xaml.Controls.TreeView? _tvFoundBooks = null;

private void windowsXamlHostTreeView_ChildChanged(object? sender, EventArgs
e)
{
    if (sender == null) return;

    var host = (WindowsXamlHost)sender;
    _tvFoundBooks = (Windows.UI.Xaml.Controls.TreeView)host.Child;
    _tvFoundBooks.ItemInvoked += _tvFoundBooks_ItemInvoked;
    _tvFoundBooks.ItemsSource = DataSource;

    const string Xaml = "<DataTemplate
xmlns=\"http://schemas.microsoft.com/winfx/2006/xaml/presentation\"><TreeVi
```

```
ewItem ItemsSource=\"{Binding Children}\" Content=\"{Binding
Name}\"/></DataTemplate>";
    var xaml = XamlReader.Load(Xaml);
    _tvFoundBooks.ItemTemplate = xaml as Windows.UI.Xaml.DataTemplate;
}
```

Don't worry so much about why `_tvFoundBooks` is a class-level variable, we'll come back to that shortly. In the preceding code sample, we have a gated check to ensure that `sender` is not `null`, and then we're forcing it to a `WindowsXamlHost` type. Once we have this type, we can get whatever is inside the host by calling the `.Child` property.

As before, we're listening to the `ItemInvoked` event (again, we'll come back to this shortly). The first really new thing here is that we're setting the `ItemsSource`, and the `ItemTemplate`. We'll come back to `ItemsSource`, but the template is worth exploring. Unlike WinForms, UWP uses XAML to define how its controls look. This means that you have control over exactly what goes into the `TreeView`; for example, each node could have an image, or text, or both. However, if you don't specify `ItemTemplate`, then the rendering engine doesn't know what to display, or how.

The preceding XAML is probably the simplest one that will display anything. You'll notice there are a few binding statements; they are binding to properties relative to the `ItemsSource`. Let's have a look at exactly what it is we're binding to.

TreeView Item model and ItemsSource

In order to bind something to a control in UWP, you need *something*. Essentially, what that means is that we need a *model*.

> A model, in .NET terms, is simply a class that holds data.

We're going to create a new class, and we'll call it `Item`:

```
public class Item
{
    public string Name { get; set; }
    public ObservableCollection<Item> Children { get; set; } = new
ObservableCollection<Item>();
    public ItemType ItemType { get; set; }
    public string FullName { get; set; }

    public override string ToString()
```

```
        {
            return Name;
        }
    }
```

> **TIP:** I would always recommend that models are held in their own file and sit in a folder called `Models`, but there's no technical reason why you couldn't add this class to the end of `ImportBooks.cs`.

Most of this class should be self-explanatory; we're holding the `Name` and `FullName` (that is, the name and path) of the file. The `ObservableCollection` is a special type of `Collection` that allows the UI framework to be notified when it changes.

> **TIP:** For the code that we're writing here, we could get away with this simply being a `List`; however, `ObservableCollection` is good practice when dealing with desktop XAML frameworks such as UWP, and this will make extensibility easier.

Finally, we're holding the type of the item, which is a new enumerated type:

```
public enum ItemType
{
    Docx,
    Docxx,
    Pdfx,
    Epubx,
    Folder
}
```

Back in `ImportBooks.cs`, we're going to set up our `ItemsSource`. The first step is to add a class-level variable called `DataSource`:

```
public ObservableCollection<Models.Item> DataSource { get; set; }
```

Our next change is in the `btnSelectSourceFolder_Click` event handler:

```
private void btnSelectSourceFolder_Click(object sender, EventArgs e)
{
    try
    {
        FolderBrowserDialog fbd = new FolderBrowserDialog();
        fbd.Description = "Select the location of your eBooks and
documents";

        DialogResult dlgResult = fbd.ShowDialog();
        if (dlgResult == DialogResult.OK)
```

```
            {
                UpdateBookList(fbd.SelectedPath);
            }
        }
        catch (Exception ex)
        {
            MessageBox.Show(ex.Message);
        }
    }
```

As you can see, the new method is hugely simplified compared to the previous version; we've extracted all the real logic into a new method, so let's see that next:

```
    private void UpdateBookList(string path)
    {
        DirectoryInfo di = new DirectoryInfo(path);
        var bookList = new List<Models.Item>();
        var rootItem = new Models.Item()
        {
            Name = di.Name
        };

        rootItem.ItemType = Models.ItemType.Folder;

        PopulateBookList(di.FullName, rootItem);
        bookList.Add(rootItem);

        DataSource = new ObservableCollection<Models.Item>(bookList);
        _tvFoundBooks.ItemsSource = DataSource.OrderBy(a => a.Name);
    }
```

Here, we're setting up the root item of our `TreeView`; however, you'll notice that the only reference that we actually have to the `TreeView` is at the end, where we refresh `ItemsSource`. `PopulateBookList` is our next port of call. As before, this method is essentially in two parts; let's see the first part:

```
    public void PopulateBookList(string paramDir, Models.Item rootItem)
    {
        if (rootItem == null) throw new ArgumentNullException();

        rootItem.FullName = paramDir;
        rootItem.ItemType = Models.ItemType.Folder;

        DirectoryInfo dir = new DirectoryInfo(paramDir);
        foreach (DirectoryInfo dirInfo in dir.GetDirectories())
        {
            var item = new Models.Item();
            item.Name = dirInfo.Name;
```

```
            rootItem.Children.Add(item);
            PopulateBookList(dirInfo.FullName, item);
        }
```

Here, we're recursively traversing the directory structure and populating our new model. Notice that we're setting the item type and the `FullName` (the directory path) at the start, and then we iterate through all the sub-directories, re-calling our method.

> **TIP** Recursion is the practice of calling a method from itself. Is can be very useful in scenarios such as this, where you wish to perform exactly the same operation on nested objects. It is faster than using a loop; however, it does have the potential to fill up the stack very quickly if used incorrectly.

For the second part of the function, we'll process any files that are in the current directory (that is, whichever directory is at the top of the recursion stack at the time):

```
        foreach (FileInfo fleInfo in dir.GetFiles().Where(x =>
    AllowedExtensions.Contains(x.Extension)).ToList())
        {
            var item = new Models.Item();
            item.Name = fleInfo.Name;

            item.FullName = fleInfo.FullName;
            item.ItemType = (Models.ItemType)Enum.Parse(typeof(Extention),
    fleInfo.Extension.TrimStart('.'), true);

            rootItem.Children.Add(item);
        }
    }
```

Our next change is to the `ItemInvoked` method; the new method should look as follows:

```
    private void _tvFoundBooks_ItemInvoked(Windows.UI.Xaml.Controls.TreeView
    sender, Windows.UI.Xaml.Controls.TreeViewItemInvokedEventArgs args)
    {
        var selectedItem = (Models.Item)args.InvokedItem;

        DocumentEngine engine = new DocumentEngine();
        string path = selectedItem.FullName.ToString();

        if (File.Exists(path))
        {
            var (dateCreated, dateLastAccessed, fileName, fileExtention,
    fileLength, hasError) =
    engine.GetFileProperties(selectedItem.FullName.ToString());

            if (!hasError)
```

```
        {
            txtFileName.Text = fileName;
            txtExtension.Text = fileExtention;
            dtCreated.Value = dateCreated;
            dtLastAccessed.Value = dateLastAccessed;
            txtFilePath.Text = selectedItem.FullName.ToString();
            txtFileSize.Text = $"{Round(fileLength.ToMegabytes(),
2).ToString()} MB";
        }
    }
}
```

Again, this is very marginally changed; instead of storing the full filename (with the path) in the node *tag* property, we're now just referencing the underlying model, so it's much clearer. Our next step is to remove the existing WinForms `TreeView` control.

Removing the existing TreeView

The following code should be removed from `ImportBooks.Designer.cs`:

```
//
// tvFoundBooks
//
this.tvFoundBooks.Location = new System.Drawing.Point(12, 41);
this.tvFoundBooks.Name = "tvFoundBooks";
this.tvFoundBooks.Size = new System.Drawing.Size(513, 246);
this.tvFoundBooks.TabIndex = 8;
this.tvFoundBooks.AfterSelect += new
System.Windows.Forms.TreeViewEventHandler(this.tvFoundBooks_AfterSelect);
```

This will remove the control itself. Later, we'll need to remove the following code that adds the `TreeView` to the controls collection:

```
this.Controls.Add(this.tvFoundBooks);
```

That's it. If you now run the project, you'll see a UWP `TreeView` control right in the middle of a WinForms application.

Tree shaking and compiling to a single executable

The main reason why web applications have grown in popularity, eclipsing their desktop cousins, is the problem of deployment. It sounds a trivial issue on the face of it, but it definitely is not. There have been many attempts to solve the problem, from technologies such as ClickOnce to the App Store model (of UWP, Apple, and Google). One of the reasons why this is so difficult in the desktop world and so simple in the web world is that, while both may have a complex tree of dependencies, the web allows those dependencies to mostly live on the server, so they don't need to be directly deployed to the client machine.

One useful feature in .NET Core 3 is the ability to bundle all of your dependencies into a single executable.

> This has previously been possible using the concept of IL weavers. This topic is beyond the scope of this book; however, because IL is not compiled, it opens the door to changing it after the project has been deployed.

In .NET Core 3, we can compile our project into a single executable by adding the following line to the `.csproj` file:

```
<PublishSingleFile>true</PublishSingleFile>
<RuntimeIdentifier>win-x64</RuntimeIdentifier>
<PublishReadyToRun>true</PublishReadyToRun>
```

When you publish the application, you'll get a single executable.

You can even reduce the size of this executable by using built-in *tree shaking*. This is the process of removing dependencies that are not used by the application; this requires the following additional line in the `.csproj` file:

```
<PublishTrimmed>true</PublishTrimmed>
```

> At the time of writing, this method did *not* copy across assets (images), so you will need to do that manually until that issue is fixed. Please see the following link for the current details on this feature: `https://docs.microsoft.com/en-us/dotnet/core/whats-new/dotnet-core-3-0`.

Summary

In this chapter, we migrated an existing WinForms application over to .NET Core 3. This means that, even though we might have an application that is 10 or 15 years old, you can update it to use the latest framework and take advantage of the performance improvements and new features afforded by .NET Core 3.

Taking advantage of the upgrade, we then investigated one of the key features of C# 8: nullable reference types. This means that, without the use of any third-party software, we were able to expose dozens of potential bugs in our legacy code base.

We didn't stop there; we then used XAML Islands to extend our application by incorporating UWP features into WinForms. This is potentially the most exciting feature, as it essentially means that you can rewrite a legacy WinForms application from the outside in.

In the final section, we took advantage of the new packaging methods available in .NET Core 3. We used the process of tree shaking to reduce the size of our output file, and compiled our code to a single executable.

Like me, you may be seeing a pattern with these features. .NET Core has, in this release, incorporated Windows-only features, meaning you can now take a legacy WinForms app and convert it to use the latest .NET Core, thereby benefiting from all the performance improvements. You can extend it by using component creating in WPF or UWP without needing to rewrite the application. Additionally, deployment is now made easier, as we can now compile into a single executable.

In the next chapter, we'll be looking ASP.NET Core 3 and creating an MVC application that uses Cosmos DB.

2
Task Bug Logging ASP.NET Core MVC App Using Cosmos DB

In this chapter, we will take a look at using Cosmos DB with ASP.NET Core MVC by creating a task/bug logging application. A personal task manager is useful, and logging bugs is especially handy when you can't attend to them immediately.

We will cover the following topics in this chapter:

- Setting up a Cosmos DB instance on Azure
- Scaling and replication features of Cosmos DB
- Creating an ASP.NET Core MVC application and integrating Cosmos DB

Cosmos DB is Microsoft's rebranding of a document database called DocumentDB. In addition to providing the facilities of a NoSQL database, it also provides a globally scalable solution with virtually no effort.

Technical requirements

The code from this chapter can be found on GitHub at `https://github.com/PacktPublishing/C-8-and-.NET-Core-3-Projects-Using-Azure-Second-Edition`.

Benefits of using Cosmos DB

It's probably worth spending some time exploring why you might choose to use Cosmos rather than one of the myriad other database engines. There are two questions here: why cloud, and why Cosmos specifically?

Why cloud? It's Microsoft's job to scale – not yours

Because Cosmos DB is managed by Microsoft, transitioning to it means that there are suddenly some things that you don't need to worry about. For example, have you ever tried to configure SQL Server to fail over, or what about if you're located in the US and your customers are in Australia? Cosmos handles all these scenarios for you on a pay-as-you-go arrangement. Obviously, if you want your data replicated on four continents and with a huge throughput, then you'll pay more. To paraphrase Winston Churchill:

> *"Using a cloud solution is the most expensive thing you can do - except for all the others!"*

If you've ever been involved in discussions around buying a decent server and managing failovers, and the cost of employing people to set up and support those servers, you'll realize that it isn't that expensive after all.

Why Cosmos? Compatibility with industry-leading APIs and global distribution

Cosmos supports what is known as a multi-model API. This means that if, for example, you had an existing app that was using DocumentDB or MongoDB, you could simply point it at the Cosmos instance and tell it that you want to use that particular API. You can ask for your data to be replicated in a region close to where the data will be accessed from, reducing latency.

Setting up Azure Cosmos DB

Throughout this book, we will be using Azure as the cloud provider of choice. If you want to follow along and do not currently have an account, then you can create one at `https://azure.microsoft.com/`. At the time of writing, you can sign up for free and receive £150/$200 of credits for the first month.

Once you've signed up, visit `https://portal.azure.com`. Here, you can manage your Azure resources and check your balance.

> TIP: All cloud providers (at least at the time of writing) have a business model whereby you will get billed for your usage. The fact that you can walk away from your machine does not necessarily mean that any processes that you may have been running in the cloud will stop. This is a very different paradigm from the days when your machine being off meant that nothing was running. At the end of each chapter that uses cloud resources will be a *Clean up* section, which will talk you through the process of tearing down all the resources that you have created.

Once you've logged into the portal, search for Cosmos DB:

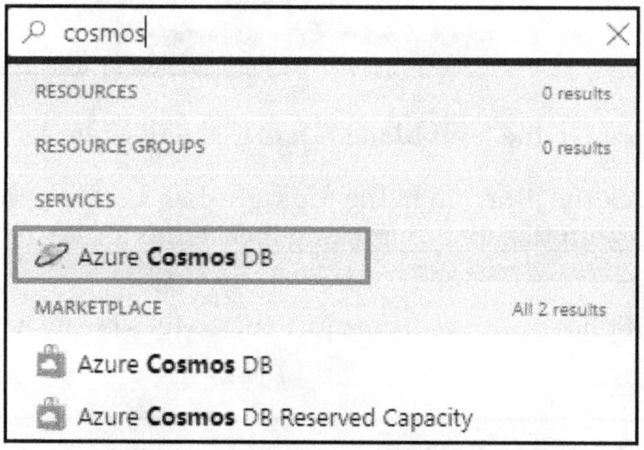

Once you select **Azure Cosmos DB**, you'll be presented with the Cosmos DB blade:

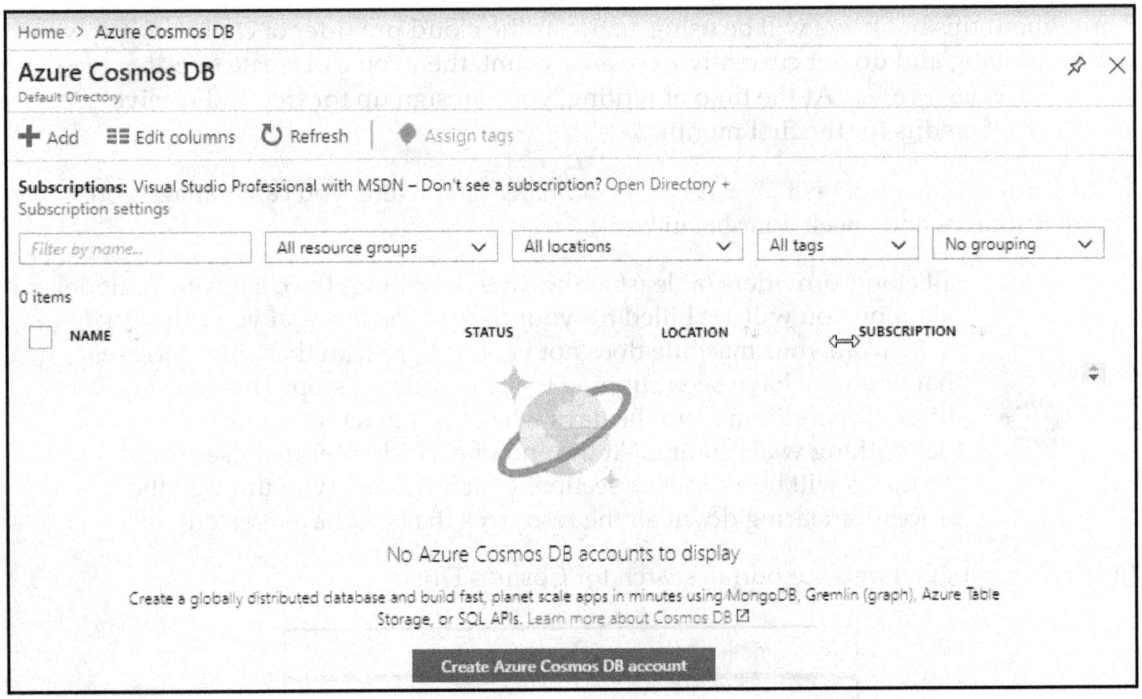

In this context, the term **blade** refers to the discrete sections of the portal.

If you click the little pin in the top right-hand corner, the blade will be added to your dashboard, making it easier to locate in the future.

As you can see, we don't have any resources just yet, so let's create a new database by selecting **Add**:

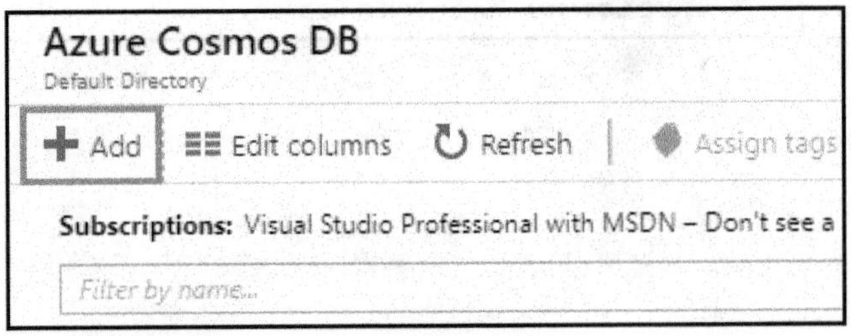

Once you click the option to add a database, you will be presented with a new screen. This gives you the chance to configure the name and location of your DB, along with the type of API you'd like to use. Let's start by creating a new resource group. We can then use this group for all future resources pertaining to this book:

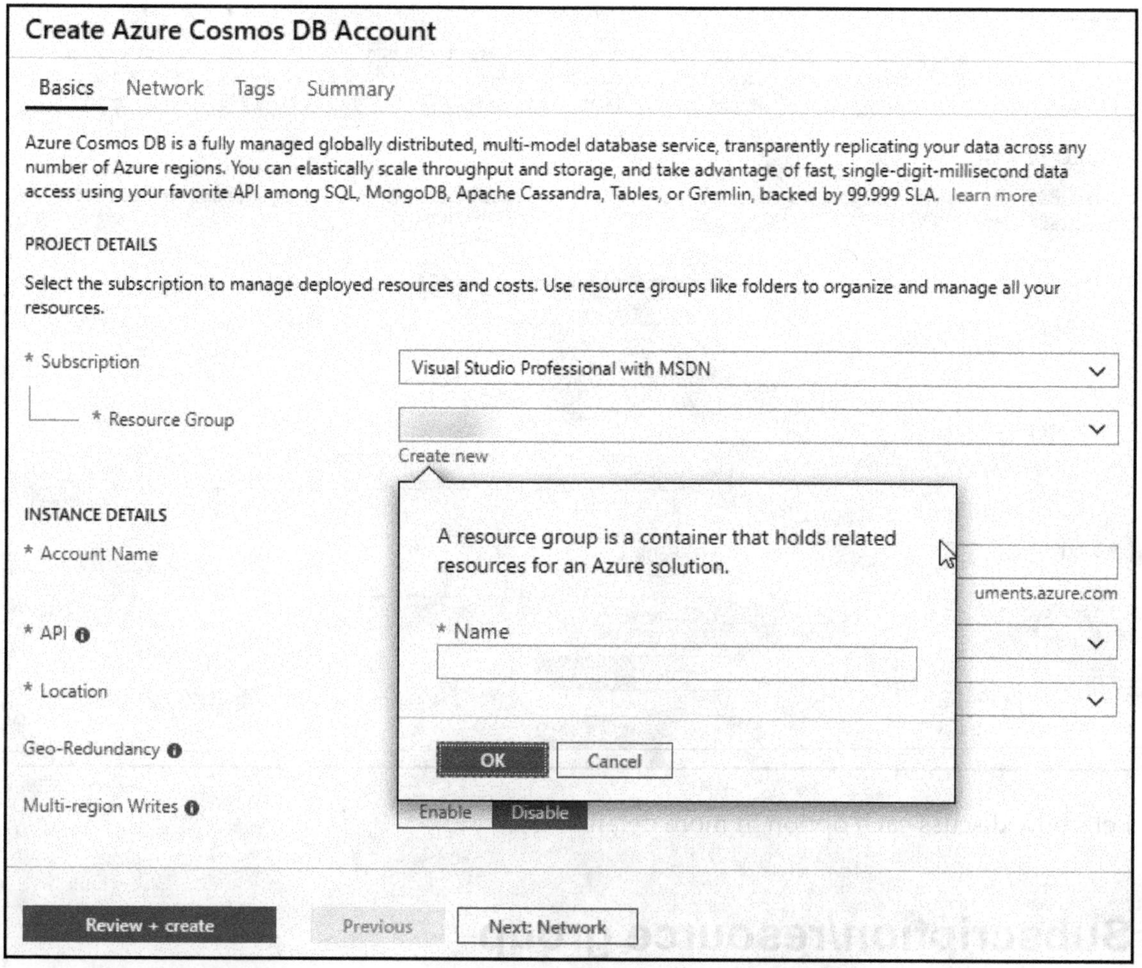

My completed form looks like this:

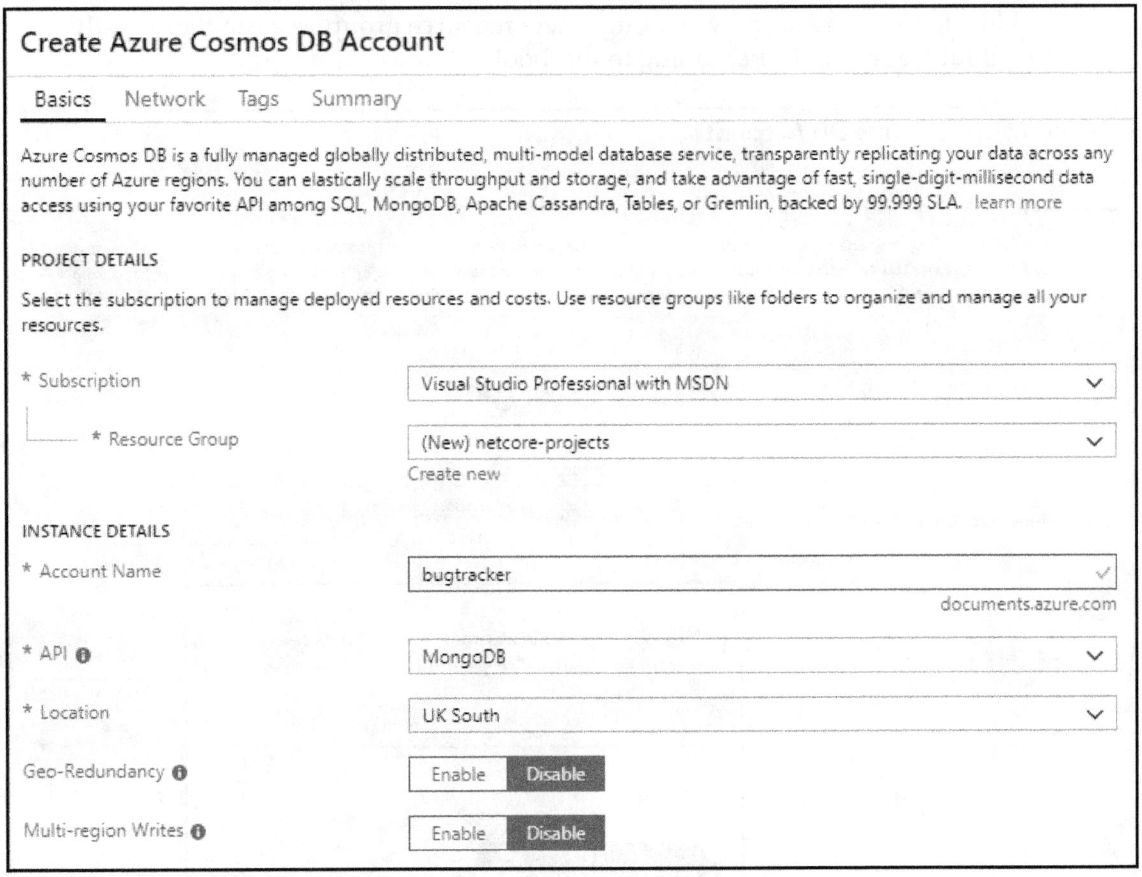

Let's now discuss each option in more detail.

Subscription/resource group

Your subscription is likely to have either been provided by your organization (for example, MyCompanyLtd Dev) or you may be running on a private MSDN subscription. Depending on your organization's size and the size of the product you're working on, you may have a subscription for the product that you're working on, a subscription for the entire company, or somewhere in between. If you're running on an MSDN account, then that will appear here, too.

At the time of writing, having an MSDN subscription entitles you to a number of Azure credits each month; the exact number depends on the subscription type.

The resource group is just that: a way to group resources together. There are no rules, but it makes sense to group resources that have a similar lifetime and purpose.

This diagram illustrates the relationship between the various hierarchical entities within Azure:

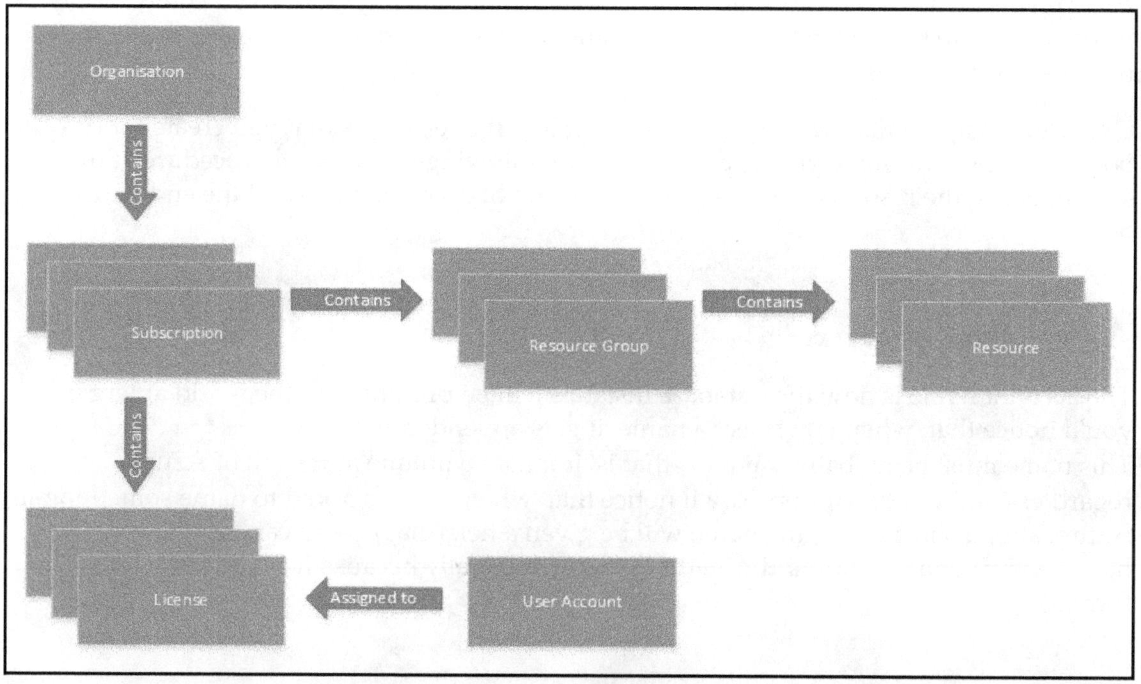

A resource is, effectively, anything that you can consume and be billed for. In our case, our Cosmos DB instance is our resource; as you can see, this exists within a resource group, and this, in turn, exists inside a subscription.

While a detailed explanation of resource groups and their management is beyond the scope of this chapter (and book), simply think of resources as tools, and a resource group as a toolbox: you might put tools that you would need for a plumbing job (wrench, pliers, etc...) into one toolbox, and tools that you might need for painting (brushes, masking tape, etc...) into another box. Resource groups are similar: a database, the application or applications that use that database, monitoring tools (Application Insights), and so on, would all go into a resource group. In a real scenario, you would probably split this by purpose as well, so you might have dev, test, and live resource groups.

Stretching the toolbox analogy to the disposal of resources, if you were finished with a particular type of job—for example, if you weren't painting anymore—you could simply throw the entire toolbox in the bin. In the same way, simply deleting a resource group will remove any resources within it.

One thing that you may wish to do is to keep all of the resources that you create for this book in a single resource group, and, instead of following the *clean-up* procedure at the end, simply delete the resource group (either at the end of each chapter, or at the end of the book).

Account name

The account name is how the database instance will be presented to the world at large; you'll notice that, when you select a name, it gets appended with `.documents.azure.com`. This name must be globally unique—that is, it must be unique across all of Azure, regardless of the subscription. You'll notice that, when you are asked to name something in Azure, after a short while, the name will be given a tick (that is, you can use the name you have chosen) or a cross (to indicate that you can't, usually because it's taken or in the wrong format).

API

The API allows you to interact with the instance in different ways—for example, we have chosen **MongoDB** here, which means that we will be able to treat the Cosmos DB instance as though it were a MongoDB instance.

> Setting the API does change the way that you interact with the database, but it does not change the underlying data. At the time of writing, it is not possible to change this selection once you have made it however; it would appear that the functionality to switch this API selection after creation is something that Microsoft would like to introduce in the future.

This is the second edition of this book, and, in the first edition, this chapter dealt with interfacing with MongoDB. By selecting a MongoDB API, we should be able to use the exact same code and simply switch the database.

Location

Location is a much bigger topic than we can cover here; however, essentially you are selecting the place where your resource will be physically located. Because information travels at a finite speed, you should consider this selection carefully; however, Cosmos does allow the opportunity to replicate the data in other physical locations. So if, as I am, you are located in the United Kingdom, you might set the location there. But if, say, 30% of your user base is located in Australia, then, with Cosmos, you can have your data replicated in that region, reducing latency.

Geo-redundancy/multi-region writes

The geo-redundancy and multi-region write settings relate to Cosmos's ability to store data in multiple physical locations simultaneously. Both are very big topics, but the basic idea is simple: make your data geo-redundant if it is important that your data is safe, and enable multi-region writes if you wish to lower your latency time and have access from multiple physical locations across the globe.

> TIP: As is the case with all Azure services, these services have a cost associated with them. The billing model is relatively complex because the services are complex. If you are concerned about cost, Microsoft provides a calculator (`https://azure.microsoft.com/en-gb/pricing/calculator`) that will give you an idea of how much any given service might cost.

Once all of these settings are complete, select **Review + Create**, then click **Create**.

> **TIP:** Creating the resource can take a few minutes, so this may be a good time to get a coffee.

Configuring the Cosmos DB instance

Now that the resource is created, we can treat this database instance as though it was MongoDB. To start with, we'll need to launch the **Data Explorer**:

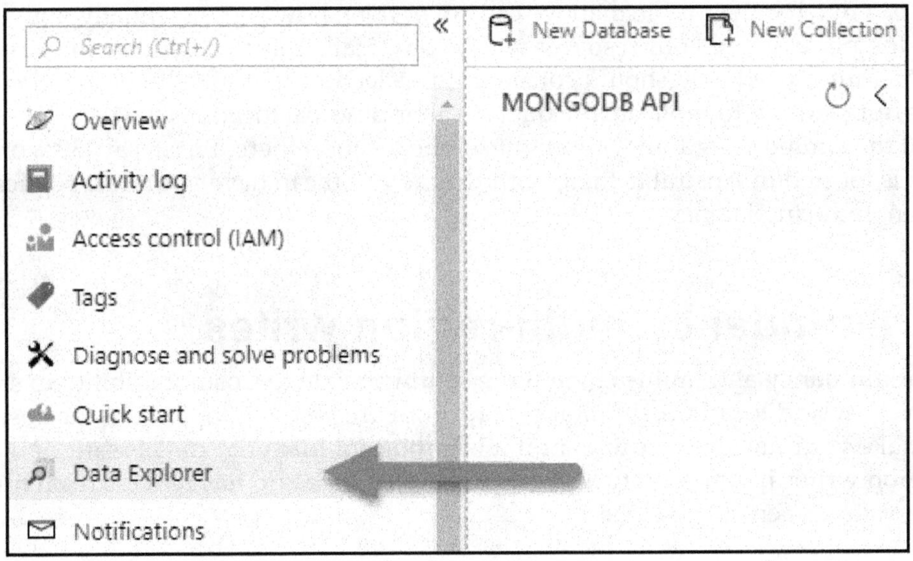

From here, we can select the following option to create a new collection:

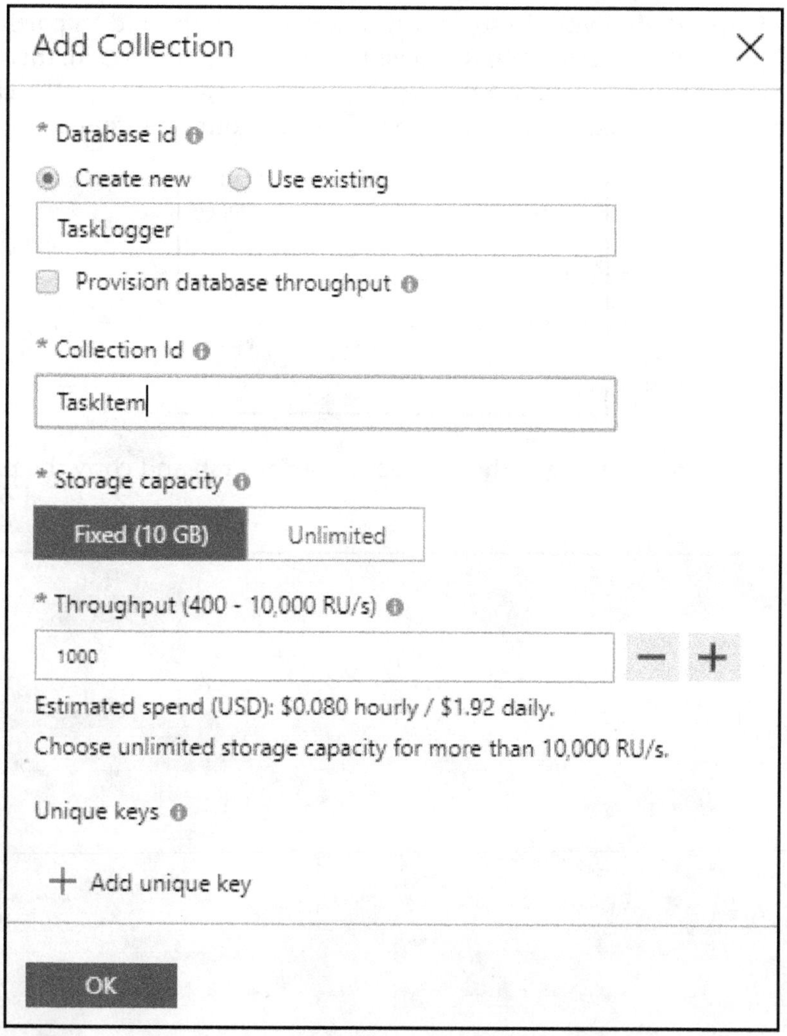

As you can see, I've left the default values here. It's worth noting that **Fixed (10 GB)** is not the recommended value, and, in a production-grade application, you would very likely want to choose **Unlimited**. If you do so, then you will need to provide a partition key. I've left the throughput as the default **1000 Request Units per second** (**RU/s**): this effectively allows you to pay for the performance that you need; the slower you go, the cheaper it is (and vice-versa)! Once created, you should be able to see your new collection:

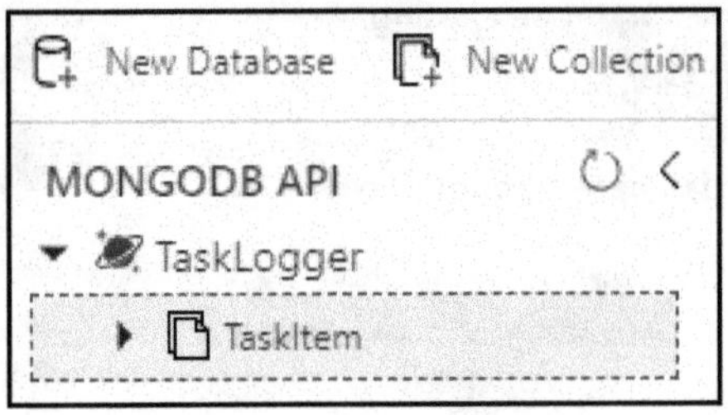

The last thing to do is to navigate to the connection strings tab and copy the primary connection string:

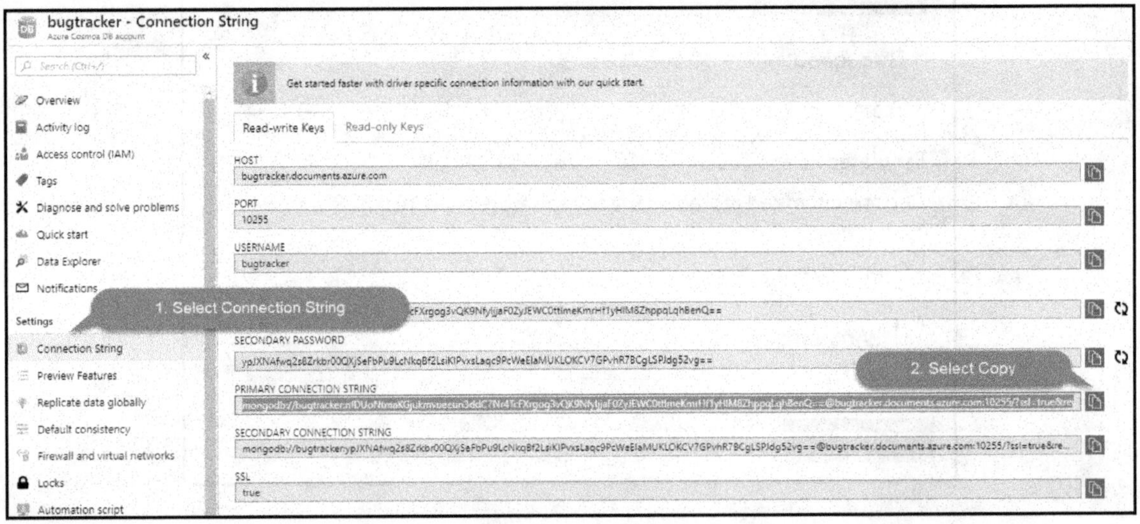

Now that our Cosmos DB instance is configured, we can move on to creating our web application and connecting to it.

Connecting your ASP.NET Core MVC application to Cosmos DB

When talking about using Cosmos DB in your application, one wonders how easy it will be to add this functionality to a new ASP.NET Core MVC application. The process is really easy. To start off, create a new project:

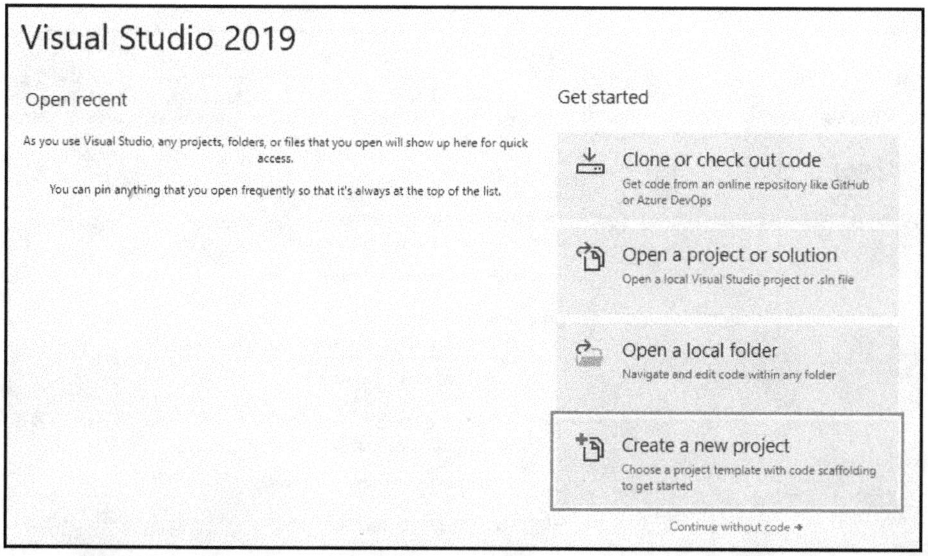

1. Name the project `BugTracker`:

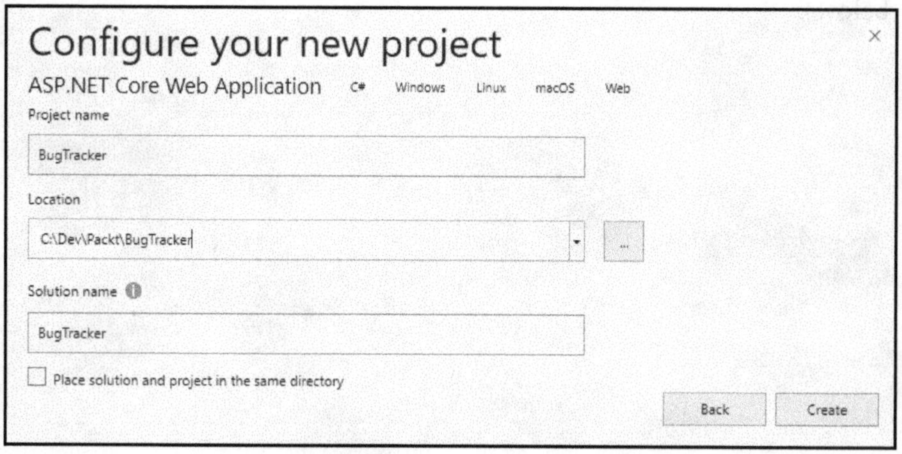

2. Select the option to create an **ASP.NET Core Web Application**:

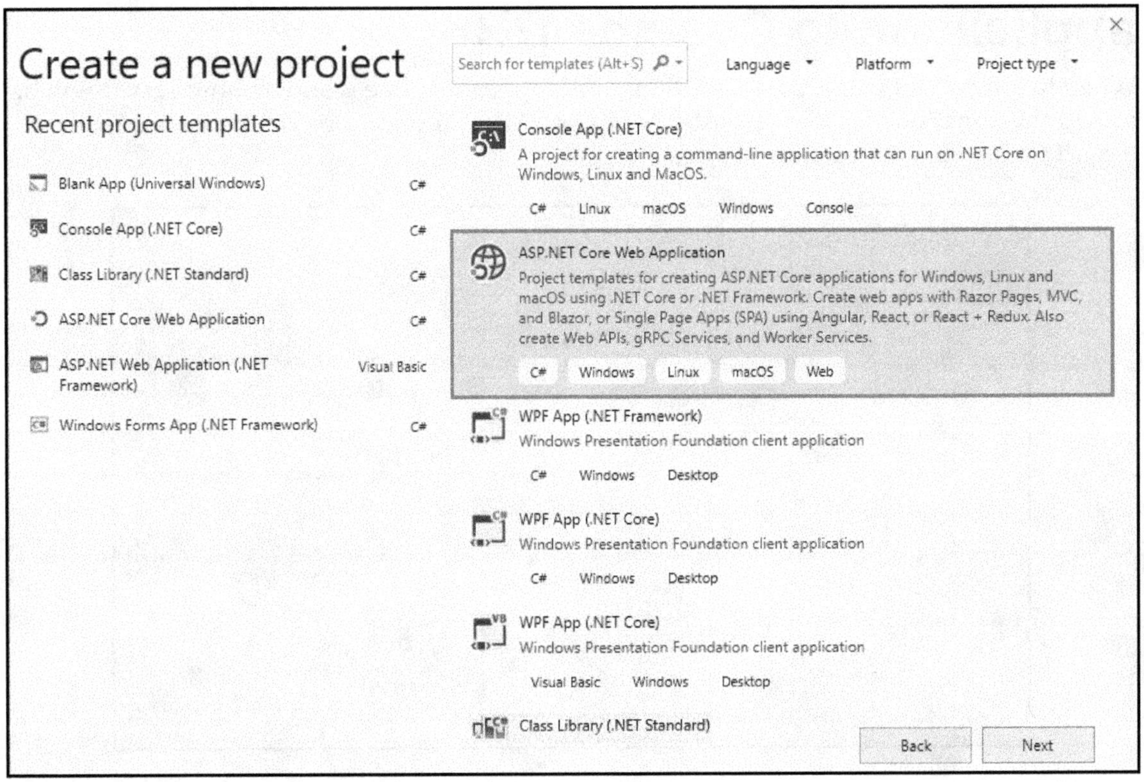

3. On the next screen, select the following options (referenced in the screenshot below):

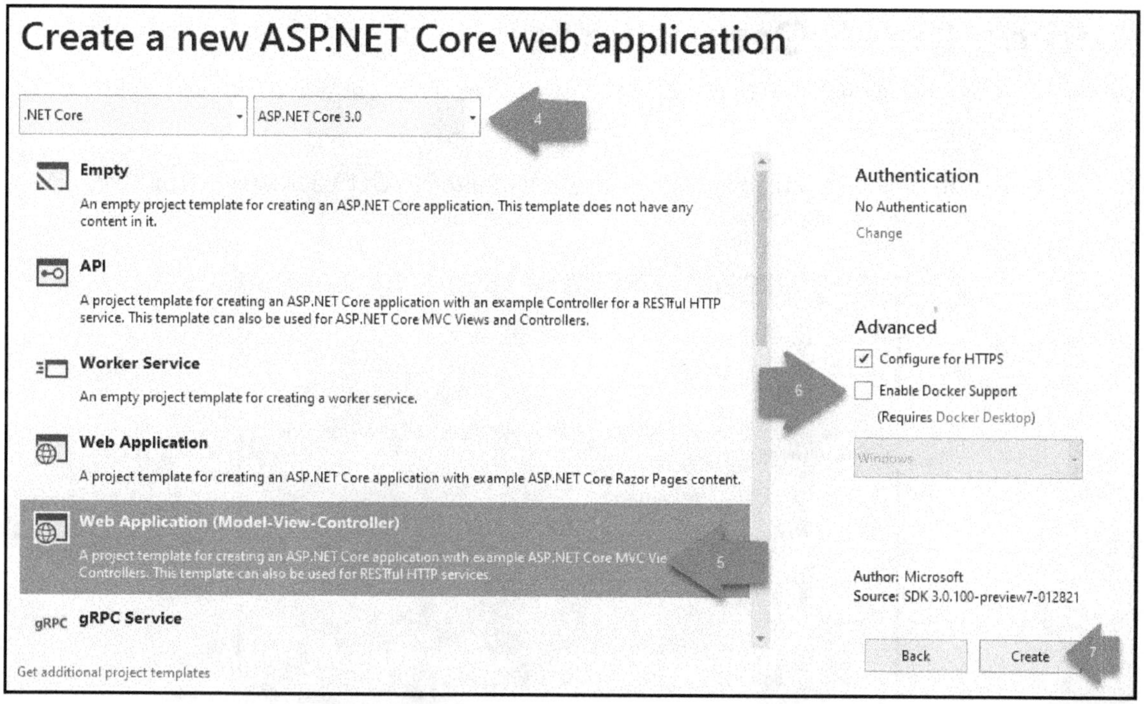

4. Select **ASP.NET Core 3.0** from the drop-down list.
5. Select **Web Application (Model-View-Controller)**.
6. Uncheck the **Enable Docker Support** option. Finally, click on the **OK** button.
7. Click **Create** and your new ASP.NET Core MVC application will be created.

> **TIP:** Enabling Docker support for your application can easily be done at creation time. You can also enable Docker support for existing applications.

We will take a look at Docker and how to make your application work with Docker in a later chapter. For now, our application does not need Docker support. Leave it unchecked and create your application as you would normally.

Adding the NuGet package

We need to add the MongoDB client API to our project. The best way to do this is by adding the NuGet package. We can do this as follows:

1. Right-click on your project and select **Manage NuGet Packages...** from the context menu, as shown in the following screenshot:

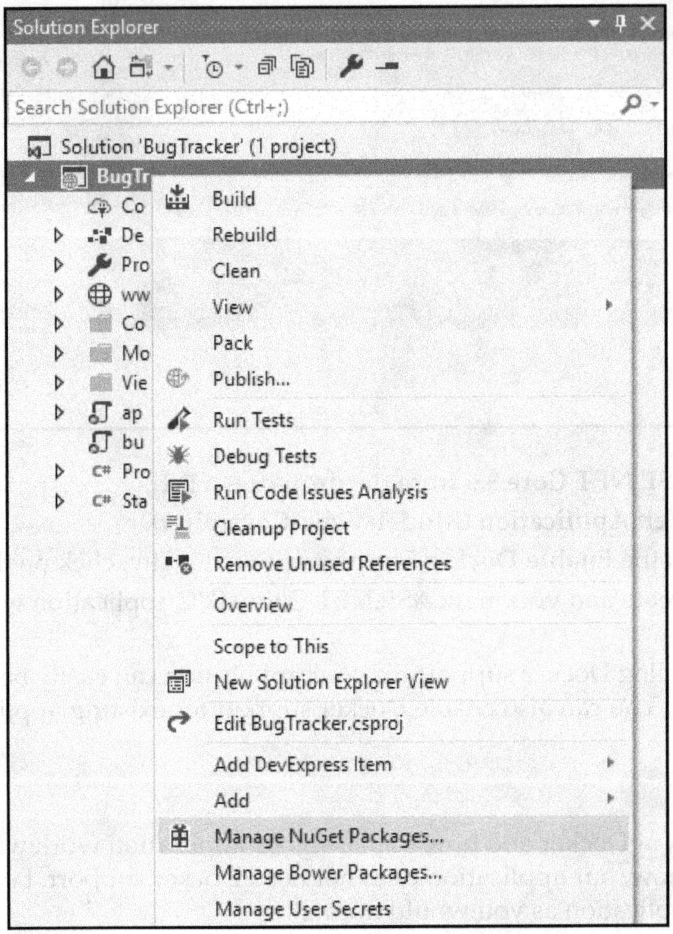

2. On the NuGet screen, select the **Browse** tab and enter `Mongodb.Driver` as the search term.
3. Select the **MongoDB.Driver by MongoDB** option.
4. Click on the **Install** button to add the latest stable package to your project. This is shown in the following screenshot:

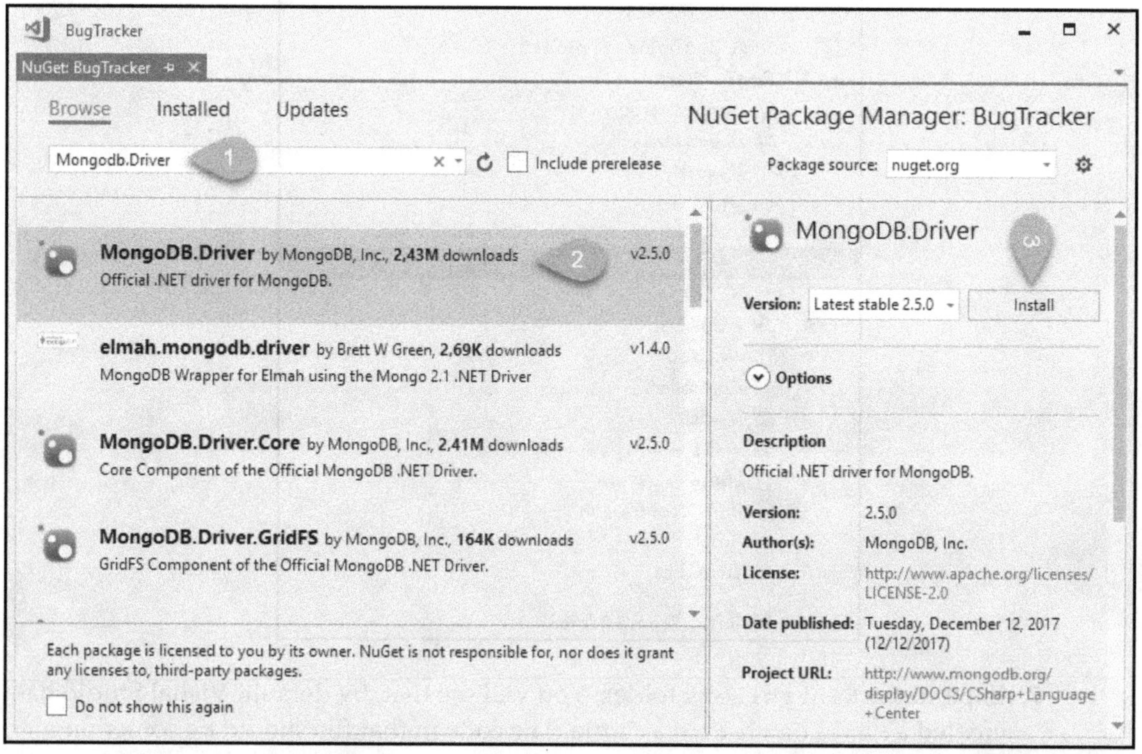

5. You can view the progress in the **Output** window of Visual Studio.

6. After MongoDB has been added to your project, you will see that **MongoDB.Driver (2.5.0)** has been added under the **NuGet** dependencies of your project, as shown in the following screenshot:

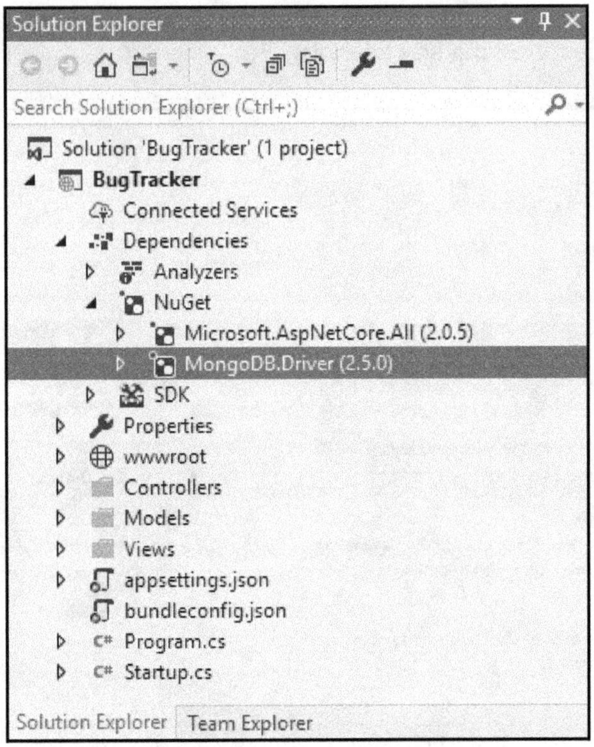

7. Expand the `Controllers` folder. You will see that, by default, Visual Studio has created a `HomeController.cs` file. The code in that file should be something like the following:

```
public class HomeController : Controller
{
    private readonly ILogger<HomeController> _logger;

    public HomeController(ILogger<HomeController> logger)
    {
        _logger = logger;
    }

    public IActionResult Index()
    {
        return View();
```

```
    }

    public IActionResult Privacy()
    {
        return View();
    }

    [ResponseCache(Duration = 0, Location =
ResponseCacheLocation.None, NoStore = true)]
    public IActionResult Error()
    {
        return View(new ErrorViewModel { RequestId =
Activity.Current?.Id ?? HttpContext.TraceIdentifier });
    }
}
```

We want to be able to connect to Cosmos DB from here, so let's create some code to connect to the Mongo client.

> You will need to add a `using` statement to your class as follows:
>
> `using MongoDB.Driver;`

The steps to connect to MongoDB are as follows:

1. Create a constructor by typing the snippet short code `ctor` and tabbing twice, or by typing in the code explicitly. Your constructor needs to create a new instance of `MongoClient`. When you have done this, your code should look as follows:

```
public HomeController()
{
    var mclient = new MongoClient();
}
```

> TIP: While this illustrates the usage of the `MongoClient`, instantiating a class inside a constructor like this is generally considered bad practice, as it makes it virtually impossible to unit test.

2. For `MongoClient` to work, we need to give it a connection string to the MongoDB instance we created. Open the `appsettings.json` file in the **Solution 'Bug Tracker'** pane, as shown in the following screenshot:

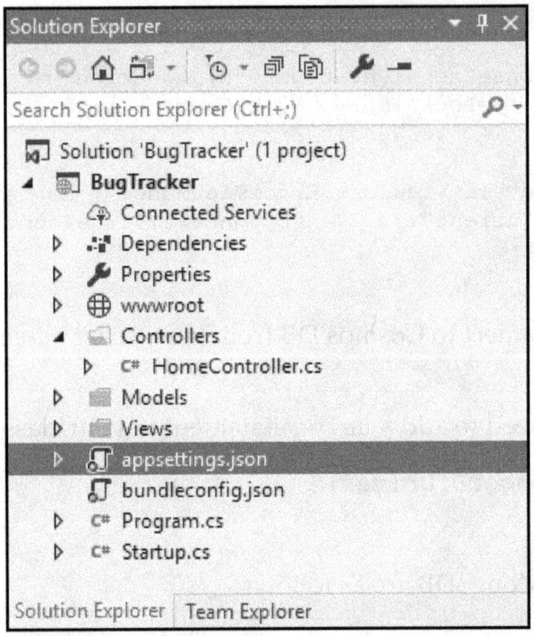

3. When you open your `appsettings.json` file, it should look as follows:

```
{
  "Logging": {
    "IncludeScopes": false,
    "LogLevel": {
      "Default": "Warning"
    }
  }
}
```

4. This is when you'll need the connection string that you copied earlier. Modify the file and add the MongoDB connection details, as follows (replacing `[connectionstring]` with the value that you copied earlier):

```
{
  "MongoConnection": {
    "ConnectionString": "[connectionstring]",
    "Database": "TaskLogger"
  },
```

```
        "Logging": {
          "IncludeScopes": false,
          "LogLevel": {
            "Default": "Warning"
          }
        }
      }
```

5. We now want to create a `Settings.cs` file in the `Models` folder, as shown in the following screenshot:

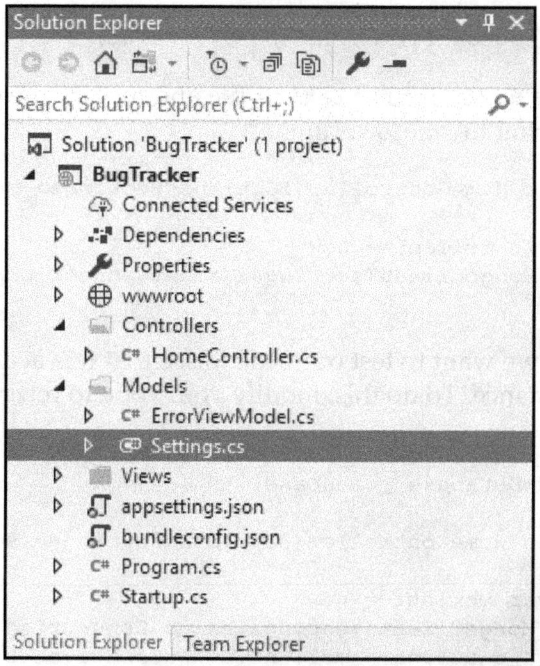

6. Open the `Settings.cs` file and add the following code to it:

```
public class Settings
{
    public string ConnectionString { get; set; }
    public string Database { get; set; }
}
```

7. We now need to open the `Startup.cs` file and modify the `ConfigureServices` method as follows, to register the service:

```
public void ConfigureServices(IServiceCollection services)
{
    services.AddControllersWithViews();
    services.AddRazorPages();

    services.Configure<Settings>(Options => {
Options.ConnectionString = Configuration.GetSection
  ("MongoConnection:ConnectionString").Value; Options.Database =
Configuration.GetSection
  ("MongoConnection:Database").Value; }); }
```

8. Go back to the `HomeController.cs` file and modify the constructor to pass the connection string to `MongoClient`:

```
public HomeController(IOptions<Settings> settings)
{
    var mclient = new
     MongoClient(settings.Value.ConnectionString);
}
```

9. At this point, we want to test our code to see that it is actually accessing my MongoDB instance. To do this, modify your code to return the cluster description:

```
IMongoDatabase _database;

public HomeController(IOptions<Settings> settings)
{
    var mclient = new
     MongoClient(settings.Value.ConnectionString);
      _database = mclient.GetDatabase(settings.Value.Database);
}

public IActionResult Index()
{
    return Json(_database.Client.Cluster.Description);
}
```

10. Run your ASP.NET Core MVC application and read the information output in the browser, as shown in the following screenshot:

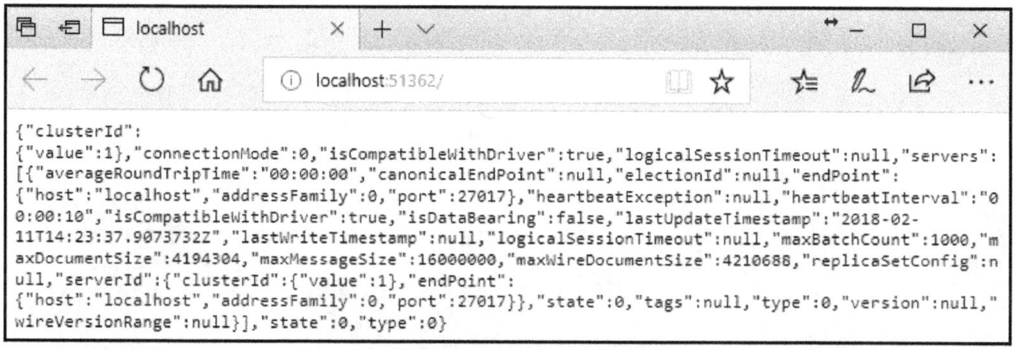
localhost
localhost:51362/
{"clusterId":
{"value":1},"connectionMode":0,"isCompatibleWithDriver":true,"logicalSessionTimeout":null,"servers":
[{"averageRoundTripTime":"00:00:00","canonicalEndPoint":null,"electionId":null,"endPoint":
{"host":"localhost","addressFamily":0,"port":27017},"heartbeatException":null,"heartbeatInterval":"0
0:00:10","isCompatibleWithDriver":true,"isDataBearing":false,"lastUpdateTimestamp":"2018-02-
11T14:23:37.9073732Z","lastWriteTimestamp":null,"logicalSessionTimeout":null,"maxBatchCount":1000,"m
axDocumentSize":4194304,"maxMessageSize":16000000,"maxWireDocumentSize":4210688,"replicaSetConfig":n
ull,"serverId":{"clusterId":{"value":1},"endPoint":
{"host":"localhost","addressFamily":0,"port":27017}},"state":0,"tags":null,"type":0,"version":null,"
wireVersionRange":null}],"state":0,"type":0}

This is all well and good, but let's look at how to separate the logic of adding the database connection into a class of its own.

Creating the MongoDbRepository class

To create a `MongoDbRepository` class, we need to go through the following steps:

1. Create a new folder called `Data` in your solution. Inside that folder, create a new class called `MongoDBRepository`:

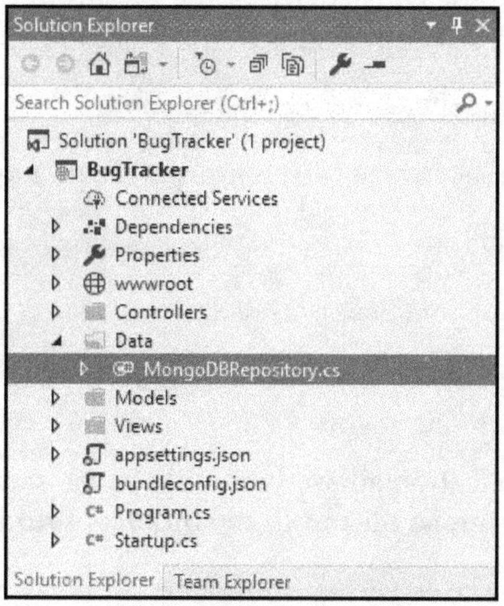

2. Inside this class, add the following code:

```
public class MongoDBRepository
{
    public readonly IMongoDatabase Database;

    public MongoDBRepository(IOptions<Settings> settings)
    {
        try
        {
            var mclient = new
             MongoClient(settings.Value.ConnectionString);
            Database =
             mclient.GetDatabase(settings.Value.Database);
        }
        catch (Exception ex)
        {
            throw new Exception("There was a problem connecting
             to the MongoDB database", ex);
        }
    }
}
```

If the code looks familiar, it's because it's the same code that we wrote in the `HomeController.cs` class; however, this time, it has a bit of error handling, and it's in its own class. This means that we also need to modify the `HomeController` class.

3. Change the code in the constructor of the `HomeController` as well as in the `Index` action. Your code needs to look as follows:

```
public MongoDBRepository mongoDb;

public HomeController(IOptions<Settings> settings)
{
    mongoDb =  new MongoDBRepository(settings);
}
public IActionResult Index()
{
    return Json(mongoDb.Database.Client.Cluster.Description);
}
```

4. Running your application again, you will see the same information displayed earlier in the browser, so output to the browser window again.

The only difference is that the code is now separated properly and makes it easy to reuse. Therefore, if any changes happen further on down the line, it only gets updated here.

Now that we've created our web application, we can move on to accessing and updating the data in our DB instance.

Reading and writing data to MongoDB

In this section, we will have a look at how to read a list of work items from the MongoDB database and how to insert a new work item into the database (I use the term work item to refer to a task or a bug). This can be done by performing the following steps:

1. In the `Models` folder, create a new class called `WorkItem`, as shown in the following screenshot:

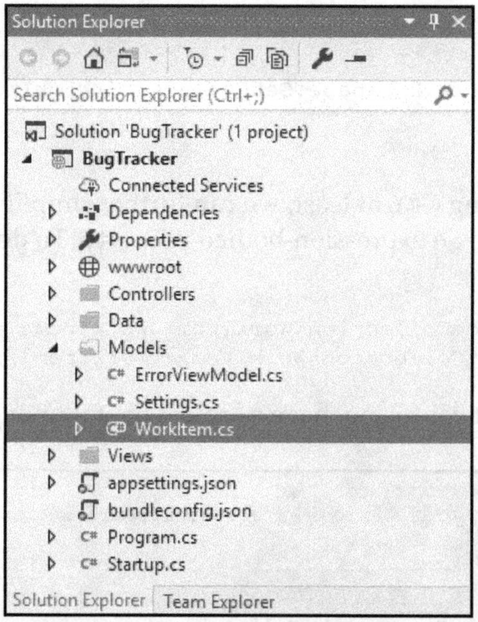

2. Add the following code to the `WorkItem` class. You will notice that `Id` is of the `ObjectId` type. This represents the unique identifier in the MongoDB document that gets created.

> You need to ensure that you add the following `using` statement to your `WorkItem` class `using MongoDB.Bson;`.

Take a look at the following code:

```
public class WorkItem
{
    public ObjectId Id { get; set; }
    public string Title { get; set; }
    public string Description { get; set; }
    public int Severity { get; set; }
    public string WorkItemType { get; set; }
    public string AssignedTo { get; set; }
}
```

3. Next, open up the `MongoDBRepository` class and add the following property to the class:

```
public IMongoCollection<WorkItem> WorkItems
{
    get
    {
        return Database.GetCollection<WorkItem>("workitem");
    }
}
```

4. Since we are using C# 6 at least, we can further simplify the `WorkItem` property by changing it to an expression-bodied property. To do this, change the code to look as follows:

```
public IMongoCollection<WorkItem> WorkItems =>
Database.GetCollection<WorkItem>("workitem");
```

5. If this looks a bit confusing, have a look at the following screenshot:

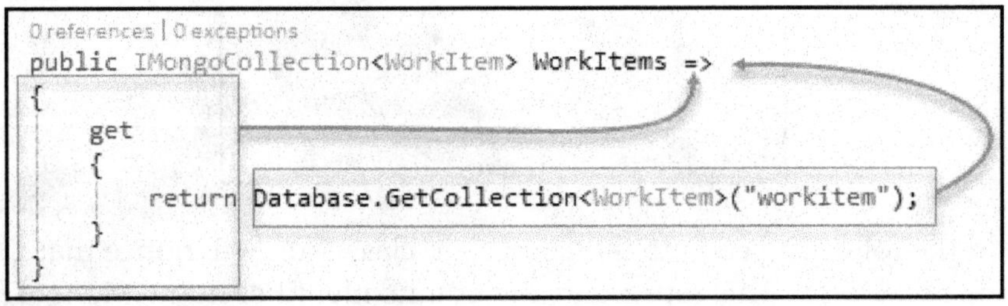

The curly braces, `get`, and `return` statements are replaced by the => lambda operator. The object being returned (in this case, the collection of `WorkItem` objects) goes after the lambda operator. This results in the expression-bodied property.

Creating the interfaces and WorkItemService

Next, we need to create an interface. To do this, we need to go through the following steps:

1. Create a new folder in your solution called `Interfaces` and add an interface called `IWorkItemService` to the `Interfaces` folder, as shown in the following screenshot:

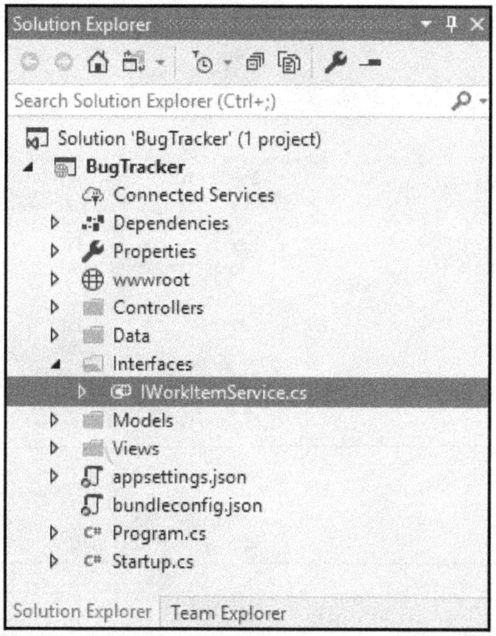

2. Add the following code to the `IWorkItemService` interface:

```
public interface IWorkItemService
{
    IEnumerable<WorkItem> GetAllWorkItems();
}
```

3. In your `Data` folder, add another class called `WorkItemService` and make it implement the `IWorkItemService` interface.

> Be sure to add the `using` statement to reference your interface. In my example, this is the `using BugTracker.Interfaces;` statement.

4. You will notice that Visual Studio prompts you to implement the interface. To do this, click on the light bulb tip and click on **Implement interface** from the context menu, as shown in the following screenshot:

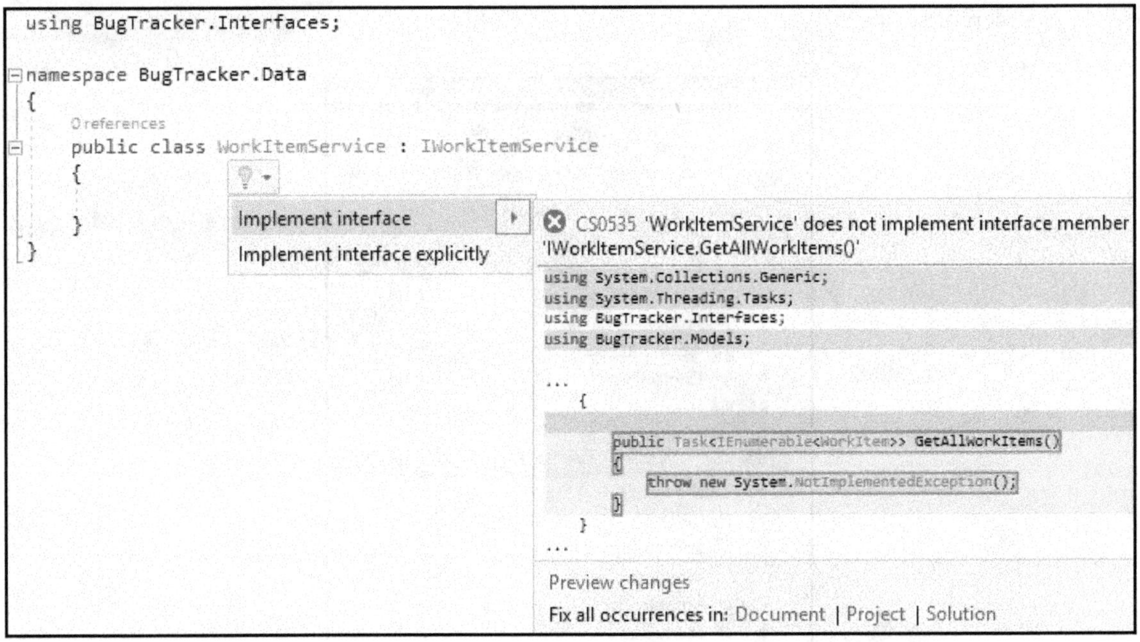

5. After you have done this, your `WorkItemService` class will appear as follows:

```
public class WorkItemService : IWorkItemService
{
    public IEnumerable<WorkItem> GetAllWorkItems()
    {
        throw new System.NotImplementedException();
    }
}
```

6. Next, add a constructor and complete the `GetAllWorkItems` method so that your class appears as follows:

```
public class WorkItemService : IWorkItemService
{
    private readonly MongoDBRepository repository;

    public WorkItemService(IOptions<Settings> settings)
    {
        repository = new MongoDBRepository(settings);
    }
    public IEnumerable<WorkItem> GetAllWorkItems()
    {
        return repository.WorkItems.Find(x => true).ToList();
    }
}
```

7. You now need to open up your `Startup.cs` file and edit the `ConfigureServices` method to add the following line of code:

```
services.AddScoped<IWorkItemService, WorkItemService>();
```

8. Your `ConfigureServices` method will now look as follows:

```
public void ConfigureServices(IServiceCollection services)
{
    services.AddMvc();

    services.Configure<Settings>(Options =>
    {
        Options.ConnectionString =
Configuration.GetSection("MongoConnection:ConnectionString").Value;
        Options.Database =
Configuration.GetSection("MongoConnection:Database").Value;
    });

    services.AddScoped<IWorkItemService, WorkItemService>();
}
```

What you have done is registered the `IWorkItemService` interface; this adds the class `WorkItemService` to the dependency injection framework. For more information on dependency injection, read the following article at `https://docs.microsoft.com/en-us/aspnet/core/fundamentals/dependency-injection`.

Creating the view

When we start our application, we want to see a list of work items. Therefore, we need to create a view for `HomeController` to display a list of work items by going through the following steps:

1. In the `Views` folder, expand the `Home` subfolder and delete the `Index.cshtml` file, if there is one.
2. Then, right-click the `Home` folder and navigate to **Add** | **View** from the context menu. The **Add MVC View** window will be displayed.
3. Name the view `Index` and select **List** as the **Template**. From the dropdown for **Model class**, select **WorkItem (BugTracker.Models)**.
4. Leave the rest of the settings as they are and click on the **Add** button:

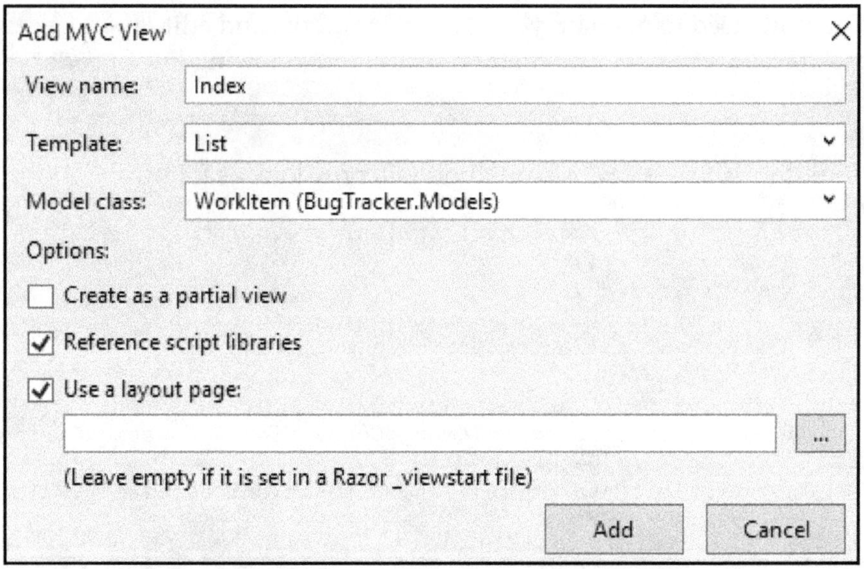

After the view has been added, your **Solution Explorer** will look as follows:

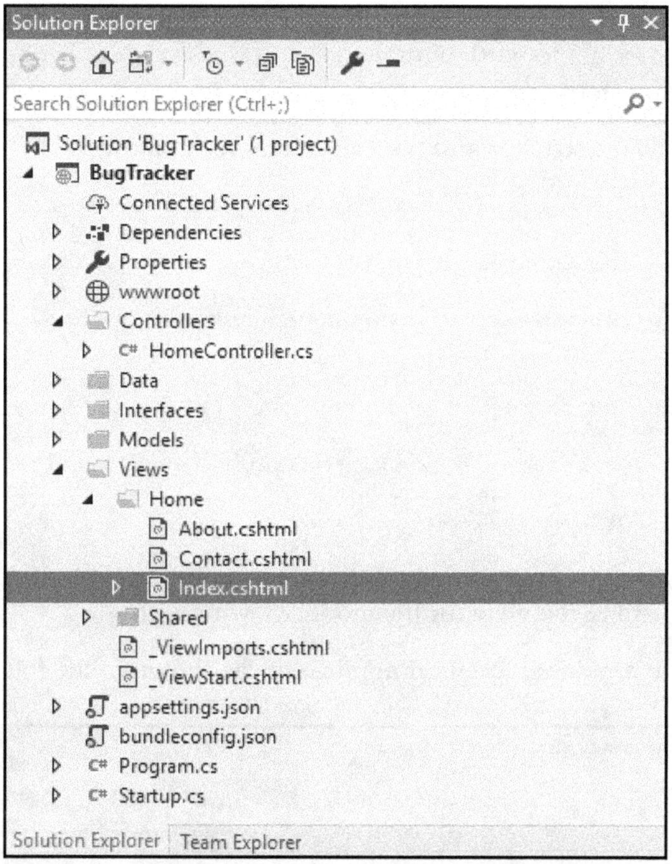

5. Taking a closer look at the view, you will notice that it uses `IEnumerable<BugTracker.Models.WorkItem>` as the model:

```
@model IEnumerable<BugTracker.Models.WorkItem>

@{
    ViewData["Title"] = "Work Item Listings";
}
```

This allows us to iterate the collection of the `WorkItem` objects returned and output them in the list. Also note that `ViewData["Title"]` has been updated from `Index` to `Work Item Listings`.

Modifying the HomeController

The last thing we need to do before we can run our application is to modify the `HomeController` class to work with the `IWorkItemService`. Let's set this up by going through the following steps:

1. Modify the constructor and the `Index` action as follows:

```
private readonly IWorkItemService _workItemService;

public HomeController(IWorkItemService workItemService)
{
    _workItemService = workItemService;
}

public IActionResult Index()
{
    var workItems = _workItemService.GetAllWorkItems();
    return View(workItems);
}
```

   With this code, we are getting all the work items in the MongoDB database and passing them to the view for the model to work with.

2. When you are done, run your application, as shown in the following screenshot:

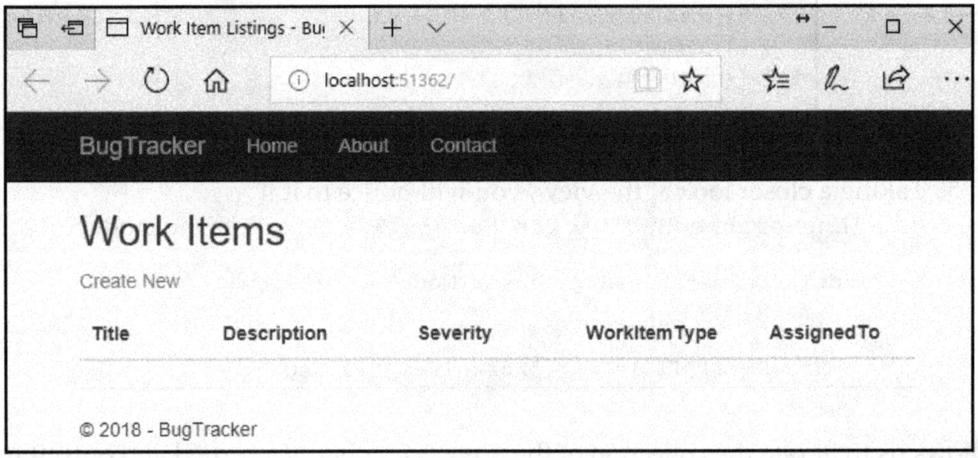

At this point, there are no work items in the database, so we see this empty list in the browser. Next, we will add the code to insert work items into our MongoDB database.

Adding work items

Let's add work items by going through the following steps:

1. To add work items, let's start off by adding a class to our `Models` folder called `AddWorkItem`, as shown in the following screenshot:

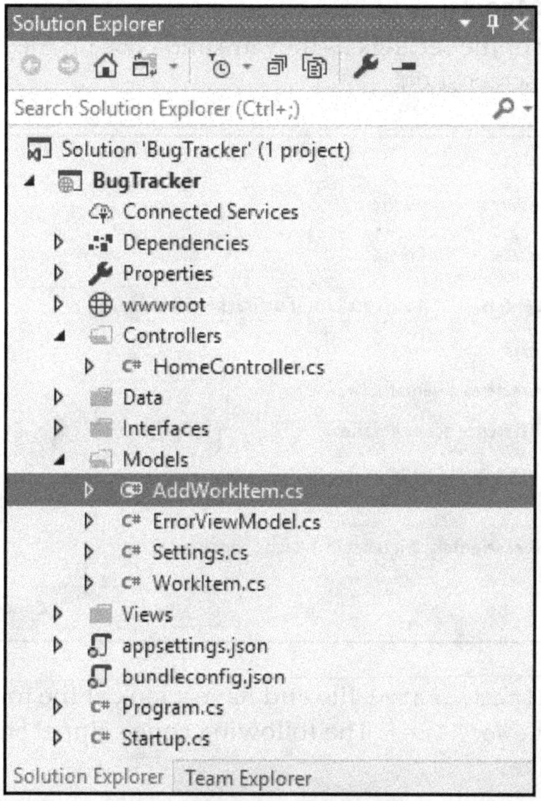

2. Modify the code in the class to essentially look like the `WorkItem` class:

```
public class AddWorkItem
{
    public string Title { get; set; }
    public string Description { get; set; }
    public int Severity { get; set; }
    public string WorkItemType { get; set; }
    public string AssignedTo { get; set; }
}
```

3. Next, create a new folder under the `Views` folder called `AddWorkItem`. Right-click the `AddWorkItem` folder, select **Add**, and then click on **View** in the context menu.
4. The **Add MVC View** window will be displayed. Call the view `AddItem` and select **Create** for **Template**.
5. From the dropdown for **Model class**, select **AddWorkItem (BugTracker.Models)**.
6. Leave the rest of the settings as they are and click on the **Add** button, as shown in the following screenshot:

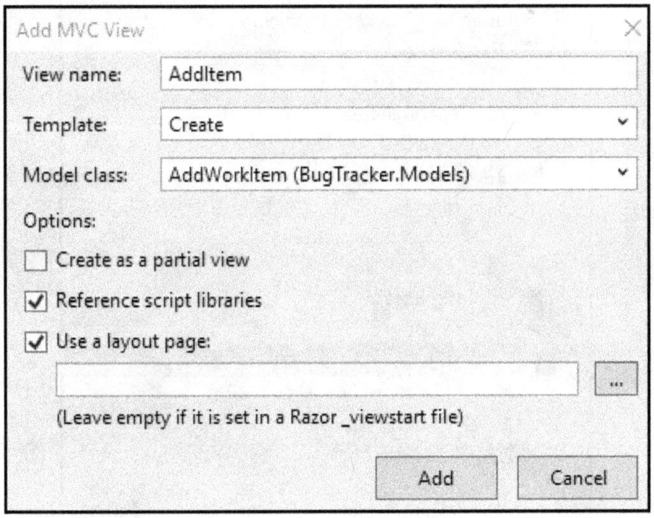

7. Open the `AddItem.cshtml` file and have a look at the form action. Ensure that it is set to `CreateWorkItem`. The following code snippet shows what the code should look like:

```
<div class="row">
  <div class="col-md-4">
     <form asp-action="CreateWorkItem">
          <div asp-validation-summary="ModelOnly" class="text-
danger"></div> @*Rest of code omitted for brevity*@
```

Your `Views` folder should now look as follows:

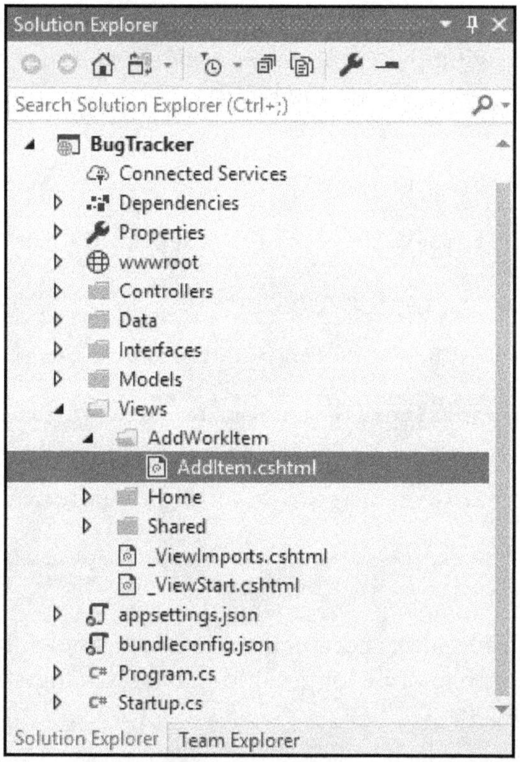

8. Now, we need to make a small change to our `IWorkItemService` interface. Modify the code in the interface to look as follows:

```
public interface IWorkItemService
{
    IEnumerable<WorkItem> GetAllWorkItems();
    void InsertWorkItem(WorkItem workItem);
}
```

We have just specified that the classes that implement the `IWorkItemService` interface must have a method called `InsertWorkItem` that takes a parameter of the `WorkItem` type. This means that we need to swing by `WorkItemService` and add a method called `InsertWorkItem`. Our code in the `WorkItemService` interface will look as follows:

```
private readonly MongoDBRepository repository;

public WorkItemService(IOptions<Settings> settings)
{
    repository = new MongoDBRepository(settings);
}
public IEnumerable<WorkItem> GetAllWorkItems()
{
    return repository.WorkItems.Find(x => true).ToList();
}

public void InsertWorkItem(WorkItem workItem)
{
    throw new System.NotImplementedException();
}
```

9. Change the `InsertWorkItem` method to add a single object of the `WorkItem` type to our MongoDB database. Change the code to look as follows:

```
public void InsertWorkItem(WorkItem workItem)
{
    repository.WorkItems.InsertOne(workItem);
}
```

10. Now, we need to modify our `WorkItem` class slightly. Add two constructors to the class, one that takes an `AddWorkItem` object as a parameter and another that takes no parameters at all:

```
public class WorkItem
{
    public ObjectId Id { get; set; }
    public string Title { get; set; }
    public string Description { get; set; }
    public int Severity { get; set; }
    public string WorkItemType { get; set; }
    public string AssignedTo { get; set; }

    public WorkItem()
    {

    }

    public WorkItem(AddWorkItem addWorkItem)
    {
        Title = addWorkItem.Title;
        Description = addWorkItem.Description;
        Severity = addWorkItem.Severity;
        WorkItemType = addWorkItem.WorkItemType;
        AssignedTo = addWorkItem.AssignedTo;
    }
}
```

The reason we have added a second constructor that takes no parameters is so that MongoDB can deserialize `WorkItem`.

During deserialization, an instance of the object is created. As a result, a parameterless constructor is necessary; otherwise, the deserialization would be unable to create the object (as it has no way of determining the relevant parameters.)

11. We now need to add another controller to our project. Right-click the `Controllers` folder and add a new controller called `AddWorkItemController`. Feel free to add this as an empty controller. We will add the code in next ourselves:

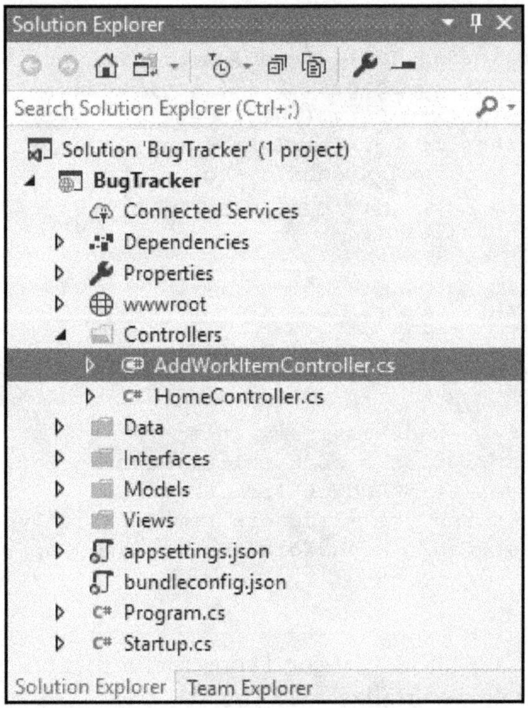

12. In the `AddWorkItemController` controller, add the following code:

```
private readonly IWorkItemService _workItemService;

public AddWorkItemController(IWorkItemService workItemService)
{
    _workItemService = workItemService;
}

public ActionResult AddItem()
{
    return View();
}

[HttpPost]
public ActionResult CreateWorkItem(AddWorkItem addWorkItem)
```

```
{
    var workItem = new WorkItem(addWorkItem);
    _workItemService.InsertWorkItem(workItem);
    return RedirectToAction("Index", "Home");
}
```

You will notice that the `HttpPost` action is called `CreateWorkItem`. This is the reason that the `AddItem.cshtml` file had a form action called `CreateWorkItem`. It tells the view what action to call on the controller when the **Create** button is clicked.

Redirecting to the list of work items

Another interesting thing to note is that, after we call the `InsertWorkItem` method on the `WorkItemService`, we redirect the view to the `Index` action on the `HomeController`. As we already know, this will take us to the list of work items. Let's wire-up a call to `AddWorkItem`:

1. Modify the `HomeController` code to add another action called `AddWorkItem`; this will call the `AddItem` action on the `AddWorkItemController` class:

    ```
    public ActionResult AddWorkItem()
    {
        return RedirectToAction("AddItem", "AddWorkItem");
    }
    Your HomeController code will now look as follows:
    private readonly IWorkItemService _workItemService;

    public HomeController(IWorkItemService workItemService)
    {
        _workItemService = workItemService;
    }

    public IActionResult Index()
    {
        var workItems = _workItemService.GetAllWorkItems();
        return View(workItems);
    }

    public ActionResult AddWorkItem()
    {
        return RedirectToAction("AddItem", "AddWorkItem");
    }
    ```

2. Now, let's modify the `Index.cshtml` view slightly. To make the list on the index view more intuitive, modify the `Index.cshtml` file.

3. Add an `if` statement to allow for the addition of new work items from the list if the list is empty.

4. Add an `ActionLink` to call the `AddWorkItem` action on the `AddWorkItemController` when clicked (note that we provide an empty area to force the action to be relative to the root and not the `HomeController`):

```
@if (Model.Count() == 0)
{
    <tr>
        <td colspan="6">There are no Work Items in BugTracker.
@Html.ActionLink(linkText: "Add your first Work Item", actionName:
"AddItem", controllerName: "AddWorkItem") now.
        </td>
    </tr>
}
else
{
    @foreach (var item in Model)
    {
    <tr>
        <td>
            @Html.DisplayFor(modelItem => item.Title)
        </td>
        <td>
            @Html.DisplayFor(modelItem => item.Description)
        </td>
        <td>
            @Html.DisplayFor(modelItem => item.Severity)
        </td>
        <td>
            @Html.DisplayFor(modelItem => item.WorkItemType)
        </td>
        <td>
            @Html.DisplayFor(modelItem => item.AssignedTo)
        </td>
        <td>
            @Html.ActionLink("Edit", "Edit", new { /*
             id=item.PrimaryKey */ }) |
            @Html.ActionLink("Details", "Details", new { /*
             id=item.PrimaryKey */ }) |
            @Html.ActionLink("Delete", "Delete", new { /*
             id=item.PrimaryKey */ })
        </td>
    </tr>
    }
}
```

5. For now, wrap the `Create New` `asp-action` in the following `if` statement:

```
@if (Model.Count() > 0)
{
<p>
    <a asp-action="Create">Create New</a>
</p>
}
```

We will be looking at this later on. To take a look at the logic of the application at this point, we can see that the `HomeControllerIndex` action lists the work items. When we click on the **Add your first Work item** link, we call the `AddWorkItem` action on the `HomeController`.

The `AddWorkItem` action on the `AddWorkItemController`, in turn, calls the `AddItem` action on the `AddWorkItemController`. This simply returns the `AddItem` view where we enter the work item details and click on the **Create** button.

The **Create** button, in turn, uses an `HttpPost`, and, because the form action on the `AddItem` view points to the `CreateWorkItem` action on the `AddWorkItemController` class, we insert the work item into our MongoDB database and redirect back to the list of work items by performing a `RedirectToAction` call to the `Index` action on the `HomeController`.

> Now, at this point, if you are thinking that this is a long-winded way to redirect back to the `HomeController` just to redirect to the `AddItem` action on the `AddWorkItemController`, then you're 100% correct. I will show you a quick way to redirect straight to the `AddItem` action on the `AddWorkItemController` when the user clicks on the link to create a new work item. For now, just bear with me; I'm trying to show you how we can interact with controllers and actions.

Now, run your application again:

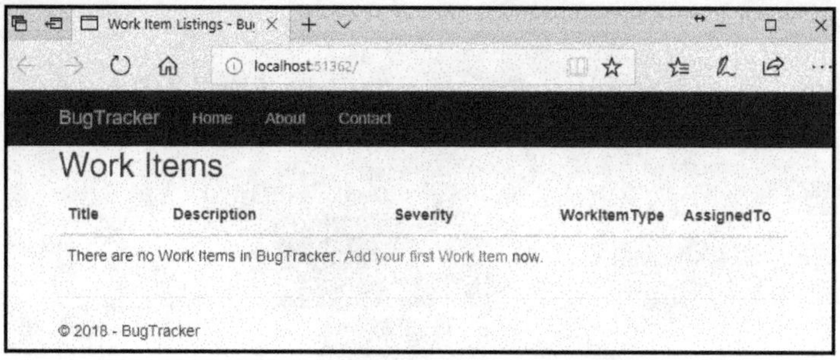

You will see that a link in the list allows you to add your first work item.

This is the link that redirects back to the `AddWorkItem` action on the `AddWorkItemController`. To run it, do the following:

1. Click on the link and you will see the output, as shown in the following screenshot:

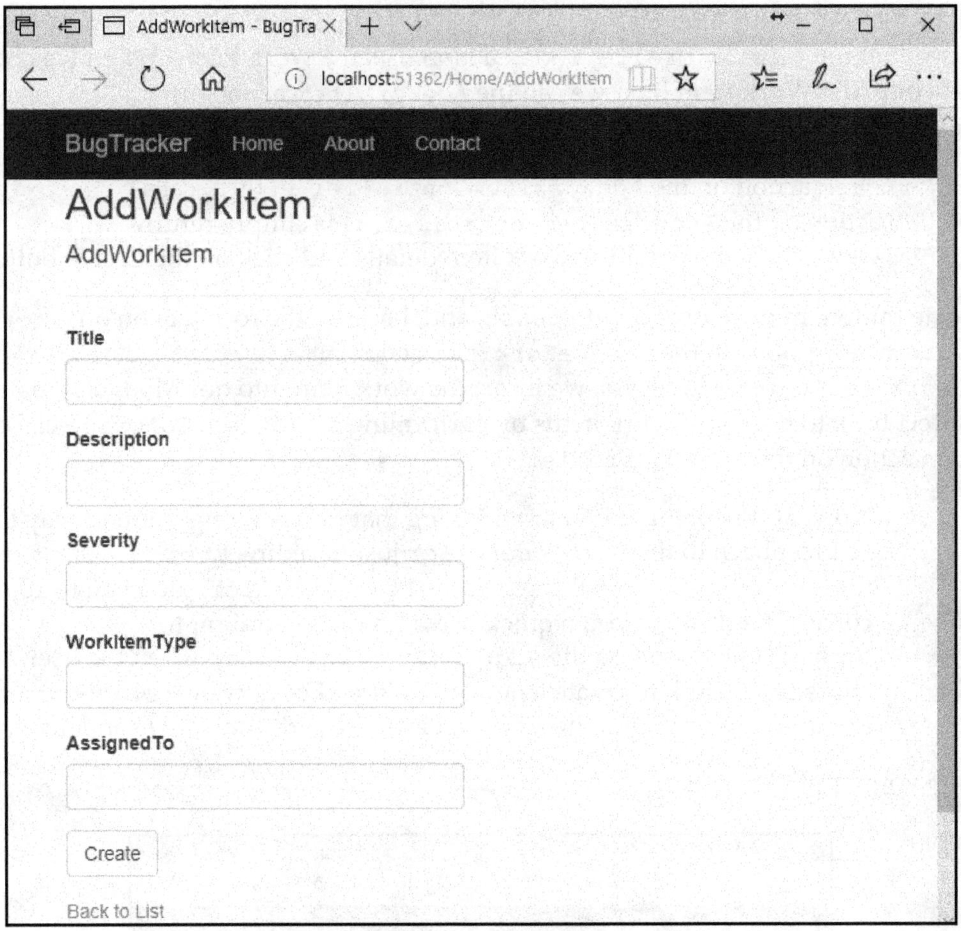

2. This will take you to the view to add a new work item. Enter some information into the fields and click on the **Create** button:

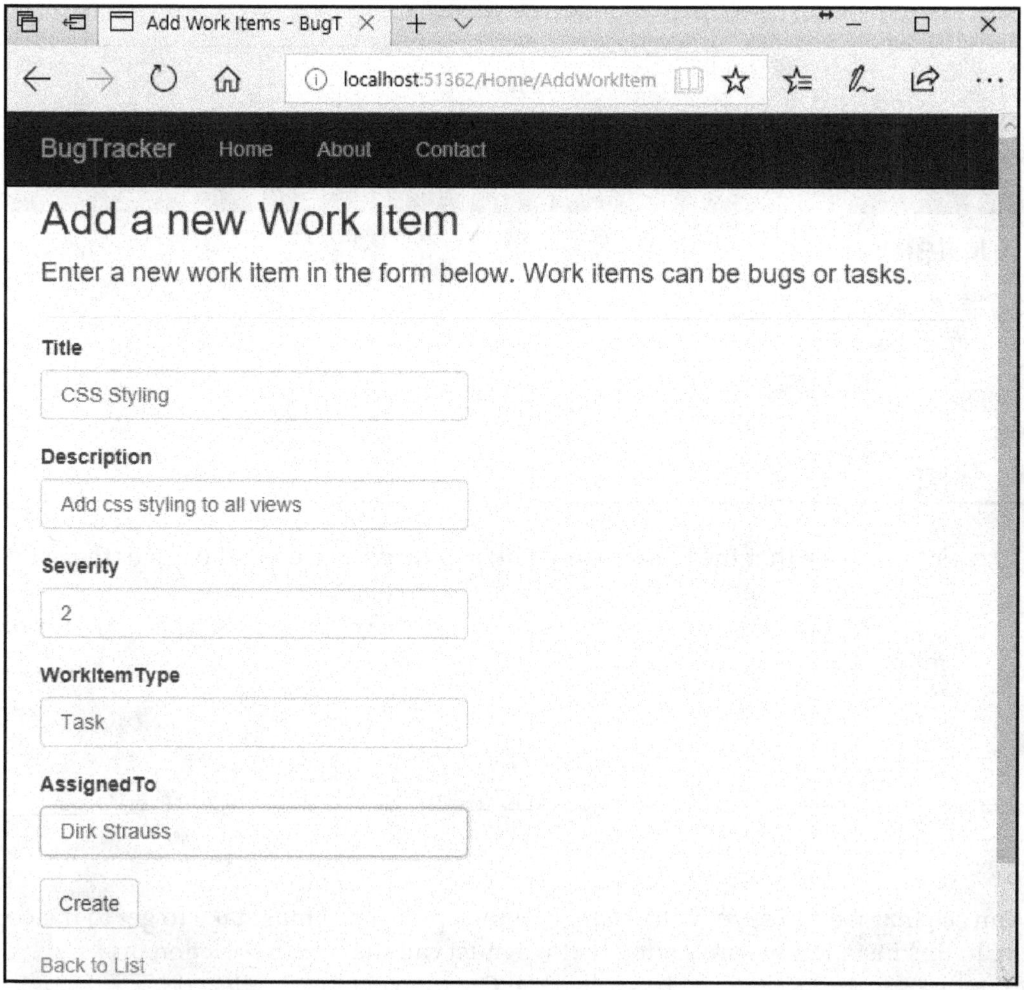

3. The **Create** button calls the `CreateWorkItem` action on the `AddWorkItemController` and redirects back to the work item list on the `Index` action of the `HomeController`:

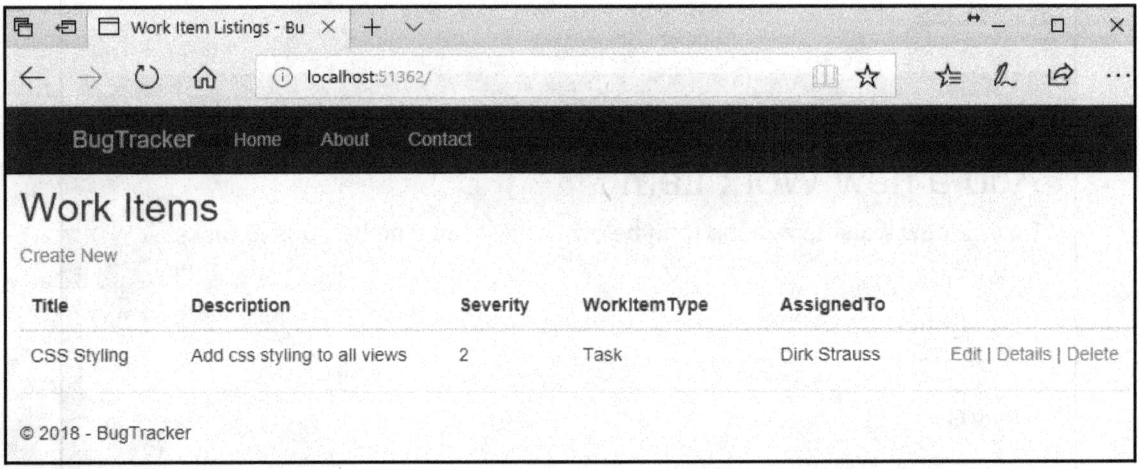

4. You can see that the **Create New** link is now displayed at the top of the list. Let's modify the `Index.cshtml` view to make that link redirect directly to the `AddItem` action on the `AddWorkItemController` class. Change the razor as follows:

```
@if (Model.Count() > 0)
{
<p>
    @Html.ActionLink("Create New", "AddWorkItem/AddItem")
</p>
}
```

You can see that we can specify the route that the application must take to get to the correct action. In this instance, we are saying that we must call the `AddItem` action on the `AddWorkItemController` class when the **Create New** link is clicked.

Run your application again and click on the **Create New** link. You will see that you are redirected to the input form that we added the work item to earlier.

The default styling of the views doesn't look too shabby, but they are definitely not the most beautiful designs out there. This, at least, gives you, as a developer, the ability to go back and style the screens with CSS, to prettify them according to your needs. For now, the dull screens are 100% functional and good enough for our purposes.

Open **MongoDB Compass** and you will see that there is a **workitem** document in there. View that document and you will see the information that we just added from our ASP.NET Core MVC application:

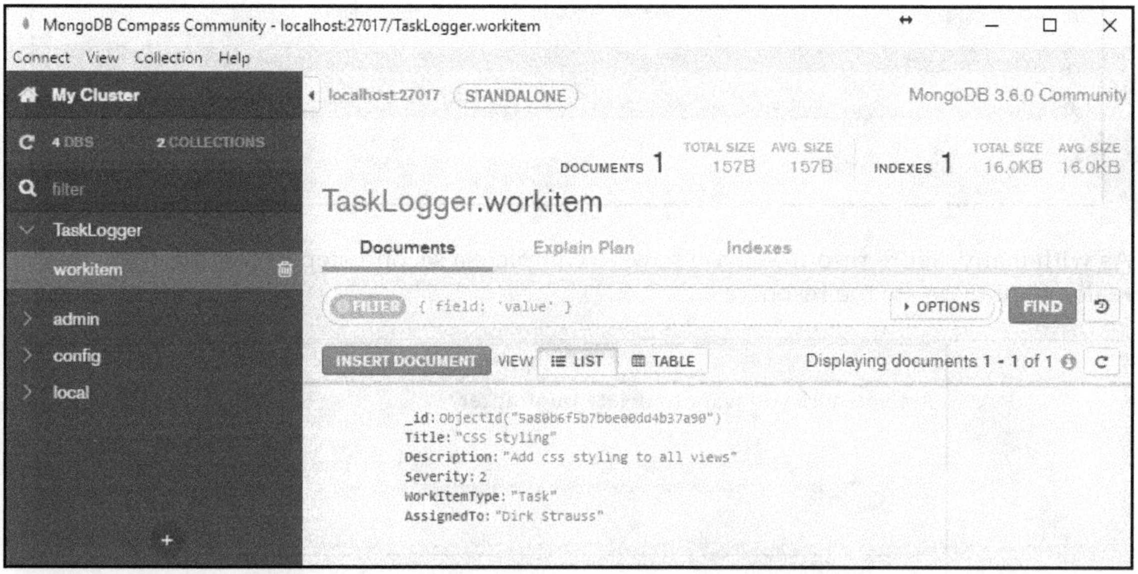

We now have a working instance of our website. If you plan on extending this application, then this will be the end of the chapter; otherwise, the following section will deal with tearing down the resources that you created.

Cleaning up the resources

As mentioned earlier, Microsoft makes their money from Azure based on your usage. In order to avoid incurring costs, you should always clean up (that is, delete) resources that you no longer need. If, like me, you named your Cosmos DB instance **bugtracker**, then you can return to the Cosmos DB blade (you may have previously pinned this to your dashboard; otherwise, you should search for this) and select the instance.

Then simply select **Delete Account**:

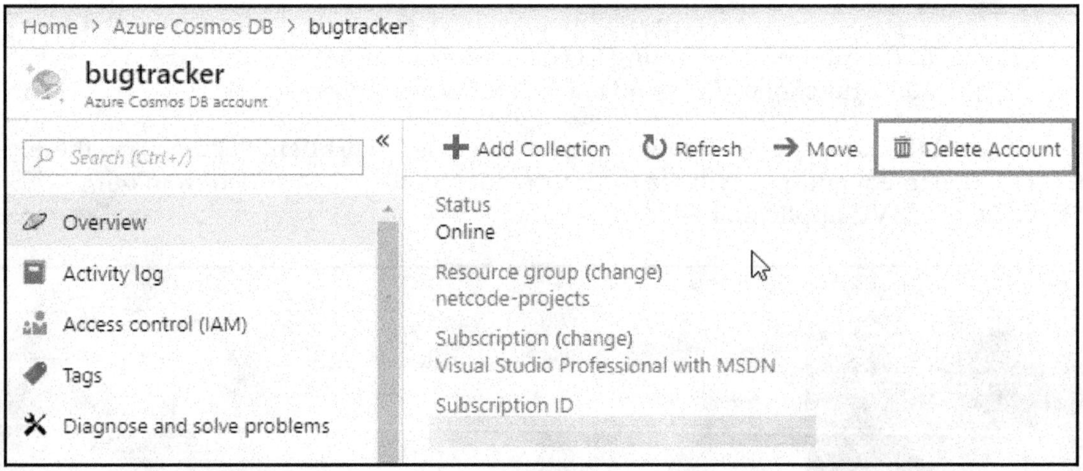

As with many Azure resources, you have to complete a second step to confirm that you really want to delete the resource:

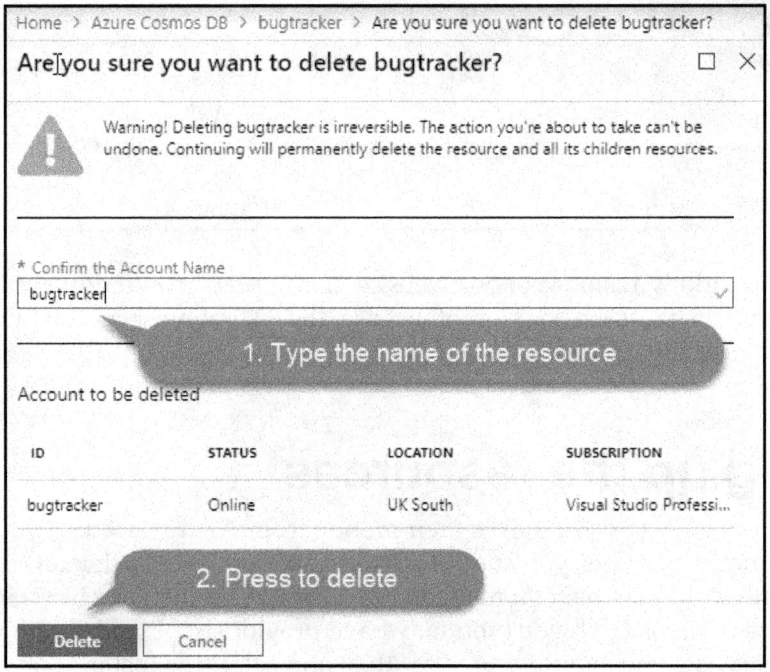

It may take a few seconds to complete, and after that, you're done.

Summary

There is still so much that you can learn when it comes to Cosmos DB and ASP.NET Core MVC. A single chapter is certainly not enough to cover it all. The days where databases sit on powerful, expensive servers that are housed in a rack in the office that only one guy has the keys to are very much numbered. This can be seen as good and bad: no-one can accidentally unplug or reboot the server, nor will a local power outage have any effect on it; however, you (or your employer) now *pay* for inefficient queries in pounds and pence (or dollars and cents).

In the next chapter, we will take a look at SignalR on Azure and how to create a real-time chat application.

3
ASP.NET Azure SignalR Chat Application

Chat applications are, in one form or another, probably as old as the internet itself. This isn't hard to believe since the original purpose of the internet was to allow communication between researchers. During those early days, this communication would have been much faster than sending a letter, but still far from instant.

In this chapter, we will create an application that allows visitors to a website to chat with each other in real time. Specifically, we will cover the following topics:

- Configuring an Azure SignalR Service
- Designing and setting up the project
- Adding the SignalR libraries
- Building the server
- Creating a client
- Running the application

Technical requirements

In this chapter, you'll need an Azure subscription (we covered briefly how to create one in the previous chapter). We'll also be using some features that are only available in the later versions of Visual Studio; at the time of writing, 15.8.7 is the latest version, but any version later than 15.8.0 should be sufficient.

The code from this chapter can be found on GitHub at: `https://github.com/PacktPublishing/C-8-and-.NET-Core-3-Projects-Using-Azure-Second-Edition`.

Introducing SignalR

Typically, in a client-server relationship, such as accessing a website, communication is instigated by the client. You may visit a website that shows share prices, click on a particular stock code, and the website goes and retrieves the price of that stock for you. Once you've got the price, you might leave the page open and return in an hour. The price of the stock is exactly the same; you refresh the web page and the stock price is re-fetched and now displays correctly.

One possible way to solve this problem would be to have the server send information to the client as and when it is ready. SignalR provides this capability. However, SignalR is not a single technology – it is actually a stack of technologies, abstracted away. This is completely transparent, so as the consumer, you'll simply call a SignalR method to send or receive a message and, internally, SignalR will use a range of available technologies to enable this message transfer. At the time of writing, this stack is as follows:

- WebSockets
- Server sent events
- Forever frame
- Long polling

It is beyond the scope of this book to discuss these in detail, so we'll just say that SignalR will use the best technology available to it.

It is possible to host SignalR yourself inside your server; however, Microsoft Azure now allows you to consume SignalR Service hosted by Microsoft. The benefit here is that Azure will handle the scaling, but also that this service can be used as part of the Azure serverless ecosystem; for example, you could use SignalR with Azure Functions so that a server-side offline process could kick off a function, which in turn would call SignalR to update clients and the updates could be pushed to thousands, or tens of thousands, of clients.

To showcase the capabilities of SignalR, we'll build a simple ASP.NET Core SignalR chat application. Our application will be self-hosted but will use Azure SignalR Service.

SignalR project

In this section, we will configure and create our web application. The first step is to configure SignalR Service.

Configuring Azure SignalR

The first step is to create our SignalR instance in Azure:

1. Search for SignalR and select **SignalR Service** from the results:

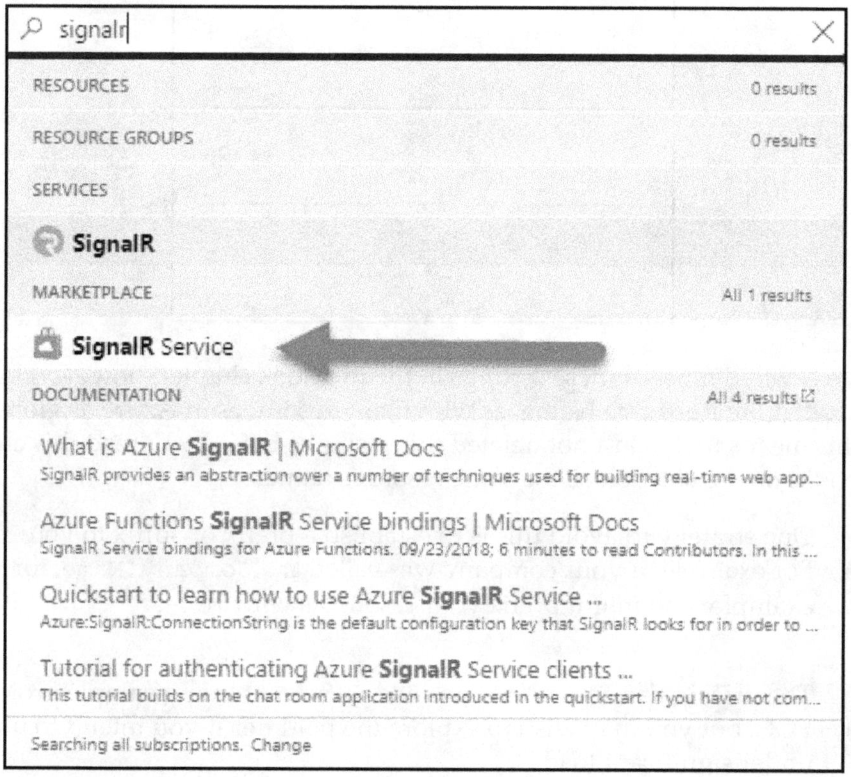

2. Once you select this, you'll be presented with the SignalR creation page:

We covered most of these settings in the previous chapter; however, I will point out that the **Resource Name**, as with many resources in Azure, is globally unique. This means that, had I not deleted this resource before you read this chapter, you would not be able to use the same resource name.

One strategy to avoid this is to establish a prefix or suffix to your naming. For example, if your company was called `My Company Name`, for example, you might prefix your resources with `mcn-`.

The pricing tier here is free, and it's sufficient for an example project or a POC, but you may wish to explore the paid tier if you intend to use this under significant load.

3. If you click **Create**, the resource will be created after a couple of minutes. Once the deployment has finished, visit the **Keys** section and make a copy of the **Primary** connection string:

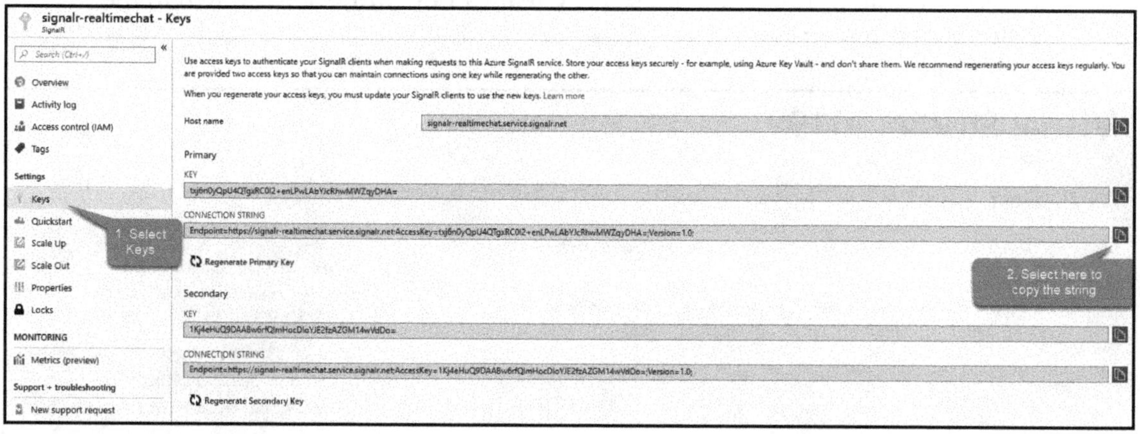

You'll need the connection string later, so paste it into Notepad or a similar tool for now. Let's move on to creating our project.

Creating the project

For this project, we'll need the following elements:

- **An Azure SignalR instance**: This will manage the SignalR messages.
- **Chat server**: This will be our server-side C# code that will process and direct the messages sent from the client(s).
- **Chat client(s)**: A client will consist of JavaScript functions for sending messages to and receiving messages from the server, as well as HTML elements for display.

We'll start with setting up Azure, then the server code, and move over to the client, building a simple bootstrap layout and calling some JavaScript functions from there.

As a bonus, we'll include a method to archive our conversation history as a text file.

Setting up the project

Let's set up this project:

1. Open Visual Studio 2019 and select **Create a new project**, as shown in the following screenshot:

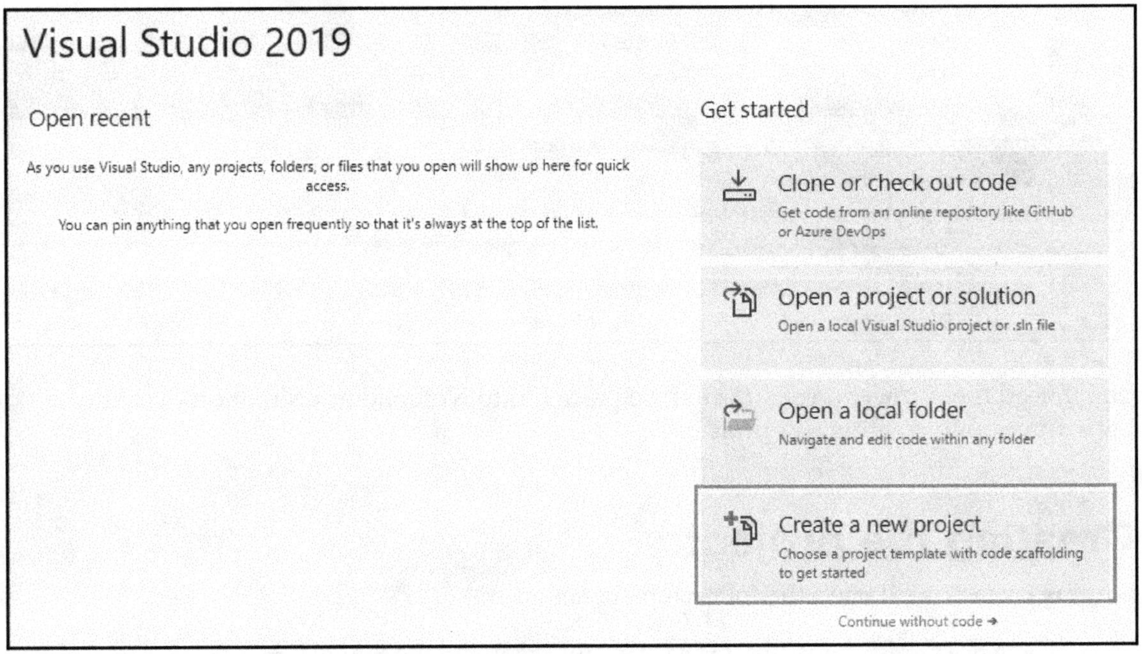

2. Select **ASP.NET Core Web Application**:

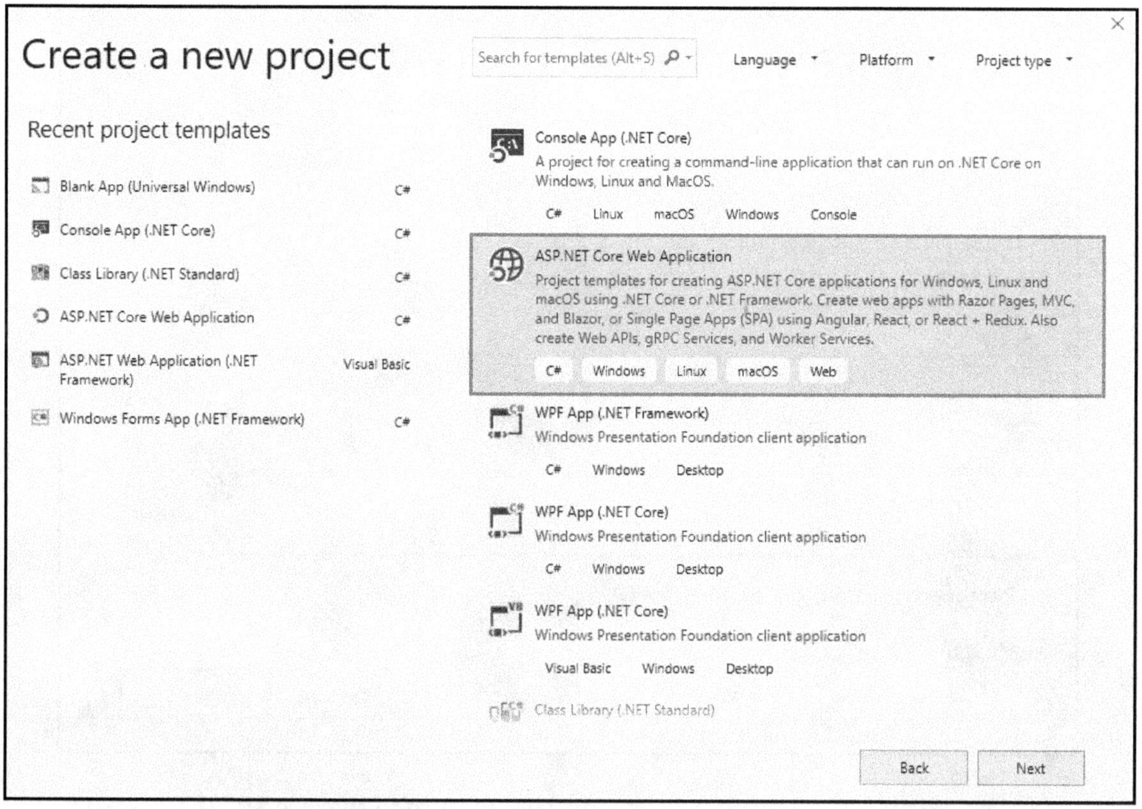

3. Configure the project (that is, decide on a name and location):

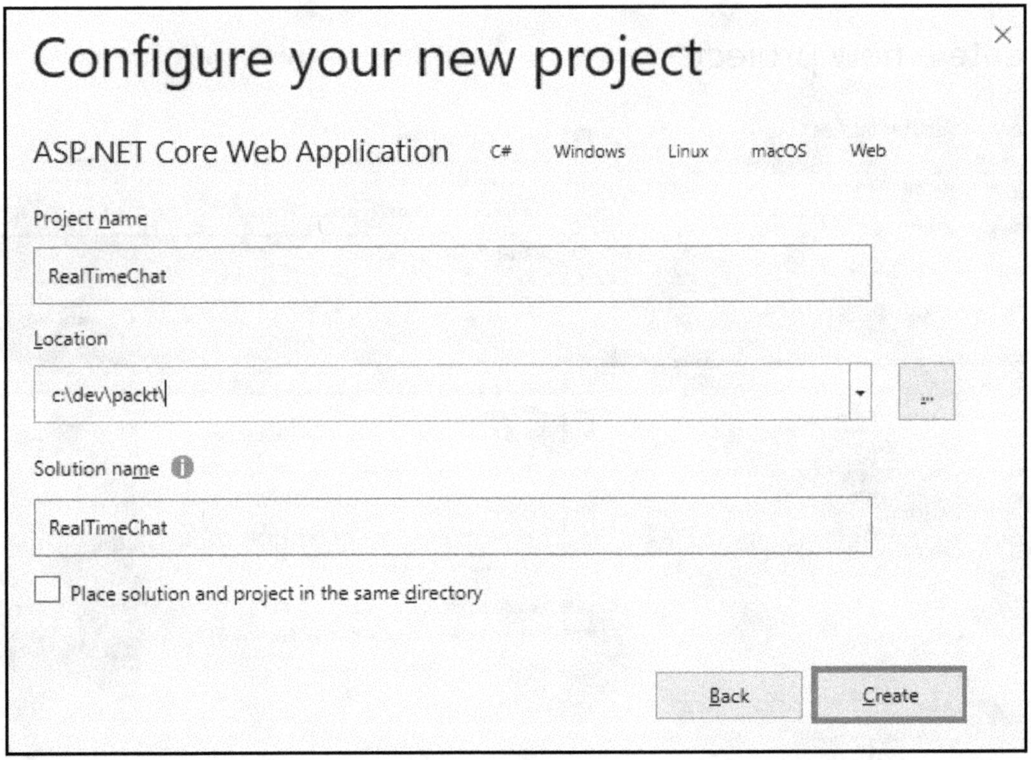

4. We'll go with an empty project template. Be sure to select **ASP.NET Core 3.0** from the dropdown:

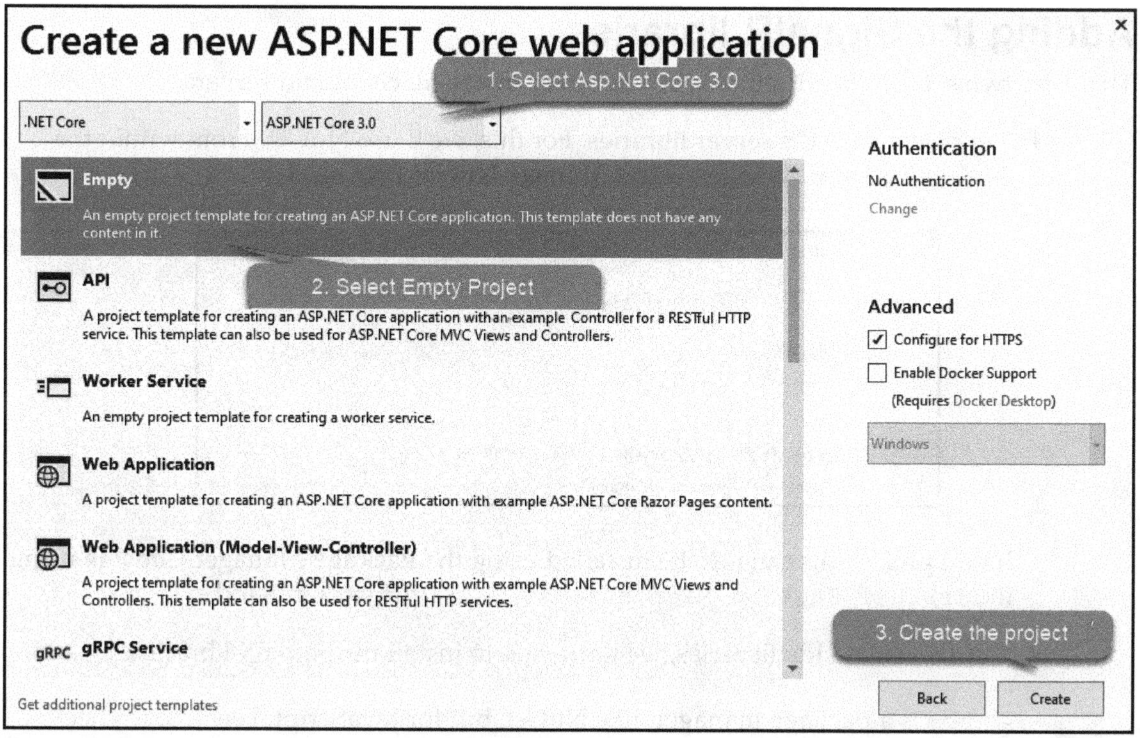

The project will be created and will look as follows:

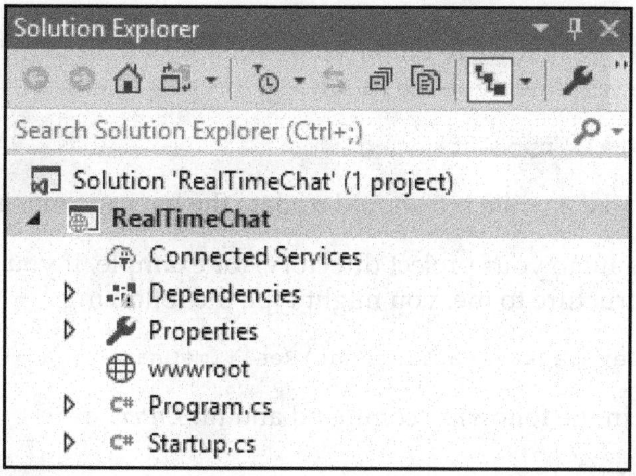

In order to use SignalR, we'll need to add some additional libraries; we'll do that next.

Adding the SignalR libraries

There are two sets of libraries that will need to be installed, client and server:

1. Let's start with the server libraries. For this, we'll use NuGet. From within the NuGet Package Manager, select **Manage NuGet Packages**:

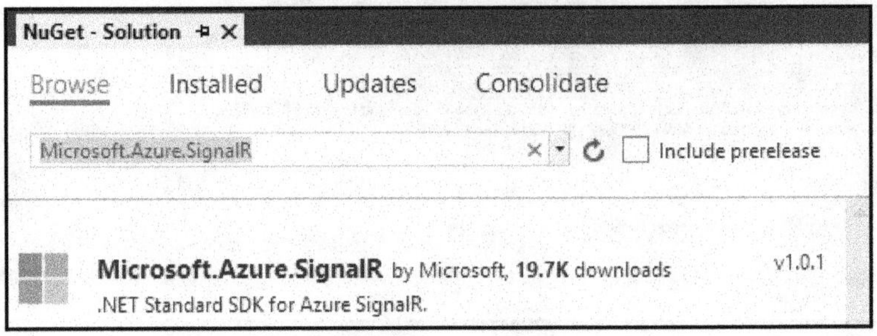

   If you prefer, this can also be installed using the **Package Manager Console** using the `Install-Package Microsoft.Azure.SignalR` command.

2. For the client-side libraries, we'll use `npm` to install the SignalR libraries.

> TIP: `npm` is a package manager, like NuGet, but for JavaScript. Feel free to check it out at `https://www.npmjs.com`.

3. Let's make sure that we're on the latest version of `npm`; launch PowerShell and, in the console window, type the following:

```
npm install npm@latest -g
```

   This might take a while but should update the package manager.

4. Now, navigate to your project directory; for example, if you had a similar directory structure to me, you might type the following:

```
cd C:\Dev\packt\RealTimeChat\RealTimeChat
```

5. Now, type in the following command and hit *Enter*:

```
npm init
npm install @aspnet/signalr
```

`npm init` will create a file called `package.json` in your project; this file determines which files are needed and will download any packages specified in this file to a `node_modules` folder within the root directory of the project. As you're initializing node modules, you'll be asked a series of questions, to which you can just press *Enter* in response.

6. You can confirm that the download was successful if the `node_modules` directory exists; this won't be included in your project, so you may have to select to show all files:

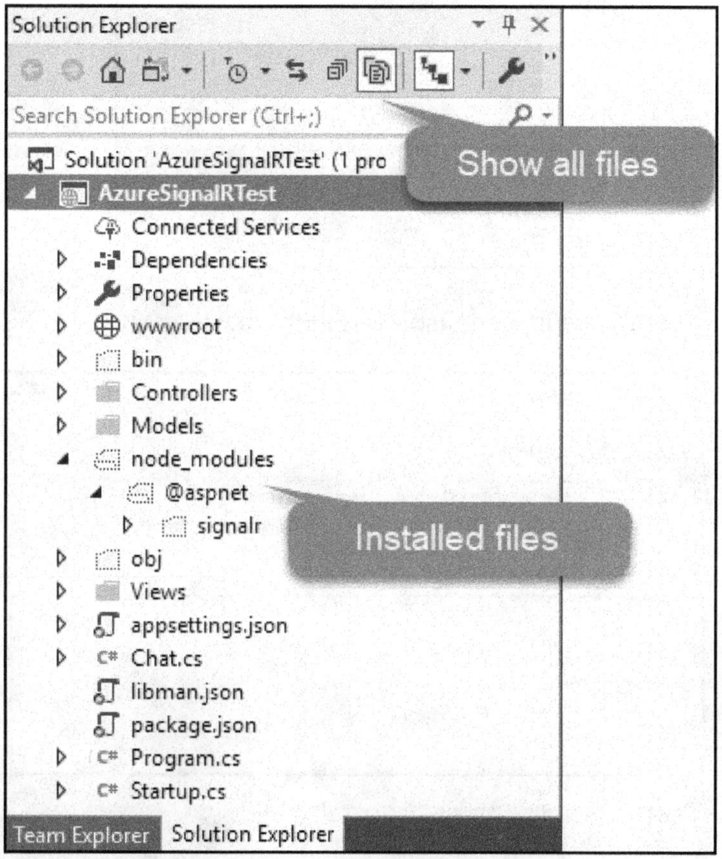

While `npm` is a widely used package manager, it does have a slight issue with .NET applications. The problem is that it downloads the files into the `node_modules` directory (as you can see in the preceding screenshot). This is not ideal as you won't be able to access anything outside `wwwroot`. Additionally, it's not actually included in your project by default.

7. Fortunately, since Visual Studio 15.8.0, we have a tool that enables the installation and maintenance of these libraries. While you can use this independently of `npm`, here, we'll use it to put the node modules into the correct location. Right-click on the project and select **Client-Side Library...**:

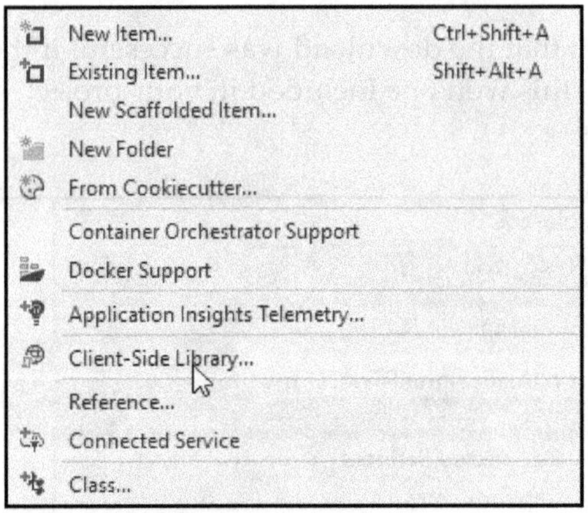

The dialog that is then displayed looks like this:

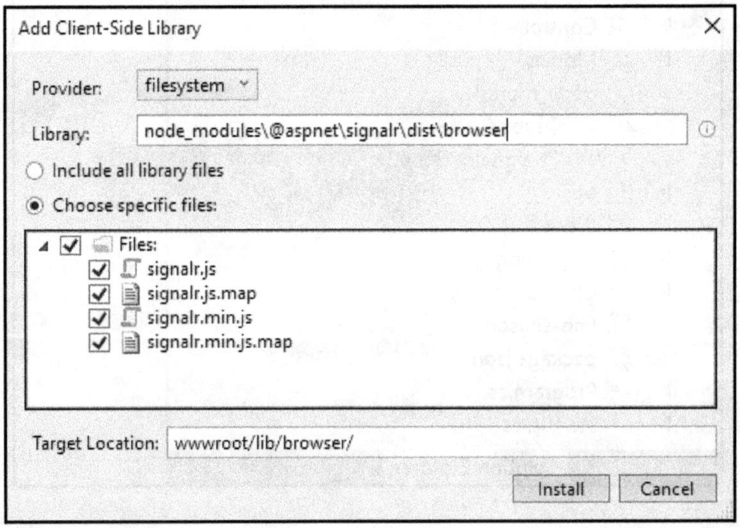

8. At the time of writing, the provider can be set to one of three options: for now, set this to **filesystem**. **Library** should be set to the source for your library: in our case, that's the directory of the `node_modules` folder and is where the SignalR files are located.

9. As you can see, the added bonus here is that you can pick and choose which files you need. Once you click **Install**, you'll be able to see the packages almost instantly appear in the correct location.

With our packages in place, we can (finally) start writing some code.

Building the server

We'll need to build a server for our chat program, which will contain the methods we want to call from our connected clients. We'll use the SignalR Hubs API, which provides the methods that we need for connected clients to communicate with our chat server.

SignalR Hub subclass

Now, we need to create the SignalR Hub. Let's learn how we do this, step by step:

1. Add a class to your project to handle the server side of the chat. We'll call it `Chat`:

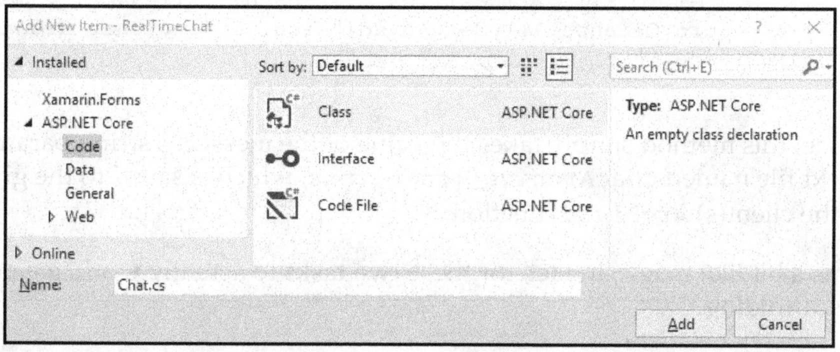

This will need to be a subclass of the SignalR `Hub` class. Make sure to add the using directive for `Micosoft.AspNetCore.SignalR`. Visual Studio's Quick Actions works well for this:

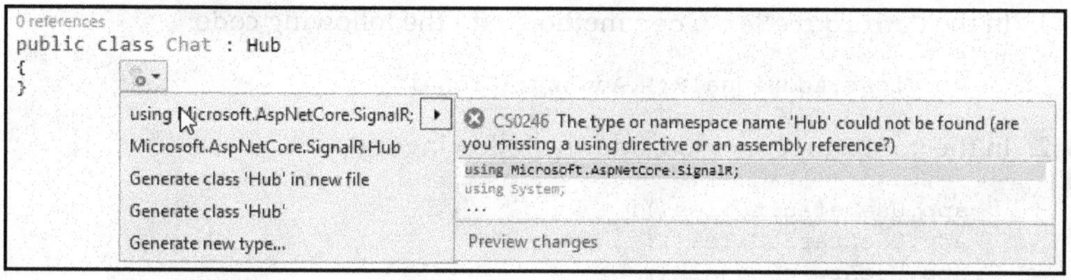

TIP: *Ctrl-.* is the keyboard shortcut for this (currently, it's possibly the second most useful one available in Visual Studio).

2. Now, add a method to the class to handle sending the messages:

```
public Task Send(string sender, string message) =>
    Clients.All.SendAsync("UpdateChat", sender, message);
```

This method will cause any connected clients to invoke the `UpdateChat` method while passing through the sender and message parameters.

3. Now, add a method to handle the archive functionality:

```
public Task ArchiveChat(string archivedBy, string path, string
messages)
{
    string fileName =
$"ChatArchive_{DateTime.Now.ToString("yyyy_MM_dd_HH_mm")}.txt";
    System.IO.File.WriteAllText($@"{path}\{fileName}", messages);
    return Clients.All.SendAsync("Archived", $"Chat archived by
{archivedBy}");
}
```

As you can see, this method simply takes the value of the messages string parameter, writes it to a new text file named `ChatArchive_[date].txt`, which is saved to the given path, and invoke the client(s) `Archived` function.

This all seems a bit like magic; in fact, for these two tasks to actually work, we need to do some more scaffolding.

Configuration changes

In the `Startup.cs` file, we need to add the SignalR Service to the container, as well as configure the HTTP request pipeline. Let's get started:

1. In the `ConfigureServices` method, add the following code:

```
services.AddSignalR().AddAzureSignalR();
```

2. In the `Configure` method, add the following code:

```
app.UseDefaultFiles();
app.UseStaticFiles();
app.UseAzureSignalR(r =>
```

```
{
    r.MapHub<Chat>("/chat");
});
```

Note that we have added `app.UseStaticFiles()` to the `Configure` method. Static files are assets that an ASP.NET Core app serves directly to clients. Examples of static files include HTML, CSS, JavaScript, and images. The call to `app.UseDefaultFiles()` (which must be called prior to `app.UseStaticFiles()`) tells the middleware to search for a predefined list of HTML files, including `index.html`.

That's our server done.

3. Finally, we'll need to tell the SignalR Services how to connect to Azure; create a new file in the project called `appsettings.json`:

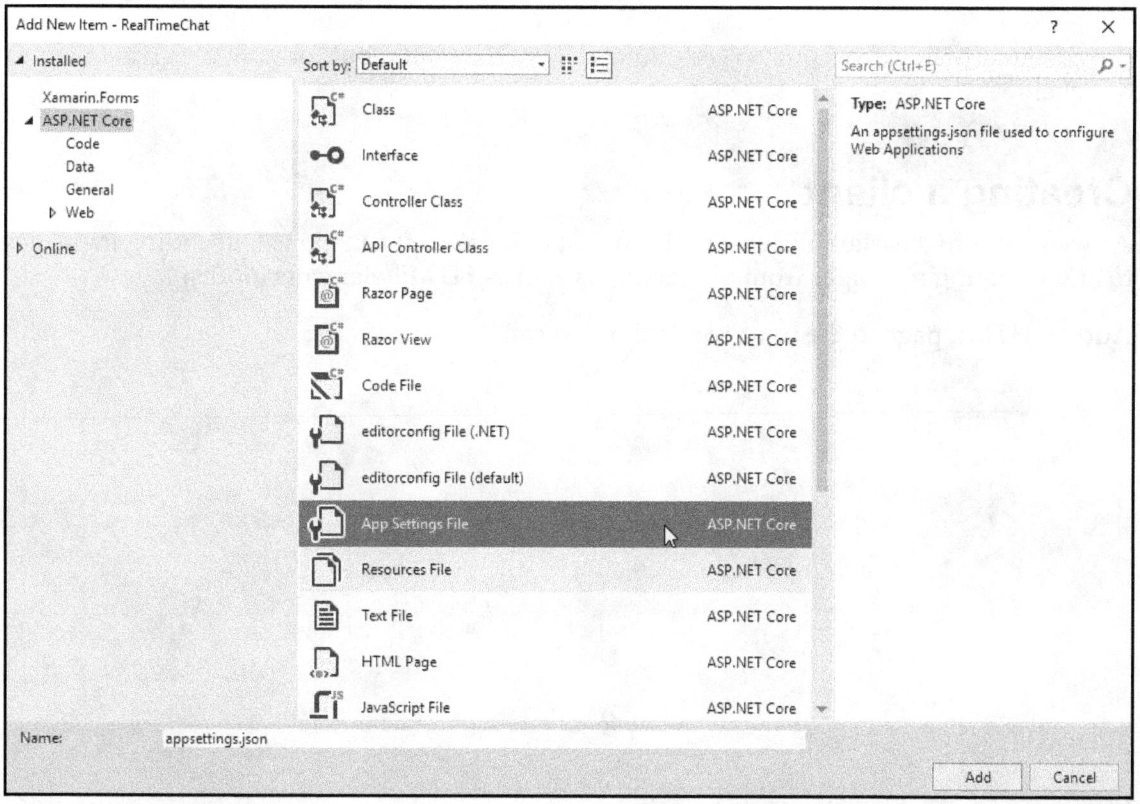

4. Remember the connection string that we copied earlier; it needs to go into this file:

```
{
  "Azure": {
    "SignalR": {
      "ConnectionString":
"Endpoint=https://signalr-realtimechat.service.signalr.net;AccessKe
y=accesskeyhere;Version=1.0;"
    }
  }
}
```

Make sure that you update the connection string to reflect your connection string.

We can (and will) extend our server's functionality a bit later, but for now, let's head over to our client.

Creating a client

As we mentioned earlier, the client will consist of JavaScript functions for sending messages to and receiving messages from the server, as well as HTML elements for display.

Add an HTML page to the `wwwroot` folder and call it `index.html`:

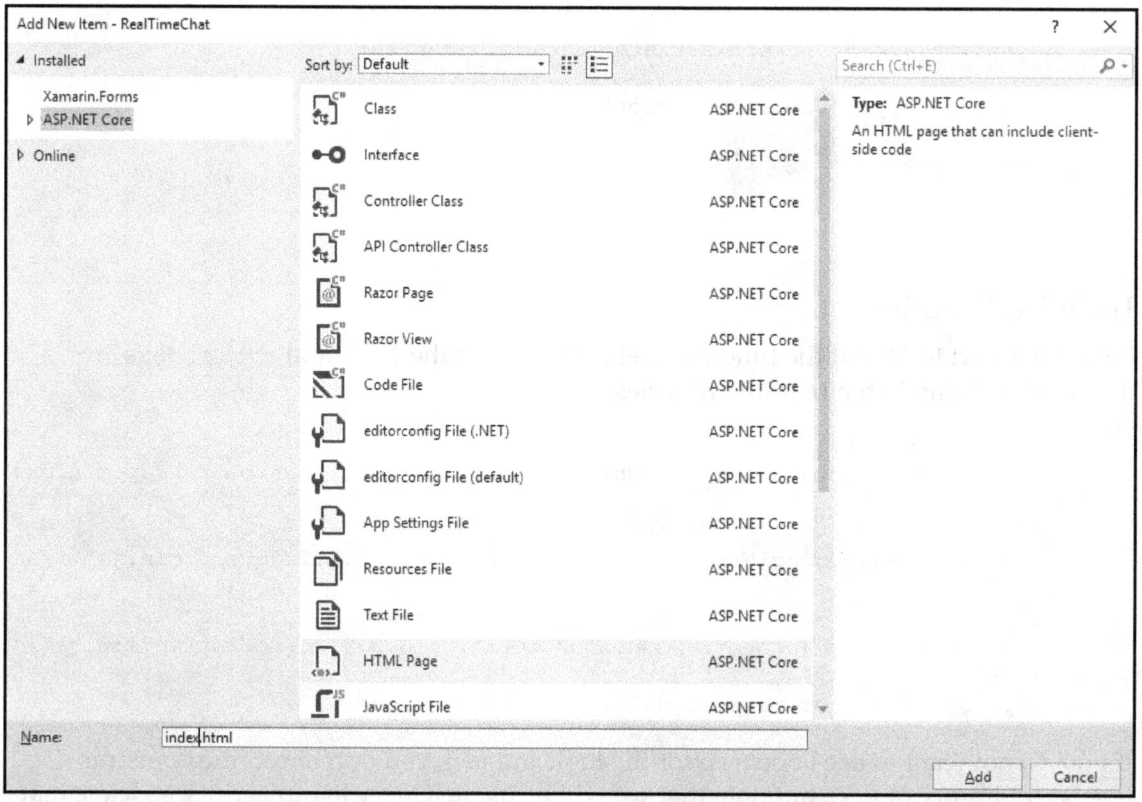

We'll keep the client page really simple. I'm using `div` tags as panels to show and hide the different sections of the page. I'm also using bootstrap to make it look nice, but you can design it whichever way you like. I'm also not going to bore you with the basics, such as where to specify your page title. We'll stick to the relevant elements.

We'll create a skeleton page and fill in the functions as we go:

```
<!DOCTYPE html>
<html>
<head>
    <title>Realtime Chat</title>
    <link rel="stylesheet"
href="https://maxcdn.bootstrapcdn.com/bootstrap/3.3.7/css/bootstrap.min.css
">
    <script
src="https://ajax.googleapis.com/ajax/libs/jquery/3.2.1/jquery.min.js"></sc
ript>
    <script
src="https://maxcdn.bootstrapcdn.com/bootstrap/3.3.7/js/bootstrap.min.js"><
```

```
/script>
    <script src="/lib/browser/signalr.min.js"></script>

    <script type="text/javascript">

    </script>

</head>
```

Included libraries

Before we start to fill out the functions, let's cover what the `link` and `script` tags are doing. They bring in the required libraries:

```
<link rel="stylesheet"
href="https://maxcdn.bootstrapcdn.com/bootstrap/3.3.7/css/bootstrap.min.css
">
<script
src="https://ajax.googleapis.com/ajax/libs/jquery/3.2.1/jquery.min.js"></sc
ript>
<script
src="https://maxcdn.bootstrapcdn.com/bootstrap/3.3.7/js/bootstrap.min.js"><
/script>
<script src="/lib/browser/signalr.min.js"></script>
```

If you do not want to use bootstrap for the look and feel, you don't need the bootstrap JavaScript library or CSS, but note that we will be using jQuery in our scripts, so leave that one in. We're also referencing the SignalR library from the `lib/browser` directory that we added it to earlier.

JavaScript functions

The following code will all go inside the `<script>` tags.

Our client will need some code to send and consume messages to and from the server. I've tried to keep the JavaScript as simple as possible, opting for jQuery code for readability:

1. Create a variable (I've named mine `connection`) for our SignalR Hub Server and call its `start` function:

```
var connection = new signalR.HubConnectionBuilder()
    .withUrl('/chat')
    .build();

connection.start();
```

The `'/chat'` parameter for `.withUrl` refers to our `Chat.cs` class, which inherits the Hub interface from SignalR.

2. Add the `UpdateChat` and `Archived` methods, which will be invoked by the server:

```
connection.on('UpdateChat', (user, message) => {
    updateChat(user, message);
});
connection.on('Archived', (message) => {
    updateChat('system', message);
});
```

We simply pass the parameters we get from the server onto our `updateChat` method. We'll define that method further down.

3. Define an `enterChat` function:

```
function enterChat() {
    $('#user').text($('#username').val());
    sendWelcomeMessage($('#username').val());
    $('#namePanel').hide();
    $('#chatPanel').show();
};
```

We set the text of our `user` label from the value of the username input element, pass it through to our `sendWelcomeMessage` method (which we'll define in a bit), and toggle the display of the relevant panels.

4. Define a `sendMessage` function:

```
function sendMessage() {
    let message = $('#message').val();
    $('#message').val('');
    let user = $('#user').text();
    connection.invoke('Send', user, message);
};
```

We set the `message` variable from the `message` input element, before clearing it for the next message, and the `user` variable from the user label. Then, we call the `Send` method on our server by using the `connection.invoke` method and pass through our variables as parameters.

5. Define a `sendWelcomeMessage` function:

```
function sendWelcomeMessage(user) {
    connection.invoke('Send','system',user+' joined the chat');
};
```

Just like the `sendMessage` function we described in the previous step, we will use the `connection.invoke` function to call the `Send` method on our server. This time, though, we pass through the `'system'` string as the user parameter and a little informational message about the user that just joined.

6. Define an `updateChatPanel` method:

```
function updateChatPanel(user, message) {
    let chat = '<b>' + user + ':</b> ' + message + '<br/>'
    $('#chat').append(chat);
    if ($('#chat')["0"].innerText.length > 0) {
        $('#historyPanel').show();
        $('#archivePanel').show();
    }
};
```

`updateChat` is just our custom function that's used to update the chat history panel. We could have done this inline in the two `connection.on` functions, but that means we would have repeated ourselves. As a general rule in any coding, you should try not to repeat code.

In this function, we set the `chat` variable to however we want each chat history line to look in terms of styling. In this case, we simply style our user (with a colon) bold with the message unstyled afterward and a line break at the end. A few lines of chat will look something like this:

```
John: Hello people
Sarah: Hi John
server: Peter joined the chat
John: Hi Sarah, Hello Peter
Peter: Hello Everyone
```

We also need to check the chat `div` `innerText` property to determine whether the chat history and archive panels should be visible.

Define the `archiveChat` function:

```
function archiveChat() {
    let message = $('#chat')["0"].innerText;
    let archivePath = $('#archivePath').val();
    connection.invoke('ArchiveChat', archivePath, message);
};
```

Like everything else, I've tried to keep this as simple as possible. We take the `innerText` of our chat panel (`div`) and the path specified in the `archivePath` input and pass it through to the server's `ArchiveChat` method.

Of course, we have a small window for error here: if the user does not type in a valid path for the file to be saved, the code will throw an exception. I'll leave it to your own creativity to sort that one out. I'm just here for the SignalR functionality.

Let's see the outline of the `body` section:

```
    <body>
        <div class="container col-md-10">
            <h1>Welcome to Signal R <label id="user"></label></h1>
        </div>
        <hr />

    </body>
</html>
```

The following code will all go sequentially after the horizontal line.

Naming section

Let's have a look at the naming section first, and then drill into some of the details:

```
<div id="namePanel" class="container">
    <div class="row">
        <div class="col-md-2">
            <label for="username" class="form-label">Username:</label>
        </div>
        <div class="col-md-4">
            <input id="username" type="text" class="form-control" />
        </div>
        <div class="col-md-6">
            <button class="btn btn-default"
                    onclick="enterChat()">
                Enter
            </button>
```

```
            </div>
        </div>
    </div>
```

We'll need to know who our chatroom attendee is. Here, we're adding an input element to capture the username and a button to call the `enterChat` function:

- `<input id="username" type="text" class="form-control" />`
- `<button class="btn btn-default" onclick="enterChat()">Enter</button>`

Chat input

The chat section allows the user to type a message and see what has been typed:

```
<div id="chatPanel" class="container" style="display: none">
    <div class="row">
        <div class="col-md-2">
            <label for="message" class="form-label">
                Message:
            </label>
        </div>
        <div class="col-md-4">
            <input id="message" type="text" class="form-control" />
        </div>
        <div class="col-md-6">
            <button class="btn btn-info"
                    onclick="sendMessage()">
                Send
            </button>
        </div>
    </div>
    <div id="historyPanel" style="display:none;">
        <h3>Chat History</h3>
        <div class="row">
            <div class="col-md-12">
                <div id="chat" class="well well-lg"></div>
            </div>
        </div>
    </div>
</div>
```

The following elements allow our user to type a message (input) and post it to the server (the event button for `sendMessage`):

- `<input id="message" type="text" class="form-control" />`
- `<button class="btn btn-info" onclick="sendMessage()">Send</button>`

We also have a `div` tag called `<div id="chat" class="well well-lg"></div>` with an ID of `"chat"`. We are using this as a container for our conversation (chat history).

Archive function

Finally, we have the archive section:

```
<div id="archivePanel" class="container" style="display:none;">
    <div class="row">
        <div class="col-md-2">
            <label for="archivePath" class="form-
             label">Archive Path:</label>
        </div>
        <div class="col-md-4">
            <input id="archivePath" type="text" class="form-control" />
        </div>
        <div class="col-md-6">
            <button class="btn btn-success"
                    onclick="archiveChat()">
                Archive Chat
            </button>
        </div>
    </div>
</div>
```

Here, we allow our user to specify a path where the archive file needs to be saved (input) and post the messages to the server (the event button for `archiveChat`):

- `<input id="archivePath" type="text" class="form-control" />`
- `<button class="btn btn-info" onclick="archiveChat()">Archive Chat</button>`

> TIP: If you are going to use this application as a base and extend it, I recommend moving the JavaScript code to a separate `.js` file. It is easier to manage and is another good coding standard to follow.

Now that we've created the application, let's build and test what we've done.

Building and running the project

We've created our project, so let's build it. On the top menu in Visual Studio, click the **Build** menu button:

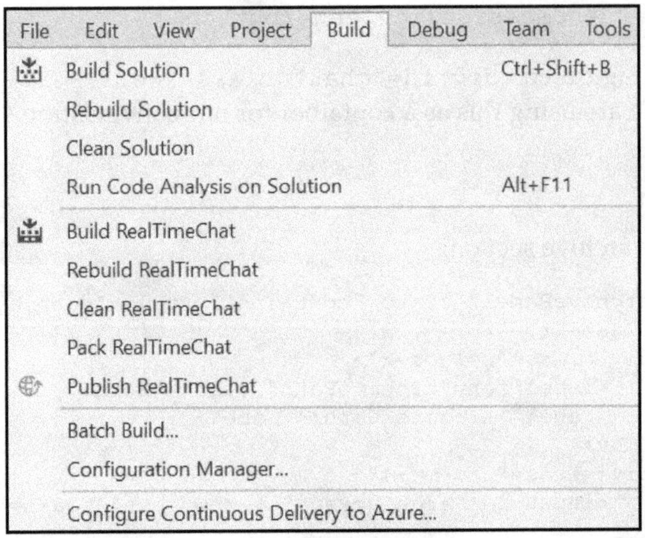

You can choose to either build the entire solution or an individual project. Since we only have one project in our solution, we can choose either. You can also use the keyboard shortcut *Ctrl* + *Shift* + *B,* but bear in mind that if you have multiple projects, this will only build the startup project and its dependent libraries.

You should see some (hopefully successful) build messages in the **Output** window:

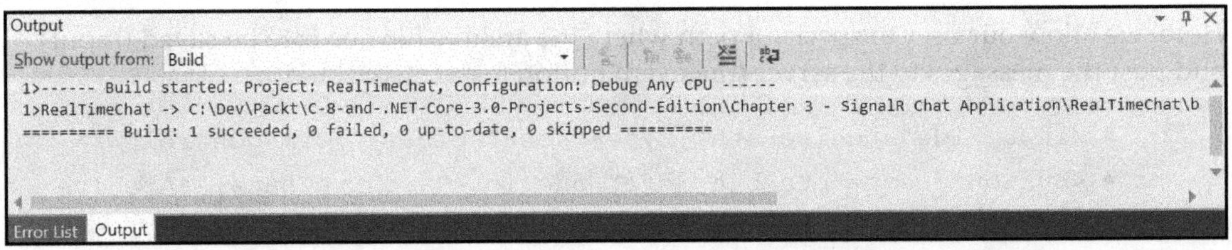

If you get any errors, go through this chapter again and see whether you have missed something.

Let's run the application and check that it does what we expect.

Running the application

Running the application is quite straightforward; however, testing requires a little ingenuity:

1. To run the app, hit *F5* (or *Ctrl* + *F5* to start without debugging):

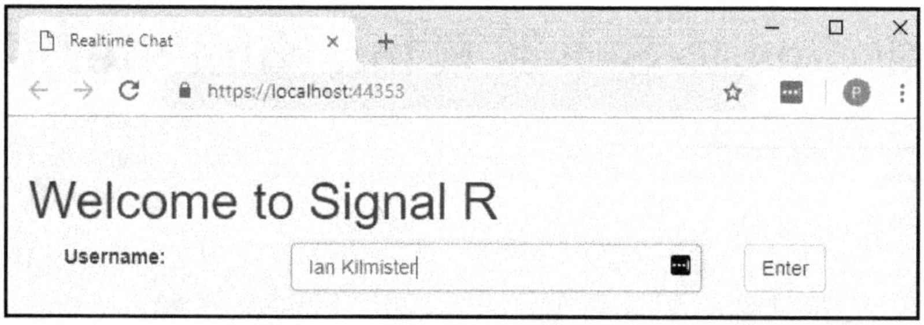

TIP: Running the application without debugging can have a significant improvement in terms of performance.

2. Now, we can start chatting. Type in a username and hit *Enter:*

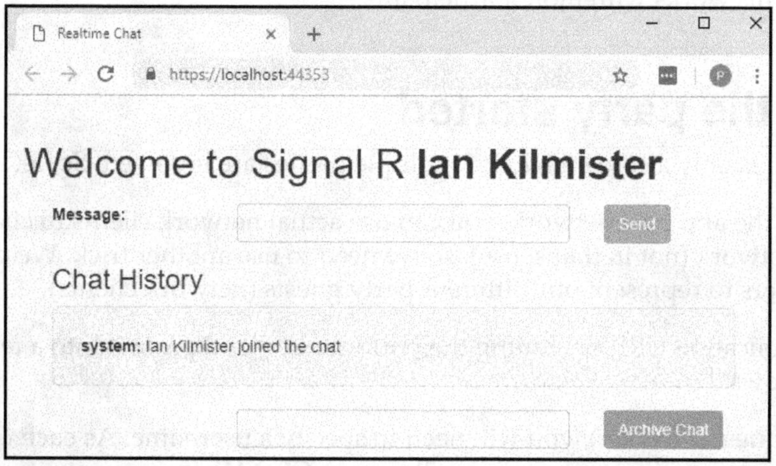

As you can see, our name panel is now hidden and our chat and archive panels are showing. Our server was also kind enough to inform us that we joined the chat, thanks to our `sendWelcomeMessage(user)` function.

3. Every time we send a message, our **Chat History** will be updated:

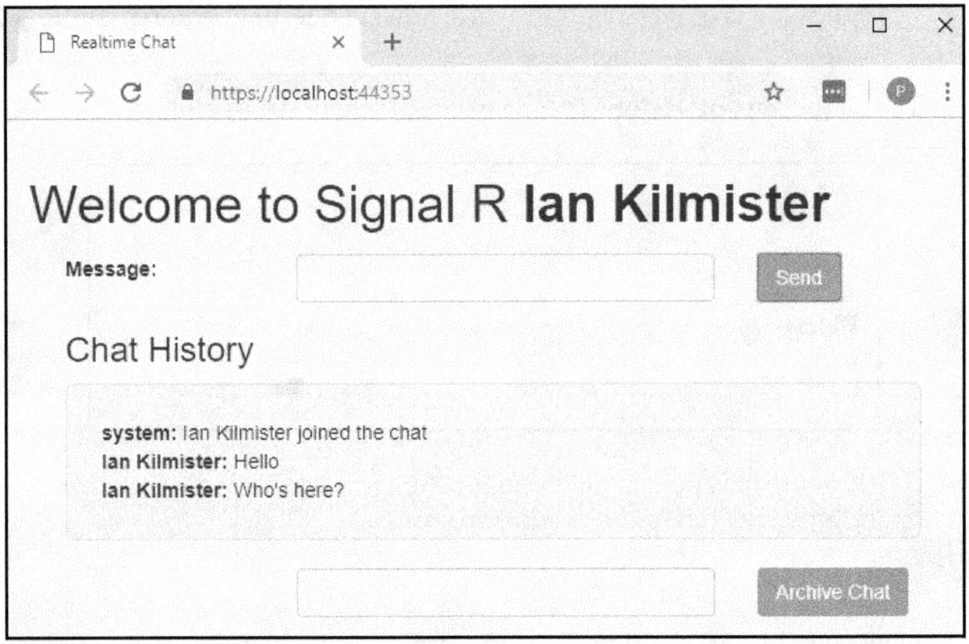

Let's see how this works with more participants.

Getting the party started

A conversation is only a conversation if multiple parties are involved. So, let's start a party.

If you publish the app on a network, you can use actual network clients to chat with, but I'm not on a network (not in that sense), so we need to use another trick. We can use various browsers to represent our different party guests (network clients).

Copy your application URL (including the port number) and paste it into a few other browser windows.

For each new guest (browser), you will need to specify a username. As each of them enters the chat and starts sending messages, you'll see our **Chat History** grow.

You can tile the browsers (or move them to other monitors if you have extra) to see how many messages sent by one person get delivered to all instantaneously, which is the whole point of SignalR.

We started with **Ian Kilmister** in Microsoft Edge, so we'll continue with him there:

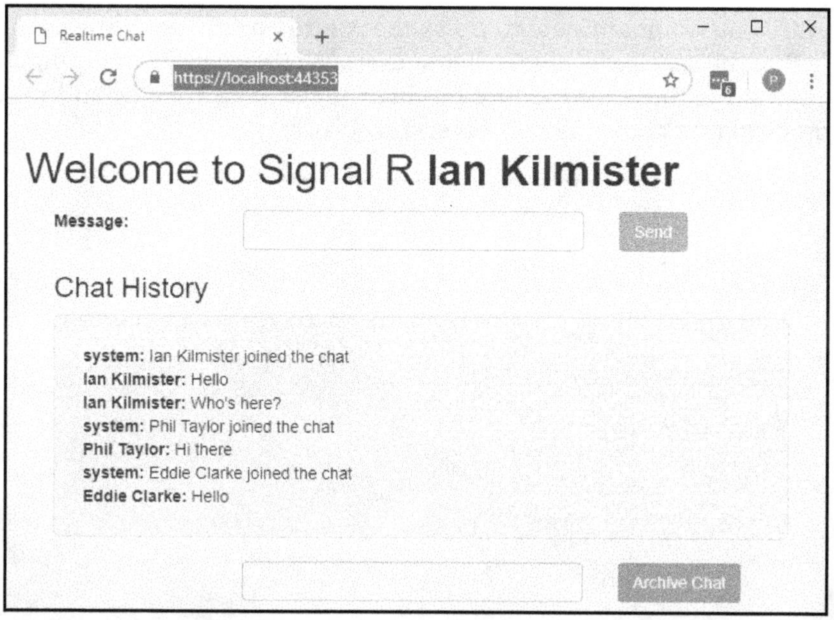

You'll also notice that each guest's chat history only starts when they join the chat. This is by design. We don't send historical chats to clients when they join.

Archiving the chat

To save the chat history to a text file, enter a valid local folder path in the `archivePath` input element and hit the **Archive Chat** button:

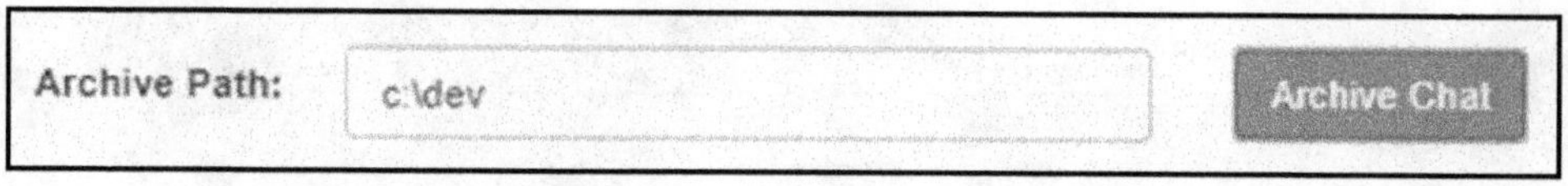

As we mentioned earlier, we haven't built in proper validation for our path, so make sure you test it using a valid path. If successful, you should see a message in the chat window like this:

```
system: Chat archived by Ian Kilmister
```

You will also find the newly created text file in the specified path with the `ChatArchive_[date].txt` naming convention.

The Azure service

At this stage, let's pause for a minute to check the Azure portal. Using the portal, we can easily identify that the service is, in fact, being used. While we've been typing away and testing this application, the Azure service has been registering activity, and we can see that by having a quick glance at the SignalR **Overview** blade:

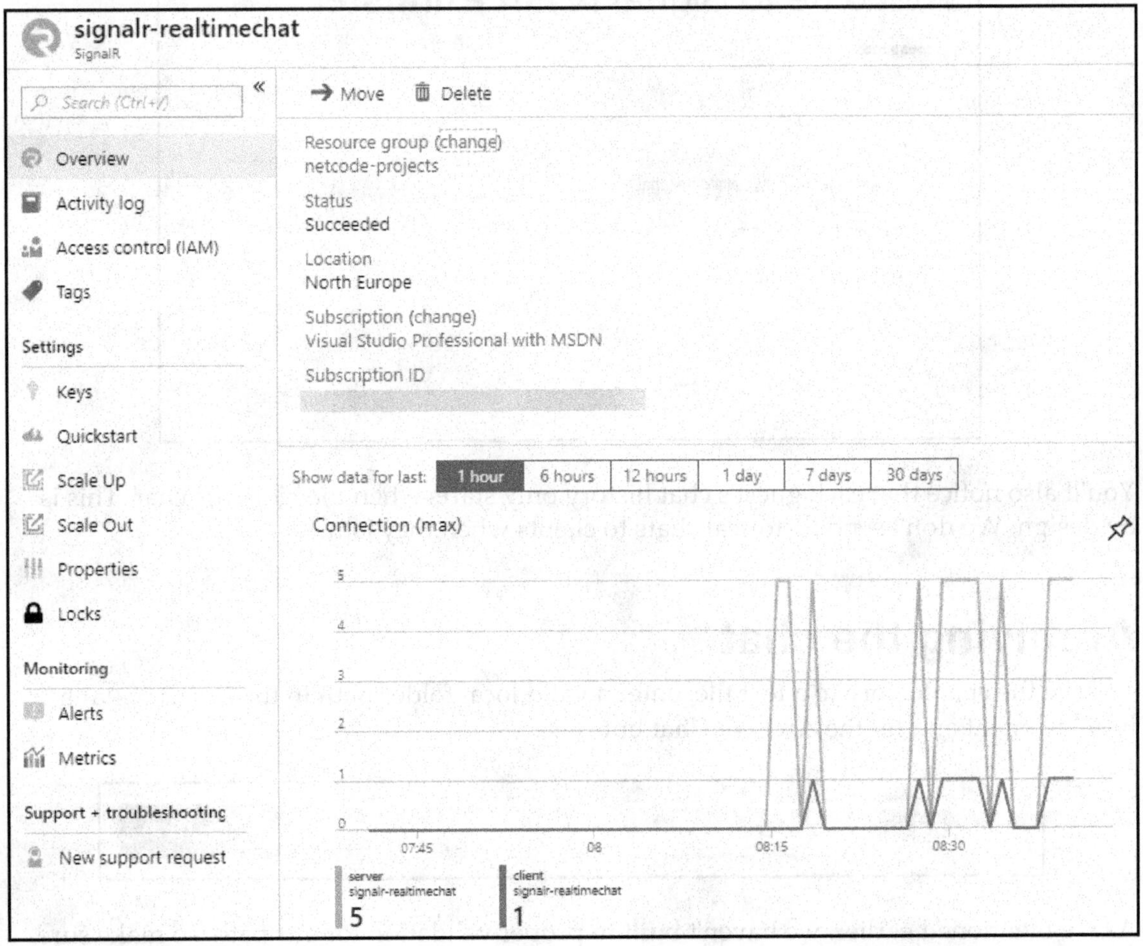

As you can see, our activity is being routed through the SignalR service on Azure. Now that we've built our application, let's clean up the resources we used.

Cleanup

Now that we have a working solution, we'll need to tidy up. In the case of Azure SignalR, if you're using the free tier, then there shouldn't be any financial implications to leaving it as is; however, as you start playing around with Azure more, you'll see your dashboard gradually fill up and become unmanageable.

Inside the SignalR blade, simply select **Delete**:

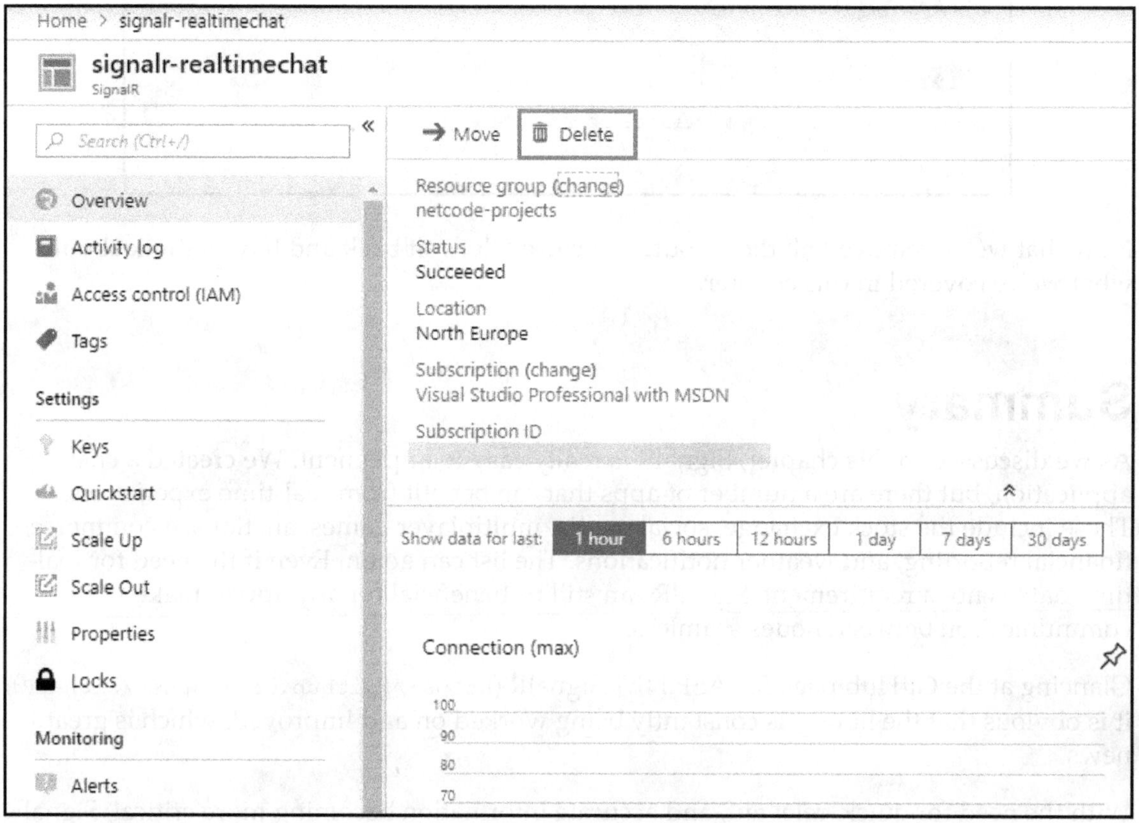

You'll be asked to confirm the deletion. Then, a few seconds later, you should receive a notification to tell you that it was successful:

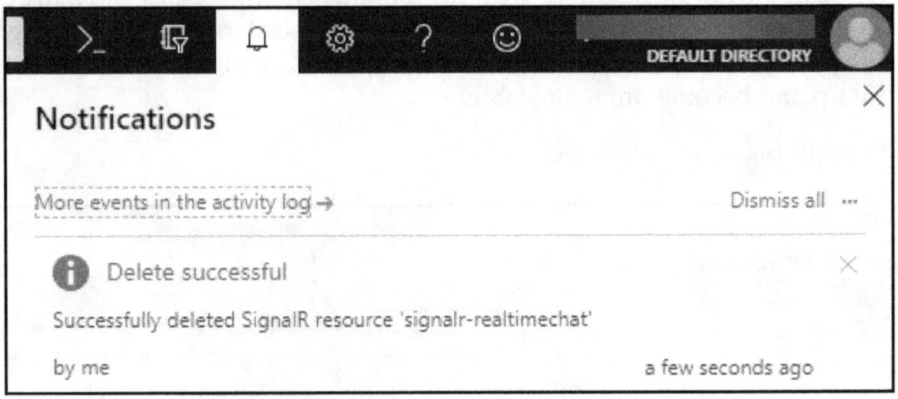

Now that we've removed all the resources we used, let's sit back and have a think about what we've covered in this chapter.

Summary

As we discussed in this chapter, SignalR is really easy to implement. We created a chat application, but there are a number of apps that can benefit from real-time experiences. These include the stock exchange, social media, multiplayer games, auctions, e-commerce, financial reporting, and weather notifications. The list can go on. Even if the need for real-time data is not a requirement, SignalR can still be beneficial for any app to make communication between nodes seamless.

Glancing at the GitHub page for ASP.NET SignalR (`https://github.com/aspnet/SignalR`), it is obvious that the library is constantly being worked on and improved, which is great news.

With the need for quick, relevant, and accurate information becoming more critical, SignalR is a useful tool to be aware of, especially since, with Azure, you can simply hand off the problem of scaling to Microsoft.

In the next chapter, we'll have a look at data access using Entity Framework Core.

4
Web Research Tool with Entity Framework Core

"The biggest lie I tell myself is that I don't need to write it down, I'll remember it."

– Unknown

So, you've got a few minutes to catch up on your feeds. As you scroll through, you come across a link to an article that someone shared about new ways to remember your guitar chords. You really want to read it, but you don't have enough time now. *I'll read it later,* you tell yourself, and later becomes never. Mainly because you did not write it down.

There are various applications out there that cater to your need to save links for later use. But we're developers. Let's just have some fun writing our own!

In this chapter, we will look at the following topics:

- **Entity Framework** (**EF**) Core history
- Code-First versus Model-First versus Database-First approach
- Developing a database design
- Setting up the project
- Installing EF Core
    - Creating the models
    - Configuring the services
    - Creating the database
    - Seeding the database with test data
    - Creating the controller
    - Running the application

- Testing the application
- Deploying the application

That is quite a mouthful, but don't fret, we'll take it one step at a time. Let's take a walk.

Entity Framework (EF) Core history

One of the most frustrating parts of developing an application that needs to read data from and write data to some sort of database is trying to get the communication layer between your code and the database established.

At least, it used to be, until Entity Framework came into the picture!

Entity Framework is an **object-relational mapper** (**ORM**). It maps your .NET Code objects to relational database entities. As simple as that. Now, you don't have to concern yourself with scaffolding the required data access code just to handle plain CRUD operations.

When the first version of Entity Framework was released with .NET 3.5 SP1 in August 2008, the initial response wasn't that great—so much so that a group of developers signed a *vote of no confidence* with regard to the framework. Thankfully, most of the concerns that were raised were addressed and the release of Entity Framework 4.0, together with .NET 4.0, put a lot of the criticisms around the stability of the framework to bed.

Entity Framework Core was a complete rewrite. Microsoft has stated that they are not trying to attain parity between EF6 and EF Core; while they are supporting many of the same features, EF Core has given the opportunity to address some of the original decisions that might not make as much sense anymore.

Code-First versus Model-First versus Database-First approach

With Entity Framework, you had a choice between three approaches of implementation. However, in Entity Framework Core, there is, effectively, only one: Code-First. Although the concept of Database-First does exist, it's a one-way ticket: that is, you can reverse-engineer a code mode from the database, but from then on, you generate the database model from the code.

Developing a database design

We can't know what we're doing until we know what we're doing. Before we jump in and create a solution with our database, models, and controllers, we need to figure out how we want to design the database.

According to Microsoft's TechNet, there are five basic steps we can follow to plan a database:

1. Gather information
2. Identify the objects
3. Model the objects
4. Identify the types of information for each object
5. Identify the relationships between objects

Our requirement is pretty simple. We only need to save a web link to navigate to later, so we won't have multiple objects with relationships between them.

We do, however, need to clarify the types of information we'd like to save for our object (web link). Obviously, we need the URL, but what else do we need? Make sure you understand what information is required for your solution and how it will be used.

Think about it in everyday terms—if you write an address for a friend's house, you might want something more than just a street; possibly your friend's name or a note of some kind.

In our solution, we want to know what the URL is, but we also want to know when we saved it and have a place to capture a note so that we can add more personal detail to an entry. Therefore, our model will contain the following:

- `URL`
- `DateSaved`
- `Notes`

We'll go into more detail when we start creating our models, but let's not jump the gun. We still need to create our project.

Setting up the project

Using Visual Studio 2019, create an **ASP.NET Core Web Application**:

1. Create a new **ASP.NET Core Web Application**:

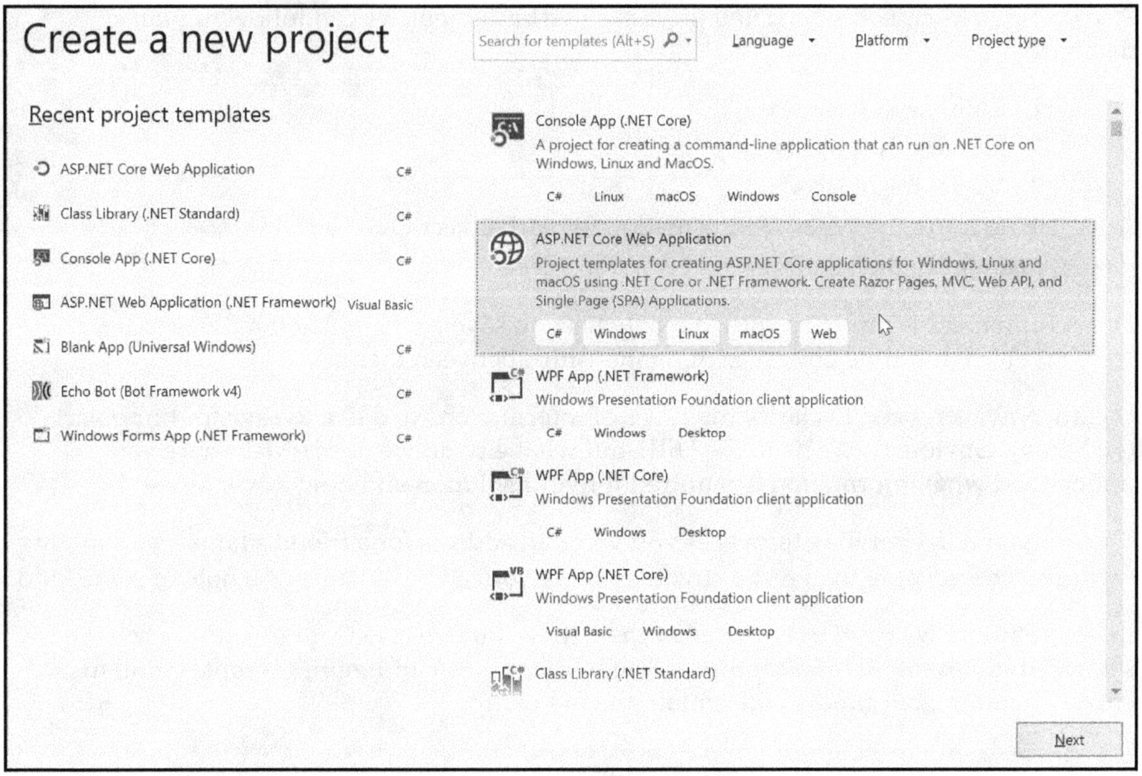

2. Let's call the application `WebResearch`. This is shown in the following screenshot:

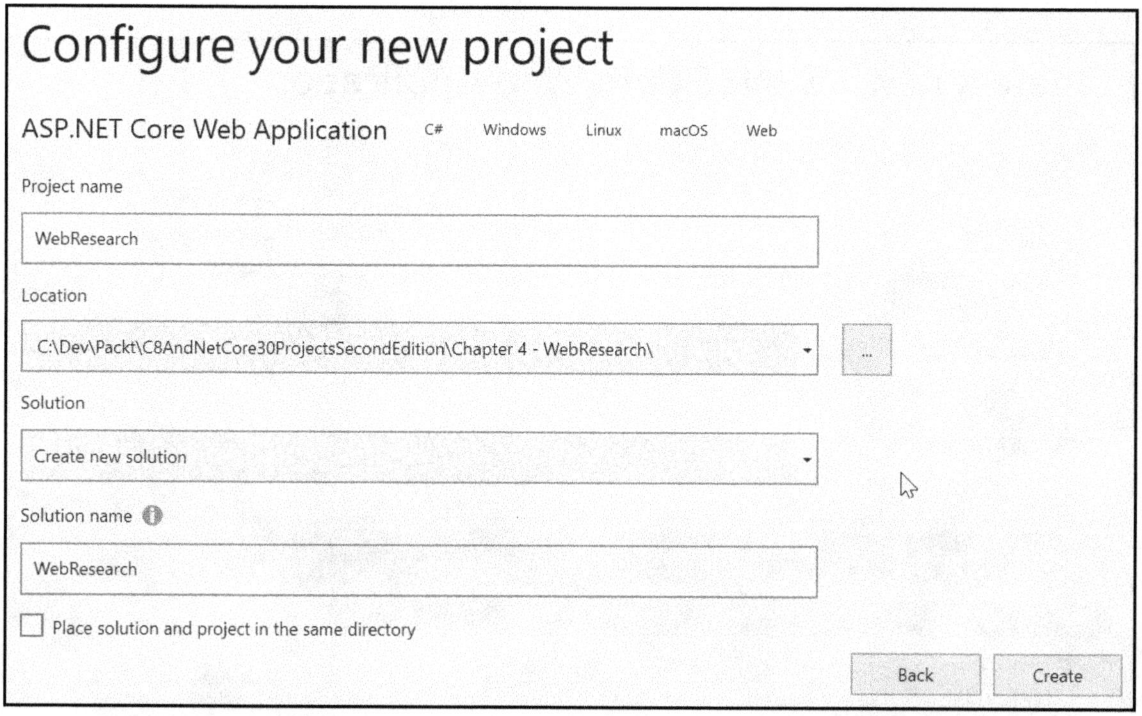

3. On the next screen, choose **Web Application (Model-View-Controller)** as a project template. To keep things simple, keep the authentication as **No Authentication**. Refer to the following screenshot:

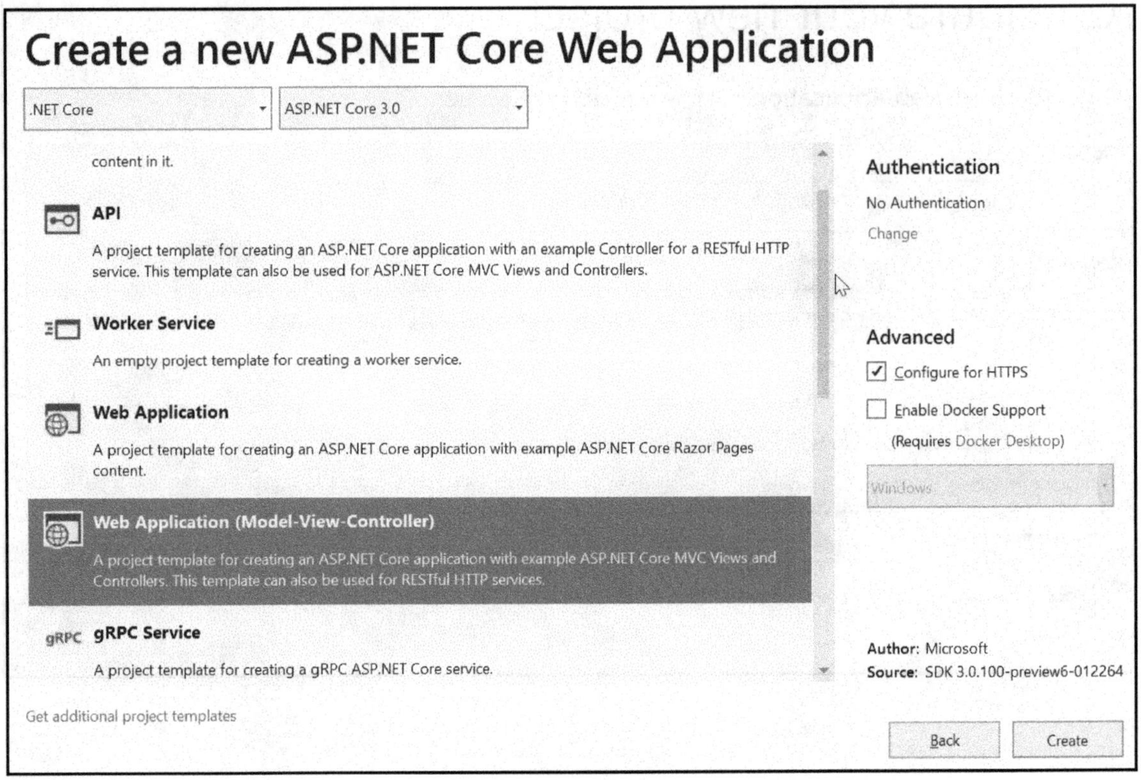

4. The created project will look as follows:

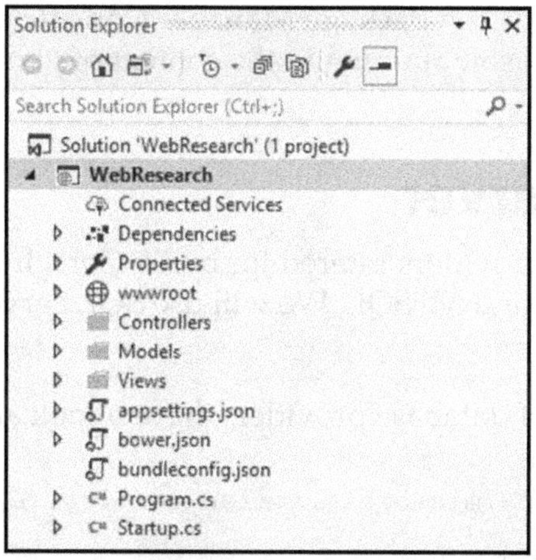

Now that we've set up the project, let's install the required packages!

Installing the required packages

We need to install three NuGet packages for our solution that will assist us in our quest. This is done through the **Package Manager Console**.

Go to **Tools** | **NuGet Package Manager** | **Package Manager Console**:

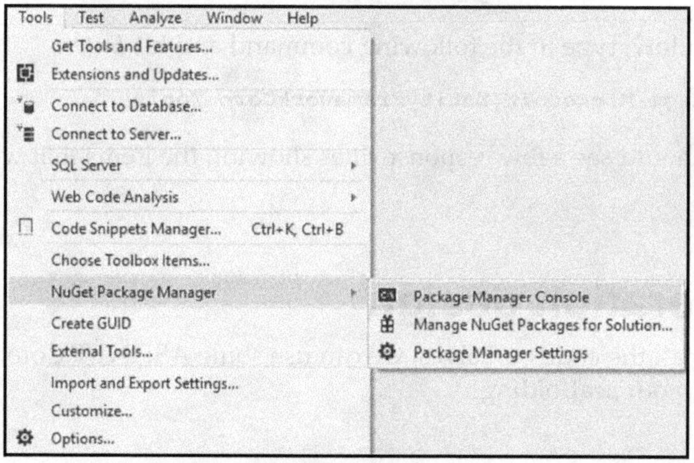

We saw the **Package Manager Console** previously; however, it's worth pointing out that this is more than it seems (or at least more than its name would suggest). The **Package Manager Console** is, effectively, a PowerShell console running in the context of your solution.

EF Core SQL Server

There are various database providers catered for by EF Core, including Microsoft SQL Server, PostgreSQL, SQLite, and MySQL. We will use SQL Server as a database provider here.

For a full list of database providers, have a look at the official Microsoft documentation at `https://docs.microsoft.com/en-us/ef/core/providers/index`.

In the console window, type in the following command and hit *Enter*:

```
Install-Package Microsoft.EntityFrameworkCore.SqlServer
```

You should see a few response lines showing the items that were successfully installed.

EF Core tools

Next up, we'll install some EF Core tools that will assist us with creating our database from our models.

In the console window, type in the following command and hit *Enter*:

```
Install-Package Microsoft.EntityFrameworkCore.Tools
```

Once again, you should see a few response lines showing the items that were successfully installed.

Code generation design

Instead of writing all the code ourselves, we can use some ASP.NET Core code generation tools to aid us with our scaffolding.

In the console window, type in the following command and hit *Enter*:

```
Install-Package Microsoft.VisualStudio.Web.CodeGeneration.Design
```

As usual, check to see that you get the `Successfully Installed` items.

> **TIP:** If you have problems installing any NuGet packages, this may be pointing to an access control issue. As a general rule, I set up my Visual Studio to run as administrator, which sorts out most of those sorts of problems.

After installation, our solution will reflect the added NuGet packages under the **Dependencies** section, as follows:

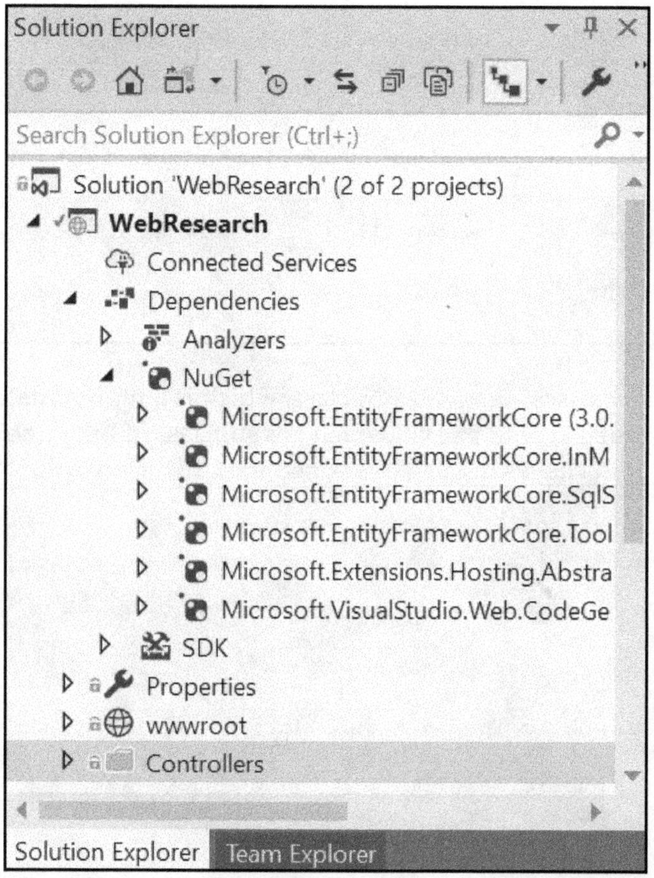

Creating the models

Right-click on the **Models** folder in your project and add a class called `ResearchModel.cs`:

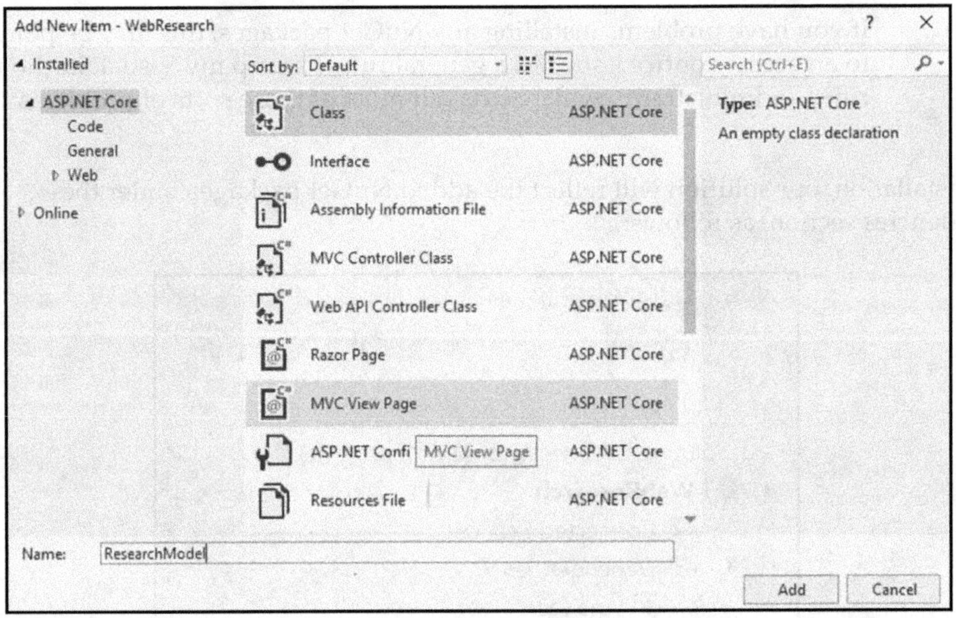

We actually need two classes – a `Research` class, which is a representation of our `entity` object, and another, `ResearchContext`, which is a subclass of `DbContext`. To keep things simple, we can put both classes in our `ResearchModel` file. Here's the code:

```
using Microsoft.EntityFrameworkCore;
using System;

namespace WebResearch.Models
{
    public class Research
    {
        public int Id { get; set; }
        public string Url { get; set; }
        public DateTime DateSaved { get; set; }
        public string Note { get; set; }
    }

    public class ResearchContext : DbContext
    {
        public ResearchContext(DbContextOptions<ResearchContext>
```

```
                options) : base(options)
                {
                }

                public DbSet<Research> ResearchLinks { get; set; }
            }
        }
```

Let's break it down as follows:

- First, we have our `Research` class, which is our `entity` object representation. As we mentioned in the *Developing a database design* section, for each link, we will save the URL, the date, and a note. The ID field is standard practice for a database table that holds information.
- Our second class, `ResearchContext`, is a subclass of `DbContext`. This class will have an empty constructor taking `DbContextOptions` as a parameter and a `DbSet<TEntity>` property for our data collection.

I could give you a brief overview about `DbSet<Entity>` here, but I'd rather let Visual Studio help us out. Let's look at the following screen:

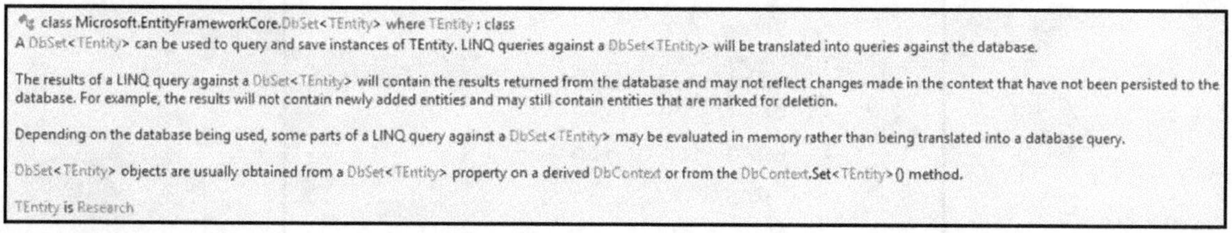

If you hover over `DbSet`, you'll get an informational popup with everything you need to know!

Configuring the services

In the `Startup.cs` class, in the `ConfigureServices` method, add the `DbContext` service with the following code:

```
string connection =
Configuration.GetConnectionString("LocalDBConnection");
services.AddDbContext<ResearchContext>(options =>
options.UseSqlServer(connection));
```

As you can see, we set a connection string variable from the configuration and then pass that in as an `options` parameter for `SqlServer` for our `DbContext`.

But hold on. Where does `LocalDBConnection` come from? We haven't set anything in our configuration. Not yet, anyway. Let's get that done now.

Open the `appsettings.json` file in the root of the project:

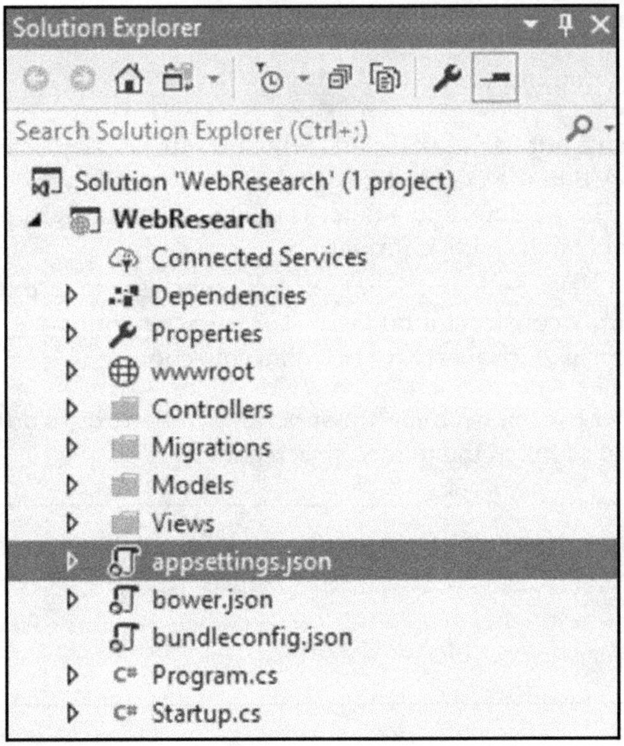

By default, you should see a logging entry. Add your `ConnectionStrings` section after the `Logging` section with a `LocalDBConnection` property.

The full file should look like this:

```
{
  "Logging": {
    "IncludeScopes": false,
    "LogLevel": {
      "Default": "Warning"
    }
  },

  "ConnectionStrings": {
    "LocalDBConnection": "Server=(localdb)\mssqllocaldb;
```

```
            Database=WebResearch;
            Trusted_Connection=True"
        }
    }
```

Later on, we will look at how to connect to an existing database, but for now, we are just connecting to a local `db` file.

Creating the database

During the development phase of any application, there is a fairly high probability that your data model will change. When that happens, your EF Core model differs from the database schema and you have to delete the outdated database and create a new one based on the updated model.

This is all fun and games until you've done your first live implementation and your application runs in a production environment. You cannot go and drop a database just to change a few columns. You have to make sure the live data persists when you make any changes.

EF Core migrations is a nifty feature that allows us to make changes to the database schema instead of recreating the database and losing production data. There is a lot of functionality and flexibility that's possible with migrations, and it is a topic well worth spending time on, but we'll just cover some of the basics for now.

We can use EF Core Migration commands in the Package Manager Console to set up, create, and, if needed, update our database.

In the Package Manager Console, we will execute the following two commands:

- `Add-Migration InitialCreate`
- `Update-Database`

The first command will generate the code in the `Migrations` folder of the project, which is used to create the database. The naming convention for these files is <timestamp>_InitialCreate.cs.

The second command will create the database and run the `Migrations`:

There are two methods of `Note` in the `InitialCreate` class: `Up` and `Down`. Simply put, the `Up` method code executes when you upgrade the application and the `Down` method code is run when you downgrade the application.

Let's say we want to add a Boolean property to our `Research` model, called `Read`. To persist this value, we would obviously need to add that column to our table as well, but we don't want to drop the table just to add a field. With migrations, we can update the table rather than recreate it.

We'll start by altering our model. In the `Research` class, add the `Read` property. Our class will look as follows:

```
public class Research
{
    public int Id { get; set; }
    public string Url { get; set; }
    public DateTime DateSaved { get; set; }
    public string Note { get; set; }
    public bool Read { get; set; }
}
```

Next, we'll add a migration. We'll use the migration name as an indication of what we're doing. Execute the following command in your Package Manager Console:

```
Add-Migration AddReseachRead
```

You will notice that we have a new class in our `Migrations` folder:

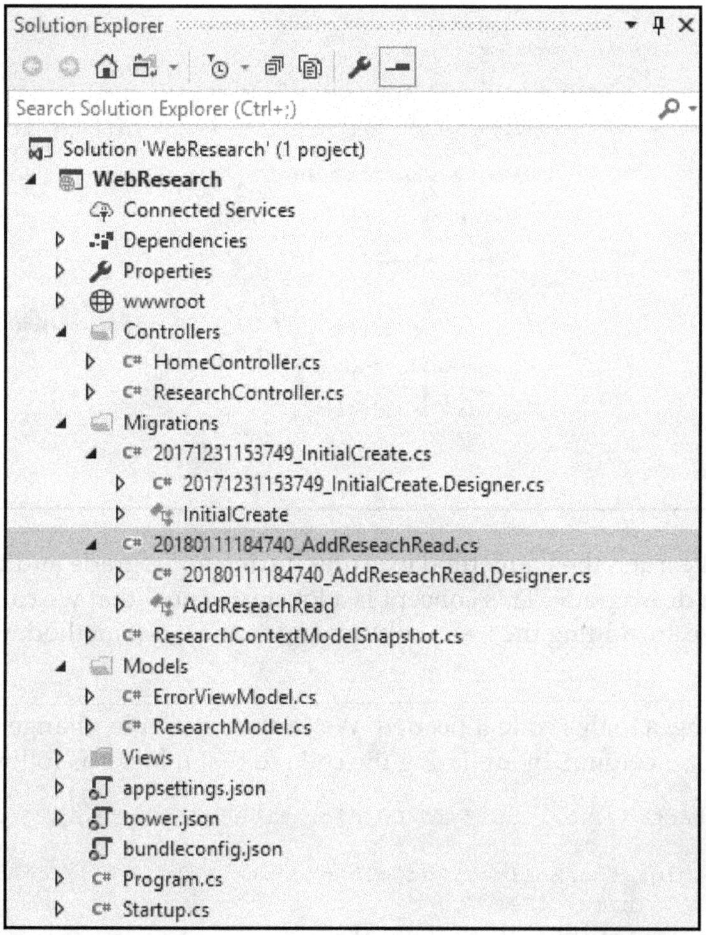

Let's have a look under the hood. You will see that our `Up` and `Down` methods aren't as empty as they are in the `InitialCreate` class:

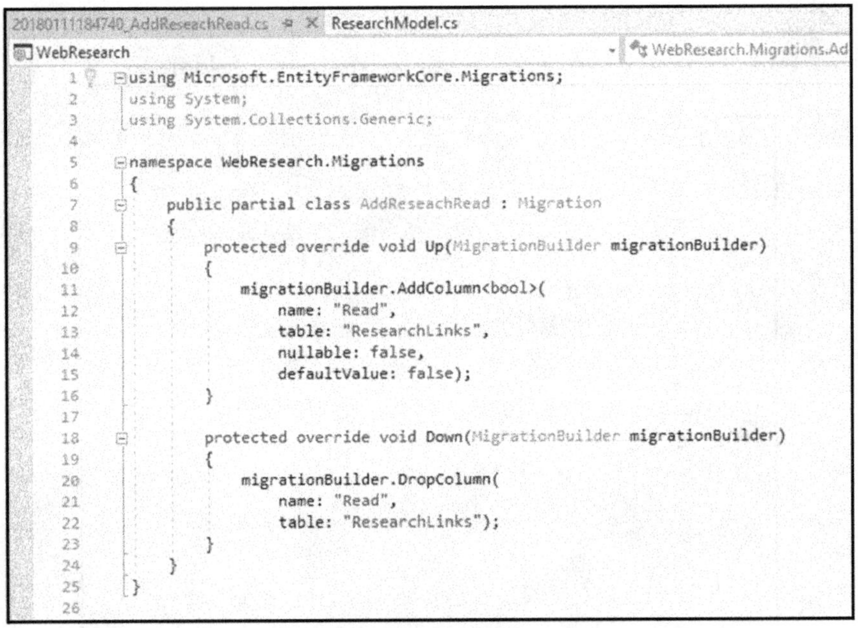


```
using Microsoft.EntityFrameworkCore.Migrations;
using System;
using System.Collections.Generic;

namespace WebResearch.Migrations
{
    public partial class AddReseachRead : Migration
    {
        protected override void Up(MigrationBuilder migrationBuilder)
        {
            migrationBuilder.AddColumn<bool>(
                name: "Read",
                table: "ResearchLinks",
                nullable: false,
                defaultValue: false);
        }

        protected override void Down(MigrationBuilder migrationBuilder)
        {
            migrationBuilder.DropColumn(
                name: "Read",
                table: "ResearchLinks");
        }
    }
}
```

As we mentioned earlier, the `Up` method executes during an upgrade and the `Down` method executes during a downgrade. This concept is a lot clearer now that we can see the code. In the `Up` method, we are adding the `Read` column and in the `Down` method, we are dropping the column.

We can make changes to this code if needed. We can, for example, change the `nullable` attribute of the `Read` column, by updating the code so that it looks as follows:

```
protected override void Up(MigrationBuilder migrationBuilder)
{
    migrationBuilder.AddColumn<bool>(
        name: "Read",
        table: "ResearchLinks",
        nullable: true,
        defaultValue: false);
}
```

We can also add a custom SQL query that will update all the existing entries to `Read`:

```
migrationBuilder.Sql(
    @"
```

```
            UPDATE Research
            SET Read = 'true';
        ");
```

I know this is not a great example, as you wouldn't want all your `Research` entries to be marked as `Read` every time you update the database, but hopefully you understand the concept.

This code hasn't yet been executed, though. So, at the moment, our model and database schema are still out of sync.

Execute the following command again and we'll be all up to date:

```
Update-Database
```

Seeding the database with test data

Now that we have an empty database, let's fill it with some test data. To do this, we'll need to create a method that we will call after our database creation:

1. Create a folder in your project called `Data`. Inside this folder, add a class called `DbInitializer.cs`:

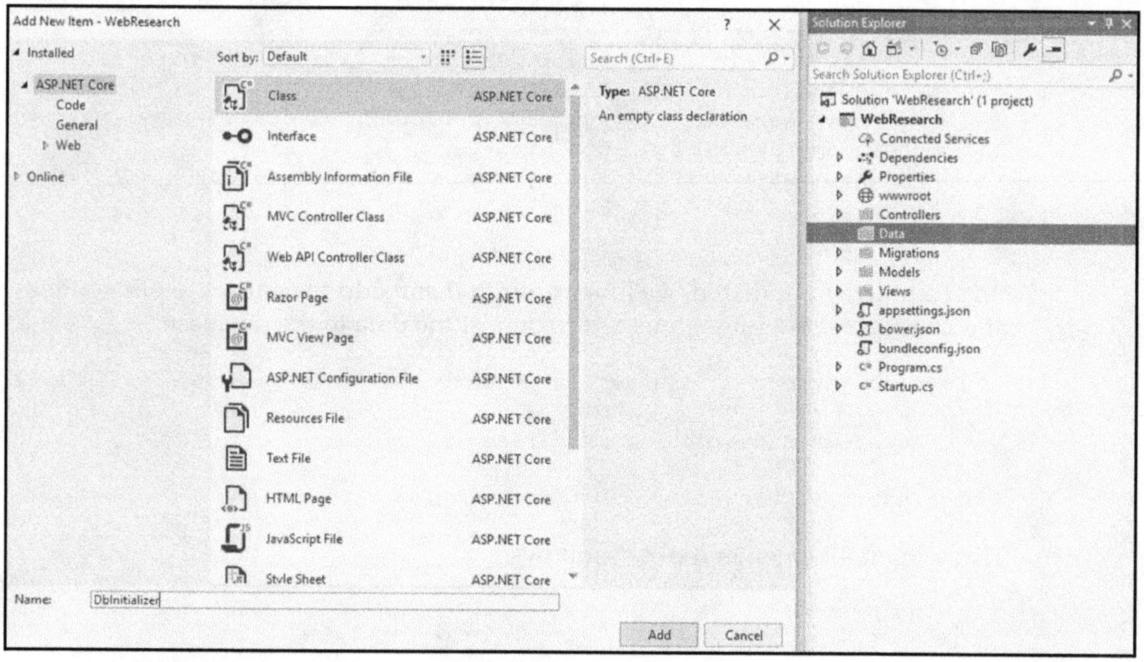

This class has an `Initialize` method that takes our `ResearchContext` as a parameter:

```
public static void Initialize(ResearchContext context)
```

2. In the `Initialize` method, we call the `Database.EnsureCreated` method to make sure the database exists and creates it if not:

```
context.Database.EnsureCreated();
```

3. Next up, we do a quick `Linq` query to check if the `ResearchLinks` table has any records. The argument is that if the table is empty, we want to add some testing data:

```
if (!context.ResearchLinks.Any())
```

4. Then, we create an array of the `Research` model and add some test entries. The URLs can be anything you like. I just went with a few of the most common sites out there:

```
var researchLinks = new Research[]
{
 new Research{Url="www.google.com", DateSaved=DateTime.Now,
  Note="Generated Data", Read=false},
      new Research{Url="www.twitter.com", DateSaved=DateTime.Now,
  Note="Generated Data", Read=false},
      new Research{Url="www.facebook.com", DateSaved=DateTime.Now,
  Note="Generated Data", Read=false},
      new Research{Url="www.packtpub.com", DateSaved=DateTime.Now,
  Note="Generated Data", Read=false},
      new Research{Url="www.linkedin.com", DateSaved=DateTime.Now,
  Note="Generated Data", Read=false},
};
```

5. With our array populated, we loop through it and add the entries to our context and call the `SaveChanges` method to persist the data to the database:

```
foreach (Research research in researchLinks)
{
    context.ResearchLinks.Add(research);
}
context.SaveChanges();
```

6. Throwing it all together looks as follows:

```
using System;
using System.Linq;
```

```
using WebResearch.Models;

namespace WebResearch.Data
{
    public static class DbInitializer
    {
        public static void Initialize(ResearchContext context)
        {
            context.Database.EnsureCreated();

            if (!context.ResearchLinks.Any())
            {
                var researchLinks = new Research[]
                {
                    new Research{Url="www.google.com",
                     DateSaved=DateTime.Now, Note="Generated Data",
                      Read=false},
                    new Research{Url="www.twitter.com",
                      DateSaved=DateTime.Now, Note="Generated
                      Data",
                       Read=false},
                    new Research{Url="www.facebook.com",
                     DateSaved=DateTime.Now, Note="Generated Data",
                      Read=false},
                    new Research{Url="www.packtpub.com",
                     DateSaved=DateTime.Now, Note="Generated Data",
                      Read=false},
                    new Research{Url="www.linkedin.com",
                     DateSaved=DateTime.Now, Note="Generated Data",
                      Read=false},
                };
                foreach (Research research in researchLinks)
                {
                    context.ResearchLinks.Add(research);
                }
                context.SaveChanges();
            }
        }
    }
}
```

Creating the controller

Controllers are a fundamental building block of how ASP.NET Core MVC applications are built. The methods inside a controller are referred to as actions. Therefore, we can say that a controller defines a set of actions. The actions handle requests and these requests are mapped to the specific actions through routing.

> To read more on the topic of controllers and actions, see the Microsoft documentation at `https://docs.microsoft.com/en-us/aspnet/core/mvc/controllers/actions`. To read more on routing, see the Microsoft documentation at `https://docs.microsoft.com/en-us/aspnet/core/mvc/controllers/routing`.

Follow these steps:

1. Right-click on the **Controller** folder and choose **Add** | **Controller**.
2. On the scaffolding screen, choose **MVC Controller with views, using Entity Framework** and click **Add**:

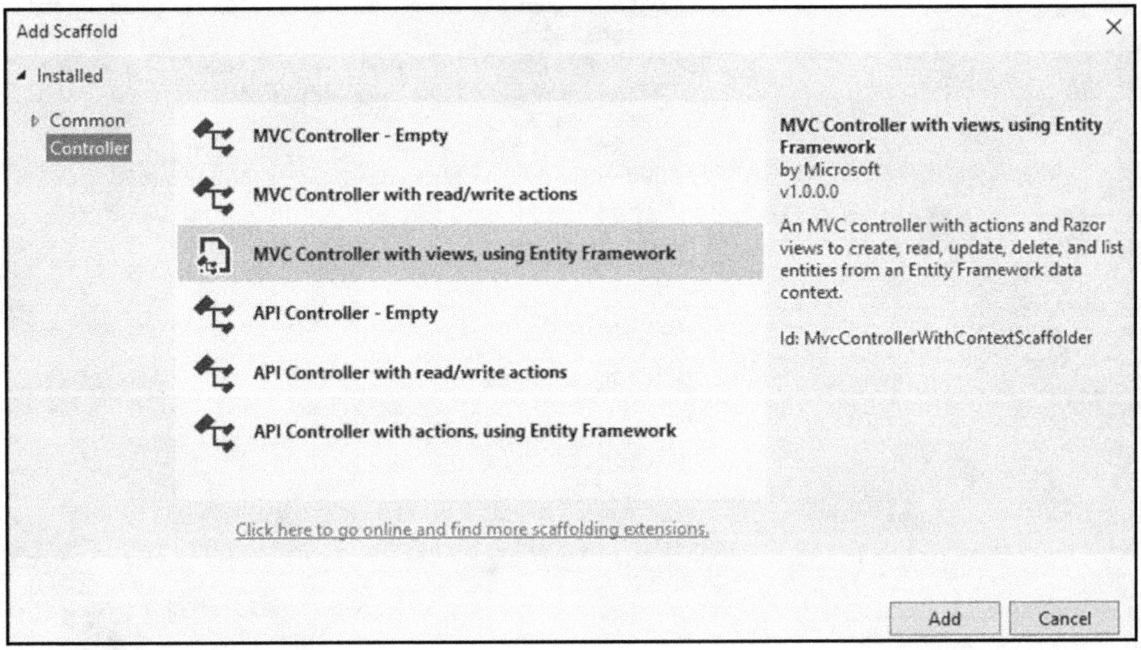

3. On the next screen, select our **Research** model for the **Model class** and **ResearchContext** for the **Data context class**. You can leave the rest as is unless you'd like to change the **Controller name**:

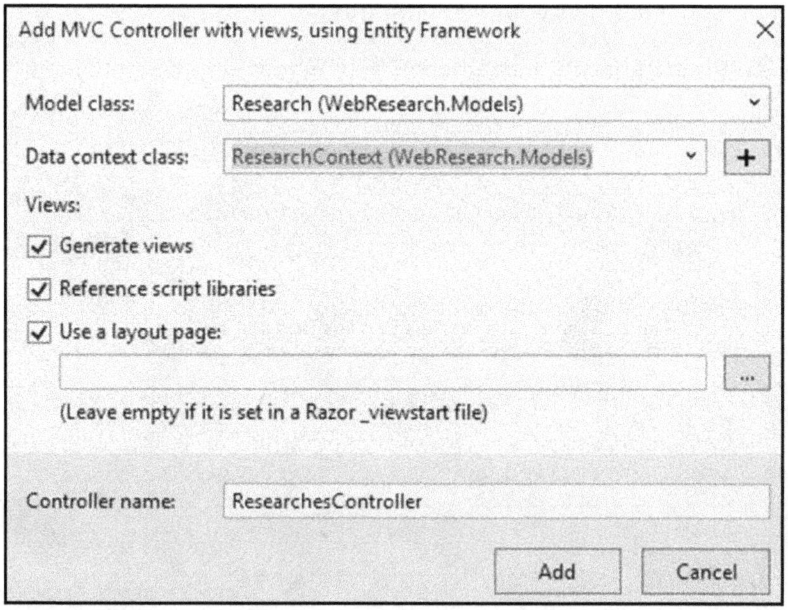

A brief look at the created controller shows us that we now have our basic **create, read, update, and delete** (**CRUD**) tasks in place. Now, it's time for the main event.

Running the application

Before we jump in and run the application, let's make sure our new page is easily accessible. The simplest way to do that is to just set it as the default home page:

1. Have a look at the `Configure` method in `Startup.cs`. You'll notice that the default route is specified as the `Home` controller.
2. Simply change the controller to your `Research` controller, as follows:

```
app.UseEndpoints(endpoints =>
{
    endpoints.MapControllerRoute(
        name: "default",
        pattern: "{controller=Research}/{action=Index}/{id?}");
    endpoints.MapRazorPages();
});
```

If you're familiar with ASP.NET 2.x, you'll have expected to see `UseMvc` here. In fact, `UseMvc` is deprecated, in favor of manually building the MVC middleware that you require.

3. Lastly, make sure that your `Main` method looks as follows:

```
public static void Main(string[] args)
{
  var host = BuildWebHost(args);
  using (var scope = host.Services.CreateScope())
  {
    var services = scope.ServiceProvider;
    try
    {
      var context = services.GetRequiredService<ResearchContext>();
      DbInitializer.Initialize(context);
    }
    catch (Exception ex)
    {
        var logger =
services.GetRequiredService<ILogger<Program>>();
        logger.LogError(ex, "An error occurred while seeding the
database.");
    }
  }
  host.Run();
}
```

4. Now, hit *Ctrl* + *F5* to run the application and see the fruits of your labor:

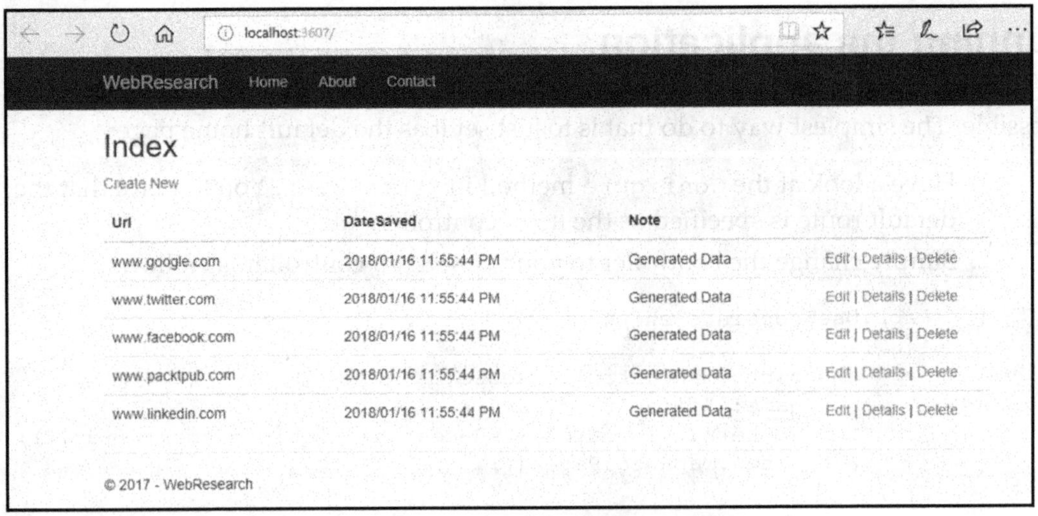

5. As you can see, our test entries are available for us to play with. Let's have a quick look at the available functionality:
6. Click on **Create New** to see the entry form for our links:

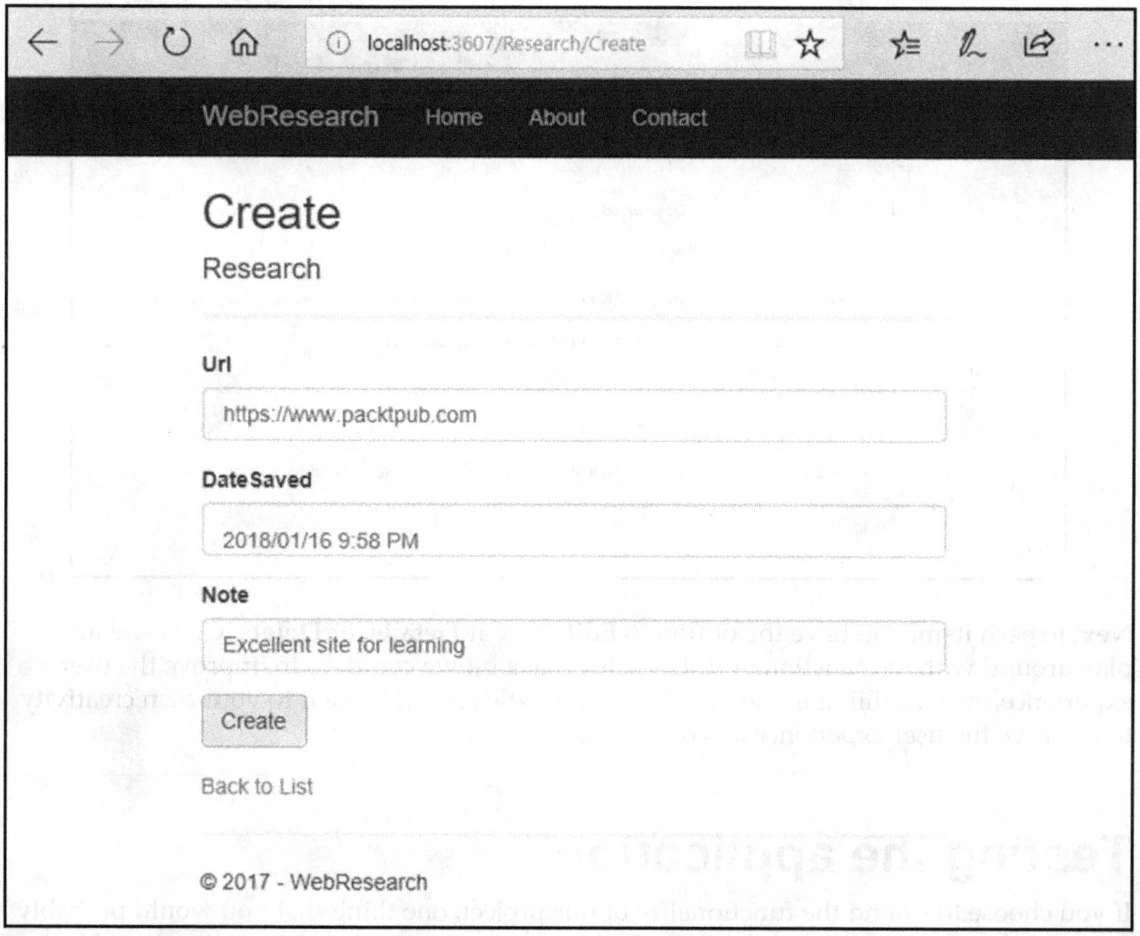

7. Enter some interesting data and hit the **Create** button. You'll be redirected to the list view and see that our new entry has been added to the bottom of the list:

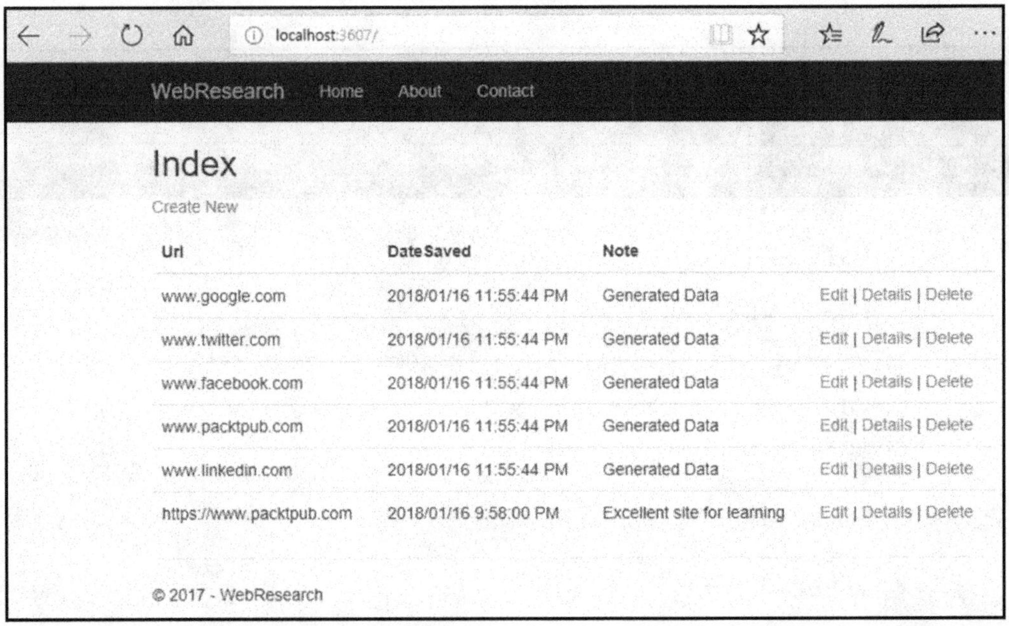

Next to each item, you have the option to **Edit**, look at **Details**, or **Delete**. Go ahead and play around with the functionality. There is quite a bit we could do to improve the user experience, such as filling in the date field automatically. I'll leave it to your own creativity to improve the user experience as you see fit.

Testing the application

If you choose to extend the functionality of this project, one thing that you would probably want to add is some automated testing. Let's get some terminology out of the way: this section concerns automated testing, but not unit testing. It's easy to get into debates and discussions regarding exactly what a test is, but for the purpose of this section, we are adding *automated* testing.

Since this application is very much a basic data access application, automated testing often gets omitted. It certainly could be argued that, since there is very little logic, you're effectively testing EF Core. Another main reason for not testing a basic CRUD application has always been how difficult it is. Testing database-centric applications has always been a difficult, time-consuming, and thankless task.

Firstly, many unit test purists would argue that you cannot include the data access in your test and so you should mock out the data access. This would typically be done by creating a repository pattern to abstract the data access or even by multiple layers of abstraction, but once we do this, we must simulate what a call to the database would return, which, while adhering to the principles of unit testing, doesn't offer us much assurance that our application works.

Secondly, database operations are typically not idempotent; that is, once you've run a test on a real database, running it again will typically have different results because the data has changed. In the past, people have gotten around this by recreating the database each time, by writing scripts to revert the operation, or by running the test inside a transaction and then rolling it back. One thing that all of these have in common is that they are all very slow.

Entity Framework itself is a kind of repository pattern and you can certainly abstract away the `DbContext`; however, with EF Core, you have the concept of something called an **in-memory database**. There have been a number of open source projects that have tried to provide this for EF6 by maintaining the data changes inside a dictionary or similar.

Let's create a couple of automated tests (I won't call them unit tests because they clearly don't test a single unit of functionality):

1. The first step is to create a `Test` project:

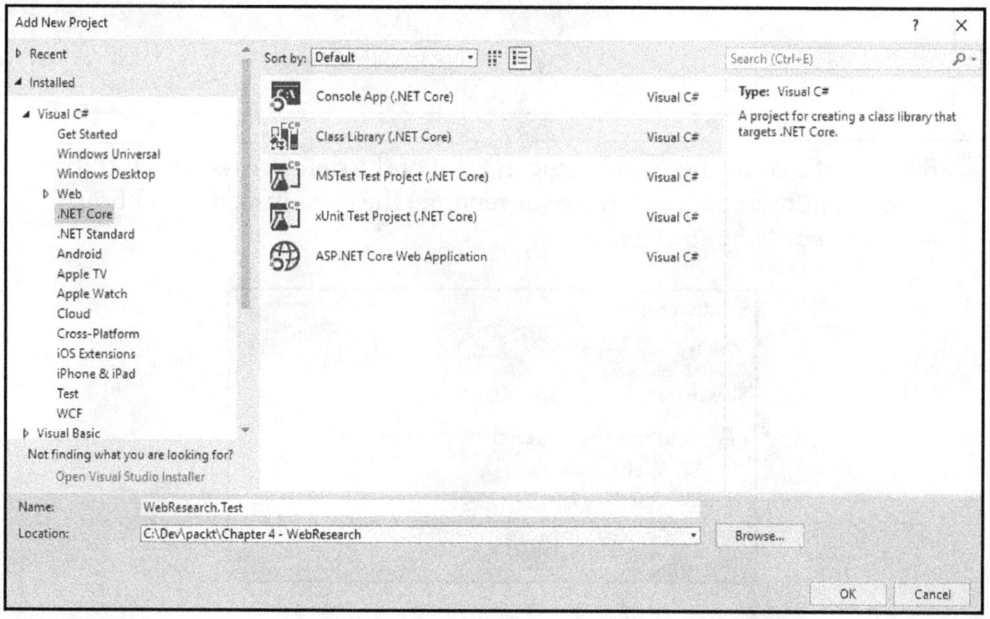

We'll create the project as a class library for now. For this particular test, we'll use `XUnit`, but you should be able to substitute this for any of the main testing libraries without any difficulty.

2. Once the project has been created, we can install the test library using the Package Manager Console (ensure that you have the correct `Test` project selected):

```
Install-Package XUnit -ProjectName WebResearch.Test
```

We'll need some more libraries:

```
Install-Package Microsoft.EntityFrameworkCore -ProjectName
WebResearch.Test
Install-Package XUnit.Runner.VisualStudio -ProjectName
WebResearch.Test
```

3. Next, we'll need to add a reference to the project that we're testing:

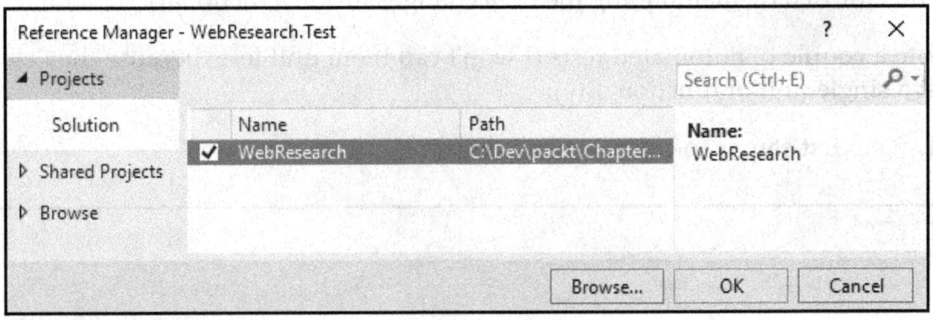

Because the controller is the logic in front of the data access, let's test the `ResearchController`. Create (or rename) the class in your test library as `ResearchControllerTests`:

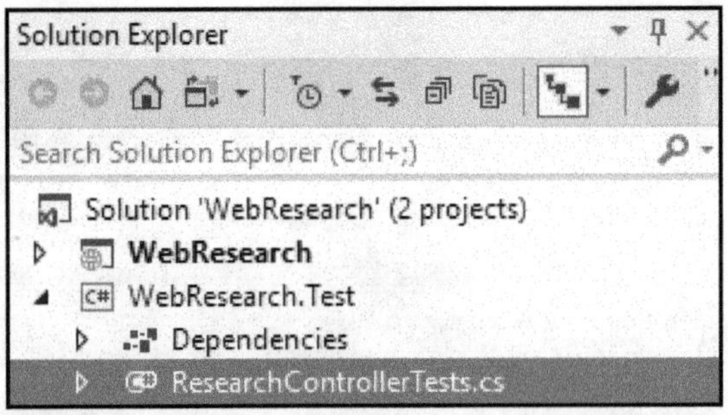

4. Lastly, we'll need to add a NuGet package to the test project that allows us to use an in-memory database:

```
Install-Package Microsoft.EntityFrameworkCore.InMemory
```

We'll come back to exactly what this is later in this chapter.

Let's look at the code for the test. Then, we can walk through what it's doing:

```
[Fact]
public async Task RetrieveDetails_DetailsCorrect()
{
    // Arrange
    var testUrl = "www.pmichaels.net";
    var options = new DbContextOptionsBuilder<ResearchContext>()
        .UseInMemoryDatabase(Guid.NewGuid().ToString())
        .EnableSensitiveDataLogging()
        .Options;
    var researchContext = new ResearchContext(options);
    var researchController = new
ResearchController(researchContext);
    var research = new Research()
    {
        Id = 1,
        DateSaved = new DateTime(2018, 10, 24),
        Note = "Useful site for programming and tech information",
        Read = false,
        Url = testUrl
    };

    var createResult = await researchController.Create(research);

    // Act
    var detailsResult = await researchController.Details(1);

    // Assert
    var viewResult = (ViewResult)detailsResult;
    var resultsModel = (Research)viewResult.Model;
    Assert.Equal(testUrl, resultsModel.Url);
}
```

5. Once you've created the test, launch the **Test Explorer**:

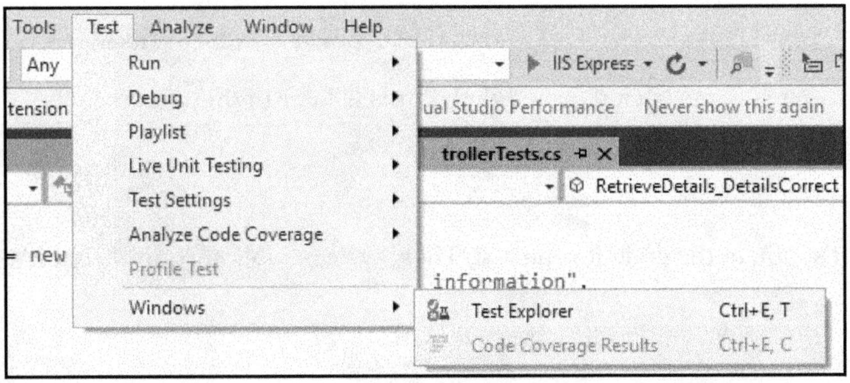

6. Once this appears, run all (or, at the minute, our single) tests:

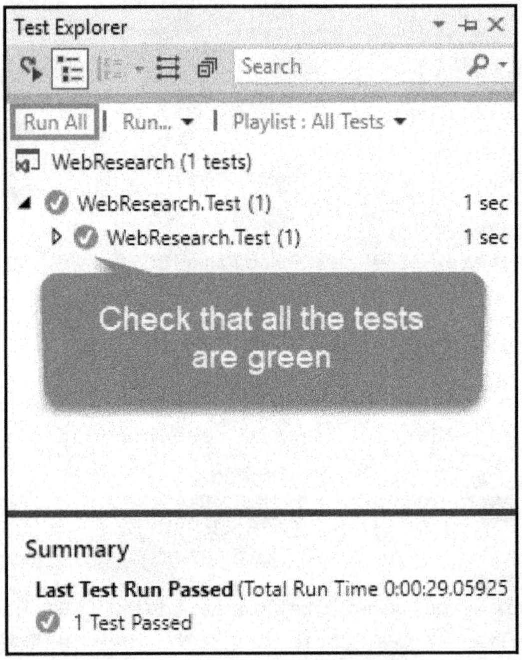

A full explanation of unit tests and `XUnit` is beyond the scope of this chapter and book; however, I'll cover some of the more salient points in the test, just for the sake of completeness.

Arrange/act/assert

Unit tests obviously don't require these comments, but I have found that, when I use them, I can clearly identify what I'm testing, and that I'm testing a single action. Since this isn't strictly a unit test, there's more than one statement that executes code; however, only one is being tested. This helps when you're trying to name your test and to identify what you have covered in your testing.

In-memory database

The following code sets up the in-memory database inside the `DbContext` options and creates a new context using these options. This is exactly the same `DbContext` that is created when the program runs with real data, but is stored in memory:

```
var options = new DbContextOptionsBuilder<ResearchContext>()
        .UseInMemoryDatabase(Guid.NewGuid().ToString())
        .EnableSensitiveDataLogging()
        .Options;
var researchContext = new ResearchContext(options);
var researchController = new ResearchController(researchContext);
```

What are we testing?

It is always worth asking yourself this question. Tests are code, which means they take time to write and to maintain, so make sure they are earning their keep. Whether this test is doing that is actually debatable. What we are doing is creating a record and then retrieving that record. There is an amount of logic between those two steps, so the test is definitely testing something. Let's add a second test so that we can ensure that we don't retrieve records that aren't there:

```
[Fact]
public async Task RetrieveInvalidRecord_DetailsCorrect()
{
    // Arrange
    var testUrl = "www.pmichaels.net";
    var options = new DbContextOptionsBuilder<ResearchContext>()
            .UseInMemoryDatabase(Guid.NewGuid().ToString())
            .EnableSensitiveDataLogging()
            .Options;
    var researchContext = new ResearchContext(options);
    var researchController = new ResearchController(researchContext);
    var research = new Research()
    {
```

```
            Id = 1,
            DateSaved = new DateTime(2018, 10, 24),
            Note = "Useful site for programming and tech information",
            Read = false,
            Url = testUrl
        };

        var createResult = await researchController.Create(research);

        // Act
        var detailsResult = await researchController.Details(2);

        // Assert
        Assert.IsType<NotFoundResult>(detailsResult);
    }
```

As you can see, this is exactly the same as the previous test, except that we test for an `Id` of `2` instead of `1`. Then, we assert that we expect this to not be found.

Speed

The tests that we're discussing here do adhere to most **FIRST** test principles (short for **Fast**, **Isolated**, **Repeatable**, **Self-validating**, **Thorough**); however, they will not be as fast as a typical unit test, so they should sit near the top of your testing pyramid:

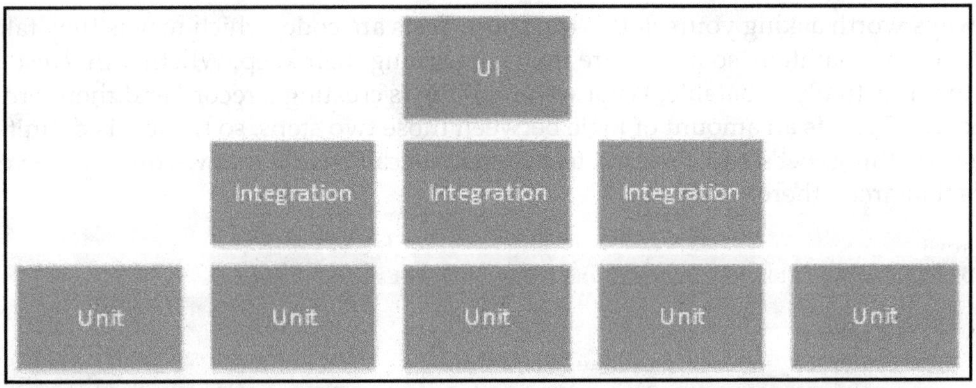

Now that we've covered how we might test our application, let's move on to how it can be deployed.

Deploying the application

Once your application is ready for deployment, there are a few options available that you can use, including the following:

- **Microsoft Azure App Service**
- Custom targets (**IIS, FTP, etc**)
- **Folder**
- **Import profile**

Under the **Build** menu item in Visual Studio, click on **Publish WebResearch** (or whatever you decided to name your project):

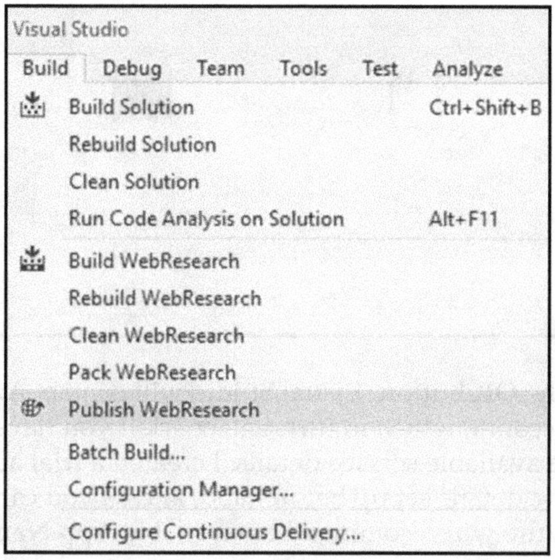

You should be presented with a screen showing you the available publishing options. Let's take a closer look.

Microsoft Azure App Service

Microsoft Azure takes care of all the infrastructure requirements that are needed to create and maintain a web application. This means that us developers don't need to worry about things such as server management, load balancing, or security. With the platform being improved and extended almost daily, we can also be fairly confident that we'll have the latest and greatest functionality available to us.

We're not going to go into too much detail about Azure App Service as a whole book could be written about it, but we can surely have a look at the required steps to publish our web app to this cloud platform:

1. Select **Microsoft Azure App Service** as your publishing target. If you have an existing site that you want to publish to, you can choose **Select Existing**. For now, I'll assume you need to **Create New**:

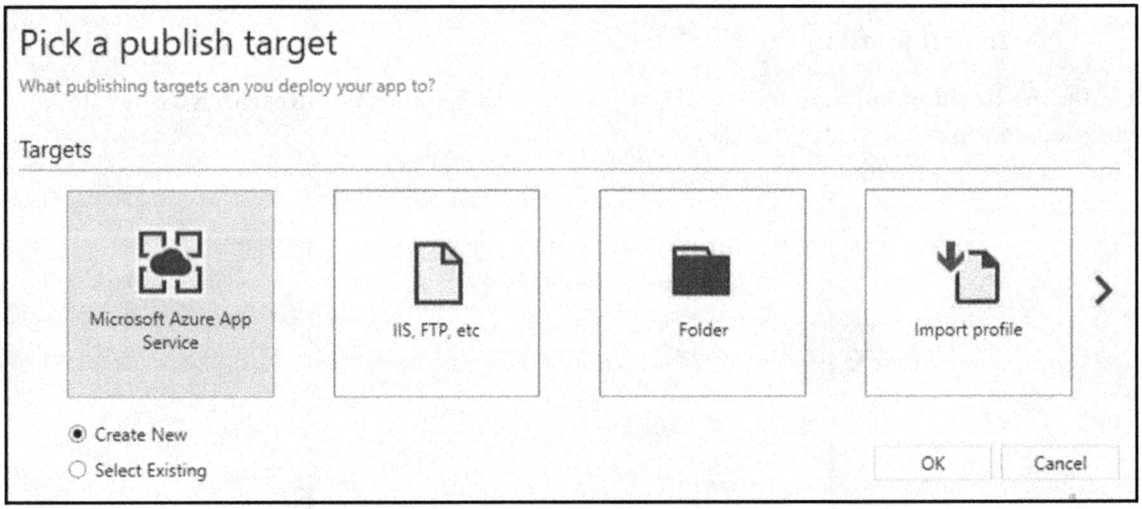

2. After hitting the **OK** button, Visual Studio will contact Azure with your logged-in Microsoft account, which in turn will check if you have an Azure account and will return the available service details. I created a trial account for this blueprint with no specific details set up beforehand, and as you can see from the following screenshot, Azure will recommend an available **App Name** and **App Service Plan** for you.

3. The **Resource Group** is optional and will have a unique group name if you do not specify anything:

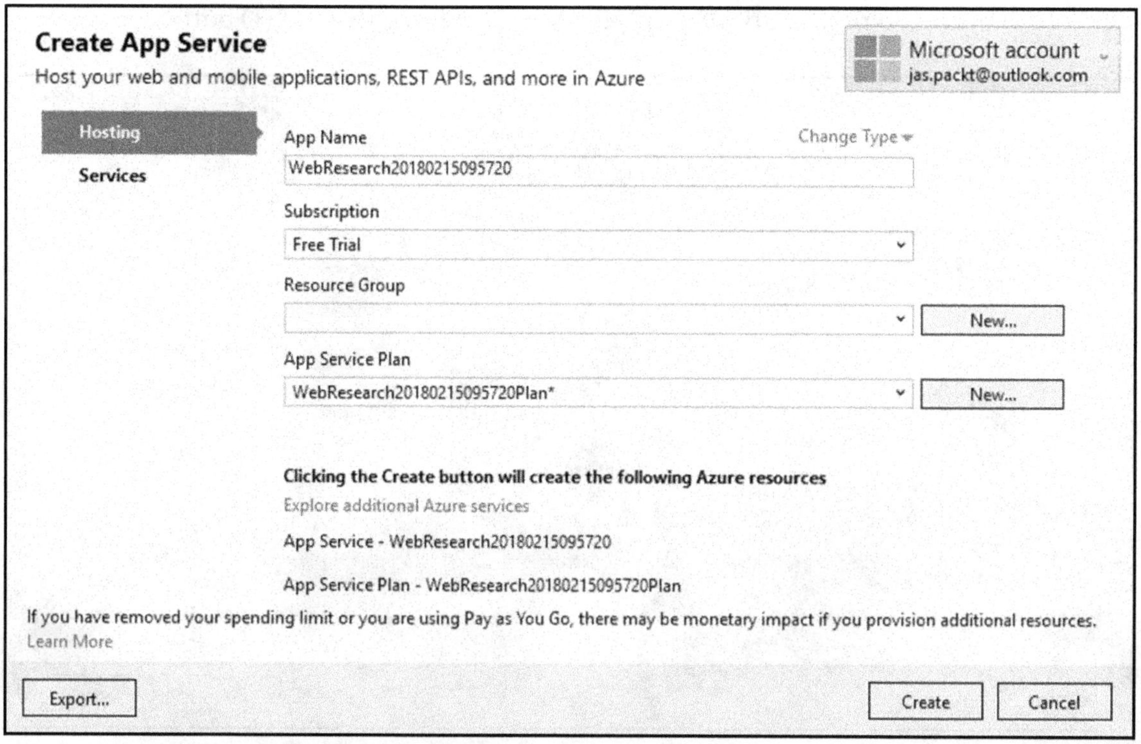

4. You can change the type of application you want to publish under the **Change Type** option. In our case, we'll obviously go with **Web App**:

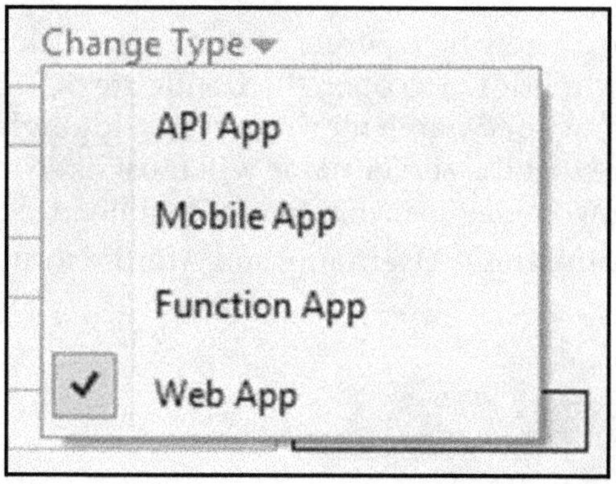

5. Click on **Services** on the left-hand side to see the services that will be set up with your publication. The first box shows any **Recommended** resource types your application might benefit from. In our case, a **SQL Database** is recommended, and we do need it, so we'll simply add it by hitting the add (+) button:

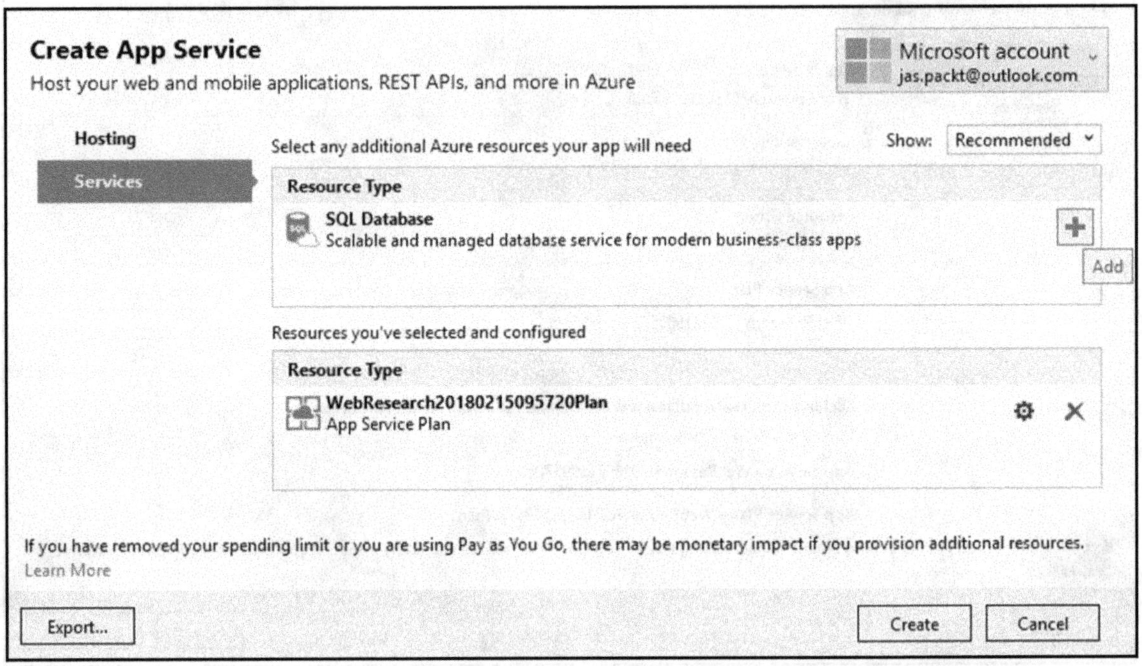

Azure will take care of the SQL installation, but we need to give it the required information, such as which server to use if you already have one on your profile, or to create a new one if you haven't.

6. We will configure a new SQL Server in this case. Click the **New** button next to the **SQL Server** dropdown to open the Configure SQL Server form. Azure will provide a recommended name for the server. Although you can provide your own, chances are that the server name will most likely not be available, so I recommend that you just use what they recommend.
7. Provide an **Administrator Username** and **Administrator Password** for the server and hit **OK**:

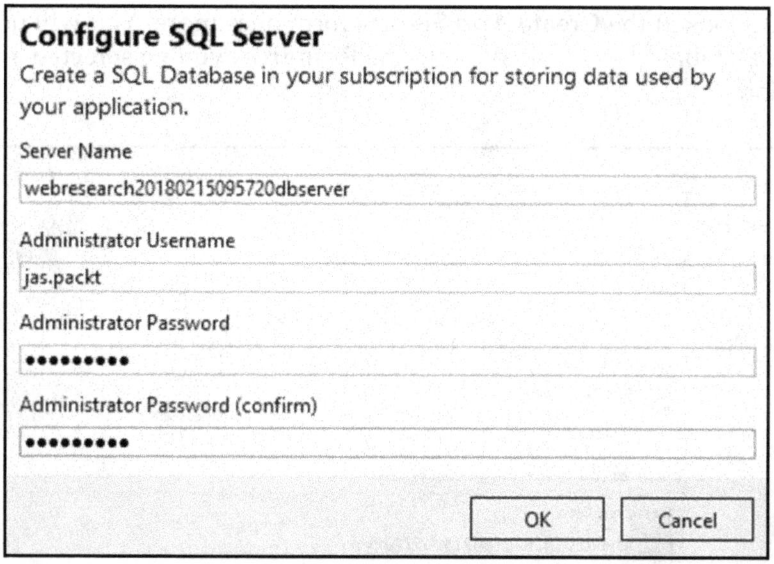

8. Doing this will bring you back to the **Configure SQL Database** form, where you need to specify the **Database Name**, as well as the **Connection String Name**:

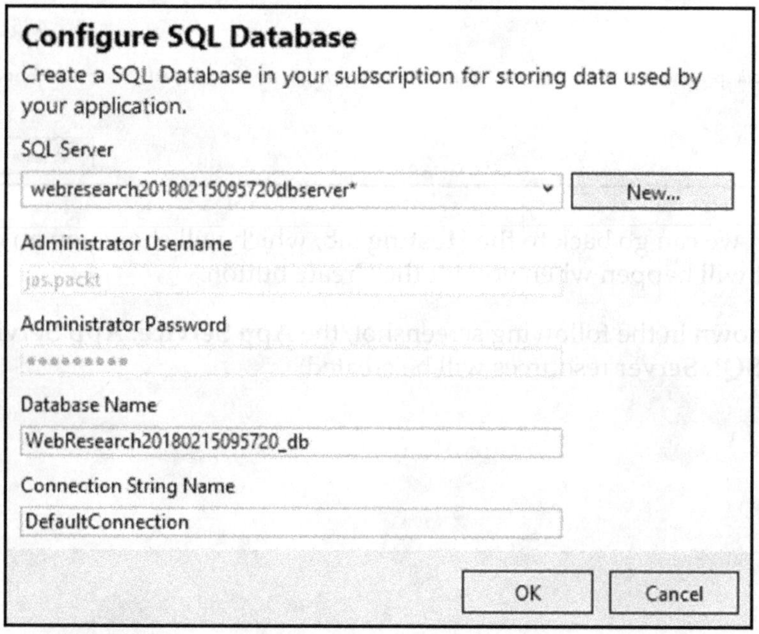

9. Take a look at the **Create App Service** form once more. You will notice that the **SQL Database** has been added to the **Resources you've selected and configured** section:

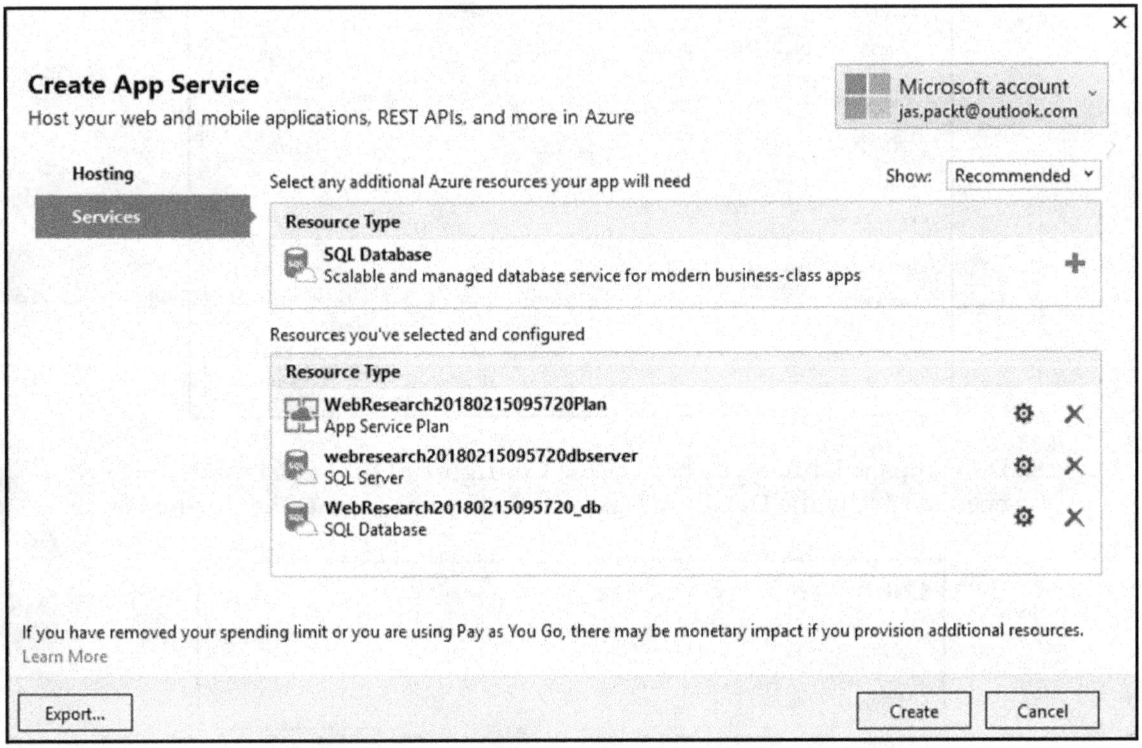

10. Now, we can go back to the **Hosting** tab, which will show you an overview of what will happen when you hit the **Create** button.

11. As shown in the following screenshot, the **App Service**, **App Service Plan**, and **SQL Server** resources will be created:

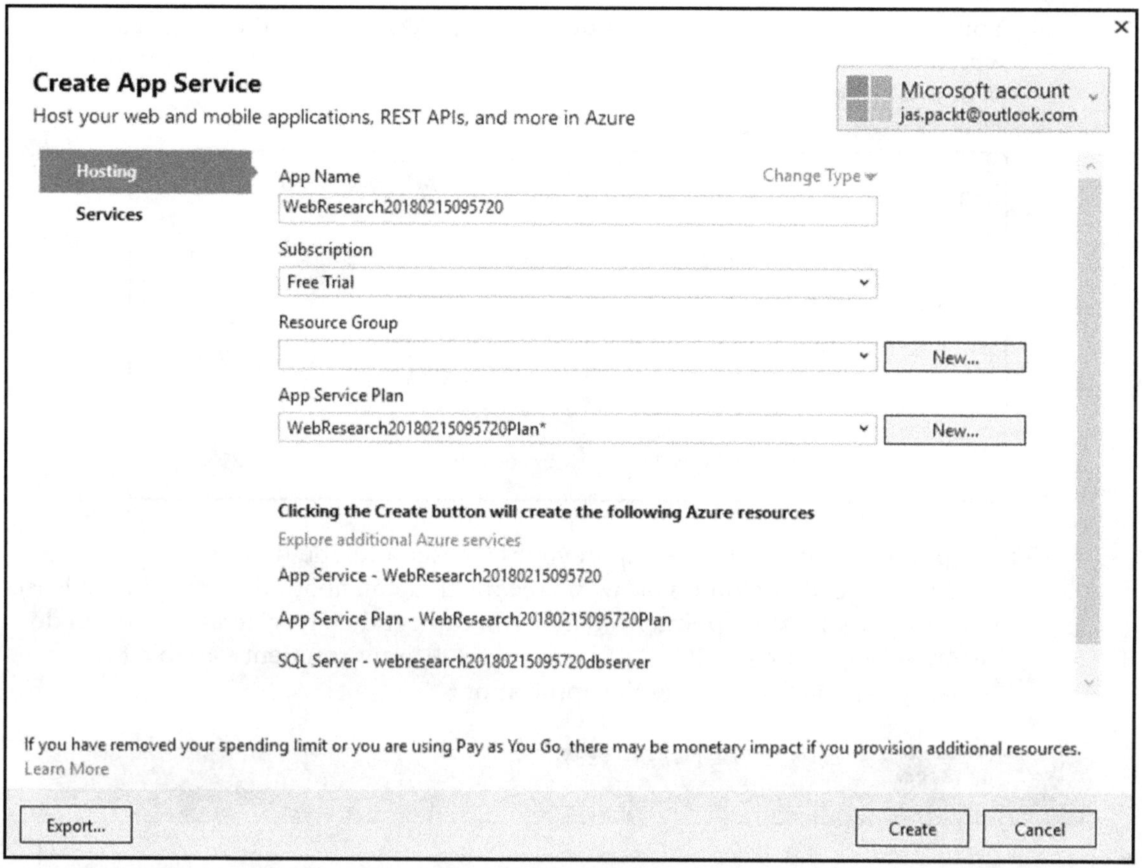

12. After creation, we can publish our new Azure profile by hitting the **Publish** button.
13. You will see some **Build** messages in your output window and should end up with the following:

```
Publish Succeeded.
Web App was published successfully
http://webresearch20180215095720.azurewebsites.net/
========== Build: 1 succeeded, 0 failed, 0 up-to-date, 0 skipped
==========
========== Publish: 1 succeeded, 0 failed, 0 skipped ==========
```

14. You can have a look at your dashboard on the Azure portal (`portal.azure.com`), which will show you the resources that have been enabled on your account due to our **Service** creation:

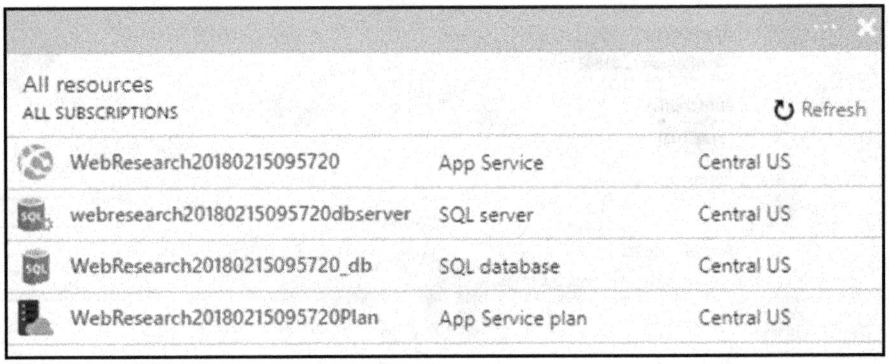

15. The published app will open up in your browser and you'll most likely see an error message. By default, you won't see much detail about the error, but at least Azure gives you some pointers so that you can get the error details. You can do this by setting your `ASPNETCORE_ENVIRONMENT` environment variable to `Development` and restarting the application:

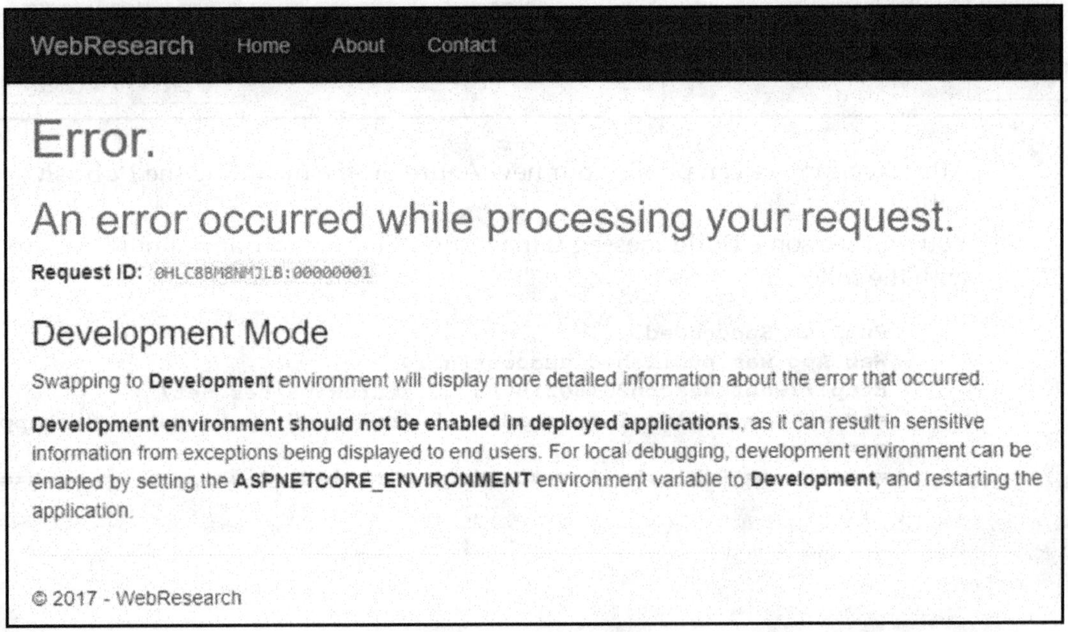

16. When you log in to your Azure portal, you can navigate to your **App Service** and then, in the **Application settings**, add the `ASPNETCORE_ENVIRONMENT` setting with the value of `Development` and restart your app:

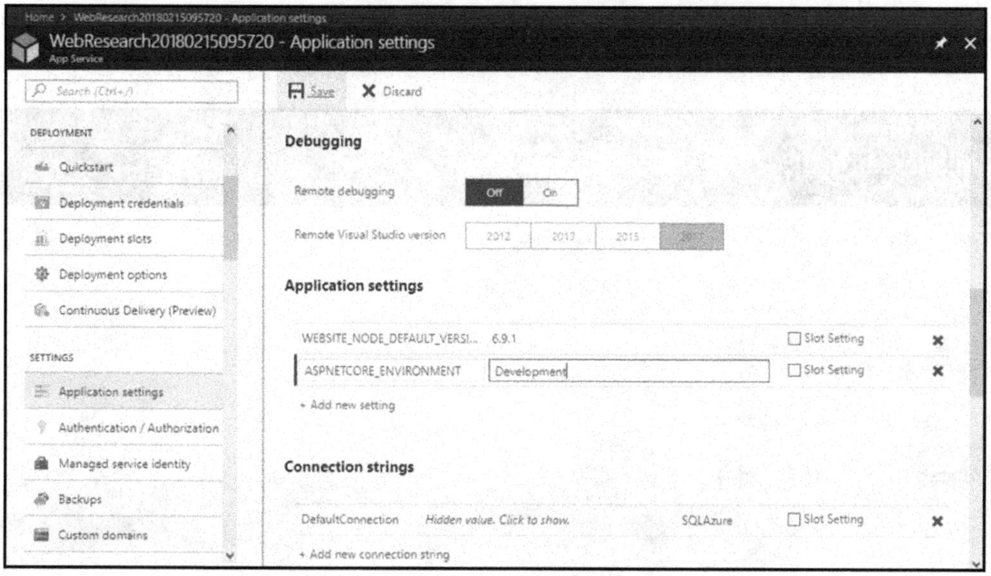

17. Now, we can refresh the site. We should see a bit more detail about the underlying error:

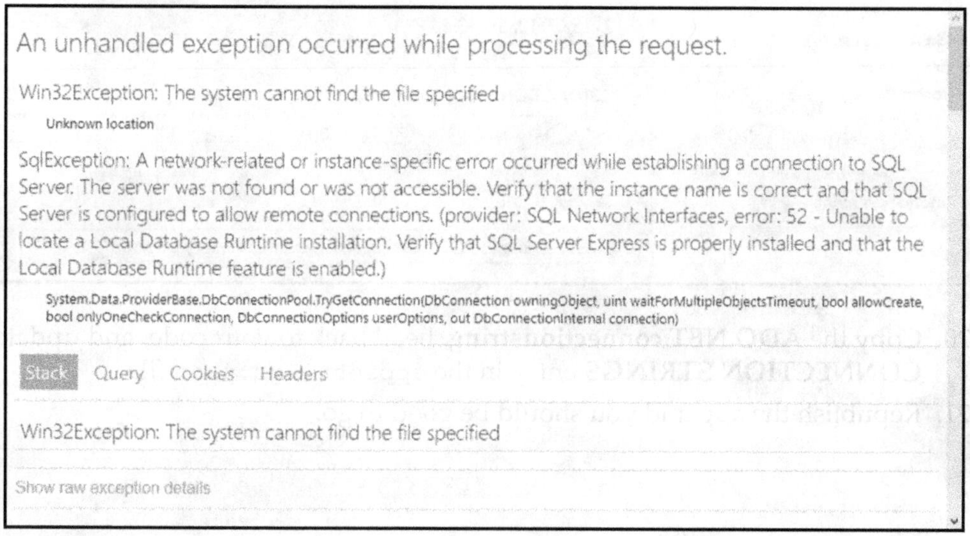

18. Ah, yes! We are still pointing to our local DB and we don't have access to that from the publish environment. Let's update our `appsettings.json` so that it points to our Azure DB.
19. Navigate to the SQL Server from your Azure dashboard and then to **Properties**. On the right-hand pane, you should see an option to **Show database connection strings**:

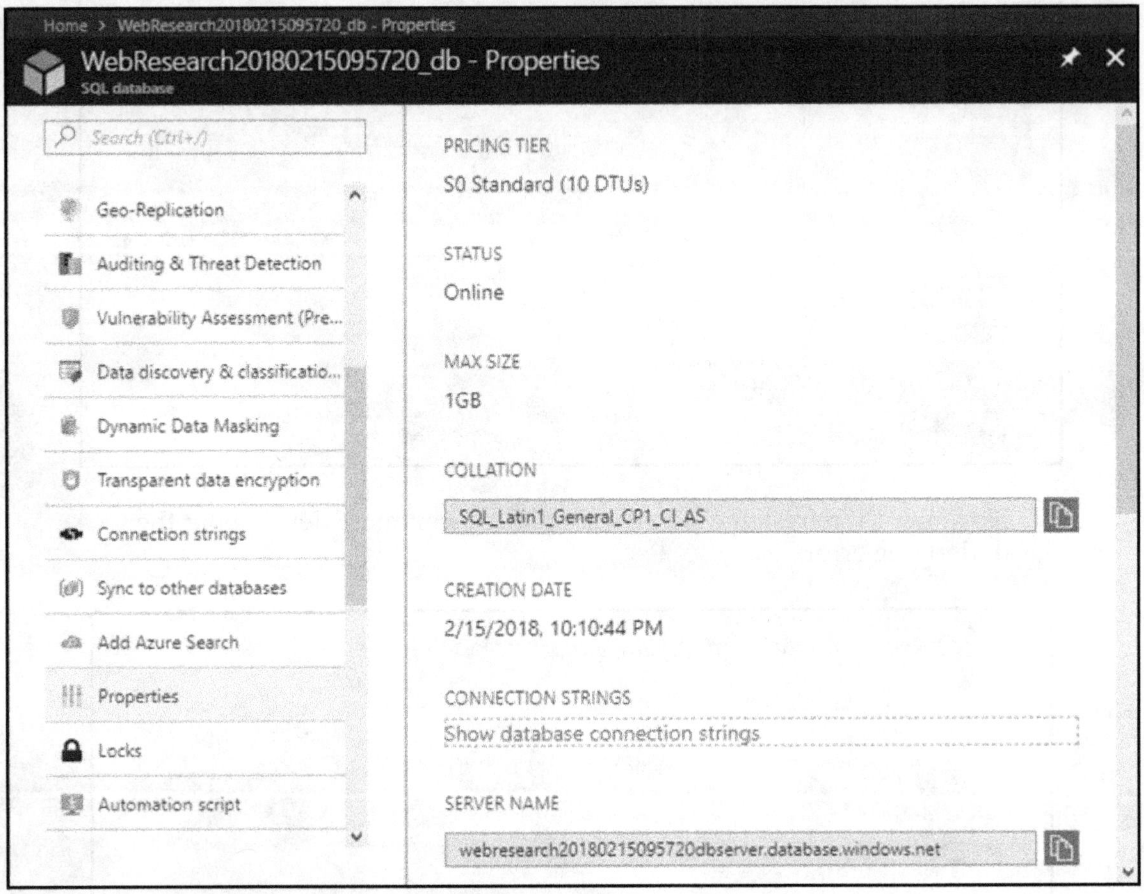

20. Copy the **ADO.NET connectionstring**, head back to your code, and update the **CONNECTION STRINGS** entry in the `appsettings.json` file.
21. Republish the app and you should be good to go!

Custom targets

The next publishing option is generally referred to as custom targets.

This option basically includes anything that is not Azure or a local filesystem. After hitting the **OK** button, you get to choose a publish method:

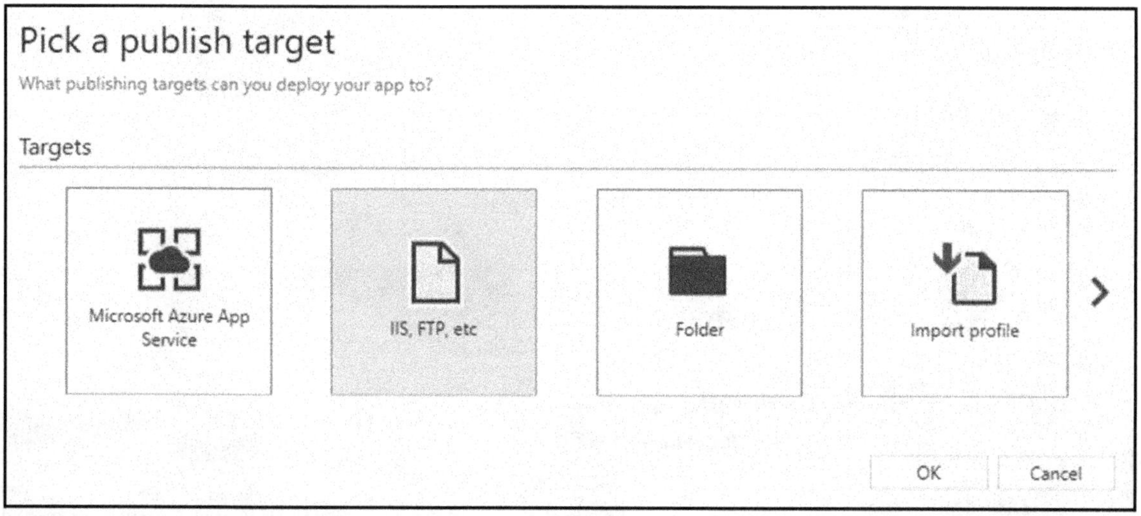

There are four publish methods—or custom targets—available, with each having its own requirements:

- FTP
- Web Deploy
- Web Deploy Package
- File System

We also have a **Settings** tab, which is applicable to all four methods. Let's have a quick look at what our options are there:

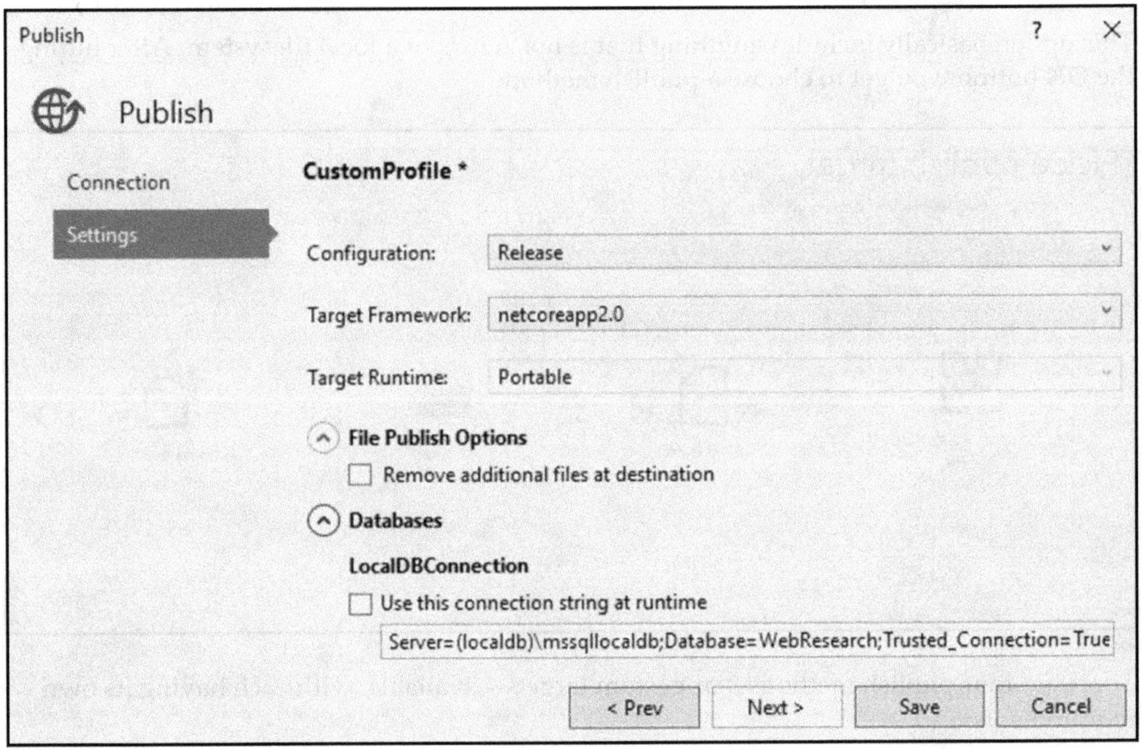

The **Configuration** option can be set to either **Debug** or **Release**.

With **Debug**, your generated files are debuggable, meaning that it is possible to hit specified breakpoints. But it also means that there is a performance decrease.

With **Release**, you won't be able to debug on the fly, but will have an increase in performance as your application is fully optimized.

In our case, the only available target framework is **netcoreapp2.0**, but in standard .NET applications, this is where you could set the target to .NET 3.5 or .NET 4.5, or whichever is available.

You can also specify the target runtime, choose to have Visual Studio clean up the destination folder, and specify a connection string specifically for runtime.

As we mentioned previously, these settings are applicable to all four publishing methods, which we will have a look at now.

FTP

The FTP publish method allows you to publish to a hosted FTP location. For this option, you need to provide the following:

- **Server URL**
- **Site path**
- **User name**
- **Password**
- **Destination URL**

It also allows you to validate the connection from the entered details:

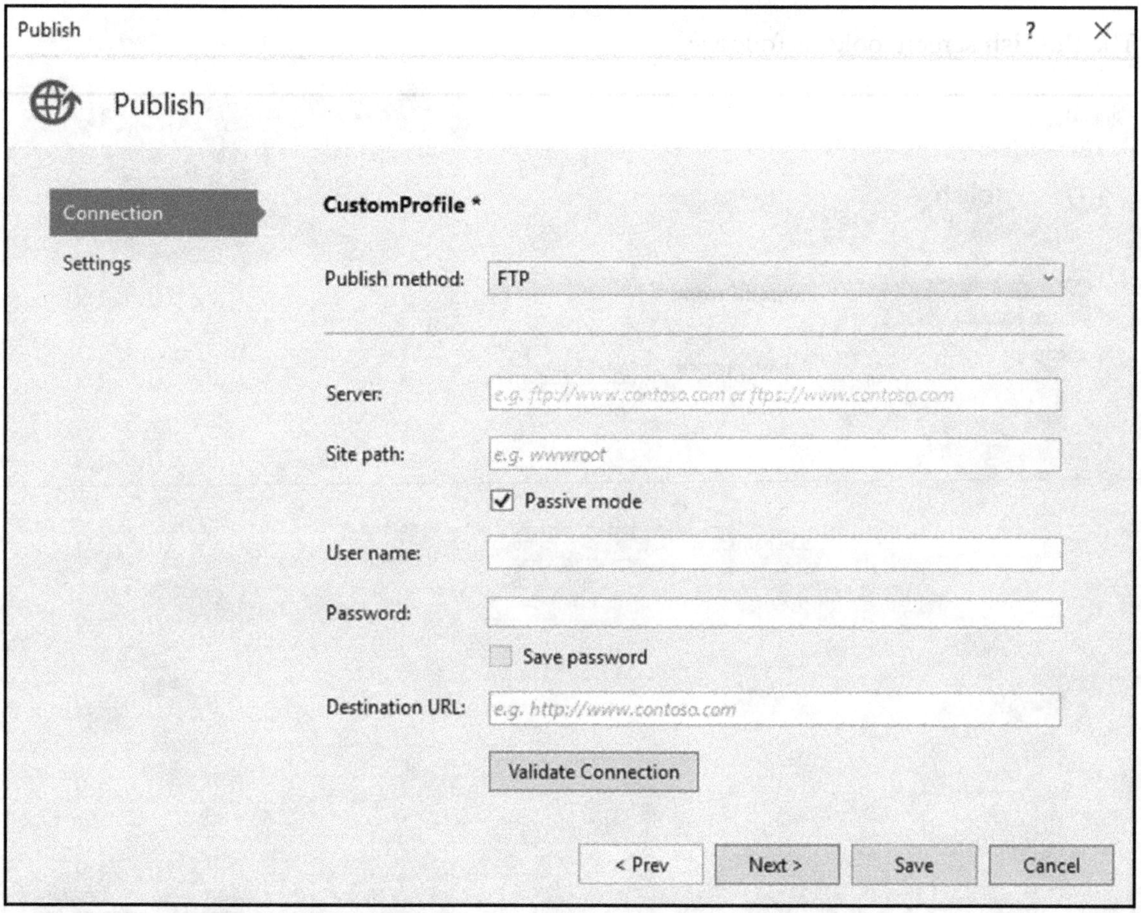

Web Deploy

Looking at the forms of both **Web Deploy** and **FTP**, you would be excused if you believe they're the same thing. Well, both result in basically the same thing in that you publish directly to a hosted site, but with **Web Deploy**, you get quite a few extra benefits, including the following:

- **Web Deploy** compares the source with the destination and only syncs required changes, resulting in a significant decrease in publishing time compared to **FTP.**
- Even though **FTP** also has its secure cousins, SFTP and FTPS, **Web Deploy** always supports secure transfers.
- Proper database support, which allows you to apply SQL scripts during the sync process.

The **Publish** screen looks as follows:

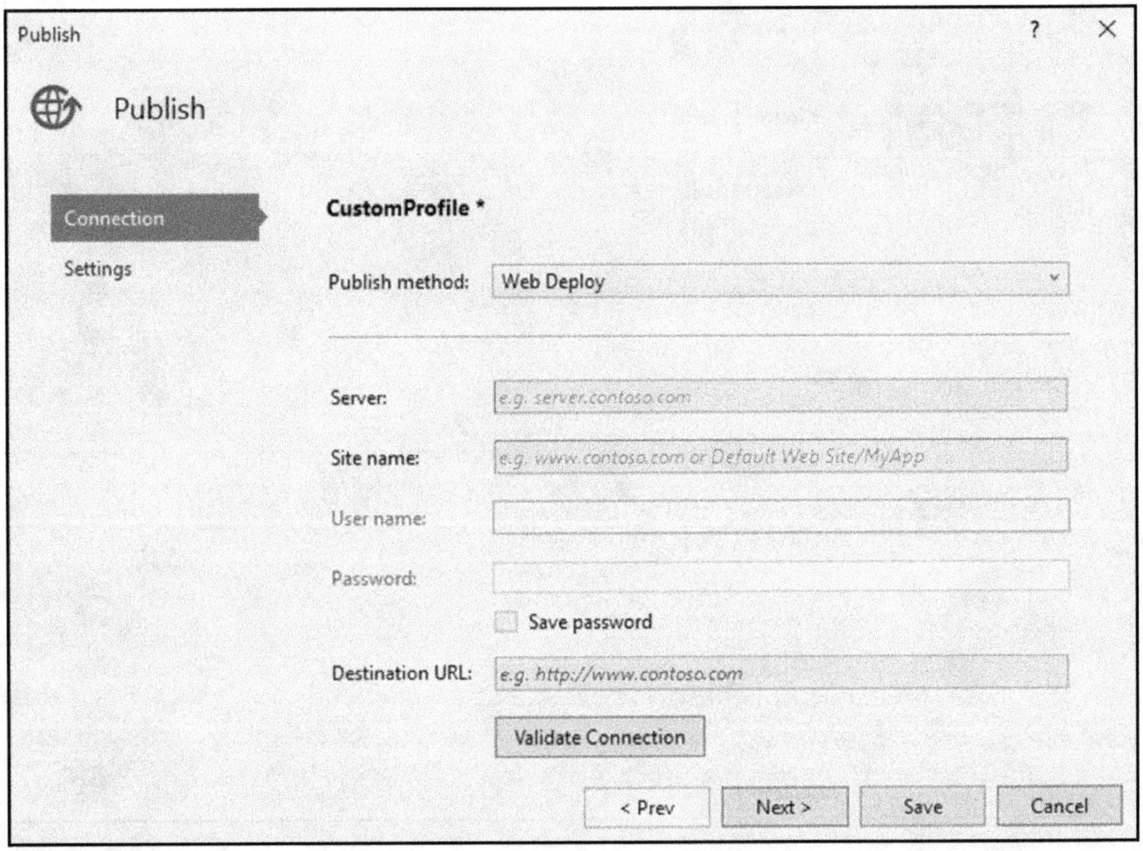

Web Deploy Package

The **Web Deploy Package** option is used to create a deployment package that you can use to install your application wherever you choose afterward. Refer to the following screenshot:

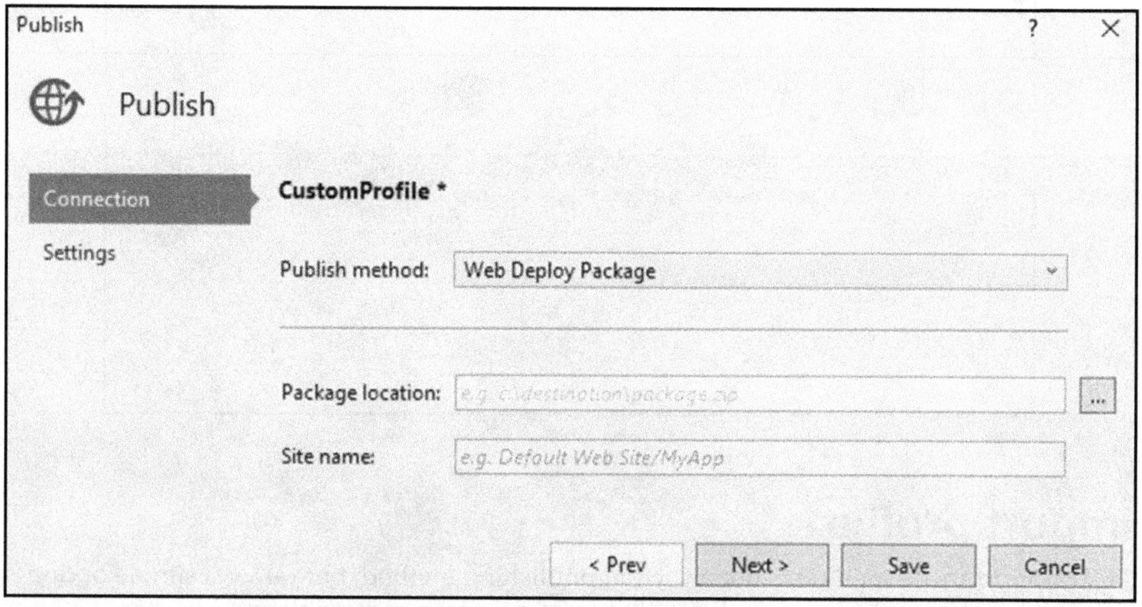

Folder

Used by old-school developers the world over, mainly due to the fact that we still don't really trust some of the available tools enough, this option allows you to publish to a folder location of your choice and then go and copy it over to the publish environment manually.

Just specify the folder location and hit **OK**:

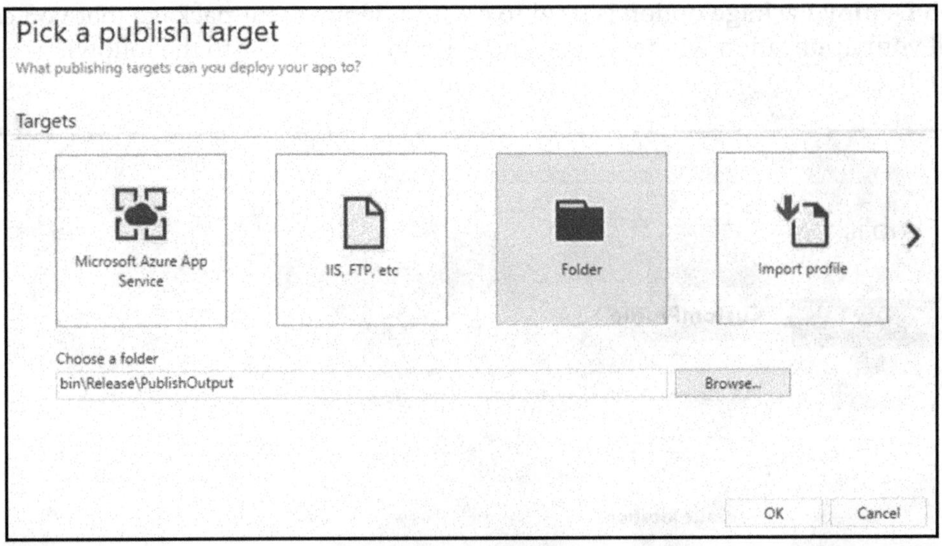

Import profile

The **Import profile** method is not an actual publishing method, but rather a simple option to import a previously saved profile, either from a backup or possibly used to share a publishing profile between a team of developers:

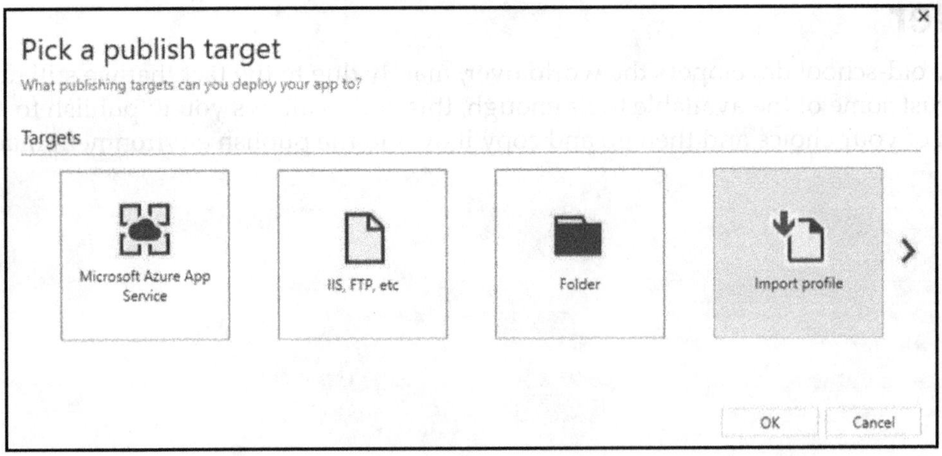

Selecting the **Import profile** option will prompt you to find a saved profile (`*.publishsettings`). Obviously, when you create one of the previous profiles, you can save it. Sometimes, it can make sense to store multiple publish profiles: this is typically something you would do locally because, in modern software development, it is unusual to find anybody manually deploying an application; instead, they will set up a CI/CD pipeline, which is triggered directly from a GitHub repository check-in.

Now that we have successfully published our application, we have come to the end of this chapter. Let's review what we've covered.

Summary

In this chapter, we've taken a bit of a guided tour around the EF Core neighborhood. We started off at the museum and looked at the history of Entity Framework before visiting the school district to discuss some of the differences between the Code-First, Model-First, and Database-First implementation approaches. There was even a quick visit from TechNet, who offered some ideas around designing a database.

Afterward, we spent some time building our own EF Core solution and looked at the various ways of deploying our application. We also had a look at populating our new building with some test data to see how it will hold up once opened up to the public.

The tour concluded with a visit to the distribution district so that we could get an overview of the available deployment options.

The visit was far too brief to cover all that is available and possible in the world of Entity Framework Core since it is a framework with a large community constantly working on improving and extending its already extensive functionality.

It is great to know that the development community does not settle for any mediocrity and constantly works toward improving and extending functionality, such as Entity Framework, which might seem quite mature and extensive already.

In the next chapter, we will investigate the Logic Apps from Azure. The chapter will guide you through the creation of a logic application, integrating the application to Twitter, and allowing you to enter data into a spreadsheet and have it automatically posted on Twitter.

Summary

5
Building a Twitter Automated Campaign Manager Using Azure Logic Apps and Functions

The purpose of computing, since the very first computer was conceived of by Charles Babbage over 200 years ago, was automation and accuracy. That is, we want computers to do things that we can do, but faster and with fewer mistakes. Things have moved on considerably since the days of analogue computers, and now we have systems that hold petabytes of data, and we typically carry computers in our pockets that would put to shame the computers that sent a man to the moon 50 years ago! The premise to all this, though, is the same: we just want computers to do the same things that we could, but faster and with fewer mistakes.

The particular problem that we are addressing in this chapter is very much an automation one: imagine that you've just started at a new company and, as your first job, you're logged into Twitter, and told that the company would like to launch a marketing campaign to sell their new product. Your task is to send out tweets at regular intervals to let people know about the new products that they have. You could just sit there and manually type in these entries every half hour, but what if you could automate this process in less than half an hour?

In this chapter, we'll discuss Microsoft's workflow engine, logic apps, and we'll see how with very little code, we can generate a fully automated system that can perform relatively complex tasks.

The following topics will be covered in this chapter:

- Creating a Microsoft logic app from scratch
- Integrating a Microsoft logic app with an Azure function and with Microsoft Excel for additional functionality

In this chapter, we will build a logic app that will read a Microsoft Excel spreadsheet, and post a tweet based on the content. While most of the functionality that we need will be available in logic apps, we will need to call out to an Azure function for some of the date calculations.

Technical requirements

As with previous chapters, you will need an Azure subscription. You'll also need a copy of Excel, or access to Office Online. Finally, you'll need a OneDrive account—these are free to set up and can be found here: `https://onedrive.live.com/`.

Since we're using Twitter in this project, you will need a valid Twitter account. If you don't have one, then you can create one here: `https://twitter.com/signup`.

The code for this chapter, as with other chapters in this book, can be found here: `https://github.com/PacktPublishing/C-8-and-.NET-Core-3-Projects-Using-Azure-Second-Edition`.

An overview of workflow engines, logic apps, and Functions

Workflow engines have been around for some time. Basically, the idea is that you have a very high-level system where you can plug complex, independent components together. Microsoft's implementation of this has a very intuitive graphical interface and can be written either in the web browser or in a Visual Studio. When you cannot find a pre-built component that does what you need, you can call out to an HTTP endpoint, allowing the workflow to seamlessly integrate with Azure Functions or, indeed, with another cloud provider.

Azure functions are what is known as **serverless**; this isn't because they are magical and run without any hardware, but simply that you, as the developer, need not care what they are running on. They are intended to be small units of functionality—think of a single method in C#—it typically accepts an argument and returns a value; that's exactly what you get with an Azure function.

We've established (or at least we will by the end of the chapter) that using Azure Functions and logic apps makes it faster to write than setting all this functionality up from scratch, but what else do you get?

The main thing that you get is scale; your software is running on exactly as much hardware as it needs, so if you're not using the software, you don't pay. If you experience a spike in usage, Microsoft will provide more hardware to meet the needs of your software.

Creating an Excel table

The first thing we'll need to do is create a readable Excel spreadsheet. An explanation of Excel in any kind of detail is out of the scope of this chapter (and book); however, in Excel, create a new spreadsheet and insert a table as follows:

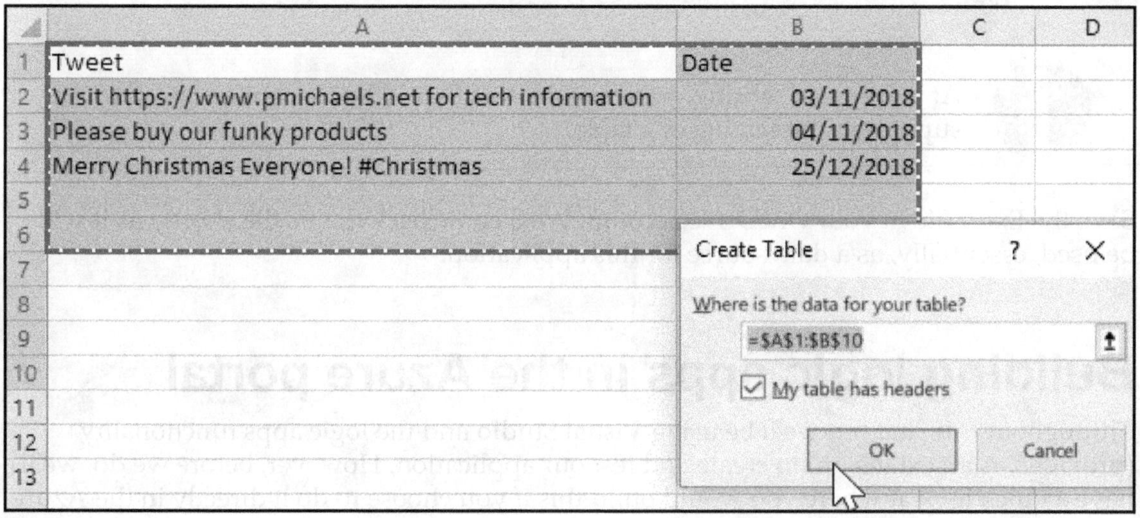

Rename the table (this will make it easier to identify later):

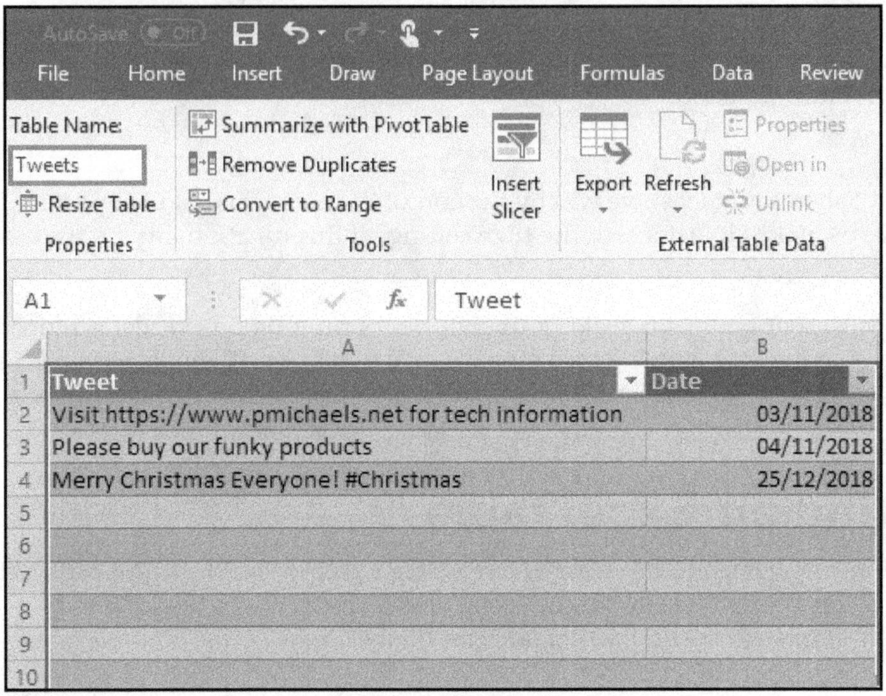

At the time of writing, some versions of Excel (the free online ones) don't support the renaming of a table.

Save the Excel file in your OneDrive account. We'll come back to this file shortly as it will be used, essentially, as a data source for this application.

Building logic apps in the Azure portal

Throughout this chapter, we'll be using Visual Studio and the logic apps functionality (provided as an extension) to create and test our application. However, before we do, we'll have a quick look at where you would build this if you choose to do it directly in the Azure portal.

In the Azure portal, search for `logic apps`, and then pick the **Logic apps** service as follows:

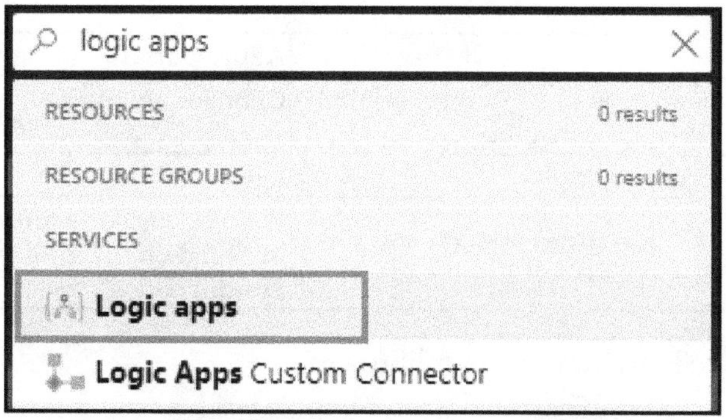

TIP

Remember that once the blade has launched, you can pin it to your dashboard using the pin icon on the top right-hand corner.

When the blade launches, you'll see any logic apps that you currently have in your subscription; if you have none, then you'll simply see a button inviting you to create one as shown in the following screenshot:

From this point on, the process of creating the logic app in the Azure portal is basically the same as with Visual Studio. There are advantages of creating the app in the Azure portal, and advantages with using the Visual Studio plug-in, as outlined in the following table:

Visual Studio	Azure portal
Source control is easy, and changes to logic apps, related functions, and web jobs can be kept together	Changes are tracked, but source control is not as easy
Features lag behind the portal slightly	Latest features
Requires the installation of the Azure Workload and the logic apps extension	Requires no software whatsoever to be installed on the local machine (not even Visual Studio)

From here onwards, we'll switch to Visual Studio.

Building logic apps in Visual Studio

There are a few installation steps that we need to go through before we can start this; the first is to install the Azure workload in Visual Studio.

Azure development workload

In order to start this, run the Visual Studio Installer, and select **Modify** on the version that you're running as follows:

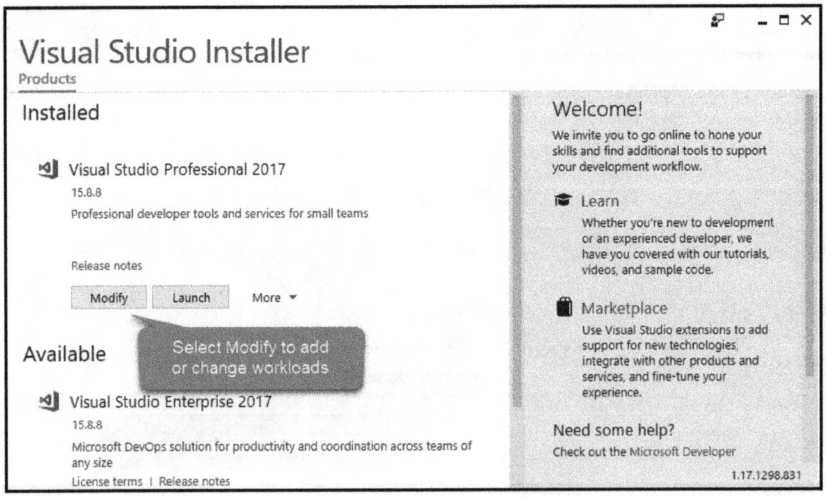

The Visual Studio Installer is a part of the initial installation and is where you change or update your installation of Visual Studio.

Select (or tick) the **Azure development** workload and select **Modify**:

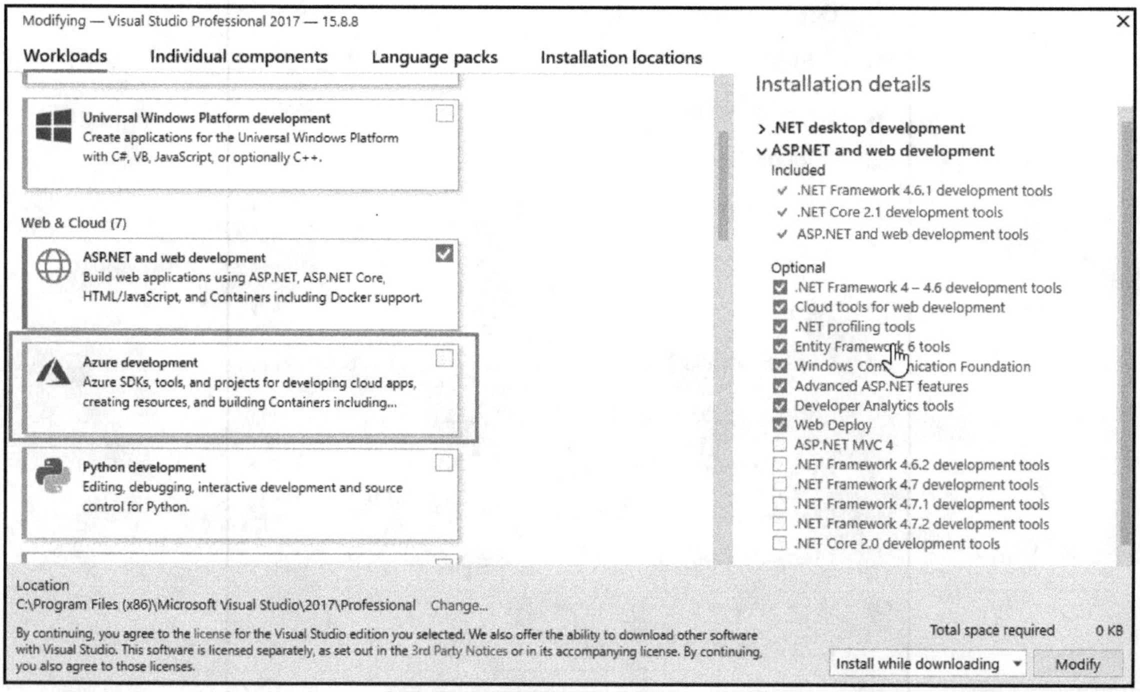

If you're currently running Visual Studio, then you'll need to close it while the update takes place. The download and installation can take a few minutes, so this might be a good time to get a coffee!

Workloads are collections of features that allow Visual Studio to perform certain tasks, or be aware of certain languages.

The logic apps extension

To install this extension, start by launching **Extensions and Updates...** from the **Tools** menu in Visual Studio as follows:

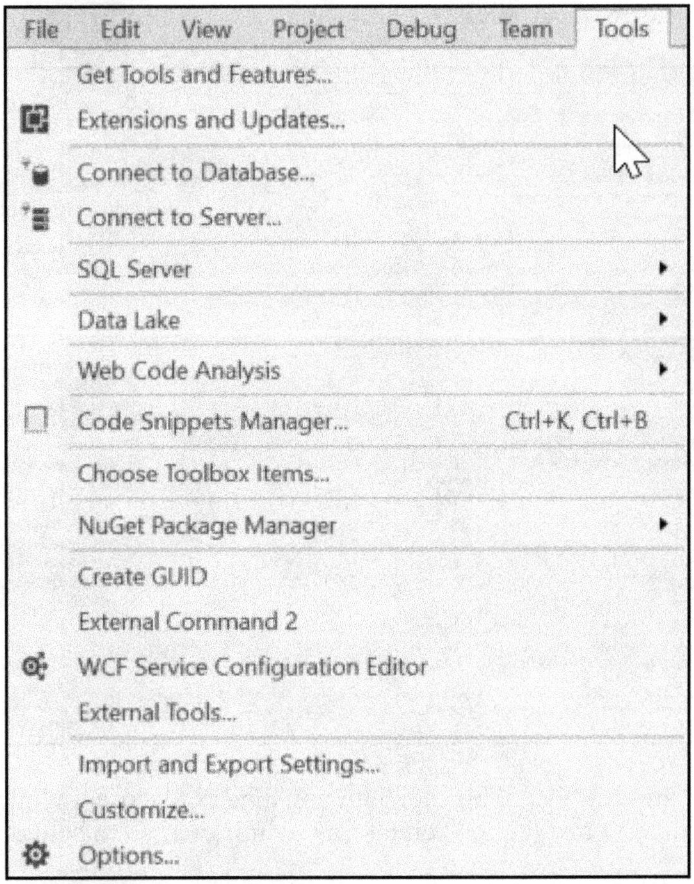

This is where you can manage extensions to Visual Studio. We'll search here for our logic apps extension as follows:

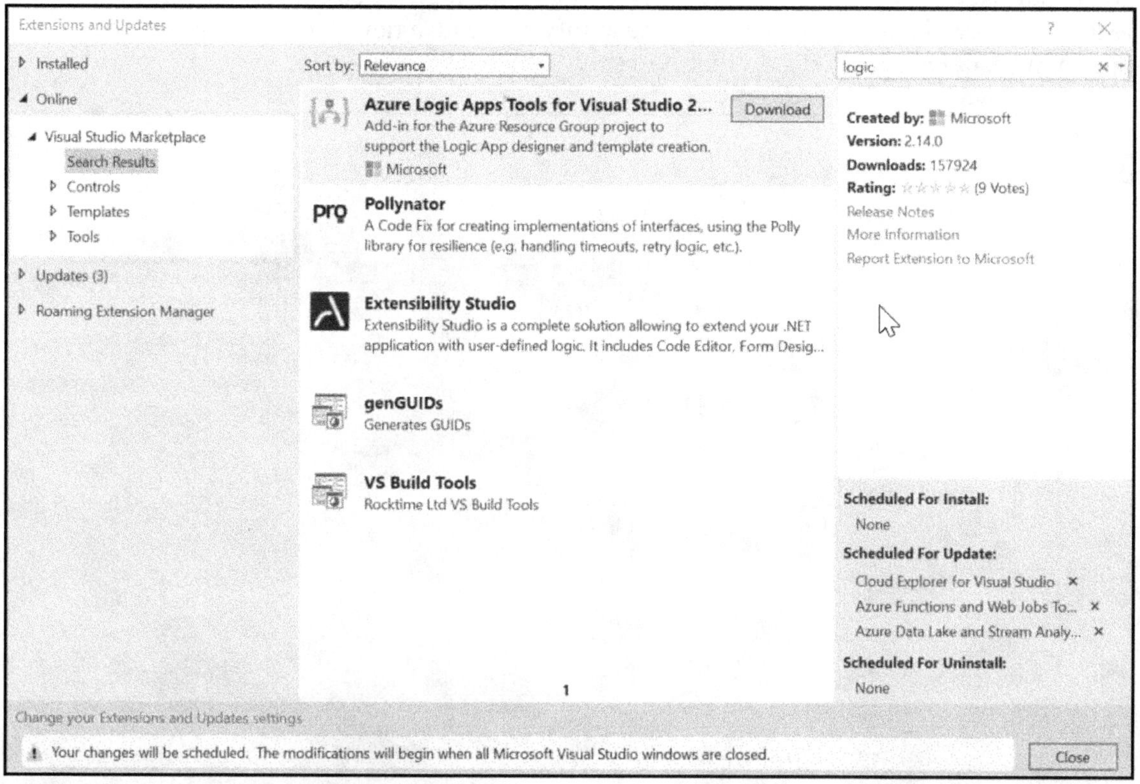

Once you've installed this, you'll need to restart Visual Studio, and once you've done so, you should be ready to start the development of our logic app.

Creating a resource group

Now that we've installed the Azure workload and the logic apps extension, a few more features are available; one of which is the ability to create a new project of type: a resource group in Visual Studio. Let's do that now:

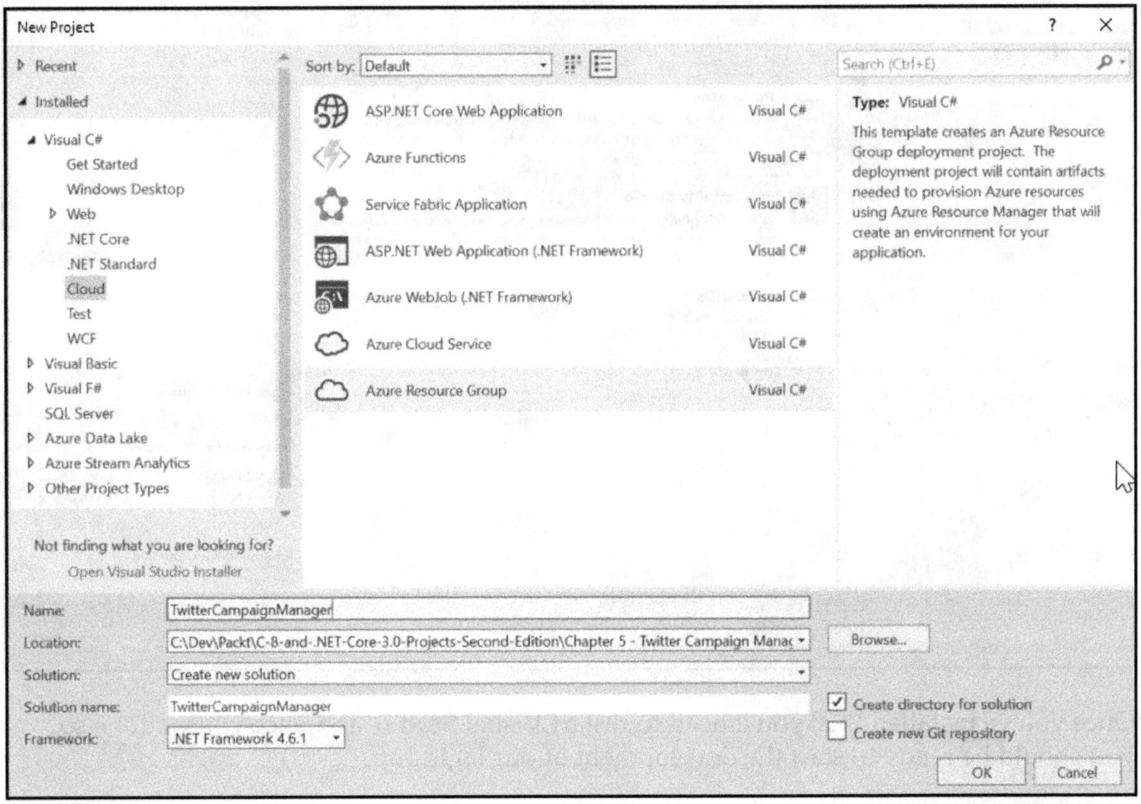

Once this is created, you'll be presented with a second dialog asking exactly what you want to create. Select **Logic App**, as shown in the following screenshot:

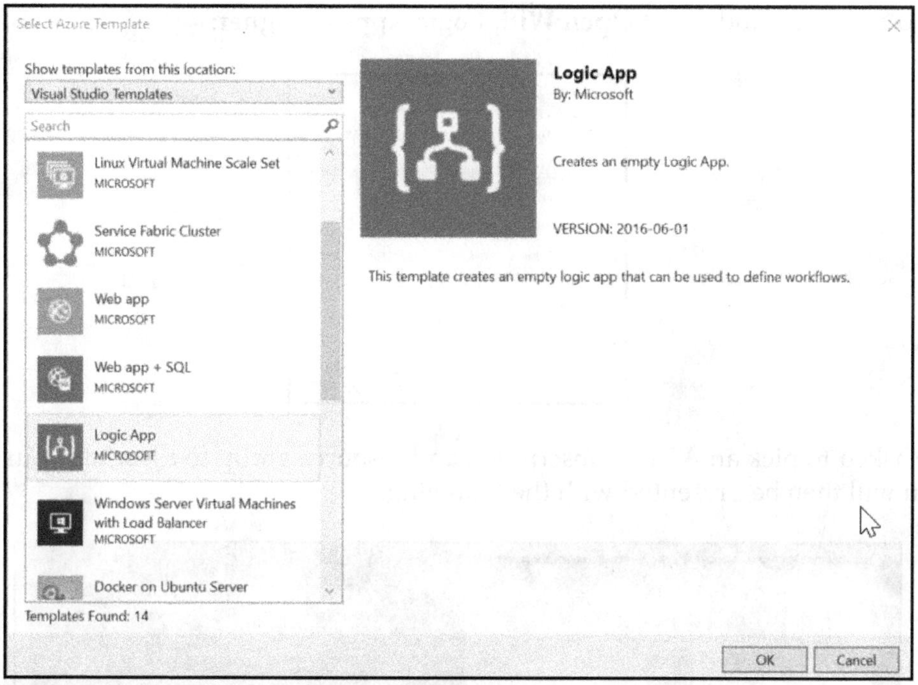

The project that is created has three files and will look like this:

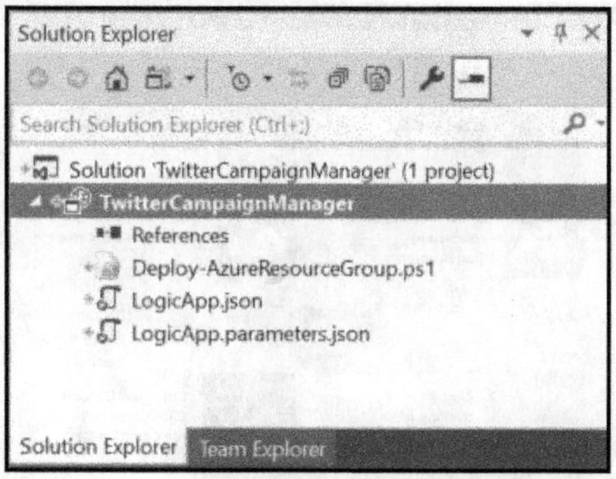

`Deploy-AzureResourceGroup.ps1` is a PowerShell script that will deploy your logic app into Azure. The other two files are the logic app template itself, described as JSON.

If you wish, you can edit the JSON directly. This works well if you have a very small change to make, or if you wish to compare or merge changes, but trying to create your logic app like this would be challenging to say the least! Instead, right-click on the `LogicApp.json` file and select **Open With Logic Apps Designer**:

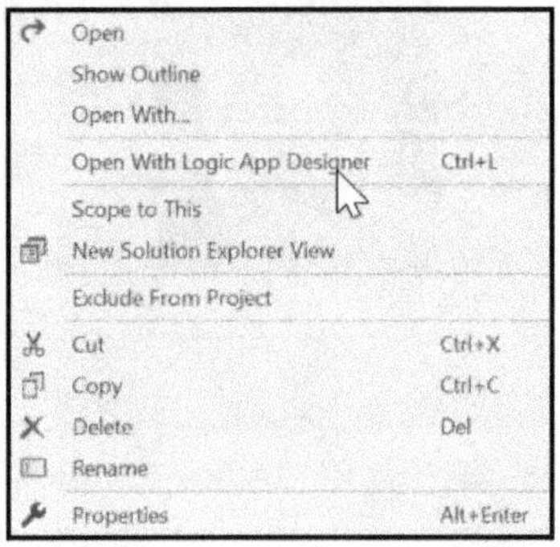

You'll be asked to pick an Azure subscription and resource group to associate your app with. You will then be presented with the following:

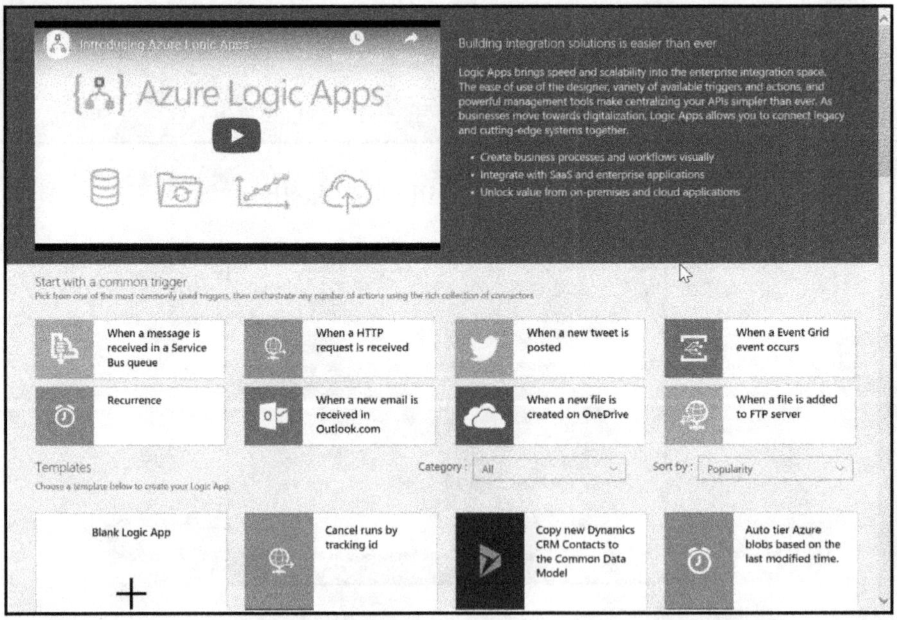

As you can see, there's a useful little video to get you started, some pre-built trigger templates, and some templates that are almost ready to go.

Creating the workflow

The basic flow here will be to interrogate the Excel file on each recurrence, and where we find an eligible row, send a tweet with the text found on that row, and then delete the row. We'll just create a blank logic app so that we can investigate each step.

Step 1 – Choosing a trigger

Once you've selected a blank logic app, you'll be presented with the template designer and you'll need to choose the trigger:

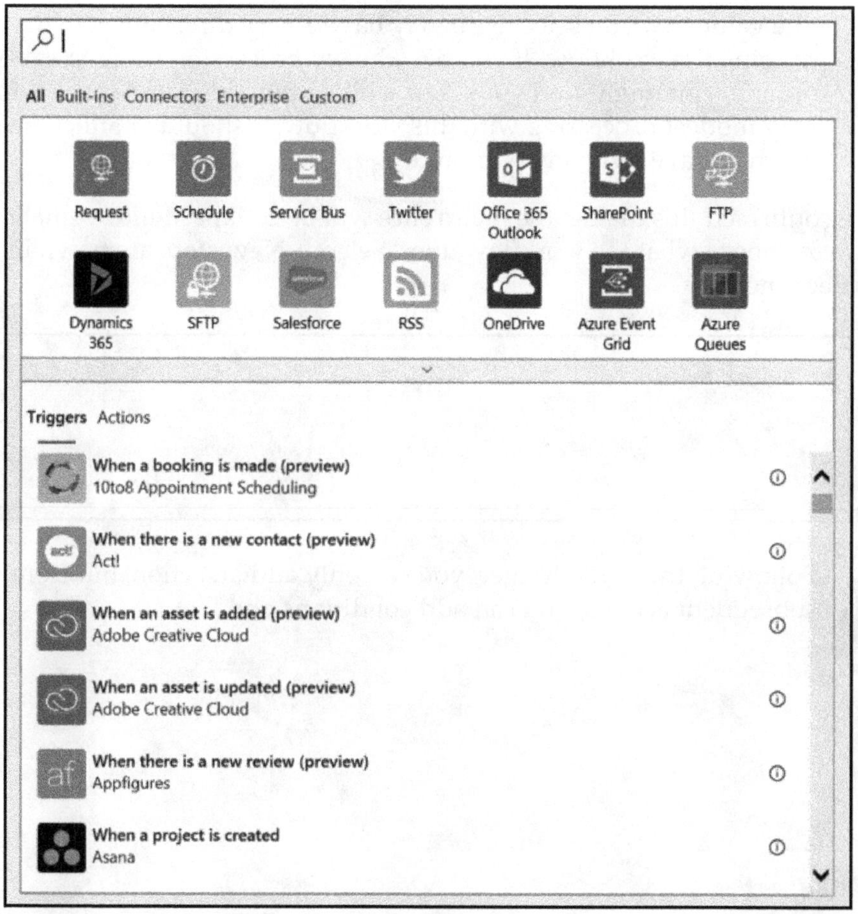

A trigger is simply something that will cause the workflow to begin. This could be an event from another system, a file appearing in storage, a message being put on a queue, or just a schedule.

For our case, we'll just choose **Schedule**, after which, you'll be given an option as to the type of schedule. At the time of writing, there is only one option available here, **Recurrence**, so let's choose that.

Finally, you'll be given the choice of how frequently you want the workflow to run. While we're creating the workflow, leave this at the default of one hour; however, when we've completed it, we'll set it to something a little more responsive.

The value that you select here may have a very direct effect to the cost of running the workflow. If you have heavy processing running every minute, you might find your Azure bill getting higher. As we're doing very modest processing with this workflow, it shouldn't affect the cost too much to have it run every minute.

Once you've confirmed this dialog, the recurrence will be collapsed into a smaller box and you'll be able to choose what the workflow does. Select **+ New step**, as shown in the following screenshot:

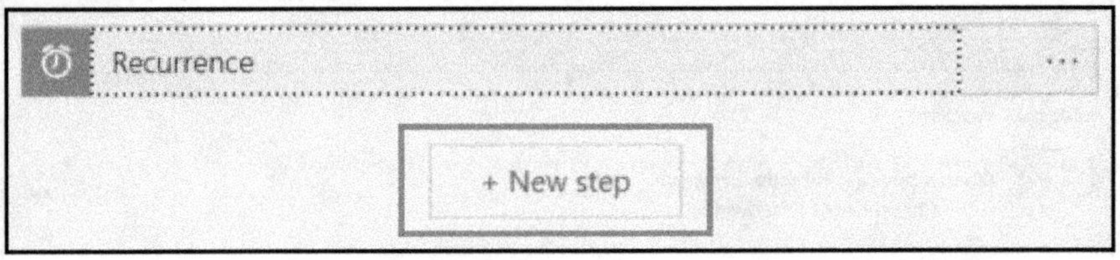

Following the initial trigger, you can only add an action, but from subsequent actions, you can add conditions and loops.

Step 2 – Reading the Excel file

After selecting **New step**, you'll be presented with a list of hundreds of possible actions. Search for `Excel` and select **Excel Online (OneDrive)**:

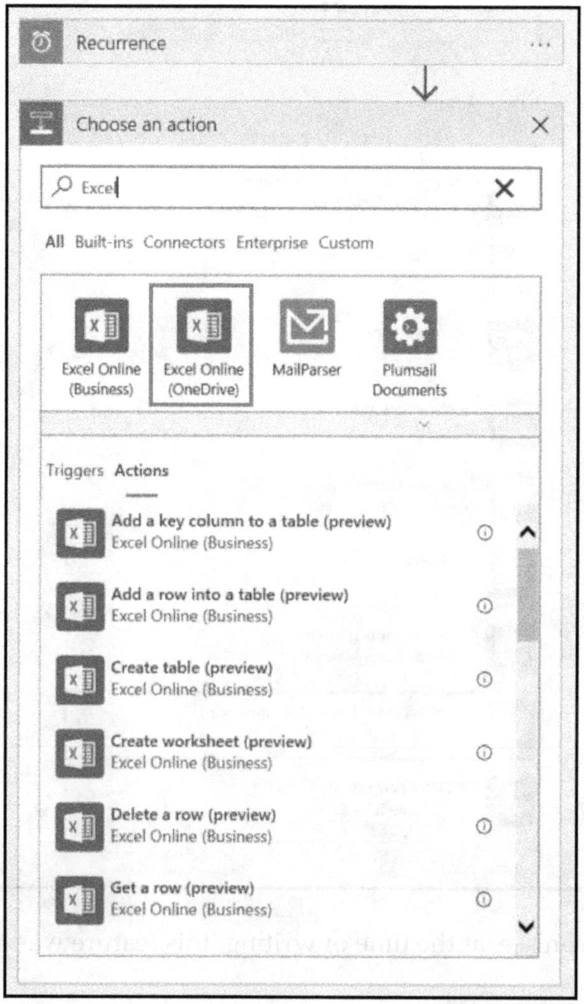

Once you select the Excel category, the list will be reduced. In the resulting list, select **List rows present in a table (preview)**:

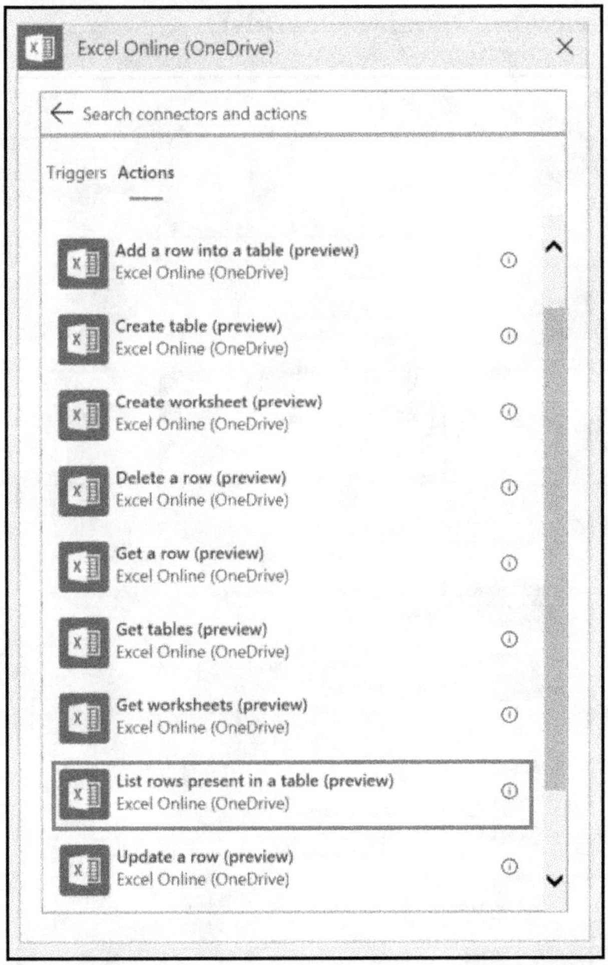

As you can see, at the time of writing, this feature was still in preview.

Once you select this, you'll be asked to sign in to OneDrive. This is a one-time event but it is necessary for each action that requires credentials. Your credentials will then be stored securely.

You'll now need to select the Excel file you stored in OneDrive and the table you created:

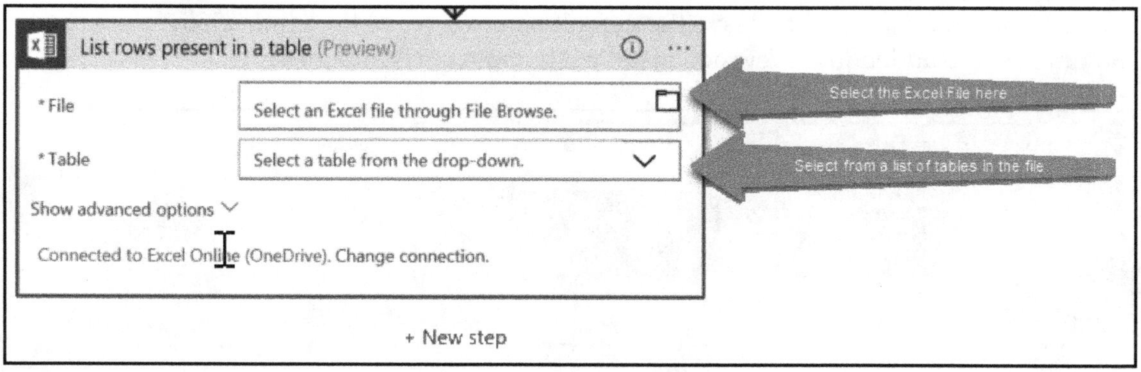

> **TIP**
> If you're using the online free version of Excel, then you won't have been able to rename your table. It will, however, still be visible here, but will be named something like `Table1`. Where you to have more than one table, it would be difficult to identify the correct one.

In the following screenshot, you can see my file and table:

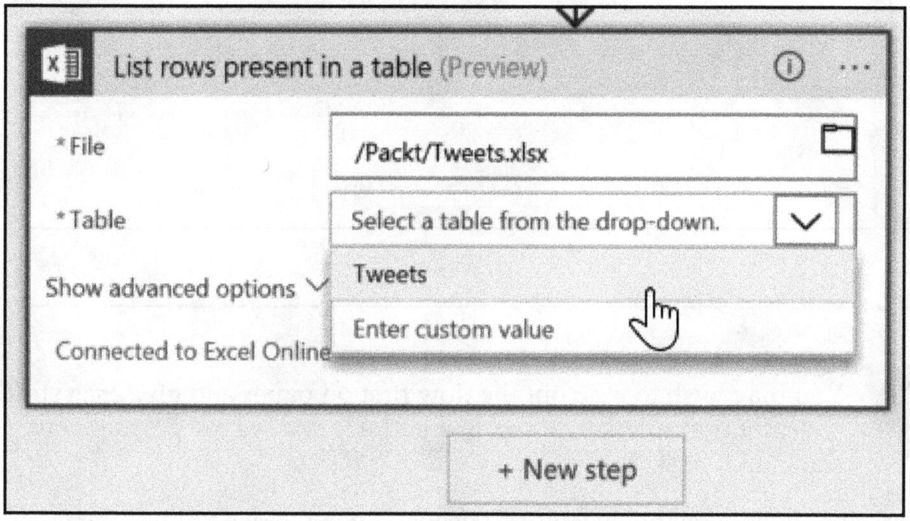

As you progress through the development of logic apps, one thing to be aware of is that the quantity of actions builds quickly. As with UI designers that use default names such as `Button1` and `Button2`, if you leave the default naming, you'll find yourself in a mess by the time you've added just a few actions. We'll rename our action here:

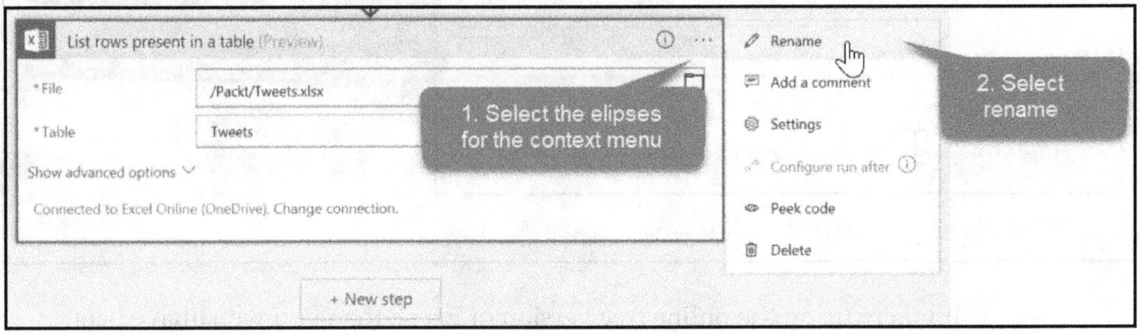

It's important to name it something that will identify it:

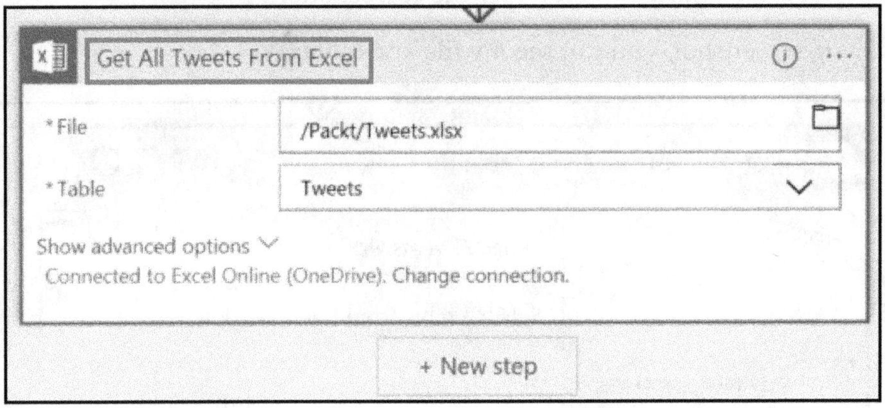

You may wish to map out the flow first on paper and give each step a code, for example, `001 GetData` and `002 Write File`; that way, you can map it back.

As my workflow will be relatively simple, I've just given it a descriptive name.

The next step is to iterate through the dates in the spreadsheet and determine which ones are in the past; however, at the time of writing, logic apps didn't handle dates very well, especially Excel dates. For this kind of thing, having the ability to invoke an Azure function is extremely useful. Typically with very high-level systems like this, once you reach something it doesn't deal with, you're stuck. However, the beauty of logic apps is that you can simply drop down to normal code whenever the need arises. Let's create an Azure function now.

New Azure function

We'll create our new function in the same solution. This enables us to keep all the functionality together for the logic app:

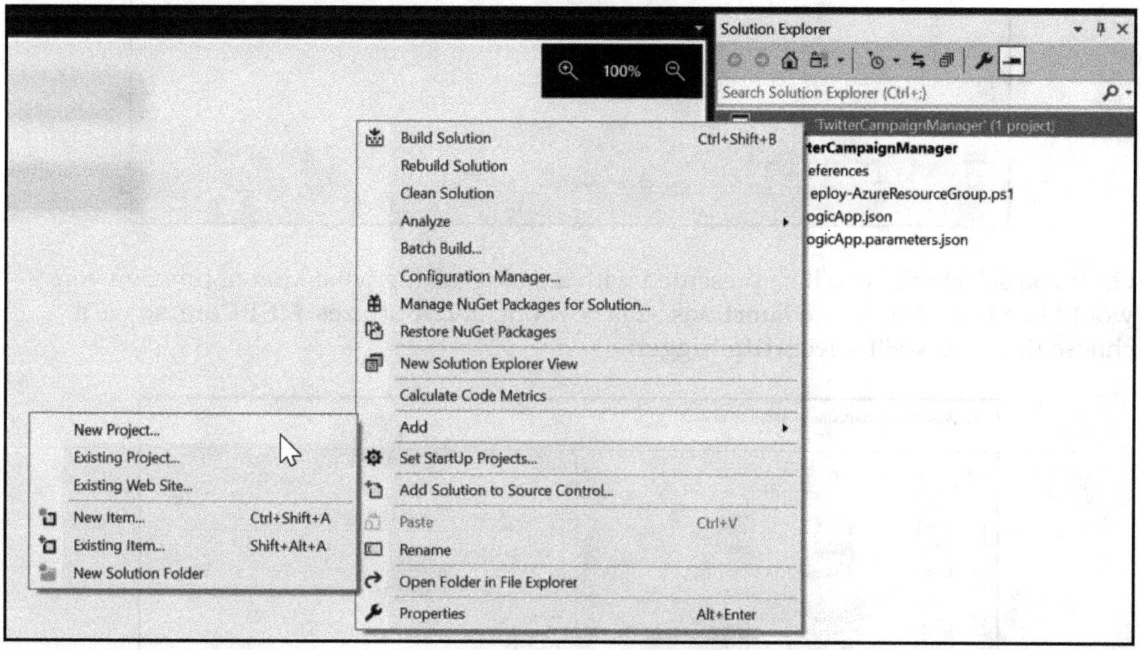

The project type that we're creating is one of the new ones that was added by the Azure workload—it's **Azure Functions**:

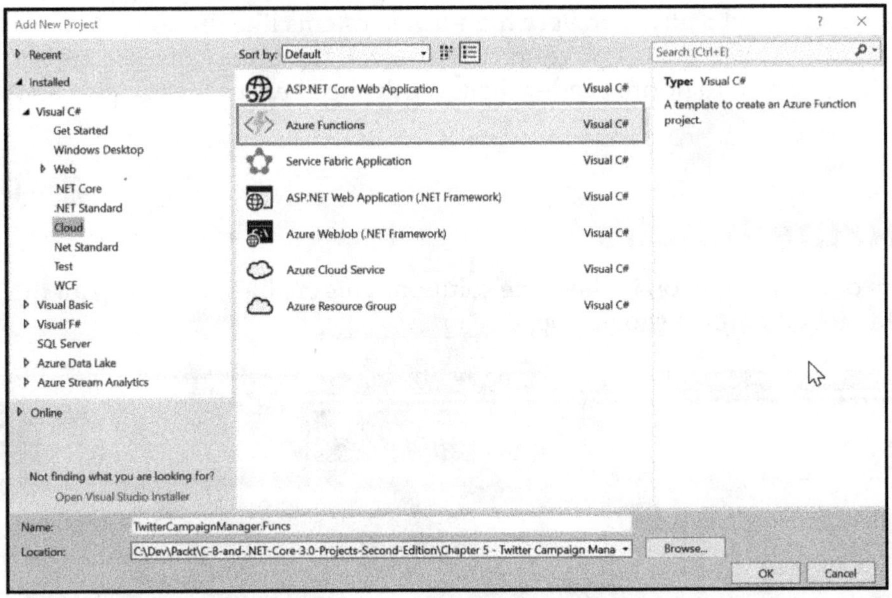

Once you select this, you'll be presented with a dialog asking what kind of function you would like to create. Azure Functions v2 is now out, and it utilizes .NET Core, so we'll choose that, and we'll select **Http trigger**:

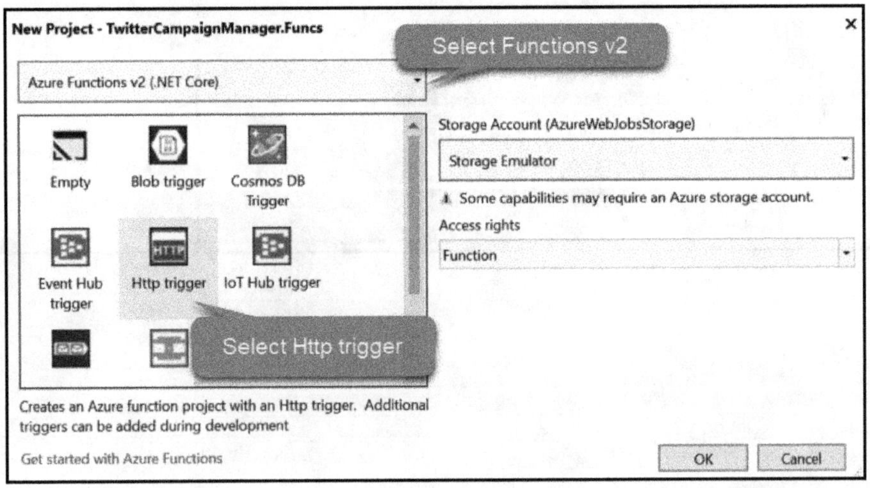

A full and detailed explanation of Azure functions and exactly what they can and cannot do is beyond the scope of this book. However, put simply, a function is a stateless piece of functionality that can be invoked, and is capable of automatically scaling.

However, if you've ever worked with web APIs, the code that's generated by default shouldn't look too unfamiliar. The first thing we should do is change our class name from **Function1**:

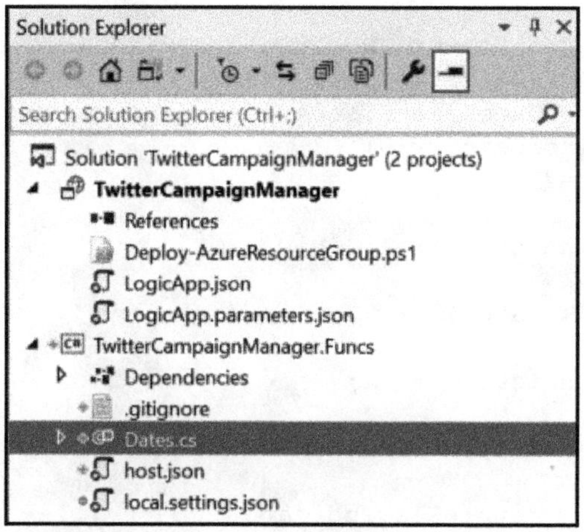

Our new class will represent a single Azure function. The following code is the function code that you'll need, so replace the default function with this:

```
[FunctionName("DatesCompare")]
public static IActionResult Run([HttpTrigger(AuthorizationLevel.Function,
"get", "post", Route = null)]HttpRequest req, ILogger log)
{
    log.Log(LogLevel.Trace, "C# HTTP trigger function processed a
request.");
    string requestBody = new StreamReader(req.Body).ReadToEnd();
    return ParseDates(requestBody);
}
```

As you can see, the function doesn't do too much here other than to log the fact that it's been called and call `ParseDates` with the request body. The important things to note here are all in the method signature.

Although the function itself is called `Run`, the decorator indicates that it will be referred to as `DatesCompare` from elsewhere; you'll see more of this when we plug it into the logic app.

`HttpTrigger` indicates when the function is called. In the case of `HttpTrigger`, the function is effectively exposed as an endpoint to the web at large; however, there are other triggers that can be used; this list is constantly changing and can be found here: `https://docs.microsoft.com/en-us/azure/azure-functions/functions-triggers-bindings`.

Let's have a look at the `ParseDates` method as follows:

```
public static IActionResult ParseDates(string requestBody)
{
    dynamic data = JsonConvert.DeserializeObject(requestBody);
    DateTime date1 = (DateTime)data.date1;
    DateTime date2 = DateTime.FromOADate((double)data.date2);
    int returnFlagIndicator = 0;
    if (date1 > date2)
    {
        returnFlagIndicator = 1;
    }
    else if (date1 < date2)
    {
        returnFlagIndicator = -1;
    }
    return (ActionResult)new OkObjectResult(new
    {
        returnFlag = returnFlagIndicator
    });
}
```

This method actually does very little in terms of functionality as it's effectively just a conditional check. The important thing to note here is `DateTime.FromOADate`. This will take a date from Excel and turn it into a standard .NET `DateTime` format.

We're also making use of the `dynamic` data type; effectively, this tells the C# runtime to not type the variable statically. This is a double-edged sword; like with JavaScript, it means that you can make use of structures that you don't need the compiler to know about at compile time. Furthermore, like JavaScript, it means that if you were to spell a variable name wrong, you might get a runtime exception or bug that would be difficult to diagnose.

The `dynamic` data type should not be confused with the `var` keyword. The `var` keyword does represent a static data type; it's merely a way to have the compiler infer that type itself. A `dynamic` type is not known by the compiler until the code is executed.

Deploying and testing the function

Now that we have written the function, we'll need to deploy it so that the logic app designer can see it. We'll publish the function manually; right-click the function project and select **Publish...**:

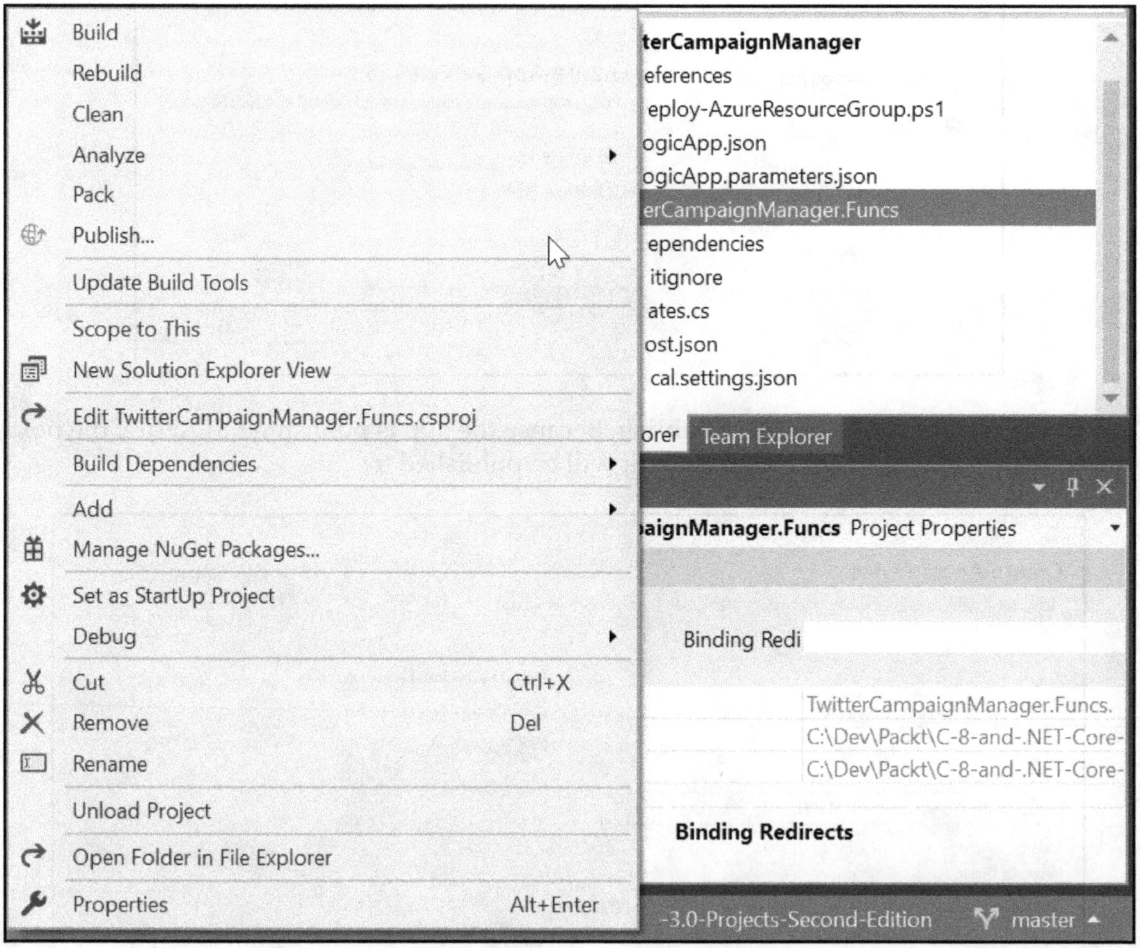

You'll be presented with a dialog offering you the chance to publish the function locally to a directory or to Azure:

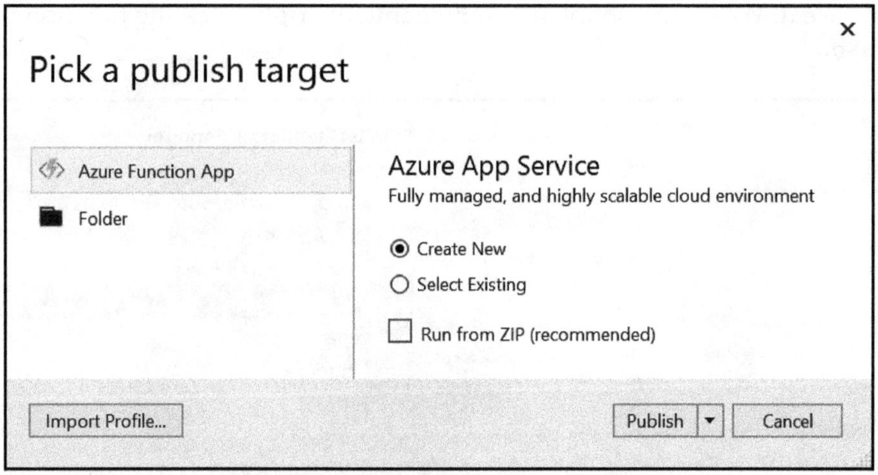

Ignore the rest for now and select **Publish**. Because the app is publishing to Azure, the next screen relates to exactly where in Azure it will be published to:

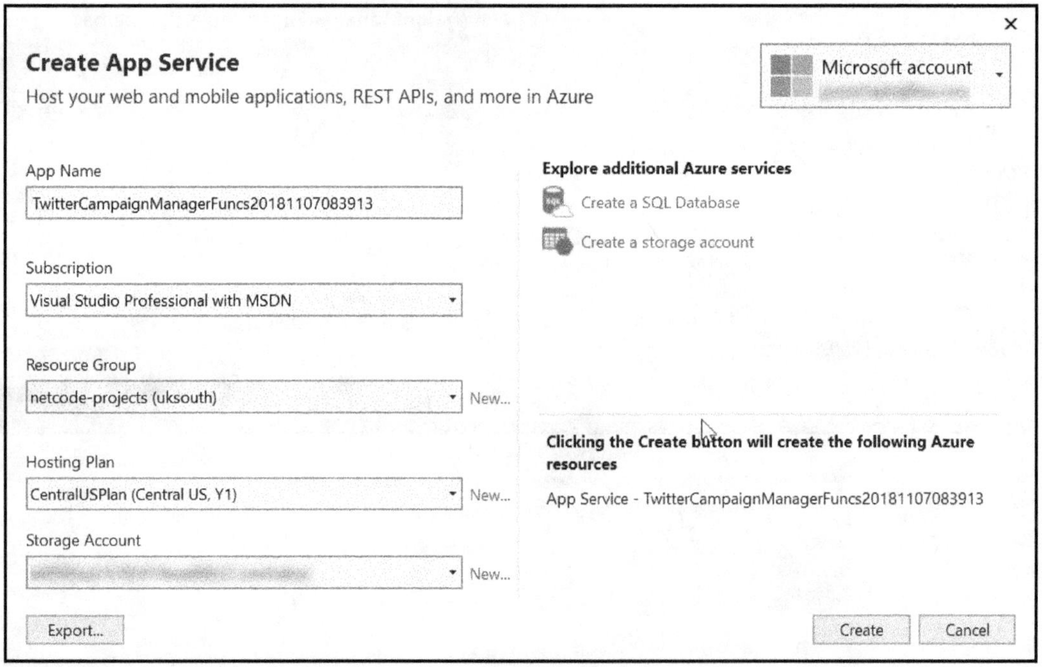

Once this has successfully deployed, you should be presented with the following screen. As you can see, there is a link to the URL that the function was deployed to:

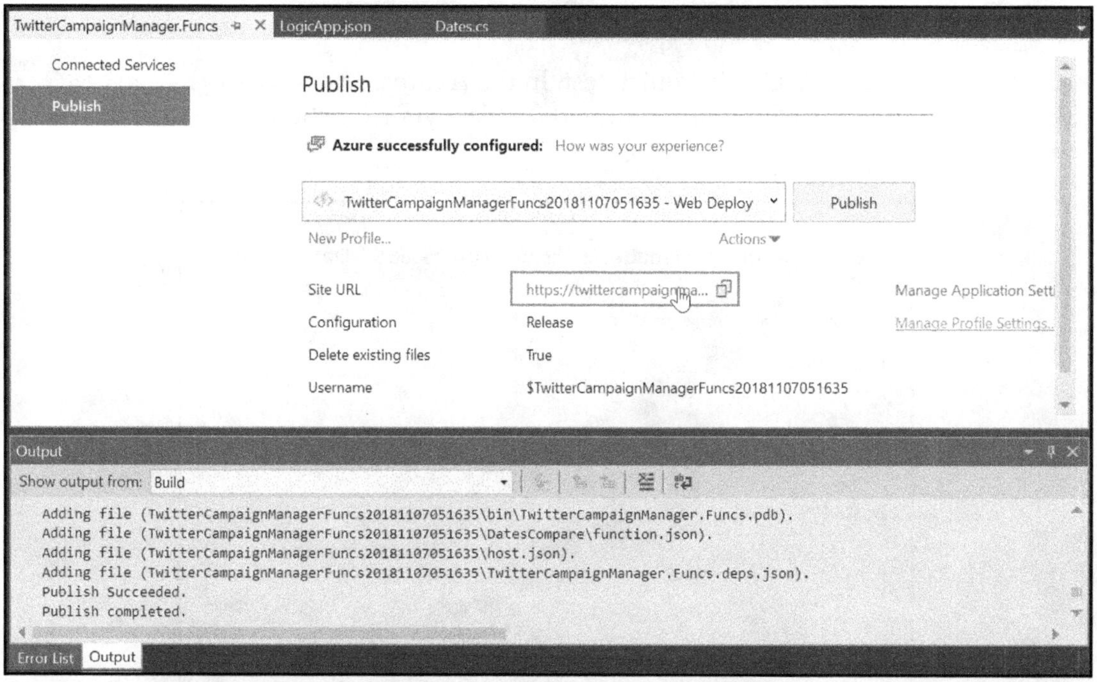

If you click this link, you should reach a website that reassures you that your function is, indeed, running and accessible:

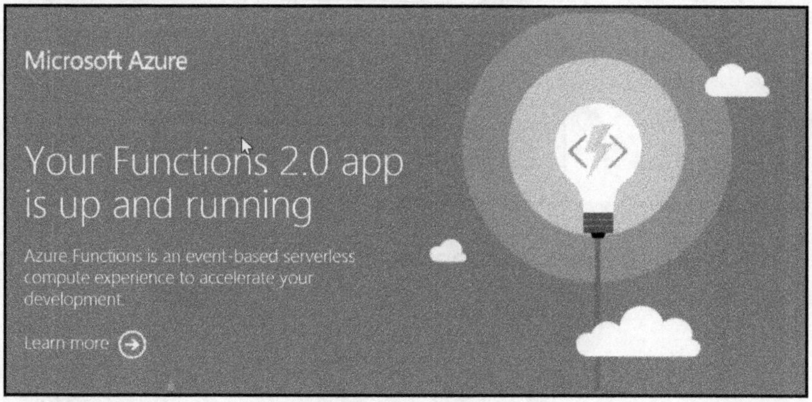

You can use this endpoint just like any other HTTP endpoint; for example, you could construct a call to it using Postman or another similar tool.

Okay, so it's running; let's give it a quick test. In the Azure portal (`www.portal.azure.com`), search for your function. Once you've located it, select your function name (in my case, it's `DatesCompare`):

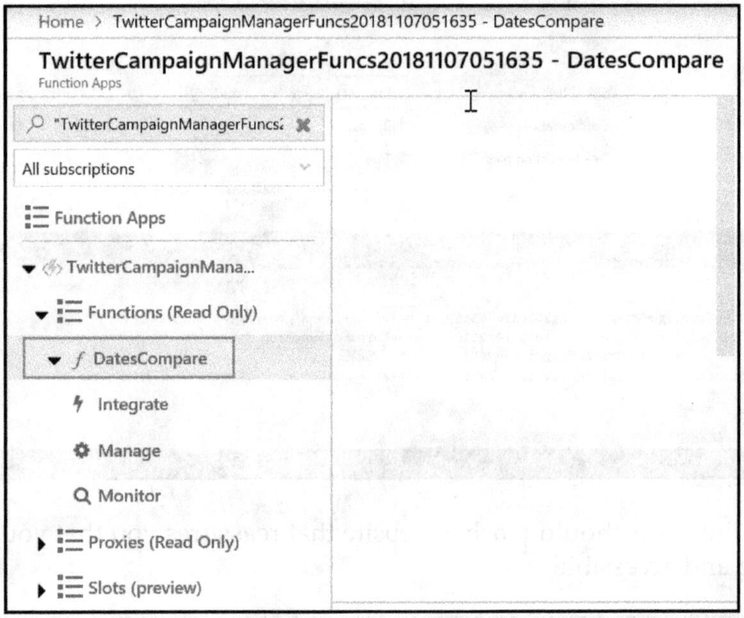

If you scroll over to the right-hand side, you'll see a small tab panel that looks like this:

Select **Test** and a whole new panel will appear. This will allow you to test your function in situ.

As with many things on the Azure portal, unless you have an enormous screen, you'll spend a lot of time scrolling around.

To test the function, enter an example JSON body and select **Run**:

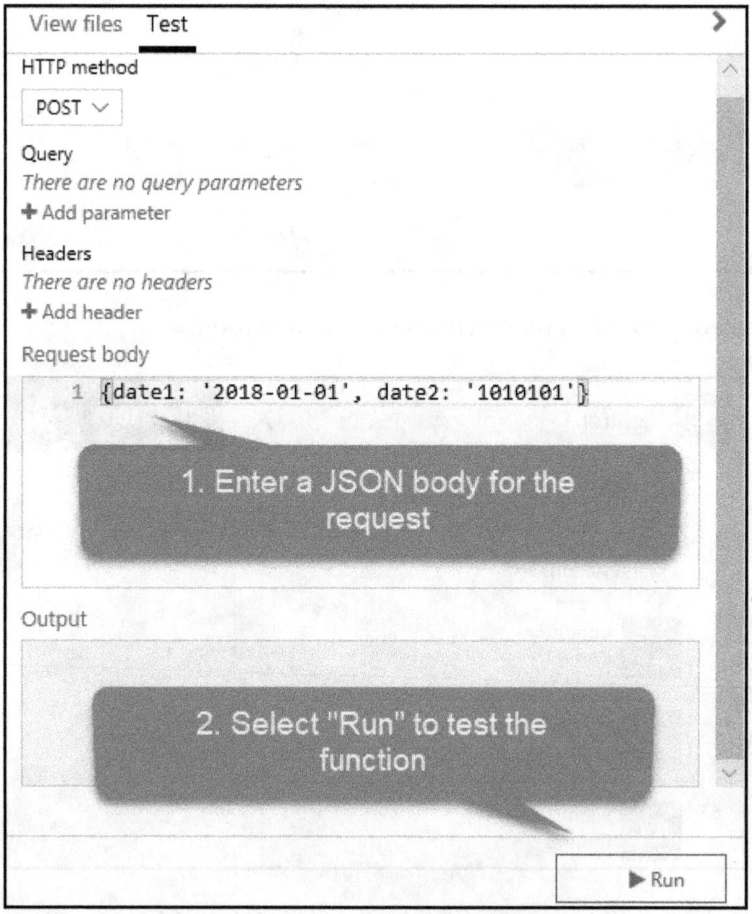

Now that our function is up and running, let's return to the logic app and plumb it in.

Iterating through the spreadsheet

Logic apps provides most of the functionality you would find in a standard programming language; in addition to actions, you have loops and conditions. The next thing we'll need is a loop. In the logic app designer, select **New Step**, and choose the **Control** category:

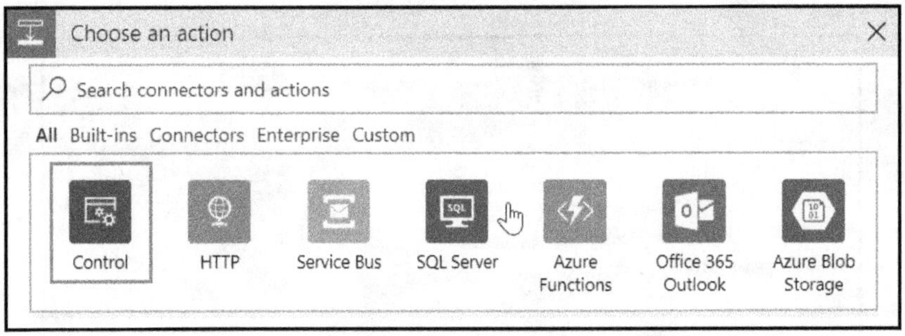

Once this is selected, you'll be able to choose a **For each** loop:

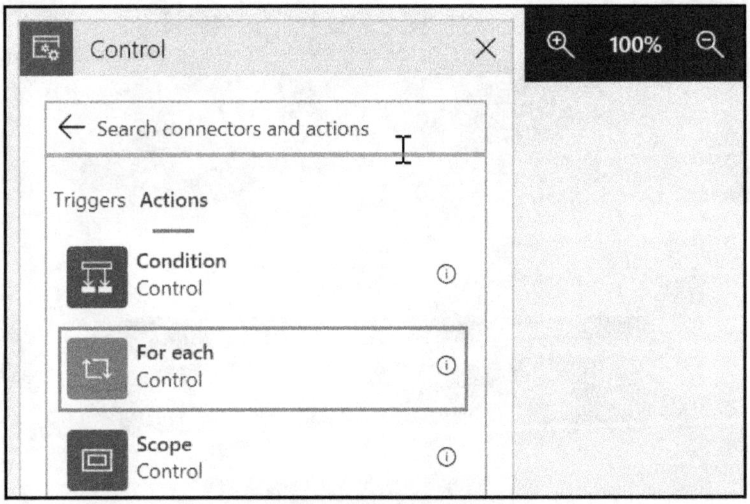

The loop will iterate over each element of the table every time it is invoked. It's worth bearing this in mind, especially if you don't have any conditions that will exclude already processed records.

Once we've created the loop, we can add an action *inside* the loop, that is, an action that will execute on each iteration:

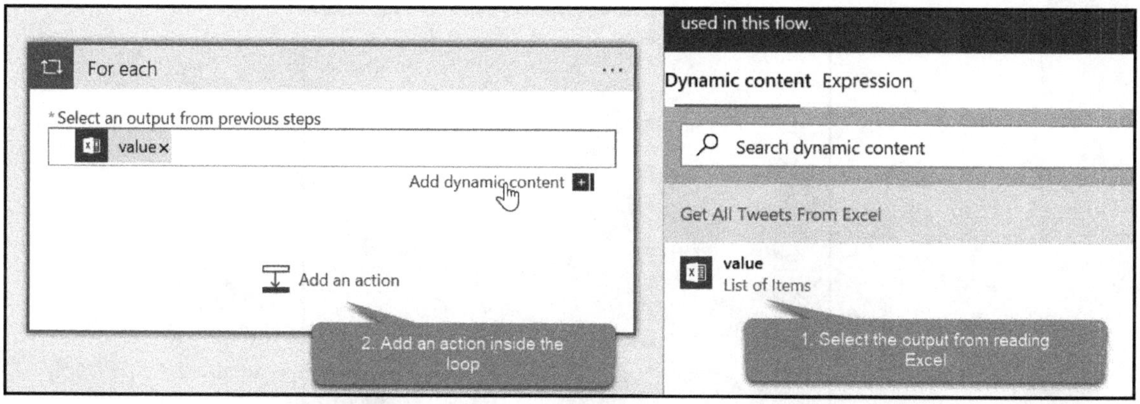

This brings us to the crux of what we are doing, which is to send a tweet.

Sending a tweet

The preceding section should leave you with a dialog box prompting you to choose an action:

1. Search for Twitter, as shown in the following screenshot:

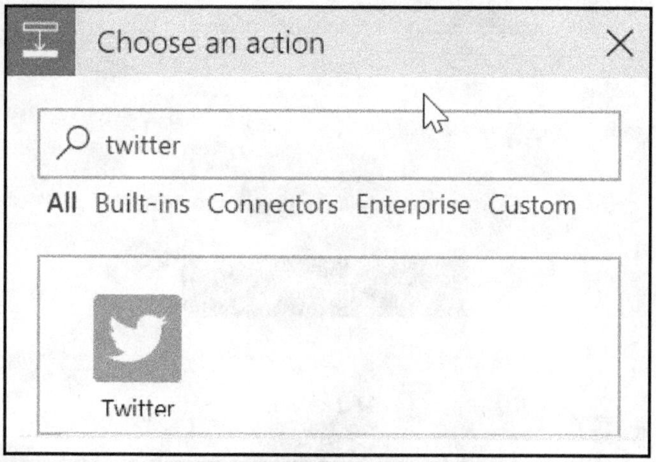

2. Once selected, you'll see a number of actions available for Twitter, but we only want to post a tweet, so we'll select that one:

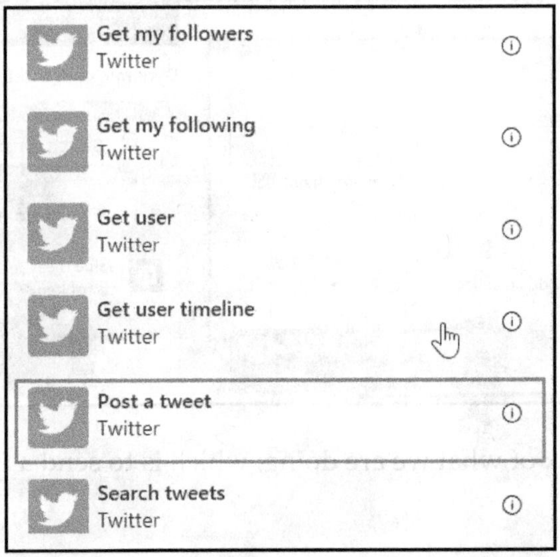

3. Having selected that, you'll be prompted to sign in to Twitter:

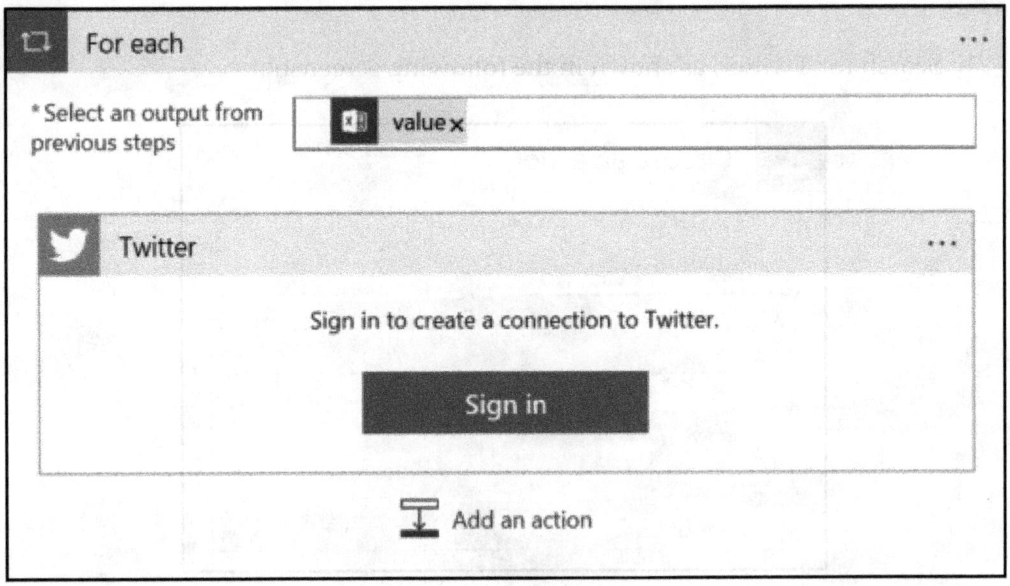

4. Once you've signed in, you'll be asked what text you would like to post. We already have this in the spreadsheet table and it's easily available:

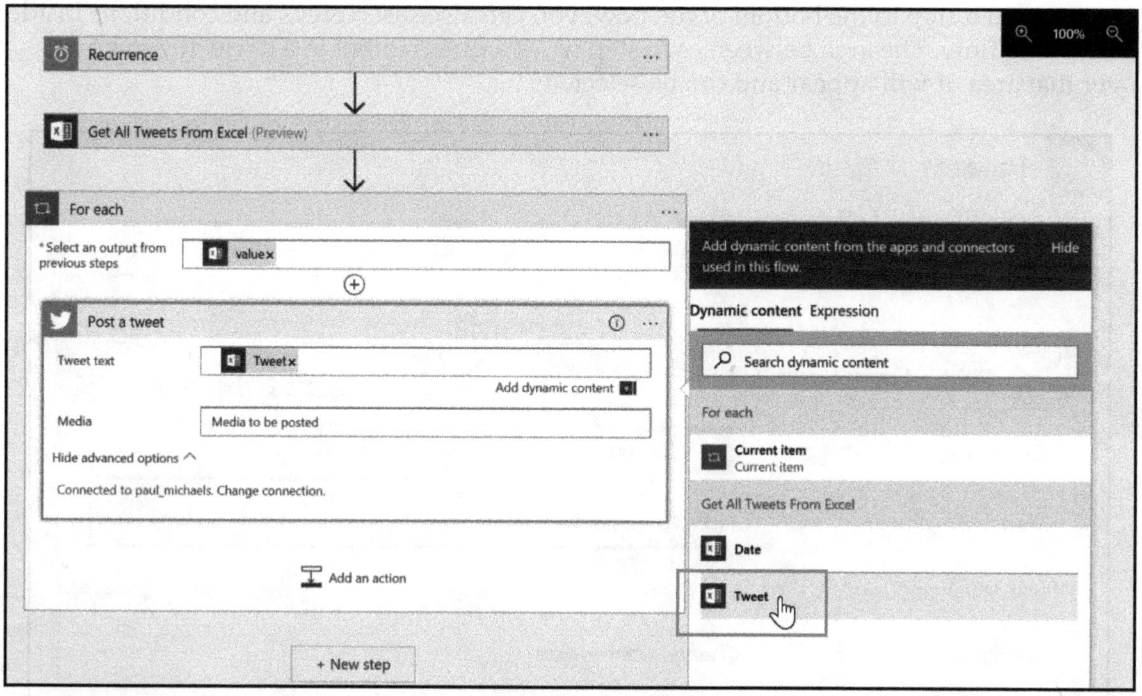

Believe it or not, that's it. As it stands, the workflow will run every hour, iterate through the list, and send any tweets that it finds. However, we're currently a little too zealous. We still need the functionality to only pick up tweets that have the correct date and we need to remove the row once the tweet is sent (otherwise we'll keep sending it once the date has passed).

Adding a condition and removing the current row

Let's start with the condition and this brings us to a very useful feature of logic apps; while you can add a step to the bottom of the flow, you can also insert steps and conditions inside an existing flow. The area between each step hides a plus symbol in a circle; if you hover over that area, it will appear and can be selected:

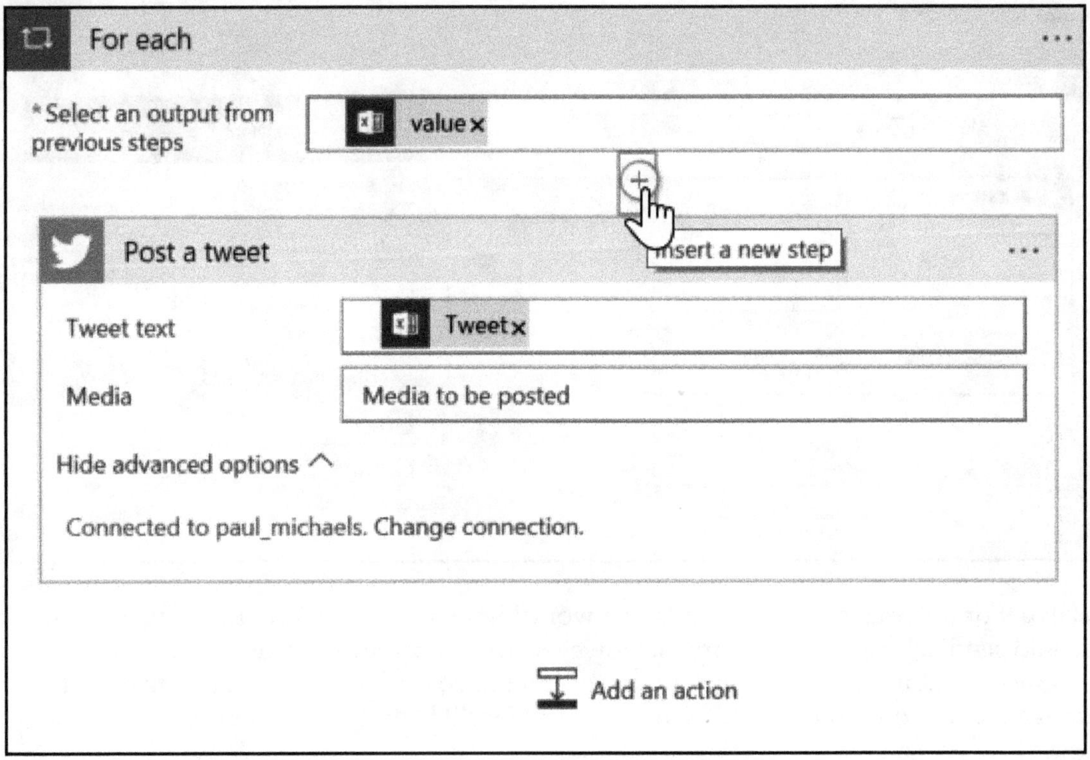

In this case, we'll select the area just above the posting of the tweet. Once you select it, a context menu will appear, allowing you to **Add an action**. If you select that, you'll be presented with the (by now) familiar dialog, allowing you to select an action. In this dialog, select **Control**, as shown here:

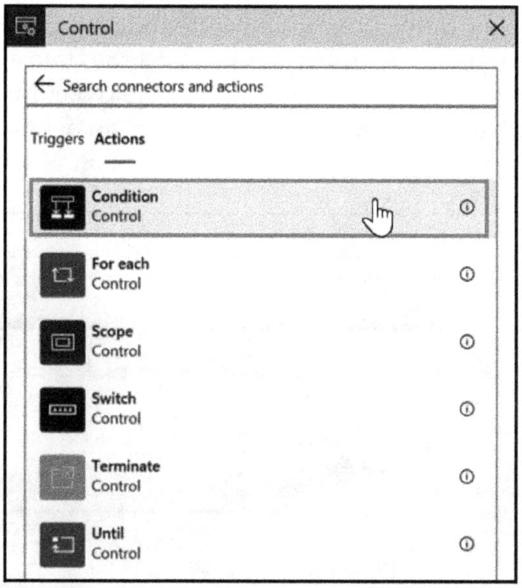

This time, we're going to select **Condition**. When you select **Condition**, you're presented with what, on the face of it, seems like a complex set of options; however, it's actually very simple.

Each condition must be a test that results in a *yes* or *no* answer; there cannot be any middle ground. For example, if the test were `Is it 5pm GMT?`, then the answer would either be `Yes, it is exactly 5pm GMT`, or it would be `No, it is not exactly 5pm GMT`. The logic app needs to know what, if anything, to do in each of these cases:

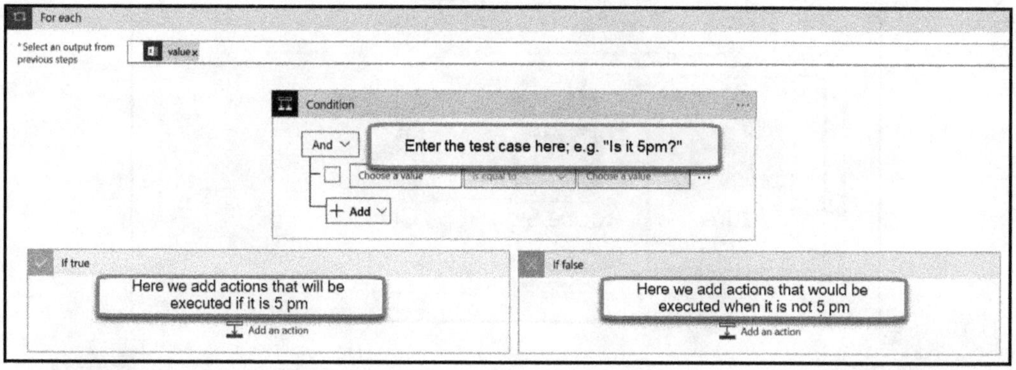

In our case, our condition is simply a call to our function using the current date and time (that is, the date and time when this function runs), and the date and time on the spreadsheet (that is, the date and time when we wish the tweet to send). So, before we can add the test, we'll need to call our function. Again, insert an action above the condition as shown here:

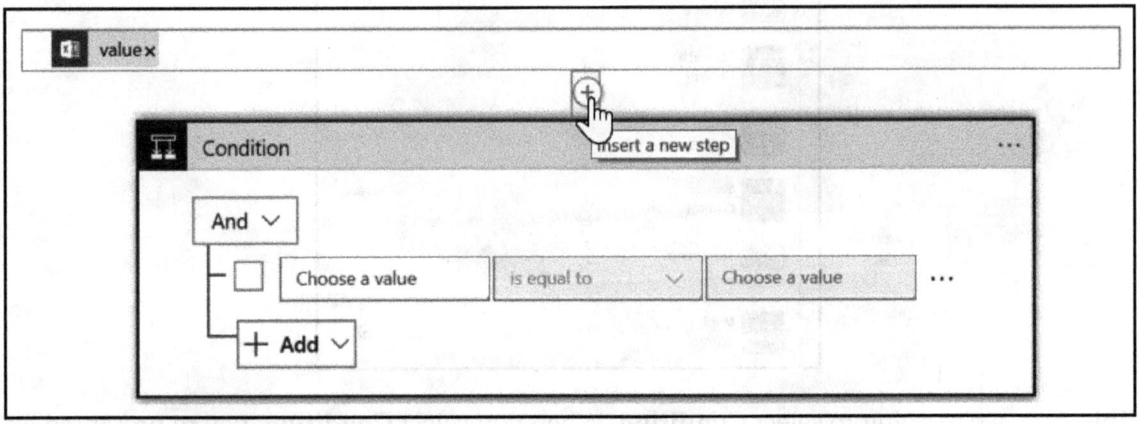

Now, it's simply a matter of selecting **Azure Functions** as the action type:

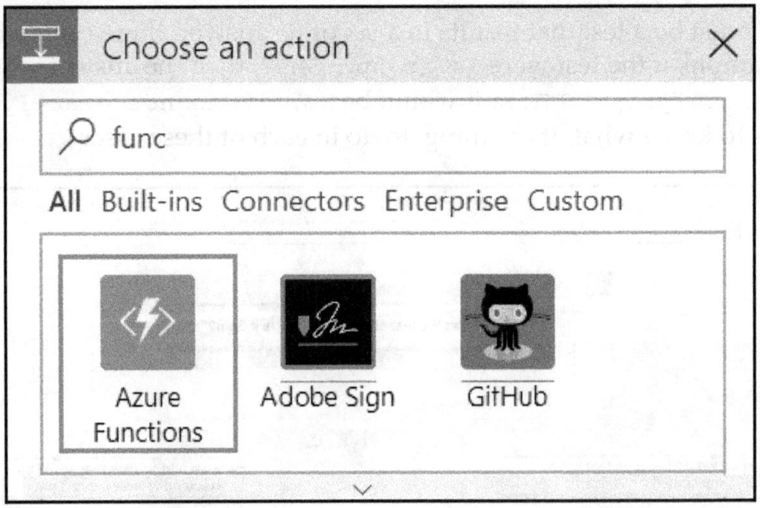

A list of available functions should now appear, like so:

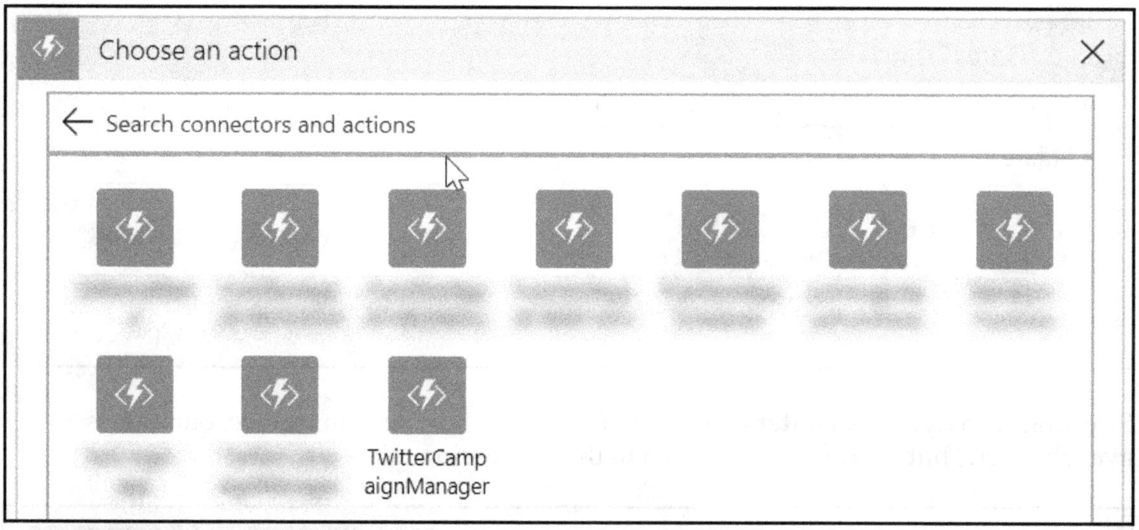

If you don't see your function here, then the likelihood is that there was a problem while publishing the function.

Once this is selected, you'll be presented with a list of functions inside your function app.

A single function app can contain many functions; however, each function is scaled independently.

Passing parameters to a function

The next bit of using the Designer is not a particularly nice experience. Essentially, we have to format for request body as JSON; this means part manual typing and part selecting built-in functions. Once you're used to this, you may find yourself dropping down to the raw JSON to add this in; however, let's step through it.

The finished JSON for the request body will need to look like this:

```
{ date1: '[Current Date]', date2: '[Date from Spreadsheet]' }
```

In the request body, enter the first part of the JSON, then select **Add dynamic content**:

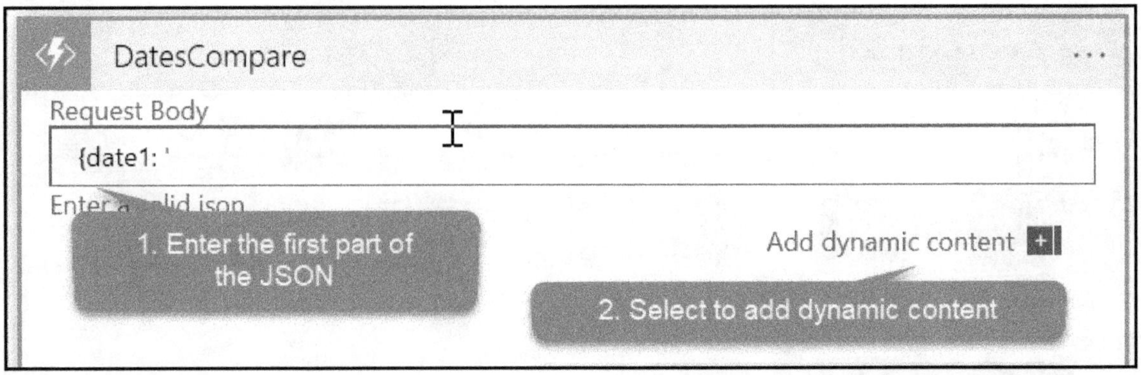

Selecting **Add dynamic content** will pop out a dialog box. As you can see, our date is available here, but for now, we'll switch to the **Expression** tab:

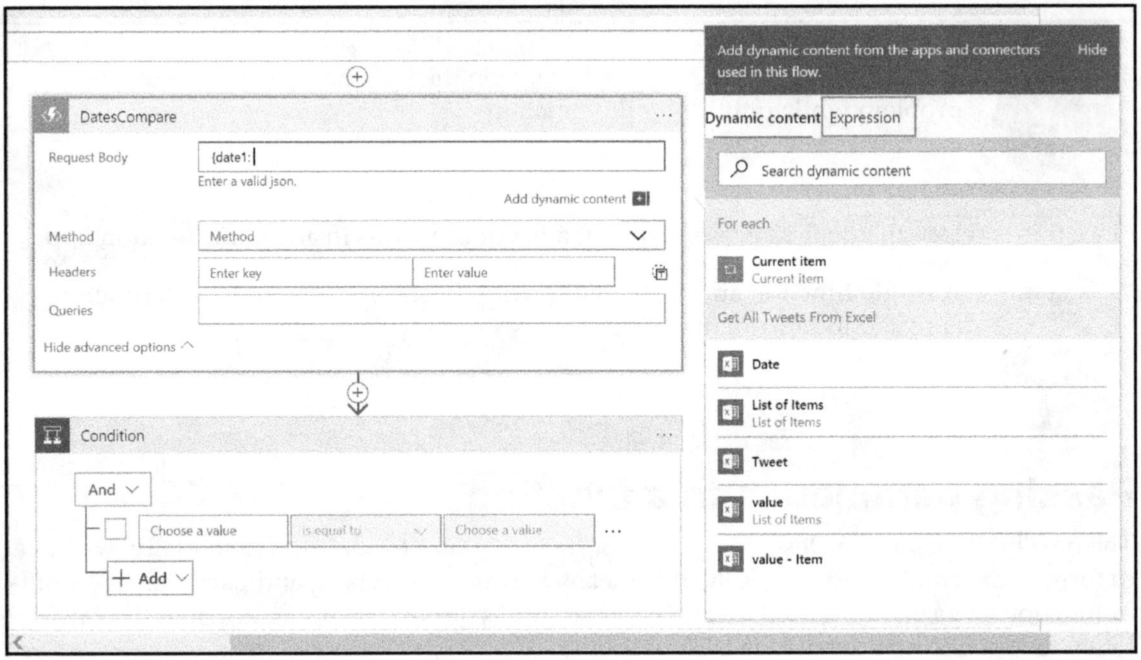

In the **Expression** tab, you'll find a number of built-in functions, and you'll see **utcNow()**:

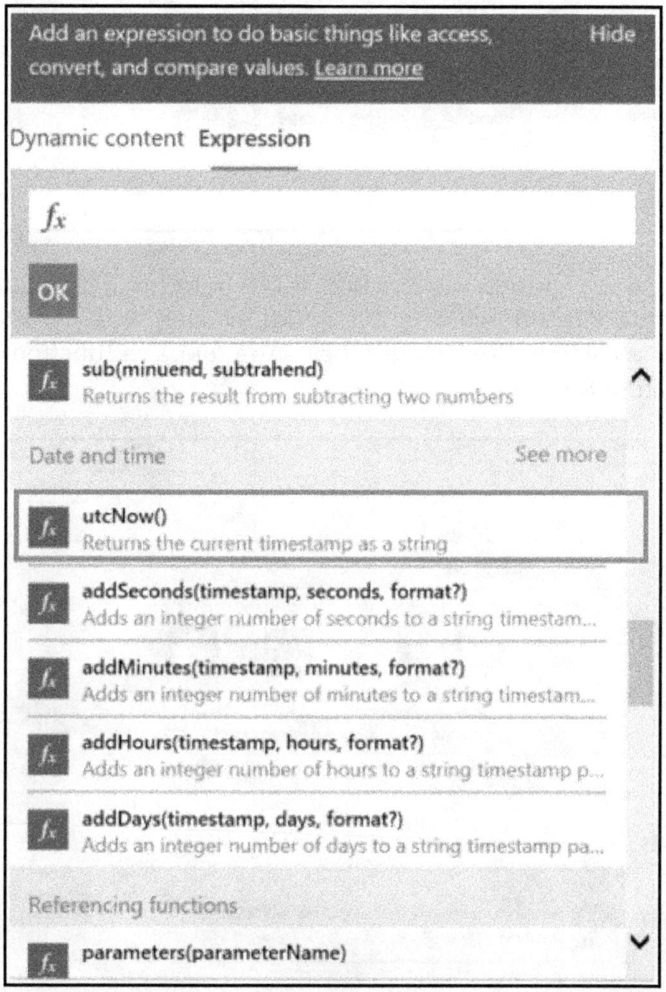

TIP

UTC is a time zone that is unaffected by daylight savings or regional variations, which means that if you're dealing with date and times, you should be doing so in UTC (you may convert to the local time zone for display of input purposes).

Once the function is selected, we'll need to finish the JSON and pass the date from Excel (as you saw earlier). The finished JSON should look like this:

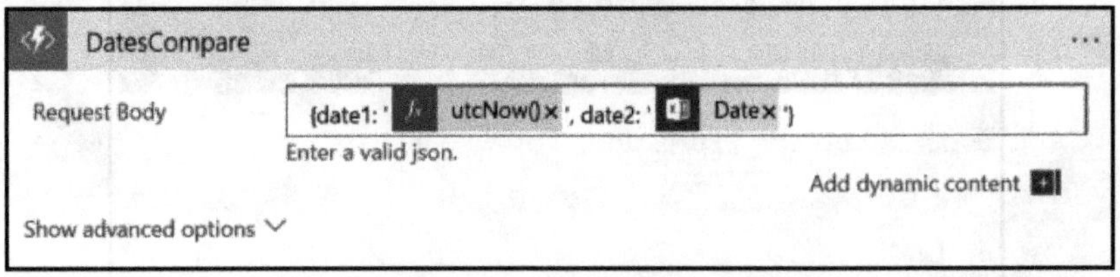

As we saw earlier when we tested the function, this will return a JSON document. If we wish to use the output of this function in the workflow later, we'll need to *parse* the JSON output. If you insert an action directly after the `DatesCompare` function call, you'll be able to select a special action for this:

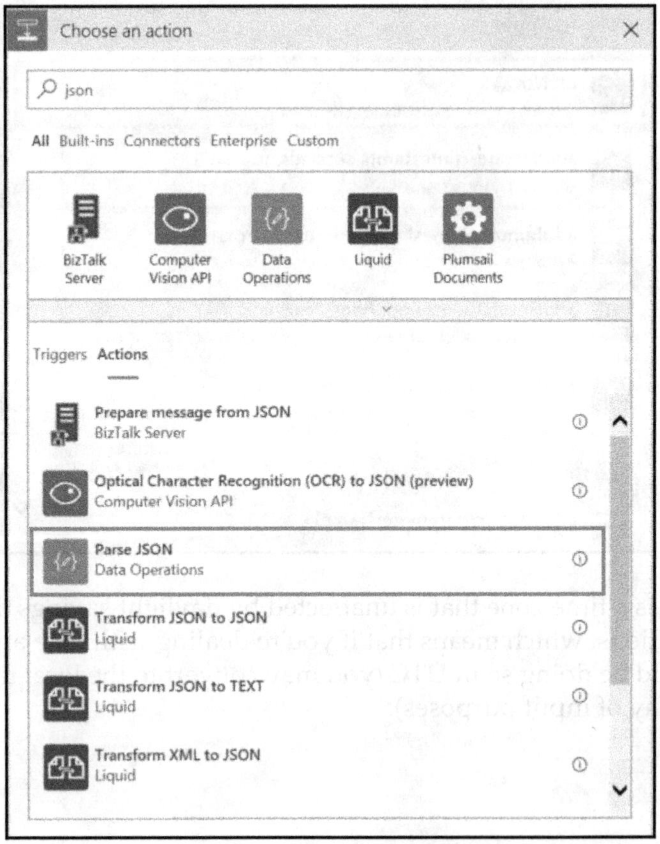

If you're wondering why you would ever *not* want to use the output of a function, it's worth remembering that functions can simply perform tasks; for example, you could have a function that updates a database or writes to a text file.

We have the output from the function called `Body`. As it stands, that's standard JSON, so you could simply dissect that yourself; however, we'll pass that to our **Parse JSON** function.

We'll also need to specify the schema as it's unlikely that anyone will be able to reel off a JSON schema. There's a nifty little function that allows you to just give it the JSON output (which you can get directly from the test screen that we saw earlier):

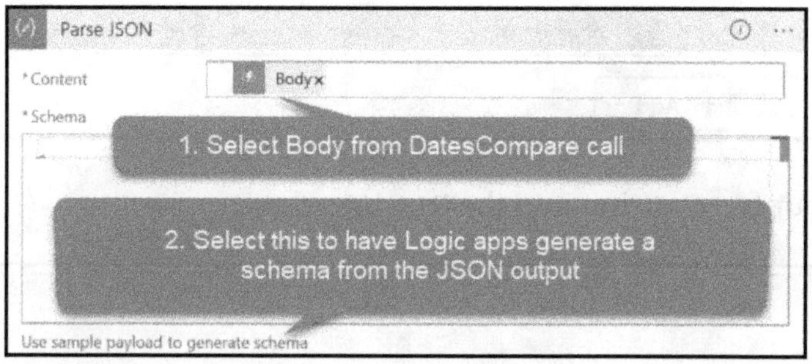

TIP: Try going back to the earlier part of the chapter and copying the output to paste into here.

The resultant schema should look like this:

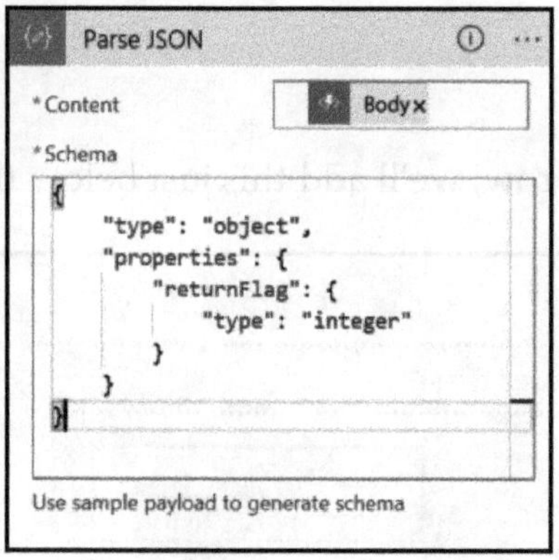

We now have a date comparison, so let's return to our condition.

Back to our condition

We can simply plug in the values. Remember that `Date1` was our current UTC date and `Date2` was our Excel date. So the logic should test if the current date is equal to or later than the Excel date; on this date, we can post the tweet:

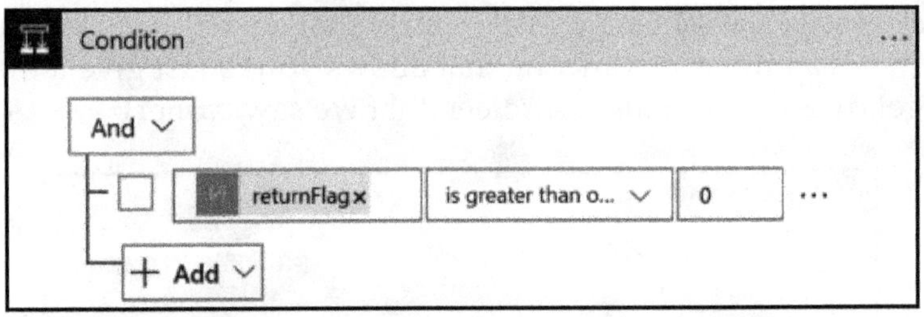

Finally, let's drag our tweet action into the true branch:

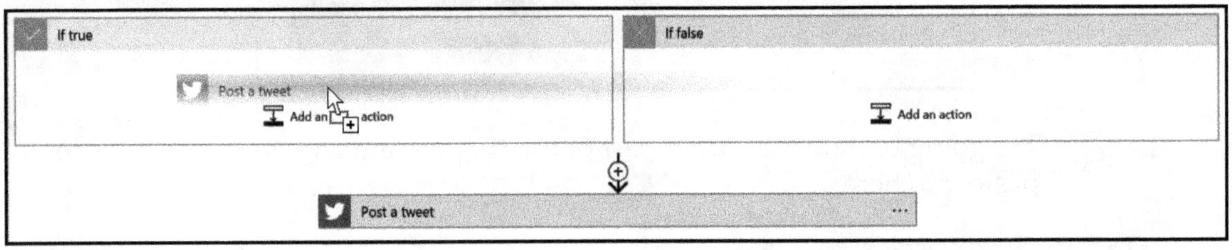

That's essentially the functionality done. We should now have the tweet successfully posting.

Deleting the row

The next step is to remove the row; we'll add this just below the tweet:

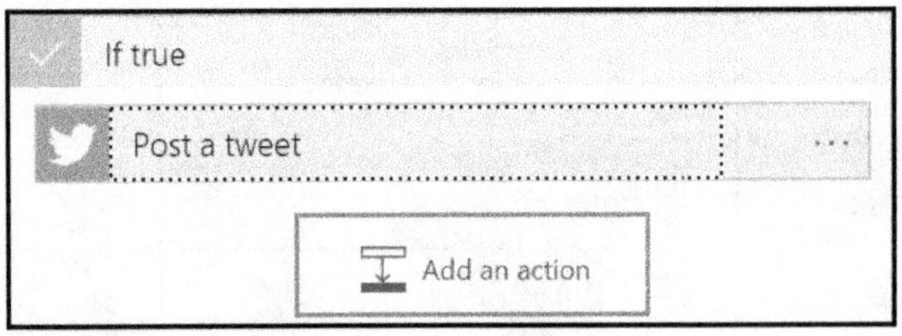

Again, we'll search for `Excel` and select **Excel Online (OneDrive)**. Finally, we'll select to **Delete a row (preview)**:

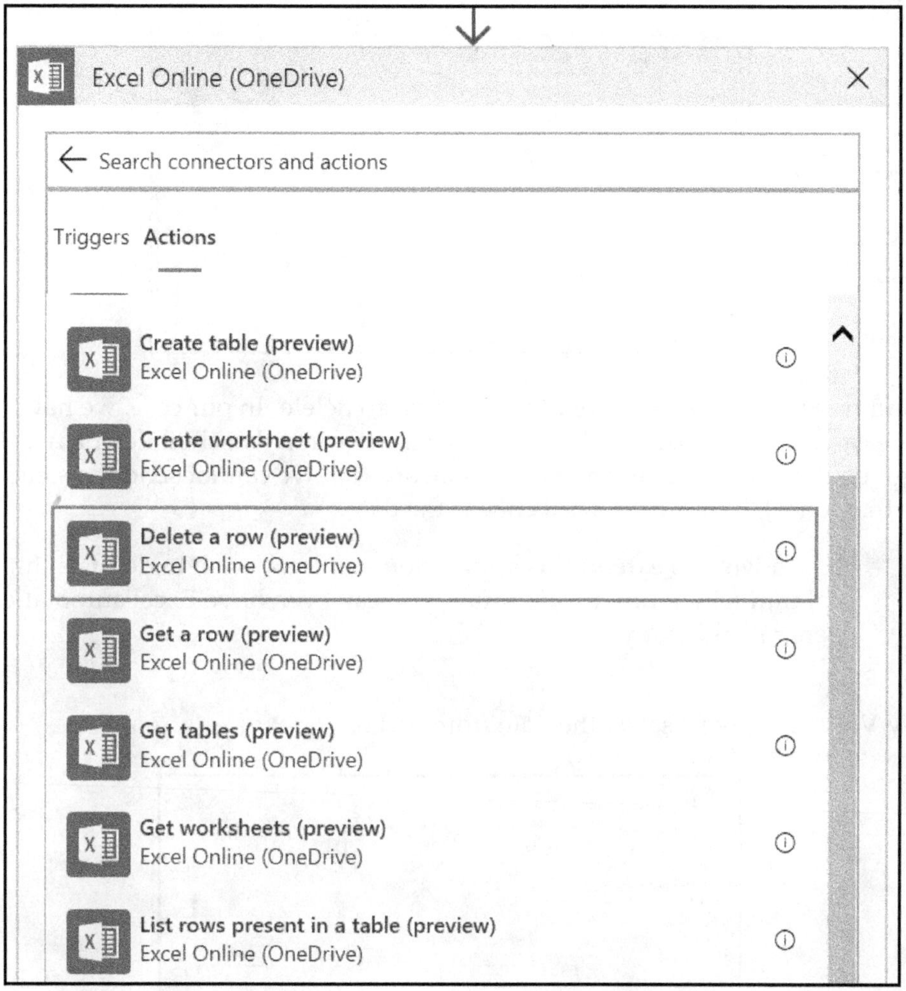

In the dialog screen that appears, the same spreadsheet and table need to be selected; then, you'll be asked to select a key column and value:

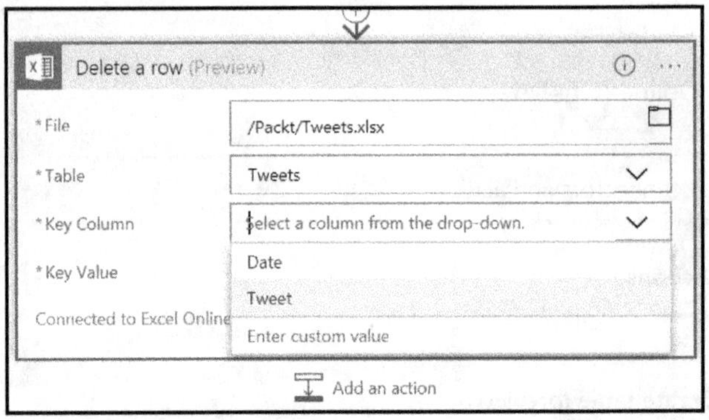

These columns are used to uniquely identify a row to delete. In our case, we have only two choices: we can choose the date (which means that we can only schedule one tweet to be sent at a given date), or the tweet text (which means that we cannot send the same tweet text more than once). In our case, we'll choose the date.

If you were to extend this application, you may wish to define a third column with a unique identifier (you can even have Excel automatically generate this for you).

In the **Key Value** box, we'll select the date from earlier:

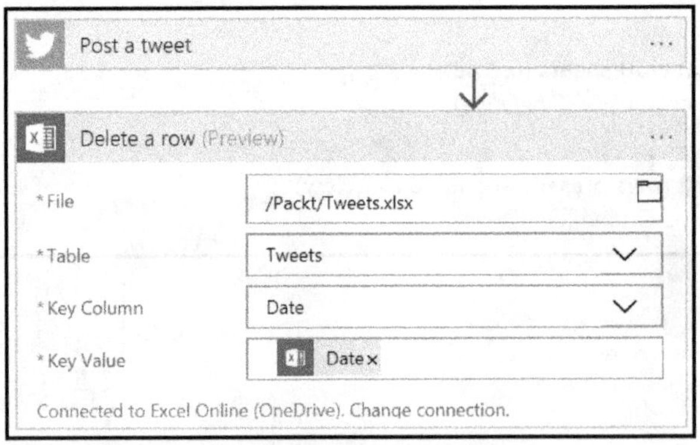

We can now move on to publishing the logic app.

Publishing the logic app

We're on the home stretch now. All that remains is to publish the app to Azure. Right-click on the logic app, select **Deploy**, and then **New...**:

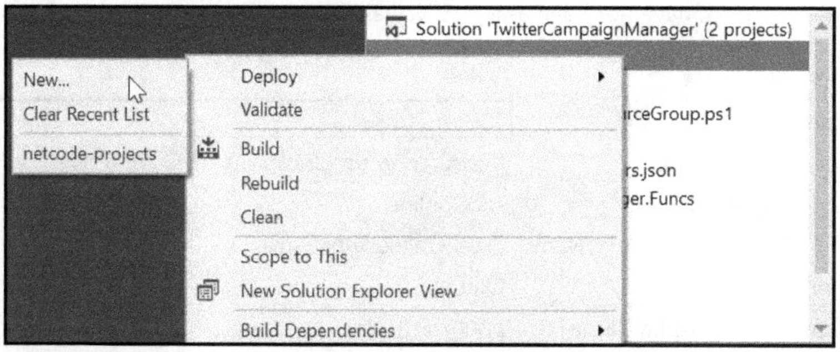

As you can see from this screenshot, once you've deployed the project, a shortcut will be created to deploy to the correct resource group.

In the dialog that appears, you're asked to select a resource group:

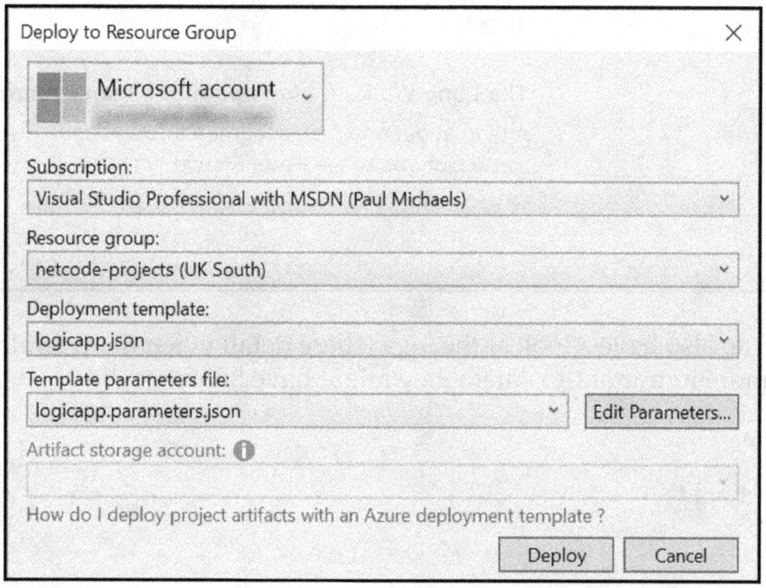

Finally, you'll be asked to fill in any missing parameters; in our case, that's just the name of the app:

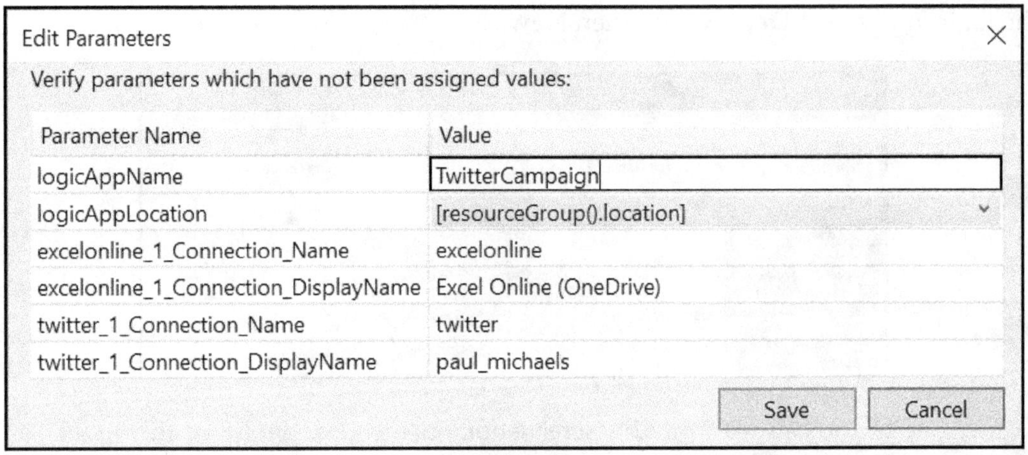

Once it is published, you can check that the workflow was successful by checking your Twitter account and by checking the spreadsheet:

However, you can also have a look at the logs. These detail when the workflows have executed and, more importantly, where they might have failed.

Failure

In fact, if you have copied the previous steps exactly, you'll see that, despite doing what it's supposed to do, the app is reporting as failing:

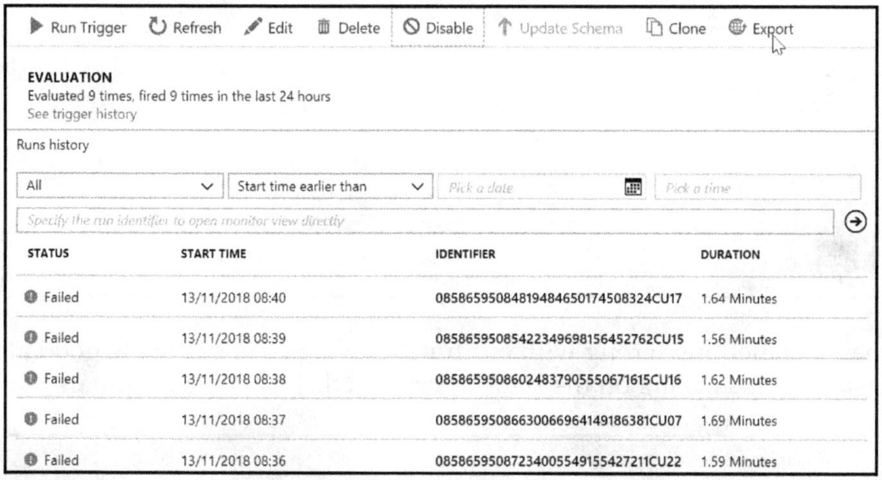

Let's see if we can find out why; click on one of the failures and you'll see exactly how far the logic app got before it threw an error:

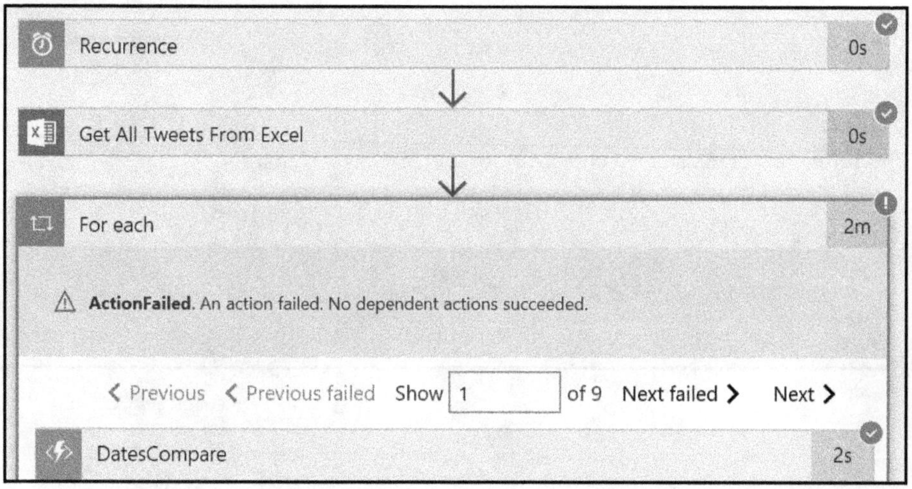

So, we can see that we got as far as `ForEach` and that something has failed, but at first glance, it looks like it succeeded. Select the **Next failed** option to jump to the issue:

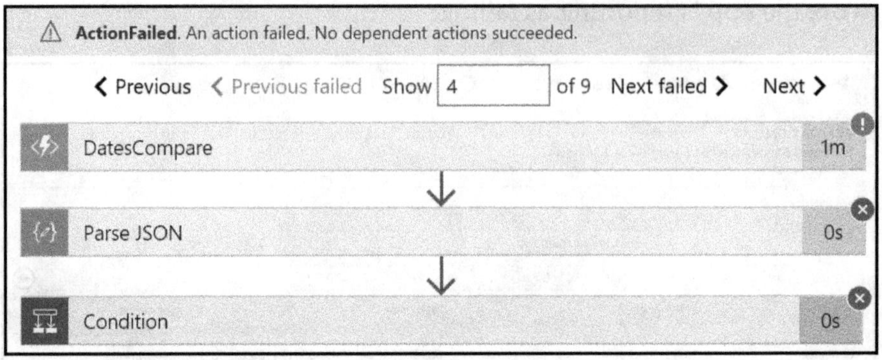

Okay, so there's something wrong with our function. Logic apps is really good at helping diagnose issues; keep clicking on the steps to drill in (click on **DatesCompare**):

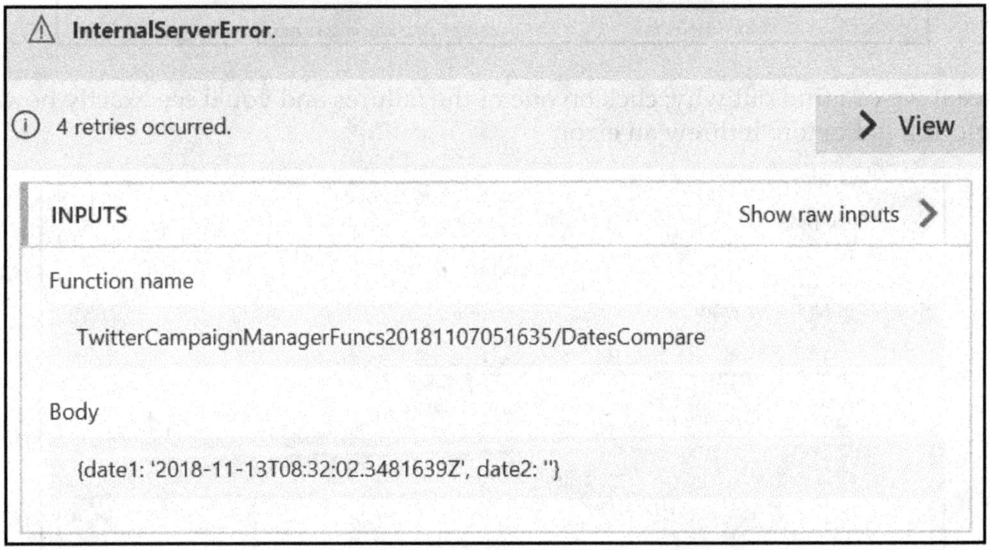

So, we're passing a blank string. The reason, of course, is because our Excel table contains blank entries. You could either solve this by simply reducing the size of the table to the available data or change the function to filter out blank rows; either way, we now have success:

STATUS	START TIME	IDENTIFIER	DURATION
Succeeded	13/11/2018 18:04	08586594746326782372134683960CU07	9.02 Seconds
Succeeded	13/11/2018 18:03	08586594746938763376847245421CU06	7.81 Seconds
Succeeded	13/11/2018 18:02	08586594747548182867614267521CU13	9.99 Seconds
Succeeded	13/11/2018 18:01	08586594748162566775079526679CU01	16.79 Seconds
Succeeded	13/11/2018 18:00	08586594748800656461473187008CU22	13.79 Seconds
Succeeded	13/11/2018 17:59	08586594749411363881593582417CU03	9.44 Seconds
Succeeded	13/11/2018 17:58	08586594750015904695702940037CU04	8.63 Seconds
Succeeded	13/11/2018 17:57	08586594750618289008112806929CU13	10.56 Seconds
Failed	13/11/2018 08:40	08586595084819484650174508324CU17	1.64 Minutes

We now have a working logic app. Let's tidy up the resources used in this chapter.

Cleaning up the Azure resources

We've only used two resources in this chapter; let's start by cleaning the logic app:

1. In the Azure portal, select the logic apps blade:

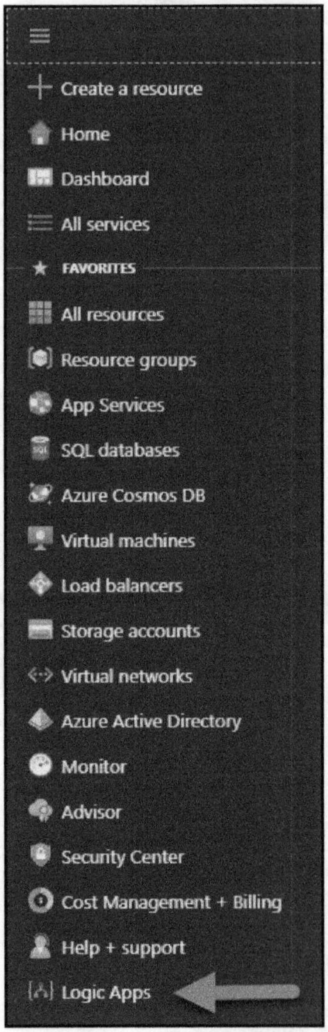

2. In this screen, you should now be able to see your app:

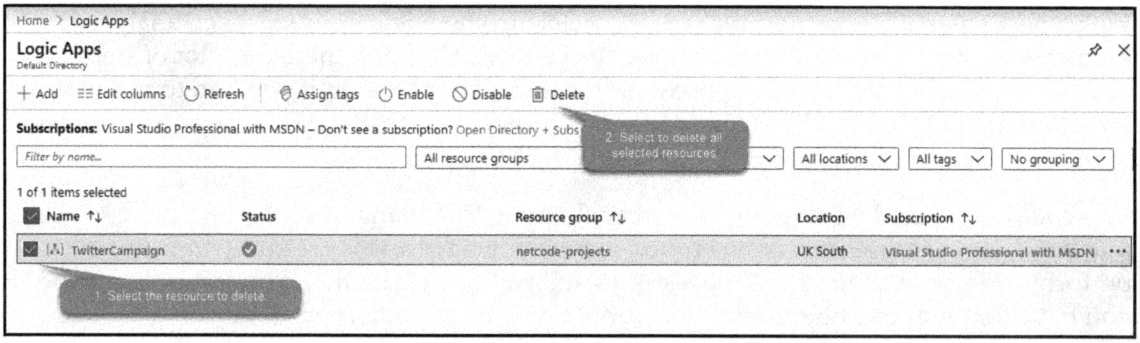

3. Next, we can find our function in a similar manner—select the **Functions** blade, either from the menu options (as you can see, my options don't have **Functions**), or just search for `Functions`. The same process applies:

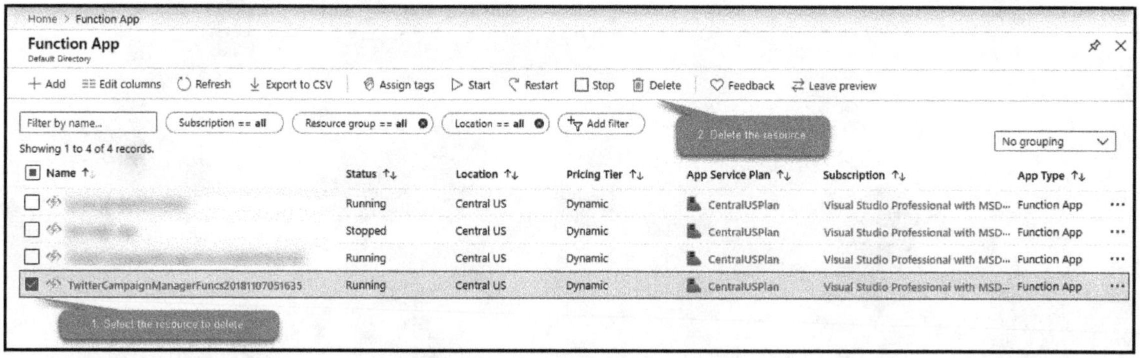

TIP: If you don't tidy the function app, then it is unlikely you will be charged. Functions only execute when they are invoked; however, the logic app is designed to run at a set interval. If you chose not to tidy it, then you will probably incur charges.

Now that we've disposed of our resources, let's review the chapter.

Summary

We've now created a logic app that retrieves data from an Excel spreadsheet, analyzes that data and, based on the result, interfaces with Twitter. Although there are a lot of steps, I hope you can see that the development of this is much faster than if you had to write all of these interfaces yourself. What's more, you get every single call to your Logic App logged, so you can easily diagnose any issues.

You could easily add an error handling capability to this so that it sent an e-mail if it failed; maybe you want to raise an issue on Jira; maybe you have a website and you want to perform a test on it every day to check if it's still running and e-mail you if it isn't; maybe you have a service bus queue and you want to notify someone every time you get a dead-lettered message. All of these things are possible with no or very little code.

In the next chapter, we'll be discussing how to implement authorization in your apps using Identity Server 4.

6
Stock Checker Using Identity Server and OAuth 2

In modern development, establishing a reliable and secure interface with which to authenticate your users is absolutely essential. OAuth 2 has pretty much emerged as the de facto standard here; however, because of its history, what exactly OAuth 2 means depends on who you ask (that is, if you ask Google, they may tell you a slightly different thing from Twitter).

In fact, should you wish to have someone simply log on with a secure interface, and you have little interest in the specifics of that login process, you could do a lot worse than using one of these companies to provide your identity services. For example, users could be able to log into your website with their Twitter credentials.

In this chapter, we will be developing a stock checking application. Our application will be very basic: we'll allow people to type in a stock code and get a stock figure, and we'll allow other people to update the stock figure. We cannot rely on access to the internet, so we will not be able to use an online identity service.

In order to achieve this, we'll use an open source framework called IdentityServer (`https://identityserver.io/`).

> TIP
>
> It's worth bearing in mind that what we are about to build, using IdentityServer, may be overkill for your specific usage scenario. If all you want is to authenticate a user, then you may find that Twitter, Google, or Microsoft's pre-built implementations of OAuth 2 are better suited to your needs. What we will do here is build a custom identity server, albeit using a framework, but it is still more work than using a pre-built offering.

In this chapter, we will cover the following topics:

- Using IdentityServer to secure an API
- Implementing a simple role-based permissions model
- **Universal Windows Platform** (**UWP**) applications
- Creating an ASP.NET Core 3.0 API
- Entity Framework Core
- Creating a certificate for development purposes

Technical requirements

In this chapter, we'll be using EF Core and SQL Server. During this chapter, I'll be assuming that you're running a version of SQL Server you've installed locally. There should be no difference (other than the connection string) should you choose to connect to a different SQL Server instance. The download page for SQL Server can be found here: `https://www.microsoft.com/en-gb/sql-server/sql-server-downloads`.

SQL Server Developer edition is free to use for developing and testing software (like you will be doing here). You can also use SQL Server Express or even a commercial version of SQL Server; however, one of the free versions will be sufficient for this project, as far as it goes.

You will also need a method of testing the API. Postman is one such tool that can be used for this and can be found here: `https://www.getpostman.com/`.

You can find the documentation for Postman (including some introductory tutorials) here: `https://learning.getpostman.com/docs`.

Visual Studio Installer – new workloads

Additional workloads can be installed via the Visual Studio Installer by selecting the **Modify** option.

In order to create the UWP application, you'll need to install the UWP workload:

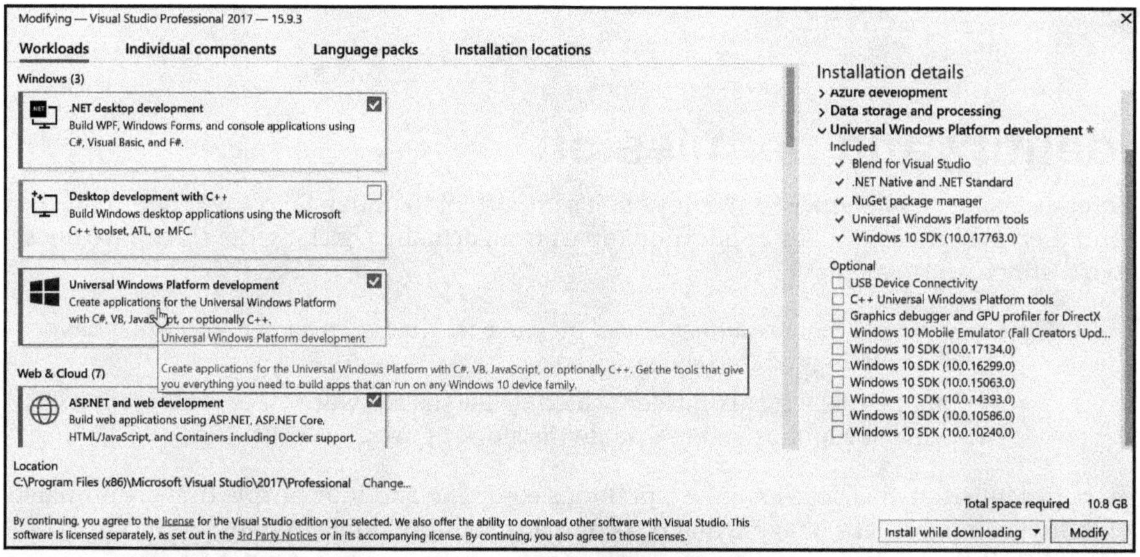

You may wish to download the data tools for Visual Studio:

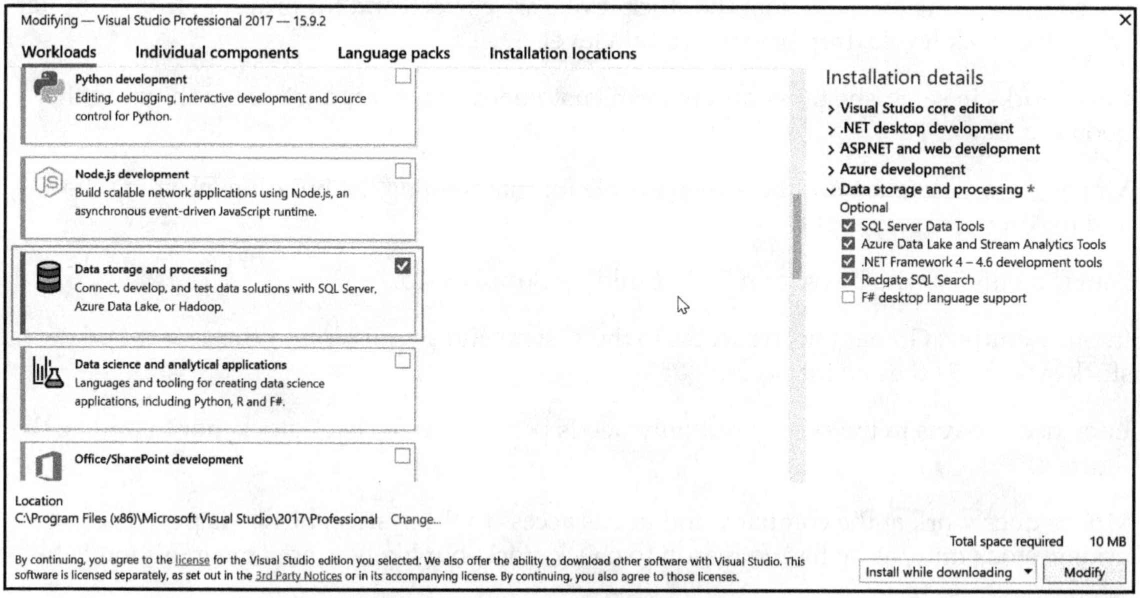

Alternatively, you could download SQL Server Management Studio, which can be found here: `https://docs.microsoft.com/en-us/sql/ssms/download-sql-server-management-studio-ssms`.

Identity and permission

Before we start to implement our solution, it's important to understand these two concepts (and their synonyms). In our application (apart from actually checking the stock), we have two distinct requirements:

- Only people that are *authenticated* may use it. That is, as a user, you must have successfully logged into the system.
- Among people who **are** authenticated to use the software, only a subsection of those may be authorized to update the stock figures.

To better illustrate this, let's imagine a fictitious company and four people that are affiliated with that company; let's imagine that our company sells building supplies: we'll call it **PCM Building Supplies Co.**.

Graham is a site manager at the company; he is responsible for everything that happens at the site, including checking that the stock levels are correct, and for ordering from suppliers when the stock levels drop below a certain level.

Lucy works in sales: she takes orders from customers and is responsible for shipping the goods.

Morris is the caretaker, and he is responsible for maintaining the building, cleaning the site, and locking up every night.

Sam is a builder who buys from PCM Building Supplies Co..

In our example, Graham needs access to the system and permission to check and update stock since he is the site manager.

Lucy needs *access* to the system but only needs permission to check stock, not to update the figures.

Morris does work at the company and needs access to the system; he needs permission to update stock only, as he has no reason to check stock, but likely uses some in his job.

Finally, Sam needs neither access nor permission as she does not work for the company.

This company is a fictitious one. We'll use it throughout this chapter for the purpose of testing data to illustrate our product working in these scenarios.

Having never worked at a building supply company, these examples may not reflect reality. If you're thinking that what I've said makes no sense in a real building supply company, then I would ask that you suspend belief as this is purely for the purpose of illustration. Having said that, the principles here are applicable, regardless of the industry you apply them to: this system could easily be applied to a newsagent, a greengrocer, or a clothes shop.

Now that we've discussed the concepts behind the key topics in this chapter, let's move on to the project itself.

Project overview

Since one of our requirements is that this solution should work, as far as possible, without a connection, and where not, with only a connection to the local network, our project will consist of a locally hosted ASP.NET Core API and a UWP application. Each person that needs access to this application will be given a tablet where they can either check or update stock. The architecture of our system will look something like this (not exactly an original architecture):

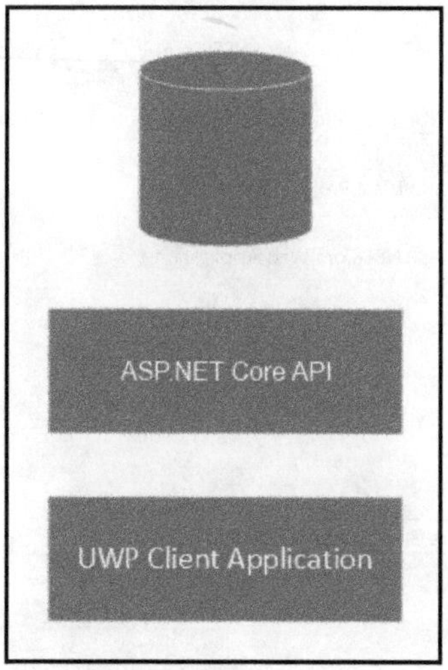

The UWP client application app will be given to all members of staff, which means that, in addition to authenticating the user, the application will need to prevent certain users from accessing certain functionality.

Stock checker application API

To start with, we'll create our stock checker application with all its functionality enabled for everyone, we'll use IdentityServer to lock down the application to only users that are authenticated, and finally, we'll enable only the correct functionality for the user.

Setup

The first stage will be to create our API. In .NET Core, the concept of an `ApiController` is replaced with a simple `Controller`; that is, there is no distinction between a controller method serving data and one serving a web page other than the return type.

Let's create our new project:

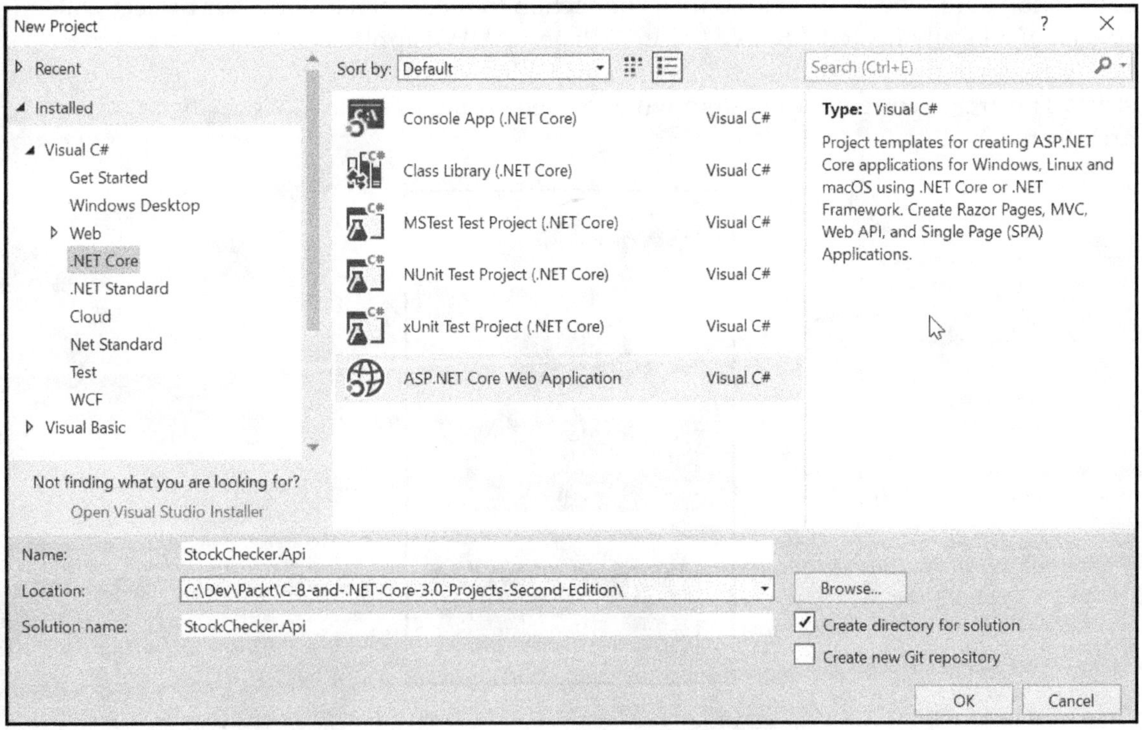

We'll create an empty application and add the API manually (targeting .NET Core 3.0):

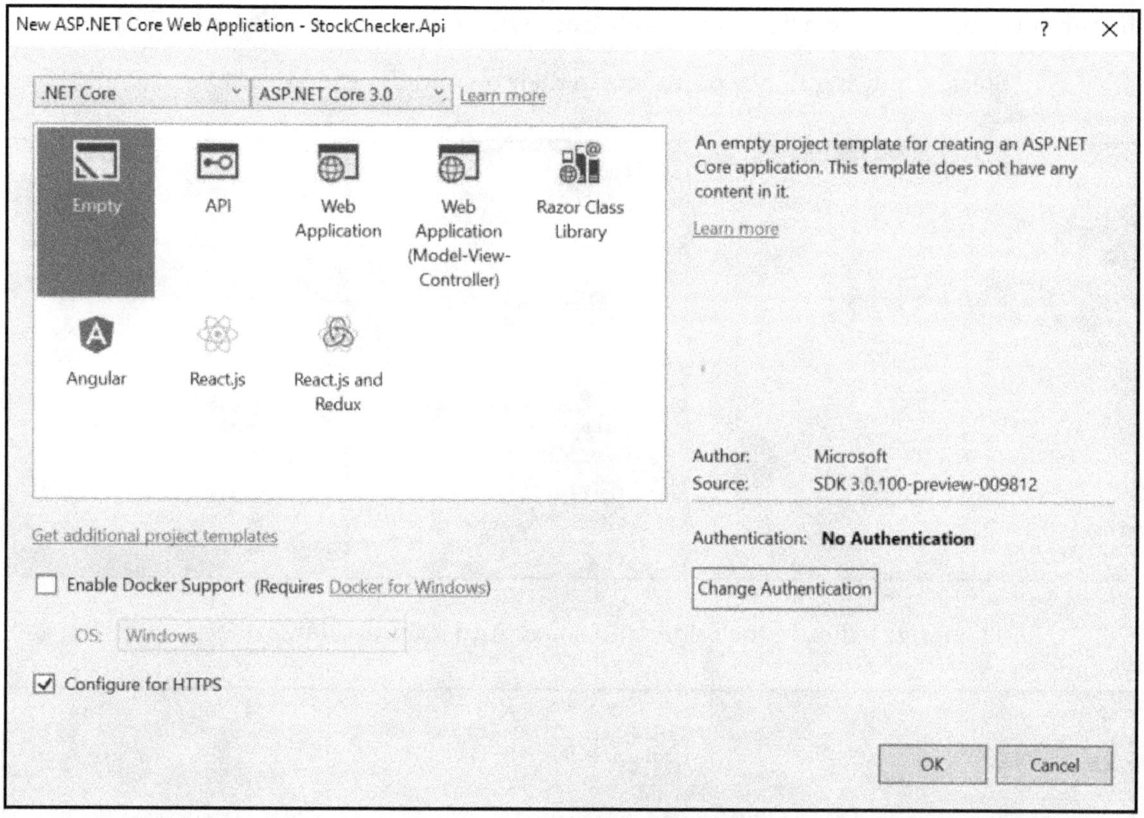

This should give you a bare-bones web application; now, we can put some meat on those bones by adding a new controller.

Adding the controller and routing

In our new application, we'll need to create our own controller. Let's see how:

1. Start by putting these controllers in their own folder called `Controllers`:

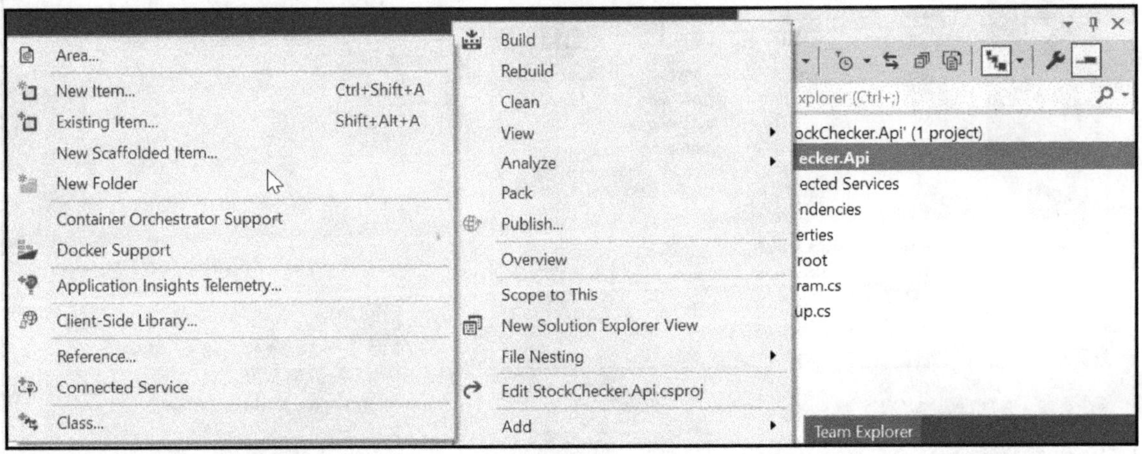

2. Then, right-click in the folder and select **Add** | **Controller...**:

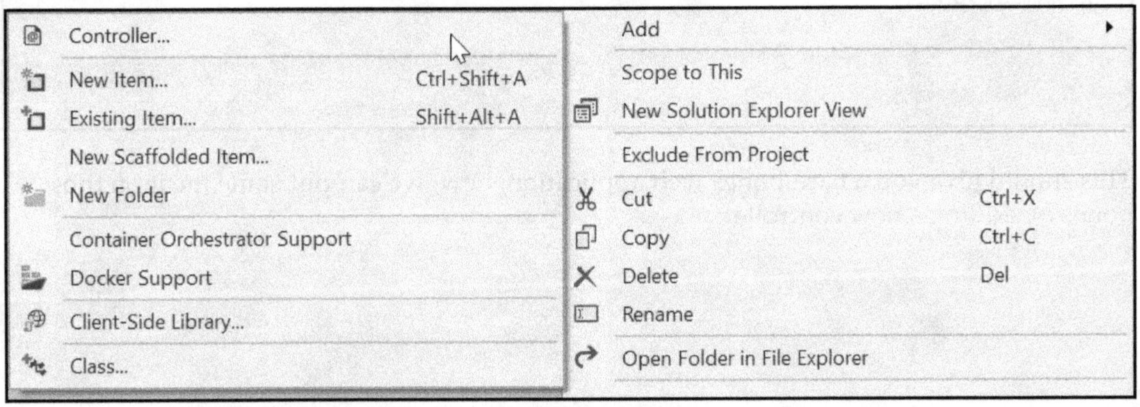

3. You can have Visual Studio create your controller for you but, again, let's roll our own and pick **Empty**:

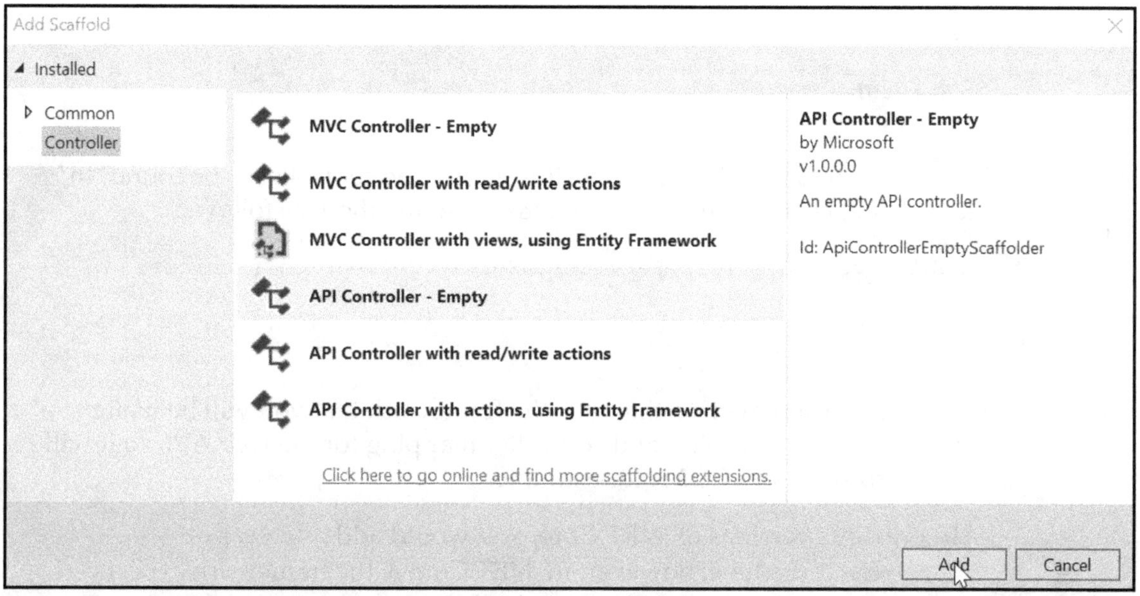

The new controller inherits from `ControllerBase`. This is because the `Controller` class (which itself inherits from `ControllerBase`) adds some functionality for binding views that relates only to an MVC controller. You could change this to inherit from `Controller` and it would work fine (although you would be including some functionality that you won't need). You'll notice that the new controller is decorated as an `ApiController`. Again, this is optional, but it adds some basic validation for you.

Your initial `controller` method should, therefore, look like this:

```
[Route("api/[controller]")]
[ApiController]
public class StockController : ControllerBase
{
}
```

4. So that we can get it working, let's add some very basic code to have it return something:

```
[HttpGet]
public string Get()
{
   return "test";
}
```

5. Now, we need to plug in some middleware for the controller to be found. In `startup.cs`, change the `ConfigureServices` method, as follows:

```
public void ConfigureServices(IServiceCollection services)
{
    services.AddControllers();
}
```

This is an extension method that tells the framework that you will be using services related to controller and controller mapping for the web API, so it will add authorization and CORS, for example.

> TIP: In previous versions of .NET Core, you would add `.UseMvc` or `.UserMvcCore` here; however, in .NET Core 3, the framework expects you to add only the parts that you need. This means that your code will never include middleware that isn't necessary. Clearly, the downside is that there's slightly more work to do initially to set up the API.

6. In the `Configure` method, tell the application to use the services that we added earlier:

```
public void Configure(IApplicationBuilder app, IHostingEnvironment
env)
{
    if (env.IsDevelopment())
    {
         app.UseDeveloperExceptionPage();
    }

    app.UseRouting();
    app.UseAuthorization();
    app.UseEndpoints(endpoints =>
    {
        endpoints.MapControllers();
    });
}
```

7. Now, you should be able to run the application and navigate to the controller; the exact address of this depends on your port, but it may, for example, be as follows:

```
https://localhost:44371/api/stock
```

Now that we have a controller, we can create our stock functionality. We have two requirements: checking stock levels and updating stock levels. We'll need to persist this information as well, so we'll use EF Core.

Reading stock levels

Let's look at how we might persist this to a SQL Server database using Entity Framework Core:

1. Because we're persisting all this to a database, we'll install Entity Framework Core in our API:

```
Install-Package Microsoft.EntityFrameworkCore.SqlServer
Install-Package Microsoft.EntityFrameworkCore.Tools
```

This installs both the *Entity Framework* libraries and tools that are required.

2. The next step is to create our model; that is, create a map of the database in a C# class. Your model could look something like this:

```
public class Product
{
    public int Id { get; set; }
    public string Description { get; set; }
    public int StockCount { get; set; }
}
```

It should sit somewhere visible to your application. I've added mine to a subfolder called `Models`.

For larger applications, it can make sense to take all of the data access logic and move it to its own library, but since this is a very small project, the extra overhead is probably not warranted at this time. If you maintain an abstraction between the data access and the business logic, moving the code later should be a trivial task. By default, Entity Framework Core uses any fields suffixed with `Id` to create a primary key. In our case, `Id` will be treated as a primary key.

Database performance, indexes, and keys are beyond the scope of this chapter and book; however, if you decide to extend this project, it is very likely that, for any volume of data, you would need to consider such things.

3. The next step is to create a data context. This is effectively a mapping class to tell EF Core which classes to use and map to your database. Ours needs to look like this at present:

```
public class StockContext : DbContext
{
    public StockContext(DbContextOptions<StockContext> options)
        : base(options) { }
    public DbSet<Product> Products { get; set; }
}
```

   There are two important parts to this class: declaring `DbSet`, which tells Entity Framework Core what we'd like to persist, and what it inherits from, that is, `DbContext` (its constructor).

4. Finally, we need to tell ASP.NET Core that we want to use Entity Framework Core, where to find `DbContext`, and where to find the database. This is all located inside `ConfigureServices`:

```
public void ConfigureServices(IServiceCollection services)
{
    services.AddMvcCore();
    var connection =
@"Server=(localdb)\MSSQLLocalDb;Database=StockCheckerDB;Trusted_Con
nection=True;ConnectRetryCount=0";
    services.AddDbContext<StockContext>(options =>
options.UseSqlServer(connection));
}
```

> **TIP:** You may wish to move the connection string into the config file and use SQL Server security rather than a trusted connection.

5. Now that we've configured our data, we'll create a migration to update the database to reflect our model. In the Package Manager Console, type the following:

```
Add-Migration InitialMigration
```

This should create a new folder, called `Migrations`, and two new files in your project. If you have a quick look at the migration file, you'll see that it consists of two functions: `Up`, which tells EF what to do when you migrate forward, and `Down`, which should revert those changes.

> **TIP:** Although this is generated code, it is not continually generated, which means that you can change it if you wish. Be aware that if you change `Up`, but not `Down`, you may find that you can't revert a migration, or worse, that reverting the migration leaves you in a new state: neither new nor old.

6. The next step is to update the database (which just runs the migration):

```
Update-Database
```

Now that our database exists, is accessible, and is up to date, we'll need our controller function to access that data.

You could simply access the `DataContext` from anywhere in the application; however, this would cause problems for unit testing; that is, if your controller function directly accesses the database, it's difficult to test a *unit* of functionality. Further, if you decided to replace Entity Framework with another data access method at a later time, this would make it much more difficult.

In order to solve these issues, we'll inject the dependency into our controller. Let's see how:

1. In order to inject the dependency into our controller, the first step is to abstract our `DbContext` class into an interface:

```
public interface IDbContext
{
    DbSet<Product> Products { get; set; }
}
```

You might be wondering why we would create an interface and not pass the class in directly. In fact, there is nothing preventing this; however, what this would mean is that we would always need to pass in a class of the `DbContext` type. Creating an interface means that we can replace our `DbContext` class with a dummy class, or even a completely different class that implements the same interface.

This may seem like abstraction for the sake of it, but consider how you would write a unit test for any method that referenced this `DbContext`.

For our project, we will simply pass the `DbContext` around; however, the best practice is to completely abstract the data access, so rather than passing in `DbContext`, you may pass in an `IDataAccess` class, which in turn accepts the `IDbContext`. This means that, should you decide to replace EF Core with another ORM, you would simply change the implementation of this class.

2. Now that we have an interface, we can inject that into our controller:

```
public StockController(IDbContext dbContext)
```

If you're using Visual Studio, pressing *Ctrl-.* on `DbContext` will give you the opportunity to create and populate a field in the class, saving you from adding the class-level variable:

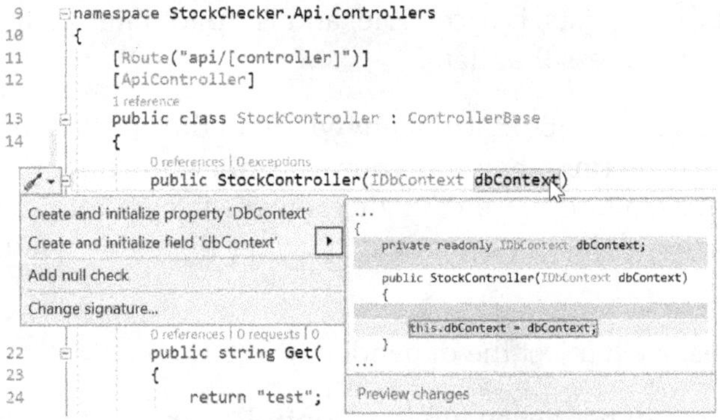
namespace StockChecker.Api.Controllers
[Route("api/[controller]")]
[ApiController]
public class StockController : ControllerBase
public StockController(IDbContext dbContext)
Create and initialize property 'DbContext'
Create and initialize field 'dbContext'
Add null check
Change signature...
private readonly IDbContext dbContext;
public StockController(IDbContext dbContext)
this.dbContext = dbContext;
Preview changes
public string Get(
return "test";

3. Finally, we'll return data from the database when the `Get` method is called:

```
[HttpGet("{id}")]
public ActionResult<int> Get(int id)
{
```

```
        Product product = dbContext.Products.FirstOrDefault(a => a.Id
== id);
        if (product == null) return NotFound();

        return Ok(product.StockCount);
    }
```

Your `StockController` should now look like this:

```
[Route("api/[controller]")]
[ApiController]
public class StockController : ControllerBase
{
    private readonly IDbContext dbContext;

    public StockController(IDbContext dbContext)
    {
        this.dbContext = dbContext;
    }

    [HttpGet("{id}")]
    public int Get(int id)
    {
        Product product = dbContext.Products.FirstOrDefault(a =>
a.Id == id);
        if (product == null) return NotFound();

        return Ok(product.StockCount);
    }
}
```

4. We now have a dependency injected into our controller; however, we'll need something to do the injecting for us. This is where an IoC container comes in. Before ASP.NET Core, you might have used something like Unity for this. You still can if you wish, but ASP.NET Core 3 has a built-in IoC container:

```
public void ConfigureServices(IServiceCollection services)
{
    services.AddControllers();

    var connection =
@"Server=(localdb)\MSSQLLocalDb;Database=StockCheckerDB;Trusted_Con
nection=True;ConnectRetryCount=0";
    services.AddDbContext<StockContext>
  (options => options.UseSqlServer(connection));
    services.AddTransient<IDbContext, StockContext>();
}
```

There are many IoC containers available for free. If you choose to use a third-party one, then I would advise that you have a reason to do so; while some of the options out there do offer features that the built-in version does not, you should consider whether that functionality is something that you actually need. Furthermore, outside of experimentation, I would advise against writing your own IoC container as this leaves you with the responsibility of maintaining it in the future.

So, we should now be able to run this and get a stock figure; let's try that. Execute the API; it should launch a browser that will bring up a 404 error (that's fine – there's just nothing at the base address). Navigate to the following address:

```
https://localhost:44371/api/stock/1
```

Your port may be different—if it is, then simply substitute your port.

You should now be able to navigate to the following address:

```
https://localhost:44371/api/stock/1
```

The browser should return the stock figure correctly (which is `0`).

Updating stock levels

Now that we can read the stock levels, let's add the functionality to change them. Now that the retrieval is done, updating is relatively trivial; your `Update` method should look something like this:

```
[HttpPut("{id}")]
public IActionResult Update(int id, [FromBody]int stockCount)
{
    Product product = dbContext.Products.FirstOrDefault(a => a.Id == id);
    if (product == null) return NotFound();
    product.StockCount = stockCount;
    dbContext.SaveChanges();
    return NoContent();
}
```

As you can see, the code is very similar to the retrieval; we simply update the stock count on the `dbContext` and call `SaveChanges()`.

In order to test this, we'll need to use Postman (if you haven't installed this, then refer to the *Technical requirements* section):

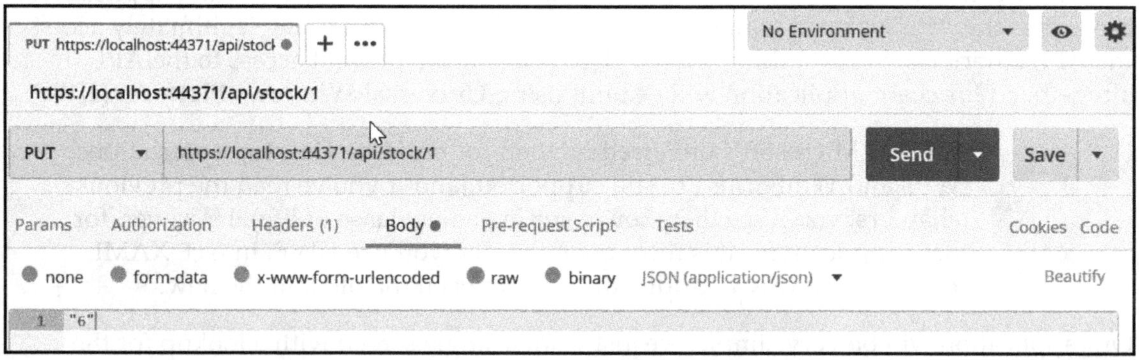

You should find that this updates the stock level for item `1` to a quantity of `6`. You can prove this by looking at the database, or you can simply navigate to the endpoint to check the stock levels (either using Postman or a browser, as you did previously).

> **TIP:** You may have noticed that we have not built in any functionality to add new products. This is intentional; if you wish to do so as an extension, I would urge you to consider whether it fits in the `Stock` controller or whether that should be handled separately.

Permissions

So far, so good. We now have the basic functionality for our stock checker application; that is, it checks stock levels and allows us to update stock levels. However, there is an issue with this. With our example, any of the users would be able to easily update the stock levels. This can (and should) be locked down on the client; however, we should implement this security on the API as well; after all, access to Postman, or even a web browser, is not exclusive, and the last thing we would want is for someone without permission to update our stock levels.

Let's plug in **IdentityServer 4** and make sure that the person accessing the API is, at least, authorized to do so.

Client application

Before we can introduce IdentityServer to validate that the correct people and applications can access the API, we need to have an application that we can say can legitimately access the API; otherwise, the best thing we could do is to simply prevent access to the API altogether. Our client application will be built using **Universal Windows Platform** (**UWP**).

> UWP is Microsoft's preferred method for building Desktop applications. WPF and WinForms are still supported (and if you've read the previous chapters, you'll see that they're getting a new lease of life). However, for new applications, it is recommended that you use UWP. In fact, XAML Islands are a way to bridge the gap between the old and the new.

Our application will be very simple: we just want a single screen with a lookup for the stock level and an option to update the stock levels.

> I've never claimed to be a UX designer, so if you feel you could design the screen better, that's probably because you could (and there is nothing in the functionality that will be altered if the layout of the screen is changed)!

Let's create a new project inside our solution:

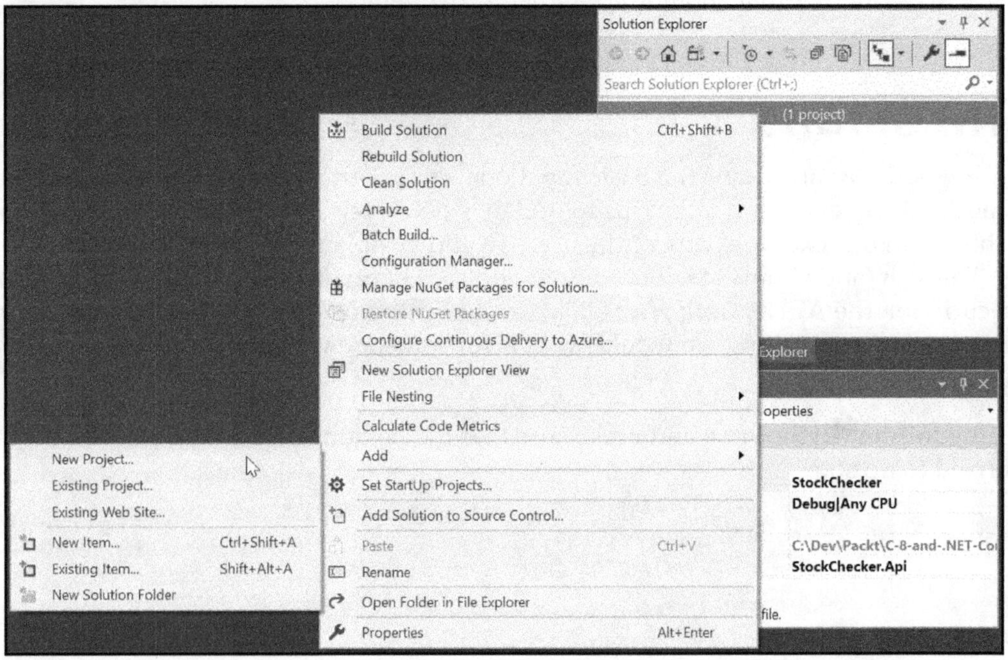

Our client application is going to be a C# UWP application:

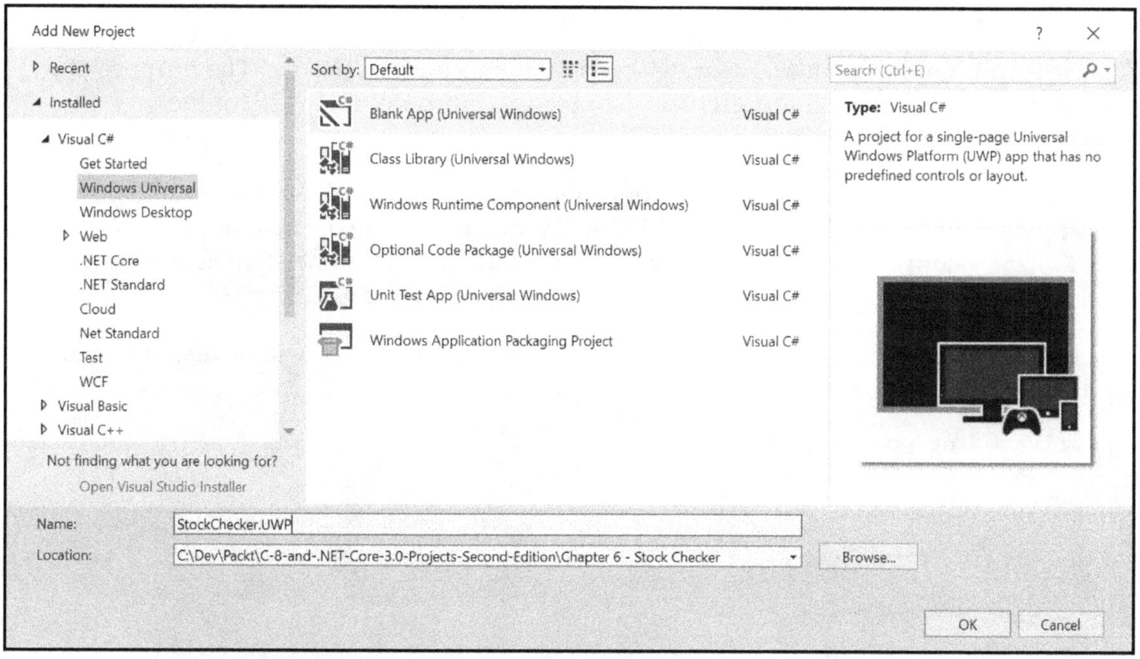

In this project, we will leverage the binding capabilities of UWP; however, it would be wrong to say that this represents an MVVM architecture. Data binding, while an important part of an MVVM architecture, is not synonymous with it. For this project, I am purposely not introducing any MVVM frameworks in order to demonstrate how the project is built; however, other than the learning opportunity that this affords, it is very much reinventing the wheel. There are several excellent MVVM frameworks out there: MVVM Cross or MVVM Light, for example. All of them will provide built-in helpers for commands, messaging, and dependency injection.

UWP allows you to simply write event handlers; so, in theory, we could handle the click event of a button, interrogate the screen, and then call the API. In fact, our UI layer is so small that this may represent the best solution; however, we will use the built-in data binding that UWP gives us out of the box. This approach also makes the solution much more extensible.

Let's start by creating a `ViewModels` folder and adding a ViewModel for our main view:

```
public class MainPageViewModel : INotifyPropertyChanged
```

We'll explain why we're implementing this particular interface shortly. The purpose of the ViewModel is to provide a representation of the view in code: that is, all of the functionality, but none of the visuals.

> TIP: You can call the ViewModel anything you choose; however, should you elect to use a particular MVVM framework, some of them use a convention that the ViewModel should have the same stem as the View; for example, `MainPageView/MainPageViewModel`.

The first thing we'll declare in our ViewModel is the fields that we will be displaying and updating; in our case, we're actually only displaying two:

```
private int _productId;
private int _quantity;
private int _originalQuantity;

public int ProductId
{
    get => _productId;
    set
    {
        if (UpdateField(ref _productId, value))
        {
            RefreshQuantity();
        }
    }
}

public int Quantity
{
    get => _quantity;
    set
    {
        if (UpdateField(ref _quantity, value))
        {
            UpdateQuantity.RaiseCanExecuteChanged();
        }
    }
}
```

Clearly, we are referencing some methods that do not exist here; `UpdateField` is simply a helper method that saves us rewriting checks that the field has changed and where it has to call `OnPropertyChanged` (more about that in a second):

```
private bool UpdateField<T>(ref T field, T value,
 [CallerMemberName] string propertyName = null)
{
    if (EqualityComparer<T>.Default.Equals(field, value))
    {
        return false;
    }

    field = value;

    OnPropertyChanged(propertyName);
    return true;
}
```

OnPropertyChanged

XAML works by rerendering the screen when it is necessary to do so. In the case of WPF and UWP, this means that we need to tell it that something has changed, and we do that by implementing a method on the `INotifyPropertyChanged` interface called `OnPropertyChanged`:

```
public void OnPropertyChanged([CallerMemberName] string propertyName =
null)
{
    this.PropertyChanged(this, new PropertyChangedEventArgs(propertyName));
}
```

When this is called, it rerenders the aspect of the screen that is bound to whatever property is passed in.

`CallerMemberName` was introduced back in .NET 4.5 and it allows you to reference the name of the caller without explicitly defining it at design time. That is, if we change the name of one of the properties, `CallerMemberName` will simply pick up the new name.

Commands and API calls

Now that we have our properties, we have two pieces of functionality that we need to introduce: the ability to update the stock quantity and the ability to retrieve the stock quantity. We've already referenced the latter, so let's add that first:

```
private async Task RefreshQuantity()
{
    Quantity = await _httpClientHelper.GetQuantityAsync(ProductId);
    _originalQuantity = Quantity;
    UpdateQuantity.RaiseCanExecuteChanged();
}
```

Again, we're clearly referencing some code that doesn't exist yet, but let's examine what we see: we're simply calling our API, assigning the quantity value to our property, and then setting the `_originalQuantity` field. The `_originalQuantity` field and `RaiseCanExecuteChanged` are closely linked, and we'll see why soon. Before that, though, let's have a look at where `_httpClientHelper` comes from. We'll add a constructor and field definition here:

```
private readonly IHttpStockClientHelper _httpClientHelper;
public RelayCommand UpdateQuantity { get; set; }

public MainPageViewModel(IHttpStockClientHelper httpClientHelper)
{
    _httpClientHelper = httpClientHelper;
    UpdateQuantity = new RelayCommand(async () =>
    {
        await _httpClientHelper.UpdateQuantityAsync(
            ProductId, Quantity);
        await RefreshQuantity();
    }, () => Quantity != _originalQuantity);
}
```

There's a lot going on here. Again, I'll ask you to hold questions about what these interfaces and variable types are for a second and have a look at what we can see: we're injecting the helper class that we saw earlier and we're instantiating a `RelayCommand`, which apparently just takes an action (something to do) and a function (something to evaluate).

That represents all the code for the ViewModel, so let's have a look at the helper classes.

Helper classes

There were two helper classes that we used here; the first was `RelayCommand`. Any command that's bound to a XAML frontend must implement `ICommand`. It's a trivial job to implement `ICommand`; you simply tell it what you want to do when it executes and the conditions under which it's allowed to. However, it does mean that you end up with a separate class for every command, and it makes passing functionality through from the ViewModel more difficult. The solution, therefore, is to generically implement a helper class that simply accepts the action and evaluation function and implements `ICommand` for you. It looks like this:

```
public class RelayCommand : ICommand
{
    private readonly Action _execute;
    private readonly Func<bool> _canExecute;
    public event EventHandler CanExecuteChanged;

    public RelayCommand(Action execute) : this(execute, null)
    {
    }

    public RelayCommand(Action execute, Func<bool> canExecute)
    {
        _execute = execute ?? throw new ArgumentNullException("execute");
        _canExecute = canExecute;
    }

    public bool CanExecute(object parameter)
    {
        return _canExecute == null ? true : _canExecute();
    }

    public void Execute(object parameter)
    {
        _execute();
    }

    public void RaiseCanExecuteChanged()
    {
        CanExecuteChanged?.Invoke(this, EventArgs.Empty);
    }
}
```

There are many versions of this that are available as open source, not least from Microsoft themselves. All of the implementations are basically the same; although if you decide to use it yourself, you might find it needs a little customization; for example, some logging will go a long way! As far as I'm aware, all of the MVVM frameworks provide a version of this that is likely to be much richer in functionality than anything you'll write yourself.

Our second helper class was `HttpClientHelper`. Let's have a look at the code. Then, we can discuss what it does and, more importantly, why it needs to be put into a separate class:

```
public class HttpClientHelper : IHttpStockClientHelper
{
    static HttpClient _httpClient;

    public HttpClientHelper(Uri baseAddress)
    {
        _httpClient = new HttpClient();
        _httpClient.BaseAddress = baseAddress;
    }

    public async Task<int> GetQuantityAsync(int productId)
    {
        string path = $"api/stock/{productId}";
        string quantityString = await _httpClient.GetStringAsync(path);
        return int.Parse(quantityString);
    }

    public async Task UpdateQuantityAsync(int productId, int newQuantity)
    {
        string path = $"api/stock/{productId}";
        var httpContent = new StringContent(newQuantity.ToString());
        httpContent.Headers.ContentType = new
MediaTypeHeaderValue("application/json");

        await _httpClient.PutAsync(path, httpContent);
    }
}
```

As you can see, we have two public methods and a constructor. Since we're calling the same service, we can configure all of that in the constructor. As you can see, we're simply calling the service by using `HttpGet` for `GetQuantityAsync` and `HttpPut` for `UpdateQuantityAsync`.

It's worth noting that both methods are doing some type conversion: it makes sense for the helper methods to expose the functionality that you expect; for example, *Update product quantity to 3*. Here, you should only need two parameters: the product and the quantity. If you're passing anything else in or out, then you're creating noise that you (or someone else) might have to sift through, should a bug occur.

So, reducing noise is the first reason for having this helper. The second is that, should we need to unit test the calling code, we can easily mock out the calls to the services.

We now have a working desktop application, so let's move on to securing the functionality. We can start with IdentityServer.

IdentityServer 4

As we mentioned earlier, IdentityServer is not a pre-built service, but a framework. Such services do exist – Google, Twitter, Facebook, Microsoft, and so on all provide pre-built services that you can simply call and get an identity back. IdentityServer is much more of a *roll your own* solution.

> TIP: It's worth considering why you might choose to roll your own in this manner. In our example here, one of the requirements is offline access, so that does weight the argument – you can't authenticate using Facebook if you're not online. It's also worth considering whether you would want to outsource the authentication of your users to a third party. I'm not saying for a minute that these aren't reliable, secure services, but they are run by companies. If you build your entire application around Facebook authentication and they suddenly withdraw the service for some reason, where would that leave you?

Let's start by creating our IdentityServer, which can just be a standard ASP.NET Core web application:

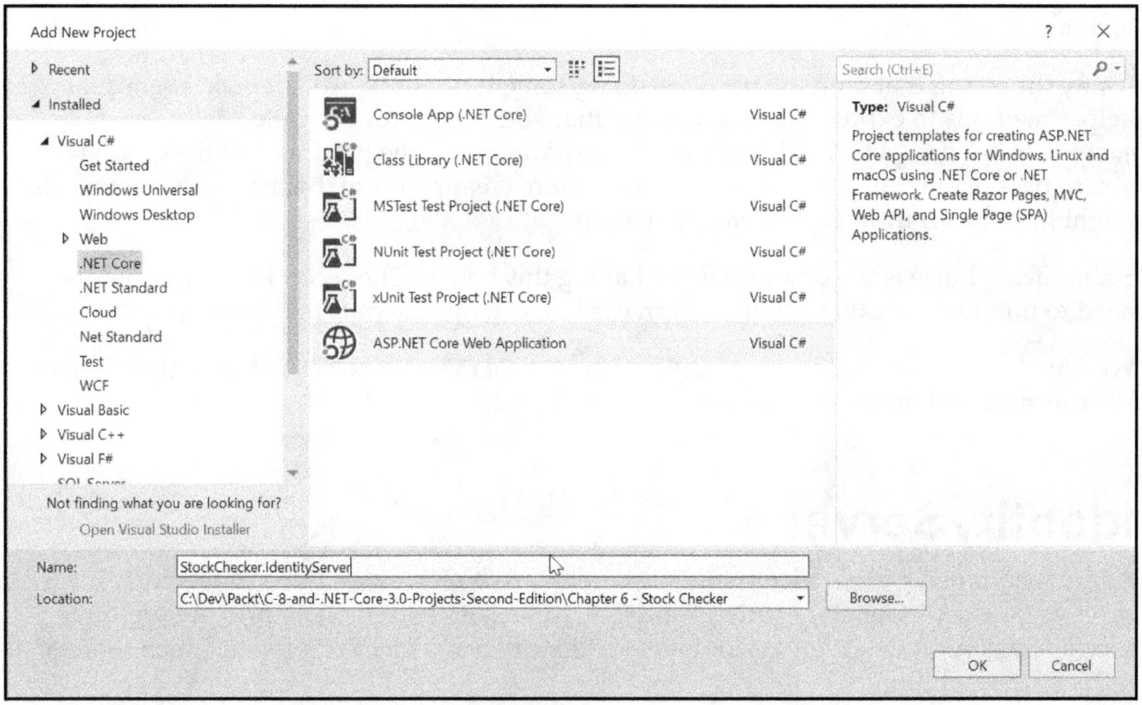

Again, we'll create an empty application so that we can see exactly how this is built up.

All of the instructions in this section relate to the new (IdentityServer) project that you have just created, unless otherwise stated.

In the Package Manager Console, we'll install the `IdentityServer4` package:

```
Install-Package IdentityServer4 -ProjectName StockChecker.IdentityServer
```

If you have decided to call your project something different than mine, then you'll need to change the preceding project name.

In `Startup.cs`, we'll need to add `IdentityServer`:

```
public void ConfigureServices(IServiceCollection services)
{
    services
        .AddIdentityServer()
        .AddDeveloperSigningCredential();
}
```

We're doing two things here: we're adding IdentityServer to the **dependency injection** (**DI**) system and we're adding some temporary credentials.

> We'll revisit this later and add some (more) valid credentials, but this will get us up and running.

Next, we'll need to register IdentityServer with the ASP.NET Core middleware pipeline:

```
public void Configure(IApplicationBuilder app, IHostingEnvironment env)
{
    if (env.IsDevelopment())
    {
        app.UseDeveloperExceptionPage();
    }
    app.UseIdentityServer();
}
```

The last thing that we need to change in order for IdentityServer to run is to tell it what will be requesting information; this can be done in `ConfigureServices` (in `Startup.cs`):

```
public void ConfigureServices(IServiceCollection services)
{
    services
        .AddIdentityServer()
        .AddDeveloperSigningCredential()
        .AddInMemoryClients(new List<Client>())
        .AddInMemoryIdentityResources(new List<IdentityResource>());
}
```

Clearly, this isn't going to let us actually authenticate anything at this stage. Essentially, in order to function correctly, IdentityServer needs to know three things:

- Who needs access (users)
- What they need access to (resources)
- How they will gain access (clients)

IdentityServer provides helper methods, such as `AddInMemoryClients`, as a way to get started. At some stage in the future, additional clients or resources may need to be added, and this could be easily refactored so that the list of each is persisted into a data store.

IdentityServer

As it currently stands, we have an identity server that runs; however, we can run our client without any credentials and use our application. Before we add resources, clients, or users to identity server, the next step is to have it refuse us entry (because we haven't set any of these things up).

Securing the API

In order to secure the API, we need to do just two things (neither of which requires IdentityServer – and one is already done for us!). The first is that we need to tell ASP.NET Core that we want to use authorization. In our startup file, we're already calling `AddControllers`. Because ASP.NET Core is now open source, we can simply look at what this does for us:

```
private static IMvcCoreBuilder AddControllersCore(IServiceCollection
services)
{
    return services
        .AddMvcCore()
        .AddApiExplorer()
        .AddAuthorization()
        .AddCors()
        .AddDataAnnotations()
        .AddFormatterMappings();
}
```

A common practice in many Microsoft products (especially .NET Core products) is to use the **Builder pattern** to allow configuration of the middleware. The premise of this pattern is simply that the method performs an action and then returns a reference to the object that it was called from. This allows for a more human-readable code flow (as shown in the preceding code).

The relevant line here is `AddAuthorization`. The next thing we'll need to do is tell ASP.NET Core what we want to secure. In the controller, add the following decorator:

```
[Authorize]
[Route("api/[controller]")]
[ApiController]
public class StockController : ControllerBase
{
```

Now, if you try to access the API, you'll get an error. Okay; so now we can't access the API at all; let's plug in the IdentityServer code. The principle here is a simple one: we will request a token from our IdentityServer that will allow us to gain access to our API. In our API, we'll install an IdentityServer package:

```
Install-Package IdentityServer4.AccessTokenValidation -ProjectName
StockChecker.Api
```

TIP: Strictly speaking, you can do this part without IdentityServer at all by adding a JWTBearer authentication. However, using IdentityServer does give you certain advantages here and, since we're already using IdentityServer, it doesn't really make sense to start rolling our own for part of the solution.

In our API, we'll need the following code in `ConfigureServices`:

```
public void ConfigureServices(IServiceCollection services)
{
    services.AddControllers();

services.AddAuthentication(IdentityServerAuthenticationDefaults.Authenticat
ionScheme)
        .AddIdentityServerAuthentication(options =>
    {
        // Base-address of our IdentityServer
        // (if you haven't purposely changed it then this is likely
correct)
        options.Authority = "https://localhost:5001";

        // Name of the API resource
        options.ApiName = "StockCheckerApi";
});
```

We'll add authentication into the pipeline:

```
public void Configure(IApplicationBuilder app, IHostingEnvironment env)
{
    if (env.IsDevelopment())
```

```
        {
            app.UseDeveloperExceptionPage();
        }
        app.UseAuthentication();

        app.UseRouting();
        app.UseAuthorization();
        app.UseEndpoints(endpoints =>
        {
            endpoints.MapControllers();
        });
    }
```

Client configuration

I appreciate that the flow of this chapter may seem a little haphazard but, in fact, there is a thought process that's gone into it. We secured the API first, which means we've protected our resource. The next thing we'll do is change the client so that it will obtain the token and correctly call the API (that's this section); obviously, this won't work yet because we haven't changed our IdentityServer. In the next section, we'll change IdentityServer, and we should see everything suddenly spring into life. The reason for doing it in this order is that I often find that it's easier to see how something works if you see it not working first (otherwise, you don't really know what you did right).

In our UWP application, we'll need another NuGet package:

```
Install-Package IdentityModel -ProjectName StockChecker.UWP
```

UWP applications (or desktop applications in general) are not like web applications in two important respects: the first is that, in a web application, you must deal with the fact that a user can simply navigate anywhere in the application. For example, the user could simply change the address bar at the login screen to the following:

```
https://www.mysecuresite.com/products/stock/1
```

As a result, when protecting a web application, you can't rely on the expected flow of the screens; however, in a desktop application, you can.

The second consideration is that the user has the code of the desktop application on their desktop. We're working in .NET, which means that reverse-engineering the code is a very trivial task; however, there are no languages that I'm aware of that can't be reverse-engineered to some extent, given sufficient will.

The takeaway here is that we're fine to expect the users to enter the login screen and keep them there with minimal effort, but we shouldn't store anything at all on the client device that might allow a user to gain access to the server.

Login screen

Let's create a new login screen; I've called my page `LoginView`. The following code goes inside the `<Page>` element:

```
<Grid HorizontalAlignment="Center" VerticalAlignment="Center">
    <Grid.RowDefinitions>
        <RowDefinition Height="Auto" />
        <RowDefinition Height="Auto" />
        <RowDefinition Height="Auto" />
    </Grid.RowDefinitions>
    <Grid.ColumnDefinitions>
        <ColumnDefinition Width="Auto" MinWidth="200" />
        <ColumnDefinition Width="Auto" MinWidth="200" />
    </Grid.ColumnDefinitions>
    <TextBlock Text="Username" Margin="5"
               Grid.Row="0" Grid.Column="0" />
    <TextBlock Text="Password" Margin="5"
               Grid.Row="1" Grid.Column="0" />
    <TextBox Text="{Binding Username, Mode=TwoWay,
UpdateSourceTrigger=PropertyChanged}" Margin="5"
             Grid.Row="0" Grid.Column="1" />
    <PasswordBox Password="{Binding Password, Mode=TwoWay,
UpdateSourceTrigger=PropertyChanged}" Margin="5"
                 Grid.Row="1" Grid.Column="1" />
    <Button Grid.Row="2" Grid.Column="0" Grid.ColumnSpan="2"
            HorizontalAlignment="Center" Margin="5"
            Command="{Binding LoginCommand}">Login</Button>
</Grid>
```

There is quite a lot of code here, but most of it is just syntax (XAML, like it's parent, XML, is quite verbose). As you can see, we're using data binding here, as we did previously. There is a single button on the form (as the user either logs in or closes the application).

At this stage, we have not set up the binding or any functionality, so the view will do nothing. We also need to tell the UWP app to launch into this view instead of the main one that we created earlier in `App.xaml.cs` (in the `OnLaunched` method):

```
if (e.PrelaunchActivated == false)
{
    if (rootFrame.Content == null)
    {
```

```
            // When the navigation stack isn't restored
            // navigate to the first page,
            // configuring the new page by passing required
            // information as a navigation parameter
            rootFrame.Navigate(typeof(LoginView), e.Arguments);
        }
        // Ensure the current window is active
        Window.Current.Activate();
    }
```

We're changing the code here, not adding anything. In fact, the only actual change is the text for `LoginView` (assuming that you named your view the same as me).

Let's create the ViewModel. We'll start with the same boilerplate code that we used for the main view:

```
public class LoginViewModel : INotifyPropertyChanged
{
    public event PropertyChangedEventHandler PropertyChanged;
    private bool UpdateField<T>(ref T field, T value,
            [CallerMemberName] string propertyName = null)
    {
        if (EqualityComparer<T>.Default.Equals(field, value)) return false;
        field = value;
        OnPropertyChanged(propertyName);
        return true;
    }

    public void OnPropertyChanged([CallerMemberName] string propertyName =
null)
    {
        this.PropertyChanged(this, new
PropertyChangedEventArgs(propertyName));
    }
}
```

TIP: If this were a production application, these two classes should inherit from a common base ViewModel. If you choose to extend this application, I would strongly advise that you start there.

The next thing we'll need is some new properties to reflect the username and password:

```
private string _username;

public string Username
{
```

```
        get => _username;
        set
        {
            UpdateField(ref _username, value);
        }
    }

    private string _password;

    public string Password
    {
        get => _password;
        set
        {
            UpdateField(ref _password, value);
        }
    }
```

The last two things we need are the `LoginCommand` wiring up and the data context setting; let's start with `LoginCommand`:

```
    public LoginViewModel()
    {
        LoginCommand = new RelayCommand(() =>
        {
            DoLogin();
        });
    }

    private void DoLogin()
    {
        throw new NotImplementedException();
    }

    public RelayCommand LoginCommand { get; set; }
```

Let's set the data context. Then, we should be able to see the login screen do everything bar actually logging in (inside `LoginView.xaml.cs`):

```
    public LoginView()
    {
        this.InitializeComponent();
        ViewModel = new LoginViewModel();
        DataContext = ViewModel;
    }

    public LoginViewModel ViewModel { get; set; }
```

Running this should show the **Login** screen when you launch, allow you to enter a username and password, and then throw a `Not Implemented` exception when you press the `Login` button. Now, we can call IdentityServer, get our token, and access the API.

Calling IdentityServer

Calling IdentityServer is really just a matter of filling in the command that we created behind the login button. Let's change our command in `LoginViewModel` so that it looks something closer to this:

```
public LoginViewModel(IHttpStockClientHelper httpStockClientHelper)
{
    _httpStockClientHelper = httpStockClientHelper;
    LoginCommand = new RelayCommand(() =>
    {
        DoLogin();
    });
}

private async Task DoLogin()
{
    bool loggedIn = await _httpStockClientHelper.Login(Username, Password);
    if (loggedIn)
    {
        var frame = Window.Current.Content as Frame;
        frame.Navigate(typeof(MainPage), null);
    }
}
```

TIP: We are calling an `async` method from a synchronous one. The effect of this is that the code will not await the result of the operation. Should you decide to extend this application, adding a `RelayCommandAsync` would be a good addition; however, this will serve for our specific purpose.

As you can see, we're now calling a new helper method that doesn't exist just yet and we're passing in the username and password; once we establish that the login was successful, we can navigate to that screen.

TIP: You may notice that, as I write code, a lot of times, I'll refer to methods that are yet to exist and then create them. If you practice **Test-Driven Development** (**TDD**), you start to get used to this method of working. It does have the advantage that you don't end up scaffolding a lot of infrastructure code that you'll never use.

All we need now is to write our helper method to log in. If you use *Ctrl-.* to create the stub, it should create an interface definition for you inside `IHttpClientHelper.cs`:

```
Task<bool> Login(string username, string password);
```

The new method (in `HttpClientHelper`) will look like this:

```
private static string _accessToken;

public async Task<bool> Login(string username, string password)
{
    var disco = await _httpClient.GetDiscoveryDocumentAsync(new
DiscoveryDocumentRequest
    {
        Address = "https://localhost:5001"
    });

    var response = await _httpClient.RequestPasswordTokenAsync(new
PasswordTokenRequest
    {
        Address = disco.TokenEndpoint,
        ClientId = "StockChecker",
        ClientSecret = "secret",
        Scope = "StockCheckerApi",
        UserName = username,
        Password = password
    });

    if (response.IsError)
    {
        // ToDo: Log error
        return false;
    }

    _accessToken = response.AccessToken;
    return true;
}
```

There's quite a lot here, so let's go through it line by line. However, before we do, you might have entered this code and realized that some of these methods (for example, `RequestPasswordTokenAsync`) do not exist on the `HttpClient` object. These are extension methods that are added by the `IdentityModel.Client` library, so make sure you've added a `using` statement for this at the top of your file.

The first thing to notice is that we have a token, which we're holding in the class. Although we're not using it at the minute, we will need that later in order to call the API (which means we will revisit this file shortly).

What we're doing here is, effectively, a three-step process; step one is to get the token endpoint from IdentityServer. The discovery document is a part of the OpenID specification, and is just that: a document that tells you where all the resources for the authentication server can be found; it's always at the same (relative) location, too, so you can go and look at the discovery document for the big identity providers, such as Microsoft, Google, and Twitter; it's always here:

```
https://baseaddress/.well-known/openid-configuration
```

`GetDiscoveryDocumentAsync` gives us a nice wrapper so that we can pull this document apart without parsing the JSON. We've given it the base address – that's it for now. You may find that you need to revisit this and set the `Policy` variable if you choose to extend the program.

The next step is to request a token from the endpoint that we've just been given. In order to do this, we have to provide valid credentials. We won't discuss these settings now as we'll need to return to them inside IdentityServer itself. For now, the important thing to note is that we're passing the username and password.

Finally, if all that works, we're caching the token and returning a flag to indicate success.

Capabilities

UWP applications are distributed as trusted applications. What that means is that anything they do must be clear; that is, you need to tell the application what you need access to and what you need permission for. This is not related to identity permissions, but we need to tell the application that it can access localhost (obviously, only while we're in development), that we can use a certificate, and so on. This is all achieved in the `Package.appxmanifest` file. If you simply double-click on it in Visual Studio, you'll be given a user interface that allows you to select assets, capabilities, declarations, and more; it's beyond the scope of this chapter to discuss everything that is found here, but you will need to add three capabilities:

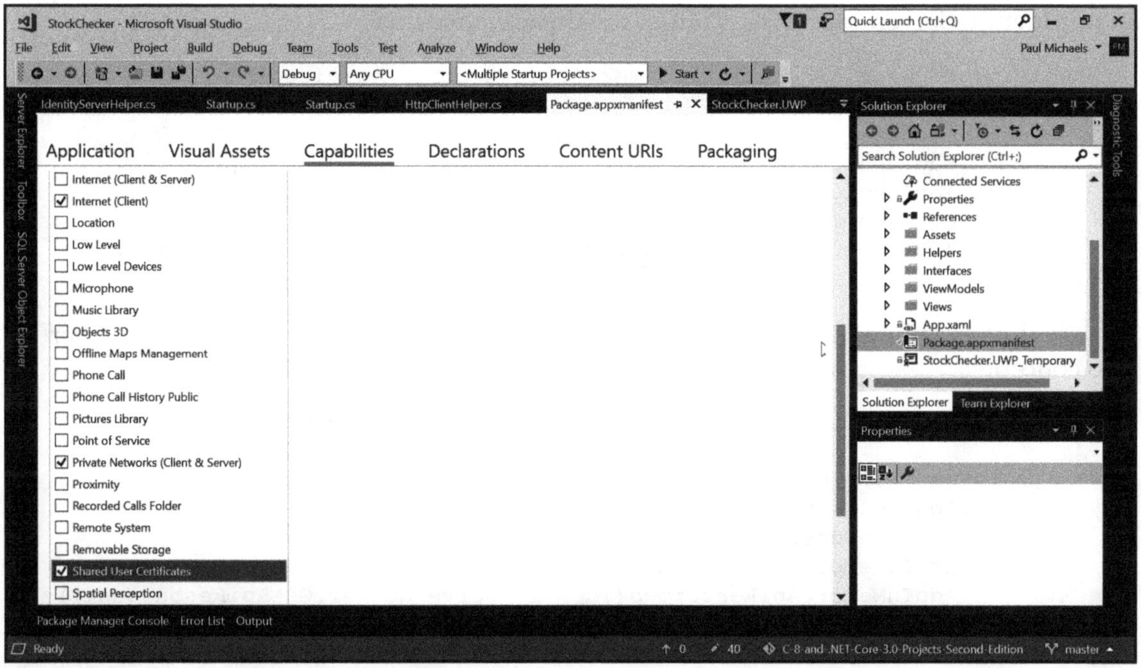

Everything should now be in place for us to correctly configure IdentityServer and have the whole login system spring to life.

Setting up IdentityServer

Setting up IdentityServer is typically the first part of this puzzle; however, I feel it better illustrates how everything works when you slot in the other parts first.

There are three concepts that we need to be aware of to set up IdentityServer, and we've already briefly come across them:

- Users (who can access the resource – in our example, Lucy would be a *user*)
- Resources (the resource that they wish to access – our resource is our *API*)
- Clients (the method by which the user is trying to access the system – in our case, this is our *UWP Application*)

In order to function, IdentityServer needs to be given a valid list of each of these. Typically, especially for users, you would link this up to a database; however, in the interests of simplicity, we'll simply tell the system what each of these is.

In our IdentityServer `services.cs` file, we already have this:

```
public void ConfigureServices(IServiceCollection services)
{
    services
        .AddIdentityServer()
        .AddDeveloperSigningCredential()
        .AddInMemoryClients(new List<Client>())
        .AddInMemoryIdentityResources(new List<IdentityResource>());
}
```

We are already telling IdentityServer about our list of clients, so let's introduce the other two concepts:

```
public void ConfigureServices(IServiceCollection services)
{
    services
        .AddIdentityServer()
        .AddDeveloperSigningCredential()
        .AddInMemoryClients(IdentityServerHelper.GetClients())
        .AddInMemoryApiResources(IdentityServerHelper.GetApiResources())
        .AddTestUsers(IdentityServerHelper.GetUsers())
        .AddInMemoryIdentityResources(new List<IdentityResource>());
}
```

Now, we have introduced our three concepts. As is becoming the standard, we have used some methods (and a class) that don't exist yet.

TIP: The method to add the users is not called `AddTestUsers` by accident. Although what we are doing here will work, it is not very extensible, and defining a data store for the users in the system is something that should be high up on the list of things to do to extend this project.

Our first method will be to add the clients:

```
public static class IdentityServerHelper
{
    internal static IEnumerable<Client> GetClients()
    {
        var clients = new List<Client>
        {
            new Client
            {
                ClientId = "StockChecker",
                AllowedGrantTypes = GrantTypes.ResourceOwnerPassword,
                ClientSecrets =
                {
```

```
                    new Secret("secret".Sha256())
                },

                AllowedScopes = { "StockCheckerApi" }
            }
        };
        return clients;
    }
}
```

Remember that we said a client was the method by which you access the resource. In our case, our client is our UWP application; however, it could be a web application, a console application, or even an application written in Python or Go – it doesn't have to be .NET.

You'll recognize the client ID and the client secret from the client (typically, you would set the server up first and then use that information for the client, not the reverse, like we've done here).

We've set the grant type – we'll return to this later and discuss it in more detail – and we've set the scope. The scope tells IdentityServer what this client is allowed to do. This means that you can have multiple clients logging onto a system and restrict access purely based on the client.

Next, we'll add resources to the same class:

```
internal static IEnumerable<ApiResource> GetApiResources()
{
    var resources = new List<ApiResource>
    {
        new ApiResource("StockCheckerApi", "Stock Checker API")
    };

    return resources;
}
```

The resource here and the scope inside the client are the same concept but with a different angle. This is a comprehensive list of all the resources that the server provides access to, whereas the client specifies which of those resources it needs.

Finally, and in the same class, we'll add the users:

```
internal static List<TestUser> GetUsers()
{
    var users = new List<TestUser>
    {
        new TestUser
        {
```

```
                SubjectId = "1",
                Username = "Lucy",
                Password = "password123"
            },
            new TestUser
            {
                SubjectId = "2",
                Username = "Morris",
                Password = "password123"
            },
            new TestUser
            {
                SubjectId = "3",
                Username = "Graham",
                Password = "password123"
            }
        };

        return users;
    }
```

At the start of this chapter, we gave a scenario where the company had four separate people they needed to consider and, as you can see, there are three users. If you go back, you'll see it's actually Sam that's missing. Sam doesn't work for the company and is a customer and, as a result, doesn't need access to the system. She is, however, an important concept; that is, a user that indirectly interacts with the system but does not need access.

> TIP: If you are thinking of extending this project, then you might consider this: as a customer, Sam may like to access a web portal, but not the UWP application. As a result, in addition to a proper user store, as we mentioned earlier, you would need to create a website and add that as a client.

Okay, so that's our setup complete. If you run all three projects now, you should be able to enter the credentials for Lucy (her password is `password123`) and have them log in.

You should also be able to see them being rejected from logging in if, for example, you tried a password of `password1`.

Calling the API

You can now log in; however, should you attempt to access any of the resources, you'll find that the system throws an exception. The reason is that we secured the API, which means that when we call the API, we need to pass a token to prove we are who we say we are.

Inside `HttpClientHelper.cs`, we can simply add a call to a method that will pass the bearer token:

```
public async Task<int> GetQuantityAsync(int productId)
{
    string path = $"api/stock/{productId}";
    _httpClient.SetBearerToken(_accessToken);
    string quantityString = await _httpClient.GetStringAsync(path);
    return int.Parse(quantityString);
}
```

Finally, we can add a similar line for the `update` method, and our API should work securely:

```
public async Task UpdateQuantityAsync(int productId, int newQuantity)
{
    string path = $"api/stock/{productId}";
    _httpClient.SetBearerToken(_accessToken);
    var httpContent = new StringContent(newQuantity.ToString());
    httpContent.Headers.ContentType = new
MediaTypeHeaderValue("application/json");

    await _httpClient.PutAsync(path, httpContent);
}
```

So, our identity system now validates that users are valid in our system. We still have an issue, though: our users can access all the features of the system. We need to lock that down, and we will, but let's tidy up a couple of loose ends first.

Grant types

The first loose end we have is the grant type. We're not going to change this, but we are going to investigate why we should (or at least why we should consider changing it). The grant type that we're using is Resource Owner Password; what this gives us is the ability to capture a user's username and password and then send that off to IdentityServer, along with a key. We then get back a token, and we can use that token to communicate with our resource. In our case, the resource is an API. This is a secure system *to an extent*.

Let's put our black hats on and have a think about how we might compromise such a system. Remember that we're dealing with desktop software, and in the case of .NET, as we've previously stated, it is extremely easy to reverse-engineer a .NET assembly or executable. We're storing the secret inside the compiled code, so an attacker could access the secret. Granted, this doesn't give access to anything without a username and password.

Further issues with this grant type are that, should we introduce a second access point (say we decided to develop a web portal for Sam the builder – see the preceding section if you've forgotten who she is), we would need to create another screen to accept the username and password.

So, what's the solution?

Well, one way around this is to host a web page inside the desktop application. That way, even though we're on the desktop, the code that's dealing with the security is hosted on the server. Windows 10 provides a **web authentication broker** for this purpose.

> When dealing with security, it should always be remembered that there is no such thing as *totally secure*. There are always ways to get into a system – no matter how locked down you make it, it is always possible to get in: you should think of it a little like securing your house. Different houses have different levels of security: your house probably has a door – just closing your door offers more security than leaving it wide open; locking the door gives more security still; having multiple locks more security still; and a reinforced door even more. However, banks have vaults, with dozens of locks and keys and security guards, alarms, and so forth, and yet if I told you someone had robbed a bank, you wouldn't think of it as a unique thing to happen.

Security, therefore, is a trade-off: how valuable is what you're trying to protect (what's the worst thing that could happen if your system was compromised?), how usable is the system if you implement that protection, and how costly is it to add that protection?

In our case, since we have a very specific and limited requirement, we'll leave our grant type as is. However, this is an excellent point for extension, should you wish to improve this system.

Creating and using a valid key

The last loose end is our key. We're currently using a development key. This works great while we're writing the software, but we obviously need to generate a real key before shipping the system. While generating a production certificate falls outside the scope of this chapter, we'll quickly cover how we can generate and use a self-signed certificate.

> This solution is not meant for production. Before deploying to production, you should get a certificate from a certificate provider. There are several such providers and some (at least one that I'm aware of) provide a free certificate.

In order to produce our certificate, let's generate it. Start by launching Windows PowerShell (ensure to do this as administrator) and enter the following command:

```
> New-SelfSignedCertificate -Subject "CN=testcert" -KeySpec "Signature" -
CertStoreLocation "Cert:\CurrentUser\My"
```

This will generate a personal certificate in your certificate store. Once it's been generated, it will give you a `Thumbprint` – make a note of that value as you'll need it in a few minutes:

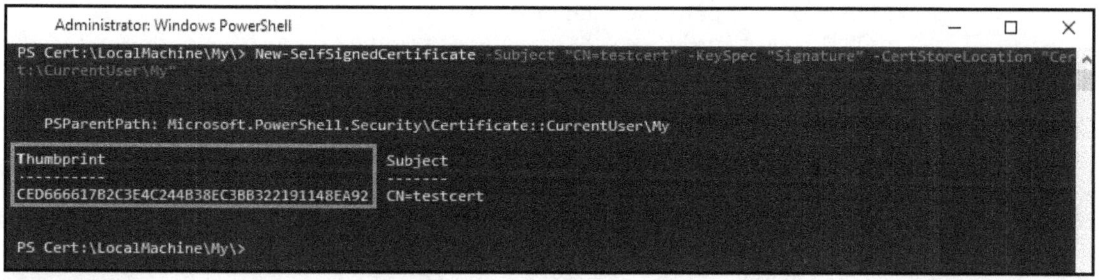

If you wish to view this, then you can do so with ease. If you're running Windows 10, press the Windows key and type the following:

```
mmc.exe
```

This should bring up the management console. Here, you can select **Personal** store and see all of your certificates:

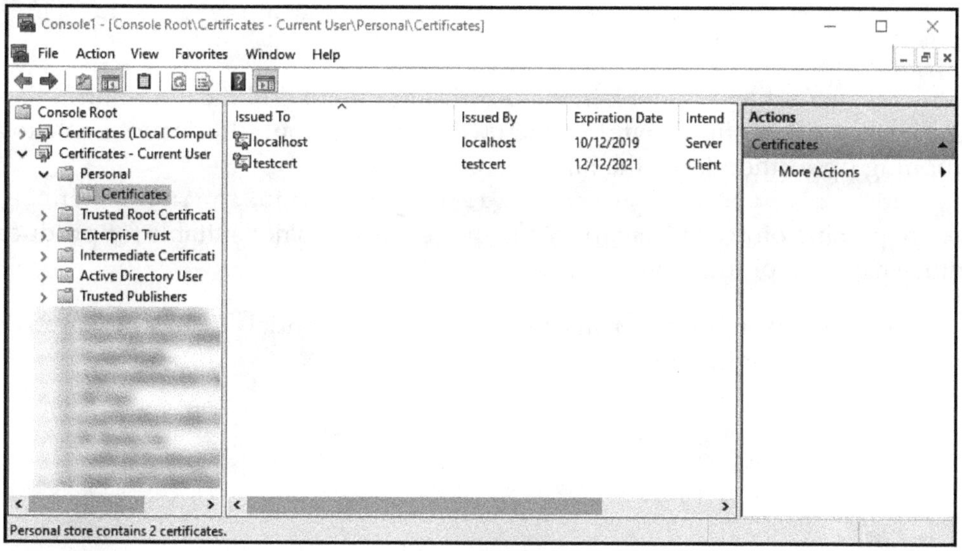

We need to make a slight change to the code. In the IdentityServer `startup.cs` file, change the `ConfigureServices` method so that it looks like this:

```
public void ConfigureServices(IServiceCollection services)
{
    X509Certificate2 x509Certificate2 = null;
    using (var certStore = new X509Store(StoreName.My,
StoreLocation.CurrentUser))
    {
        certStore.Open(OpenFlags.ReadOnly);
        var certCollection = certStore.Certificates.Find(
        X509FindType.FindByThumbprint,
        "CED666617B2C3E4C244B38EC3BB322191148EA92", // Thumbprint
        false);

        if (certCollection.Count == 0)
            throw new Exception("No certificate found");

        x509Certificate2 = certCollection[0];
    }

    services
        .AddIdentityServer()
        //.AddDeveloperSigningCredential()
        .AddSigningCredential(cert)
        .AddInMemoryClients(IdentityServerHelper.GetClients())
        .AddInMemoryApiResources(IdentityServerHelper.GetApiResources())
        .AddTestUsers(IdentityServerHelper.GetUsers())
        .AddInMemoryIdentityResources(new List<IdentityResource>());
}
```

As you can see, we're having a look in the certificate store to find the thumbprint that we noted earlier. If we don't find anything, then we're crashing out (this is preferable to an error cropping up further down the line). Finally, we're changing `AddDeveloperSigningCredential` to plain old `AddSigningCredential`, which we're passing our certificate to. While the certificate is not suitable for production, this is much closer to production code.

Now, we'll have a look at how we can check the user's credentials to allow them to access different parts of the application.

Authorization

Authorization is the policy that you apply to a user *after* they have been authenticated. That is, we now know who the user is: at least, we know that they have a valid username and password and that they are using an approved client. The next stage is to ensure that each user only has access to the correct parts of the system.

> Some of these permissions may not be completely realistic, but they do have the advantage of covering the various possibilities. A quick note on PolicyServer: PolicyServer (found here: `https://policyserver.io/`) is a framework, written by the same people that created IdentityServer. It offers very similar functionality. If you are intending to extend this application, then I would strongly encourage you to consider using it. It is an open source and commercial offering.

There are three parts to this change: changing the users to have the relevant permissions, changing the infrastructure to pass this through, and changing the client to display the correct controls.

Users and roles

Essentially, in order to make our app work for our different users, we will introduce the concept of *roles*. This is a very common concept when dealing with permissions; it means that, instead of creating a code path that identifies the username "Graham" and then enables all features, we can give each user a role and give permissions based on that.

I see this as the stick house of authorization (this is a reference to a children's story about three little pigs, who tried to protect themselves from a wolf by building different types of houses). The straw house (that is, the least extensible) is to explicitly check for a specific user each time (for example, checking that the user name is Graham). The brick house (that is, the most extensible) is a further abstraction, where you introduce the concept of a policy; each role may have one or more policies, and it is the policy that governs what can be accessed.

Let's start there and give each user a role. In `IdentityServerHelper.cs`, we currently have a method entitled `GetUsers`; we'll add the role here:

```
internal static List<TestUser> GetUsers()
{
    var users = new List<TestUser>
    {
        new TestUser
```

```
            {
                SubjectId = "1",
                Username = "Lucy",
                Password = "password123",
                Claims = new List<Claim>()
                {
                    new Claim(JwtClaimTypes.Role, "Sales")
                }
            },
            new TestUser
            {
                SubjectId = "2",
                Username = "Morris",
                Password = "password123",
                Claims = new List<Claim>()
                {
                    new Claim(JwtClaimTypes.Role, "Maintenance")
                }
            },
            new TestUser
            {
                SubjectId = "3",
                Username = "Graham",
                Password = "password123",
                Claims = new List<Claim>()
                {
                    new Claim(JwtClaimTypes.Role, "Administrator")
                }
            }
        };
        return users;
    }
```

There's a lot of code here, but as you can see, there's only five or six lines of new code: we are just allocating a new set of claims to the user, and each has a particular role.

> TIP: As we mentioned earlier, this is not an ideal way to store the users, but it does mean that as we make changes such as this, it's obvious what we've changed. If these users were held in a database, then the change would be obscured.

Unfortunately, we can't just allocate new information to the user and have it immediately propagate through: there are a number of supporting changes that we require.

IdentityServer

The next stop is our client. We need to tell IdentityServer that the client is allowed to access an additional resource; inside the `IdentityServerHelper.cs` file, we will change the `GetClients` method so that it looks like this:

```
internal static IEnumerable<Client> GetClients()
{
    var clients = new List<Client>
    {
        new Client
        {
            ClientId = "StockChecker",
            AllowedGrantTypes = GrantTypes.ResourceOwnerPassword,
            ClientSecrets =
            {
                new Secret("secret".Sha256())
            },
            AllowedScopes =
            {
                "StockCheckerApi",
                "roles",
                IdentityServerConstants.StandardScopes.OpenId
            }
        }
    };
    return clients;
}
```

Again, we've only added two new lines of code here; we've specified that we *can* return `OpenId` and a new resource called `roles`.

`OpenId` is a standardized method of dealing with identification. In order to return anything at all about the user, we need to specify this.

Now that we've said we can return something called `roles`, let's define what this is; this takes the form of a new helper method in this file (we'll call it in the next section):

```
internal static IEnumerable<IdentityResource> GetIdentityResources()
{
    return new List<IdentityResource>
    {
        new IdentityResource
        {
            Name = "roles",
```

```
                UserClaims = new List<string> { JwtClaimTypes.Role }
            },
            new IdentityResources.OpenId()
        };
    }
```

Up until now, we've only seen an `ApiResource`; however, here, we are declaring that we'll return a resource related to the identity. In fact, we're returning two: `OpenId` and our new `roles` resource.

Let's quickly revisit the `startup.cs` file in `IdentityServer`; the `ConfigureServices` method needs to be changed, as follows:

```
services
    .AddIdentityServer()
    //.AddDeveloperSigningCredential()
    .AddSigningCredential(x509Certificate2)
    .AddInMemoryClients(IdentityServerHelper.GetClients())
    .AddInMemoryApiResources(IdentityServerHelper.GetApiResources())
    .AddTestUsers(IdentityServerHelper.GetUsers())
.AddInMemoryIdentityResources(IdentityServerHelper.GetIdentityResources());
}
```

The entire method is not included here, but we have only changed one line: `AddInMemoryIdentityResources()` now has our new helper method passed into it.

That's all there is to it. Now, let's have a look at what client-side changes (by far the biggest part of this change) are needed.

Client

Here, we'll update the client so that users can only see the functions that are relevant to them.

> TIP: It's worth noting that the changes we're making here do not prevent a user from manually calling the API and performing functions that are not available on the screen. Again, this project is a starting point, and when extending it, you should think carefully about what you are protecting and who you are protecting it from.

Within the client changes, there are three stages: the logic changes to actually allow the users to see and change the controls they have access to, the changes to the server call to bring back the additional data, and finally, the need to retrieve some additional information from the server and pass that through to the relevant ViewModel. Let's start with the logic changes.

Logic changes and UI changes

Let's start with the `MainPage.xaml` file of our UWP application. At present, there is only one change here (we will have a second that we'll come back to later). What we need to do is make the quantity not visible when the user doesn't have access to view it. Locate the `TextBox` quantity within the XAML:

```
<TextBox Grid.Row="1" Grid.Column="1" Text="{Binding Quantity, Mode=TwoWay,
UpdateSourceTrigger=PropertyChanged}" Visibility="{Binding CanViewQuantity,
Converter={StaticResource BooleanToVisibilityConverter}}"/>
```

Who would have thought that such a small amount of code would raise so many questions? However, the answer is simple: we don't have any of the new things referenced here yet – they're coming. However, we do need to quickly discuss exactly what is being bound to here.

One of the main advantages of using data binding is that you separate your business logic (in MVVM terms, your ViewModel) from your view. Here, we are binding to a Boolean property called `CanViewQuantity`; however, we want to bind that to the `Visible` property of our control. We could have `CanViewQuantity` return an enumerated `Visibility` object (that the view would understand directly), which would work; however, we would never be able to use the model outside of a Windows environment. Consequently, we need to create a converter.

> In fact, if you use the new x:Bind syntax, `BooleanToVisibility` conversion is now baked into the system; this is, however, only available in Windows 10 since release 1607. Check out the following link for further details: `https://docs.microsoft.com/en-us/windows/uwp/xaml-platform/x-bind-markup-extension`.

Let's do so now by creating a new file and naming it `BooleanToVisibilityConverter`:

```
class BooleanToVisibilityConverter : IValueConverter
{
    public object Convert(object value, Type targetType, object parameter,
string language)
    {
```

```
        return (bool)value ? Visibility.Visible : Visibility.Collapsed;
    }

    public object ConvertBack(object value, Type targetType, object
parameter, string language)
    {
        throw new NotImplementedException();
    }
}
```

This, along with other useful extensions, tools, and controls can also be found in the Windows Community Toolkit: `https://docs.microsoft.com/en-gb/windows/communitytoolkit/`.

This code file doesn't really warrant much explanation; we're just returning `Visible` where the Boolean value is true. It's worth bearing in mind that the conversion can be as complex as you need it to be, although you should refrain from putting business logic in here: it should always be a way to bind a primitive type to a complex view concept (such as `true` to `visible`).

Let's return to `MainPage.Xaml` briefly. Before we move on, we will need to declare that we wish to use a converter; the declaration section should look similar to this:

```
<Page
    x:Class="StockChecker.UWP.MainPage"
    xmlns="http://schemas.microsoft.com/winfx/2006/xaml/presentation"
    xmlns:x="http://schemas.microsoft.com/winfx/2006/xaml"
    xmlns:local="using:StockChecker.UWP"
    xmlns:d="http://schemas.microsoft.com/expression/blend/2008"
    xmlns:mc="http://schemas.openxmlformats.org/markup-compatibility/2006"
    mc:Ignorable="d"
    Background="{ThemeResource ApplicationPageBackgroundThemeBrush}"
    xmlns:converters="using:StockChecker.UWP.Converters">
    <Page.Resources>
        <converters:BooleanToVisibilityConverter
x:Key="BooleanToVisibilityConverter" />
    </Page.Resources>
```

We've added two things here: an XML namespace reference (`xmlns`) to include the `converters` file and the specific converter that we wish to use as a resource.

We're now done with the XAML, so let's have a look at what we'll need to change in the ViewModel. `MainPageViewModel` needs three new properties: the user's role, whether the user should be able to view the quantity, and whether the user should be able to update the quantity. Let's add the local variables first:

```
private bool _canViewQuantity;
private bool _canUpdateQuantity;
private string _userRole;
```

`CanViewQuantity` and `CanUpdateQuantity` are very simple properties:

```
public bool CanUpdateQuantity
{
    get => _canUpdateQuantity;
    set
    {
        UpdateField(ref _canUpdateQuantity, value);
    }
}

public bool CanViewQuantity
{
    get => _canViewQuantity;
    set
    {
        UpdateField(ref _canViewQuantity, value);
    }
}
```

However, in `UserRole`, we'll decide what the user can do:

```
public string UserRole
{
    get => _userRole;
    set
    {
        if (UpdateField(ref _userRole, value))
        {
            CanViewQuantity = UserRole == "Administrator" || UserRole ==
"Sales";
            CanUpdateQuantity = UserRole == "Administrator" || UserRole ==
"Maintenance";
        }
    }
}
```

TIP

This is a very simple example; should you wish to make it more complex, I would strongly recommend that you extract this logic into a separate class or even a separate library that is responsible for permissions. One possible way to address this is to use decorators.

We have just one change left in the ViewModel, and that is to ensure that the **Update Quantity** button is only enabled for those with permission. The constructor should be changed like so:

```
public MainPageViewModel(IHttpStockClientHelper httpClientHelper)
{
    _httpClientHelper = httpClientHelper;
    UpdateQuantity = new RelayCommand(async () =>
    {
        await _httpClientHelper.UpdateQuantityAsync(ProductId, Quantity);
        await RefreshQuantity();
    },
    () => Quantity != _originalQuantity && CanUpdateQuantity);
}
```

All we've done here is add a single additional check so that the command (and therefore the button) is only enabled when `CanUpdateQuantity` is true.

Next, we'll change the login process to get additional information and pass it into the ViewModel.

Login and navigation changes

The **Login** view itself doesn't need to change; however, we will need to change the **Login** ViewModel so that we can retrieve the data related to the user. In `LoginViewModel.cs`, we'll change the `DoLogin()` method, as follows:

```
private async Task DoLogin()
{
    bool loggedIn = await _httpStockClientHelper.Login(Username, Password);
    if (loggedIn)
    {
        string userRole = await _httpStockClientHelper.GetUserRole();
        var frame = Window.Current.Content as Frame;
        frame.Navigate(typeof(MainPage), userRole);
    }
}
```

We've done two things here: first, we've made a call to a new method on the helper class (the method itself to follow soon), and secondly, we've passed that information into `MainPage`. The second part of this change is in the `MainPage` code behind (`MainPage.xaml.cs`), where we will add a new method:

```
protected override void OnNavigatedTo(NavigationEventArgs e)
{
    base.OnNavigatedTo(e);
    var viewModel = DataContext as MainPageViewModel;
    viewModel.UserRole = e.Parameter.ToString();
}
```

In the constructor, we set the data context of the view to be the ViewModel. As a result, we can simply cast the data context back to a ViewModel here.

> TIP
> Having too much code in the code is usually an indication that the project doesn't have a good base architecture and that the business logic and UI are too tightly coupled. As you can see here, we are coupling the two. If you must breach their separation, then referencing the ViewModel from the view is the better approach.

That concludes the changes we need to make to the logic and navigation. Our last change is to the server calls.

Server calls

The most obvious change here is that we need a new method. We referenced it earlier, and so the code won't compile as it is currently. If you select the method call that is unrecognized and use *Ctrl-.*, you should see that the following method definition has been created in the interface (or you could simply copy it from here into `IHttpClientHelper.cs`):

```
Task<string> GetUserRole();
```

The implementation for this new method is in `HttpClientHelper.cs` and needs to look like this:

```
public async Task<string> GetUserRole()
{
    var userInfo = await _httpClient.GetUserInfoAsync(new UserInfoRequest()
    {
        Address = _discoveryResponse.UserInfoEndpoint,
        Token = _accessToken
    });
```

```
        string role = userInfo.Claims.First(a => a.Type ==
JwtClaimTypes.Role).Value;
        return role;
    }
```

`GetUserInfoAsync()` is an extension method from the IdentityServer 4 libraries. Essentially, it allows you to get some information about the authenticated user. This call is why we need to allow `OpenId`.

This will return, in addition to information about the user, any *claims* they have, which is our role definition.

> TIP: It's worth bearing in mind that information about a user should be *about that user*. For example, a user's age, gender, hair color, and role are all examples of information about the user, whereas whether or not the user has access to update the quantity field is most emphatically not information about the user; it is a logical decision based on that information.

Before we finish, we just need to make a couple more small changes to this same file. First, we'll need to change the `Login` method:

```
public async Task<bool> Login(string username, string password)
{
    _discoveryResponse = await _httpClient.GetDiscoveryDocumentAsync(new
DiscoveryDocumentRequest
    {
        Address = "https://localhost:5001",
        Policy =
        {
            ValidateIssuerName = false,
        }
    });

    var response = await _httpClient.RequestPasswordTokenAsync(new
PasswordTokenRequest
    {
        Address = _discoveryResponse.TokenEndpoint,
        ClientId = "StockChecker",
        ClientSecret = "secret",
        Scope = "openid roles StockCheckerApi",
        UserName = username,
        Password = password
    });

    if (response.IsError)
    {
```

```
            // ToDo: Log error
            return false;
        }

        _accessToken = response.AccessToken;
        return true;
    }
```

In fact, there are only really two changes here. The first is in the scope – we're declaring that we'd like to return information about the user and the roles. The second is that we've renamed the discovery response variable. In fact, we're going to give that variable class-level scope:

```
static DiscoveryResponse _discoveryResponse;
```

This is just so that we can hang onto the information after we've made the initial discovery call.

And that's it. Now, if you run the application, you should find that everything works as expected... with one tiny exception.

How to update the quantity when you can't see it

It turns out that we have a slight glitch in the logic here: Morris, our caretaker, needs to be able to update the stock, but not view the current level. However, our program hides the stock figure for him and so he can't update it. In order to get around this, we'll need to add some additional commands and buttons. Essentially, what we want Morris to be able to do is use an item of stock, so a decrease stock button would be ideal; let's add the button to `MainPage.xaml` now (we'll put it just underneath the `Update Quantity` button):

```
        <Button Command="{Binding UpdateQuantity}"
             Grid.Row="2" Grid.Column="0">
            <TextBlock Text="Update Quantity" />
        </Button>
        <Button Command="{Binding DecreaseQuantity}"
             Grid.Row="2" Grid.Column="1">
            <TextBlock Text="Decrease Quantity" />
        </Button>
    </Grid>
```

We can add this new command to our ViewModel (`MainViewModel.cs`):

```
public RelayCommand DecreaseQuantity { get; set; }
```

Finally, let's create the logic for the new command in the constructor, which should now look like this:

```
public MainPageViewModel(IHttpStockClientHelper httpClientHelper)
{
    _httpClientHelper = httpClientHelper;
    UpdateQuantity = new RelayCommand(async () =>
    {
        await _httpClientHelper.UpdateQuantityAsync(
            ProductId, Quantity);
        await RefreshQuantity();
    },
    () => Quantity != _originalQuantity && CanUpdateQuantity);

    DecreaseQuantity = new RelayCommand(async () =>
    {
        await _httpClientHelper.UpdateQuantityAsync(
            ProductId, Quantity - 1);
        await RefreshQuantity();
    },
    () => Quantity > 0 && CanUpdateQuantity);
}
```

Okay, so what are we doing here? In fact, it's almost the same as the update quantity; we're simply telling it that we wish to reduce the quantity by one, and in `CanExecute`, we're checking that we have at least one item left. The very final thing we need to do is force the app to refresh `CanExecute` on `RefreshQuantity`:

```
private async Task RefreshQuantity()
{
    Quantity = await _httpClientHelper.GetQuantityAsync(ProductId);
    _originalQuantity = Quantity;
    UpdateQuantity.RaiseCanExecuteChanged();
    DecreaseQuantity.RaiseCanExecuteChanged();
}
```

Again, this is just a single extra line to ensure that we can only decrease the quantity where there is a quantity to decrease:

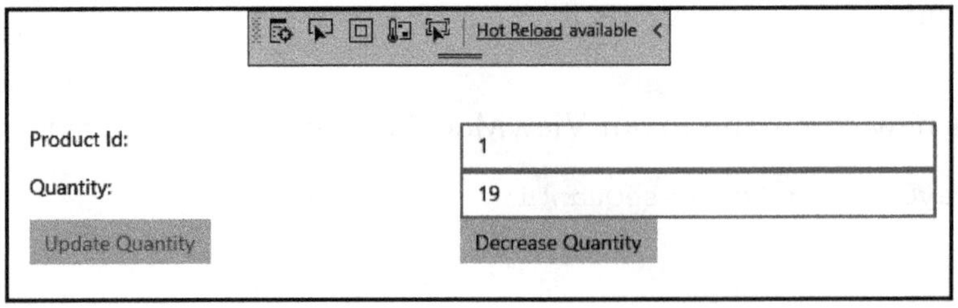

Now that we have completed the project, let's have a look back at what we've covered here.

Summary

That was a mammoth ride. We set up a functional application for our small company, we secured access using IdentityServer 4, and we implemented permissions using roles.

I've said it a few times in this chapter, but just to conclude: when it comes to identity, and indeed security in general, there is no one right answer. IdentityServer makes sense in this case because we used an application and API owned and maintained by the company, we needed offline access, and we were supporting a desktop application. If you change just one of those parameters, it might make sense to use Google OAuth or Azure B2C.

To reiterate something else that I've also stated several times: security of any kind isn't an absolute. Your system might be very secure as it may use encrypted traffic and firewalls. However, you may have put your application through penetration testing and it came out with not a scratch on it, and then one of your staff may share their password with somebody. Suddenly, you might as well have not bothered with any of that.

In the next chapter, we will look at creating a Windows service using .NET Core 3. We will create an application that will back up photos on your PC to an Azure Storage account.

Suggested improvements

Should you wish to pick this application up and improve it, I have a few suggestions for where to start (if you've been paying close attention, you may have noticed some of these along the way):

1. Change the credentials flow to implicit. To do this, you'll need to host a web view inside the desktop application and create the login website.
2. Add a user store. Our users are clearly not suitable for production; that is, unless we can categorically guarantee that they will never employ or lose any staff. Also, storing a password in plain text in code is clearly never a good idea (even if it is on the server).

3. Do any of the following:
    - Take the XAML from the UWP application and convert it into `Xamarin.Forms`, then compile and release an Android version.
    - Take common areas of code and combine them to create a mini framework for your application.
    - Implement an MVVM framework. Most MVVM frameworks now also support cross-compiling to some extent.
4. Link the stock system to a frontend website that allows users to log on and purchase items that are in stock.
5. Create a stock item image; you could store these images in Azure Storage. In fact, our next chapter is all about that.

Further reading

At the time of writing this book, the IdentityServer documentation was in a state of flux. However, it is still very useful and contains many examples. It can be found here: `docs.identityserver.io`.

The OpenID Specification can be found here: `https://openid.net/developers/specs/`.

The OAuth 2 specification can be found here: `https://oauth.net/2/`.

7
Building a Photo Storage App Using a Windows Service and Azure Storage

Computing has gone through some interesting changes since 1997 when I started my first job, and even more since the early 1980s when I got my first computer (a Spectrum ZX81). On the Spectrum, if you wanted to save some information, you recorded it on a cassette tape; a typical game would take around 5 to 10 minutes to load from the tape. Of course, at the time, more sophisticated computers were in use, but much of the heavy storage was actually still done on tape. Even after I got my first PC, I remember buying a tape drive for it so that I could store up to a gigabyte of information (a gigabyte of information was a lot of data back then).

These days, your phone has far more storage than that, and it's still not enough: you go on holiday and maybe take 100 pictures; long gone are the days of taking two 24 exposure reels on holiday with you. Of course, after a while, you realize that these hundreds and hundreds of high-resolution pictures of yourself eating breakfast are filling up your phone.

Some phone manufacturers offer additional storage capacity for under £1 per month. This certainly doesn't seem a lot, considering that this provides a backup for all of your images; however, it's probably more than you would pay if you were to put your images in the cloud yourself.

That's exactly what we intend to do in this chapter, where we'll write a Windows Service to monitor a directory on your computer, upload anything in it to the Azure Cloud, and then remove it from the source directory if it's over a certain age. That way, you can keep your latest pictures with you and archive the rest.

The following topics will be covered in this chapter:

- Creating a Windows Service using .NET Core 3
- Installing and using the Windows Compatibility Pack
- Uploading files to Azure Blob Storage

Technical requirements

The Azure Storage Explorer can be found here: `https://azure.microsoft.com/en-gb/features/storage-explorer/`. This is an open source piece of software maintained by Microsoft; the GitHub repository for it can be found here: `https://github.com/Microsoft/AzureStorageExplorer`.

> TIP: This isn't a necessity, but it would greatly help with the development and testing stages.

Windows Services and Windows Compatibility Pack

In this project, we'll be using the Windows Compatibility Pack in order to create a Windows Service. We'll discuss why later, but, in this section, I wanted to quickly discuss what these things were.

Windows Services

Most operating systems have the equivalent of a Windows Service. Essentially, this is an application that runs all the time and does something in the background. If you have a quick look at the services currently running on your machine, you'll see that there are many and that they're varied; to do so, in Windows 10, simply press the start button and type `Services`. Then, select the top match. You should be presented with the following application:

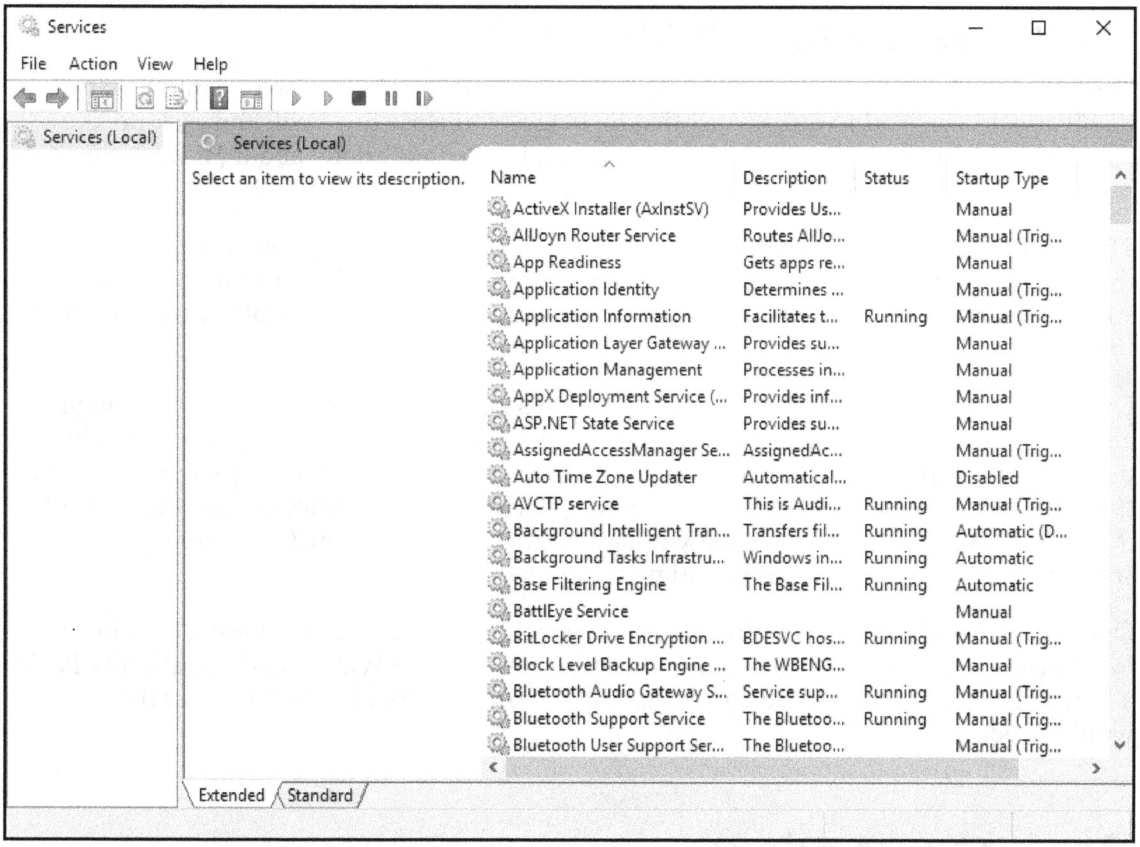

It's very likely that you'll have a different set of services, but the principle is the same. These applications all run in the background and do something. Every single one of these services that are marked as running is consuming resources from your computer, so, when you install a service, you should consider whether you need it to be running all the time (otherwise, simply disable it).

> Disabling some Windows Services can cause your machine to behave differently, or even stop some functionality, so be careful if you intend to disable services that were installed when you arrived.

If we're *writing* a service, this is true twice over: people will notice very quickly if it is your application that has slowed their machine down, so performance is a huge consideration here.

Windows Compatibility Pack

The history behind .NET Core is an interesting one and one that I won't go into exhaustive detail about here (had to quickly get that in, before you close this book and pick up something by Stephen King!). I would, however, like to talk briefly about (at least one of the reasons) why Microsoft chose to create .NET Core.

The .NET Framework has been around since 2002, and you can still run an application now that was written then. At the time of writing, this means that the .NET Framework needs to support nearly 20 years of assumptions and code, based on the technical landscape *at that time*.

Due to this, Microsoft found themselves stuck in a position where they couldn't change anything fundamental because they couldn't risk breaking the thousands, or even millions, of applications that were out there, untouched, but still running. The only solution, therefore, was to create a brand new framework with no dependency on the original: enter .NET Core. However, the price that you pay for that is that the new framework doesn't support all the functionality of the original framework.

One such example was, ironically, Windows-specific functionality (including creating a Windows Service). However, in 2017, Microsoft released the Windows Compatibility Pack: a NuGet package that provided access to most of the functionality of Windows that you would need.

Project overview

Essentially, our project is going to center around a Windows Service that will monitor a given folder on the machine's hard drive. Once a file has been detected, we'll read some of the properties, such as size, date, and name, and we'll do a quick search in the Azure cloud; if it doesn't exist, we'll upload it. Once we're sure it's safely in the cloud, we'll check the date, and anything over a certain age will be removed from the hard drive.

Configuring Azure Storage

Setting up an Azure Storage account is quite a straightforward process; you'll need to start by signing in to Azure. If you don't have an account, then you can create one here: `https://azure.microsoft.com/`. Once you've signed up, visit `https://portal.azure.com`.

Most cloud providers have a storage model and it wouldn't be difficult to use an alternate provider; however, you would need to change some of the code that interfaces with Azure.

Start by selecting the storage blade from the Azure portal:

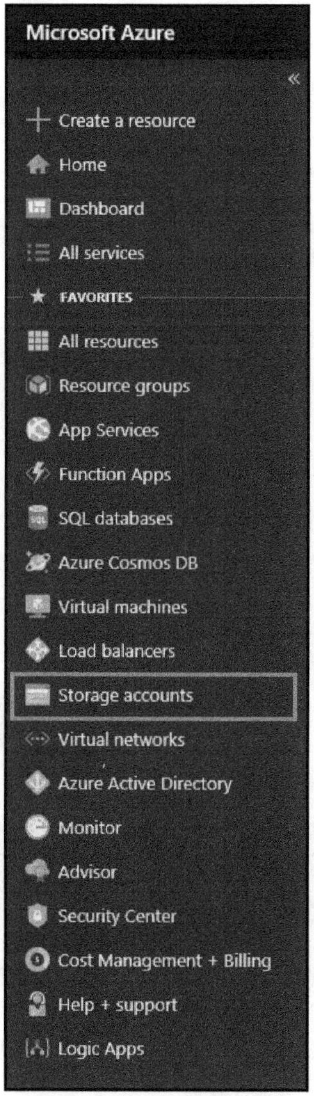

Alternatively, you could just search for `Storage`. Once the blade appears, select **Add** and fill in the details for your new account:

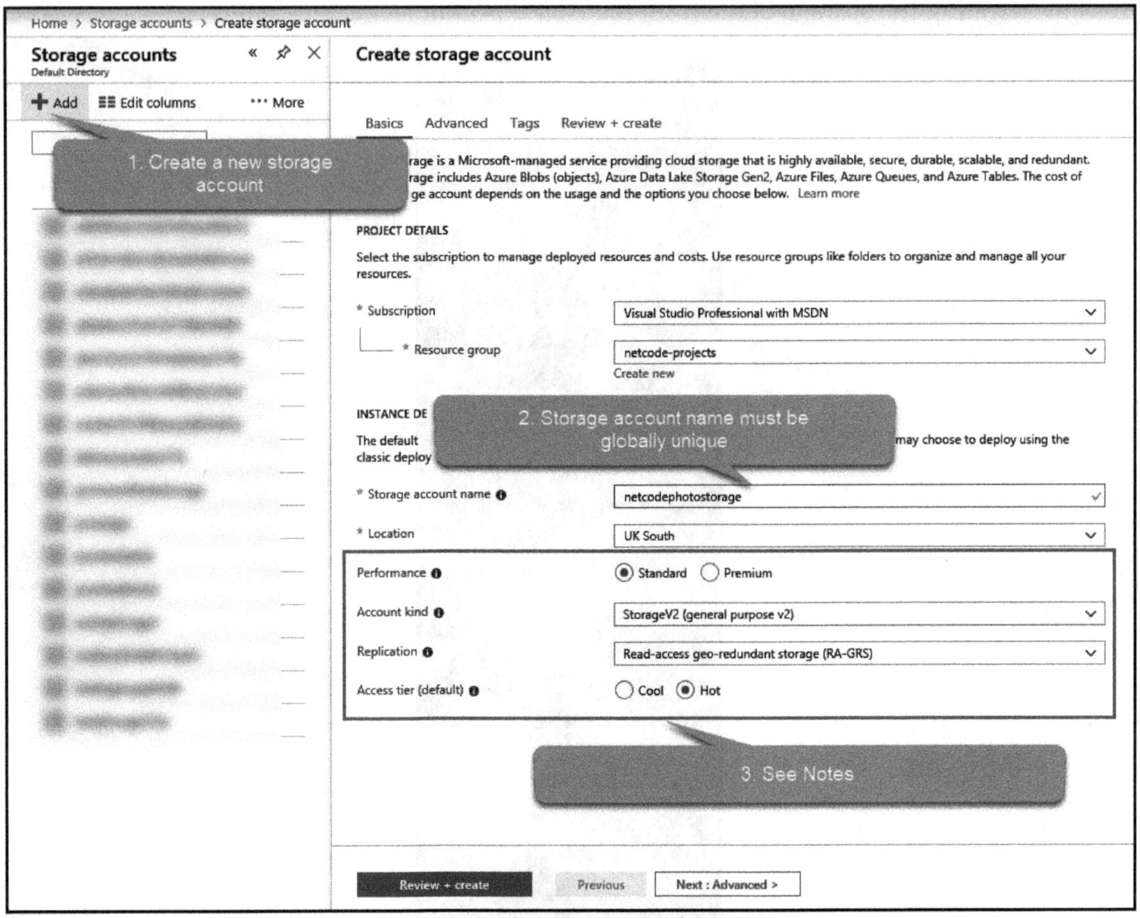

If you've already gone through the rest of this book, you'll be familiar with most of this screen; however, the preceding section, labeled **3. See Notes**, denotes a section of the storage account that directly affects the cost, performance, and the safety of the data. Essentially, if you want to access the data quickly, you'll pay more; if you want the data to be secure (backed up in other regions), then you'll pay more.

I won't go into the specific detail about these options (mainly because by the time you read this, they'll probably be different). However, there are two concepts here that are used across all cloud platforms:

- Hot and cold storage
- Storage redundancy

Let's start with the former.

Hot and cold storage

Typically, cloud providers offer the concept of storage, which is optimized for reading or optimized for writing. Although we've set our storage model to *hot* here, it may be that this particular model suits *cold* storage better; that is, it costs more to read and write the data, but costs less for the actual storage. *Hot* storage is the opposite: it costs more for the storage, but less to access the information.

Some cloud providers (including Microsoft) offer a tier that's similar to cold but even more optimized for storage: this is the type of storage you might use for backups or files that you expect won't need to be retrieved at all.

For an application such as ours, you might find it useful to use hot for the development and testing phase and substitute a cold storage account when it's in use in a live system.

Finally, a note on premium: Microsoft offer solid-state drives for this, meaning that your access speed is increased; however, this is more expensive than either of the other two options.

Storage redundancy

It's worth remembering at all times that the cloud is just another way of saying *someone else's computer*; in our case, that could be read as *Microsoft's computers*. Obviously, storing your data in Azure is more secure than storing it on the computer of your next-door neighbor, but many of the concepts are the same; this includes the fact that your neighbor may have a break-in, a flood, or a fire.

Microsoft faces the same risks, which they attempt to mitigate against with more security, fire safety, and waterproofing than your neighbor probably has. However, it is still possible that the machine that has your data goes up in smoke.

Different vendors have slightly different versions of this concept, but they all essentially offer the same thing: the ability to replicate your data somewhere else. Out of the box, you typically get the data written to more than one physical machine, so a single machine failure will not lose your data.

The next level is usually your data being replicated outside of the physical building, or even a collection of buildings. The final level is that the data is replicated outside of the area (typically in a different country).

As I mentioned previously, different cloud providers give these concepts different names and they change the terminology; however, it broadly comes down to what has to happen for you to lose your data, that is, multiple machine failure, a country-wide disaster, or a world-wide disaster. It's worth noting that, while cloud providers will give you a percentage of durability, none of them will go to 100%; that is, they will not guarantee the safety of your data. They'll simply say that it is unlikely that it will get lost.

Storage account

Back in our storage account, we have four storage concepts: **Blobs**, **Files**, **Tables**, and **Queues**. For the purpose of this project, we'll be using **Blobs**.

> In brief: files provide replication of local storage for legacy applications, tables provide a simple key-value pair data storage mechanism, and queues provide basic message queue functionality. Full details on these other types fall outside the scope of this chapter.

Inside our storage area, we need to create a container. Inside **Blobs**, choose to create a container:

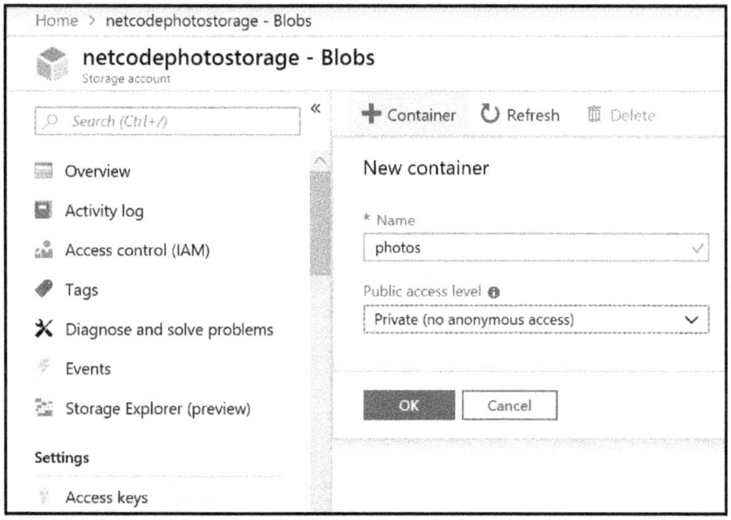

The access level relates to how you can access the container. Setting anonymous access means that you're pretty much granting access to anyone that knows where your container is.

The next thing we'll need (well, not exactly need, but it does help with testing) is the Azure Storage Explorer. If you have installed it, then launch it now:

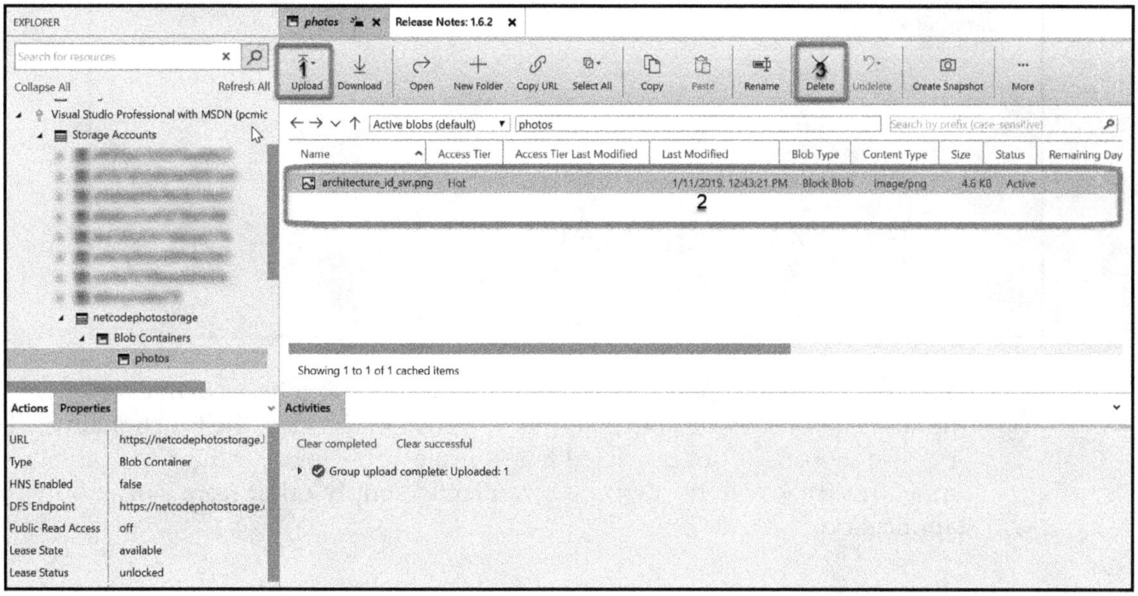

As you can see, in this utility, you can upload a file to the container (**1**), view its contents (**2**), and delete it again (**3**).

The tool also allows you to manage files, but, for now, we'll just use these three features.

> **TIP:** If you have chosen to not install this tool, you can still follow along with this chapter; however, determining whether your project is working correctly or not will not be easy. Having said that, by the end of this project, you should have sufficient knowledge to write a small utility that will list the contents of the container.

Once you've played with the tool, we can move on and create our Windows Service.

Creating our Windows Service

To create the Windows Service, let's start with a new .NET Core 3 console application:

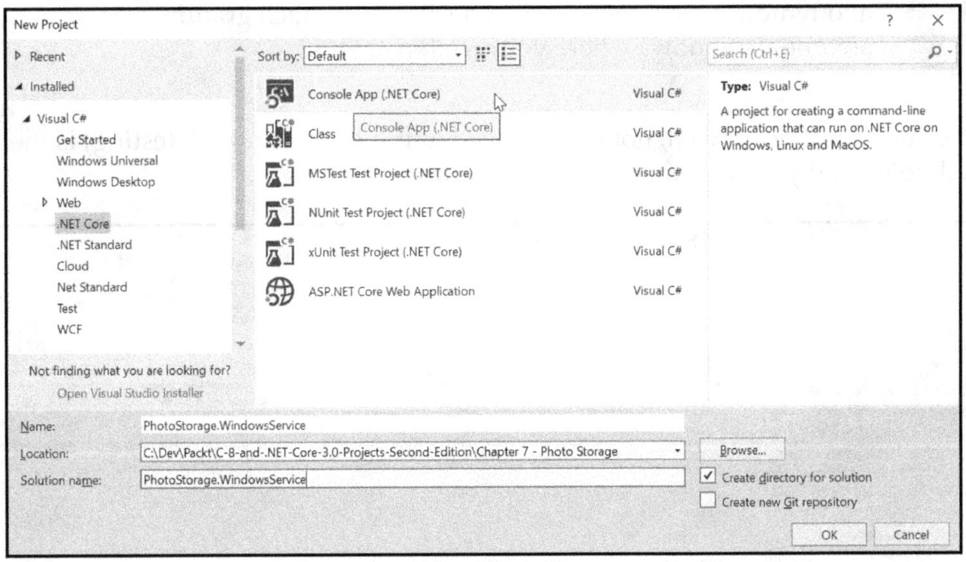

> **TIP:** You may wish to separate parts of this application into their own class libraries if you choose to extend this application. Clearly, the functionality that we're using is not restricted to a console application. If the functionality was in its own class, you could simply call it from a desktop application.

The next step is to install the Windows Compatibility NuGet package:

```
Install-Package Microsoft.Windows.Compatibility
```

This will allow us to create a Windows Service.

> It's worth noting at this stage that, despite being .NET Core, this application will not be cross-platform; in fact, any application using the Windows Compatibility Pack will not be.

Now that we've installed this, we can create the service. We'll need a class similar to this:

```
public class PhotoService : ServiceBase
{
}
```

You should be able to use *Ctrl* + . `ServiceBase` as it's part of the compatibility pack. We'll need to override some functions inside here (namely `OnStart` and `OnStop`):

```
public class PhotoService : ServiceBase
{
    protected override void OnStart(string[] args)
    {
        base.OnStart(args);
    }

    protected override void OnStop()
    {
        base.OnStop();
    }
}
```

We'll also need to tell the console application to run the service. Here, we can use another feature of C# 8—the implicitly scoped using statement. Essentially, instead of explicitly wrapping the disposable object in a using statement, it is now possible to simply declare it, and the object will be disposed of when it goes out of scope:

```
class Program
{
    static void Main(string[] args)
    {
        using var service = new PhotoService();
        ServiceBase.Run(service);
    }
}
```

That's basically our service done. The astute among you may have noticed it doesn't actually *do* anything just yet, but as it stands, it's a legitimate service.

The service needs to do essentially three things: scan a folder on the hard drive for new files, upload files to the container on Azure, and scan the Azure container. Let's start with a useful little class that monitors the filesystem for us: `FileSystemWatcher`. This is now available to .NET Core through the magic of the compatibility pack. It makes sense to put all of this code into a separate class, so let's just create and destroy the class in our service. Then, we can see what that class might look like a little later on:

```
public class PhotoService : ServiceBase
{
    private FileMonitor _fileMonitor;

    protected override void OnStart(string[] args)
    {
        _fileMonitor = new FileMonitor("c:\tmp");
    }

    protected override void OnStop()
    {
        _fileMonitor.Dispose();
    }
}
```

TIP: I'll be using the `c:\tmp` path a lot in this chapter. It's just a directory that I typically use for testing such things. If you don't want to use this, then you can use any path that you choose (although I recommend that you make it short). We will make this configurable later on.

Just use the keyboard shortcut *Ctrl* + . on the undefined new class, `FileMonitor`, which will create the class stub for you. Let's have a look at what it needs to look like:

```
public class FileMonitor : IDisposable
{
    private FileSystemWatcher _fileSystemWatcher;

    public FileMonitor(string path)
    {
        _fileSystemWatcher = new FileSystemWatcher(path);
        _fileSystemWatcher.Filter = "*.*";
        _fileSystemWatcher.EnableRaisingEvents = true;

        _fileSystemWatcher.Changed += new
FileSystemEventHandler(OnChanged);
        _fileSystemWatcher.Created += new
```

```
FileSystemEventHandler(OnCreated);
            _fileSystemWatcher.Renamed += new RenamedEventHandler(OnRenamed);
        }

        private void OnRenamed(object sender, RenamedEventArgs e)
        {
            throw new NotImplementedException();
        }

        private void OnCreated(object sender, FileSystemEventArgs e)
        {
            throw new NotImplementedException();
        }

        private void OnChanged(object sender, FileSystemEventArgs e)
        {
            throw new NotImplementedException();
        }

        public void Dispose()
        {
            _fileSystemWatcher.Dispose();
        }
    }
```

As you can see, there's not too much here: the `FileSystemWatcher` class itself is probably beyond the scope of this chapter in any serious detail, but essentially, you point it as a path and tell it to let you know when anything happens there; then, you get an event. `Filter` and `EnableRaisingEvents` need to be set so that the class knows what to look out for and what to do when it finds anything. We've implemented the `IDisposable` pattern so that we can dispose of `FileSystemWatcher` when the service is stopped.

TIP: The `IDisposable` pattern tends not to be implemented as much these days. Essentially, it gives you a chance to tidy up your resources. If you're doing anything that requires file access or database access, then you really should consider using it. The `Using` statement gives you a very nice way to have the system automatically dispose of your object for you, even when an error occurs.

Testing the class

One of the advantages of using a console application here is that we can simply run the project.

There's a myriad of ways to do this, but the preceding code will simply sit in an infinite loop with the `FileMonitor` class instantiated. If you create a file in `c:\tmp`, you should see the program crash with `NotImplementedException`. This proves that our `FileMonitor` class works so far.

The next step is to tell the class what to do. In this case, we'll use a new dependency class called `AzureStorageClientService`. This will provide the Azure Storage interface functionality. However, before we get into the messy business of writing it, let's use it. Start by creating a bank interface (you may choose to put this in a directory called `AzureClient` like I have):

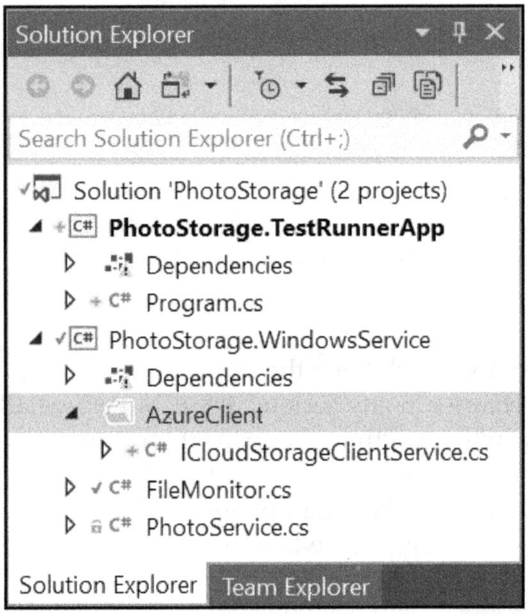

The astute among you may notice that I haven't called the interface `IAzureStorageClientService`, but `ICloudStorageClientService`. The reason for this is that, in addition to enabling testing, having a dependency injection such as this allows you to easily switch out one piece of functionality for another. For example, say you decided you wanted to use Google Cloud Platform instead of Azure—you could simply create `GoogleCloudStorageClient` that implemented the same interface and inject that instead.

Let's use our interface by declaring a variable at the top of our class:

```
public class FileMonitor : IDisposable
{
    private FileSystemWatcher _fileSystemWatcher;
    private ICloudStorageClientService _cloudStorageClientService;

    public FileMonitor(string path, ICloudStorageClientService
cloudStorageClientService)
    {
        _cloudStorageClientService = cloudStorageClientService;

        _fileSystemWatcher = new FileSystemWatcher(path);
        _fileSystemWatcher.Filter = "*.*";
        _fileSystemWatcher.EnableRaisingEvents = true;

        _fileSystemWatcher.Changed += new
FileSystemEventHandler(OnChanged);
        _fileSystemWatcher.Created += new
FileSystemEventHandler(OnCreated);
        _fileSystemWatcher.Renamed += new RenamedEventHandler(OnRenamed);
    }
```

As you can see, we're injecting it into our class using the constructor. We'll use it further down within our class:

```
private async void OnRenamed(object sender, RenamedEventArgs e)
{
    if (_cloudStorageClientService.FileExists(e.Name))
    {
        await _cloudStorageClientService.RenameFile(e.Name, e.OldName);
    }
    else
    {
        await _cloudStorageClientService.UploadFile(e.FullPath);
    }
}

private async void OnCreated(object sender, FileSystemEventArgs e)
{
    await _cloudStorageClientService.UploadFile(e.FullPath);
}

private async void OnChanged(object sender, FileSystemEventArgs e)
{
    await _cloudStorageClientService.UploadFile(e.FullPath);
}
```

If you so wish, you can use *Ctrl* + . to create the interface definitions; however, the methods do need to be asynchronous. The resultant definitions for the interface are as follows:

```
public interface ICloudStorageClientService
{
    Task RenameFile(string name, string oldName);
    Task UploadFile(string fullPath);
    Task<bool> FileExists(string name);
}
```

Finally, we'll need to implement the service.

Using the Azure Storage Client

We'll start by uploading a file into Azure Storage. The first step is to download the NuGet package for client access to Azure Storage:

```
Install-Package WindowsAzure.Storage
```

Then, we can create the method to upload the file:

```
public async Task UploadFile(string fullPath)
{
    string fileName = Path.GetFileName(fullPath);
    var blob = GetBlockBlobReference(fileName);

    using (var fileStream = System.IO.File.OpenRead(fullPath))
    {
        await blob.UploadFromStreamAsync(fileStream);
    }
}
```

The preceding code is basically getting a reference to the file in Azure (even though it doesn't exist) and uploading the stream. We should probably have a look at the helper method, that is, `GetBlockBlobReference`:

```
private CloudBlockBlob GetBlockBlobReference(string fileName)
{
    if (CloudStorageAccount.TryParse(_connectionString, out
CloudStorageAccount storageAccount))
    {
        var client = storageAccount.CreateCloudBlobClient();
        var container = client.GetContainerReference("photos");
        var blob = container.GetBlockBlobReference(fileName);
        return blob;
    }
```

```
        else
        {
            throw new Exception("Unable to parse the storage account");
        }
    }
```

This helper method does have quite a bit of code, so let's unpack it and see what we're actually doing. For the minute, don't question where `_connectionString` comes from – we'll return to that shortly. The first thing that we're doing is using a static method on the `CloudStorageAccount` class that's helpfully allowing us to create a new instance of `CloudStorageAccount` based on the connection string.

> TIP: Should you wish to extend this, you might consider an alternative to throwing an exception where the connection string is not valid.

We then, in turn, get the container inside the storage account based on its name; then, we get a reference to the Blob based on its name (which is our file name). It's worth noting that the Blob doesn't need to actually exist in order to return a Blob object.

> **Blob** is an abbreviation of **Binary Large OBject**. Essentially, in this context, this represents anything that can be stored on a computer in a single file.

Before we can test this, we need to return to `_connectionString`, which I asked you to briefly suspend questions on until now.

Configuring our Service to Access Azure Storage

Essentially, this needs to represent a connection string to the storage account. You can easily find the correct value for this in the Azure portal, under **Access keys**:

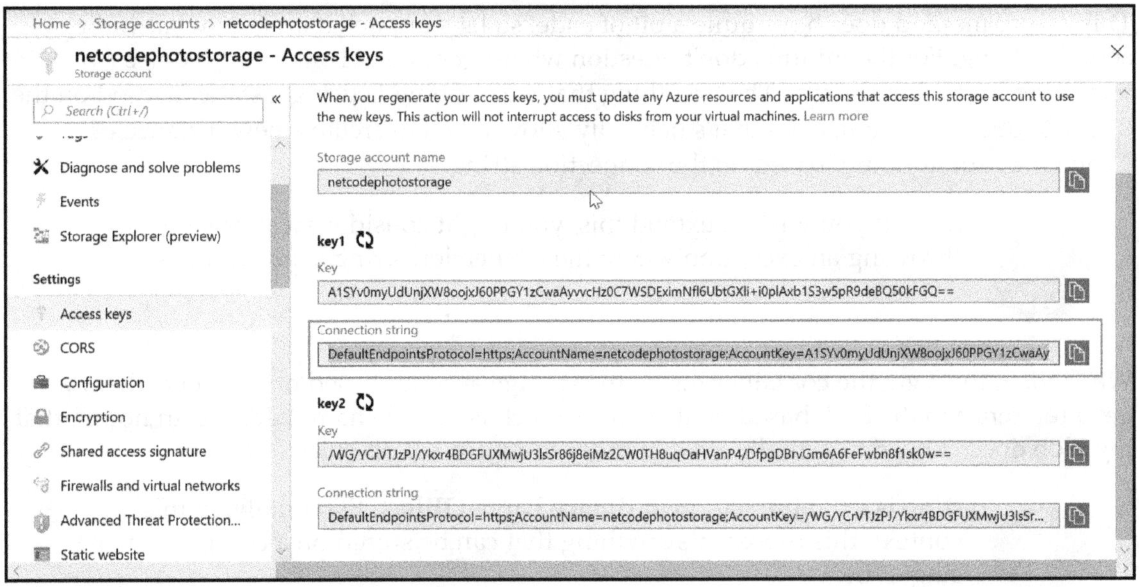

We could simply copy this and paste it directly into the code by assigning the `_connectionString` variable to it. However, instead, we're going to use `ConfigurationBuilder`. Before we can make a start on this, we'll need some NuGet packages:

```
Install-Package Microsoft.Extensions.Configuration -ProjectName
PhotoStorage.WindowsService

Install-Package Microsoft.Extensions.Configuration.Json -ProjectName
PhotoStorage.WindowsService
```

This should allow us to build our configuration using JSON files, so the next step is to create one. We'll add a file called `appsettings.json` to our project:

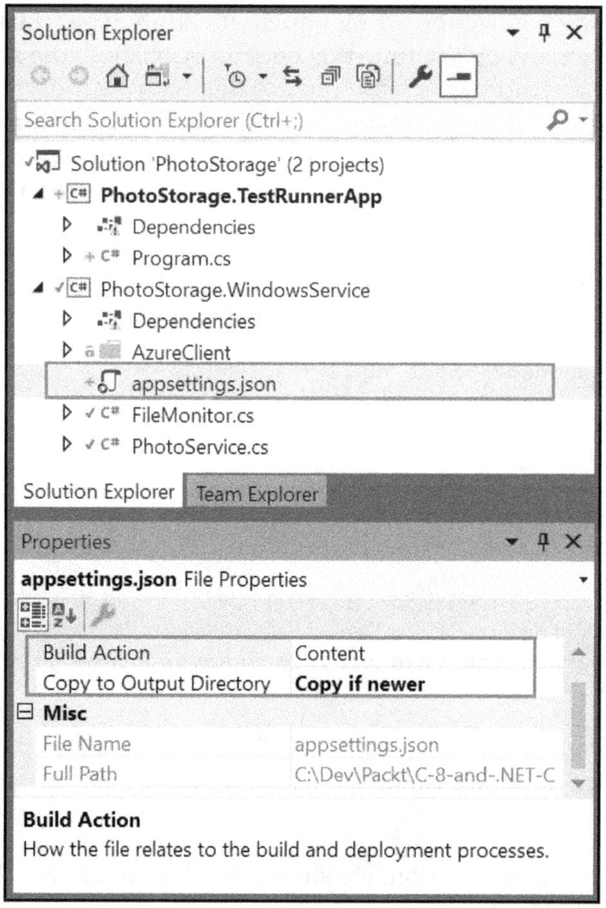

As you can see, not only have we created the new file, but we've set the **Build Action** and **Copy to Output Directory** so that the file will be copied to the home directory of the application when it is running.

Let's see what the file itself looks like:

```
{
    "ConnectionStrings": {
        "netcodephotostorage":
"DefaultEndpointsProtocol=https;AccountName=netcodephotostorage;AccountKey=
A1SYv0myUdUnjXW8oojxJ60PPGY1zCwaAyvvcHz0C7WSDEximNfl6UbtGXli+i0plAxb1S3w5pR
9deBQ50kFGQ==;EndpointSuffix=core.windows.net"
    }
}
```

> I've left my connection string here to illustrate what the string would look like; obviously, by the time this book is published, the storage account will not exist anymore, so please replace this with your own connection string; otherwise, it will not connect. In truth, you can structure this file differently if you so wish; by looking at `ConfigurationBuilder`, you'll see that, providing it's in a key-value pair structure, it makes little difference.

Now, let's look at how we can extract that configuration. Inside `AzureStorageClientService`, we'll create a constructor:

```
private string _connectionString;

public AzureStorageClientService()
{
    var builder = new ConfigurationBuilder()
        .SetBasePath(Directory.GetCurrentDirectory())
        .AddJsonFile("appsettings.json");

    var configuration = builder.Build();
    _connectionString =
configuration["ConnectionStrings:netcodephotostorage"];
}
```

All we're doing here is using `ConfigurationBuilder` to load and parse the JSON file that we've just created. Once done, we can use the resultant `configuration` property to extract key-value pairs.

Now, if we run the console application, we should be able to see that the file has been uploaded to the Azure Cloud Storage:

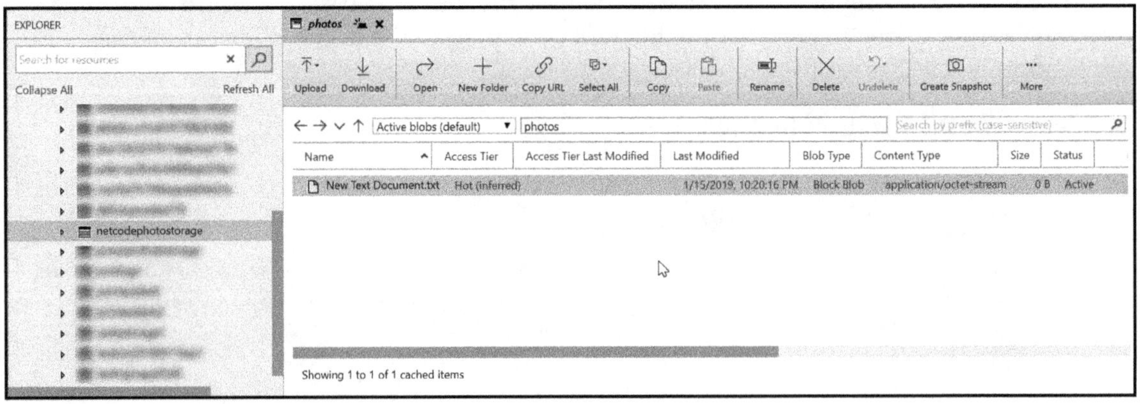

We can see that the storage client code now works. There are a few methods left to fill in, so let's do that next.

Finishing off the Cloud Storage Client

We will start with an easy method, that is, `FileExists`:

```
public async Task<bool> FileExists(string name)
{
    var blob = GetBlockBlobReference(name);

    return await blob.ExistsAsync();
}
```

We're reusing the same helper method from the `Upload` function, but, this time, we're simply calling a built-in method, `ExistsAsync`, to determine whether or not the file is there.

Finally, we have the `RenameFile` method:

```
public async Task<bool> RenameFile(string name, string oldName)
{
    var blobNew = GetBlockBlobReference(name);
    var blobOld = GetBlockBlobReference(oldName);

    if (await blobNew.ExistsAsync()) return false;

    await blobNew.StartCopyAsync(blobOld);
    await blobOld.DeleteAsync();

    return true;
}
```

Since there is no built-in method to rename a file, we just copy the contents and delete the original. Obviously, should the new name already exist, the task would fail.

Further configuration

Our next task is to move our only remaining hard coded variable into the `appsettings.json` file. Let's have a quick look at what that might look like in the configuration file:

```
{
    "ConnectionStrings": {
```

```
        "netcodephotostorage":
"DefaultEndpointsProtocol=https;AccountName=netcodephotostorage;AccountKey=
A1SYv0myUdUnjXW8oojxJ60PPGY1zCwaAyvvcHz0C7WSDEximNfl6UbtGXli+i0plAxb1S3w5pR
9deBQ50kFGQ==;EndpointSuffix=core.windows.net"
    },
    "MonitorPath": "c:\\tmp"
}
```

Okay, so our next stage will be to use it. There are a number of ways to achieve this; we could read each configuration value as it's needed or, as we will do here, we could read all the configuration at the beginning and pass the values around. Let's create a new class to hold these values. I've added mine to a new folder called `Models`:

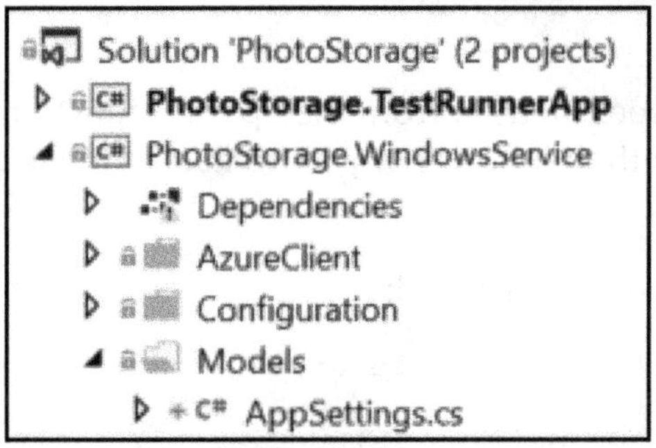

The idea here is that we have a single class that holds all of the configuration for the application; therefore, we can simply pass this to any other class that needs that configuration. The code for the class itself looks like this:

```
public class AppSettings
{
    public string ConnectionString { get; set; }
    public string MonitorPath { get; set; }
}
```

Our next step is to add some code to read this configuration. In order to achieve this, I've created a new service:

```
public class ConfigurationService
{
    public AppSettings Load()
    {
        var builder = new ConfigurationBuilder()
            .SetBasePath(Directory.GetCurrentDirectory())
            .AddJsonFile("appsettings.json");

        var appSettings = new AppSettings();
```

```
        var configuration = builder.Build();

        appSettings.ConnectionString =
configuration["ConnectionStrings:netcodephotostorage"];
        appSettings.MonitorPath = configuration["MonitorPath"];

        return appSettings;
    }
}
```

Because we have created a service to load the configuration settings, we can pass that into `AzureStorageClientService`. Here's the revised constructor and class variables for that file:

```
private readonly AppSettings _appSettings;
public AzureStorageClientService(AppSettings appSettings)
{
    _appSettings = appSettings;
}
```

I think you'll agree that this looks much cleaner now we're not loading configuration inside the service; `GetBlockBlobReference` also needs updating like so:

```
private CloudBlockBlob GetBlockBlobReference(string fileName)
{
    if (CloudStorageAccount.TryParse(_appSettings.ConnectionString, out
CloudStorageAccount storageAccount))
    {
        var client = storageAccount.CreateCloudBlobClient();
        var container = client.GetContainerReference("photos");
        var blob = container.GetBlockBlobReference(fileName);

        return blob;
    }
    else
    {
        throw new Exception("Unable to parse the storage account");
    }
}
```

Our `PhotoService.cs` class will need to instantiate this new configuration service on startup:

```
private FileMonitor _fileMonitor;
private AppSettings _appSettings;

protected override void OnStart(string[] args)
{
```

```
        var configurationService = new ConfigurationService();
        _appSettings = configurationService.Load();

        var cloudStorageClientService = new
    AzureStorageClientService(_appSettings);
        _fileMonitor = new FileMonitor(_appSettings.MonitorPath,
    cloudStorageClientService);
    }
```

Finally, if you created a console application for testing, you'll need to update that, too (in `Program.cs`):

```
    static void TestFileMonitorNewFile()
    {
        var configurationService = new ConfigurationService();
        var appSettings = configurationService.Load();

        var cloudStorageClientService = new
    AzureStorageClientService(appSettings);

        using var fileMonitor = new FileMonitor(appSettings.MonitorPath,
    cloudStorageClientService);
        for (; ; ) { }
    }
```

With that, we're done. Now, the application should read the configuration from the `appsettings.json` file and, should we create or drop a file into the `c:\tmp` folder, we should see it uploaded into the cloud. When it is changed, the changed version is uploaded; however, we are missing three key pieces of functionality.

The next thing we'll need to add is logging. The unfortunate reality about Windows Services or, indeed, services of any kind, is that they are notoriously difficult to debug.

Secondly, if we run our application and the target destination is empty, all the files that were dropped into that directory will be transferred over to the cloud; however, what if we point this at an existing directory, already full of our photos? And finally, as it currently stands, we're backing up all our files, whereas we're only interested in image formats.

Let's address these three remaining pieces of functionality.

Logging

Ultimately, logging is just writing information to a persistent store, which means you can log to a database or to a file. You can even log to the screen, although you then have the problem that the persistence may not be sufficient. In our case, we'll just output the text to a file. Let's have a look at the logging code:

```
public class FileLogger : ILogger
{
    private readonly string _loggingPath;

    public FileLogger(string loggingPath)
    {
        _loggingPath = loggingPath;
    }

    public void Log(string message)
    {
        File.AppendAllText($@"{_loggingPath}\PhotoStorage.Log.txt",
$"{DateTime.Now} : {message}{Environment.NewLine}");
    }
}
```

Here, we're implementing an `ILogger` interface, which we'll come to shortly. There's not a great deal of complexity to this class—we simply accept a path and then output to a file in the path. Let's see what the interface looks like:

```
public interface ILogger
{
    void Log(string message);
}
```

Again, there's probably not too much to explain about this except its existence. Logging is one of those features that you definitely want to be able to switch out for unit testing, so an interface is crucial. I won't detail every place that I'm logging, but let's look at the `PhotoService` constructor:

```
private readonly string _path;
private readonly ILogger _logger;
private FileMonitor _fileMonitor;
private AppSettings _appSettings;

public PhotoService(string path, ILogger logger)
{
    ServiceName = "PhotoService";
    AutoLog = true;
    _path = path;
```

```
        _logger = logger;
    }
```

As you can see, we're passing the logger in; therefore, we're instantiating it in the `Main` method:

```
    static void Main(string[] args)
    {
        var path = args[0];
        var logger = new FileLogger(path);

        using var service = new PhotoService(path, logger);
        ServiceBase.Run(service);
    }
```

This has had a little re-jig: now, we're taking the argument and storing it in the `path` variable.

Now, we have the capability to log; if you want to see a couple of log messages, try putting one in `OnStart` and one in `OnStop`.

> Although I'm not going to list all the logging places, you're free to download the GitHub repository for this book and have a look. Should you encounter any issues when following along, this logging capability will be invaluable; however, there is a section later on *Testing and debugging* if you want to find out more.

Only uploading images

In order to determine whether we have an image, we'll simply add a check before we process any files. Here's our revised methods for `OnCreated` and `OnChanged`:

```
    private async void OnCreated(object sender, FileSystemEventArgs e)
    {
        if (!FileHelper.IsImage(e.Name)) return;
        await _cloudStorageClientService.UploadFile(e.FullPath);
    }

    private async void OnChanged(object sender, FileSystemEventArgs e)
    {
        if (!FileHelper.IsImage(e.Name)) return;
        await _cloudStorageClientService.UploadFile(e.FullPath);
    }
```

As you can see, we just have a very basic gated check that returns whether we are dealing with an image. Of course, we're going to need to write that method. Here, we've come to one of the new C# 8 features that we haven't mentioned yet. Prior to C# 8, the method may have looked like this:

```
public static bool IsImage(string fileName)
{
    string ext = Path.GetExtension(fileName);
    switch (ext)
    {
        case "png":
        case "jpg":
        case "jpeg":
        case "bmp":
        case "gif":
            return true;
        default: return false;
     };
 }
```

However, with the new `switch` statement, we can write that method like this:

```
public static bool IsImage(string fileName)
{
    string ext = Path.GetExtension(fileName);
    return ext switch
    {
        "png" => true,
        "jpg" => true,
        "jpeg" => true,
        "bmp" => true,
        "gif" => true,
        _ => false
    };
}
```

We could make it even terser if we included a `GetExtension` call in the `switch` statement itself, but, generally, it reads easier.

> **TIP:** The new `switch` statement is actually more powerful than this and, in fact, supports pattern matching.

Let's have a look at how we can upload any images that we find in the directory on startup.

Uploading existing images

Once started, our app will monitor any new files that are created or changed inside the directory, but what if we start the application and point it to a directory that's already full? We can change our `OnStart` code so that it calls a method that will scan the directory for us. Presumably, we'll need to pass information on where it can scan and what to do once it finds something:

```
protected override void OnStart(string[] args)
{
    var configurationService = new ConfigurationService();
    _appSettings = configurationService.Load(_path);

    var cloudStorageClientService = new
AzureStorageClientService(_appSettings);

    _fileDiscoverer.DiscoverFiles(_appSettings.MonitorPath, (file) =>
cloudStorageClientService.UploadFile(file));
    _fileMonitor = new FileMonitor(_appSettings.MonitorPath,
cloudStorageClientService, _logger);
}
```

The new line here is a call to a new object called `_fileDiscoverer`. Here, we're passing through the directory that we're monitoring and a callback to the `UploadFile` method. To begin with, let's add this dependency to the constructor:

```
private readonly string _path;
private readonly ILogger _logger;
private readonly IFileDiscoverer _fileDiscoverer;
private FileMonitor _fileMonitor;
private AppSettings _appSettings;

public PhotoService(string path, ILogger logger, IFileDiscoverer
fileDiscoverer)
{
    ServiceName = "PhotoService";
    AutoLog = true;
    _path = path;
    _logger = logger;
    _fileDiscoverer = fileDiscoverer;
}
```

As with all good dependency injections, we're using an interface to pass the object in; let's see what our interface needs to look like:

```
public interface IFileDiscoverer
{
```

```
    void DiscoverFiles(string directory, Action<string> action);
}
```

> **TIP:** You can have Visual Studio automatically generate this for you by simply using the *Ctrl* + . shortcut on all the preceding unknown methods and interfaces.

Before we create the method itself, let's have a look at the `Program.cs` code that passes this in:

```
static void Main(string[] args)
{
    var path = args[0];
    var logger = new FileLogger(path);
    var fileDiscoverer = new FileDiscoverer(logger);

    using var service = new PhotoService(path, logger, fileDiscoverer);
    ServiceBase.Run(service);
}
```

We're just instantiating the object and passing it in.

> **TIP:** You may notice that this is starting to look like we would benefit from an IoC container. I'm purposely not using one because it detracts from the code that we're demonstrating; however, should you decide to extend this project, that would be an excellent place to start.

We'll need a method of scanning the directory for files that are already present. To this end, we'll be able to use a feature that was introduced in .NET Core 2.1 called `FileSystemEnumerable`. This builds on the work that was done in .NET Core 2.1 to introduce `Span` and, therefore, provides some performance benefits over the previous `System.IO` alternatives. Let's have a look at the `IFileDiscoverer` implementation:

```
public class FileDiscoverer : IFileDiscoverer
{
    private readonly ILogger _logger;

    public FileDiscoverer(ILogger logger)
    {
        _logger = logger;
    }

    public void DiscoverFiles(string directory, Action<string> action)
    {
        var enumerationOptions = new EnumerationOptions()
```

```
        {
            RecurseSubdirectories = false,
            AttributesToSkip = FileAttributes.Directory
             | FileAttributes.Device | FileAttributes.Hidden
        };

        var files = new FileSystemEnumerable<FileInfo>(directory,
            (ref FileSystemEntry entry) =>
(FileInfo)entry.ToFileSystemInfo(), enumerationOptions)
        {
            ShouldIncludePredicate = (ref FileSystemEntry entry) =>
                FileHelper.IsImage(entry.FileName.ToString())
        };

        foreach (var file in files)
        {
            action.Invoke(file.FullName);
        }
    }
}
```

We're passing in the `ILogger` so that we can see what files have been found and uploaded; however, it's not relevant to the functionality of the class, so I've left its usage out of the preceding code.

`FileSystemEnumerable` allows us to traverse a directory in various ways. As you can see, we can filter certain files and file types by using a combination of `EnumerationOptions` and `ShouldIncludePredicate`. Once we have our list, we can simply iterate it as we would any collection; in our case, we're calling the method that we passed in and passing back the filename.

A full and detailed explanation of `FileSystemEnumerable` is beyond the scope of this chapter (and book); however, a good source of information for the .NET Core API's functions is the Microsoft online documentation, which can be found here: `https://docs.microsoft.com/en-us/dotnet/api/`.

Installing the Windows Service

The installation of a Windows Service, especially for .NET Core (at least at the time of writing), is a very manual process. Furthermore, because we are using a configuration file, we'll need to make some slight tweaks so that the service will know where to look for the config file.

Code changes

When we install the service, we'll need to tell it where to look for the config file. We can do that by simply passing the parameter into the service. There are actually two ways to do this; the first (and the one that we're interested in) is to pass the parameter in during the installation of the service. This gets passed into the `Main` method. The second is passed in via the service management utility; the arguments are passed into the `OnStart` method of the service.

In our case, we're interested in changing the `Main` method:

```
static void Main(string[] args)
{
    using (var service = new PhotoService(args[0]));
    ServiceBase.Run(service);

}
```

Clearly, we'll need to accept that parameter in the constructor of `PhotoService`:

```
private readonly string _path;
private FileMonitor _fileMonitor;
private AppSettings _appSettings;

public PhotoService(string path)
{
    ServiceName = "PhotoService";
    AutoLog = true;
    _path = path;
}
```

As you can see, we're storing the parameter in a class-level variable. Finally, we'll need to change the `OnStart` method so that it uses that path:

```
protected override void OnStart(string[] args)
{
    var configurationService = new ConfigurationService();
```

```
    _appSettings = configurationService.Load(_path);

    var cloudStorageClientService = new
AzureStorageClientService(_appSettings);
    _fileMonitor = new FileMonitor(_appSettings.MonitorPath,
cloudStorageClientService);
}
```

All we need to do now is issue the install command and we're done.

Installation command

With all of that finished, we can install our service.

> **TIP:** If you choose to extend this project so that it needs distributing, then this method of deployment would be insufficient. There are a number of options for installation and, I imagine, a number more by the time this book is released. However, creating a simple console application that runs the command in this section might be the easiest and quickest option.

In order to install our service, we're going to use a tool called Service Control: it's part of the Windows SDK. Launch a Command Prompt with elevated privileges. You'll need to use the following command:

```
c:\windows\system32\sc.exe create PhotoService binpath= [Full Path and
Filename for PhotoStorage.WindowsService.exe] [Full Path to the
appsettings.json] start= auto
```

If you wish to get the path to the executable from Visual Studio, you can simply copy it from the output window when the project compiles (note that you need to supply the executable and not the DLL):

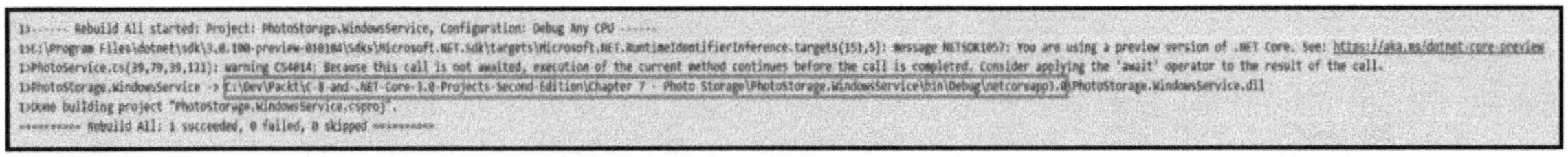
1>------ Rebuild All started: Project: PhotoStorage.WindowsService, Configuration: Debug Any CPU ------
1>PhotoService.cs(39,79,39,121): warning CS4014: Because this call is not awaited, execution of the current method continues before the call is completed. Consider applying the 'await' operator to the result of the call.
1>Done building project "PhotoStorage.WindowsService.csproj".
========== Rebuild All: 1 succeeded, 0 failed, 0 skipped ==========

The path to `appsettings.json` can be anything; however, initially, it will be the same path as the one to the executable. This is also where the log will be written to.

> **TIP**
>
> It's worth noting that, depending on how your service runs, and your own permissions, you may not have access to anywhere on the hard drive.

In my case, the full command looks like this:

```
c:\windows\system32\sc.exe create PhotoService binpath=
"\"C:\Dev\Packt\C-8-and-.NET-Core-3.0-Projects-Second-Edition\Chapter 7 -
Photo
Storage\PhotoStorage.WindowsService\bin\Debug\netcoreapp3.0\PhotoStorage.Wi
ndowsService.exe\" \"C:\Dev\Packt\C-8-and-.NET-Core-3.0-Projects-Second-
Edition\Chapter 7 - Photo
Storage\PhotoStorage.WindowsService\bin\Debug\netcoreapp3.0\" " start= auto
```

The screenshot showing the preceding command is as follows:

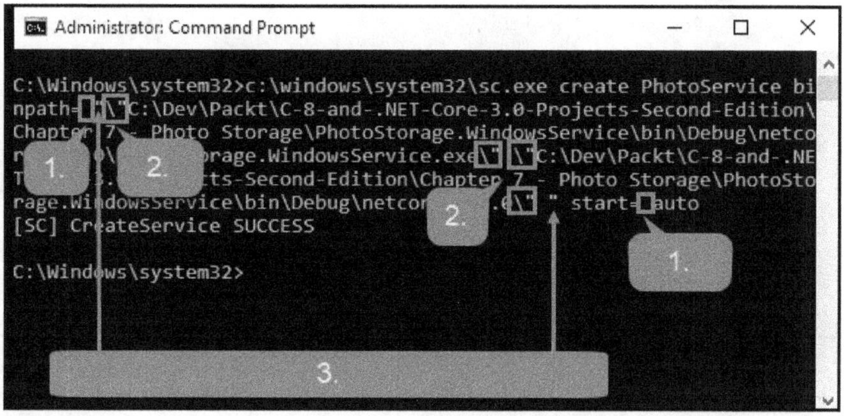

The command in the preceding screenshot can be explained as follows:

1. The spaces after the parameters are not cosmetic, but bizarrely necessary!
2. Any quotation marks inside the `binpath` parameter must be escaped.
3. These denote the opening and closing quotation marks for the `binpath` parameter.

Once you have created your service, you should be able to see it and start it:

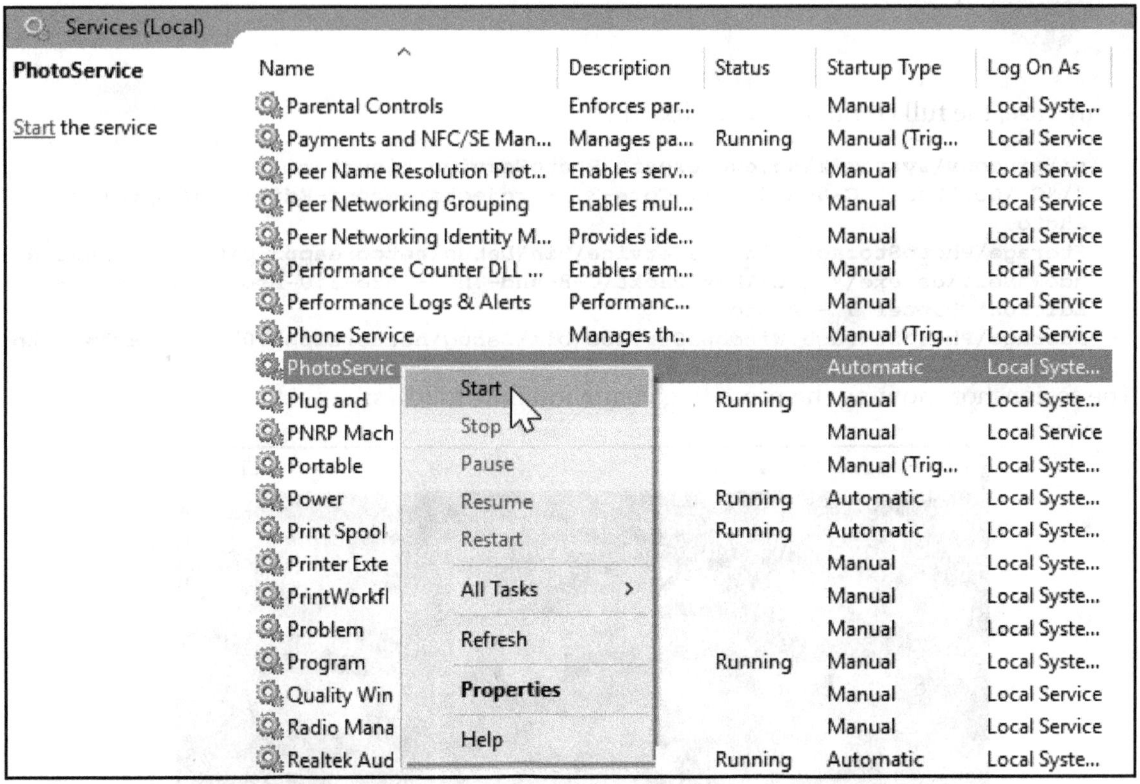

That's it. Now, you should be able to drop files into the specified directory and see them magically upload to the cloud (which you can check using the Azure Storage Explorer, as we mentioned earlier in this chapter).

That's excellent, but what if it doesn't work?

Testing and debugging

If you pull the repository, you'll see that I've added a number of unit tests to cover some of the basic functionality. If you find something isn't working, then writing a unit test that exposes that issue is often the fastest way to fix it. However, it is sometimes the case that the application will run, the unit tests pass, but still, something isn't working. I've composed some steps that you can follow to try to debug the service, should it not work.

Step 1 – check the service is running

It sounds simple, but the most obvious explanation for something not doing what you expect it to, is that it isn't doing anything at all. You can easily check whether the service is running by going to the Services application:

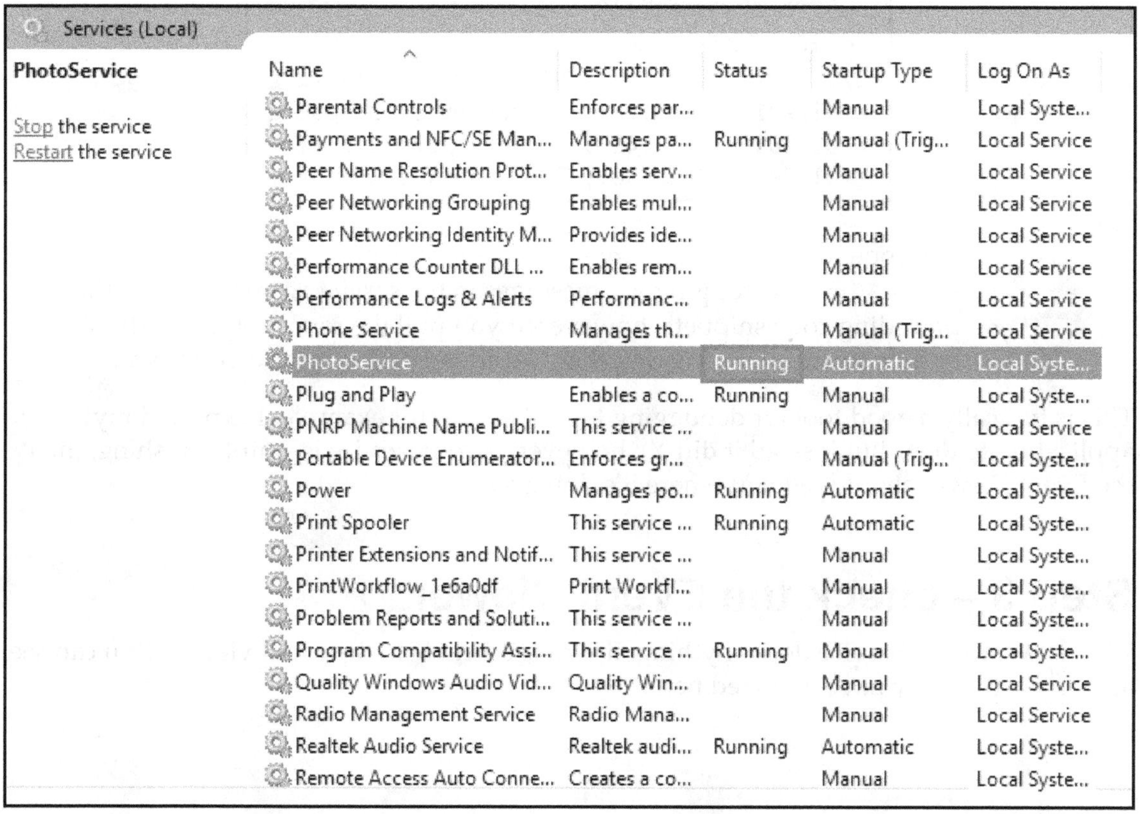

Services (Local)

PhotoService

Stop the service
Restart the service

Name	Description	Status	Startup Type	Log On As
Parental Controls	Enforces par...		Manual	Local Syste...
Payments and NFC/SE Man...	Manages pa...	Running	Manual (Trig...	Local Service
Peer Name Resolution Prot...	Enables serv...		Manual	Local Service
Peer Networking Grouping	Enables mul...		Manual	Local Service
Peer Networking Identity M...	Provides ide...		Manual	Local Service
Performance Counter DLL ...	Enables rem...		Manual	Local Service
Performance Logs & Alerts	Performanc...		Manual	Local Service
Phone Service	Manages th...		Manual (Trig...	Local Service
PhotoService		Running	Automatic	Local Syste...
Plug and Play	Enables a co...	Running	Manual	Local Syste...
PNRP Machine Name Publi...	This service ...		Manual	Local Service
Portable Device Enumerator...	Enforces gr...		Manual (Trig...	Local Syste...
Power	Manages po...	Running	Automatic	Local Syste...
Print Spooler	This service ...	Running	Automatic	Local Syste...
Printer Extensions and Notif...	This service ...		Manual	Local Syste...
PrintWorkflow_1e6a0df	Print Workfl...		Manual	Local Syste...
Problem Reports and Soluti...	This service ...		Manual	Local Syste...
Program Compatibility Assi...	This service ...	Running	Manual	Local Syste...
Quality Windows Audio Vid...	Quality Win...		Manual	Local Service
Radio Management Service	Radio Mana...		Manual	Local Service
Realtek Audio Service	Realtek audi...	Running	Automatic	Local Syste...
Remote Access Auto Conne...	Creates a co...		Manual	Local Syste...

If the service doesn't say **Running**, as shown in the preceding screenshot, then it isn't. There can be a number of reasons for this and, unlike most other similar situations, simply starting it is very unlikely to work. Often, the quickest way to find out why is to check the log file or the Event Viewer.

Step 2 – check the log file

Initially, the log file will be written to the same directory as the executable (unless you specify a different directory for the config file). The log file may look something like this:

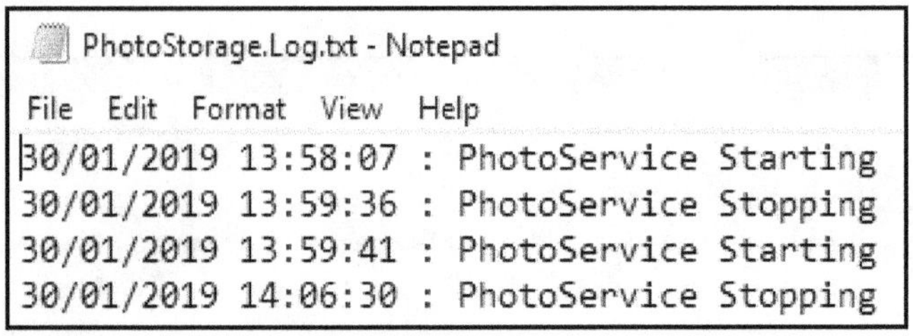

PhotoStorage.Log.txt - Notepad

File Edit Format View Help

```
30/01/2019 13:58:07 : PhotoService Starting
30/01/2019 13:59:36 : PhotoService Stopping
30/01/2019 13:59:41 : PhotoService Starting
30/01/2019 14:06:30 : PhotoService Stopping
```

TIP

The code to create the `PhotoService` starting and `PhotoService` stopping log messages in the service were left out of the preceding code snippets; however, if you pull the repository, you should be able to see all the logging that I've added and even add your own.

This is typically a good tool for debugging logical errors (for example, I expected my application to do X, but instead it did Y); however, if your service is simply crashing, then the Event Viewer should tell you where it's doing so.

Step 3 – check the Event Viewer

When a Windows Service does anything, it writes an entry to the event viewer. You can see any errors that may have occurred here:

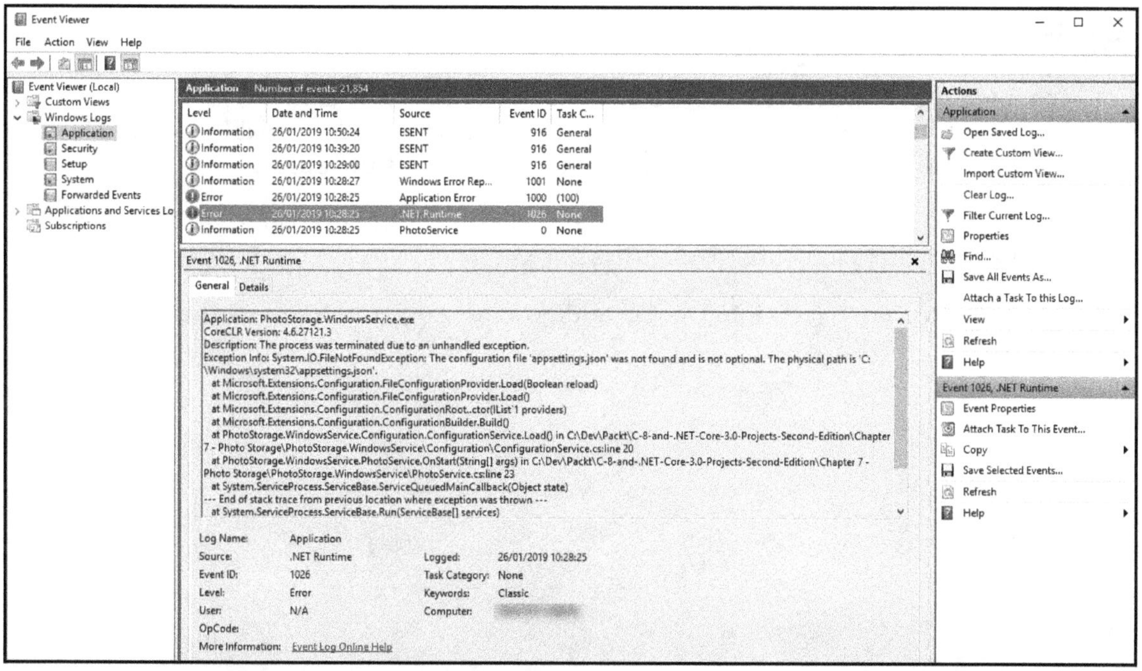

As you can see, in the preceding case, the service was unable to find the configuration file.

It's not possible to cover every possible error and solution here; however, broadly speaking, a Windows Service obeys the same rules as any other program. If the Windows Service works in the test harness and the unit tests pass, then the likely issue is with the environment, that is, the deployed directory, permissions, or runtime resources that are needed.

If the program can't find the configuration file (or any dependency), then open the directory that it's looking in and see if you can find the log file (or dependency) yourself. In this example, the `appsettings.json` file simply needed copying to the output directory. You can have Visual Studio do this by changing the *Build Action* and *Copy to Output Directory* parameters.

The Event Viewer is a really useful tool and it gives you the entire call stack, meaning that you can isolate the specific line that's failing.

Summary

In the chapter, we created a Windows Service using .NET Core 3 and the Windows Compatibility Pack. We also used the new switch statement that's available in C#8. Then, we used Azure Blob Storage as a mechanism to upload and store our files.

We now have a little service that will sit in the background and upload our files to the cloud as we drop them into a particular directory.

In the next chapter, we'll look into Docker and how we can build a service that can be hosted in Azure on AKS.

8
A Load-Balanced Order Processing Microservice Using Docker and Azure Kubernetes Service

It's not so long ago that, when glancing through job adverts, the term *n*-tier architecture would crop up as something that potential candidates needed to be familiar with. The principle behind this architectural paradigm was that there was a data store that was typically held on a company-owned server; then, there was a service (or several services) that would interrogate that data at the behest of either the client application, or of another service, and you would have a client application (be that a desktop or web client) that communicated with the service. The architecture is typically illustrated as follows:

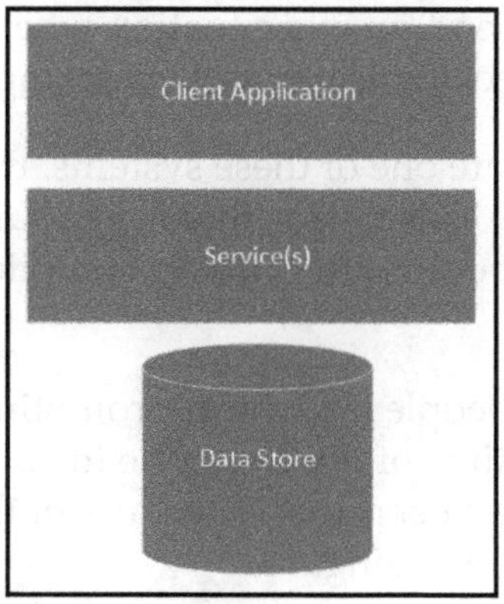

The term *n*-tier overtook three tier as the service in that diagram could actually call another service and so there could, feasibly, be several layers between the client and the server.

There were a number of advantages to this approach: you could keep your UI and business logic separate and it could be (if done correctly) agnostic of (or at least not irrevocably tied to) the data store. All your code could exist in a single solution (if you were using .NET) and you knew that whatever was in your database was how things were at any given time.

However, there are downsides to this architectural approach that are related to scale of one kind or another, as well as reliability.

The first is usage: if you increase traffic, then at a certain point, your architecture can't deal with that level of traffic.

The data store that we mentioned earlier has a defined limit because, ultimately, it's reading and writing to a disk. This can be improved: the data can be spread across multiple disks, which greatly improves performance. There is also the issue that, where the data in a database is being updated, records must be locked, and finally, there is the physical time that it takes to insert a new record, update the indexes, and so forth.

The service has a similar issue: there is a limit to the amount of traffic it can ingest at a single time, especially if it is communicating with the database and performing a transaction. You can, of course, increase the number of services, but they are all competing for the same data store.

The next issue of scale is that of development: imagine that you want to simultaneously work on several parts of the application. Of course, with modern source control, this is mechanically very easy; however, your sales order system may have a dependency on your stock checking system. You may end up in a situation where the sales order team is unable to progress because the stock checking team is still working on a given feature.

Furthermore, if you want to update one of these systems, then you need to test them all and change them all at the same time. This means that every part of your system changes (maybe some parts only change because they are re-compiled, but they do change) for every deployment.

So, what's the solution? A lot of people have been promoting the idea of distributed systems as of late (at least at the time of writing). The idea is that you break your entire system into loosely coupled parts or services. The parts of the system typically communicate via some form of messaging.

For the purpose of this chapter, we're going to work on the premise that our system is being designed for a large DIY store chain.

In this chapter, we'll explore the use of a microservice using Azure Kubernetes Service to scale and orchestrate the service. We'll cover the following topics:

- Creating storage queues in Azure
- Creating a new service and deploying it to **Azure Container Registry** (**ACR**) and then to **Azure Kubernetes Service** (**AKS**)
- Demonstrating that the system is load-balanced by killing a pod
- Testing our service under load using JMeter

Microservices and containers are buzzwords at the minute:

Technical requirements

We're going to be using **Azure Kubernetes Service** (**AKS**), so the first thing you'll need is the Azure CLI. You can install it by going to `https://aka.ms/installazurecliwindows`.

You will also need an Azure account; if you don't have one, then you can create one here: `https://azure.microsoft.com/`.

At the time of writing, you can sign up for free and receive £150/$200 of credit for the first month.

Once you've signed up, visit `https://portal.azure.com`. Here, you can manage your Azure resources and check your balance.

JMeter

This is an optional step, and I'll explain how you can skip this later. If you choose to skip this, then you can also skip to the end of this section.

In order to test our microservice under load, we'll use a tool called JMeter; it can be downloaded from `http://jmeter.apache.org/download_jmeter.cgi`.

In addition, you'll need to install the Java SE Development Kit; you can do so here: `http://www.oracle.com/technetwork/java/javase/downloads/index.html`.

Installing the JRE is beyond the scope of this chapter, although there are many online tutorials for this; if you have installed it correctly, you should be able to type the following into Command Prompt and see the version that you've installed:

```
java -version
```

Microservices

Many years ago, I used to work on an **Electronic Data Interchange** (**EDI**) system. This system worked by the sales order system writing a summary of the sales for the current day to a text file; then, another process would pick up that text file and process those orders. This was, in essence, a distributed system: each part of the system functioned independently of the other. The sales order system could be turned off, and any files it had already written would still be processed.

These days, this form of data exchange has changed into using message brokers: either maintained on-premises or in the cloud. I'll explain more about why this is the case a little later on.

TIP: At the time of writing, RabbitMQ and ActiveMQ are two well-known message brokers that are typically run on-premises. All of the big cloud providers offer a message broker of one form or another, including Azure, Google, and AWS (which use ActiveMQ).

Microservices are simply a type of distributed system, and they fit well with using containers. The idea is that you encapsulate the smallest level of functionality inside a self-contained process. The key thing here is that the process is self-contained – while there doesn't appear to be an official document that declares what microservices are, it would be wrong to call something a microservice if you simply had a process that had a direct dependency on another process.

It's worth considering the term dependency here. In my EDI example, clearly, a dependency exists in a logical process sense. The test here is whether you can turn one of these processes off and the other(s) continue (obviously with limited effect).

We've covered what creating a distributed system does for us, but let's consider the downsides to this approach, as there are many: you definitely should not create a distributed system unless you *need* one. I've compiled a (non-exhaustive) list of negatives here (each of these can be mitigated to an extent, but the purpose of this list is to illustrate that this isn't a silver bullet):

- **Data integrity**: In a system with a single data store, you can simply rely on the transactional model of your DBMS of choice to ensure that when you, for example, create a sales order, your stock is reduced. With a truly distributed system, these may be separate, independent services, and you can't execute these as a single transaction; the net effect of this is that you cannot guarantee that, at any specific given time, your data is correct.
- **System complexity**: Once you start creating many services, you'll find that you have a web of logical dependencies (similar to the physical dependencies you may have in a monolithic or *n*-tier system, as we mentioned previously).

Speed: The fastest possible way to write a set of data to a database is to do so in a single transaction. Once you introduce a service bus into the middle of this process, you reduce its speed significantly.

- **Maintenance**: While one of the advantages of using this architectural style is that you can independently update individual components, it is also one of the downsides. If you have 50 different components, then you need to track 50 different versions.

In this chapter, we will do the following:

- Create a very simple sales order processing system. There will be no frontend, but we will feed it a list of sales orders.
- Wrap our system in a Docker container and add it to a Kubernetes cluster hosted on **Azure Kubernetes Service** (**AKS**).
- Demonstrate that, even though we may kill an instance of that service, or it may crash, Kubernetes can self-heal and our orders will continue to be processed.

I've mentioned both Docker and Kubernetes, but what exactly are these technologies? It's easiest to start by exploring Docker.

Exploring Docker

Docker is a container engine: what that means is that you can encapsulate all the dependencies of the process (the executable) into a single entity. I often think that it helps to analyze the journey that ended with (or has currently reached) containers.

At one time, in the Microsoft development world (before .NET), we would write an application that still had dependencies on DLLs. Windows provided a registry that told the program where the DLL would be. When it was time to ship the product, you would have to create an installer that added your dependencies into the registry; however, because all the DLLs were held centrally, you then had an issue where another program could depend on the same DLL, but a different version of that DLL. Needless to say, this caused untold issues, and we simply didn't know what code was running on-site and were never confident that anything would install. Registry cleaners and install tools sprung up left, right, and center, and finally Microsoft moved away from the registry model.

When .NET was released, there were two ways to ship your dependencies: you could install them to the **Global Assembly Cache** (**GAC**) or just put them in the same directory as the executable. The GAC had its own issues (it was quite close to the registry model), but the *package up dependencies that I needed and used* worked quite well; however, what happens when you want to use a system dependency (.NET Framework, for example)? Well, again, Microsoft was quite good in that they would allow you to add this to an installer, but we are back to the principle that we're taking a piece of software and running it in a different environment than it was tested in. For example, what version of SQL Server did you write your data access against, and is that the version that's on the target machine?

What started to spring up was the principle of creating a virtual machine and then taking the entire virtual machine and simply copying it to the destination; that way, you can be absolutely sure what's running because it's essentially the same machine that the testing was done on. This was a good solution, but it (arguably) went too far. There are now a number of virtual machines with operating systems and licenses that need to be updated and maintained. What was needed was a container for the application where you could store the application and its dependencies, but the whole thing needed to be abstracted from the operating system.

That's essentially what Docker is – a container just like that.

Kubernetes and orchestration

For all intents and purposes, Kubernetes came out around 2016. This was inspired by an internal Google product that they had been using for some years internally. To illustrate what Kubernetes allows us to do, I invite you to walk through a little scene.

You're in a queue at a supermarket. The tills are, unfortunately, very problematic and are constantly breaking down. There is a man that works for the supermarket who has the job of keeping the queue flowing: his name is Winston, and so each time a till breaks down, he redirects the next person in the queue to another till, fixes the till, and then reopens it.

Suddenly, the queue gets very big: 200,000 people all join the queue together. Winston has instructions that, should this happen, he should "scale out" and so he quickly builds another 500 tills to cope with the strain; it takes a few minutes, but the tills quickly come online and the queue flows again:

Kubernetes acts as our Winston: it can create new containers, upgrade existing containers with no downtime, and route traffic.

Creating our microservice

We should consider what our microservice is, and what it is not: the most important thing here is that the service needs to be autonomous. If we create a service that needs other services in order to run, then it is not a microservice.

> We shouldn't confuse this with creating a service that requires other services to function. For example, our sales order processing system must have sales orders, and these come from an external source. This is fine because we're not dependent on that external source: if we don't get a list of sales orders, then our service will still run; it just won't do anything.

Let's start by creating our new service!

Remember that what we mean here by *service* is a process that performs a task: it should not be confused with specific usages of the word service, such as a REST service. What we want is simply an independent process.

Bear in mind that, like Winston, our busy supermarket employee, Kubernetes can scale your application by *replicating* the container. You can only replicate a container or process if that process is written in such a way to allow it. What this means for us is that we need to communicate with our service using a mechanism that allows multiple processes to read from a single queue, which needs to be maintained.

If we return to our example involving Winston the super supermarket employee, each person in the queue approaches the till only when they are called; if they all try to approach the till together, then the till operator will not be able to serve them. Alternatively, imagine a situation where the till operator comes to the queue and scans the items of the person at the front, but then leaves that person there: the next available till operator may do the same. Winston creating new tills only works if there is a mechanism in place for the customers to approach the tills in an orderly fashion.

The same is true of our containers: if you design a microservice in the wrong way, then it simply can't be scaled.

Queues

In order to get around this situation, we'll use Azure Service Bus to provide a queue for our feed into the system; because we don't need guaranteed delivery order, we can use storage queues rather than service bus queues.

It's worth bearing in mind that, in the case of sales order processing, the order that processes the messages is probably not too important; however, this is not always the case. You should carefully consider whether the order of delivery is critical in your own case.

Let's start by configuring our queue:

1. The first thing we need to do is create a new storage account. In the Azure portal, select **Storage accounts** from the menu, or simply search. Once the **Create storage account** blade appears, select the option to add a new storage account:

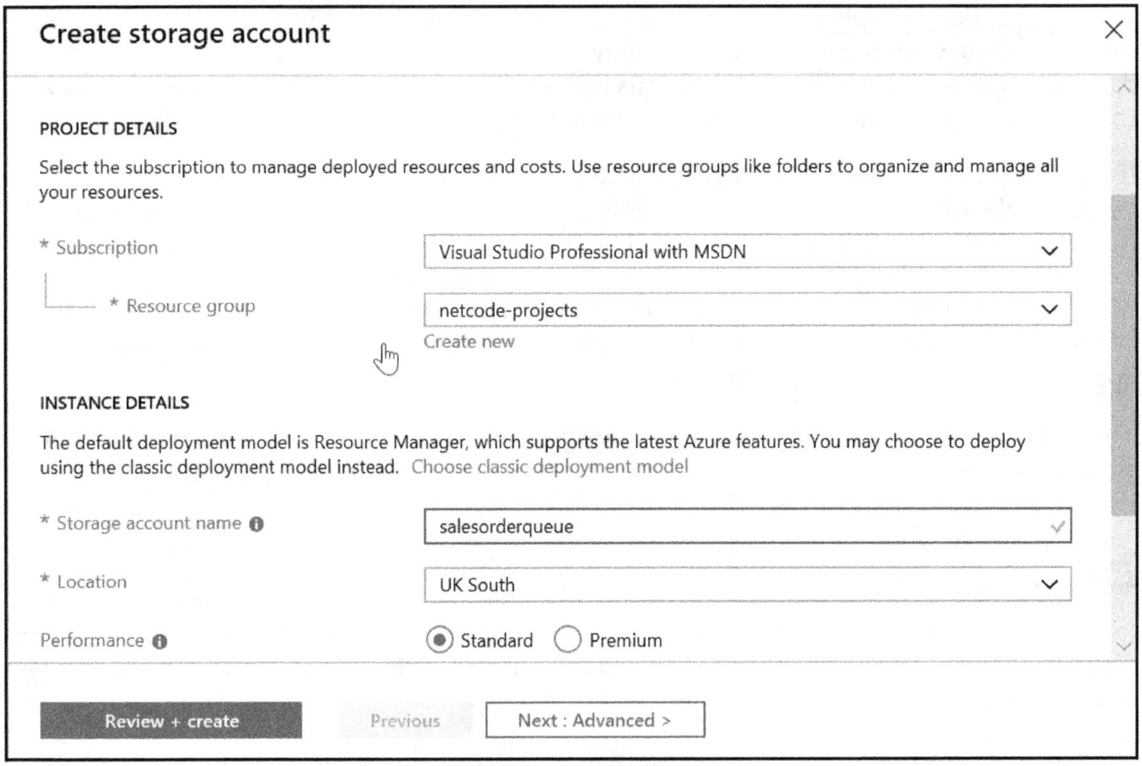

2. At the time of writing, there are four services available when creating a storage account: Blobs, Files, Tables, and Queues. We want **Queues** for what we're doing, so select that from the list:

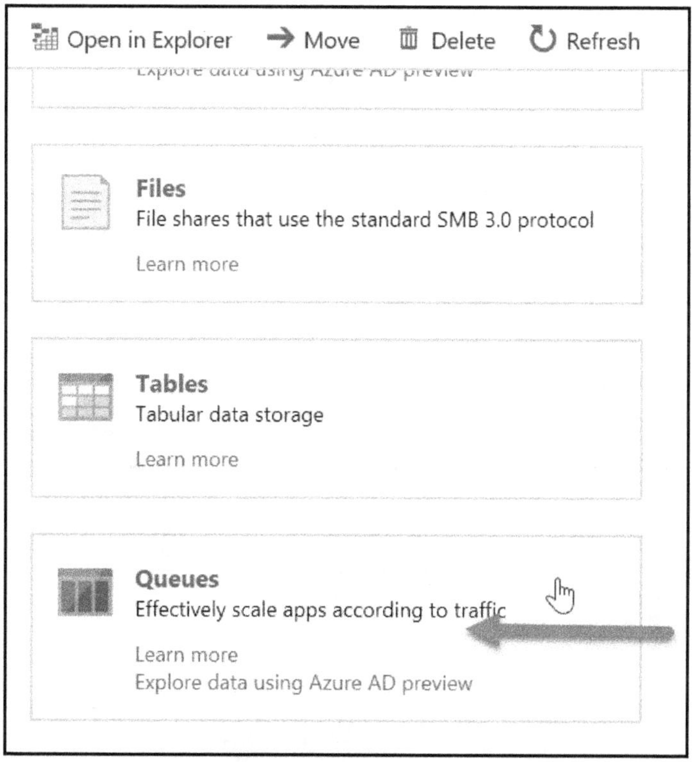

3. Once you select **Queues**, you'll be presented with a list of queues that are currently set up. It's initially quite lonely in here, so let's create a new queue:

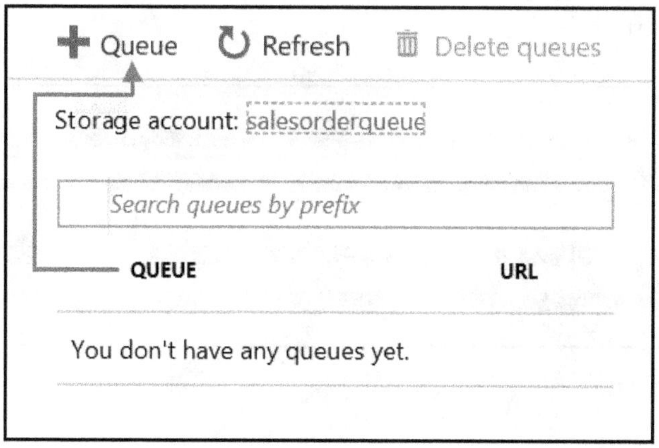

You'll be asked to name your queue here:

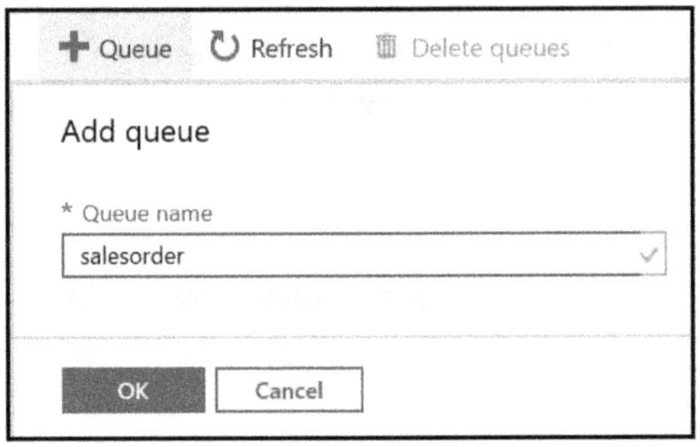

5. Once the new queue has been created, make a note of the URL as we'll need it later on:

6. Next, navigate to **Access keys** and copy the **Connection string** (again, we'll need this later on):

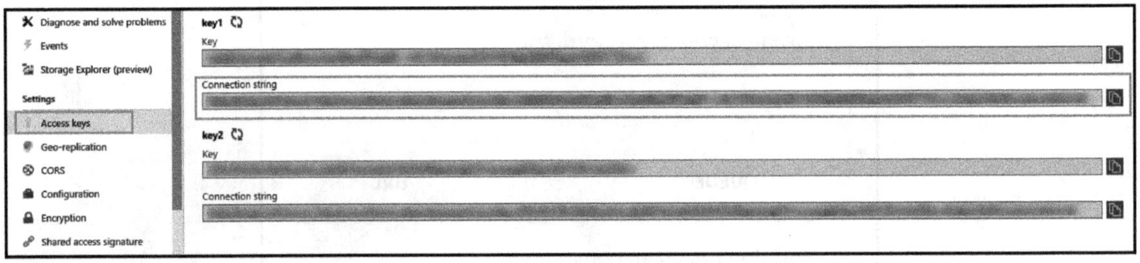

We have configured our queue and it's time to investigate how we can simulate sales orders being created.

Sales order generator

Because we don't have a website with thousands of orders coming in, we'll create a new process to generate a new sales order message. Then, we'll use a tool called JMeter to call this process enough times to simulate a heavy load. Let's build our application to create new messages first; the first step is to create a new .NET Core 3 console application.

> **TIP:** If you have decided to not use JMeter, then follow through anyway, and I'll explain which sections you should skip.

Because we're going to write to and read from a storage queue, we'll put that code inside a separate helper library. For now, we'll simply write the code as though the helper exists. Let's start with the console's main method:

```
static void Main(string[] args)
{
    // How many to create?
    int salesOrderCount = int.Parse(args[0]);

    // Set-up Helpers and Dependencies
    var serviceBusHelper = new ServiceBusHelper();
    var productRepository = new ProductRepository();
    var productService = new ProductService(productRepository);
    var salesOrderRepository = new SalesOrderRepository();

    // Process sales orders - will run forever
    var generateSalesOrders = new GenerateSalesOrders(serviceBusHelper,
productService);
    generateSalesOrders.Run(salesOrderCount);
}
```

As you can see, we're following the standard of manually building our dependencies, rather than using a third-party library.

```
public class GenerateSalesOrders
{
    private readonly IServiceBusHelper _serviceBusHelper;
    private readonly IProductService _productService;
    private Random _rnd = new Random();
    public GenerateSalesOrders(IServiceBusHelper serviceBusHelper,
IProductService productService)
    {
        _serviceBusHelper = serviceBusHelper;
        _productService = productService;
    }
}
```

We're just accepting some basic dependencies here: `serviceBusHelper` and `productService`. We'll go into the details of these classes shortly.

For now, I'd like to draw your attention to the `_rnd` variable. Outside of writing games, it's rare that you'll find random numbers in code. I felt that it made sense here because we're generating example data. Clearly, any test that uses a random number doesn't adhere to FIRST testing principles.

The next part of the class is the `Run` method:

```
public void Run(int salesOrderCount)
{
    for (int i = 0; i < salesOrderCount; i++)
    {
        var newOrder = CreateSalesOrder();
        _serviceBusHelper.SendToSalesOrderMessageQueue(newOrder);
    }
}
```

This simply calls a method to create a sales order and then uses the service bus helper to put the message on the queue. We'll come back to the service bus in the next section, but for now, let's have a look into the `CreateSalesOrder()` method to see what it does:

```
private SalesOrder.Models.SalesOrder CreateSalesOrder()
{
    var products = _productService.GetProductData();
    var product = products.ElementAt(_rnd.Next(products.Count() - 1));
    var salesOrder = new SalesOrder.Models.SalesOrder()
    {
        ProductCode = product.ProductCode,
        UnitPrice = product.UnitPrice,
        Quantity = _rnd.Next(1, 5)
    };
```

```
        return salesOrder;
    }
```

There's a bit more to this method, but essentially all we're doing is calling the product service to retrieve a list of products and then picking one at random. Finally, we're creating a sales order with a random quantity.

The product service reads a list of products from a product repository; for the sake of completeness, I'll list both the product service and its interface here. However, since it only calls through to the product repository, I won't go into any further explanation of the code:

```
public interface IProductService
{
    IEnumerable<Models.Product> GetProductData();
}
```

The implementation is as follows:

```
public class ProductService : IProductService
{
    private readonly IProductRepository _productRepository;
    public ProductService(IProductRepository productRepository)
    {
        _productRepository = productRepository;
    }

    public IEnumerable<Models.Product> GetProductData()
    {
        return _productRepository.GetProductData();
    }
}
```

Again, I'll list the repository interface, but it doesn't warrant any explanation:

```
public interface IProductRepository
{
    IList<SalesOrder.Models.Product> GetProductData();
}
```

The interesting part here is in the implementation. However, before we go into that, I'll show you where these components are in my solution, along with the data that I'll be using for the product data:

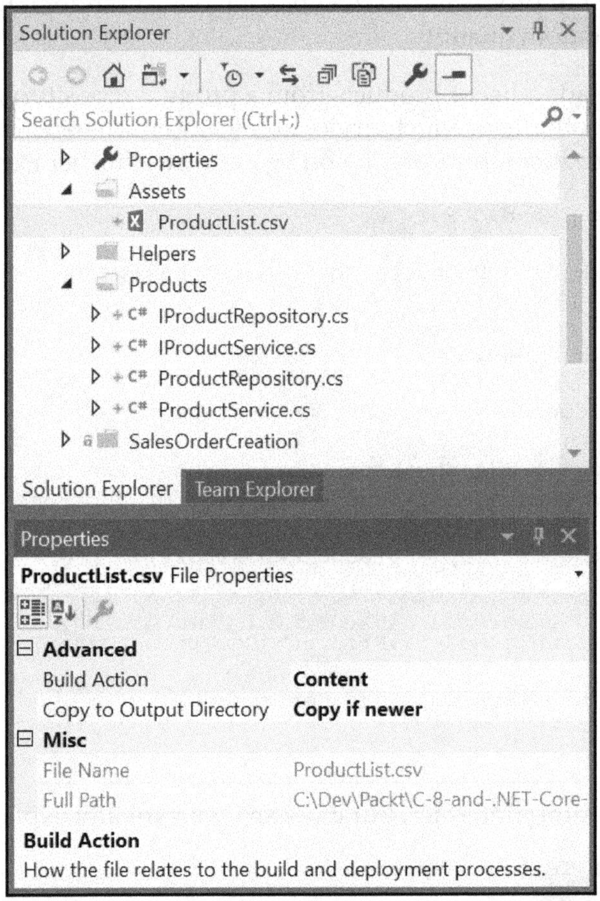

The `ProductList.csv` file is included as a content file. I won't list the full contents here, but if you would like to see it, then I would encourage you to download it from the GitHub repository. However, I will list the first few lines to give you a feel for the format of the file (after all, I'm sure you're just as capable of making up product codes and prices as I am!). The file should be in the following format:

```
SCREW025MMX50,1.72
HARDWOODSQMT,0.45
SLEDGEHAMMER,34.56
```

The product repository method looks like this:

```
public IList<SalesOrder.Models.Product> GetProductData()
{
    string data = File.ReadAllText($"Assets/ProductList.csv");
    var products = new List<Models.Product>();
    string[] productLines = data.Split(Environment.NewLine);
    foreach(var productLine in productLines)
    {
        string[] productData = productLine.Split(",");
        var product = new Models.Product()
        {
            ProductCode = productData[0],
            UnitPrice = decimal.Parse(productData[1])
        };

        products.Add(product);
    }

    return products;
}
```

This file does have quite a lot in it, starting with a call to read all the text from the data file. First, we're splitting that into lines and then, in turn, with commas. Finally, we're creating a new product class object and reading the data in.

This code isn't very resilient: you should be able to break it quite easily with some poorly formatted data. Should you choose to extend this project, you may wish to start here, either to improve the code by adding some defensive checks, or even to move the data to a database; for any serious extension, the latter is advised.

TIP: Should you wish to improve the reliability of the code, you may choose to use the following NuGet package, which I created: `https://www.nuget.org/packages/Castr/`.

Now that we've finished with our services and repositories, let's have a look at the Service Bus helper.

The Service bus helper library

As you saw in the preceding section, we're referring to a service bus helper. For the generation routine, we'll just have a single method in the service bus helper. I would strongly encourage you to put this code in its own project: that way, you can limit your dependency on Azure to a single project. Here's the overview of my solution as it currently stands:

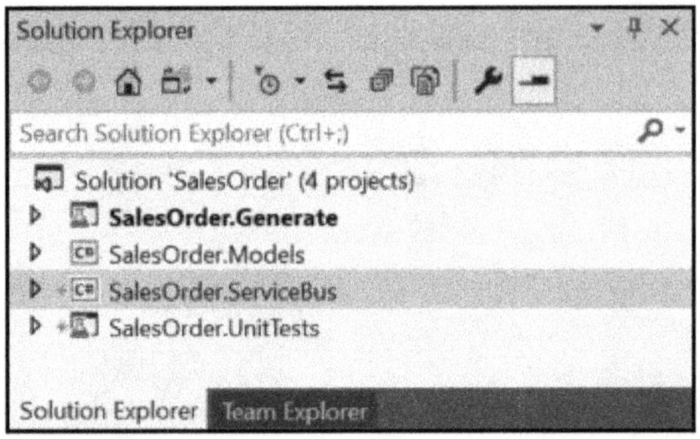

As you can see, we've separated the service bus interaction. Let's have a look at the interface that we've been using so far:

```
public interface IServiceBusHelper
{
    Task SendToSalesOrderMessageQueue(SalesOrder.Models.SalesOrder
salesOrderData);
}
```

Inside our new project, we'll need to reference a Microsoft NuGet library:

```
Install-Package WindowsAzure.Storage
```

Once we've done this, we can implement our helper method:

```
public async Task SendToSalesOrderMessageQueue(Models.SalesOrder
salesOrderData)
{
    CloudStorageAccount storageAccount =
CloudStorageAccount.Parse("DefaultEndpointsProtocol=https;AccountName=sales
orderqueue;AccountKey=...;EndpointSuffix=core.windows.net");

    CloudQueueClient queueClient = storageAccount.CreateCloudQueueClient();
    CloudQueue queue = queueClient.GetQueueReference("salesorder");
    CloudQueueMessage message = new
CloudQueueMessage(JsonConvert.SerializeObject(salesOrderData));
```

```
        await queue.AddMessageAsync(message);
    }
```

Before we delve into an explanation of what this is doing, note that the string that's passed to `CloudStorageAccount.Parse()` is the connection string that we made a note of earlier. As you can see, I've put the connection string directly into the code. Needless to say, this is bad practice; however, as in previous chapters, I feel that it illustrates, the software that we are actually writing better, and more directly.

So, what is this code doing? Well, initially, we create a `CloudStorageAccount` instance; this effectively connects to the Azure storage account and acts as the basis for our future calls. Next, we're asking for a `CloudQueueClient` and then getting a reference to the queue itself using `GetQueueReference`. Finally, we build up a new message by simply serializing our class data and adding that to the queue.

TIP

A message should contain all the information that's necessary to deal with that message. You should think carefully about the size of your message; however, on storage queues, you have a limit of 200 GB!

Testing our sales order generator and JMeter

Before we proceed, let's give our generator a quick test. There are two ways to do this; the first is to compile and run the software in the command line, but you can also simply provide a parameter in the project properties:

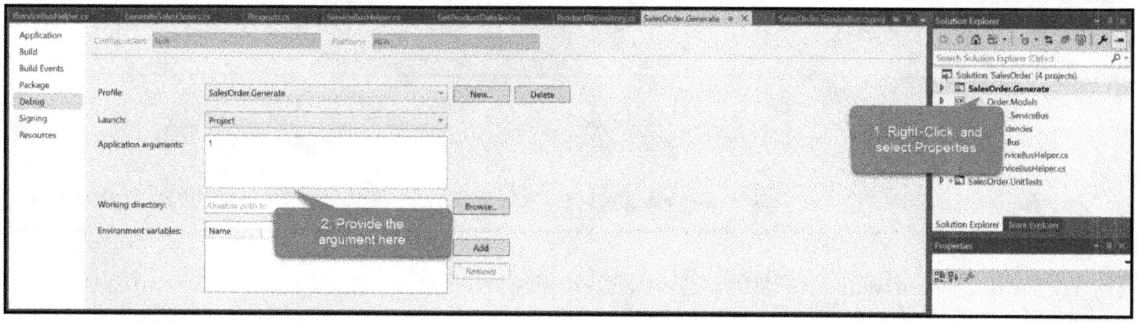

As you can see, I've chosen to create a single order. It's always best to try creating a single item first, just to check it runs correctly. Once you know this works, you can up it to, say, 10 or 20.

How do you know it works? Helpfully, Microsoft has the Storage Explorer application, which you can download for free; you can find it here: `https://azure.microsoft.com/en-us/features/storage-explorer/`.

Furthermore, at the time of writing, Microsoft has released a preview of the same tool inside the portal:

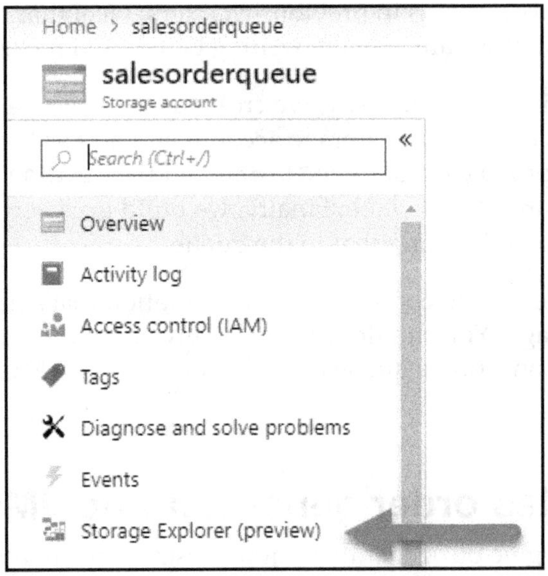

Whichever way you decide to look at the queue, once you've run the sales order generator, you should see a message in the queue (the following screenshot is from the desktop version):

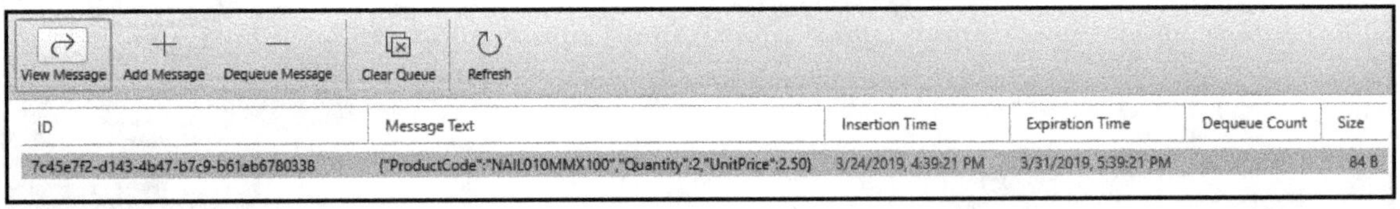

Try running the software for 10 or even 100 messages, just to check that it generates them as expected.

Our next step will be to call our program from JMeter so that we can simulate many orders being placed simultaneously.

JMeter

To simulate a heavy load, one option is simply to compile the application and run several instances of it together. This is what tools like JMeter do for you: I mentioned in the *Technical requirements* section that JMeter was optional; if you would rather not use JMeter, then simply run your application several times, with the number set to around 100. The following DOS command will do this for you:

```
for /l %x in (1, 1, 10) do start SalesOrder.Generate.exe 10
```

In this case, we're calling the `Generate` routine 10 times. This will add 100 messages to the queue almost instantly. You'll find a batch script in the GitHub repository that performs this same action. If you don't wish to use JMeter, then feel free to skip to the next section, entitled *Logging*.

Back to JMeter and, assuming you have successfully installed the JDK (see the *Technical requirements* section), you should be able to simply extract the ZIP file to somewhere on your local drive and run `jmeter.bat`. You can find this in the following subdirectory of the extraction: `apache-jmeter-5.1\bin`.

If you have successfully run the software, you should be presented with a screen similar to this:

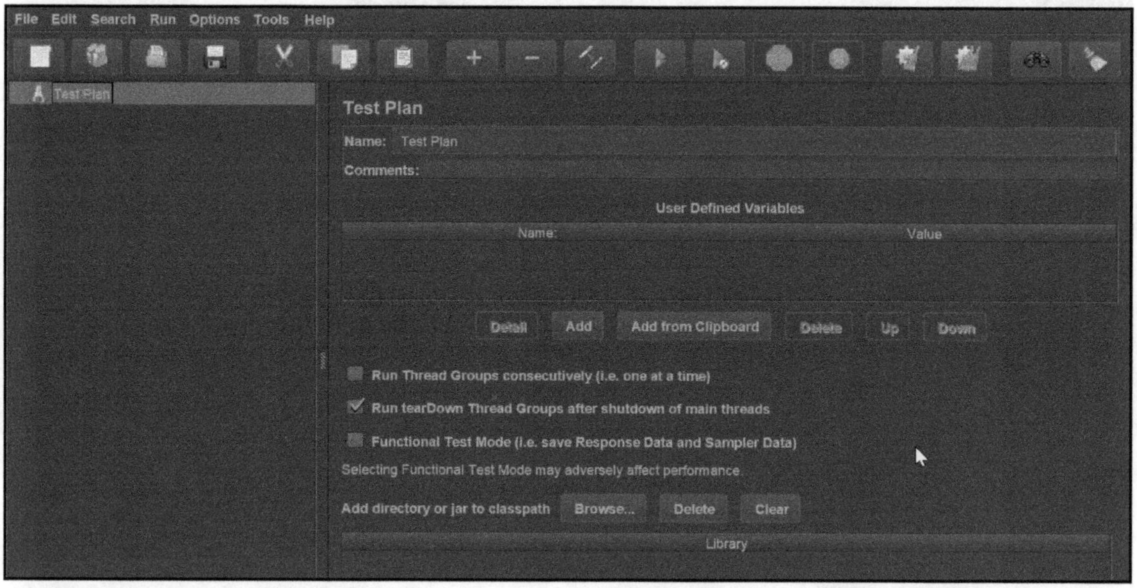

It's worth bearing in mind that, depending on when you are reading this, the user interface for JMeter may have changed.

The first step is to add a **Thread Group**:

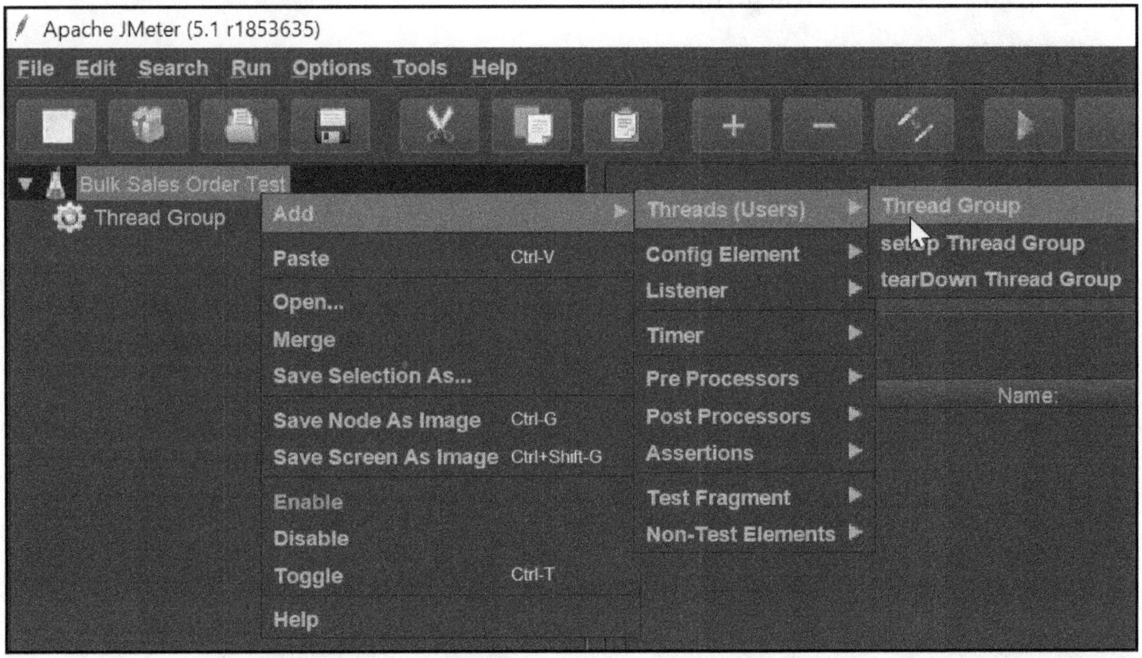

A thread group is a way to represent a set of users performing an action. Let's set up 10 users who will execute our generation app 10 times each.

10 users running the app 10 times and the app generating 10 orders for each invocation means that 1,000 orders will be generated.

Here's how we might configure the preceding scenario on the threads screen:

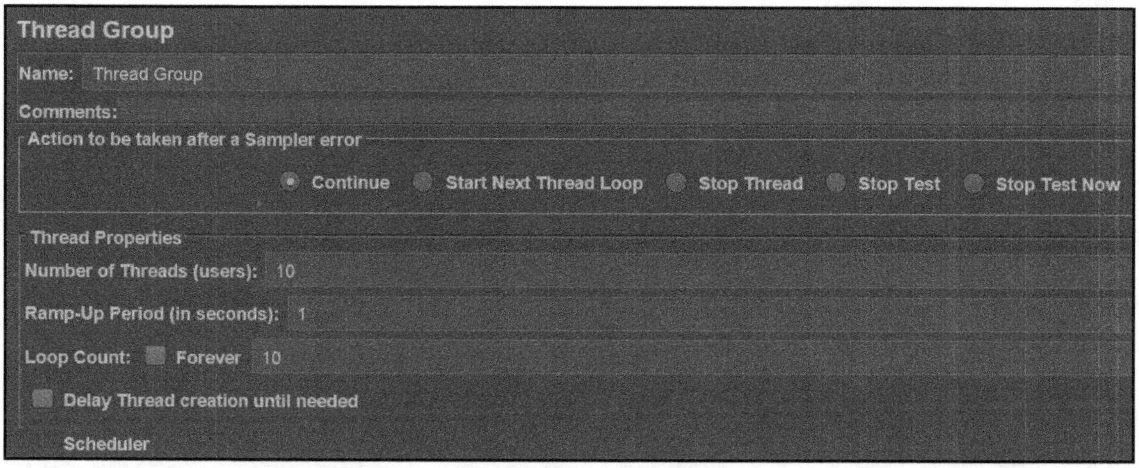

Finally, we'll add a new sampler to call our executable:

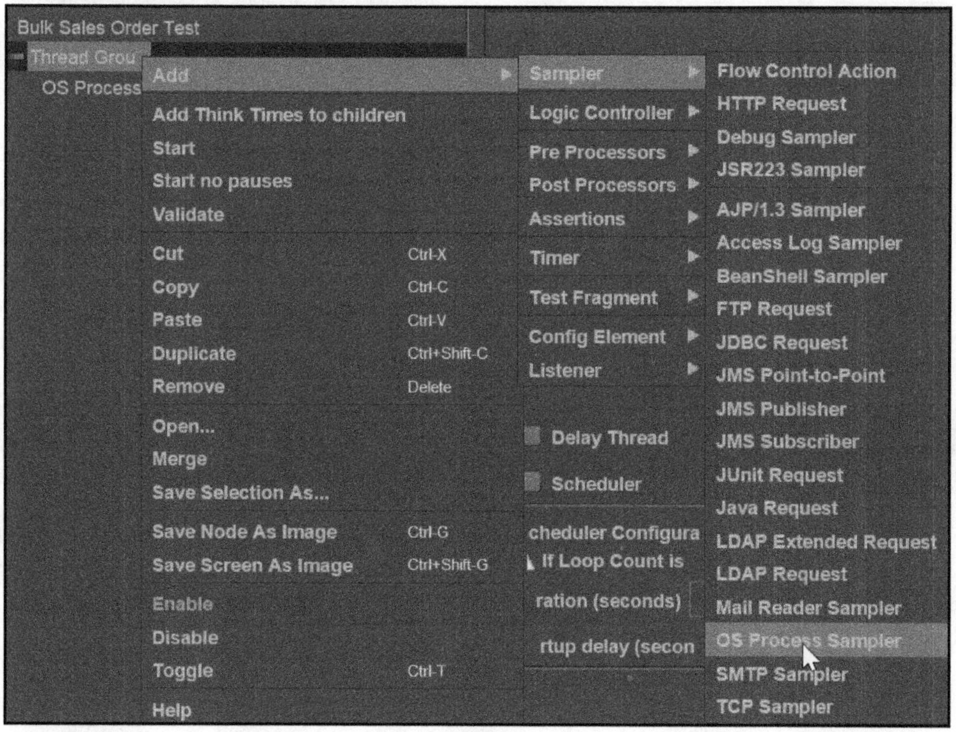

Once we've added that, we can ask it to call our executable from the new sampler and we're done:

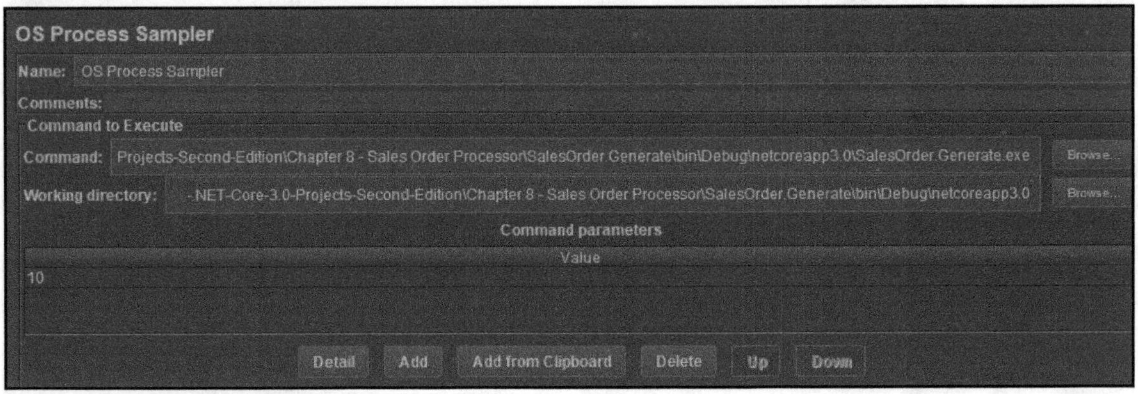

We're ready to go. Simply press the play button. 10 users should instantly start placing orders at a rate of knots!

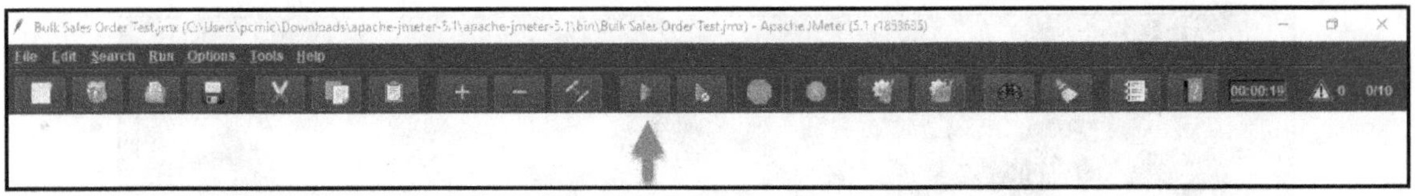

Logging

Before we progress any further, we should consider logging. Using a single application, logging is quite an easy process – you log everything to a log file (typically located on the server) and, since all the calls are to services on that single server, everything is logged in one place. Among other problems that we create when moving to microservices, we create one of logging. Exactly which service is logging, and where is it logging to? In a container system, you can't simply log to the local filesystem because it's not necessarily persisted.

It is far beyond the scope of this chapter to create an aggregated logging system; however, should you wish to do so, I would strongly suggest that you look at some of the offerings from the main cloud providers. Application Insights from Microsoft offers a logging capability.

Another option would be to simply create a logging queue and write all your log messages to a queue (then, you could, optionally, write a consumer than converted this into a single file). Remember that you could potentially have multiple log messages written at exactly the same time, so you should have a way to separate these processes.

Creating a new microservice

Now that we have a queue and some data, we can create our new microservice.

> Our microservice will be technology-agnostic. It will be written in .NET Core 3.0 and it will be running inside a Linux container; however, it will not have any hard dependencies on any external hosting, so we should be able to take it out of AKS and drop it into Google-hosted Kubernetes. If you are developing microservices (or anything), you should ask yourself why you are using the technology (and architecture) that you've chosen. An answer such as *to gain exposure to that technology* is an acceptable reason if it's a personal project, but if you are being paid to produce a piece of software, saying this may not be acceptable to the person paying you. Kubernetes is an excellent container orchestrator, but bear in mind that if you simply write an Azure WebJob or function, you may get all of the benefits that you need with less of the overhead.

Our service itself is very simple. We'll just monitor the queue and, where we find a message, we'll process it. Obviously, a complete, fully functional sales order processing system would be far too much code for a single chapter; however, we will produce a complete process that will do the following:

- Add a new sales order to the database
- Add a message to another queue for the dispatch system to pick up

You may have realized from the architecture that this process is a disjointed one; that is, when the user places an order, the process to check whether there's enough stock to fulfill the order happens offline. This is intentional: it's how systems such as this can deal with sudden surges of traffic; however, it means that you have to rethink your user experience. Say the user has placed the order and then, at some point in the future, the order is rejected. There are ways to deal with this; for example, if stock is your only potential issue, you could simply factor in the time it would take to restock the item into the lead time so that every order has a delivery window of 10 days, but most are delivered in 2. In short, it's a business logic problem, but perhaps one that you wouldn't have with a more conventional architecture.

Now, we have to create our microservice. The logic of this is actually relatively simple; the service should do the following:

- Check the sales order queue for a new request; if there are no requests, then the service should check again in a period of time (we'll go for 1 minute)
- Where a message is found, the service should add the sales order to the database
- The service should put a message on a new queue to say that the order was successful

Clearly, this flow is abridged, but it is fully functional in and of itself.

Creating our new Docker Container

Let's start by creating a new console application; we are going to compile and run this in a Linux container. The console application is created exactly like any other console application, although since we're dealing with Linux, the naming must be in lowercase and cannot contain dots. This makes our solution look a little messy, but nevertheless, let's create `salesorder-process`:

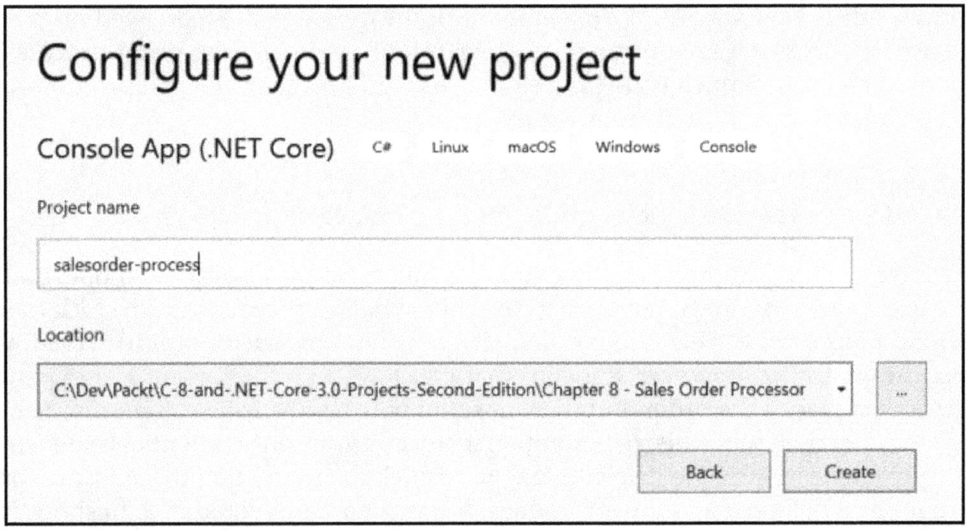

Our next step is to add Docker support. Here, you could simply create a Docker file manually, but Visual Studio kindly helps us along with this. By right-clicking the project, there is now an **Add | Docker Support** option:

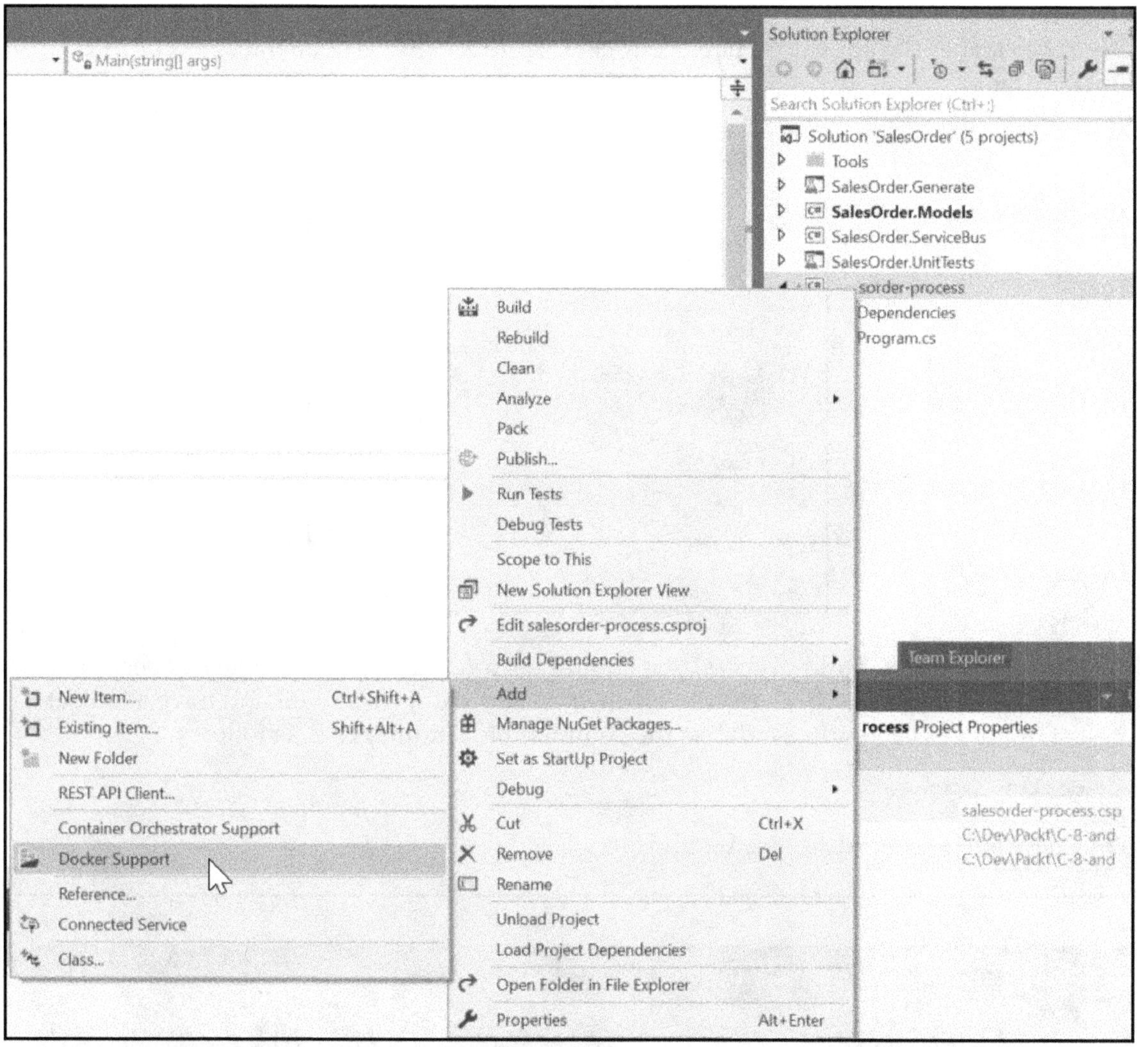

You'll be presented with an option to create either a Windows or Linux container; we'll select Linux. This will create your Dockerfile for you.

Docker for Windows either runs Linux or Windows containers, but at the time of writing, it cannot run both (you can switch). It looks like Microsoft is going all-in on Linux containers, so my advice would be going for Linux and staying with them. Of course, this is just my personal opinion.

Once the Docker file appears, a new right-click context menu is available. Select **Build Docker Image**:

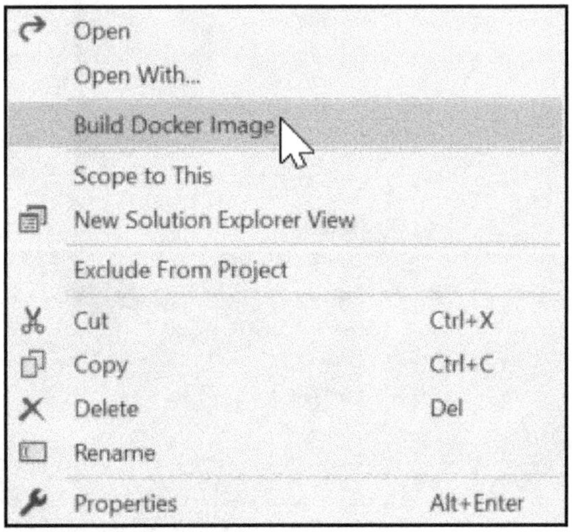

After a fairly lengthy build process, you should get a report that the image has been successfully created. To check this, let's run an instance of PowerShell and have a look at the list of images currently available; the command to list images is as follows:

```
docker images
```

Your new image should be listed at the top:

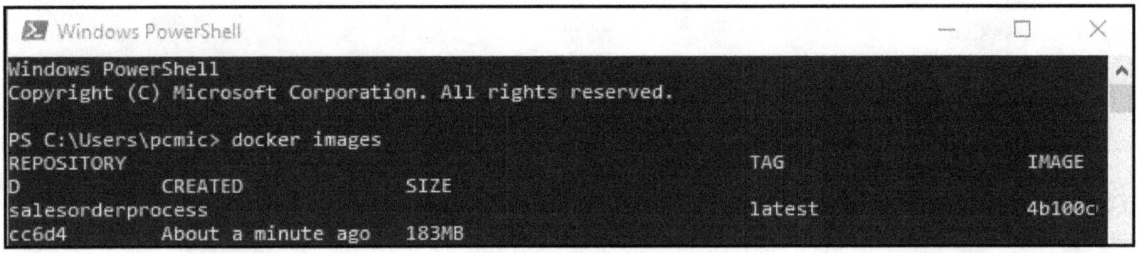

Now, we can run this image, just to check that it's built correctly. To do so, use the following command:

```
docker run salesorderprocess
```

You should be presented with the output of the console application; since we haven't changed anything yet, this is the default `Hello World`.

Now that we have successfully created the container, let's start by adding the logic that will make up the microservice.

Creating the microservice logic

The logic itself is relatively straightforward; however, you'll notice some gaps in here where we are using methods and classes that either don't exist or are not accessible. We'll start by putting our logic into a separate class; to make the class easy to understand, we'll create a public function called `Run`:

```
public async Task Run()
{
    while (true)
    {
        if (!await ProcessEachMessage())
        {
            await Task.Delay(60000);
            continue;
        }
    }
}
```

The logic here is that we try to get the next message from the service bus; when we are not successful, we wait for a minute and try again. Let's see what `ProcessEachMessage` looks like:

```
public async Task<bool> ProcessEachMessage()
{
    SalesOrder.Models.SalesOrder? salesOrder = await
_serviceBusHelper.GetNextOrderFromMessageQueue();

    if (salesOrder == null) return false;

    _salesOrderService.Create(salesOrder);
    await _serviceBusHelper.ConfirmSalesOrderToMessageQueue(salesOrder);

    return true;
}
```

If we do get a sales order from the queue, we call a service method to create the sales order; then, we add a confirmation message to the queue.

> This is the basis of this kind of design; where you need to communicate with other parts of the system, you need to do so via a mechanism that doesn't require that part of the system to respond immediately (or, indeed, at all). In this case, if we stopped this service and then ran the generator, the generator would not fail because this service was not running.

We're using a separate class so that we can inject our dependencies; as you can see, we're using a few here, and they are mostly non-existent at the minute. We'll cover those shortly, but let's just cover the constructor of our new class first:

```
private readonly IServiceBusHelper _serviceBusHelper;
private readonly IProductService _productService;
private readonly ISalesOrderService _salesOrderService;

public SalesOrderProcessor(IServiceBusHelper serviceBusHelper,
                           IProductService productService,
                           ISalesOrderService salesOrderService)
{
    _serviceBusHelper = serviceBusHelper;
    _productService = productService;
    _salesOrderService = salesOrderService;
}
```

You'll need to add a reference to the `SalesOrder.ServiceBus` and `SalesOrder.Models` projects at this stage. We've now reached the stage where most of the code inside `SalesOrder.Generate` should be brought into its own project so that it can be accessed from elsewhere. Because most of this is moving code from one project to another, I won't detail each class, but simply show the structure of the new and old project; here's the `SalesOrder.Generate` project after the move:

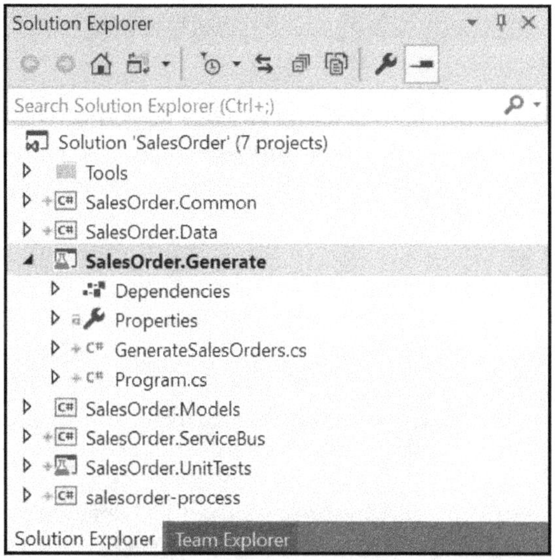

As you can see, we've moved almost everything out of `SalesOrder.Generate` and shifted it into a new project: `SalesOrder.Data`. Let's have a look at what we have in `SalesOrder.Data`:

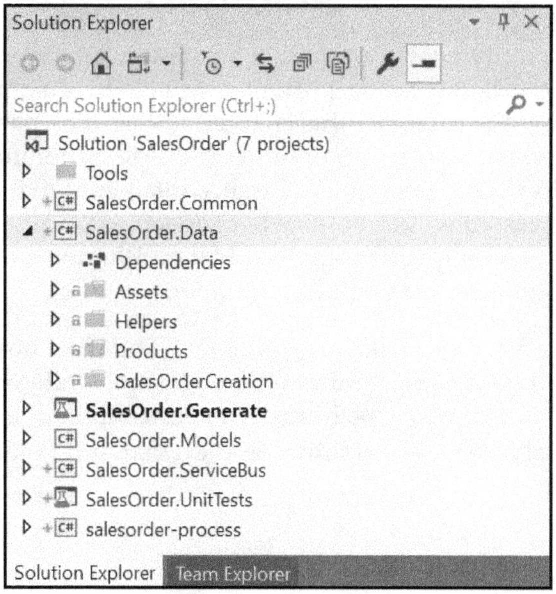

As you can see, we have simply taken the files from the one project and pasted them into the other. The only other step that was necessary was to rename the namespace; for example, the namespace for `ProductService` would now be `SalesOrder.Data.Products`.

> **TIP:** In cases like this, *Ctrl* + *Shift* + *H* is your best friend and will allow you to replace all the instances of the old namespace with the new one.

You'll also need to add some project references; the `SalesOrder.Generate` project should now reference the `SalesOrder.Data` project. The new `SalesOrder.Data` project, in turn, has a dependency on `SalesOrder.Models`.

Now that we have that out of the way, we can start filling in our stub functions; let's start with the `SalesOrder` service.

> **TIP:** For the sake of illustration, we grouped the service and data repository classes inside a single project. Generally, this should be avoided; should you decide to extend this project, separating the repository and the services may be a good idea.

Creating a new Azure SQL database

When you're writing for containers, especially when you want a smooth development experience, it's becoming less and less important to be able to remember the Docker commands; in fact, during the course of this chapter, it would be possible to not touch the command line until we start moving the container into AKS. Therefore, it is easy to forget that you're running inside a container, and a Linux container at that. EF Core allows you to connect to a SQL instance, so it would be easy to connect to (LocalDB). However, you won't be able to access this from within your container as it's a Windows-only concept and, of course, exists on the host machine, not in the container.

So, can we access SQL Server from within a container? And if so, how? The answer is that you can access it, but you need to remember where you are: while you're inside the container, your localhost is not your machine – it's your container. If you wanted to host your own SQL Server instance, you certainly could do that, but you would need to connect via your external IP address.

In our case, we intend to move this onto AKS, so it would make sense to have our database hosted in Azure. Let's quickly create a new SQL Azure database and server. From Azure, select the **SQL databases** blade:

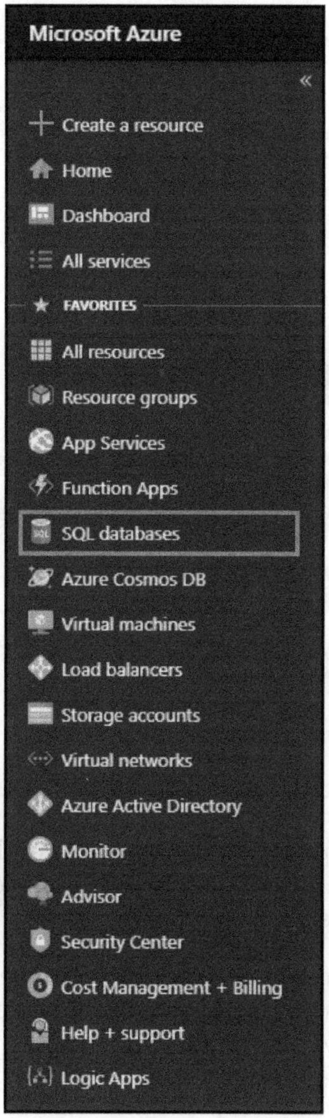

As usual, you can simply search for this as well. When selected, click **Add** to create a new database:

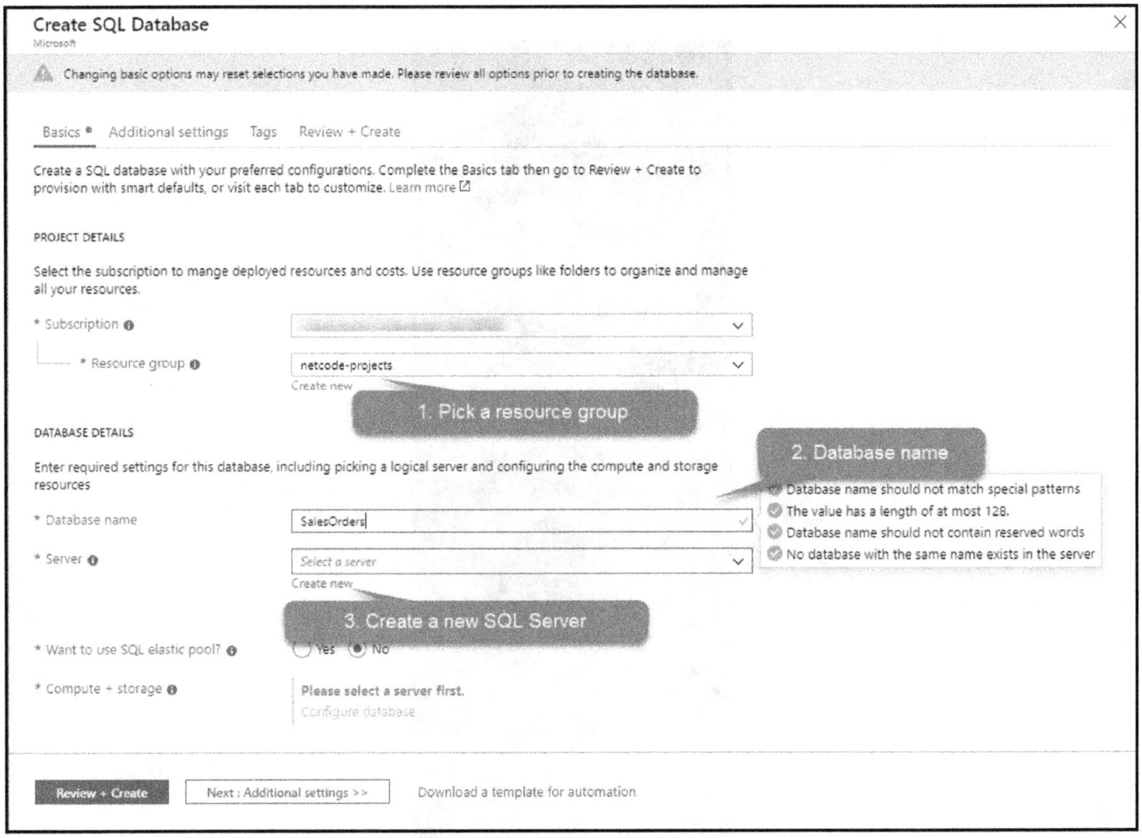

This screen is probably looking quite familiar by now. All the parts are broadly the same: **Subscription** and **Resource group** determine where your resource lives. The **Database name** should be unique per server.

Unless you already have a server set up, select the link labeled **Create a new SQL server**. This will open a window on the right-hand side of the screen, allowing you to create a new server. Once you've done so, it will populate that value for you.

> **TIP:** You'll be given a default Standard S0 compute and storage model. The compute and storage model that you choose is something that only you will know; however, if you are simply following along to learn how this works, I would recommend selecting the hyperlink to configure the database and selecting the **Basic** tier. At the time of writing, this comes in at under £5/month.

Once the resource has been created, select **Connection strings** from the **Overview** and keep a copy of the connection string – we'll need it shortly.

Entity Framework Core

At this stage, we'll need to introduce a data persistence layer. For this, we'll use **Entity Framework Core** (**EF Core**). The first step is to add EF Core to the data project:

```
Install-Package Microsoft.EntityFrameworkCore -ProjectName SalesOrder.Data
Install-Package Microsoft.EntityFrameworkCore.Tools -ProjectName
SalesOrder.Data
Install-Package Microsoft.EntityFrameworkCore.SqlServer -ProjectName
SalesOrder.Data
Install-Package Microsoft.EntityFrameworkCore.Design -ProjectName
salesorder-process
```

Once we've installed the necessary packages, we need a few classes so that EF Core can create our database; let's put them all in a new folder called `Entities` inside the `SalesOrder.Data` project. In fact, the first thing we'll need is a `SalesOrder` entity:

```
public class SalesOrderEntity : SalesOrder.Models.SalesOrder
{
    [DatabaseGenerated(DatabaseGeneratedOption.Identity)]
    public int Id { get; set; }
}
```

As you will see, we are just inheriting from our model. This process of having model classes that can be passed around agnostic of the database and then inheriting from them in order to create a database entity is not uncommon. You could simply tell EF to use the model class, but this method provides an abstraction so that you can mask updates to the model class and not have them proliferate to the database. We have also declared an auto-generated primary key here, too, which clearly has no place in our model.

Next, we'll need to create a database context:

```
public class SalesOrderContext : DbContext
{
    public SalesOrderContext(DbContextOptions<SalesOrderContext> options) :
base(options)
    {
    }

    public DbSet<SalesOrderEntity> SalesOrders { get; set; }
}
```

Here, we are simply saying that we want a single table to hold sales orders. The rest of the functionality is helpfully provided for us by EF Core (notice that we inherit from `DbContext`). Finally, we'll need a design context so that EF Core knows where to create our database:

```
public class SalesOrderContextFactory :
IDesignTimeDbContextFactory<SalesOrderContext>
{
    public SalesOrderContext CreateDbContext(string[] args)
    {
        var optionsBuilder = new
DbContextOptionsBuilder<SalesOrderContext>();
        optionsBuilder.UseSqlServer(@"Data Source=[ConnectionString]");

        return new SalesOrderContext(optionsBuilder.Options);
    }
}
```

This is simply so that EF Core can connect to our database and create or update it. You'll need to replace the `[ConnectionString]` placeholder with the connection string that you made a note of earlier.

TIP: The connection string has absolutely no place in this file; once you're familiar with how this works, I would encourage you to put this into a configuration file.

That's all the infrastructure that we need. The next step is to add the migration:

```
Add-Migration InitialCreation -Project SalesOrder.Data -StartupProject
salesorder-process
```

> **TIP:** You can call this command from PowerShell, or wherever you choose, but using the Package Manager Console inside Visual Studio gives you a nice little PowerShell interface directly inside the IDE.

This should create a `Migrations` folder in the `SalesOrder.Data` project and provide a migration that will create the database. To have it actually create the database, we need another command:

```
Update-Database -Project SalesOrder.Data -StartupProject salesorder-process
```

A quick look inside the SQL Server Object Explorer in Visual Studio should verify that the database has, in fact, been created. We can now proceed to our code and populate it from the message queue.

> **TIP:** There are ways that you can have your program automatically call the migration when it runs. There are advantages to doing this either way; this method provides more control (you won't be able to run the software if the database isn't up to date), however, having to manually run an update script might not make sense in your deployment scenario.

Creating the sales order

In creating the sales order, we effectively have two layers of abstraction: a service and a repository class. The idea here is that the repository is responsible for the data access and the service for the business concept. In our case, these are the same because it's such a simple application, but should you start to extend this project, keeping these differences in mind will help the code remain clean and concise.

> **TIP:** Abstraction, for the sake of it, is the enemy of simplicity. If you *know* that your application will always be just a UI over a database and that you will always use Entity Framework, then access the data context directly. Although this does reduce your ability to create unit tests that don't include data access, it could be argued that, in such a scenario, those tests were unnecessary anyway.

From the code that we created in the `Main` method previously, we have two new methods to create in the sales order service; we'll start with the creation of a sales order. `SalesOrderService` needs a single method called `Create`. Here's the amended interface:

```
public interface ISalesOrderService
{
    void Create(SalesOrder.Models.SalesOrder salesOrder);
}
```

Not much to look at, I'll grant you. The implementation of this is not much more complicated:

```
public void Create(SalesOrder.Models.SalesOrder salesOrder)
{
    var salesOrderEntity = new SalesOrderEntity()
    {
        ProductCode = salesOrder.ProductCode,
        Quantity = salesOrder.Quantity,
        Reference = salesOrder.Reference,
        UnitPrice = salesOrder.UnitPrice
    };
    _salesOrderRepository.Create(salesOrderEntity);
}
```

Our repository method accepts an entity of the `SalesOrderEntity` type (we covered this earlier), and this means that we have to convert the object here. We're injecting the repository into this class; here's the constructor and class variable for completeness:

```
public class SalesOrderService : ISalesOrderService
{
    private readonly ISalesOrderRepository _salesOrderRepository;

    public SalesOrderService(ISalesOrderRepository salesOrderRepository)
    {
        _salesOrderRepository = salesOrderRepository;
    }

    . . .
```

Our next step is to fill in the methods in the `StorageQueueHelper`.

The storage queue

We have two methods that need to be completed from the storage queue. Our first method is `ConfirmSalesOrderToMessageQueue`; this is responsible for posting a copy of the sales order to a new queue to indicate that we have processed it. You may start to notice a similarity between this and the method we wrote earlier to send a message to the queue in the first place:

```
public async Task ConfirmSalesOrderToMessageQueue(Models.SalesOrder
salesOrderData)
{
    CloudStorageAccount storageAccount =
CloudStorageAccount.Parse("DefaultEndpointsProtocol=https;AccountName=sales
orderqueue;AccountKey=aa8eED0s25wezSDCyj0BmukVq2zE9puEFRVq4jIR++n8L1NNSUyZZ
aJXZHVN91BgsQQ9sPE2gnlsb5MWC1TsVw==;EndpointSuffix=core.windows.net");

    CloudQueueClient queueClient = storageAccount.CreateCloudQueueClient();
    CloudQueue queue = queueClient.GetQueueReference("salesorderconfirm");
    await queue.CreateIfNotExistsAsync();
    CloudQueueMessage message = new
CloudQueueMessage(JsonConvert.SerializeObject(salesOrderData));

    await queue.AddMessageAsync(message);
}
```

Remember to replace the connection details with your own (these are not real account details).

In fact, the two methods are almost identical. The queue name is different, but clearly, the two methods could be refactored to be one, should you wish to do so. For now, I'm going to leave them separate as I think it illustrates their different functions better; however, I won't reexplain the code.

Finally, we have the code to get the next sales order from the queue, that is, `GetNextOrderFromMessageQueue`:

```
public async Task<Models.SalesOrder?> GetNextOrderFromMessageQueue()
{
    CloudStorageAccount storageAccount =
CloudStorageAccount.Parse("DefaultEndpointsProtocol=https;AccountName=sales
orderqueue;AccountKey=aa8eED0s25wezSDCyj0BmukVq2zE9puEFRVq4jIR++n8L1NNSUyZZ
aJXZHVN91BgsQQ9sPE2gnlsb5MWC1TsVw==;EndpointSuffix=core.windows.net");
    CloudQueueClient queueClient = storageAccount.CreateCloudQueueClient();
    CloudQueue queue = queueClient.GetQueueReference("salesorder");
```

```
        var message = await queue.GetMessageAsync();
        if (message == null) return null;
        string data = message.AsString;
        var salesOrder =
    JsonConvert.DeserializeObject<Models.SalesOrder>(data);

        await queue.DeleteMessageAsync(message.Id, message.PopReceipt);
        return salesOrder;
    }
```

Again, this is a very familiar set of methods; the highlights are as follows:

```
var message = await queue.GetMessageAsync();
...
string data = message.AsString;
```

This simply returns a message. Now, we can extract its content by using the `AsString` property. Then, we deserialize it back to a `SalesOrder` object:

```
await queue.DeleteMessageAsync(message.Id, message.PopReceipt);
```

This command removes the message from the queue. It's worth bearing in mind that, should something crash after this point, the message will be lost. You may wish to think about maintaining this ID, and perhaps even only deleting the message after the order is created. We could still, however, identify the order, as we would be able to determine that the sales order didn't have a confirmation.

If you run this project now, you should find that it works as expected and starts to process any messages that you have in the queue.

The final step is to upload this into Azure's AKS system, which completes the project.

Now that we've created our project, let's have a look at how we can host the project in Microsoft's Azure Kubernetes Service.

Azure Kubernetes Service

Azure Kubernetes Service (or **AKS**, as it is commonly abbreviated to) is just one of several cloud Kubernetes offerings. It acts as a kind of halfway point between creating and hosting your own Kubernetes cluster and uses specific cloud services, such as AWS Lambda and Azure Functions. The main advantages here are control (you can determine why and how your deployment scales) and portability (you should be able to up sticks from Microsoft, drop the exact same setup into Google, and continue from where you left off).

Building a Docker image

Let's create a Docker image from our code. Find the Dockerfile inside your project and select **Build Docker Image** from the context menu:

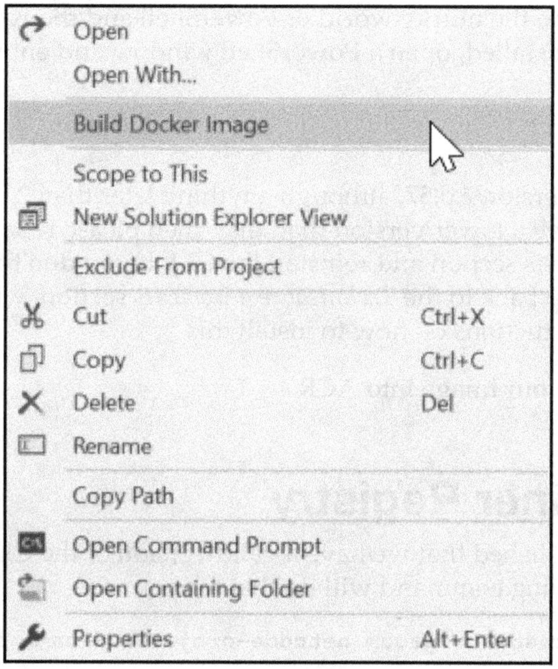

Azure Container registry

Now, you should be able to open PowerShell and type the following:

```
docker images
```

This will give you a list of any Docker images that you currently have on your machine. A container registry is essentially a remote version of this; that is, you create an image and upload it to a registry. When we're uploading to AKS, we'll need our image to be in a container registry. Although Azure does have its own container registry, you can use any; Docker has a container registry, and so do most (if not all) of the big cloud providers. In this section, we'll be uploading to **Azure Container Registry** (**ACR**).

Up until now, we've pretty much been relying on Visual Studio to manage our Docker image; at the time of writing, this is a very new feature and would previously require everything to be done in the command line. Now, we're going to need to leave the comfort of the IDE and delve into the murky world of PowerShell and the Azure CLI. To ensure that you have the CLI installed, open a PowerShell window and enter the following command:

```
az --version
```

Mine is version 2.0.57, although anything later than 2.0.55 should be fine. If you have a lower version than that, then please return to the *Technical requirements* section and reinstall the CLI. If you don't have this installed, then jump back to the *Technical requirements* section, where you'll find some instructions on how to install this.

Our first task is to push our image into ACR.

Azure Container Registry

Now that we have established that we have a valid version of the CLI, we can create our new registry; the following command will do that for you:

```
az acr create --resource-group netcode-projects --name salesorderregistry -
-sku Basic
```

`netcore-projects` is my resource group, so you'll need to replace that with your own. I've called my registry `salesorderregistry`, but providing you obey the naming rules, you can call yours anything you like. `sku` determines the performance and scale that's available.

> **TIP:** You would need to look into the specifics at the time of using this, but broadly, the more you pay, the better the performance and the easier it will scale. This is a common pattern with cloud utilization.

The response to the preceding command should look similar to this:

```
PS C:\> az acr create --resource-group netcode-projects --name salesorderregistry --sku Basic
{
  "adminUserEnabled": false,
  "creationDate": "2019-04-10T07:13:45.735754+00:00",
  "id": "/subscriptions/[redacted]/resourceGroups/netcode-projects/providers/Microsoft.Contai
erRegistry/registries/salesorderregistry",
  "location": "uksouth",
  "loginServer": "salesorderregistry.azurecr.io",
  "name": "salesorderregistry",
  "networkRuleSet": null,
  "provisioningState": "Succeeded",
  "resourceGroup": "netcode-projects",
  "sku": {
    "name": "Basic",
    "tier": "Basic"
  },
  "status": null,
  "storageAccount": null,
  "tags": {},
  "type": "Microsoft.ContainerRegistry/registries"
}
```

Make a note of the `loginServer` response as this determines how you will refer to your registry from here on in, starting with our login:

```
az acr login --name salesorderregistry
```

In the preceding command, `salesorderregistry` is, in fact, the value that was returned when we created the ACR a few moments ago (for the purposes of this command, we only need the first part of this value). You should get a response to this command, telling you that the login has succeeded.

Earlier, we had a look at the Docker images to identify the images that were present on our local system; we'll need that command again, but this time, we'll need to make a note of the image name and tag. As a reminder, the command for this is as follows:

```
docker images
```

The response should look like this:

```
PS C:\> docker images
REPOSITORY                                        TAG             IMAGE
D             CREATED             SIZE
salesorderprocess                                 dev             3071c2
fcfee         41 hours ago        183MB
salesorderprocess                                 latest          e95e57
5e62a         41 hours ago        192MB
```

First, we'll need to tag our image; the following command should do that for us:

```
docker tag salesorderprocess
salesorderregistry.azurecr.io/salesorderprocess:v1
```

If we list the images again, we should see the new tag:

```
salesorderregistry.azurecr.io/salesorderprocess                 v1              e95e574
5e62a         41 hours ago        192MB
```

Now that we have a tag, we can push this to our repository:

```
docker push salesorderregistry.azurecr.io/salesorderprocess:v1
```

This time, we should see some action; that is, as the image is pushed into the repository, you should see some status bars moving:

```
PS C:\> docker push salesorderregistry.azurecr.io/salesorderprocess:v1
The push refers to repository [salesorderregistry.azurecr.io/salesorderprocess]
e3015455a98c: Pushed
14a21ca053e7: Pushed
28faeef33b8f: Pushed
132c8212430d: Pushed
98b9d81b9b02: Pushed
5dacd731af1b: Pushing [=======================================>           ]  44.47MB/55.28MB
```

To confirm this, use the following command, which should tell you that your image is now, indeed, in ACR:

```
az acr repository list --name salesorderregistry --output table
```

Now that we have an image in the container registry, we can create our Kubernetes cluster and set up our orchestration.

Azure Kubernetes Service

We'll pretty much spend this entire section in PowerShell. In order to use Kubernetes, the first thing you'll need to do is install the CLI. To do this, log in to Azure:

```
az login
```

This should bring up a window that will allow you to enter your Azure credentials. Once you've been authenticated, you should be able to install the Kubernetes CLI:

```
az aks install-cli
```

This may take a little while to download; once it has, we can create a new Kubernetes cluster. A cluster is, essentially, what you may think of when you say *Kubernetes*. The *nodes* in the cluster are managed by a master. This means that you interact with the master and it delegates the workload to the nodes. A good way to think of this is like a crew on a building site: you may approach the foreman and ask him to build a wall, but he is unlikely to do that himself; instead, he will find some of his workers who are available and capable of building a wall and ask them to start building.

The following command should create our cluster:

```
az aks create --resource-group netcode-projects --name salesorder-cluster -
-generate-ssh-keys
```

TIP

It's worth pointing out that creating a Kubernetes cluster creates a number of virtual machines, all of which you pay for whether or not you're actually doing anything with them. In the grand scheme of things, you're looking at maybe a pound or two by the time you've completed this chapter, but remember to clean up afterward; otherwise, you may get an unexpectedly large bill!

Again, you should replace the resource group with the one that you're using for this project. You can also replace the name with... well, whichever name you wish.

TIP

The SSH keys that you've asked for will allow you to access the cluster.

When that is complete, you should get a JSON response with a lot of details about the cluster.

The next step is to point the `kubectl` tool to your new cluster:

```
az aks get-credentials --resource-group netcode-projects --name salesorder-cluster
```

`kubectl` is the main tool for interfacing with Kubernetes via the command line.

We can verify this is now working against our cluster by asking it to list our nodes:

```
kubectl get nodes
```

You should get a list of three nodes, all ready to go. The next thing we'll need to do is specify the Docker image to use in the cluster; we can do this by creating a Kubernetes deployment file (in YAML!).

Kubernetes deployment

One of the huge advantages of modern deployment techniques is that you no longer need to have someone in the company who *does the deployment*. I remember from my early professional career that you would either manually deploy software to a live environment yourself or know *someone in the office* that could do that. Needless to say, this technique was fraught with danger! Type in the wrong command and you may deploy the wrong software, or deploy the right software incorrectly or incompletely; it made diagnosing issues on-site extremely difficult because you were never quite sure what was there.

These days, there are many tools to help with this; however, Kubernetes (and the container ecosystem in general) is built with automated deployments as part of how you use it. As a result, in order to have anything deployed to Kubernetes, you must create a script (in either YAML or JSON) that tells Kubernetes what to deploy and how.

YAML is white-space sensitive, that is, the indentation levels matter.

Let's start by creating our YAML file:

```
apiVersion: extensions/v1beta1
kind: Deployment
metadata:
  name: salesorderservice
```

```
spec:
  replicas: 2
  template:
    metadata:
      labels:
        app: salesorderservice
    spec:
      containers:
      - name: salesorder-process
        image: salesorderregistry.azurecr.io/salesorderprocess:v1
        ports:
        - containerPort: 80
```

Here, we are declaring our intention to deploy our image to Kubernetes. Once this is deployed, Kubernetes will constantly try to keep this declaration correct; for example, if a node dies, it will try to create another; if we push a new image, it will try to get that image, and so forth.

TIP: It is possible to simply ask Kubernetes to return the latest image (`:latest`), but this is generally considered to be bad practice, especially in production, as this could result in changes to a production environment that weren't planned.

Now, we can use the `kubectl` tool to *apply* our deployment (you'll need to do this any time the deployment file changes – we'll come back to this later on):

```
kubectl apply -f "C:\Dev\Packt\C-8-and-.NET-Core-3.0-Projects-Second-Edition\Chapter 8 - Sales Order Processor\deployment.yaml"
```

TIP: Remember to replace the path with the path to your own YAML file.

When you run this, it should appear to work correctly. However, all this actually tells you is that the file itself is valid; what you've asked it to do may not be possible. For example, let's type the following:

```
kubectl describe pod
```

From this, we can see that the deployment was far from successful:

```
Events:
  Type     Reason     Age                 From                                Message
  ----     ------     ----                ----                                -------
  Normal   Scheduled  24m                 default-scheduler                   Successfully assigned default/salesord
erservice-699bf79b68-mdzvr to aks-nodepool1-40464275-0
  Normal   Pulling    23m (x4 over 24m)  kubelet, aks-nodepool1-40464275-0  pulling image "salesorderregistry.azur
ecr.io/salesorderprocess:v1"
  Warning  Failed     23m (x4 over 24m)  kubelet, aks-nodepool1-40464275-0  Failed to pull image "salesorderregis
ry.azurecr.io/salesorderprocess:v1": [rpc error: code = Unknown desc = Error response from daemon: Get https://sa
esorderregistry.azurecr.io/v2/salesorderprocess/manifests/v1: unauthorized: authentication required, rpc error: c
de = Unknown desc = Error response from daemon: Get https://salesorderregistry.azurecr.io/v2/salesorderprocess/ma
ifests/v1: unauthorized: authentication required]
  Warning  Failed     23m (x4 over 24m)  kubelet, aks-nodepool1-40464275-0  Error: ErrImagePull
  Warning  Failed     9m (x64 over 24m)  kubelet, aks-nodepool1-40464275-0  Error: ImagePullBackOff
  Normal   BackOff    4m (x86 over 24m)  kubelet, aks-nodepool1-40464275-0  Back-off pulling image "salesorderreg
stry.azurecr.io/salesorderprocess:v1"
```

The issue is that Kubernetes doesn't have permission to pull the image from ACR. We can get a slightly better picture of what's happening by looking at the Kubernetes dashboard. First, we'll need to let the dashboard access our cluster:

```
kubectl create clusterrolebinding kubernetes-dashboard --
clusterrole=cluster-admin --serviceaccount=kube-system:kubernetes-dashboard
```

Then, the following command will launch the dashboard:

```
az aks browse --resource-group netcode-projects --name salesorder-cluster
```

The dashboard is an invaluable tool when you're trying to diagnose issues with Kubernetes!

In fact, in order to pull from ACR, AKS requires explicit permission. We can grant that with the following command:

```
az ad sp create-for-rbac --skip-assignment
```

From this, you should get a response that's similar to the following:

```
PS C:\Users\pcmic> az ad sp create-for-rbac --skip-assignment
>>
{
  "appId": "8a970d1b-7b69-4d2e-a084-0087c9cbf5d0",
  "displayName": "azure-cli-2019-04-11-07-25-04",
  "name": "http://azure-cli-2019-04-11-07-25-04",
  "password": "1e1ddf9f-ac29-4b35-bfb4-f8bc08b588c4",
  "tenant": "03510b8c-63d4-414d-8e1e-a4cbd8bdeb99"
}
```

The highlighted value is the value of the assignee (take a note of it); we'll refer to this in a minute as `value_a`. We'll need some details from our container registry, too:

```
az acr show --resource-group netcode-projects --name salesorderregistry --
query "id" --output tsv
```

This should give you a response similar to the following:

```
PS C:\Users\pcmic> az acr show --resource-group netcode-projects --name salesorderregistry --query "id" --output
sv
subscriptions/16a7fc79-9bea-4d04-83a1-09f3b260adb0/resourceGroups/netcode-projects/providers/Microsoft.Container
gistry/registries/salesorderregistry
PS C:\Users\pcmic>
```

We'll call the highlighted value here the scope (we'll refer to this as `value_b`).

To actually assign the roles, we need to use the following command:

```
az role assignment create --assignee value_a --scope value_b --role acrpull
```

In my case, this looks as follows:

```
az role assignment create --assignee 8a970d1b-7b69-4d2e-a084-0087c9cbf5d0 -
-scope /subscription
s/16a7fc79-9bea-4d04-83a1-09f3b260adb0/resourceGroups/netcode-
projects/providers/Microsoft.ContainerRegistry/registries/salesorderregistr
y --role acrpull
```

Now, this should work correctly; however, if you are getting any issues, a good place to start diagnosing these is inside the dashboard. Selecting the button highlighted in the following screenshot will display the log file for the container, including any crash reports:

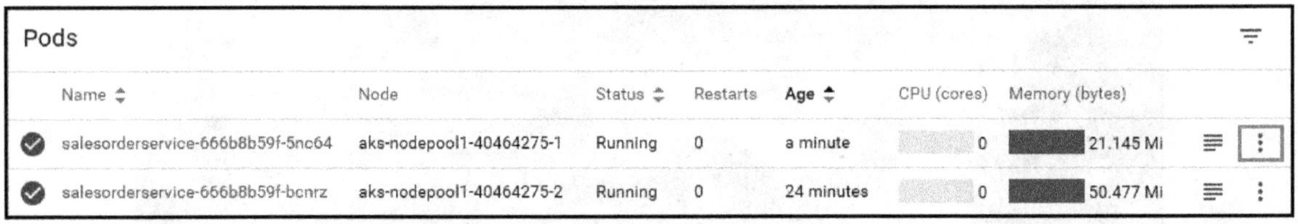

If you do discover that you have any errors, you can fix them and recreate the image (jump to the *Building a Docker image* section to learn more). Then, you can follow along by tagging the image; however, this time, tag the image as `v2`. Finally, update and reapply the `deployment.yaml` file. Now, your new YAML file may look like this:

```
apiVersion: extensions/v1beta1
kind: Deployment
metadata:
  name: salesorderservice
spec:
  replicas: 2
  template:
    metadata:
      labels:
        app: salesorderservice
    spec:
      containers:
      - name: salesorder-process
        image: salesorderregistry.azurecr.io/salesorderprocess:v2
        ports:
        - containerPort: 80
```

When your pods are running correctly, you should be able to see the following in the pod status:

```
kubectl describe pod
```

This should give you a healthy report of the pods:

```
  Type    Reason     Age   From                              Message
  ----    ------     ----  ----                              -------
  Normal  Scheduled  16m   default-scheduler                 Successfully assigned default/salesorderservice-666b8b59f-
wl58x to aks-nodepool1-40464275-1
  Normal  Pulling    16m   kubelet, aks-nodepool1-40464275-1  pulling image "salesorderregistry.azurecr.io/salesorderpro
cess:v2"
  Normal  Pulled     16m   kubelet, aks-nodepool1-40464275-1  Successfully pulled image "salesorderregistry.azurecr.io/s
alesorderprocess:v2"
  Normal  Created    16m   kubelet, aks-nodepool1-40464275-1  Created container
  Normal  Started    16m   kubelet, aks-nodepool1-40464275-1  Started container
PS C:\Users\pcmic>
```

Finally, the dashboard should show green:

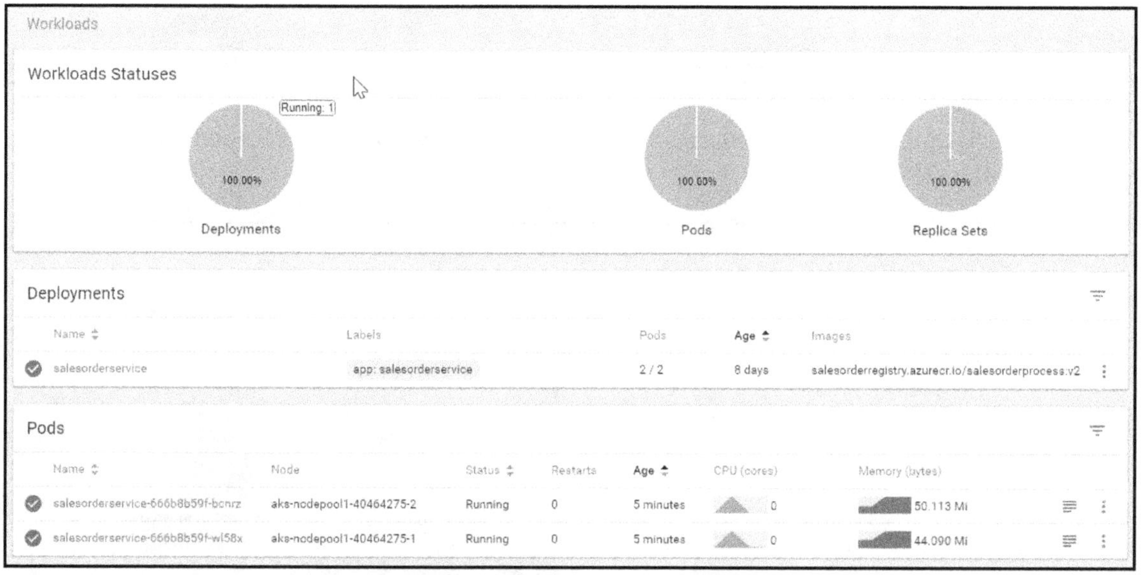

Now that we have successfully configured our Kubernetes cluster, let's go back to the title of this chapter and investigate the load balancing aspect of Kubernetes.

Load balancing

The title of this chapter is *A Load-Balanced Order Processing Microservice Using Docker and Azure Kubernetes Service*. In fact, you've already seen this since the worker pods were picking up items from the queue based on which were available. However, let's see if we can engineer a more dramatic demonstration of what that actually means. Let's go into the dashboard and delete one of the pods; select the ellipsis to the right-hand side of a pod and delete it:

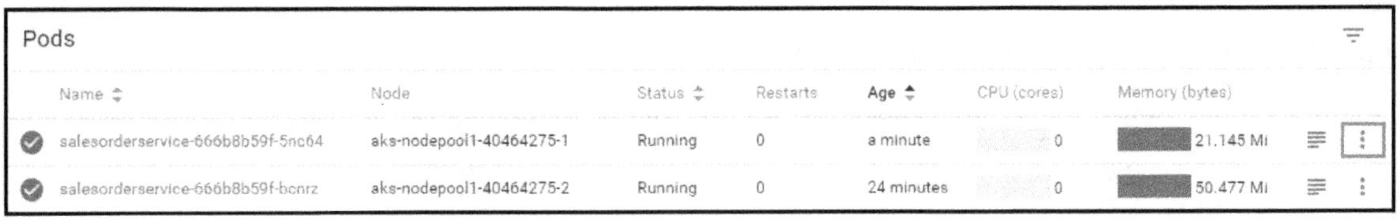

Once you've deleted the pod, you should (almost instantly) notice the screen change to look something like this:

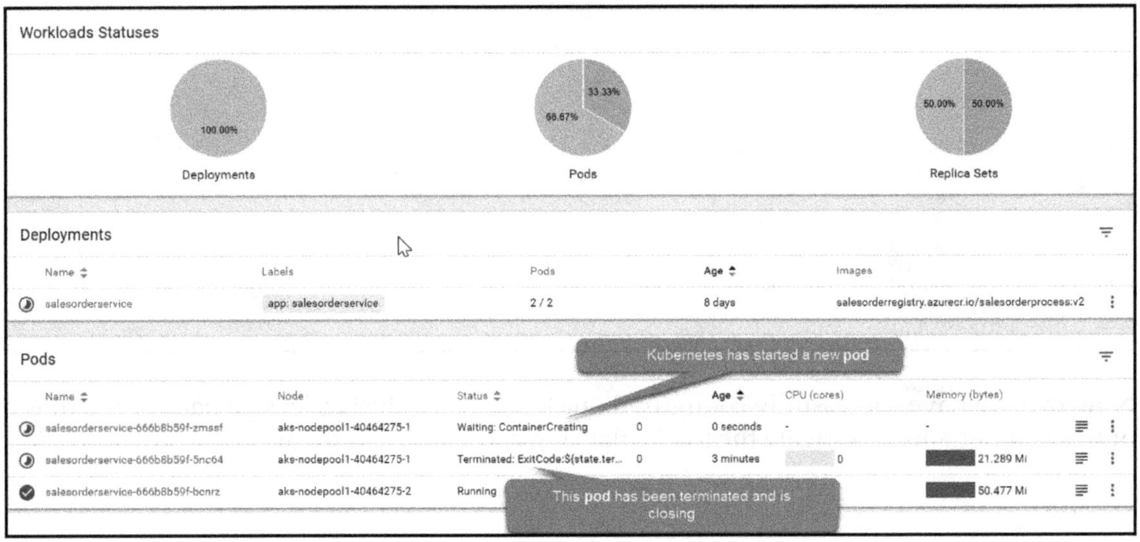

As you can see, as soon as Kubernetes realizes that you have killed one of the pods, it instantly compensates by starting a new one! How did it know to do this? Well, in our `deployment.yaml` file, we had set the replicas to be `2`. To prove this, let's increase the replicas to `3`:

```
apiVersion: extensions/v1beta1
kind: Deployment
metadata:
  name: salesorderservice
spec:
  replicas: 3
  template:
    metadata:
      labels:
        app: salesorderservice
    spec:
      containers:
      - name: salesorder-process
        image: salesorderregistry.azurecr.io/salesorderprocess:v2
        ports:
        - containerPort: 80
```

As you can see, we're changing nothing but that one field. Now, let's reapply the deployment:

```
kubectl apply -f "C:\Dev\Packt\C-8-and-.NET-Core-3.0-Projects-Second-
Edition\Chapter 8 - Sales Order
Processor\deployment.yaml"
```

Kubernetes leaps into action and spins up a new node:

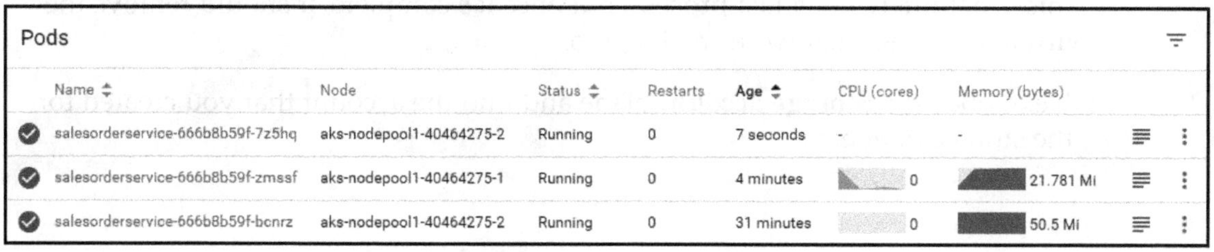

Now, we have successfully created our AKS cluster and seen it process our orders. AKS can be expensive when left running unnecessarily, so we'll tear down our resources in the next section.

Cleanup

A Kubernetes cluster can be an expensive business. To be clear, it's usually much cheaper than buying and running the services yourself; however, if you're playing around with these things, you can quickly run up a hefty bill. To remove the resources that we've created in this chapter, let's start with the cluster:

1. Start by opening the **Kubernetes services** blade and selecting your cluster:

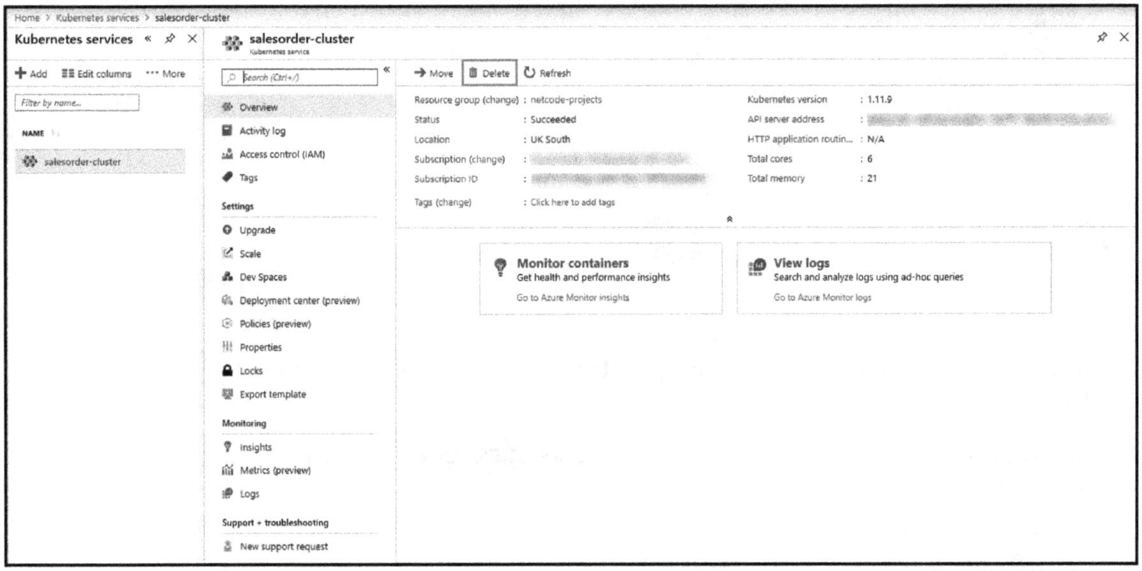

This is definitely not a fast process, but once it's complete, it should remove the virtual machines that were created, too.

2. Next, open the **Storage account** blade and find the account that you created for the storage queue:

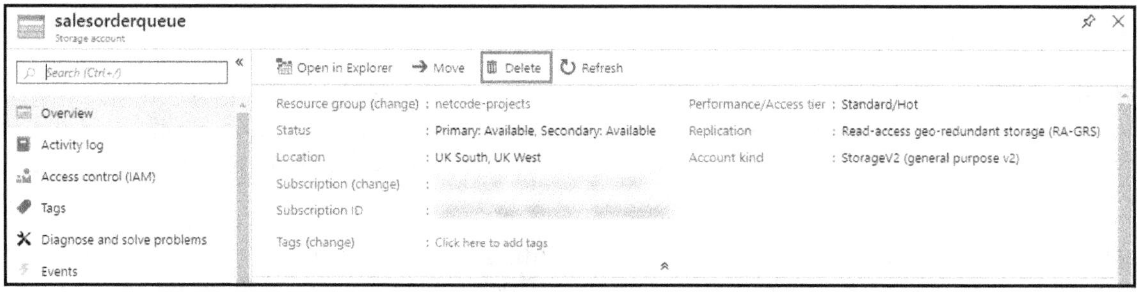

3. Our next stop is the **Container registry** blade. We'll need to locate our registry and delete that:

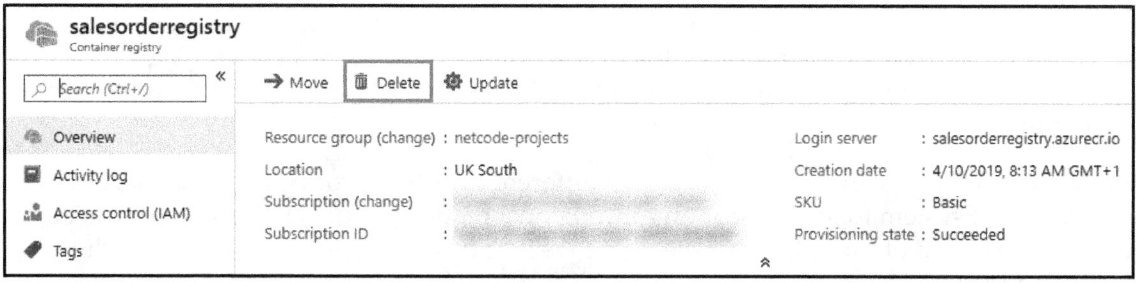

4. Last, but not least, is our database. In the **SQL database** blade, find and delete the database that we created:

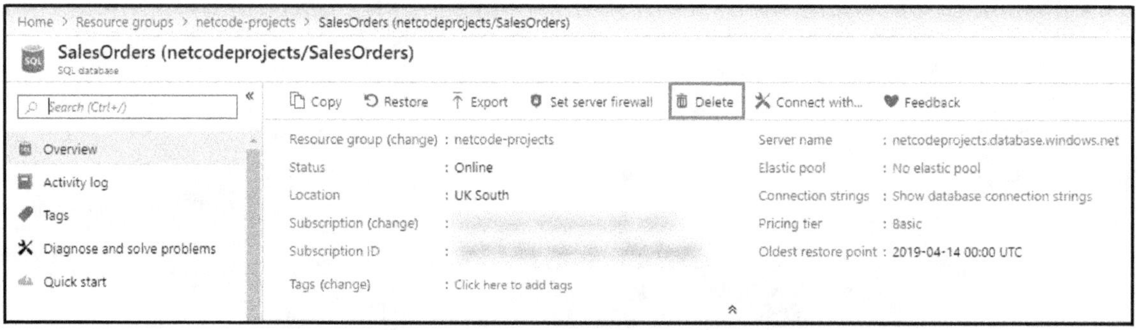

Now that we've cleaned the resources that we have created, let's talk about what we've covered in this chapter.

Summary

In this chapter, we've had a look at what a microservice is and how we can create one. We've discussed how we can separate services using a technique such as a queue, meaning that one microservice is not dependent on another. In using Kubernetes to orchestrate our service, we've seen how this can be a self-healing system.

Along the way, we've looked at Docker and building a Docker image; we've explored container registries and how you can store your Docker images in them; and we've also created and configured an AKS cluster. We've explored the use of both Service Bus and storage queues in Azure, and how they might be used in a distributed system.

As I mentioned in the introduction, this is a very seductive architectural pattern; however, we also discussed how it is not without cost, and that cost is complexity. In replacing a single piece of software with several, the interactions between them, the logging mechanism, and your ability to easily maintain the whole system suddenly become much more difficult.

In the next chapter, we will move in a very different direction, from designing a large-scale cloud-hosted system to an application running on a mobile phone. However, we won't be leaving the world of the cloud completely as we'll be leveraging some pre-built machine learning models.

9

Emotion Detector Mobile App - Using Xamarin Forms and Azure Cognitive Services

In this chapter, we will combine two technologies that have progressed massively in the past few years: mobile development and machine learning.

Machine learning was the exclusive domain of the very select few only a few years ago. It was used to predict the weather and design chess computers. For programmers outside of that specific and specialized space, it was simply beyond their reach. However, recently, with the advent of the cloud, and with quantities of data hitherto unheard of, cloud providers are offering this capability to the average programmer as a service. We will see how easy it is to upload a picture of someone's face and have Microsoft Azure send back an analysis of that face to predict whether the person is happy, sad, angry, etc.

The second topic that we'll cover is mobile development. Xamarin has made it possible to write a C# application, cross-compile it, and run it on Android, iOS, and other platforms. Microsoft's acquisition of Xamarin has turned this method of cross-platform mobile development into the default choice for most desktop developers.

The following topics will be covered in this chapter:

- Machine Learning and Azure Cognitive Services
- Cross Platform Development:
    - Creating a new Xamarin application that runs on an Android device
    - Setting up Azure Cognitive Services
    - Consuming Cognitive Services from our new Application

Technical requirements

To follow along with this chapter, you'll need to install the Xamarin Workload for Visual Studio. You should be able to find this in the Visual Studio installer:

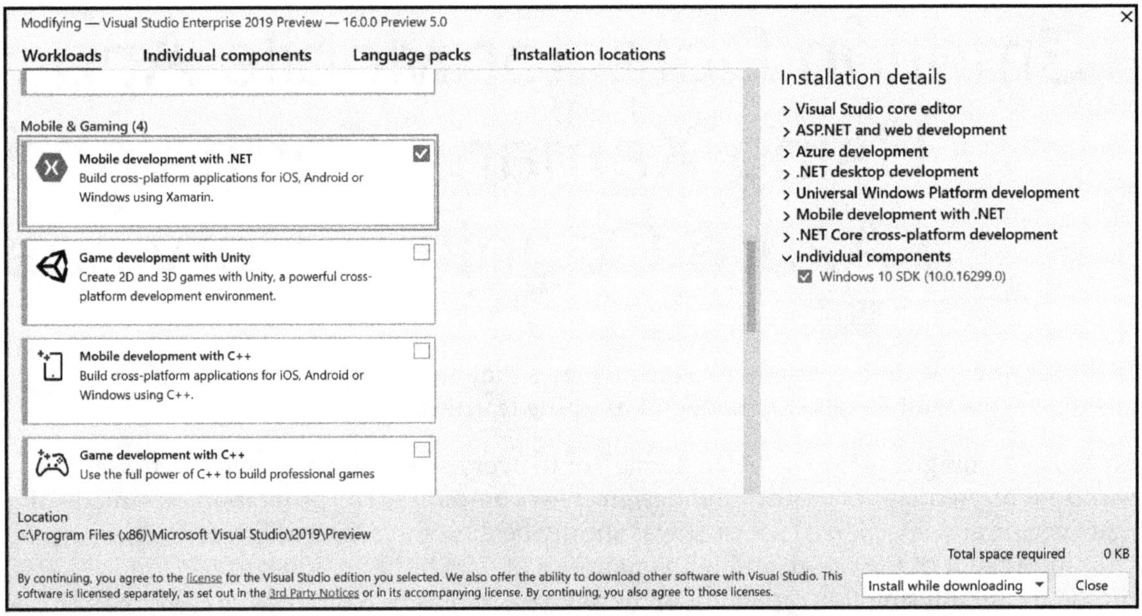

Like the previous chapters, you will also need an Azure account. Since the process of setting this up has already been covered in `Chapter 2`, *Task Bug Logging ASP.NET Core MVC App Using Cosmos DB*, we won't revisit that here.

During the testing phase of this, we will be running our application on a physical device; this means that you will need access to an Android device with an attached camera. Without this, while you can still follow along, you will not be able to see the application working.

Concepts overview

Before we start building anything, let's briefly discuss at a high level the two main concepts in this chapter.

Machine learning

This is a huge topic, and far too big to cover in any kind of sensible depth in one section. However, it's worth covering, briefly, what machine learning *is*, and what it *is not*.

In this chapter, we'll be taking an image of a face and uploading it into a machine learning service. This service will provide details regarding whether it thinks that face is happy, sad, angry, or anything else. It's important to try and not anthropomorphise this process. The algorithm will analyze the face and return percentages of certainty; however, this is based on it seeing many, many similar images and being told whether the image it was identifying was, say, happy. This means that if I start to feed images of sad people in, but tell the machine learning algorithm that these are happy people, it will gradually start to change its estimation. This is a modern-day equivalent of the old adage **Garbage In, Garbage Out** (**GIGO**).

It is possible to create your own machine learning models; in fact, all the big cloud providers have suites of tools around this. There is a trade-off here, though: creating your own model requires time and expertise in data science, but gives you complete control over the model and the questions that you want answers to. On the other hand, consuming a pre-built service means that you are reliant on the service provider to correctly train the model, and so it is less likely to suit specific needs.

Cross-platform and mobile development

When .NET was first released over 20 years ago, it was a Windows development tool. In fact, Microsoft development tools up until this point had been Windows-specific and proud of it. Microsoft used to have a business model that relied on the sale of operating systems; and, clearly, if you have programmers creating software that will only run on your operating system, you have an advantage over the competition.

This model seemed to work well until Apple released the first iPhone. While Windows still dominated the business market, people gradually started to shift toward phones and then tablets for leisure. The Microsoft dream of a computer in every home and business had come and gone and suddenly, programmers were seeing reasons to abandon .NET development and move to iOS and Android development.

Playing catch-up, Microsoft tried releasing their own phones (that is, they bought Nokia); they also started closely supporting Xamarin in an effort to get code written in .NET to run on Android and iOS. At the time of writing, Microsoft has dropped support for the ill-fated Windows phone and bought Xamarin. There are other ways to write software that runs on iOS and Android, but, to my knowledge, Xamarin is the only one that allows you to do so in C# and compiles down to the native platform.

Having said all this, as with all the technologies showcased in this book, you should consider whether you could use a simpler option; for example, would a simple website support your needs? Not every use case requires a custom application for a smartphone.

Project overview

Our project in this chapter will be a very simple application. This will have a single button that will take a picture. We'll then send that image over to Azure and display a result, indicating the emotion that we have detected in that image.

We'll be using Xamarin Forms, which is a simple UI layer that is also cross-platform: for our needs, this is ideal as the software has a very small UI component.

We'll also be creating this application for Android only. The main reason for this is that, in order to create an iOS application, you need a Mac, which I feel would exclude a good number of readers (and the author) from following along!

Configuring Azure Cognitive Services

Before we start writing any code, we'll need to configure our cognitive service. To accomplish this, you'll need an Azure account; please refer to the chapter 2 (Task Bug Logging ASP.NET Core MVC App Using Cosmos DB) if you don't have one yet.

Let's set-up Cognitive Services:

1. We'll start by navigating to the **Cognitive Services** blade in the Azure Portal; you can search for it or select it from the menu on the left-hand side. From this blade, add a new service. Once you do so, you'll be presented with a list of possible cognitive services to create:

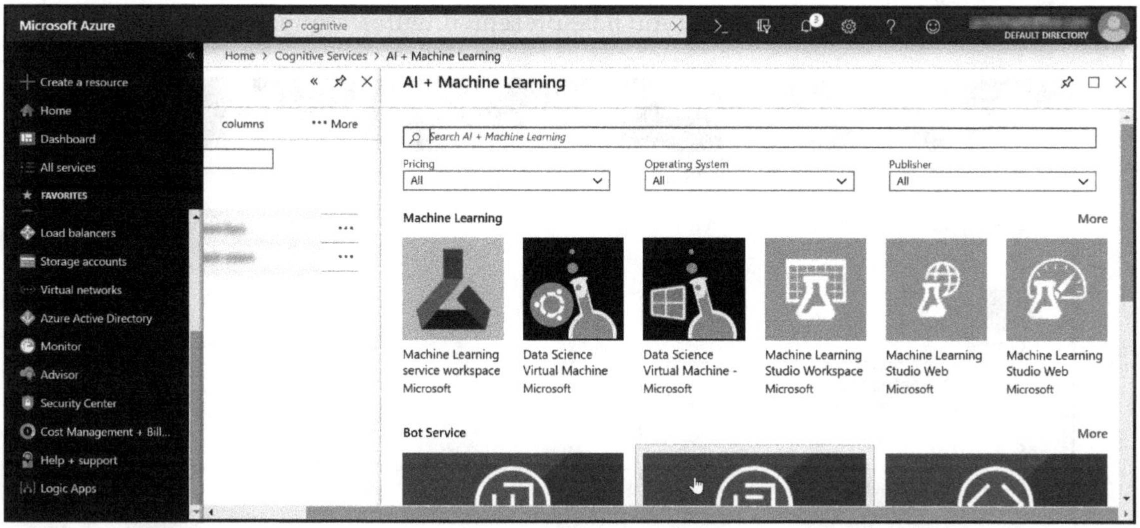

2. Again, you can either search through this list by scrolling down for the **Face** API or simply typing `Face` into the search box. This should bring up the **Face** API and allow you to **Create** it:

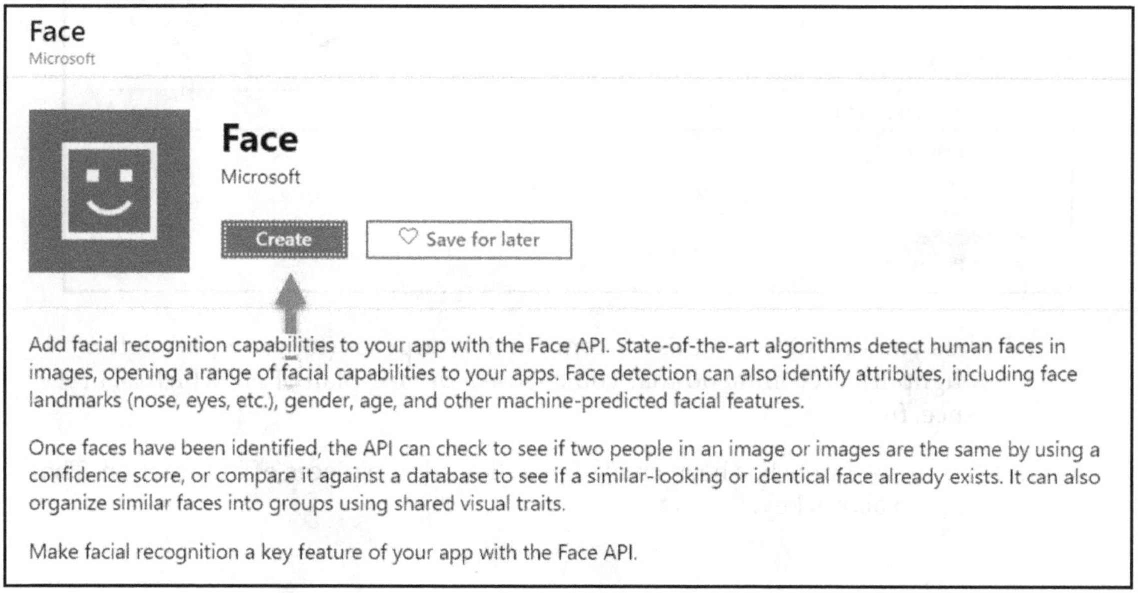

3. Once you've select **Create**, you'll be presented with a familiar list of options:

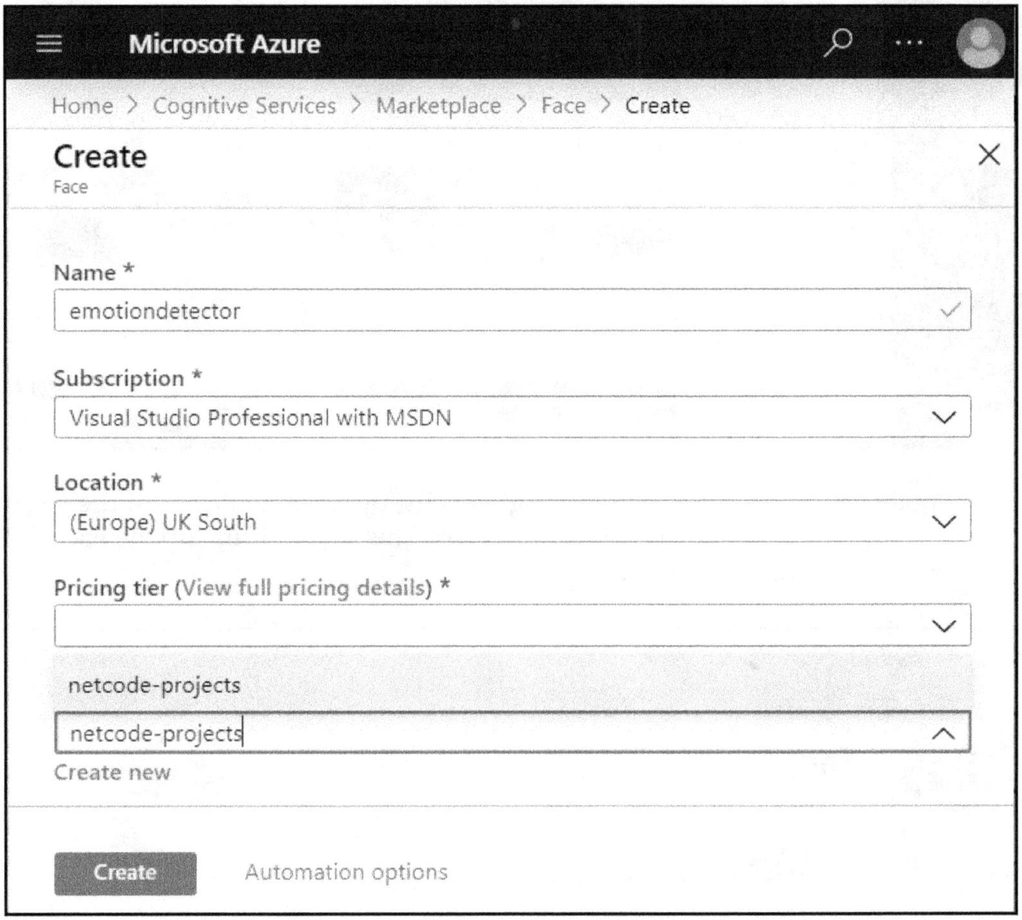

Unless you intend to use this for commercial purposes (for example, high throughput), I recommend that you choose a pricing plan of F0, which is, in essence, free.

4. After the resource has been created, you'll need two pieces of information. The first is an access key:

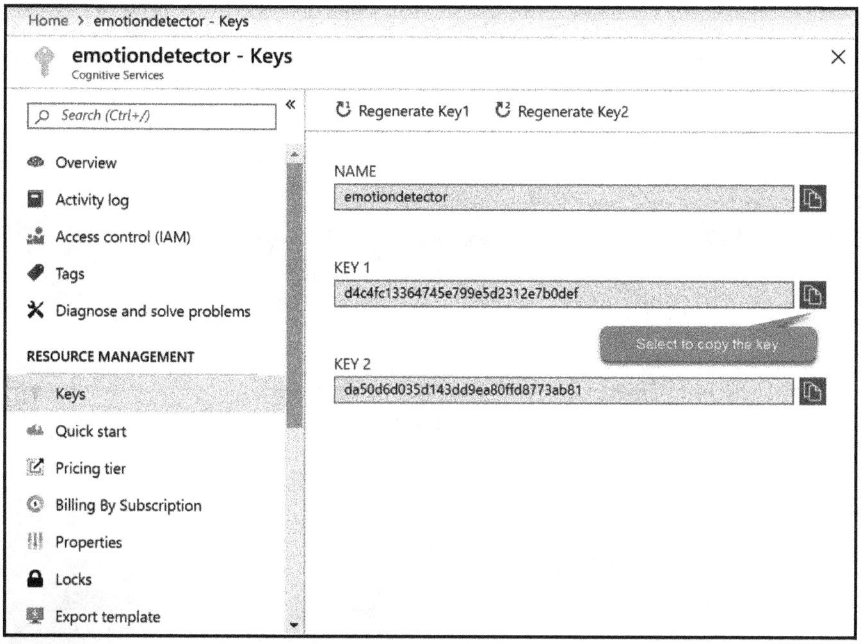

5. The second piece of information you'll need is the endpoint, which can be found on the **Overview** screen:

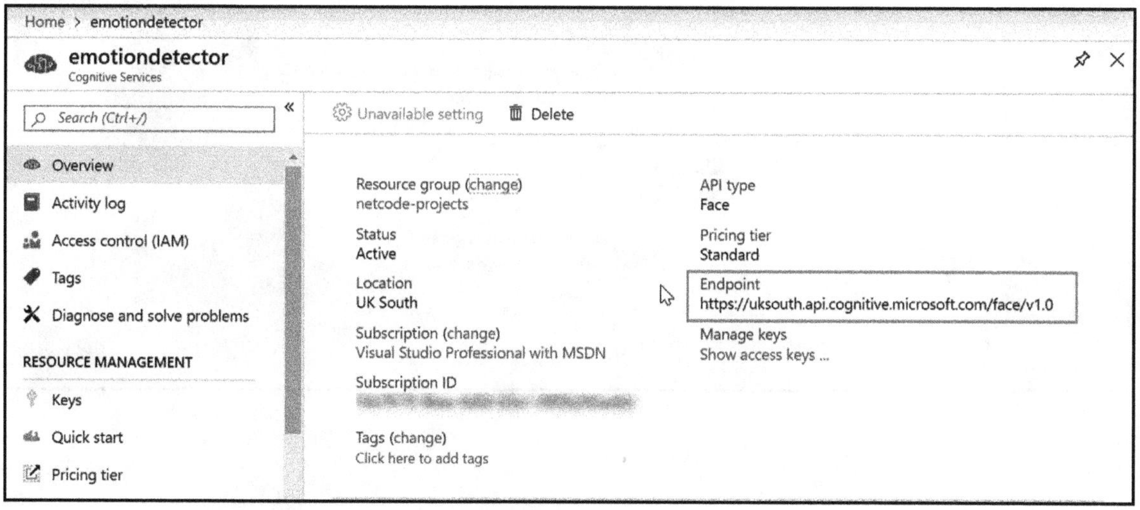

That's it! You've now configured the cognitive service. The **Quick Start** page has a wealth of resources that you can use; it is also very likely to have more up to date information than what you will find here. Now that we have configured the Azure Services, we can create our Xamarin Application.

Creating the Xamarin application

Let's create our Xamarin application. Select **File** | **New** | **Project**, and you'll be presented with the following screen:

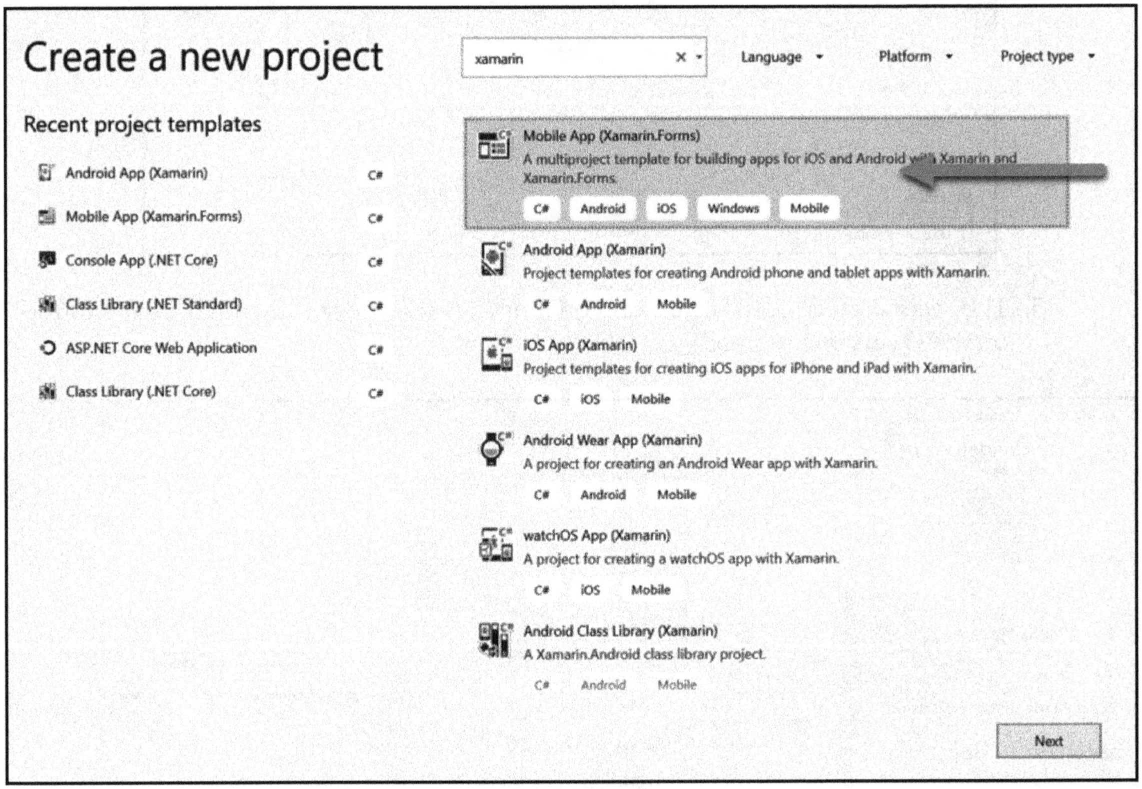

Once you've selected a Xamarin application, you're presented with a further dialog:

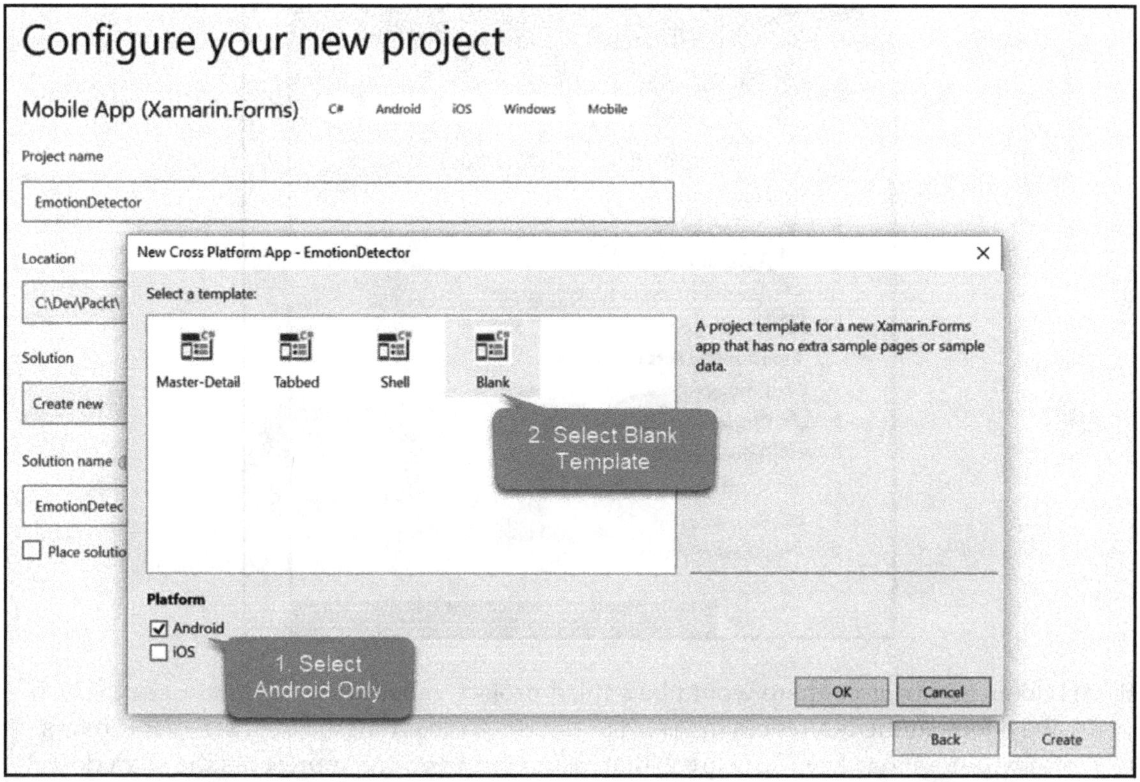

1. Select whether to create the application for iOS, Android, or both. We'll just create an Android application.
2. Select a **Blank** template, so we can see exactly what we are creating.

Now that we've configured the template, we can create our project (by selecting **Create**).

TIP

It's worth bearing in mind that there are some quite strict rules on what you can have in your path and how long that path can be. Avoid spaces, dashes, and full paths over 127 characters.

Once created, your project should look roughly like this:

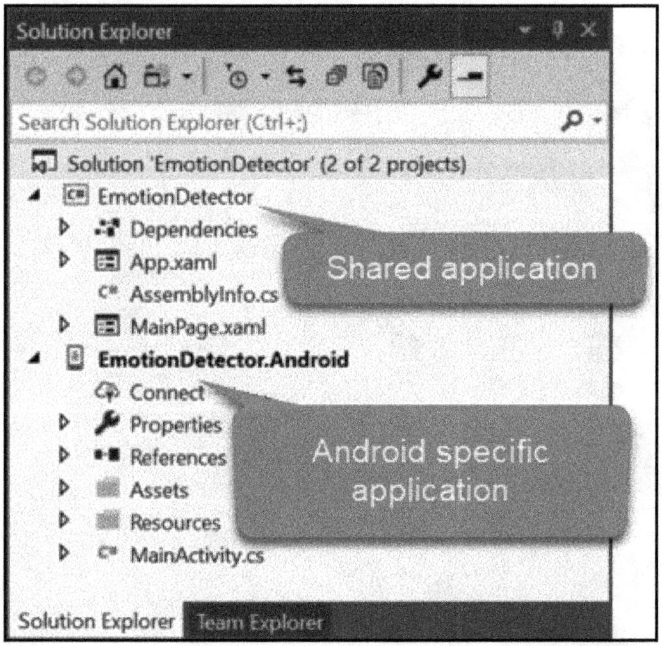

If we had an iOS project, there would be a third project, called `EmotionDetector.iOS`. If you have a look at the references in `EmotionDetector.Android`, you'll see that it refers to `EmotionDetector`. The idea here is that `EmotionDetector` represents the shared codebase; however, this functionality can be overridden per platform.

Before we do anything with the project, let's run it and see what we get in the emulator:

> **TIP:** If the emulator is showing a blank screen, ensure that it's turned on. The emulator operates like a real phone, even down to being able to power up and down.

Let's add a button that will take our picture and an image control to display that picture. In `MainPage.Xaml`, replace the XAML code with the following:

```
<?xml version="1.0" encoding="utf-8" ?>
<ContentPage xmlns="http://xamarin.com/schemas/2014/forms"
             xmlns:x="http://schemas.microsoft.com/winfx/2009/xaml"
             xmlns:local="clr-namespace:EmotionDetector"
```

```
             x:Class="EmotionDetector.MainPage">

    <AbsoluteLayout x:Name="Layout">

        <Image x:Name="DisplayedImage"
               VerticalOptions="Center"
               HorizontalOptions="Center" />

        <Button Text="Take Picture"
           HorizontalOptions="Center"
           VerticalOptions="EndAndExpand"
           Clicked="Button_Clicked"
            AbsoluteLayout.LayoutBounds=".5, .1, .5, .1"
AbsoluteLayout.LayoutFlags="All" />

    </AbsoluteLayout>
</ContentPage>
```

In the previous chapters, I spoke about using the MVVM pattern to abstract the UI layer from the logic of the application. This is possible in Xamarin Forms, too. However, I felt that creating an MVVM abstraction here would create an unnecessary additional distraction in the development.

If you do decide to extend this project, then creating (or using a third party) an MVVM infrastructure might be a good place to start.

The preceding code has two controls inside a `Layout` component. `AbsoluteLayout` is a container that will allow us to dictate exactly where our controls are positioned. Inside the layout, we have a single button that is centralized near the top of the screen and an image. The code calls for a single event handler to be present in the code behind. The `Button_Clicked` event in the code behind for `MainPage.Xaml.cs` can be empty for now:

```
[DesignTimeVisible(true)]
public partial class MainPage : ContentPage
{
    public MainPage()
    {
        InitializeComponent();
    }

    private void Button_Clicked(object sender, EventArgs e)
    {
    }
}
```

While this event handler does nothing at the minute, we need it to do three things eventually:

- Take a picture
- Upload the picture to Azure
- Display the results

Let's sketch that out in some calls to stub methods. Then, we can focus on each in turn:

```
private void Button_Clicked(object sender, EventArgs e)
{
    var image = TakePicture();
    var emotionData = GetEmotionAnalysis(image);
    DisplayData(emotionData);
}

private void DisplayData(object emotionData)
{
    throw new NotImplementedException();
}

private object GetEmotionAnalysis()
{
    throw new NotImplementedException();
}

private object TakePicture()
{
    throw new NotImplementedException();
}
```

The signatures of these methods will change, but this describes the basic flow of our logic; that is, we take a picture and pass the result to a method that calls the Azure cognitive service before we display the results. Let's go through each of these steps and fill them in one at a time.

Taking a picture

When using any (or most) platform-specific code in Xamarin, you tend to find yourself using plugins. Before we continue, we'll need to discuss *Xamarin* plugins.

Xamarin plugins

The principle behind Xamarin is that the code that you write is cross-compiled. That is, when you compile for Android, you end up with a native app targeting the Android platform, and when you compile for iOS, you end up with a native app targeting iOS. However, the Xamarin platform is unable to do this when a piece of code is platform-specific. Say, for example, I want to access the camera – this varies from platform to platform. You can't simply take the code that does this for an iPhone and compile it for Android. So, how do we create platform-specific code?

The answer is that each piece of platform-specific code needs to be created separately for each platform; the principle behind Xamarin Forms is that you call the method in a polymorphic fashion. Let's take the camera as an example (since that's what we're about to use); the code that takes a picture on Android is clearly different to that on iOS. When we install the plugin, each environment implements that plugin's code in a platform-specific way. From our point of view, though, we simply install the plugin and call a few lines of code and it works everywhere.

Media plugin

Installing the plugin itself is actually just as straightforward as adding a NuGet package:

```
Install-Package Xam.Plugin.Media -ProjectName EmotionDetector
```

TIP: It's worth bearing in mind that these plugins are constantly changing; while they are correct at the time of writing, you should follow the `readme.txt` file as a primary source.

Once you've done this, the plugin displays a `readme.txt` file with instructions on how to install it. Please follow those instructions as they are likely to change by the time you read this. I will detail the Android instructions here for completeness as some of the instructions may not be as verbose as they could be.

Let's start with `MainActivity.cs` in `EmotionDetector.Android`. The `OnRequestPermissionsResult` method should look like this:

```
public override void OnRequestPermissionsResult(int requestCode, string[]
permissions, Android.Content.PM.Permission[] grantResults)
{
Plugin.Permissions.PermissionsImplementation.Current.OnRequestPermissionsRe
sult(
        requestCode, permissions, grantResults);
}
```

Anything that you want to do in a mobile app these days has to be approved by the user; if you need access to the user's contacts, phone, or camera, then the user will be presented with a dialog indicating that your app needs these permissions. The code in this method is called after the user responds to that.

You will have to declare which permissions your app needs, and this should be automatically added by the plugin. If you have a look inside `EmotionDetector.Android.Properties.AssemblyInfo.cs`, you should see the following:

```
// Add some common permissions, these can be removed if not needed
[assembly: UsesPermission(Android.Manifest.Permission.Internet)]
[assembly:
UsesPermission(Android.Manifest.Permission.WriteExternalStorage)]

[assembly: UsesFeature("android.hardware.camera", Required = true)]
[assembly: UsesFeature("android.hardware.camera.autofocus", Required =
false)]
```

If this hasn't automatically been added, then add it now.

Note that we have slightly diverted from the instructions here, in that we have declared that the camera is required. In most applications, the functionality would still work fine without the camera, but in this case, we really do need to use it.

You should also consider whether your app can offer some degraded functionality, even if the user is unwilling to give access to requested resources. As we've mentioned previously, in this particular case, there's not too much we can do without the camera, but if you extended this application, maybe you would add the ability to upload existing pictures to the application – in which case, the app *would* still be usable *without* the camera.

The `AndroidManifest.xml` file should look like this:

```
<?xml version="1.0" encoding="utf-8"?>
<manifest xmlns:android="http://schemas.android.com/apk/res/android"
android:versionCode="1" android:versionName="1.0" package="com.companyname"
android:installLocation="auto">
    <uses-sdk android:minSdkVersion="21" android:targetSdkVersion="27" />
    <application android:label="EmotionDetector.Android">
        <provider android:name="android.support.v4.content.FileProvider"
android:authorities="${applicationId}.fileprovider"
                          android:exported="false"
                          android:grantUriPermissions="true">
          <meta-data android:name="android.support.FILE_PROVIDER_PATHS"
                          android:resource="@xml/file_paths"></meta-data>
        </provider>
  </application>
</manifest>
```

This is used to support a subdependency of the media plugin. As you can see, it references a specific resource directory, and so the next step is to create that directory. In the Android `Resources` folder, create a new `xml` folder:

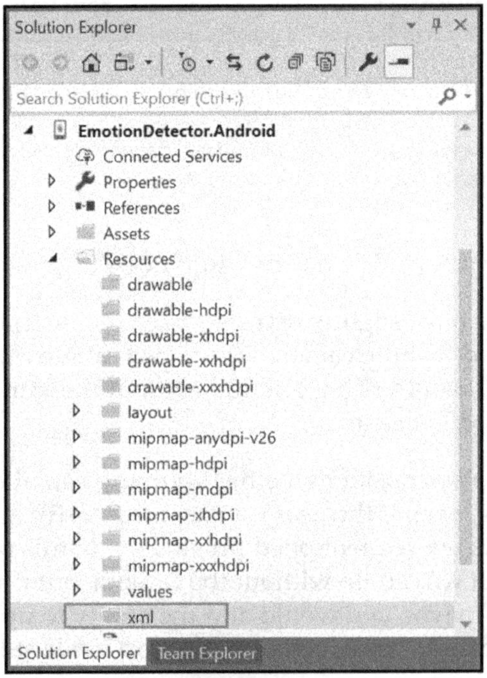

Create a file inside this folder labeled `file_paths.xml` and add the following code:

```
<?xml version="1.0" encoding="utf-8"?>
<paths xmlns:android="http://schemas.android.com/apk/res/android">
    <external-files-path name="my_images" path="Pictures" />
    <external-files-path name="my_movies" path="Movies" />
</paths>
```

Finally, the `MainActivity.cs` module needs an additional line in its `OnCreate` method:

```
protected override void OnCreate(Bundle savedInstanceState)
{
    TabLayoutResource = Resource.Layout.Tabbar;
    ToolbarResource = Resource.Layout.Toolbar;

    base.OnCreate(savedInstanceState);
    CrossCurrentActivity.Current.Init(this, savedInstanceState);

    Xamarin.Essentials.Platform.Init(this, savedInstanceState);
    global::Xamarin.Forms.Forms.Init(this, savedInstanceState);
    LoadApplication(new App());
}
```

The `CrossCurrentActivity` plugin is another plugin in the same ecosystem. It allows the media plugin to access `MainActivity`.

TakePicture()

Now that we've added the plugin, we can create the code so that we can use the camera. Let's have a quick look at this method:

```
private async Task<MediaFile> TakePicture()
{
    string fileName = $"FaceImg_{DateTime.Now.Ticks}";

    MediaFile photo = await
Plugin.Media.CrossMedia.Current.TakePhotoAsync(new
Plugin.Media.Abstractions.StoreCameraMediaOptions()
    {
        SaveToAlbum = true,
        Name = fileName
    });

    if (photo != null)
    {
        return photo;
```

```
        }

        return null;
    }
```

There's not much to this method since the plugin does the bulk of the work for us. The parameters that we're passing in allow the image to be saved, and we're declaring a unique name for it.

> TIP: During testing, you may decide to switch off the save feature; otherwise, your phone will fill up with pictures of you pulling strange faces to try to look angry, sad, or happy!

If the photograph is successfully taken, we return a `MediaFile`; otherwise, we return `null`.

GetEmotionAnalysis()

Our next method is responsible for calling the Azure API and getting a response. There is a client API for this, however. At the time of writing, it was still in preview, and seemed to have various issues. Should you wish to investigate using this instead, then a good place to start is the NuGet repository: `https://www.nuget.org/packages/Microsoft.Azure.CognitiveServices.Vision.Face/`.

However, we will be making use of only a part of this package, so let's install it now:

```
Install-Package Microsoft.Azure.CognitiveServices.Vision.Face -Version
2.4.0-preview
```

In this section, we will manually build up the call to the API; here's the code for our method:

```
private async Task<IList<DetectedFace>> GetEmotionAnalysis(Stream
imageStream)
{
    var byteData = GetImageAsByteArray(imageStream);

    return await MakeAnalysisRequest(byteData,
        "https://uksouth.api.cognitive.microsoft.com/face/v1.0/detect",
        "4a9c2b7404fd45ed9aff787f158e24c7");
}
```

`MakeAnalysisRequest` accepts three pieces of information (as you will see in a second). The first, `byteData`, is a binary representation of the image stream (we'll come back to the `GetImageAsByteArray` method shortly). The second parameter is the endpoint that you made a note of earlier; we then append `detect` to the URL, which indicates the action that we wish to take. The result is as follows:

```
$"{endpoint}/detect"
```

The third parameter is the key that you noted down earlier.

> TIP: The preceding values were my values at the time of writing; by the time you read this, the resource they were generated for will have been removed. You will need to change these to match your own values.

Before we move on, let's quickly review the `GetImageAsByteArray` method:

```
private byte[] GetImageAsByteArray(Stream stream)
{
    using BinaryReader binaryReader = new BinaryReader(stream);
    return binaryReader.ReadBytes((int)stream.Length);

}
```

The bulk of the work, however, is done by the `MakeAnalysisRequest` method. Let's see what that looks like:

```
public async Task<List<DetectedFace>> MakeAnalysisRequest(Byte[] byteData,
string uriBase, string subscriptionKey)
{
    using HttpClient client = new HttpClient();
    client.DefaultRequestHeaders.Add("Ocp-Apim-Subscription-Key",
subscriptionKey);

    string requestParameters =
"returnFaceId=true&returnFaceLandmarks=false" +
"&returnFaceAttributes=emotion&recognitionModel=recognition_01&returnRecogn
itionModel=false";

    string uri = $"{uriBase}?{requestParameters}";
    HttpResponseMessage response;

    using (ByteArrayContent content = new ByteArrayContent(byteData))
    {
        content.Headers.ContentType = new
MediaTypeHeaderValue("application/octet-stream");
```

```
            response = await client.PostAsync(uri, content);
            string contentString = await response.Content.ReadAsStringAsync();

            List<DetectedFace> faceDetails =
    JsonConvert.DeserializeObject<List<DetectedFace>>(contentString);
            if (faceDetails.Count != 0)
            {
                return faceDetails;
            }
        }
        return null;
    }
```

There's a lot going on here; however, the basis is that we are making an HTTP call and serializing the returned result into a list of `DetectedFace`. `DetectedFace` is a class that can be found in the NuGet package that we installed earlier. We are passing the access key in the header of our request and building up our parameters in the query string.

A link to the Face API documentation can be found in the **Quick Start** guide in the Azure portal. This will give you a comprehensive (and up to date) list of methods and parameters that are available to you.

The next step is to package up and send the image off to Azure for analysis. What is returned is a JSON representation of the analysis.

DisplayData()

This is the final method: we have now taken the picture using the camera and sent that image to Azure for analysis. Our final task is to display the results to the user. Before we look at the code, we should consider exactly what we are trying to achieve here.

Our specific application is designed to indicate someone's emotional state at the time of taking the picture. When we pass the image to Azure, it will not return a statement saying, *this person is happy*; instead, it will return a list of possible detected faces and a list of possible emotions for each, along with a value to indicate how much it thinks that person displays that emotion. For example, have a quick look in the mirror: how do you look? Are you happy, angry, surprised, or disgusted? Maybe you are a little of two or three of these. Because of this, the JSON that is returned is a list of values for each face and each emotion.

When displaying the data, we will need to do two things:

1. Where there is more or less than a single face, display an error to indicate this.
2. Where there is a single face, display only the highest-ranking emotion; for example, if you are angry and surprised, we need to take whichever the analysis believes to be the greater and display that.

With that in mind, let's have a look at the code:

```
private void DisplayData(IList<DetectedFace> faces)
{
    // Remove and existing labels
    var labels = Layout.Children
        .Where(a => (a.AutomationId?.Contains("emotion-label") ?? false)
        || (a.AutomationId?.Contains("error") ?? false))
        .ToList();
    foreach (var label in labels)
    {
        Layout.Children.Remove(label);
    }

    if (faces == null)
    {
        CreateLabel("Unable to get data", "error");
        return;
    }

    if (faces.Count() > 1)
    {
        CreateLabel("Multiple faces not supported in this version",
"error");
        return;
    }

    var face = faces.SingleOrDefault();
    if (face == null)
    {
        CreateLabel("No face found", "error");
        return;
    }

    CreateLabel(face.GetStrongestEmotion(), face.FaceId.ToString());
}
```

To start analyzing this, we'll begin with `CreateLabel`.

CreateLabel()

We'll have a look at the code for this shortly, but, for now, let's just accept that it dynamically creates a label, using `AutomationId` as a unique reference.

> **TIP:** `AutomationId` is really intended to provide an anchored reference to automated UI test frameworks. What we are doing here is potentially not in-keeping with that intent; in fact, there is no real reason that `AutomationId` couldn't be fixed at simply: "emotion-label", which would allow automated UI testing to work more easily with this application. The preceding code does provide slightly more information when debugging, so I would suggest this as a future enhancement, once the software is working.

As you can see, our first task is to look for any labels with a relevant `AutomationId` and remove them. What follows is a series of gated checks to determine whether a single face is returned; where one isn't, we will create an error label.

Assuming there are no errors, a label will be created based on a method that we have yet to see called `face.GetStrongestEmotion()`. This returns a string indicating the strongest emotion found (we'll get to that later). Let's return to the `CreateLabel()` method:

```
private void CreateLabel(string displayText, string id)
{
    var newLabel = new Label()
    {
        Text = displayText,
        AutomationId = $"emotion-label-{id}",
        FontAttributes = FontAttributes.Bold,
        FontSize = 20,
        HorizontalTextAlignment = TextAlignment.Center
    };

    AbsoluteLayout.SetLayoutBounds(newLabel, new Rectangle(.5, 1, .5, .1));
    AbsoluteLayout.SetLayoutFlags(newLabel, AbsoluteLayoutFlags.All);

    Layout.Children.Add(newLabel);
}
```

What we are doing here is building a UI control in code. Most of the preceding code is relatively straightforward: we're setting the font and text (we've discussed `AutomationId` already), and then we're calling a method on the `AbsoluteLayout` parent control in order to orient the control at specific coordinates:

```
AbsoluteLayout.SetLayoutBounds(newLabel, new Rectangle(.5, 1, .5, .1));
```

This method sets the boundary rectangle for the control in question, within the `AbsoluteLayout` control. The values that we pass to it vary in meaning, depending on how we call the method:

```
AbsoluteLayout.SetLayoutFlags(newLabel, AbsoluteLayoutFlags.All);
```

In our case, we are setting this to `All`, which indicates that all the values are proportional; for example, the X coordinate (that is, the first value in the `Rectangle` struct) specified that the control should be positioned exactly halfway across the `AbsoluteLayout` control.

Finally, we add the new control that we created to the `Layout` control. Next, we'll analyze the `GetStrongestEmotion()` method.

GetStrongestEmotion()

This method is simply an extension method and uses reflection to calculate the emotion with the highest score:

```
public static class FaceExtensions
{
    public static string GetStrongestEmotion(this DetectedFace face)
    {
        var emotions = face.FaceAttributes.Emotion;

        var strongest = emotions.GetType()
            .GetProperties()
            .Select(a => new { name = a.Name, value =
(double)a.GetValue(emotions) })
            .OrderByDescending(a => a.value)
            .First();

        return strongest.name;
    }
}
```

TIP: If you are not familiar with extension methods, an extension method class must be static, and the item that you're extending is indicated by the `this` keyword, before the parameter.

Button_Clicked

Finally, let's change the event handler to correctly handle the updated methods:

```
private async void Button_Clicked(object sender, EventArgs e)
{
    var image = await TakePicture();
    DisplayedImage.Source = ImageSource.FromStream(() =>
image.GetStream());
    var emotionData = await GetEmotionAnalysis(image.GetStream());
    DisplayData(emotionData);
}
```

As you can see, we needed to make our handler async, as we're calling async methods. We're setting the image source by extracting the stream from the result of `TakePicture`. Finally, we're passing the list of *faces* that we return from `GetEmotionAnalysis` over to the `DisplayData` method.

We now have a functioning application:

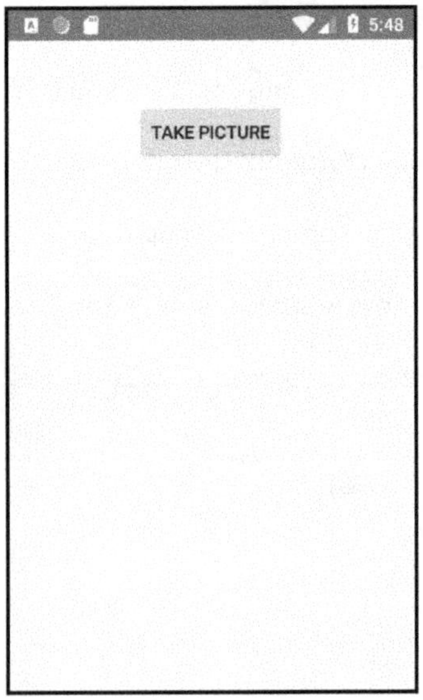

If you press the button, you'll see that the emulator lets you know that you're using the camera, but doesn't actually provide an image that makes sense for our application. We'll now need to talk about how we can test this on a physical device.

Testing and running on a physical device

Since the basis of this program is to use the camera, testing the application on a physical device is essential.

In addition, and quite bizarrely, testing on a physical device can actually be faster than testing on an emulator.

In this section, we will cover the basics of what we will need to set this up on our Android device; however, I strongly encourage you to refer to Xamarin's own guide on this: `https://docs.microsoft.com/en-gb/xamarin/android/get-started/installation/set-up-device-for-development`.

This guide is much more comprehensive and, given that it's updated frequently (whereas this book is not), is an up-to-date guide.

The instructions here relate to Android 8.x (Oreo), but should also work for later versions (at the time of writing, the latest version is 9.x, that is, Pie).

> The following screenshots have been taken from the emulator; however, they have been checked on a physical device to ensure they are accurate for this version of Android.

In order to configure your phone:

1. The first step is to configure your phone; start by loading the settings screen:

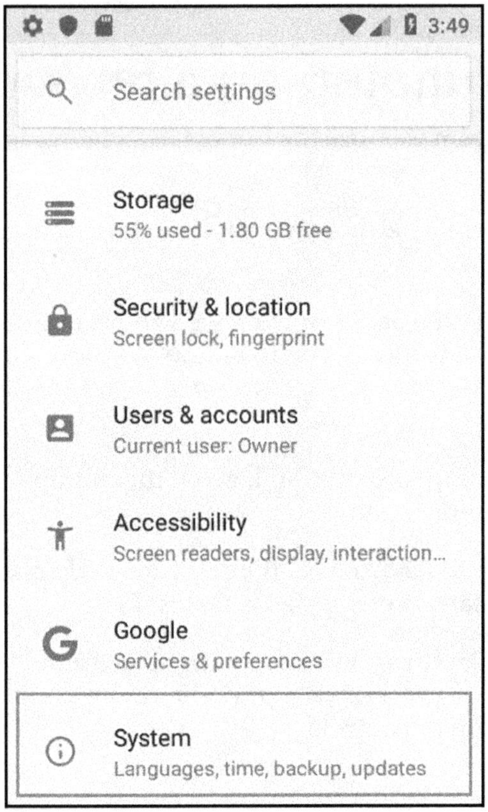

2. Inside **System**, you should see a menu option labeled **About Phone** or similar:

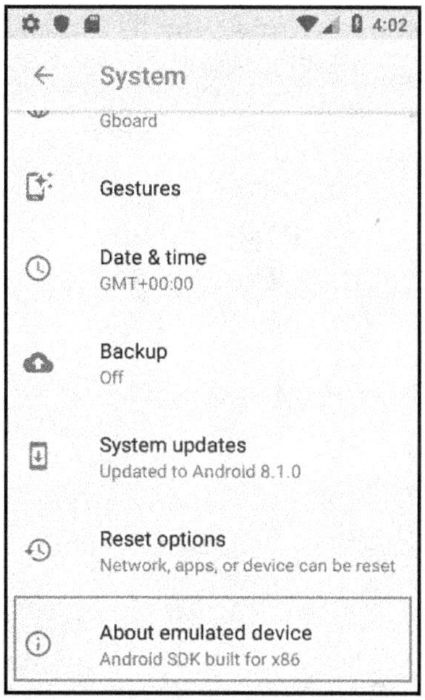

3. Locate the **Build number**:

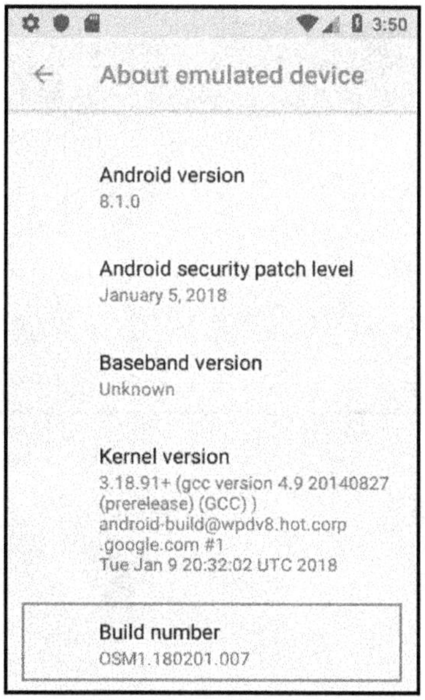

4. You'll need to tap this seven times. You'll be presented with the following message (don't blink, or you'll miss it!):

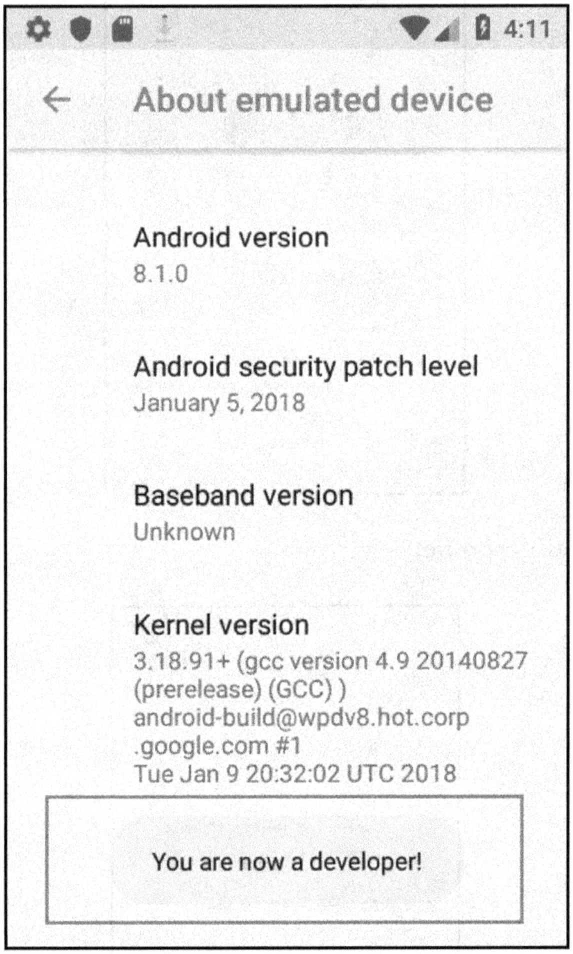

5. A new menu will appear on the **System** menu, that is, **Developer options**:

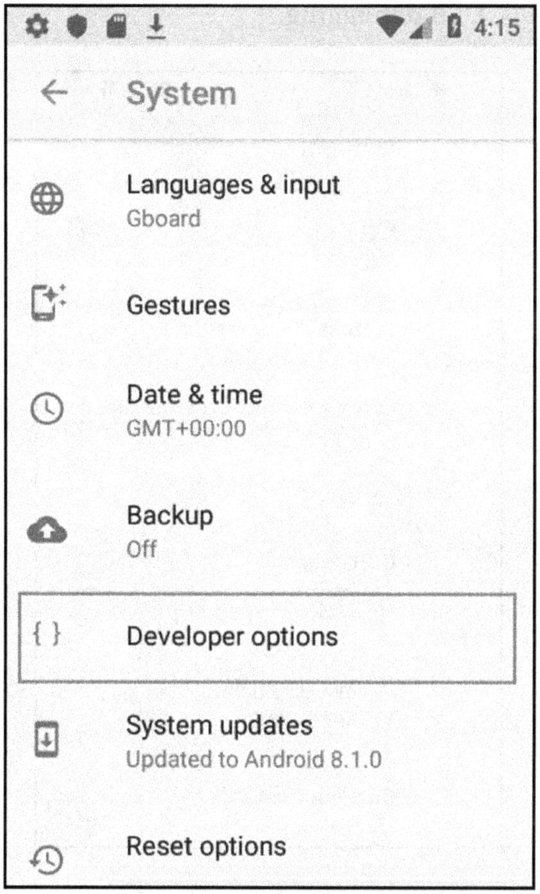

6. This new menu allows you to determine various settings that are useful while testing your software; however, there is one setting in particular that you'll need to change, that is, **USB debugging**:

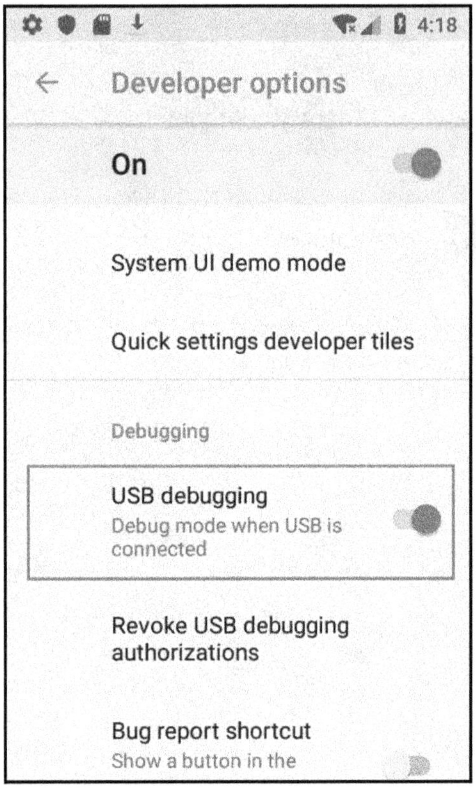

The other settings are optional. You may find that **Stay Awake** saves your sanity, but don't forget to switch it off afterward if you're using a phone.

The next step is to check the Android SDK manager. You should have (at least) the following components installed for Oreo (8.1):

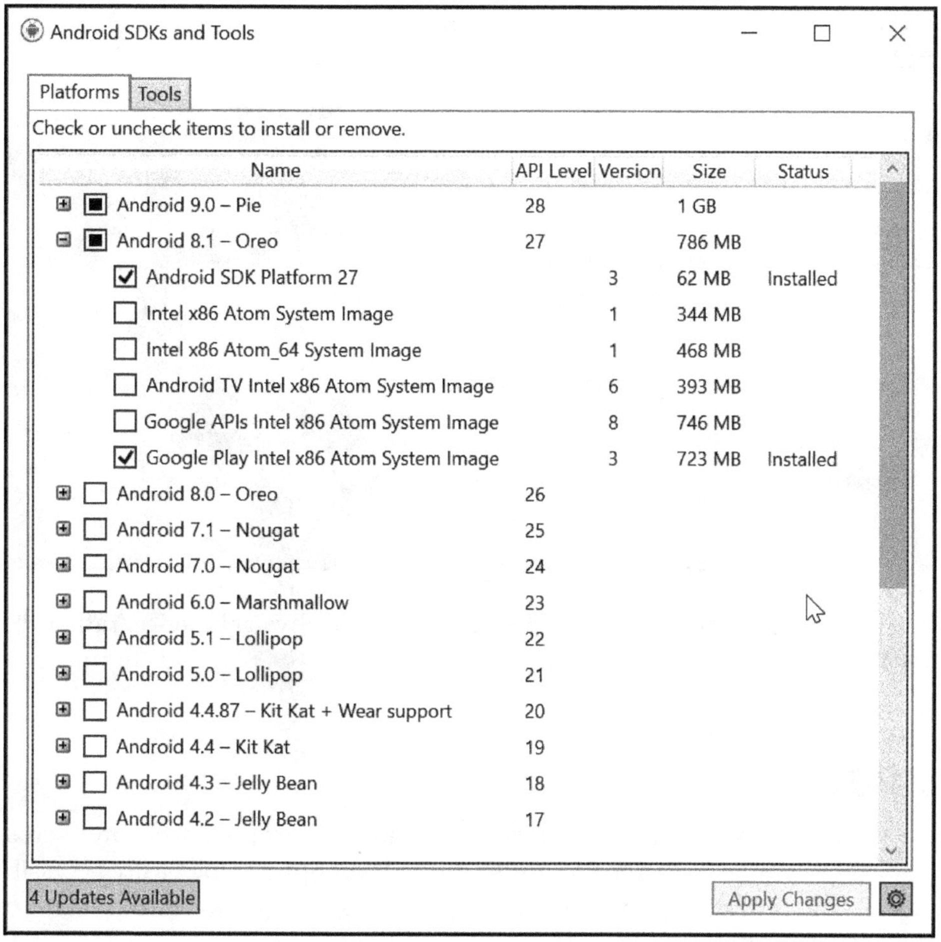

If, like me, you have several updates, you should definitely update.

That's pretty much the basics covered. Depending on your phone, you may find that you need to install some USB drivers. See the preceding link if this is the case for you.

When you plug your phone in, select to transfer files.

Visual Studio should automatically recognize that your phone is connected, and the run icon should change from the emulator to the actual phone:

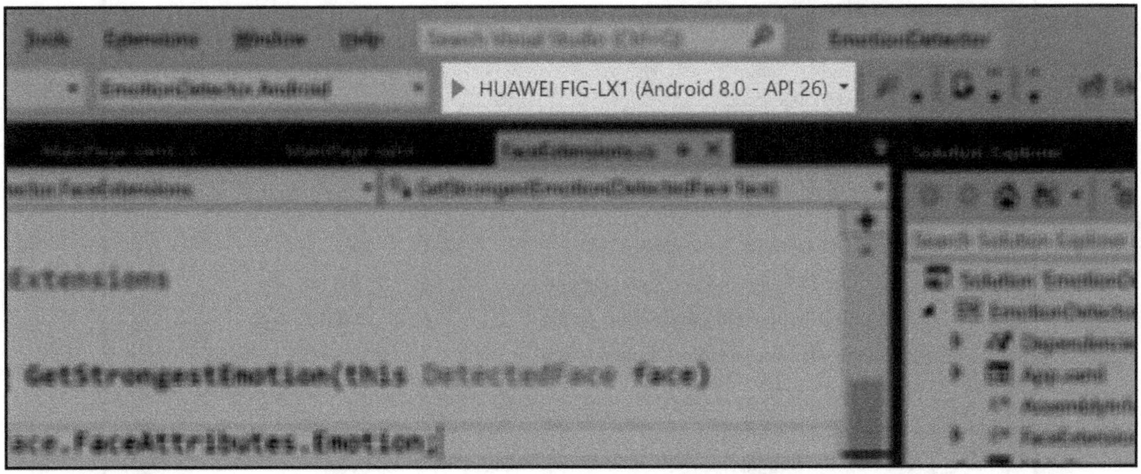

Now, when you run the project, it should launch on your physical device, rather than on the emulator.

Summary

In this chapter, we've seen how we can take two relatively complex problems – cross-platform development and machine learning – and, leveraging some easily accessible services, create an application that, until a few years ago, would have taken teams of specialists years to write.

Of course, the application *has* taken teams of specialists years to write – it's just that you now have access to the produce of their labor.

Cross-platform development is something that many companies have tried to get right: with Microsoft adopting Xamarin first into the company (by buying it) and now appearing in the code base (the 2019 build announced that, in 2020, .NET would combine Mono, .NET Core, and .NET Framework into a single .NET – at the time of writing, this is simply known as .NET 5).

Machine learning is attracting billions of dollars of research: imagine a time in the near future where your phone will be able to monitor your mood. Imagine if a camera in a shop could detect when a customer left because they were unhappy; imagine a camera in the street that could detect if the person walking past was preparing to commit a crime just by their facial expression.

In the next chapter, we'll be exploring machine learning in more detail and creating a chatbot that uses the Microsoft Language Understanding Intelligent Service in order to emulate a conversation with a human.

10
Eliza for the 21st Century - UWP and the MS Bot Framework

The Turing test was developed by Alan Turing in order to answer the question of whether machines could ever be considered as having the ability to think. In the 1960s, a program called Eliza was created, which was one of the first programs that would attempt to pass this test.

The Turing test was developed when the concept of machine learning was in its infancy (Turing himself, in fact, contributed to this field). Now, we have systems that use machine learning to detect sentiment, we have complex systems that can understand language, and we get phone calls from bots that we have entire verbal conversations with and never realize that they are not human.

Eliza was built to emulate a psychotherapist, the idea being that it picks out keywords and phrases and turns them back into questions in order to fool the human into believing they are speaking to another human.

In this chapter, we will create a version of Eliza. We'll learn how to create a client application in UWP using .NET Core 3. We'll then learn how to set up and configure LUIS, and lastly, we'll learn how to integrate this into the MS Bot Framework.

The following topics will be covered in this chapter:

- Chatbots
- The Microsoft chatbot framework
- LUIS (Microsoft's Language Understanding Service)
- Creating an application in UWP

Chatbots can be used for everything, from IT support to booking a flight (an example of which is shown in the following image):

Technical requirements

During this chapter, we will be using the default templates for creating a Microsoft bot using the Bot Framework. At the time of writing, despite the release of .NET Core 3, the Bot Framework project was still being created in .NET 2.2. In a later section, we will see how to upgrade this to .NET Core 3; however, by the time this book is released, that may have changed.

In this chapter, you'll need an Azure subscription (we briefly covered how to create one in `Chapter 2`, *Task Bug Logging ASP.NET Core MVC App Using Cosmos DB*).

The code from this chapter can be found on GitHub at `https://github.com/PacktPublishing/C-8-and-.NET-Core-3-Projects-Using-Azure-Second-Edition`.

Creating a chatbot

Let's start with the chatbot. At the time of writing, chatbots are everywhere, from when you ask for help on a website to when you phone a call center. Essentially, a chatbot is simply a complex state machine, and frameworks, such as Microsoft's Azure Bot Framework, simply hide that complexity from you. Imagine the following dialog between a human and a machine (**H** and **M**):

```
M: Hello, how can I help?
H: Hello, I'd like to check my balance, please.
M: I can help you with that. Which account is this for?
H: Current.
M: I'm sorry, I didn't get that. Which account is this for?
H: Current account.
M: What is the number of your current account?
```

Okay, so if we have a look at this exchange, we can see that it is initiated by the bot. The customer responds by saying that they'd like to check their balance—so here the bot is listening for keywords, and clearly `balance` is one. Now the machine needs to know which account the customer wants to know the balance of. Behind the scenes, it may have checked whether there is more than one account registered to the customer. At this point, the customer says `current`, and the bot needs to clarify, so it loops back and asks again. When it finally understand the answer, it moves on.

We'll create our bot using a template, which you'll need to install from `https://marketplace.visualstudio.com/items?itemName=BotBuilder.botbuilderv4`.

When you choose to create a new bot, you're given three options: **Empty Bot**, **Echo Bot**, and **Core Bot**, as shown in the following screenshot. For this project, we'll pick **Echo Bot**:

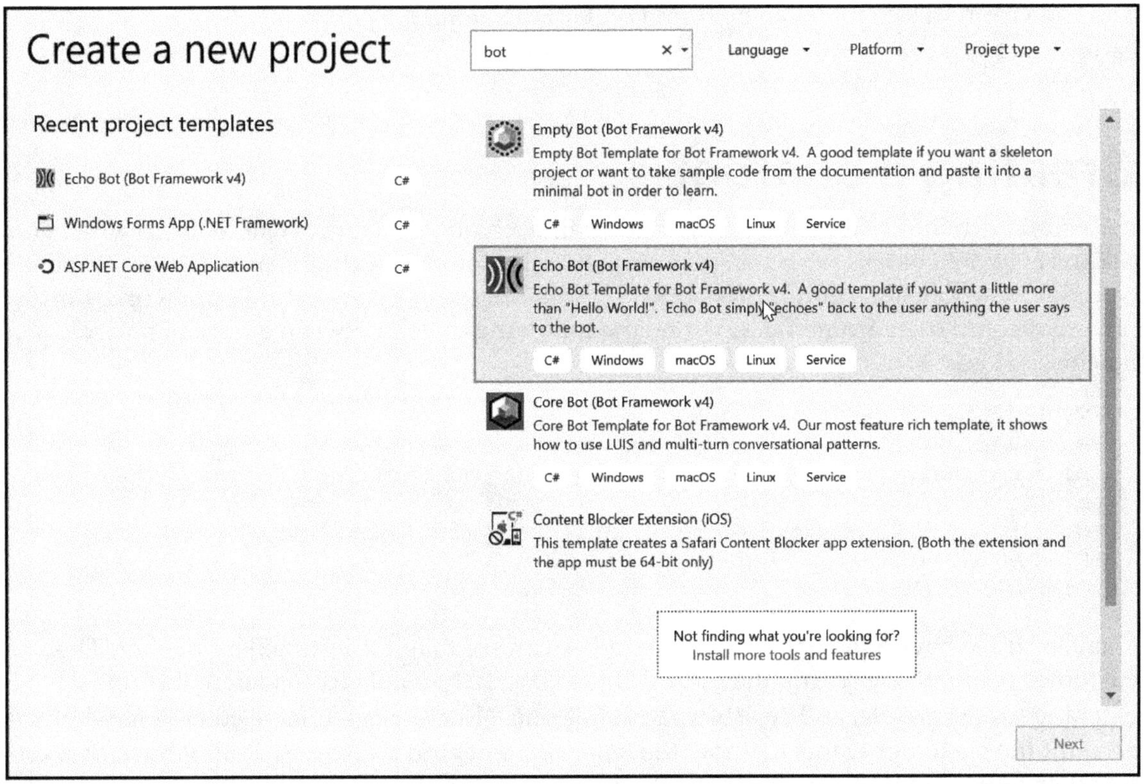

These are prebuilt templates with varying degrees of existing functionality. Obviously, the empty template has no functionality and only boilerplate code. The **Core Bot** gives you a fully functioning bot that is linked to LUIS.

We'll now choose the file location of our project:

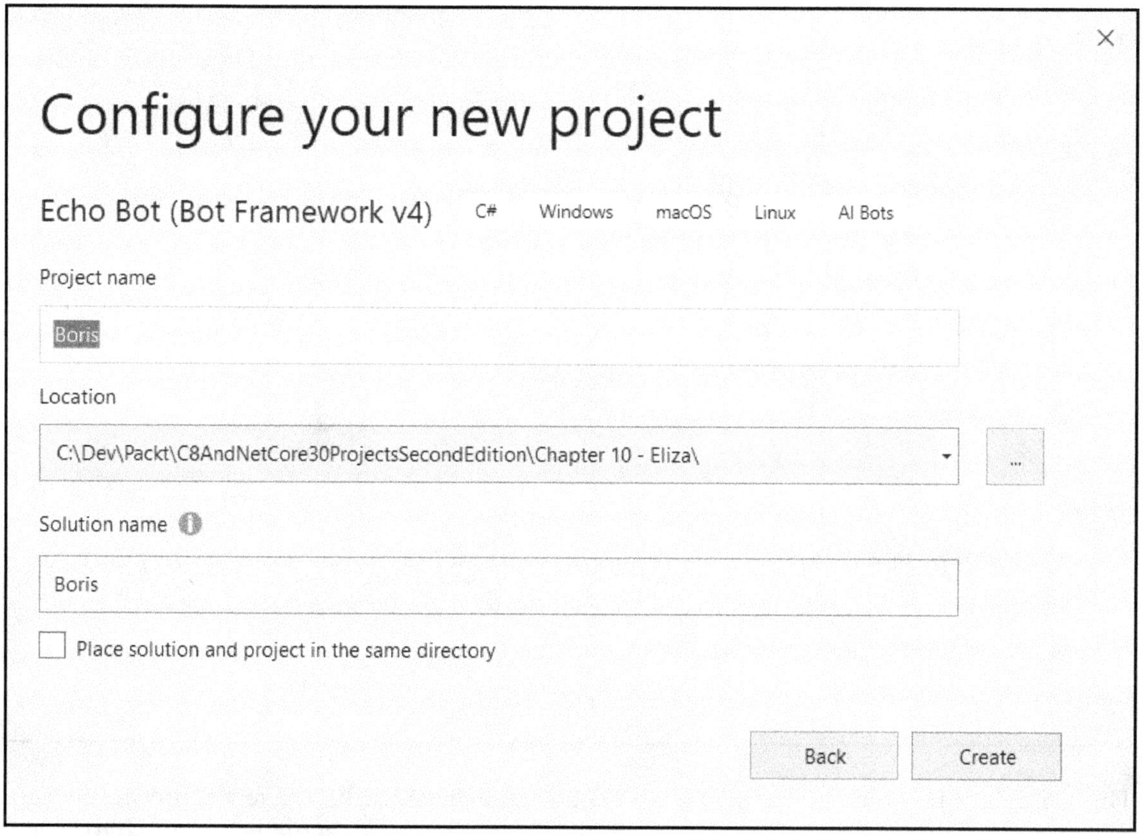

By default, the bot name will be set to the project name.

Once you've created your bot, run it up, and you should see the following screen:

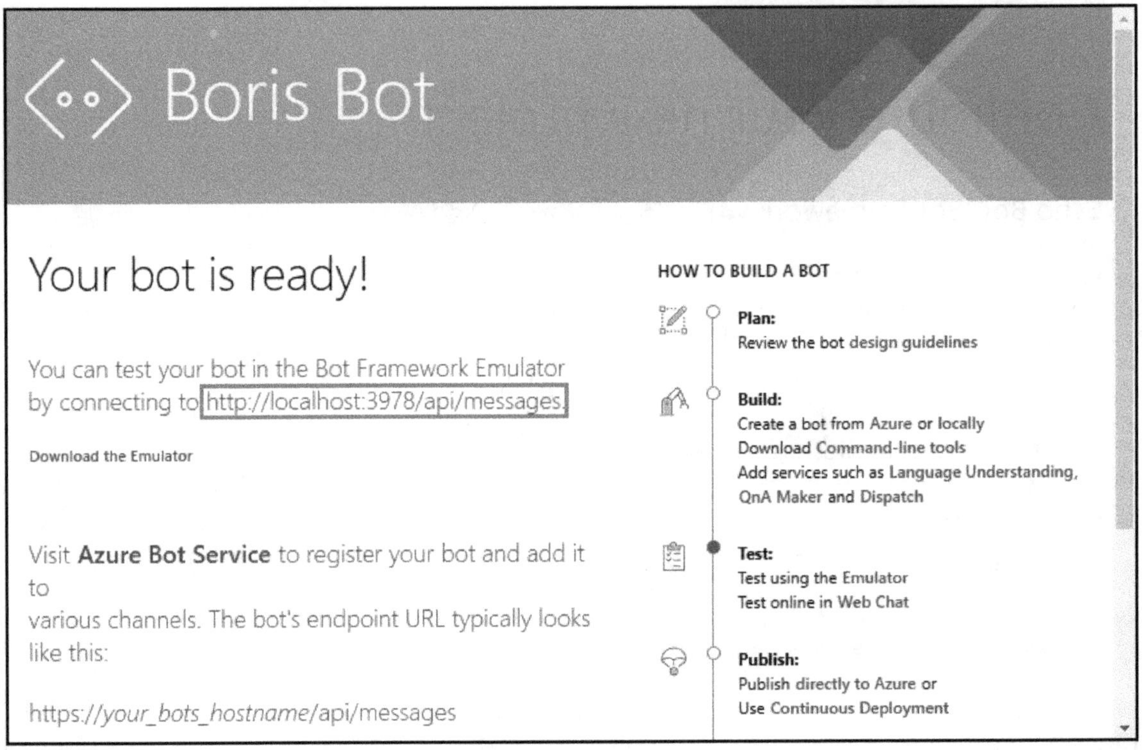

This might not be exactly what you were expecting, as we now have a few more steps to go through to see our bot in action (spoiler: at this stage, there's not actually too much to see!). Make a note of the URL in the screenshot, as we'll need it shortly.

Bot emulator

The next stage is to run an emulator. The bot that we've just created is, in fact, just a service. The emulator gives us a UI to interact with it.

At the time of writing, the latest version of the emulator was at `https://github.com/Microsoft/BotFramework-Emulator/releases/tag/v4.2.1`.

To install this, there is a self-extracting executable:

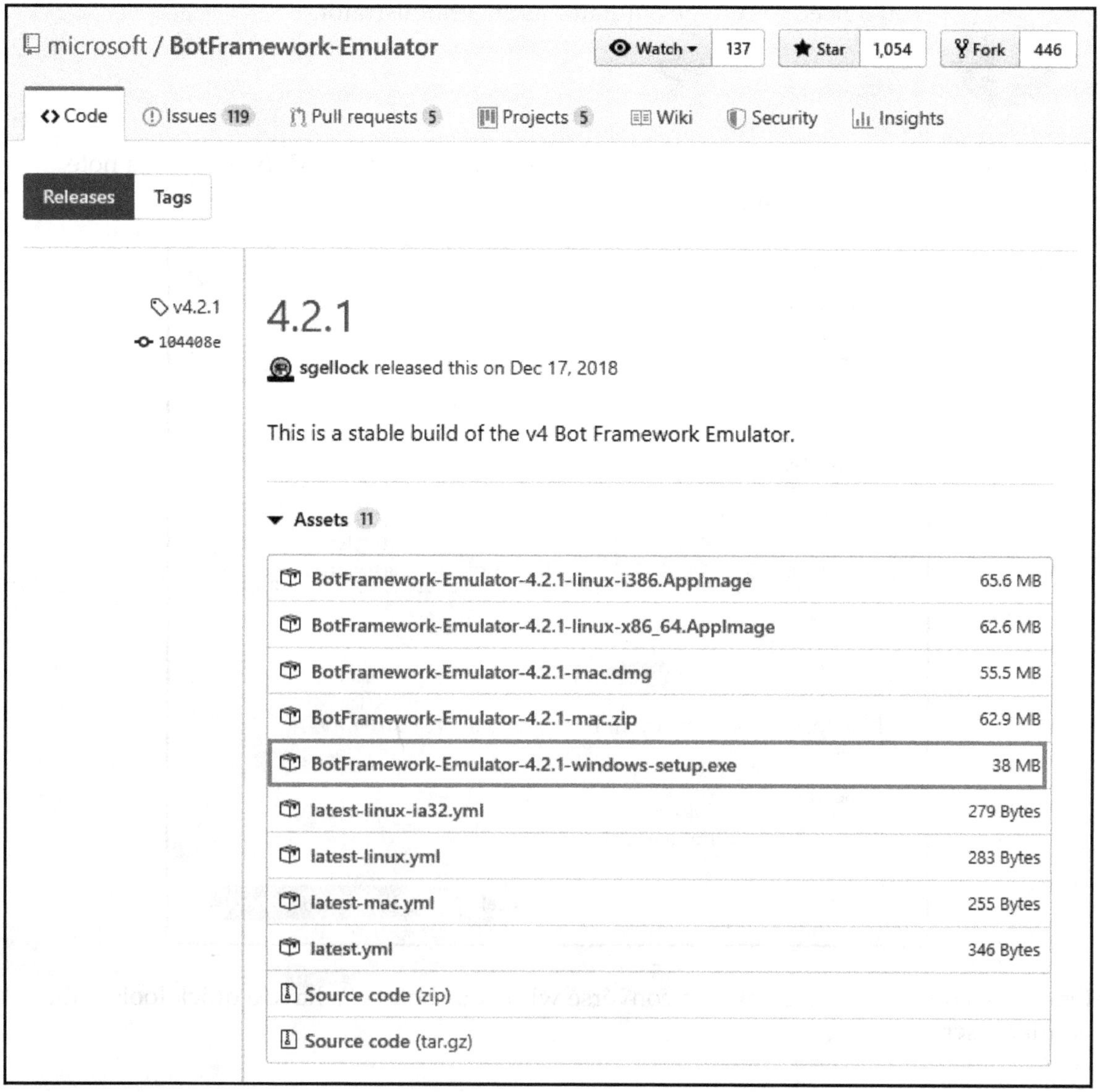

Download and install the emulator, then run it.

You'll need to run the emulator as an administrator.

When you run the emulator, you'll need to give it a name and a URL (you made a note of the URL a few moments ago, and the name can be anything):

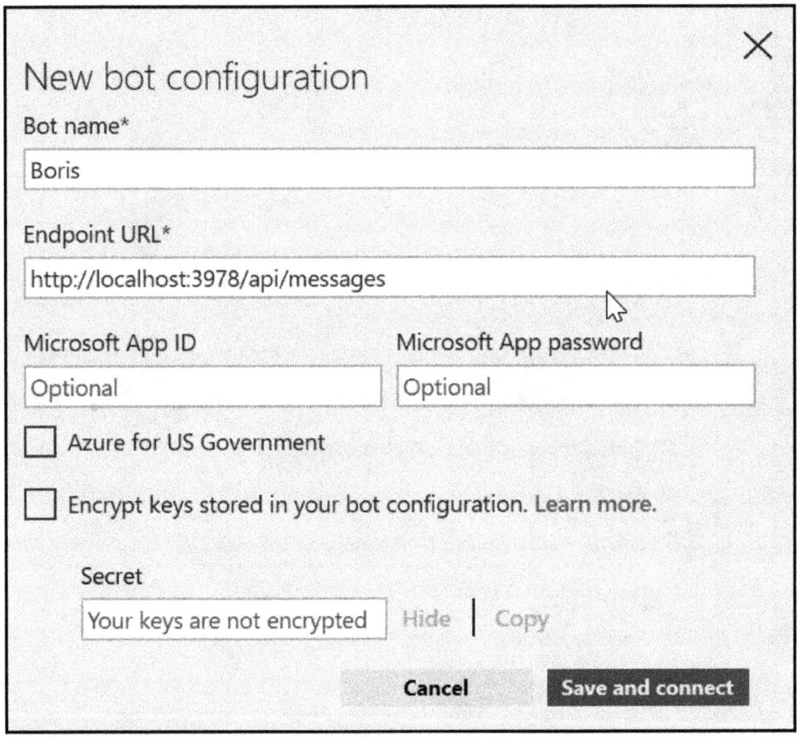

Once you connect, you'll be able to converse with your bot. Let's have a quick look at the emulator screens:

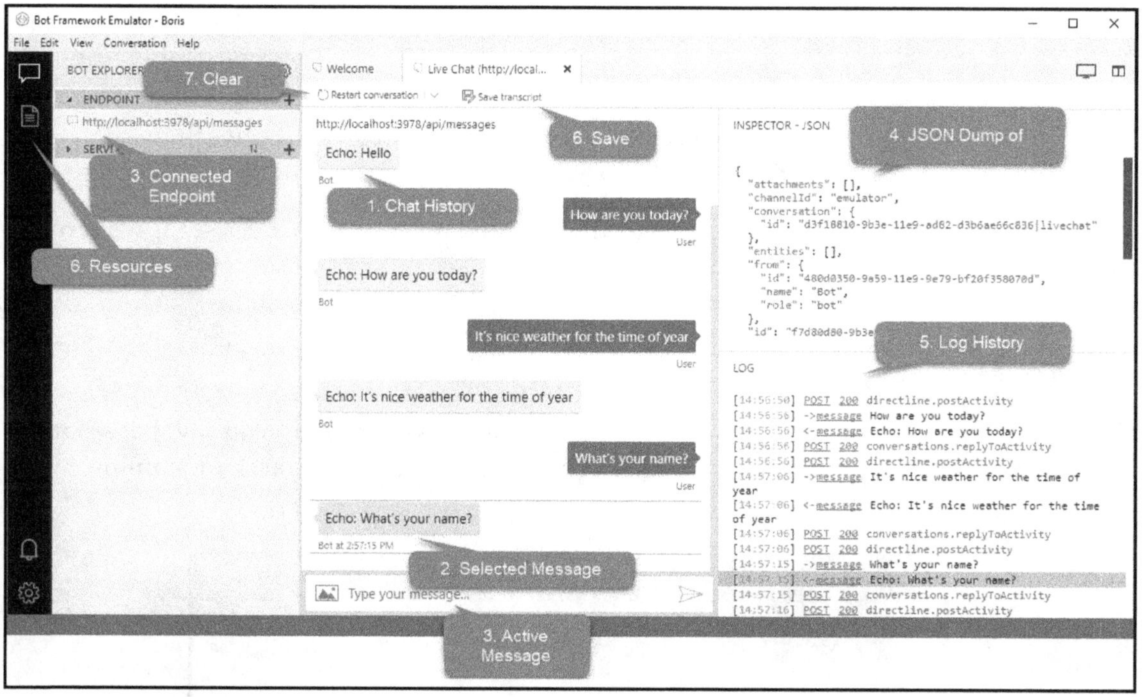

Let's see what it's actually telling us:

1. This section lists all of the messages that either you (the human) or the bot writes.
2. You can select any message in the chat history (see 4).
3. This is where you type a message to the bot.
4. This shows the message in its raw JSON form. Remember that your bot is simply an API, so communication in and out is in JSON format.
5. This gives the network history of the conversation. This is particularly useful if you're having authentication or network issues.
6. The entire chat history can be saved to a `.transcript` file. This is, essentially, a JSON representation of the conversation history. The resources icon on the left allows you to open these files and inspect old transcripts. This is useful in a support scenario, where something has gone wrong and you want to see what happened during the chat.
7. At any time, you can simply restart the chat from scratch.

8. This shows or hides the *Resources* section. This allows you to view transcripts or chat files.
9. This shows the endpoint that you are currently communicating with.
10. A history of connected endpoints is stored; you can switch between these by simply clicking through the history.

You may notice that the bot's dialog is heavily inspired by your own. Let's see if we can identify why that is and correct it slightly.

Echo Bot – Except for Hello

Currently, Echo Bot lives up to its name—it simply echoes everything you say. Let's start making it a little more Boris by adding a slight change to this. Let's start by renaming `EchoBot` to `BorisBot`:

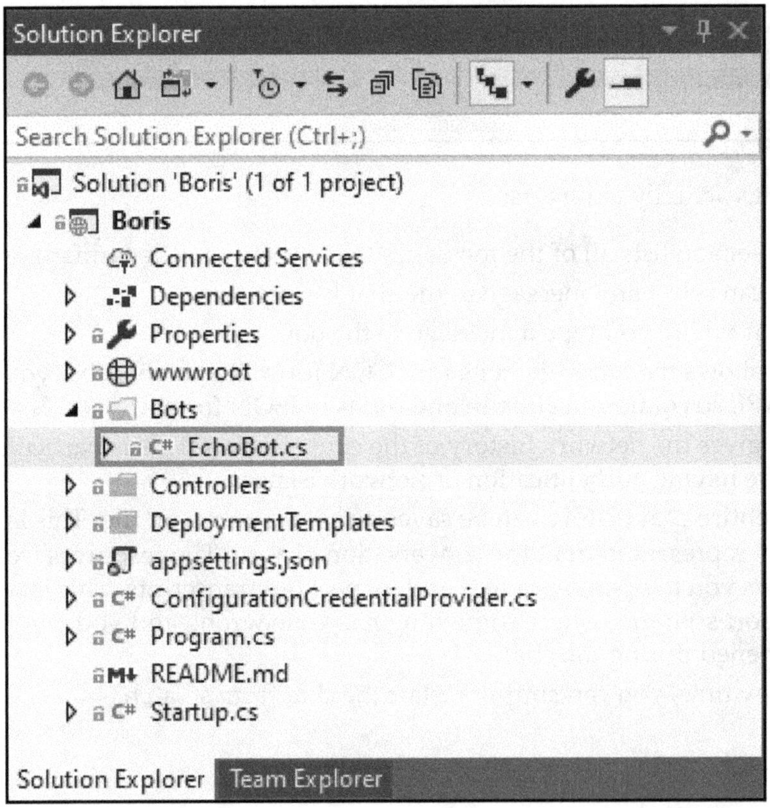

We are going to change the code for the bot slightly by going through the following steps:

1. First, let's rename the class:

```
public class BorisBot : ActivityHandler
{
    . . .
}
```

2. Next, we'll make a small change to `OnMessageActivityAsync` to capture the user typing `Hello`, and respond with a more sensible message:

```
protected override async Task
OnMessageActivityAsync(ITurnContext<IMessageActivity> turnContext,
CancellationToken cancellationToken)
{
    if (turnContext.Activity.Text == "Hello")
    {
        await
turnContext.SendActivityAsync(MessageFactory.Text($"Hello, my name
is Boris"), cancellationToken);
    }
    else
    {
        await
turnContext.SendActivityAsync(MessageFactory.Text($"Echo:
{turnContext.Activity.Text}"), cancellationToken);
    }
}
```

3. In `Startup.cs`, you'll also need to change the dependency injection to register the new bot:

```
services.AddTransient<IBot, BorisBot>();
```

Now, if we run the bot, we get a different response:

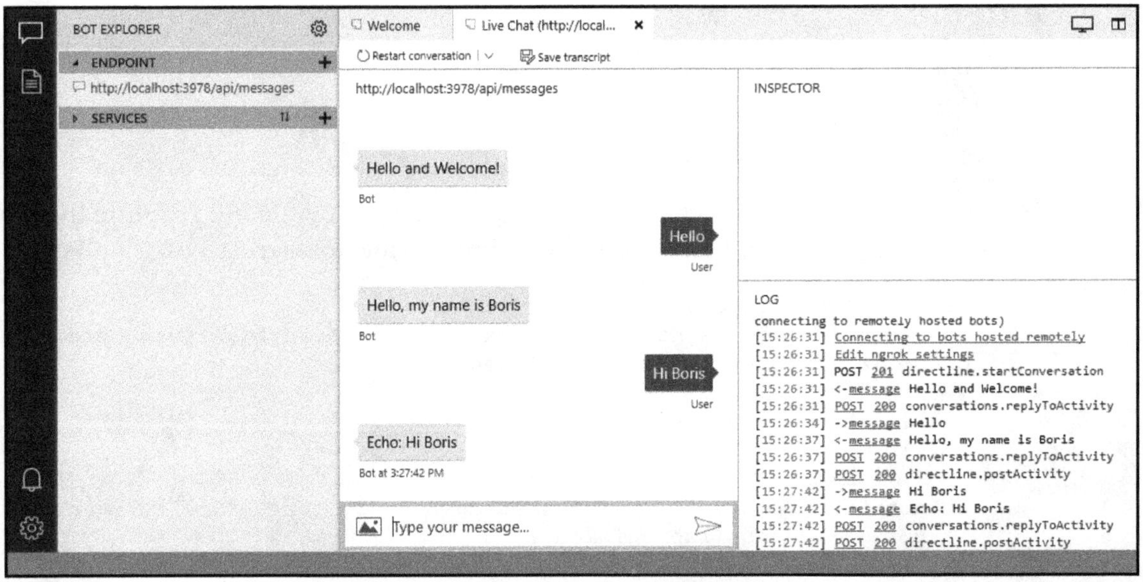

Okay, so we now get a sensible response when we type `Hello`, but anything else and we're back to **Echo**. In order to pass the Turing test, we need to improve on this. Remember, this is all about perception, so we first need to cover various ways of saying similar things, and secondly, we need to vary our responses. We could write a massive switch statement inside `OnMessageActivityAsync` and try to think of as many ways of saying `Hello` as we can. However, we could also use a tool that Microsoft has created for us, called LUIS, which does some of this for us.

Introducing LUIS

LUIS stands for Language Understanding Intelligent Service. It allows you to tap into a machine learning algorithm to train a prebuilt language model. In fact, this service (as with the Bot Framework) is far more powerful than we'll see here. For our purposes, we only need to train a simple model that has very few keywords and phrases. If you haven't done so, you'll need to start by registering at `https://www.luis.ai`.

Once you're registered, you can start building a new model:

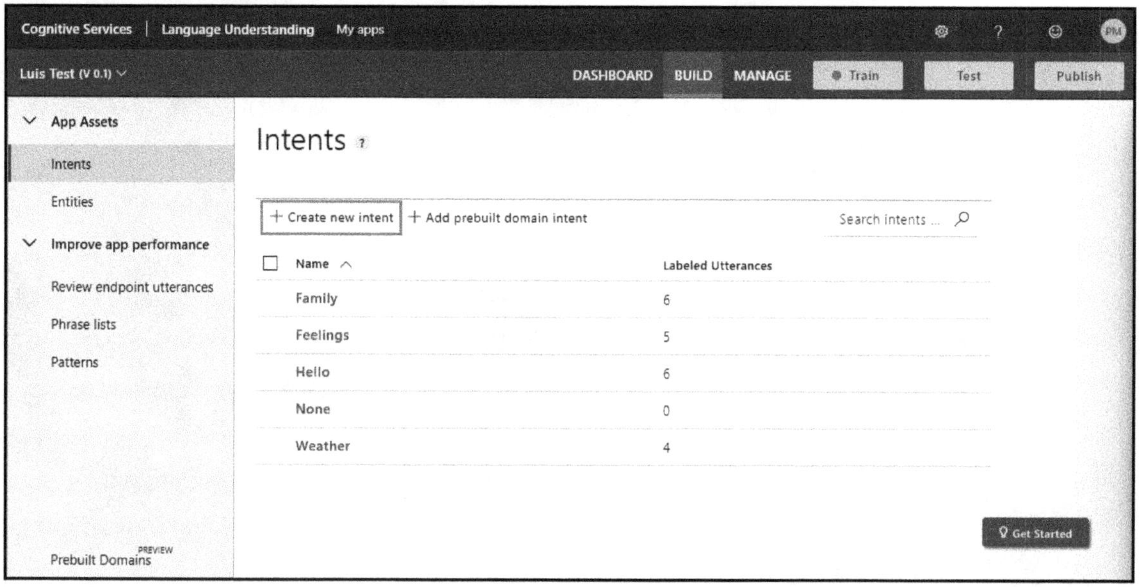

Here, if we select **Intents**, we can identify key areas of conversation; as you can see, I've identified a number of areas here. You select the **Create new intent** option, then give the intent a name (in fact, it doesn't matter what you name the intent). Once you've done so, you'll be asked to give some examples of what might be typed in—for example, for **Feelings**, you may have something like this:

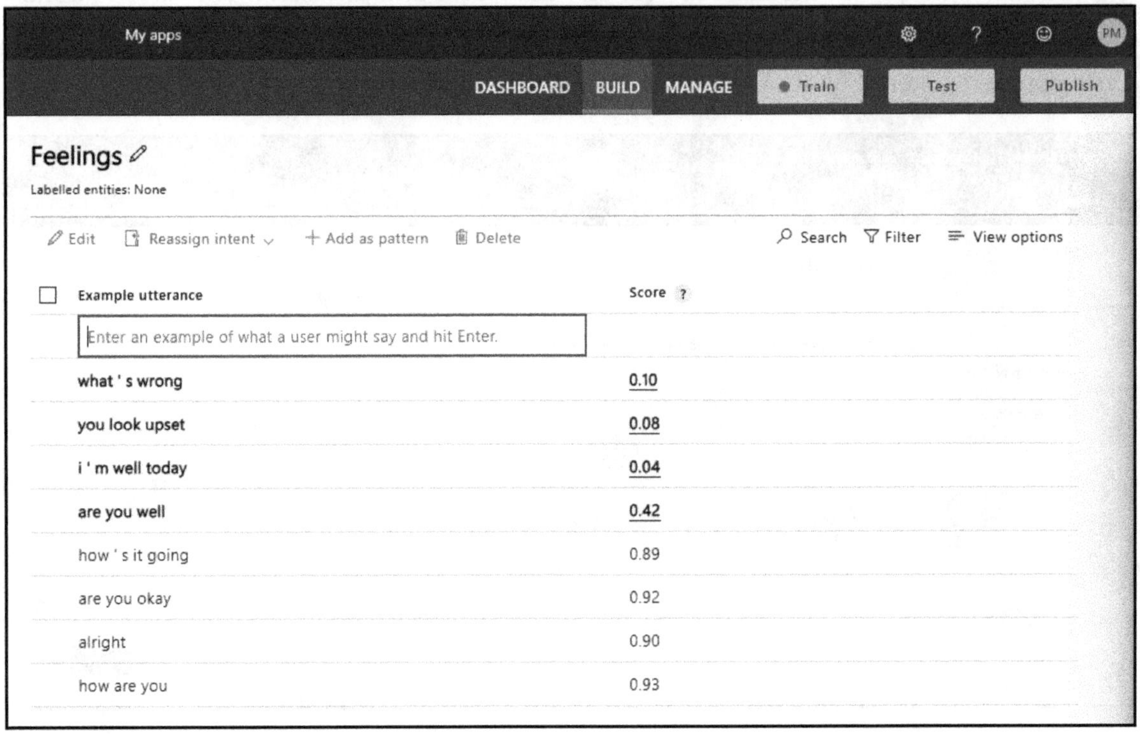

TIP

You should ensure that you add at least five phrases for each intent, but the more phrases you have, the better the model.

Once you've done this, you can train and test your model.

> You can add these examples all day, but unless you train the model, it will not change.

Let's try training and testing our model. Once you've added a number of intents (it doesn't have to be all of them, and they don't have to be the same as those listed here), select **Train**. As you can see in the preceding screenshot, you'll know when your model needs training, as a little red traffic light appears next to the **Train** button. After your model is trained, give it a test by selecting **Test**:

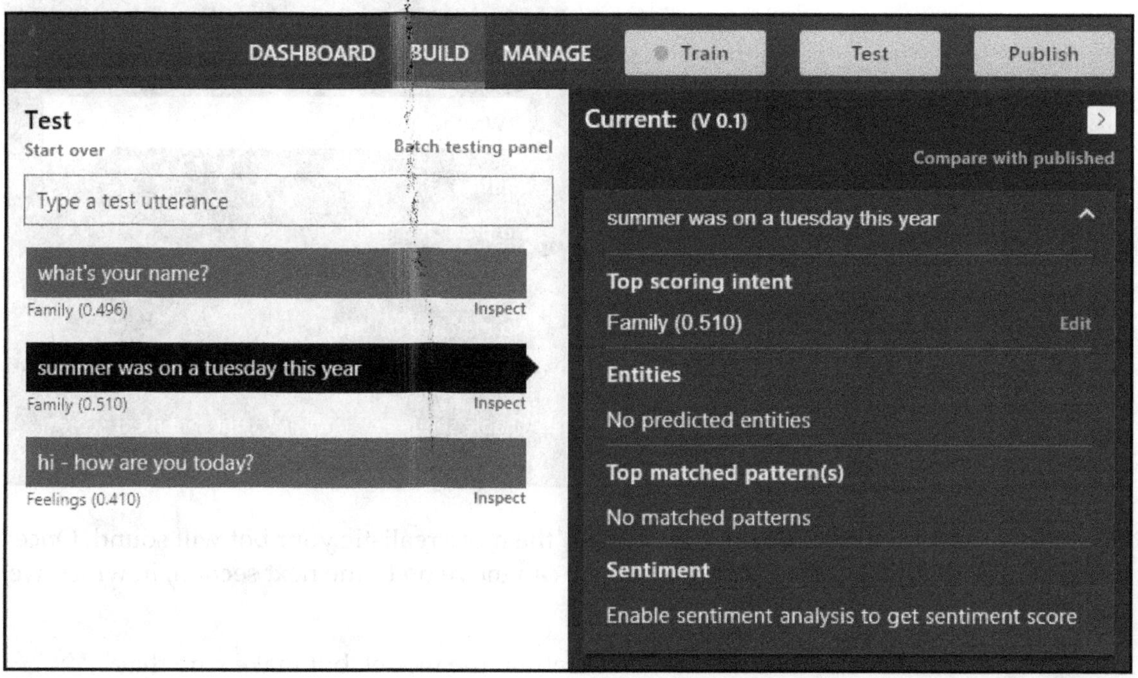

Here, I've tried three phrases. You can see that beneath each phrase it returns an intent. It seems to have entered one of them correctly, but the other two are a little off. The great thing here is that, as I'm testing, if it gets something wrong, I can simply tell LUIS it's wrong by clicking **Edit** and then telling it the correct intent:

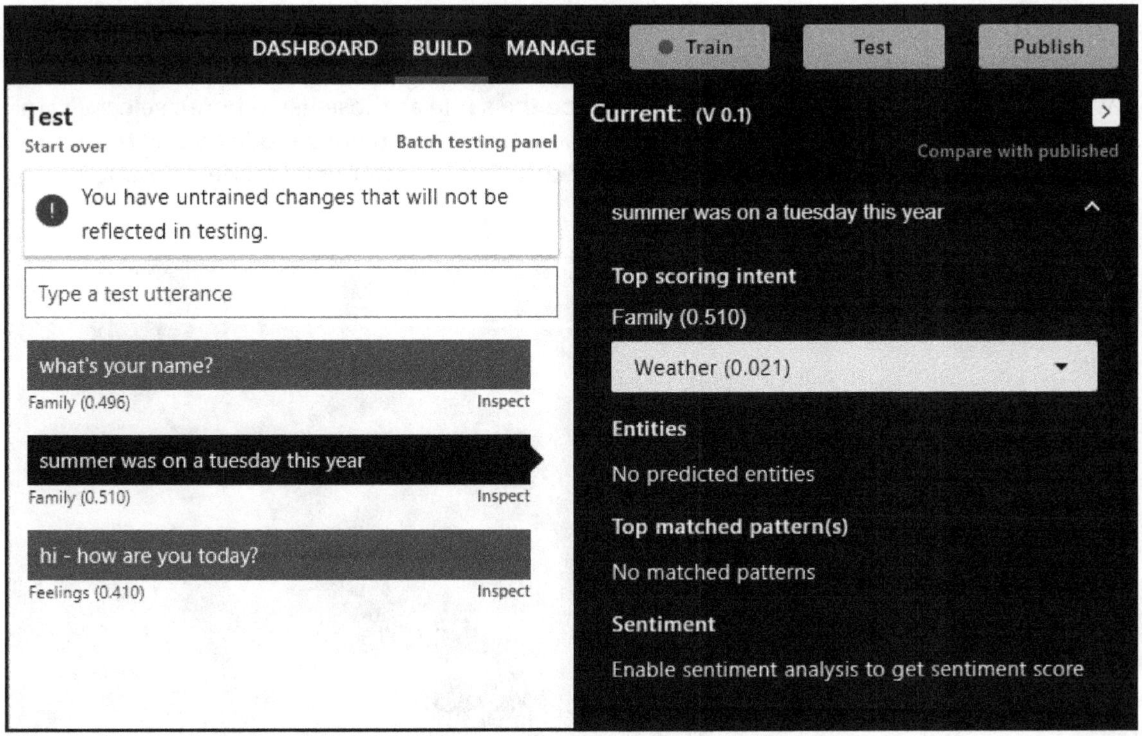

Obviously, the more fine grained your intents, the more realistic your bot will sound. Once you're happy that you've trained your bot, we can move on to the next section, in which we will integrate LUIS into our bot.

TIP

We can always come back and retrain the model, but make sure that you're happy with the intents, as we'll be coding against them.

Integrating LUIS into the Bot Framework

It's worth noting that this process is well documented by Microsoft; feel free to follow this section or to have a look at the documentation found at `https://docs.microsoft.com/en-us/azure/bot-service/bot-builder-howto-v4-luis?view=azure-bot-service-4.0tabs=csharp`.

Let's go through the following steps:

1. The first thing we need in order to integrate LUIS is to add the connection details. In the LUIS portal, select **MANAGE** and from **Application Information**, copy the **Application ID**:

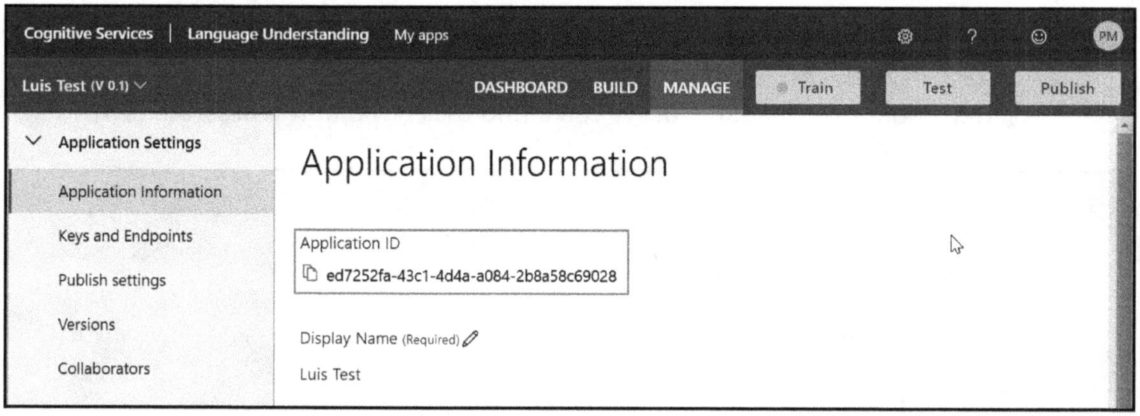

2. Add this into your `appsettings.json` file:

```
{
  "MicrosoftAppId": "",
  "MicrosoftAppPassword": "",
  "LuisAppId": "ed7252fa-43c1-4d4a-a084-2b8a58c69028",
  "LuisAPIKey": "",
  "LuisAPIHostName": ""
}
```

3. Now, select **Keys and Endpoints** and copy the **Authoring Key**:

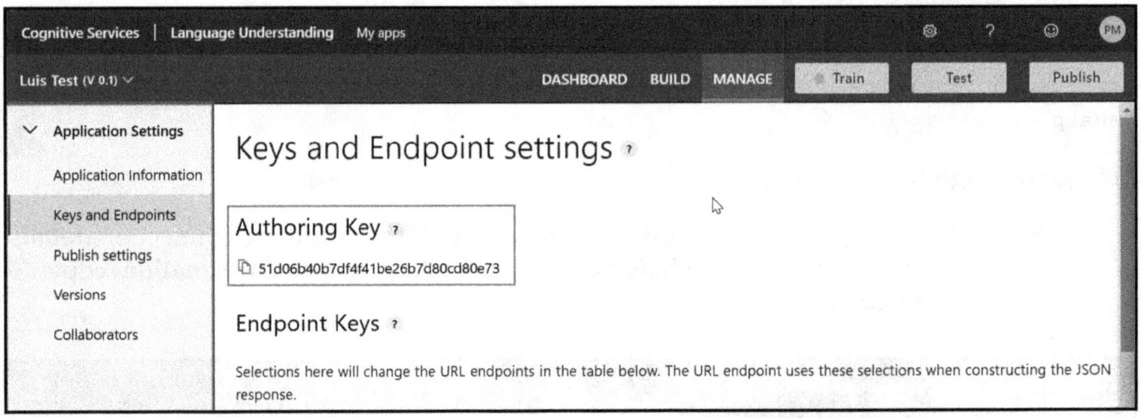

4. At the bottom of the same page, you'll find the endpoint if you scroll down:

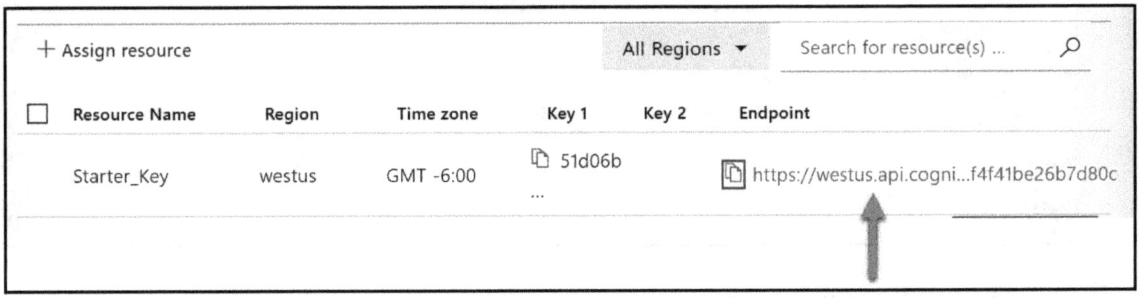

These values also need to be copied into `appsettings.json`:

```
{
  "MicrosoftAppId": "",
  "MicrosoftAppPassword": "",
  "LuisAppId": "ed7252fa-43c1-4d4a-a084-2b8a58c69028",
  "LuisAPIKey": "51d06b40b7df4f41be26b7d80cd80e73",
  "LuisAPIHostName": "https://westus.api.cognitive.microsoft.com"
}
```

Note that the hostname is trimmed after `.microsoft.com`.

5. Once this is done, you'll need to **Publish** your model:

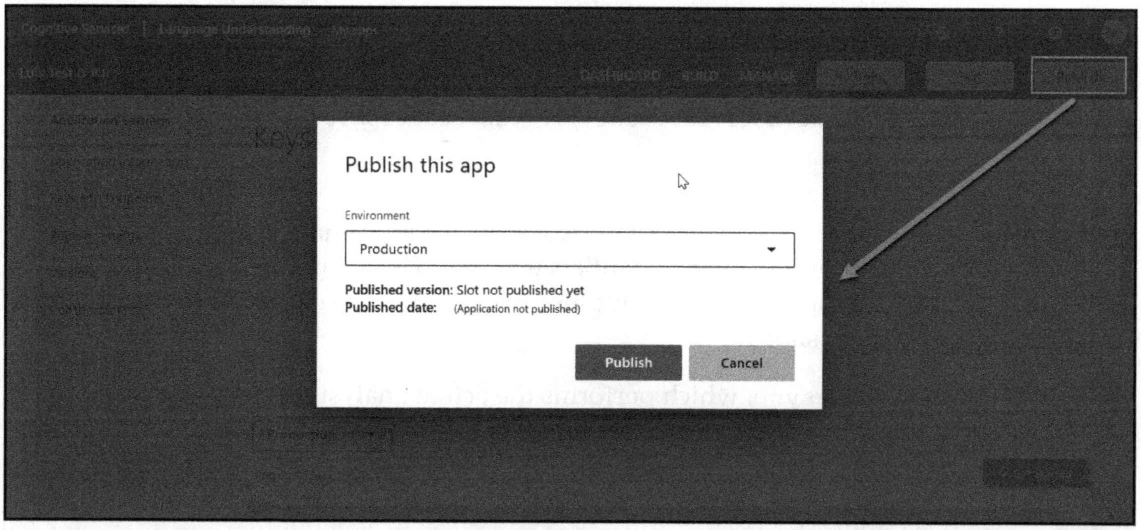

6. The next step is to install the LUIS NuGet package:

```
Install-Package Microsoft.Bot.Builder.AI.Luis
```

7. Finally, we need to plumb in the code; let's replace our check for `Hello` with a call to LUIS:

```
protected override async Task
OnMessageActivityAsync(ITurnContext<IMessageActivity> turnContext,
CancellationToken cancellationToken)
{
    var luisApplication = new LuisApplication(
                    _configuration["LuisAppId"],
                    _configuration["LuisAPIKey"],
                    _configuration["LuisAPIHostName"]
                );

    var recognizer = new LuisRecognizer(luisApplication);
    var recognizerResult = await
recognizer.RecognizeAsync(turnContext, cancellationToken);

    var (intent, score) = recognizerResult.GetTopScoringIntent();
    if (intent == "Hello")
    {
        await
turnContext.SendActivityAsync(MessageFactory.Text($"Hello, my name
```

```
is Boris"), cancellationToken);
            }
            else
            {
                await
turnContext.SendActivityAsync(MessageFactory.Text($"Echo:
{turnContext.Activity.Text}"), cancellationToken);
            }
        }
```

Let's quickly review what we've changed here. Firstly, we instantiate a new `LuisApplication` and provide the credentials that we collected in the `appsettings.json`. In order to do this, we also inject `IConfiguration` into the class, which we'll come back to shortly.

We then call `RecognizeAsync`, which performs the actual analysis of the phrase, and finally, we ask it to tell us what it thinks the intent is. Let's see what that means for the bot:

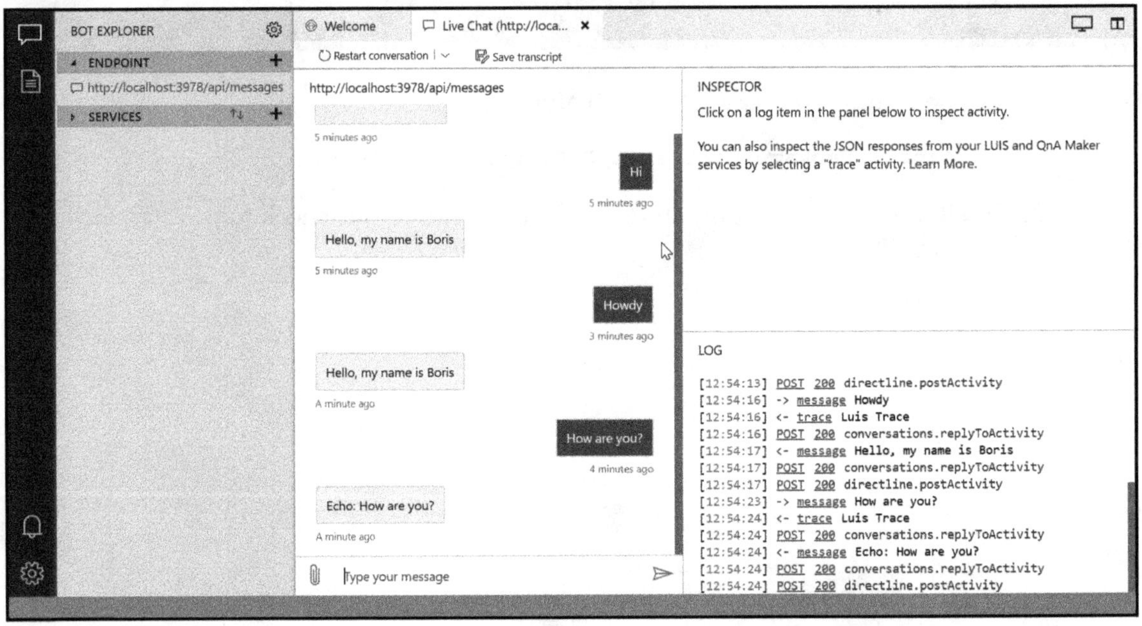

As you can see, Boris now understands a little more; however, our response is still quite wooden, and it only works for the `Hello` intent. Let's address the other intents next, but first, we injected the `IConfiguration` into the class. Let's have a look at that change:

```
private readonly IConfiguration _configuration;

public BorisBot(IConfiguration configuration)
{
    _configuration = configuration;
}
```

The next stage is to upgrade our project to use .NET Core 3.

At the time of writing, the templates use .NET Core 2.1; however, if that is not the case by the time you read this, please feel free to skip the next section.

Upgrading the template from .NET Core 2.1 to 3.0

At this stage, we'll need to bump up the version from .NET Core 2.1 to .NET Core 3.0. This will likely result in us needing to make a couple of little tweaks.

The first tweak is that `IHostingEnvironment` should be replaced with `IHostEnvironment` (for a full transcript of this method, see the following):

```
public void Configure(IApplicationBuilder app, IHostEnvironment env)
```

This is to avoid namespace conflicts introduced in 2.1.

The next change is the compatibility version: it shouldn't surprise you to learn that the app now needs to be set to be compatible with version 3:

```
services.AddMvc()
    .SetCompatibilityVersion(CompatibilityVersion.Version_3_0);
```

Now that we've added MVC to the dependency injection system, we need to register it as middleware in the application.

UseMvc

Finally, there have been a number of changes around the endpoint routing. The net effect of this is that `UseMvc` now seems to configure too many settings in one go; as a result, the `Configure` method should look more like this:

```
public void Configure(IApplicationBuilder app, IHostEnvironment env)
{
    if (env.IsDevelopment())
    {
        app.UseDeveloperExceptionPage();
    }
    else
    {
        app.UseHsts();
    }

    app.UseDefaultFiles();
    app.UseStaticFiles();

    //app.UseHttpsRedirection();
    //app.UseMvc();
    app.UseRouting();
    app.UseCors();
    app.UseEndpoints(e =>
        e.MapControllerRoute("default",
"{controller=Home}/{action=Index}/{id?}")
    );
}
```

We no longer call `UseMvc`, but instead, call the specific aspects of middleware that we need.

AllowSynchronousIO

In .NET Core 3.0, a breaking change was introduced, whereby the default of allowing synchronous calls was changed so that they were not allowed. At the time of writing, `BotFrameworkAdaptor` breaks that rule (perhaps because it's using Newtonsoft JSON serialization—in which case this may not be an issue by the time this book is published). You might get the following error when running the project:

```
System.InvalidOperationException: Synchronous operations are disallowed.
Call ReadAsync or set AllowSynchronousIO to true instead.'
```

The following changes should be implemented only if you get the preceding error when running the project:

1. In `BotController`, change the `AllowSynchronousIO` flag:

```
[HttpPost]
public async Task PostAsync()
{
    var syncIOFeature =
_httpContextAccessor.HttpContext.Features.Get<IHttpBodyControlFeatu
re>();
    if (syncIOFeature != null)
    {
        syncIOFeature.AllowSynchronousIO = true;
    }

    // Delegate the processing of the HTTP POST to the adapter.
    // The adapter will invoke the bot.
    await _adapter.ProcessAsync(Request, Response, _bot);
}
```

2. We'll need to inject `IHttpContextAccessor` into `BotController`; this is what the constructor should now look like:

```
private readonly IHttpContextAccessor _httpContextAccessor;

public BotController(IBotFrameworkHttpAdapter adapter,
    IBot bot, IHttpContextAccessor httpContextAccessor)
{
    _adapter = adapter;
    _bot = bot;
    _httpContextAccessor = httpContextAccessor;
}
```

3. Lastly, in `Startup.ConfigureServices`, add the context accessor:

```
services.AddHttpContextAccessor();
```

Your project should now compile using .NET Core 3.0. Now let's investigate broadening our code to deal with other intents.

Intent/response matrix

This section covers, essentially, the final two requirements of this API. We're going to create a JSON file that maps an intent to a possible reply (or replies). In fact, we're going to link each intent to multiple replies and then use one at random; that way, the bot will give the impression of responding uniquely to each message.

Let's start with the JSON document. Here's what it might look like:

```
{
  "Hello": [
    "Hi there!",
    "Hello, My name is Boris",
    "Nice to meet you",
    "Hello"
  ],
  "Family": [
    "Tell me more about your family",
    "Do you have any siblings?",
    "Let's talk about your family some more"
  ],
  "Feelings": [
    "It's important to talk about your feelings",
    "It's healthy to talk about how you feel",
    "Please tell me: how are you feeling"
  ],
  "Weather": [
    "How's the weather where you are",
    "In 1987, the BBC weatherman Michael Fish failed to predict a
Hurricane",
    "The weather is very unpredictable",
    "What's the forecast for tomorrow?"
  ],
  "None": [
    "I'm afraid I'm not sure what you mean",
    "That sounds interesting, please tell me more",
    "Wow - really?"
  ]
}
```

Save this inside a folder called `Data`, and change the properties to make it an **Embedded Resource**:

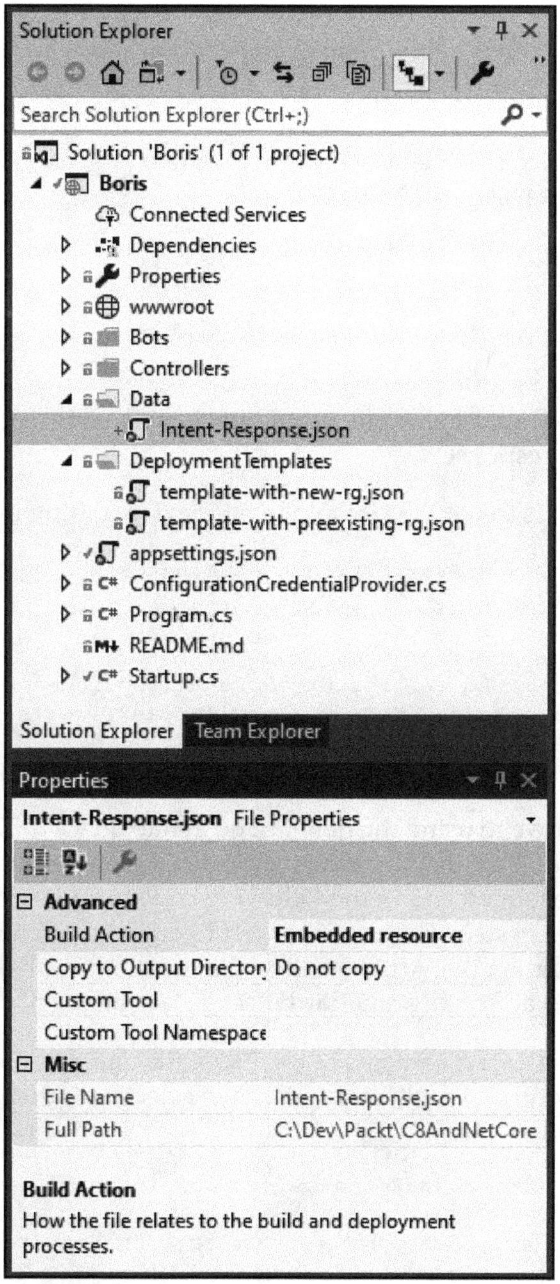

Let's plumb this in. The changes that we need are in the bot file `BorisBot.cs`. We're going to change the `OnMessageActivityAsync` method. Along the way, we'll meet another couple of new features in .NET Core 3 and C# 8:

1. Let's start by removing the code from here that we no longer require:

```
if (intent == "Hello")
{
    await turnContext.SendActivityAsync(MessageFactory.Text($"Hello, my
name is Boris"), cancellationToken);
}
else
{
    await turnContext.SendActivityAsync(MessageFactory.Text($"Echo:
{turnContext.Activity.Text}"), cancellationToken);
}
```

   We're going to replace this placeholder code with some code that generates a more realistic response.

2. Our next step is to read the JSON file into text, resulting in `result`:

```
var assembly = Assembly.GetExecutingAssembly();
var resourceName = "Boris.Data.Intent-Response.json";

using Stream stream =
assembly.GetManifestResourceStream(resourceName);
using StreamReader reader = new StreamReader(stream);

string result = reader.ReadToEnd();
```

   Note that we're using the new `using` syntax in C# 8. This is especially nice in methods such as this because without the new syntax, the method would be longer, and in the following code the `using` statements would need to be nested. The new `using` statement has an implicit scope from the declaration point to the end of the function; in all other respects, it behaves exactly like a standard `using` statement.

3. We then pass the text contents of the JSON file and the intent to a new method, which then returns a reply array. We then select a random reply from that array, and send that:

```
var response = ReadResponse(result, intent);

string selectedResponse = response[_rnd.Next(response.Length)];
await
```

```
turnContext.SendActivityAsync(MessageFactory.Text(selectedResponse)
, cancellationToken);
```

Before we talk about the new method, `ReadResponse()`, let's see how and where `_rnd` is declared. It's actually declared at the top of the class:

```
private Random _rnd = new Random();
```

A discussion about how to reliably generate random numbers in C# is probably outside the scope of this chapter (and book); however, it's worth bearing in mind that the random number algorithm uses a seed based on the time of day, meaning that if you instantiate the class twice in rapid succession and call `_rnd.Next(number)`, you will very likely get the same number back twice.

4. Finally, let's see our new method:

```
public static string[] ReadResponse(string jsonString, string key)
{
    using var document = JsonDocument.Parse(jsonString);

    var root = document.RootElement;
    var possibleResponses = root.GetProperty(key);

    return possibleResponses.EnumerateArray().Select(a =>
a.GetString()).ToArray();
}
```

Again, we are using the new `using` syntax. We're also making use of the new JSON libraries that are part of .NET Core 3. Some of the changes made during .NET Core 2.1 and 2.2 have opened the door for a new, faster .NET Core JSON parsing library.

The decision to bring this in-house wasn't entirely because Microsoft thought they could make a better JSON parsing library than JSON.NET (in fact, at the time of writing, the author of that library was working at Microsoft.) The decision may have been driven more by the fact that some of the lowest-level libraries within the framework had a dependency on JSON.NET.

Let's briefly talk about what this new JSON parsing code is doing: once we've instantiated a new `JsonDocument`, we find the `root` element, and then return the specific text that we're looking for by calling `GetProperty` on `root`. Finally, we call `EnumerateArray` and pipe that into a `Linq Select` statement to extract the strings.

The final step here is to publish the bot.

Publishing the bot

To start the publishing process, simply right-click the project file and select **Publish**. You'll be shown the following screen:

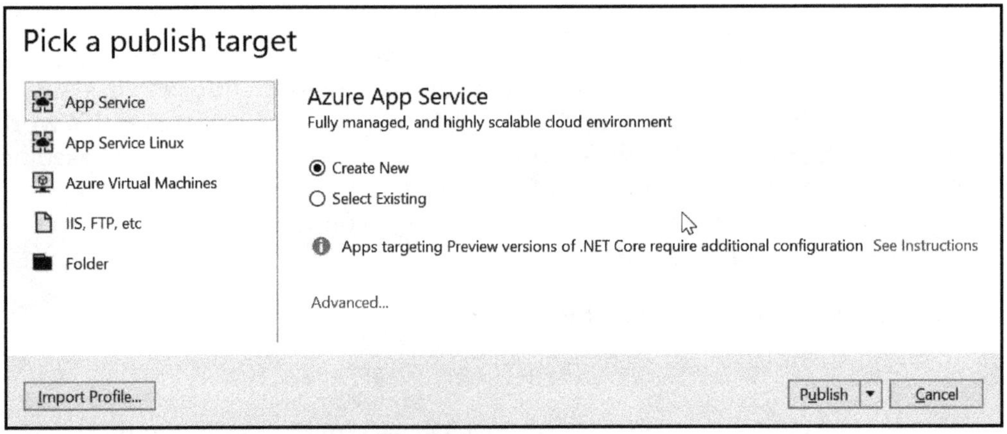

Leave the default settings as they are and select **Publish**. You'll now be asked a series of questions regarding how and where to deploy your app:

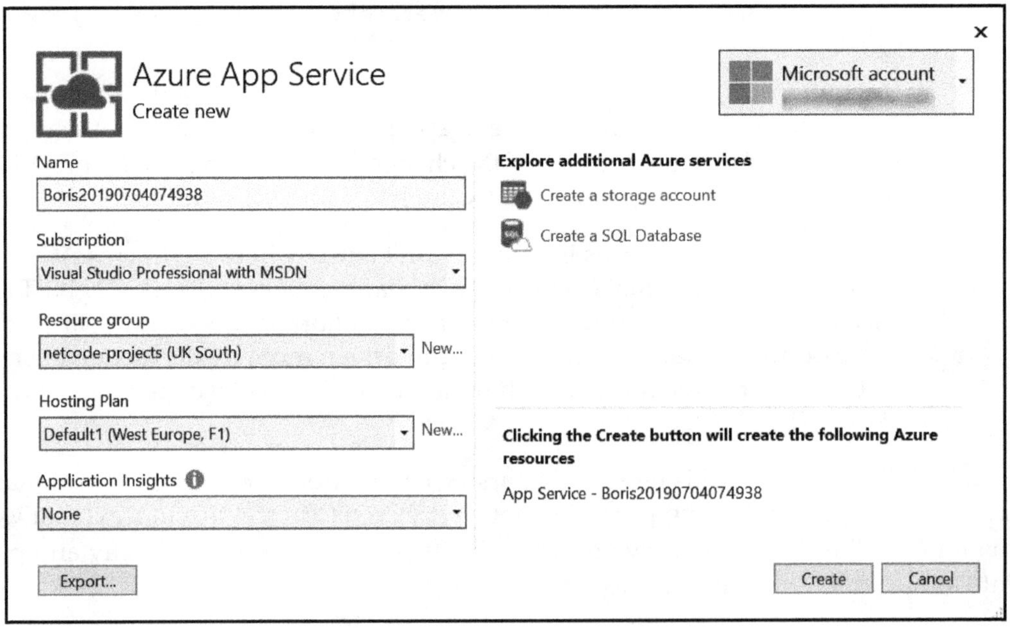

Again, you can leave these as the default and click **Create**.

At the time of writing, this prompted an error from Visual Studio, informing you that .NET Core 3.0 is not supported. While that is technically true, following the steps outlined in this chapter should result in a working bot. The team are hoping to get full .NET Core 3 support very soon.

You should be presented with a web page indicating that your bot is successfully deployed. Make a note of the URL of this page, as we'll need it shortly. In my case, it was the following:

```
https://boris20190704074938.azurewebsites.net/
```

The next stage is to create a channel registration.

TIP

Note that an alternative to creating the App Service and Channel Registration separately is to create a bot in the portal. This will create both for you, and you can then publish your bot into that service.

Creating a Channel Registration

A Channel Registration allows other applications to communicate with our bot. Let's create one. Select **Create a resource** from the Azure portal:

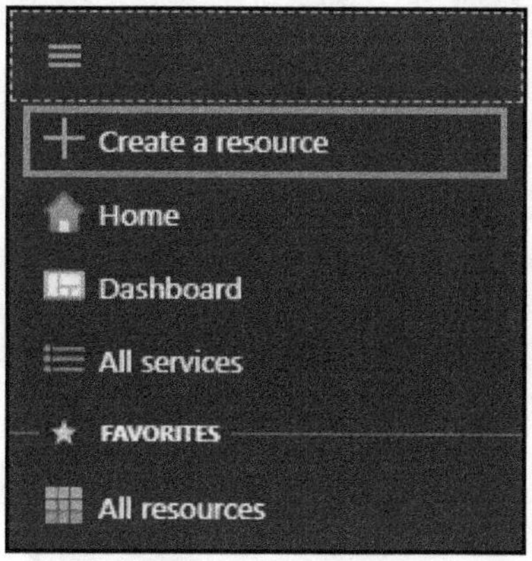

In the next screen, choose a **Bot Channels Registration**:

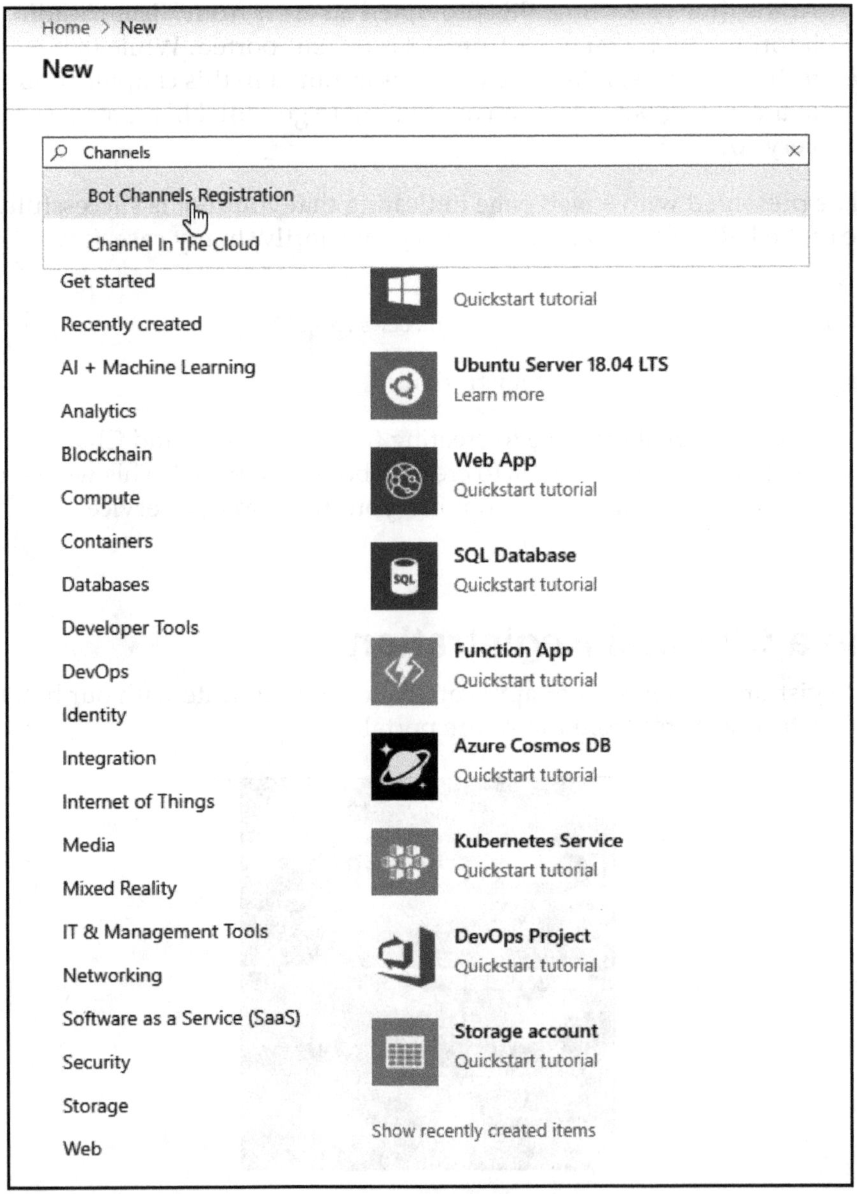

Once you have selected the option to create the bot, you'll be presented with a screen similar to the following. The labeled sections of the page are described in the list following the screenshot:

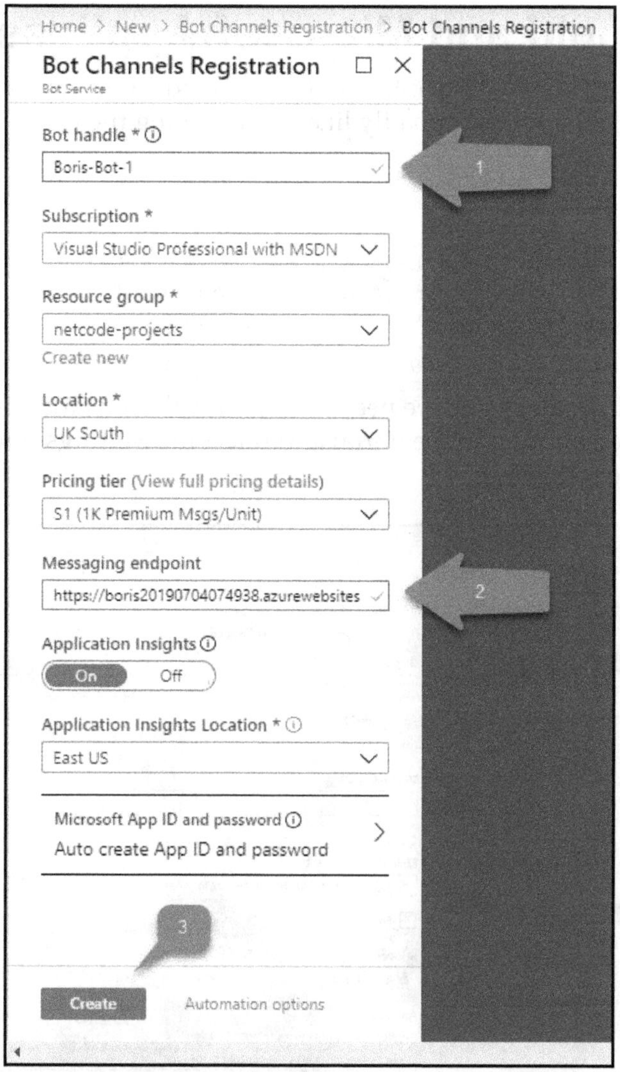

1. The **Bot handle** is a globally unique reference.
2. The **Messaging endpoint** is the URL that you noted earlier. You should append `/api/messages` to the end of the URL; in my case, this is `https://boris20190704074938.azurewebsites.net/api/messages`.
3. Once you've finished with the settings, choose the **Create the resource** option.

We now have a working, published bot integrated with LUIS. The next step is to create our UWP app.

MicrosoftAppId and MicrosoftAppPassword

Earlier in the chapter, you may remember that we created some values inside our `appsettings.json`; they looked broadly like the following the last time we saw them:

```
{
  "MicrosoftAppId": "",
  "MicrosoftAppPassword": "",
  "LuisAppId": "ed7252fa-43c1-4d4a-a084-2b8a58c69028",
  "LuisAPIKey": "51d06b40b7df4f41be26b7d80cd80e73",
  "LuisAPIHostName": "https://westus.api.cognitive.microsoft.com"
}
```

Now that we've published our bot, we need to populate those values. If you navigate to your new Channel Registration in the portal and select the **Settings** screen, you should see something akin to the following:

Make a note of the `MicrosoftAppId`. Select **Manage** to display the **Certificates & Secrets** blade:

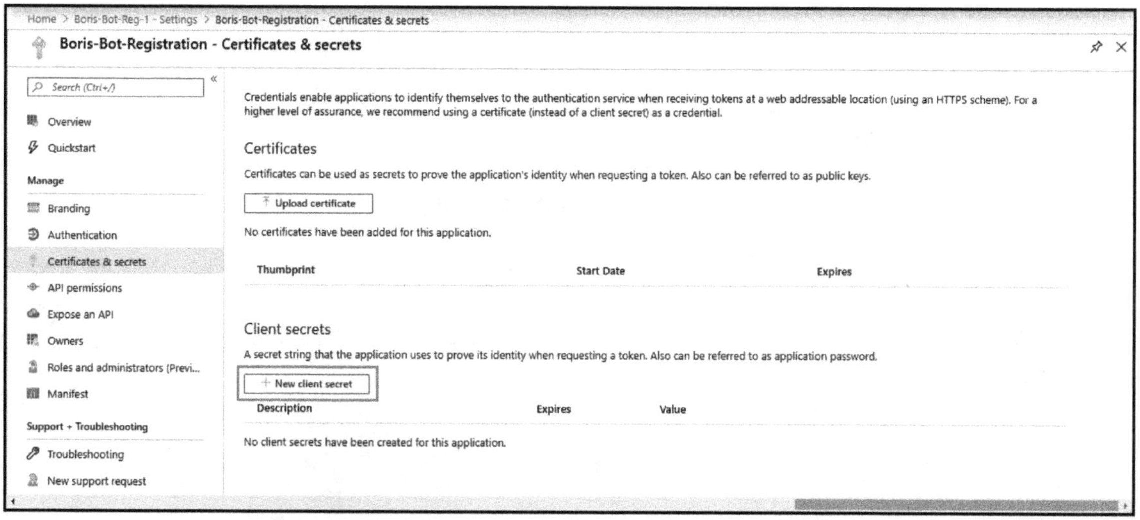

Here, we can create a new secret:

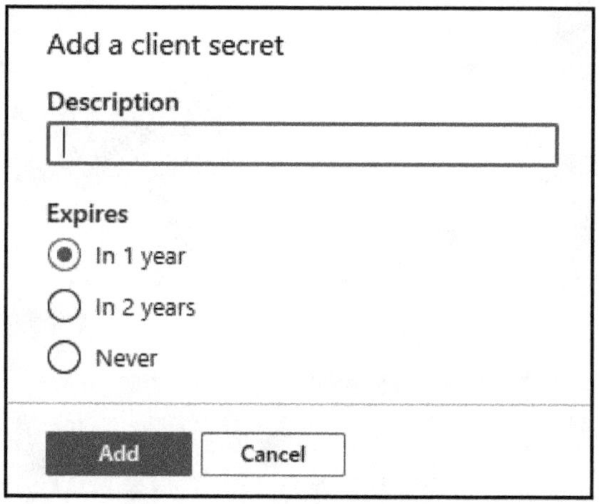

Simply provide a description and click **Add**. Once you create the secret, you will have only one chance to make a note of it; you will never see it ever again, so if you lose it, you'll need to remove and recreate it.

Once you've noted the App ID and secret, there are two options to activate them. The first (and perhaps easiest while you're debugging) is to simply paste them into the `appsettings.json` and publish the app again. However, you don't *need* to do this—you can simply navigate to the **Configuration** blade of the App Service and add an `AppSetting` there:

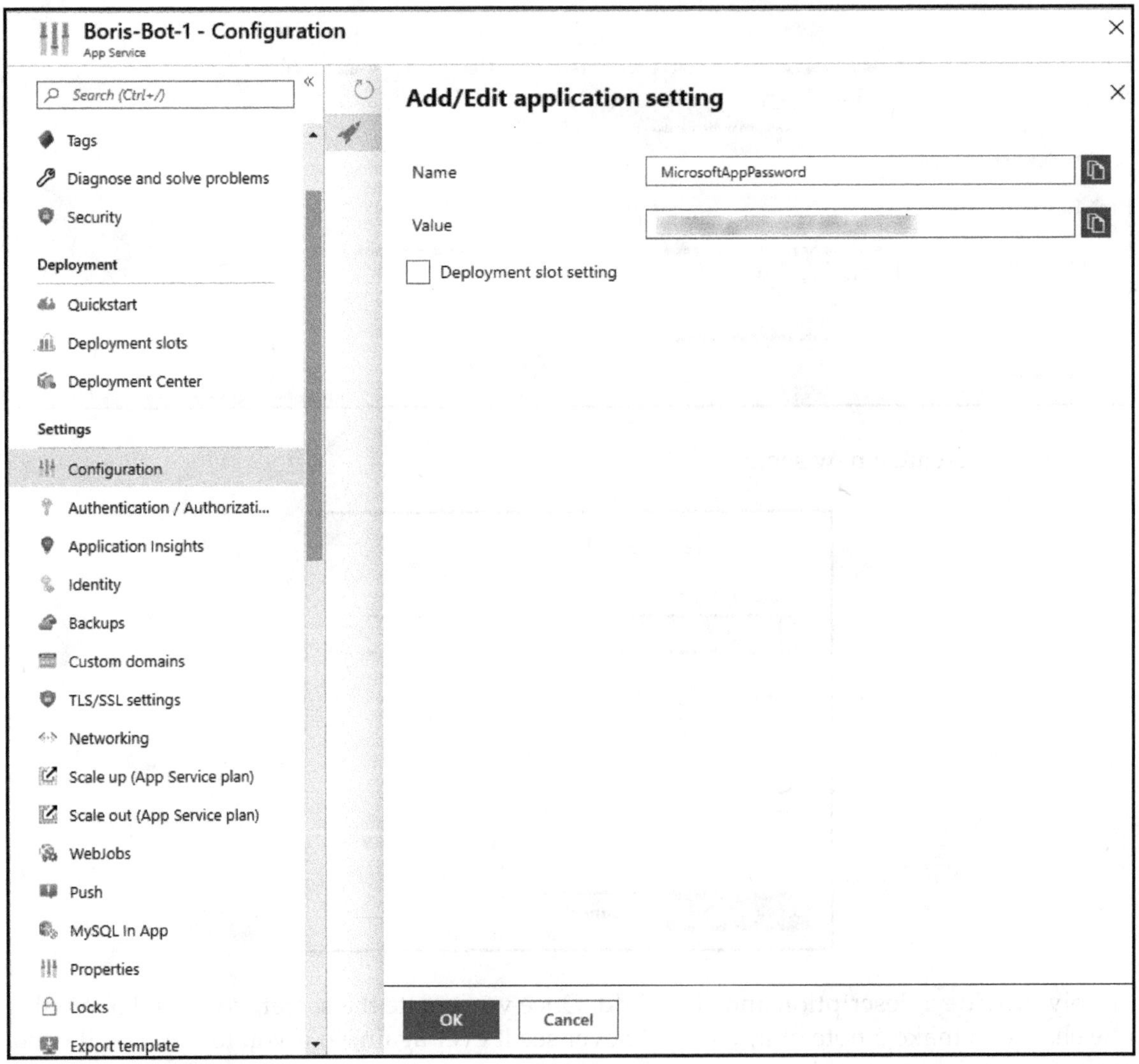

> **TIP:** This is a very useful trick: any app settings that are added here will override anything in the `appsettings.json`. This means that you don't need to keep sensitive data in your source code.

Now that we've correctly set up the registration, we can move on to creating the client application.

Creating a UWP application

Our UWP application will be very simple. We'll create a single screen that allows us to enter a message, and then a log whereby the user can see the bot's response, along with their own chat history. Firstly, let's create a new UWP application:

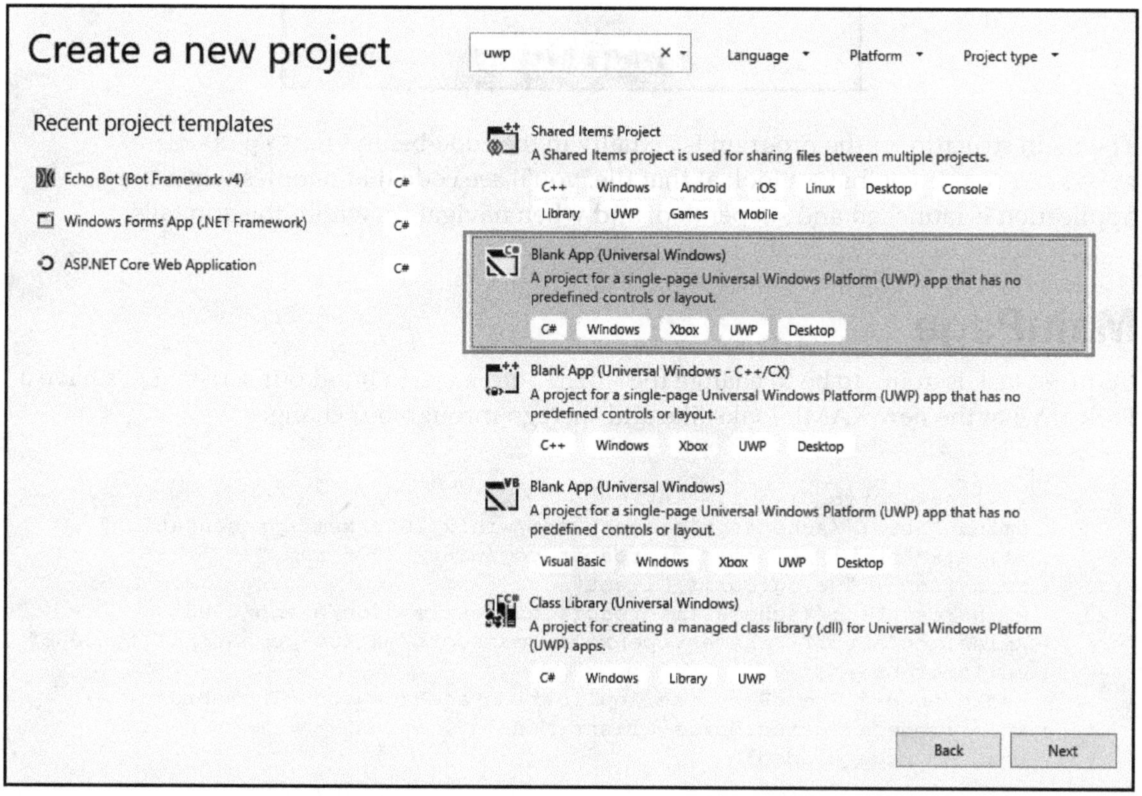

The initial application is created with two XAML files: `App.xaml` and `MainPage.xaml`:

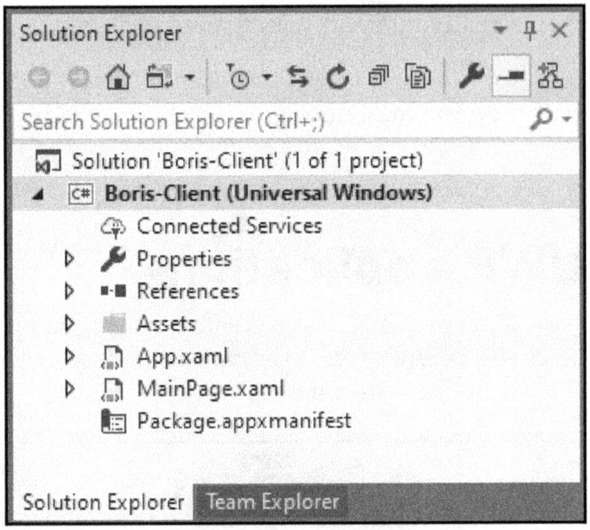

The main structure of the program is actually in the code-behind for `App.xaml`: `App.xaml.cs`. If you have a look at that file, you'll see code that handles when the application is launched and suspended, and when navigation within the app fails.

MainPage

Our first task is going to be to change the `MainPage.xaml` to build our screen. Let's have a look at what the new XAML looks like and then go through our changes:

```
<Page
    x:Class="Boris_Client.MainView"
    xmlns="http://schemas.microsoft.com/winfx/2006/xaml/presentation"
    xmlns:x="http://schemas.microsoft.com/winfx/2006/xaml"
    xmlns:local="using:Boris_Client"
    xmlns:d="http://schemas.microsoft.com/expression/blend/2008"
    xmlns:mc="http://schemas.openxmlformats.org/markup-compatibility/2006"
    mc:Ignorable="d"
    Background="{ThemeResource ApplicationPageBackgroundThemeBrush}"
    xmlns:models="using:Boris_Client.Models"
    Loaded="Page_Loaded">

    <Grid>
        <Grid.RowDefinitions>
            <RowDefinition Height="*" />
```

```
            <RowDefinition Height="Auto" />
        </Grid.RowDefinitions>

        <ListView Grid.Row="0" ItemsSource="{Binding ChatHistory}">
            <ListView.ItemTemplate>
                <DataTemplate x:DataType="models:ChatMessage">
                    <StackPanel Orientation="Horizontal">
                        <TextBlock Text="{Binding Sender}"/>
                        <TextBlock Text=":"/>
                        <TextBlock Text="{Binding Message}"/>
                    </StackPanel>
                </DataTemplate>
            </ListView.ItemTemplate>
        </ListView>

        <Grid Grid.Row="1">
            <Grid.ColumnDefinitions>
                <ColumnDefinition Width="*"/>
                <ColumnDefinition Width="Auto"/>
            </Grid.ColumnDefinitions>
            <TextBox Grid.Column="0" Grid.Row="0" x:Name="SendMsg"
Text="{Binding MessageText}"/>
            <Button Grid.Row="0" Grid.Column="1"
                    Command="{Binding SendMessageCommand}"
                    CommandParameter="{Binding ElementName=SendMsg,
Path=Text, Mode=OneWay}"
                    Content="Send" />
        </Grid>
    </Grid>
</Page>
```

We will discuss this block in detail in the next sections. Let's start by looking at the grid layout.

Row definitions

In XAML, we have a concept of a grid: essentially, each XAML page is subdivided into a grid, and you can tell the system how many rows and columns you want in your grid. In our example, the grid has two rows. The second row is as big as it needs to be (`Auto`) to fit its contents, and the first row takes up the remaining space (`*`).

TIP: Should you wish, you can have grids nested inside grids. There is no limit (except the available memory) as to how far you can nest controls. Obviously, the deeper you nest your controls, the more work there is for the UI renderer, which can have a performance impact.

Each subsequent control within the grid specifies the row that it wishes to occupy—even the subgrid. Specifying the row and column always applies to the immediate parent grid.

ListView

Next, we come to the `ListView`. The key to understanding XAML is composition: you can achieve almost any effect because you can place a control inside another control. In the case of a `ListView` control, you essentially have two elements of the control: the data that it's displaying and how it displays that data.

```
<ListView Grid.Row="0" ItemsSource="{Binding ChatHistory}">
```

We'll come back to exactly what `ChatHistory` is later, but for now, just think of it as a collection. We're binding the `ItemSource`—that is, the data source of the control—to the collection of *things*, called `ChatHistory`. That's the *what*; the next part is *how*:

```
<ListView.ItemTemplate>
    <DataTemplate x:DataType="models:ChatMessage">
        <StackPanel Orientation="Horizontal">
            <TextBlock Text="{Binding Sender}"/>
            <TextBlock Text=":"/>
            <TextBlock Text="{Binding Message}"/>
        </StackPanel>
    </DataTemplate>
</ListView.ItemTemplate>
```

Here, we're using `DataTemplate` to tell the `ListView` that each element will be of the `ChatMessage` type; again, we'll come back to what that is—the important thing is that it has at least two properties: `Sender` and `Message`. Inside the `DataTemplate`, we're declaring a `StackPanel`, and inside of that, we're declaring a number of `TextBlock` elements. This is what I mean by composition—if you want to display a list of elements in a list, then you need to define where that data is and exactly how to display it.

TIP

While this process is more verbose than other technologies, it affords a much greater degree of flexibility—for example, you could have an image control, another `StackPanel`, or even another `ListView` inside the `DataTemplate`. Additionally, the `DataTemplate` can be reused across files or even applications.

Message and command binding

Finally, we have the second row, which is simply another grid inside the first. The interesting part is shown in the following code:

```
<TextBox Grid.Column="0" Grid.Row="0" x:Name="SendMsg" Text="{Binding
MessageText}"/>
<Button Grid.Row="0" Grid.Column="1"  Command="{Binding
SendMessageCommand}"  CommandParameter="{Binding ElementName=SendMsg,
Path=Text, Mode=OneWay}"
        Content="Send" />
```

In the `TextBox`, we're binding the contents to something called `MessageText`. Again, don't worry about what `MessageText` is, although, given that it is bound to a `Text` property, we can safely assume that it is (or must be) a string.

Finally, we have a button and something called **command binding**. Unlike the other bindings, where we are, essentially, just taking data and displaying it, command binding binds to a method. Again, let's not worry too much about exactly what `SendMessageCommand` is; for now, let's just accept that it *does something*.

Data binding and view models

Now that we've created our frontend XAML file, let's have a look at the code-behind (`MainPage.xaml.cs`):

```
public sealed partial class MainPage : Page
{
    public MainPage()
    {
        this.InitializeComponent();

        DataContext = new MainViewModel();
    }
}
```

As you can see, there is very little to discuss here. In fact, we actually have only one additional line of code, which sets the `DataContext` to an instance of `MainViewModel`.

Essentially, what we are doing here is taking a class and assigning that class to the `DataContext` of the XAML code file. This means that anything in that file can now be bound to the frontend XAML.

It is entirely your choice, but at this stage, I renamed the `MainPage` file to `MainView`. The reason that I did this is that it binds to `MainViewModel`, and I find it much easier to read it if the names are aligned by convention. But don't worry: the code will still work if you don't do this.

Now that we've bound the view model, we can call methods on the `ViewModel`. Once the page is loaded, we'll call a method to initialize everything:

```
private async void Page_Loaded(object sender, RoutedEventArgs e)
{
    await ((MainViewModel)DataContext).Initialise();
}
```

We can have a look at the `ViewModel` file shortly; however, first, let's just take a minute to talk about view models as a concept. Imagine for a minute that, instead of writing an application, you're plumbing a sink. If you go down to your local DIY shop, you'll probably see dozens of types of sink, but you can pick any sink that has the correct number of fittings for your taps and take it home, confident that you can place it where your old sink was, connect a few pipes, and have running water.

How does this relate to views and view models? Well, imagine that the pipes coming into your house are view models. They carry the necessary information in its raw form—that is, water. If you didn't plumb the sink in and just turned the mains water on, you would see that information flooding out of the pipes. The sink, like the view, arranges the information, or water, in whichever form you would like to see it.

Please don't take any aspect of this analogy as reliable information on plumbing—it's for illustrative purposes only. I am not a qualified plumber!

When designing your view and view model, you should bear this in mind. If you start to see local relating to the arrangement of the data creeping into your view model, that should be a red flag that you're crossing a line and tightly coupling the two. One question to ask yourself is, if I wanted to display this differently, could I do so without changing the view model? If the answer is no, then consider a different approach.

Let's start by declaring our `ViewModel`:

```
public class MainViewModel : INotifyPropertyChanged
{
    public event PropertyChangedEventHandler PropertyChanged;

    protected void RaisePropertyChanged([CallerMemberName]string name =
```

```
null)
        {
            if (PropertyChanged != null)
            {
                PropertyChanged(this, new PropertyChangedEventArgs(name));
            }
        }
    }
```

This is the absolute minimum code that you need for a functioning UWP `ViewModel`. The `INotifyPropertyChanged` interface is an interface that has one event: `PropertyChanged`. Essentially, the purpose here is that when you change a property, you need to tell the binding system that you've done so, and then the UI can be updated. The first thing that we need in *our* `ViewModel` is a method called `Initialise`—if you remember, we actually called this further up:

```
internal async Task Initialise()
{
    await _wrapper.StartConversation();
}
```

Let's add the data that we're displaying in the app:

```
public ObservableCollection<ChatMessage> ChatHistory { get; set; } = new
ObservableCollection<ChatMessage>();

private string _messageText;
public string MessageText
{
    get { return _messageText; }
    set
    {
        _messageText = value;
        RaisePropertyChanged();
    }
}
```

The `MessageText` phrase is simply a string (as we guessed earlier it would be). As you can see, we're calling the `RaisePropertyChanged` event that we created earlier when the property was set.

> TIP: You can choose to enhance this by only raising the event when the value changes.

The second piece of data is held in a special collection, known as an `ObservableCollection`.

ObservableCollection

An `ObservableCollection` notifies the UI when its content changes. That is, every time you add or remove an item, the UI will automatically be updated. An `ObservableCollection` in every other respect behaves like any other collection (say a `List`).

> It's worth bearing in mind that, while an `ObservableCollection` will update the UI when you add or remove an item, it will not update the UI if you change the collection itself. For example, look at the following:
>
> ```
> MyCollection = new ObservableCollection<MyObject>()
> ```
>
> This would not update the UI. Furthermore, changing the contents of `MyObject` (in this case) would not update the UI.

For now, we won't worry about `ChatHistory`, although by now you've probably worked out what it will look like. Next, we'll have a look at the command.

Command binding

In the UI, we had a button that had its `Command` property set. In this section, we won't have a look at what the `Command` actually looks like. In this code, we'll be using a `wrapper` class called `RelayCommand`. We'll come back to `RelayCommand` shortly, but a command is simply any class that implements the `ICommand` interface. The `helper` class that we're using here just means that we can declare the command functionality inside the `ViewModel`.

Initially, we just declare the `RelayCommand`:

```
public RelayCommandAsync<string> SendMessageCommand { get; set; }
```

Then, we instantiate this inside the constructor:

```
public MainViewModel()
{
    SendMessageCommand = new RelayCommandAsync<string>(SendMessage);
}
```

As you can see, we're passing a method to the command as an argument. Before we look at the method itself, we need to go on a bit of a detour; otherwise, the method won't make much sense.

DirectLineWrapper

Ultimately, the purpose of this entire application is to send a message to our bot and print the reply on the screen. The next thing that we're going to introduce is a wrapper class to do just that. We'll fill in the actual class code later in the chapter, but here, we're just going to use the class as though it does everything we need. Let's start by declaring it as a class-level variable:

```
BotClientSdk.DirectLineWrapper _wrapper = null;
```

Now, we'll instantiate this in the constructor, which should now look like this:

```
public MainViewModel()
{
    SendMessageCommand = new RelayCommandAsync<string>(SendMessage);
    _wrapper = new BotClientSdk.DirectLineWrapper(PopulateHistory);
}
```

You'll notice that we're passing a variable into the `DirectLineWrapper` class; we'll come back to this method shortly.

> **TIP:** Broadly speaking, instantiating a dependency inside a constructor is bad practice. It makes testing the class very difficult; should you wish to extend this project, moving this into an injected dependency would be a good start.

The `SendMessage` method body should be changed as follows:

```
private async Task SendMessage(string message)
{
    await _wrapper.SendMessage(message);
    MessageText = string.Empty;
}
```

The `_wrapper` has a method called `SendMessage`. This calls a method inside a class that we'll create shortly. Finally, we clear the text box so that the user can enter another message.

We also need a method to populate the history:

```
private void PopulateHistory(List<KeyValuePair<string, string>> response)
{
    var ignored = Dispatcher.RunAsync(CoreDispatcherPriority.Normal, () =>
    {
        foreach (var historyItem in response)
        {
            ChatHistory.Add(new ChatMessage(historyItem.Key,
historyItem.Value));
        }
    });
}
```

This is passed into the constructor of our new `wrapper` class—that is, the entire function is passed in. The idea here is that we can update the UI from inside our `wrapper` class, but the `wrapper` class remains unaware of its calling context. There's a final tiny piece that we need to add here:

```
private CoreDispatcher Dispatcher =>
     (Window.Current == null) ?
     CoreApplication.MainView.CoreWindow.Dispatcher :
     CoreApplication.GetCurrentView().CoreWindow.Dispatcher;
```

This just allows us to use the `Dispatcher`; as we are essentially working on a background thread, without this, we would be unable to update the UI, which is, by necessity, a foreground thread.

As we iterate through this, we add it to the `ObservableCollection`; we said earlier that adding data to the collection in this way would update the UI for us.

Before we cover the details of what the wrapper looks like internally, we have a few `helper` classes and models that we've used. Let's start with the models.

Models

We've used a model to store the chat message (singular), and so we need to see what that class looks like. As I said earlier, the shape of it should not be a surprise if you've read through the chapter this far:

```
public class ChatMessage
{
    public ChatMessage(string sender, string message)
    {
        Sender = sender;
```

```
        Message = message;
    }

    public string Message { get; set; }
    public string Sender { get; set; }
}
```

Before we move on, we need to see the `RelayCommandAsync` class.

RelayCommandAsync

The code for `RelayCommandAsync` is not too onerous. We implement an interface called `ICommand`, which has just two methods. A bare-bones implementation of `ICommand` would look like this:

```
public class RelayCommandAsync<T> : ICommand
{
    public bool CanExecute(object parameter)
    {
    }

    public void Execute(object parameter)
    {
    }
}
```

Clearly, this does nothing, so let's fill in those methods. We'll start with `Execute`; we need to pass an action into the `Execute` method, and we can do that through the constructor:

```
public class RelayCommandAsync<T> : ICommand
{
    readonly Func<T, Task> _execute = null;

    public RelayCommandAsync(Func<T, Task> execute)
    {
        if (execute == null)
            throw new ArgumentNullException("execute");

        _execute = execute;
    }

    public void Execute(object parameter)
    {
        _execute.Invoke((T)parameter);
    }
```

```
        . . .
    }
```

So here, we are simply passing a function delegate into the class as a constructor, and then invoking it when `Execute` is called.

> **TIP:** The reason that we're using `Func` and not `Action` here is that we are, in fact, returning something—namely, a `Task`. If the command were synchronous, we could return an `Action`.

Finally, we'll add the `CanExecute` code:

```
public class RelayCommandAsync<T> : ICommand
{
    readonly Func<T, Task> _execute = null;
    readonly Func<T, bool> _canExecute = null;

    public RelayCommandAsync(Func<T, Task> execute)
        : this(execute, null)
    {
    }

    public RelayCommandAsync(Func<T, Task> execute, Func<T, bool>
canExecute)
    {
        if (execute == null)
            throw new ArgumentNullException("execute");

        _execute = execute;
        _canExecute = canExecute;
    }

    public bool CanExecute(object parameter)
    {
        return _canExecute == null ? true :
_canExecute.Invoke((T)parameter);
    }

    public event EventHandler CanExecuteChanged;

    public void RaiseCanExecuteChanged()
    {
        CanExecuteChanged?.Invoke(this, EventArgs.Empty);
    }

    public void Execute(object parameter)
```

```
        {
            _execute.Invoke((T)parameter);
        }
    }
```

The `CanExecute` phrase essentially returns a Boolean to say whether or not the command in question is valid to execute. By binding a UI to this, you can disable the button on your UI if this returns `False`. We're not actually using this functionality here; however, this code would work if we were.

> TIP: One of the advantages of `CommandBinding` is that you can unit test the command itself without touching the UI—that is, your unit test covers the code immediately after pressing the button.

Now that we've filled in the remaining gaps, we need to talk about Direct Line, and how to communicate with our bot.

Channels

Before we talk about Direct Line and what it is, we should discuss what a channel is in respect to a bot. Let's look at the following image:

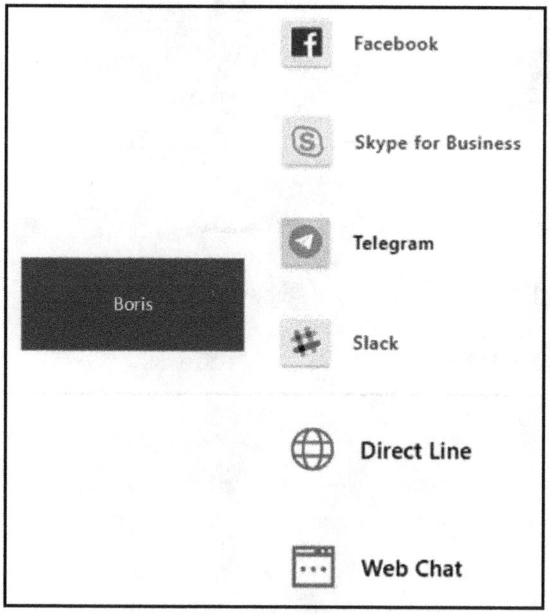

This is not intended to be an exhaustive list of channels, but it is an attempt to illustrate that a channel is simply an interface between an application and the bot—for example, you could link your bot up to Slack, should you wish to do so.

There are two channels here that stand out: Direct Line and Web Chat. Let's look at them briefly.

Direct Line and Web Chat

We've already seen Web Chat: essentially, it's a way to test your bot, and it comes for free when you register a channel, which is why you were able to use it to test your bot earlier in the chapter.

Direct Line allows you to interact with your bot directly. Let's configure a Direct Line channel now. In the Azure portal, navigate to your bot and select **Channels**:

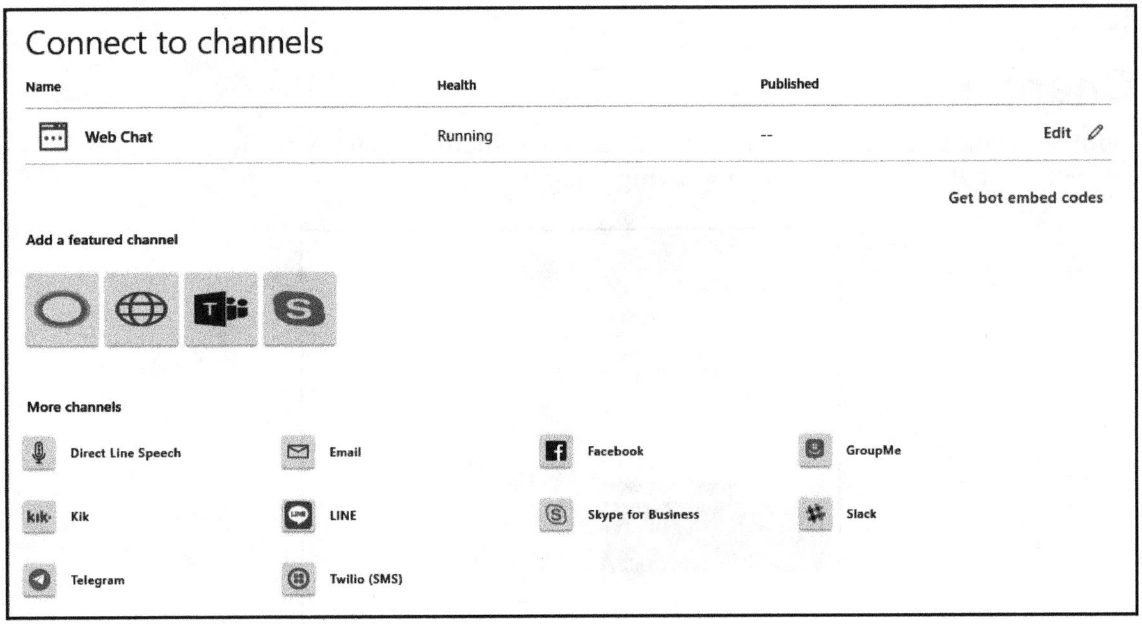

Strangely distorted graphics aside, the Direct Line channel is the globe; if you click it, you should be asked to name the site:

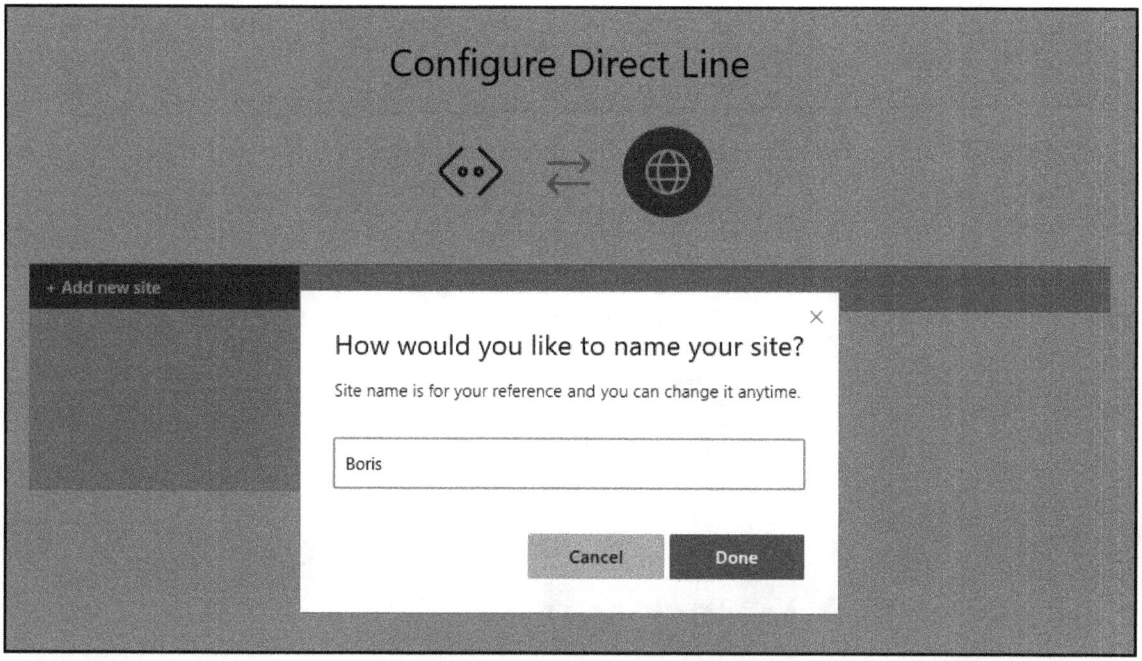

In the next screen, you'll be provided with two secret keys. Click **Show** on the first, and keep a copy of it, as we'll need it shortly. When you're done, click **Done**, and you should see that you now have two channels.

Bot client

The final step is to create the client that we referenced in our UWP application. Let's start by creating a new project and immediately reference it from the UWP application. A .NET Standard 2.0 class library will be sufficient for what we need:

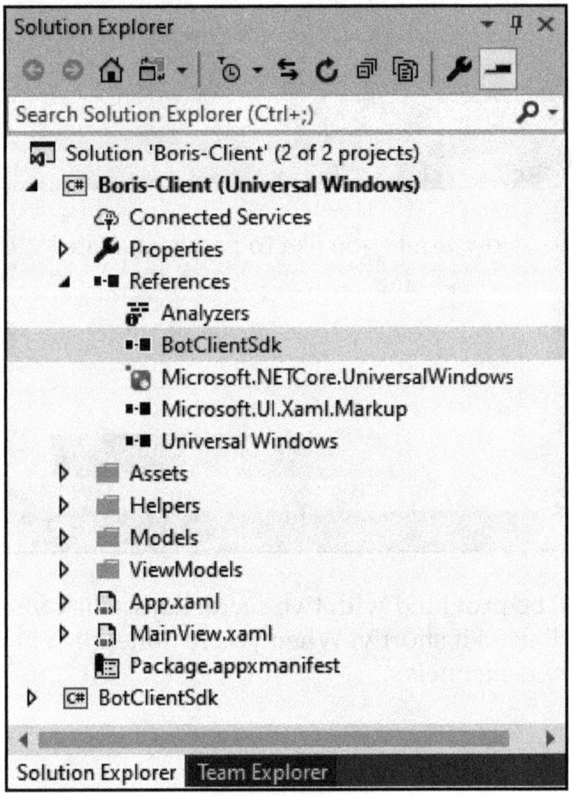

The first thing we'll need is to import two NuGet packages: the Direct Line package itself and the Rest Client Runtime:

```
Install-Package Microsoft.Bot.Connector.DirectLine
Install-Package Microsoft.Rest.ClientRuntime
```

We'll only need a single class in this project—let's call it `DirectLineWrapper`.

TIP

As a general principle, I always like to try to wrap external dependencies in a Wrapper Project to protect the main project from having too many direct external dependencies: this allows you to swap out the wrapper much easier if, for example, you wished to use a different bot service.

We'll need a handful of class-level variables, including the `DirectLineClient` itself; we'll also need to instantiate this, as follows:

```
public class DirectLineWrapper
{
    private string? _conversationId = null;
    private readonly DirectLineClient _client;
    Action<List<KeyValuePair<string, string>>> _updateMessages;

    public DirectLineWrapper(Action<List<KeyValuePair<string, string>>>
updateMessages)
    {
        _client = new
DirectLineClient("A33UCbCQoP1.QNPYS_u2Z7LhobFce9mA2ZWt47n7VzEuTjTGWHO-
aL0");
        _updateMessages = updateMessages;
    }
}
```

The string parameter that is passed into the `DirectLineClient` constructor is the secret that you made a note of earlier. We'll come back to the conversation ID shortly. As you can see, we're injecting an *action* into the class; this will allow us to update the screen with messages as they come in.

We'll need just three methods in this class, only two of which are public. Let's see the first:

```
public async Task SendMessage(string message)
{
    if (string.IsNullOrWhiteSpace(_conversationId))
    {
        throw new Exception("No active conversation");
    }

    Activity userMessage = new Activity
    {
        From = new ChannelAccount("User"),
        Text = message,
        Type = ActivityTypes.Message
    };

    var resourceResponse = await
_client.Conversations.PostActivityAsync(_conversationId, userMessage);
}
```

Here, we create a new `Activity` instance. Essentially, this is our message; however, it doesn't have to be a message—it could simply be a notification that you're still typing or a ping. There are a number of options, but we're interested in the `Message` here.

Each time you start a conversation with the bot, it gives you a Conversation ID. If you were to start a new conversation each time, you would wipe the context of the chat, so you need to maintain a reference to the ID and, where it doesn't exist, call `StartConversationAsync()`, which does just that. This brings the `usd` to our second public method:

```
public async Task StartConversation()
{
    if (string.IsNullOrWhiteSpace(_conversationId))
    {
        var conversation = await
_client.Conversations.StartConversationAsync();
        _conversationId = conversation.ConversationId;

        new System.Threading.Thread(async () => await
ReadBotMessagesAsync(_client, conversation.ConversationId)).Start();
    }
}
```

Once we've started the conversation, we start a new thread to read the messages. Our third method reads the messages in an endless loop:

```
private async Task ReadBotMessagesAsync(DirectLineClient client, string
conversationId)
{
    string watermark = string.Empty;
    var messages = new List<KeyValuePair<string, string>>();
    while (true)
    {
        var activitySet = await
client.Conversations.GetActivitiesAsync(conversationId, watermark);

        lock (_lock)
        {
            watermark = activitySet.Watermark;

            var activities = from x in activitySet.Activities
                             select x;

            messages.Clear();
            foreach (Activity activity in activities)
            {
                messages.Add(new KeyValuePair<string,
```

```
string>(activity.From.Id, activity.Text));
                }

                _updateMessages(messages);
            }

            await Task.Delay(TimeSpan.FromSeconds(1)).ConfigureAwait(false);
        }
    }
```

This essentially just reads back the activities; however, the important thing to note here is the watermark. As poorly named as this is, the watermark is a pointer to where we currently are in the activity set. If you didn't store the watermark, you would simply get the entire conversation back each time. Once we get a list of activities back, we simply call out the delegate `_updateMessages`, which updates the UI.

That pretty much concludes our project; we now have a chat client that can communicate with a user and, hopefully, deceive them into believing that they are talking to another human:

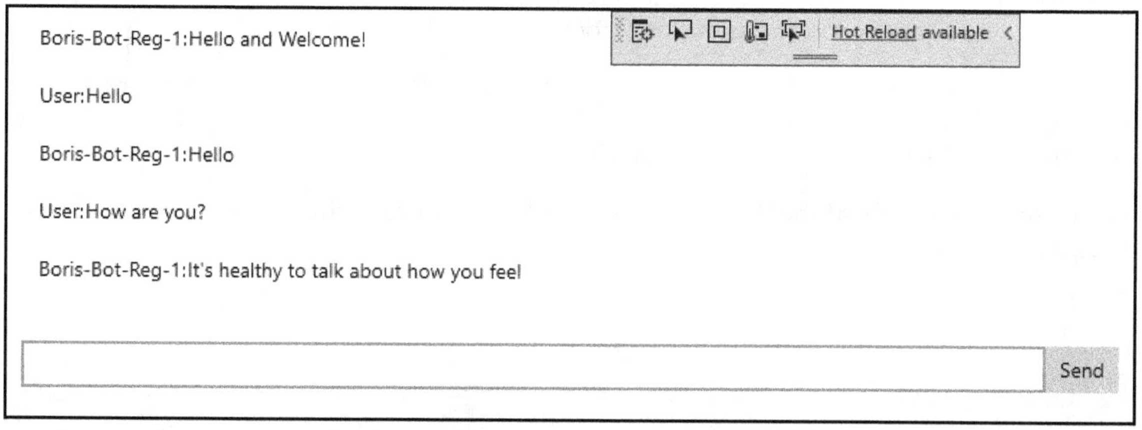

As you can see, the bot is responding to the user and, admittedly vaguely, engaging in conversation. In order to improve the quality of this exchange, we need only go back to the LUIS deployment and train it further with specific responses.

Summary

In this chapter, we created a chatbot and gave it a basic understanding of language using LUIS. We took the default template and upgraded it from .NET Core 2.2 to .NET Core 3.0, and created a UWP client app that uses the Direct Line API to communicate with the bot.

Is our version of Eliza (Boris) more likely to pass the Turing test than the original? Maybe. If you wish to improve the model in LUIS then you may give it more of a fighting chance, but the real-world applications of chatbots and language recognition stretch far beyond the ability to fool someone into thinking they are talking to a human. You could easily link this to a voice synthesizer and telephony integration software (such as Twilio), and you will have an automated call center.

The Universal Windows Platform, at least for now, is what Microsoft is touting as the desktop platform of choice. Whether that will continue and we move toward a single .NET platform, I can't say.

In this book, we covered a number of new features from the C# language. We leveraged them to make our code more readable and concise, and, in the case of nullable reference types, we actually reduced the number of potential bugs in the code.

We also looked at some of the benefits that .NET Core 3 offers, allowing us to migrate existing desktop applications to the new .NET Core 3 framework and, using XAML Islands, even use controls from newer applications in legacy software.

We looked extensively at the Azure services available for use and saw how easy it can be to integrate these services into our code base.

Appendix A: WebAssembly

WebAssembly is something that, at the time of writing, everyone is talking about. It was first introduced in 2015. Essentially, the principle is that your browser (WebAssembly is supported by all the major browsers) can run a type of compiled code (previously, you were limited to just JavaScript).

The following link shows browser support for WebAssembly: `https://caniuse.com/#feat=wasm`.

Firefox, Chrome, Edge, and Safari all support it. It's worth noting that some of the older browsers (for example, IE) don't support it, so if you're writing something that needs to be compatible with these older browsers, you may have to resort to more traditional JavaScript.

The question you may initially ask yourself is: why should I care? Hopefully, this appendix will cover the reasons why WebAssembly is braced to take over the web in the next few years.

We'll then run through two examples, one using the native WebAssembly compilation, and a second using Blazor, a technology from Microsoft that allows you to write C# and have it run in the browser.

The following topics will be covered in this chapter:

- Why WebAssembly?
- Writing WebAssembly
- Understanding Blazor

Why WebAssembly

As it currently stands, you can write JavaScript, and it will run quite happily in any browser. Given that you're reading a book on C#, you'll be (at least vaguely) familiar with the JavaScript syntax. In this section, I'll try to outline the reasons why you may choose to use WebAssembly over the possible alternatives.

Due to the nature of this comparison, it inevitably contains some opinion. For example, I'm about to extol the virtues of statically typed languages over dynamic ones. If you know and are happy with using JavaScript, you may wish to skip the sections that don't interest you.

Reason one – statically typed

One of my personal gripes with JavaScript is that it's dynamically typed. This means that you can use a variable that hasn't been explicitly declared. The knock-on effect here is that you could end up with the following code:

```
var myInt = 2;
myNum++;
```

Assuming that you intend these two numbers to be the same, you would want to have this trapped at compile time; however, with JavaScript, this will run—although it clearly will not do what you expect.

There are many tools available to help to alleviate this problem, from ESLint to TypeScript. However, this involves you including a step in your build chain to capture what, in a statically-typed language, would simply be a compilation error.

Reason two – compiled

This is a tenuous one: while JavaScript is definitely not compiled, but interpreted, WebAssemby is JIT-compiled. Having said that, the compilation process for C or C# will capture most of the issues mentioned in the previous section. Further, there is a significant speed gain in the execution of the code when compared to JavaScript (since JavaScript is interpreted). There have been claims of up to 20x speed improvement; however, as you'll see in the next section, that's not as clear-cut as it may first seem.

Reason three – speed

Like reason two, reason three is also tenuous. It would be wrong to make a blanket statement that WebAssembly is faster than JavaScript. Execution of the same code, as stated earlier, is faster than JavaScript—in fact, speed for processor-intensive code was one of the reasons for WebAssembly's existence.

However, remember that you're still running in the browser's context, so any external libraries that you may wish to use need to be downloaded. While this is less of an issue for running a C program compiled into WASM, it may be in issue for something such as Blazor, where a version of the .NET runtime must be downloaded.

> In a later section, we will look into this in more detail. As it currently stands, the version of client-side Blazor uses the Mono runtime.

Reason four – languages that you know/same language in the frontend and backend

If you know JavaScript, then you may choose to use Node.js as your backend. There may be many reasons for choosing to do this, and one of them may be that you can hire JavaScript developers for the team. Let's just delve into that for a minute: at the time of writing, there is a skills shortage in the IT industry (at least in the UK); if you can isolate a single skill that you need to recruit for, that surely makes you job easier because, in addition to the developers that program C# and JavaScript, you could employ JavaScript-only developers or developers that use Python, Ruby, VB.NET, or any backend language and use JavaScript for the frontend—in fact, anyone that programs for the web in 2019 needs to know at least a basic level of JavaScript.

Until now, if you were a C# developer (or any of the other preceding languages), you would have to learn JavaScript to write the frontend of your application: now you can write the frontend and backend in C#.

> At the time of writing, client-side Blazor was not officially part of the .NET Core ecosystem. We'll cover this in more detail later in this chapter.

It's also worth bearing in mind that, with the advent of Xamarin, this essentially means that you can program in C# for absolutely any platform.

> There is, in fact, an open source project that translates `Xamarin.Forms` code into WASM; it can be found here: `https://github.com/praeclarum/Ooui`.
>
> Uno is another project that allows you to write XAML and translates it into platform-specific code (including WASM): `https://platform.uno/`.

Reason five – existing code

Since so many languages are supported already by various tools to compile down to WASM, you may already have some code that could simply by compiled into WebAssembly. There are several anecdotal examples of this happening to great success.

Imagine that you have a game that is written entirely in C; you may be able to port this to run on the browser. I, personally, am anxiously awaiting the creation of a tool that will translate the Spectrum ZX80 Assembly language into WASM, then I can play all of the old Spectrum games on the web!

Reason six – deployment

One of the main reasons that web development is more popular than desktop development is that the web browser solves a problem that has been the bane of our lives as programmers for years: deployment. Write a desktop application, and deploy it—you'll be surprised at how difficult that becomes to deploy when you don't have total control over the target machine.

In my opinion, this reason may be the most compelling of all of the reasons: WebAssembly provides a hybrid solution between a desktop and a web development environment.

Reason seven – security

To be clear, WebAssembly runs in the same context as JavaScript, so it is no more or less secure than writing a web application in JavaScript. However, when you consider what you're doing, it is actually quite secure. It is far more secure than sending people an executable and asking them to run it on their machine.

I've listed some reasons why you may wish to use WebAssembly. It clearly has some advantages over the traditional web model for certain applications. However, as always with technology, it's about trade-offs.

In the next section, we'll look at how you might actually write some WebAssembly.

Writing WebAssembly

To try writing some WebAssembly, we'll use the WebAssembly Studio tool: `https://webassembly.studio/`.

This is an online tool that allows you to write code in various languages and have them compiled into WASM. In the WebAssembly Studio web application, if you create a new `C Hello World` application, you can very quickly get to see some WASM code by building the project:

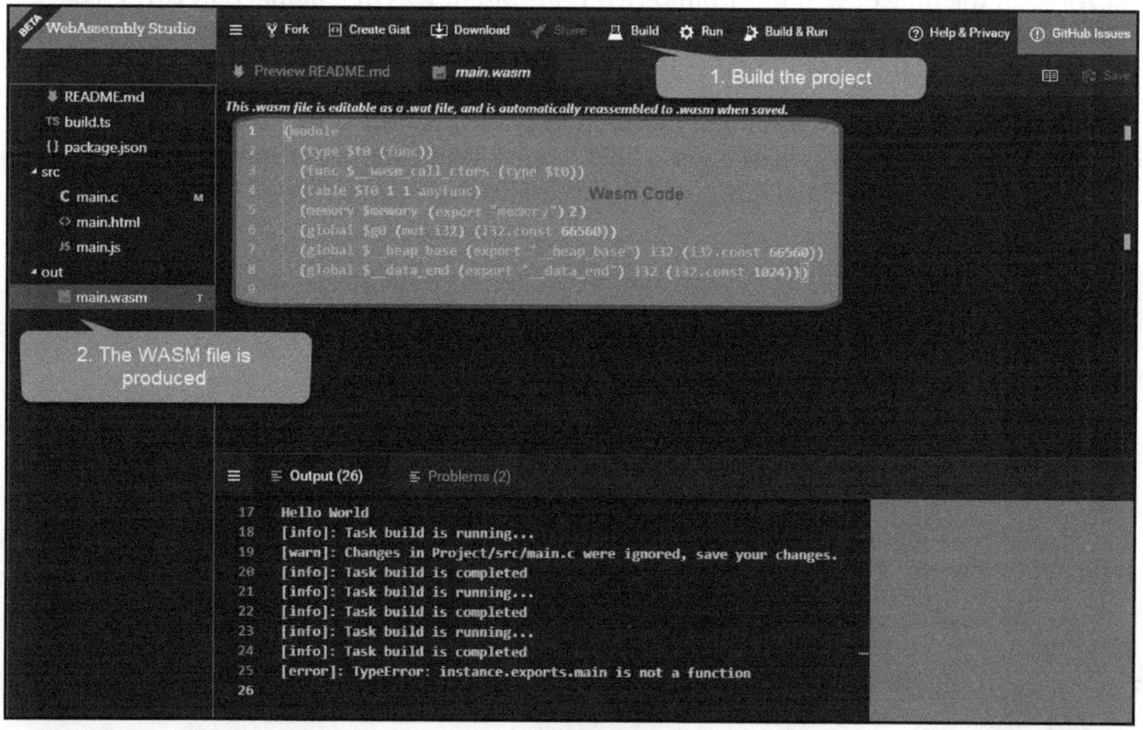

As you can see, WASM isn't exactly intuitive. However, you can write (or produce this) yourself and have the web browser run it.

This tool certainly gives an inkling of what may be possible with this technology; however, if you're not too familiar with C or Rust, you may struggle to use this beyond displaying **42** in the browser.

Fortunately, Microsoft is working on an experimental technology called Blazor that abstracts a lot of this work behind a familiar-looking project structure.

Understanding Blazor

Blazor is, at the time of writing, around two years old (it was first demoed in 2017). The idea was to take the concept of WebAssembly and mix it in with existing concepts that web developers are familiar with, such as Razor.

> Part of the reason that this section is an appendix is that only server-side Blazor was released with .NET Core 3. While the client side is in a workable state, it is not in the official release at the time of writing.

There are two flavors of Blazor: client and server. Server-side Blazor was released with .NET Core 3. It works by running the C# code on the server and then sending screen updates to the client using SignalR. Whilst this is an interesting methodology, since it does not use WebAssembly, we won't discuss it further in this chapter.

To create a Blazor project, you'll need the Visual Studio plugin: `https://marketplace.visualstudio.com/items?itemName=aspnet.blazor`.

You'll also need to install the Visual Studio Templates for Blazor; from a command line, type the following:

```
dotnet new -i Microsoft.AspNetCore.Blazor.Templates
```

> By the time this book is published, this step may no longer be necessary.

We can now create a new Blazor project:

1. Create a new **Blazor App** project from Visual Studio 2019:

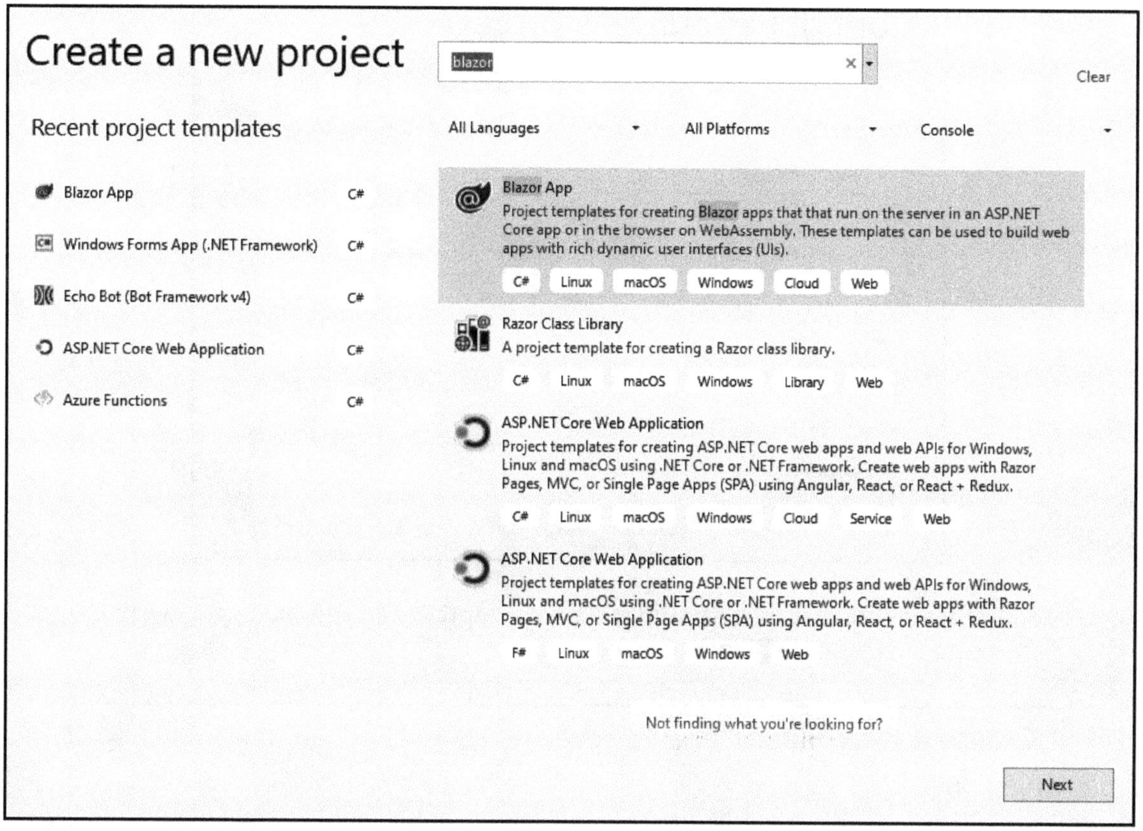

2. In the next screen, select your **Project name** and **Location**, as you would normally:

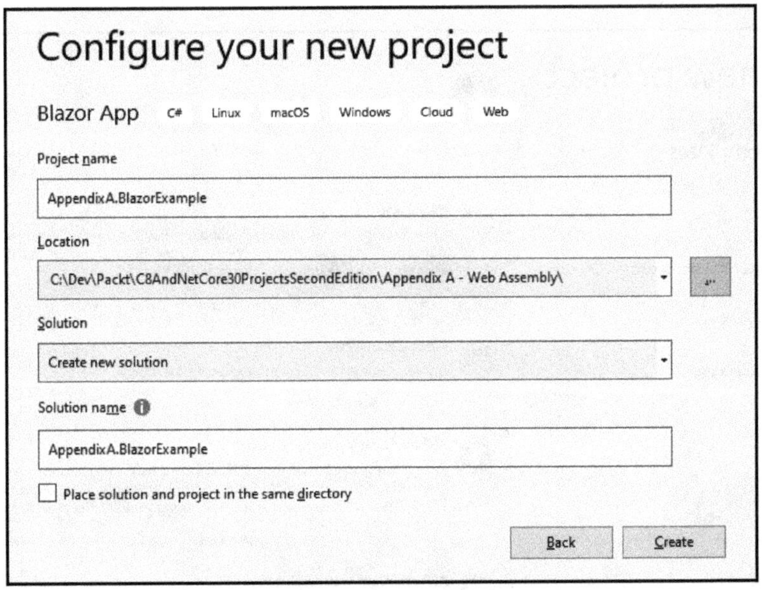

3. In the next screen, you should see several options. In this example, we're going to create a client-side Blazor application:

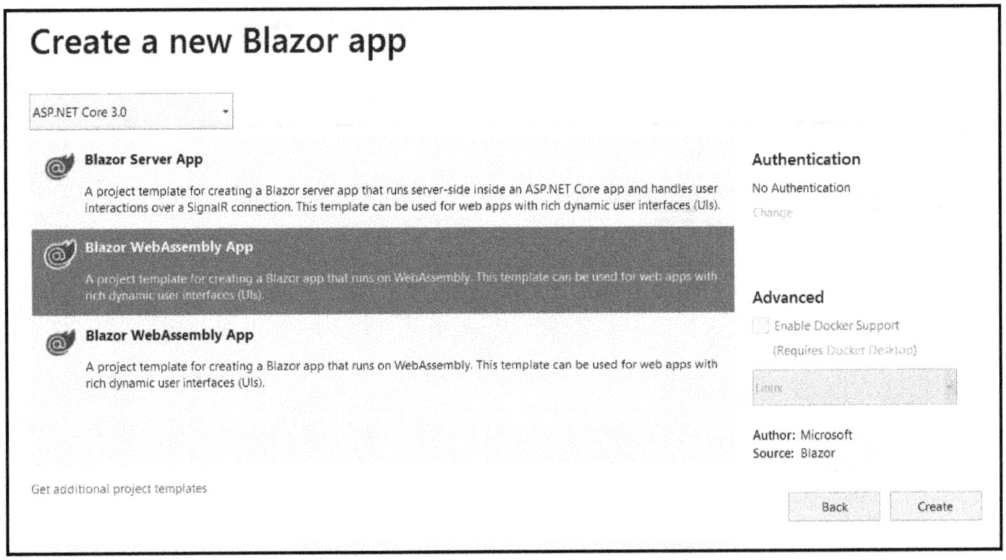

4. If you now select **Create**, you should be presented with a complete and working example of Blazor. Try running this: you should see a fully functional single-page application. If you've ever seen the React template, this structure should look very familiar to you.

   While this is true at the time of writing, the template may have changed by the time you read this.

If you click around the application, it should feel a lot like a modern single-page application. Let's look a little deeper. We'll start with the project structure:

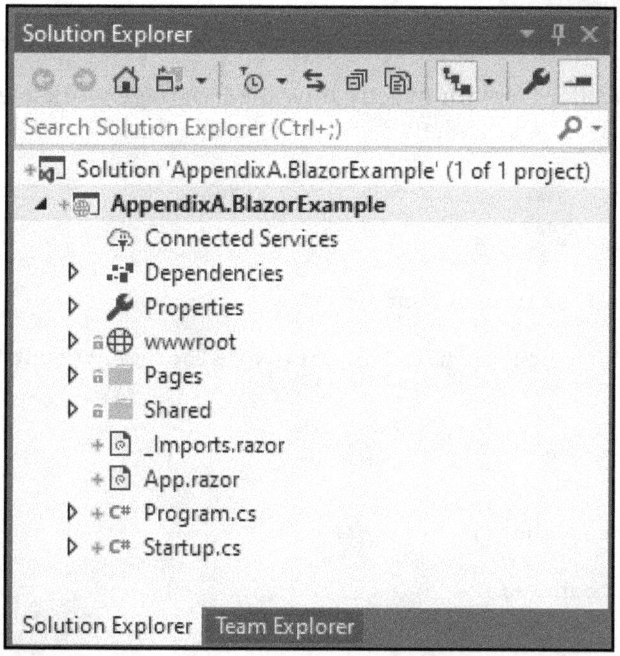

This structure should look quite familiar to you. It's worth noting the `.razor` extensions: in fact, the name **Blazor** comes from an amalgamation of the words **B**rowser and **R**azor.

For this quick overview, we won't go too far into the details, but let's have a look at the **Counter** page; when you run the application, you should see a page that allows you to click a button and increase the value:

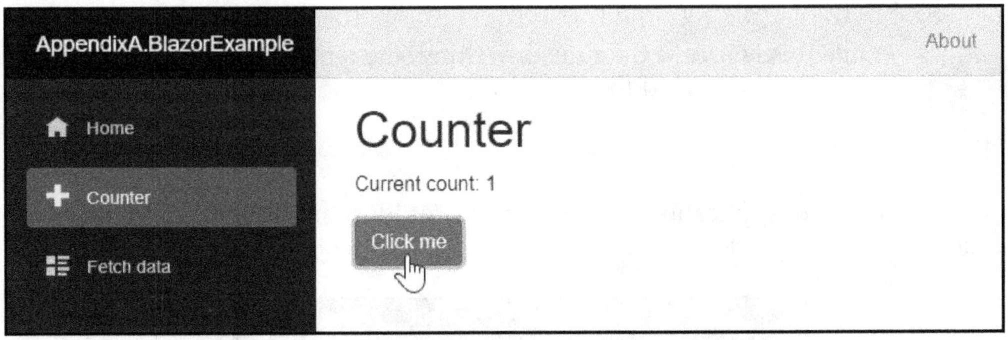

This page gives an excellent feel for exactly how the language works; let's have a look at the code that drives this. The `Counter.razor` file looks like this:

```
@page "/counter"

<h1>Counter</h1>

<p>Current count: @currentCount</p>

<button class="btn btn-primary" @onclick="@IncrementCount">Click
me</button>

@code {
    int currentCount = 0;

    void IncrementCount()
    {
        currentCount++;
    }
}
```

We have some HTML: the page header, the current count, and so on. Then, we have the Razor syntax—that's pretty much anywhere that you see an *at* symbol (`@`). Note that the button maps the *click* event handler to the method inside the `@code` block. Blazor keeps a track of the DOM, and when something changes—for example, the `currentCount`—the page is refreshed.

Let's run the application again, but this time, switch on the Developer Tools in the browser:

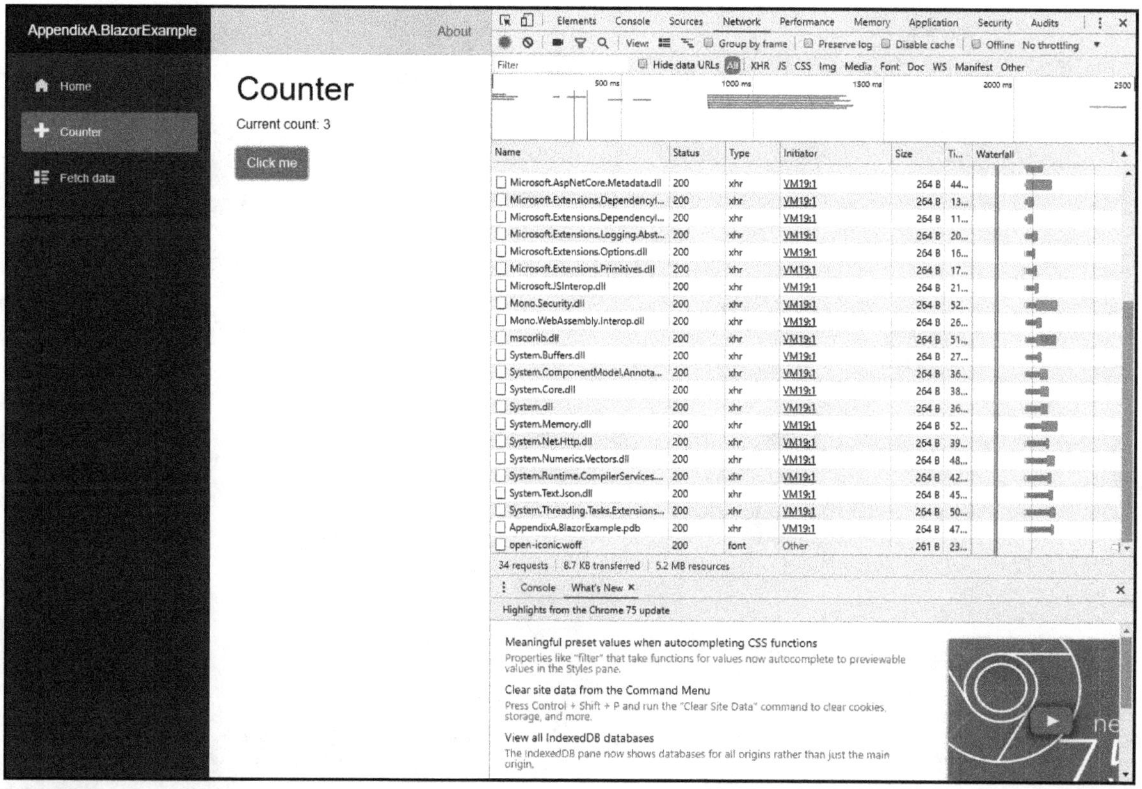

For most browsers, this can be achieved by pressing *F12*.

This tells us two things that are very important when dealing with Blazor. First, have a look at all of the DLLs that are being brought down to run the application. Essentially, this is downloading the Mono runtime. As you can see, the files aren't particularly big, but it is something to bear in mind when selecting the Blazor technology.

The second thing to note is that clicking the button does not make a server call. All of the code is executing on the client. This is the real draw of Blazor: you can write C# code and it runs in your browser.

We've had a quick look at WebAssembly in its raw form. We've discussed why WebAssembly is such an appealing, emergent web technology. We then had a look at the Blazor project to see how it simplifies the process of creating web applications.

Other Books You May Enjoy

If you enjoyed this book, you may be interested in these other books by Packt:

Hands-On Software Architecture with C# 8 and .NET Core 3
Gabriel Baptista, Francesco Abbruzzese

ISBN: 978-1-78980-093-7

- Overcome real-world architectural challenges and solve design consideration issues
- Apply architectural approaches like Layered Architecture, service-oriented architecture (SOA), and microservices
- Learn to use tools like containers, Docker, and Kubernetes to manage microservices
- Get up to speed with Azure Cosmos DB for delivering multi-continental solutions
- Learn how to program and maintain Azure Functions using C#
- Understand when to use test-driven development (TDD) as an approach for software development
- Write automated functional test cases for your projects

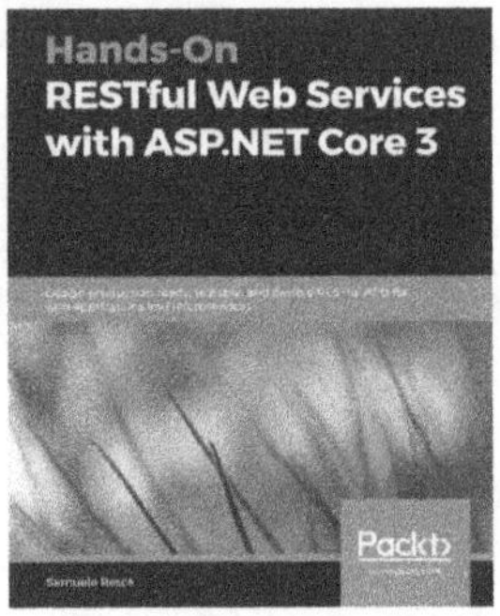

Hands-On RESTful Web Services with ASP.NET Core 3
Samuele Resca

ISBN: 978-1-78953-761-1

- Gain a comprehensive working knowledge of ASP.NET Core
- Integrate third-party tools and frameworks to build maintainable and efficient services
- Implement patterns using dependency injection to reduce boilerplate code and improve flexibility
- Use ASP.NET Core's out-of-the-box tools to test your applications
- Use Docker to run your ASP.NET Core web service in an isolated and self-contained environment
- Secure your information using HTTPS and token-based authentication
- Integrate multiple web services using resiliency patterns and messaging techniques

Leave a review - let other readers know what you think

Please share your thoughts on this book with others by leaving a review on the site that you bought it from. If you purchased the book from Amazon, please leave us an honest review on this book's Amazon page. This is vital so that other potential readers can see and use your unbiased opinion to make purchasing decisions, we can understand what our customers think about our products, and our authors can see your feedback on the title that they have worked with Packt to create. It will only take a few minutes of your time, but is valuable to other potential customers, our authors, and Packt. Thank you!

Index

B

C

D

E

N

O

P

Q

R

S

T

U

V

W

X

www.ingramcontent.com/pod-product-compliance
Lightning Source LLC
Chambersburg PA
CBHW060639060326
40690CB00020B/4453